KU-709-586

12·3·99

£81·50 set 2 vols

to Courage

ST. HELENS COMMUNITY LIBRARIES

3 8055 00662 2054

MONUMENTS
TO
COURAGE

VICTORIA CROSS
HEADSTONES AND MEMORIALS

COMM
HOSPITAL

MONUMENTS TO COURAGE

VICTORIA CROSS
HEADSTONES AND MEMORIALS

VOLUME TWO
1917 – 1982

ST. HELENS
COMMUNITY
LIBRARIES

ACC. No.

A99 160247

CLASS No. D

64

DAVID HARVEY

Published on behalf of the Author
by Kevin and Kay Patience
© David Harvey
1999

All rights reserved. No part of this publication
may be reproduced, stored in a retrieval system
or transmitted in any form or by any means,
electrical, mechanical or otherwise
without the permission of the author.

Printed by Akhbar Al Khaleej, Bahrain, Arabian Gulf

INDEX

AARON Arthur L.	1246
ABDUL HAFIZ..	1261
ABLETT Alfred	95
ACKROYD Harold	851
ACTON Abraham	566
ADAMS James W.	351
ADAMS Sir Robert	417
ADDISON Henry	287
ADDISON Williams R.F.	694
ADLAM Tom E.	759
AGANSING RAI	1279
AGAR Augustine W.S.	1149
AIKMAN Frederick R.	236
AITKEN Robert H.M.	130
ALBRECHT Herman	454
ALEXANDER Ernest W.	529
ALEXANDER John	75
ALGIE Wallace L.	1116
ALI HAIDAR	1329
ALLEN William B.	363
ALLEN William W.	747
ALLMAND Michael	1272
AMEY William	1141
ANDERSON Charles	283
ANDERSON Charles G.W.	1198
ANDERSON Eric	1234
ANDERSON John T.M.	1238
ANDERSON William	576
ANDERSON William H.	964
ANDREW Leslie W.	840
ANDREWS Henry J.	1154
ANGUS William	626
ANNAND Richard W.	1164
ANSON The Hon. Augustus	185
ARCHIBALD Adam	1142
ARTHUR Thomas	69
ASHFORD Thomas E.	359
ATKINSON Alfred	459
AUTEN Harold	1020
AXFORD Thomas L.	1014
AYLMER Sir Fenton	407
BABTIE Sir William	444
BADCOE Peter J.	1346
BADLU SINGH	1087
BAKER Charles G.	281
BALL Albert	812
BAMBRICK Valentine	268
BAMFORD Edward	987
BANKES William G.H.	246
BARBER Edward	577
BARKER William G.	1134
BARRATT Thomas	839
BARRETT John C.	1088
BARRON Colin F.	912
BARRY John	497
BARTER Frederick	618
BARTON Cyril J.	1260
BASKEYFIELD John D.	1295
BASSETT Cyril R.G.	637
BATES Sidney	1285
BATTEN-POOLL Arthur H.H.	710
BAXTER Edward F.	698
BAXTER Frank W.	414
BAZALGETTE Ian W.	1284
BEACH Thomas	31
BEAK Daniel M.W.	1037
BEAL Ernest F.	946
BEATHAM Robert M.	1029
BEATTIE Stephen H.	1204
BEAUCHAMP-PROCTOR Andrew F.W	1021
BEELEY John	1191
BEES William	508
BEESLEY William	1002
BEET Harry C.	472
BELCHER Douglas W.	617
BELL David	329
BELL Donald S.	726
BELL Edward W.D.	4
BELL Eric N.F.	714
BELL Frederick W.	500
BELL Mark S.	340
BELLEW Edward D.	588
BENNETT Eugene P.	766
BENT Philip E.	887
BENT Spencer J.	552
BERESFORD Lord William	380
BERGIN James	335
BERRYMAN John	16
BEST-DUNKLEY Bertram	841
BHANBHAGTA GURUNG	1319
BHANDARI RAM	1302
BINGHAM The Hon. Edward	702
BIRKS Frederick	876
BISDEE John H.	487
BISHOP William A.	827
BISSETT William D.	1132
BLACKBURN Arthur S.	734
BLAIR James	149
BLAIR Robert	186
BLAKER Frank G.	1280
BLOOMFIELD William A.	745
BOGLE Andrew C.	144
BOISRAGON Guy H.	408
BONNER Charles G.	854
BOOTH Anthony C.	374
BOOTH Frederick C.	774
BORELLA Albert C.	1017
BORTON Arthur D.	915
BOUGHEY Stanley H.P.	932
BOULGER Abraham	140
BOULTER William E.	728
BOURCHIER Claude T.	49
BOURKE Roland R.L.	1004
BOYD-ROCHFORT George A.	636
BOYES Duncan G.	321
BOYLE Edward C.	609
BRADBURY Edward K.	537
BRADFORD George N.	988
BRADFORD Roland B.	761
BRADLEY Frederick H.	507
BRADSHAW Joseph	63
BRADSHAW William	177
BRENNAN Joseph C.	254
BRERETON Alexander P.	1030
BRILLANT Jean	1022
BRODIE Walter L.	554
BROMHEAD Gonville	364
BROMLEY Cuthbert	591
BROOKE James A.O.	549
BROOKS Edward	813
BROOKS Oliver	672
BROWN Donald F.	752
BROWN Francis D.M.	207
BROWN Harry	860
BROWN Peter	383
BROWN Walter E.	1016
BROWNE Edward S.	379
BROWNE Henry G.G.	151
BROWNE Sir Samuel	277
BROWNE-SINGE-HUTCHINSON Edward D.	488
BRUCE William A.M.	563
BRUNT John H.C.	1303
BRYAN Thomas	792
BUCHAN John C.	947
BUCHANAN Angus	692
BUCKINGHAM William	572
BUCKLEY Alexander H.	1055
BUCKLEY Cecil W.	65
BUCKLEY John	114
BUCKLEY Maurice V.	1080
BUDGEN Patrick J.	885
BULLER Sir Redvers	376
BURGES Daniel	1081
BURGOYNE Hugh T.	66
BURMAN William F.	877
BURSLEM Nathaniel G.	298
BURT Alfred A.	666
BURTON Alexander S.	641
BURTON Richard H.	1297
BUSHELL Christopher	960
BUTLER John F.P.	556
BUTLER Thomas A.	239
BUTLER William B.	853
BYE Robert J.	842
BYRNE James	257
BYRNE John	32
BYRNE Thomas	427
BYTHESEA John	2
CADELL Thomas	122
CAFE William M.	266
CAFFREY John J.	679
CAIN Robert H.	1292
CAIRNS George A.	1258
CAIRNS Hugh	1139
CALDWELL Thomas	1138
CALVERT Laurence	1076
CAMBRIDGE Daniel	98
CAMERON Aylmer S.	249
CAMERON Donald	1249
CAMPBELL Frederick W.	627
CAMPBELL Gordon	776
CAMPBELL John C.	1192
CAMPBELL John V.	753
CAMPBELL Kenneth	1177
CAMPBELL Lorne M.	1235
CARLESS John H.	916
CARLIN Patrick	259
CARMICHAEL John	872
CARNE James P.	1341
CARPENTER Alfred F.B.	989
CARROLL John	833
CARTER Herbert A.	520
CARTER Nelson V.	713
CARTON de WIART Sir Adrian	724
CARTWRIGHT George	1054
CASSIDY Bernard M.	971
CASTLETON Claude C.	738
CATES George E.	781
CATHER Geoffrey St. G.S.	715
CATOR Henry	793
CHAFER George W.	706
CHAMPION James	278
CHANNER George N.	341
CHAPLIN John W.	299
CHAPMAN Edward T.	1325
CHARD John R.M.	365
CHARLTON Edward C.	1331
CHASE William St. L.	358
CHATTA SINGH	685
CHAVASSE Noel G	743(& after 852)
CHERRY Percy H.	786
CHESHIRE Geoffrey L.	1283
CHHELU RAM	1236
CHICKEN George B.	279
CHOWNE Albert	1324
CHRISTIAN Harry	676
CHRISTIE John A.	940
CLAMP William	896
CLARE George W.B.	924
CLARK-KENNEDY William H.	1051
CLARKE James	1140
CLARKE Leo	751
CLARKE Wilwood A..	1239
CLEMENTS John J.	498
CLIFFORD Sir Henry	33
CLOGSTOUN Herbert M.	289
CLOUTMAN Sir Brett	1148
COBBE Sir Alexander	515
COCHRANE Hugh S.	251
COCKBURN Hampden Z.C.	490
COFFEY William	56
COFFIN Clifford	843
COGHILL Nevill J.A.	360
COLEMAN John	94
COLLEY Harold J.	1046
COLLIN Joseph H.	977
COLLINGS-WELLS John S.	955
COLLINS John	911
COLLIS James	357
COLTMAN William H.	1108
COLUMBINE Herbert G.	956
COLVIN Hugh	878
COLVIN James M.C.	420
COLYER-FERGUSSON Thomas R.	844
COMBE Robert G.	818
COMMERELL Sir John	110
CONGREVE Sir Walter	445
CONGREVE William La T.	729
CONNOLLY William	135
CONNORS John	99
CONOLLY John A.	22
COOK John	344
COOK Walter	288
COOKE Thomas	736
COOKSON Edgar C.	669
COOPER Edward	861
COOPER Henry	68
COOPER James	330
COPPINS Frederick G.	1031
CORBETT Frederick	397
CORNWELL John T.	703
COSENS Aubrey	1313
COSGROVE William	608
COSTELLO Edmond W.	416
COTTER William R.	689
COUGHLAN Cornelius	121
COULSON Gustavus H.B.	501
COUNTER Jack T.	986
COURY Gabriel G.	742
COVERDALE Charles H.	888
COWLEY Charles H.	699
COX Christopher A.	784
CRAIG James	97
CRAIG John M.	829
CRANDON Harry G.	504
CREAGH Sir O'Moore	348
CREAN Thomas J.	510

Name	No.
CRICHTON James	1103
CRISP Thomas	857
CROAK John B.	1023
CROSS Arthur H.	965
CROWE John J.	985
CROWE Joseph P.H.	148
CRUICKSHANK John A.	1282
CRUICKSHANK Robert E.	1001
CRUTCHLEY Sir Victor	990
CUBITT William G.	128
CUMMING Arthur E.	1197
CUNINGHAME Sir William	50
CUNNINGHAM John (1916)	767
CUNNINGHAM John (1917)	803
CURREY William M.	1056
CURRIE David V.	1288
CURTIS Albert E.	461
CURTIS Henry	76
CURTIS Horace A.	1125
CURTIS Philip K.E.	1342
CUTLER Sir Roden	1185
DALTON James L.	366
DALZIEL Henry	1015
DANAHER John	391
DANCOX Frederick G.	897
DANIEL Edward St. J.	34
DANIELS Harry	578
D'ARCY Henry C.D.	381
DARTNELL Wilbur T.	650
DARWAN SING NEGI	558
DAUNT John C.C.	192
DAVEY Philip	1013
DAVIES James L.	845
DAVIES John T.	963
DAVIES Joseph J.	731
DAVIES Richard B.	681
DAVIS Gronow	100
DAVIS James	261
DAWSON James L.	674
DAY George F.	107
DAY Sidney J.	871
DAYKINS John B.	1126
DEAN Donald J.	1089
DEAN Percy T.	991
DEASE Maurice J.	523
DE L'ISLE Viscount	1256
DE MONTMORENCY The Hon. Raymond	428
DEMPSEY Denis	147
de PASS Frank A.	559
DERRICK Thomas C.	1252
DE WIND Edmund	948
DIAMOND Bernard	188
DICK-CUNYNGHAM William H.	352
DICKSON Sir Collingwood	11
DIGBY-JONES Robert J.T.	455
DIMMER John H.S	555
DINESEN Thomas	1034
DIVANE John	152
DIXON Matthew C.	60
DOBSON Claude C.	1151
DOBSON Frederick W.	545
DONNINI Dennis	1307
DONONHOE Patrick	189
DOOGAN John	392
DORRELL George T.	536
DOUGALL Eric S.	980
DOUGHTY-WYLIE Charles H.M.	607
DOUGLAS Campbell M.	331
DOUGLAS Henry E.M.	441
DOUGLAS-HAMILTON Angus F.	663
DOWELL George D.	89
DOWLING William	133
DOWN John T.	309
DOWNIE Robert	765
DOXAT Alexis C.	489
DOYLE Martin	1063
DRAIN Job H.C.	532
DRAKE Alfred G.	682
DRESSER Tom	823
DREWRY George L.	599
DRUMMOND Geoffrey H.	1005
DUFFY James	941
DUFFY Thomas	178
DUGDALE Frederic B.	499
DUNBAR-NASMITH Martin E.	621
DUNDAS James	325
DUNLAY John	217
DUNN Alexander R.	17
DUNSIRE Robert	664
DUNSTAN William	643
DUNVILLE John S.	835
DURRANT Thomas F	1205
DWYER Edward	585
DWYER The Hon. John	884
DYNON Denis	193
EARDLEY George H.	1298
EDMONDSON John H.	1178
EDWARDS Alexander	852
EDWARDS Frederick J.	757
EDWARDS Hughie	1186
EDWARDS Thomas	402
EDWARDS Wilfred	862
EDWARDS William M.M.	398
EGERTON Ernest A.	879
ELCOCK Roland E.	1124
ELLIOTT Keith	1214
ELLIOTT-COOPER Neville B.	925
ELPHINSTONE Sir Howard	77
ELSTOB Wilfrith	949
ELTON Frederick C.	57
EMERSON James S.	937
ENGLEHEART Henry W.	465
ENGLISH William J.	503
ERSKINE John	708
ERVINE-ANDREWS Harold M.	1168
ESMONDE Eugene	1199
ESMONDE Thomas	79
EVANS Arthur	1064
EVANS George	739
EVANS Lewis P.	889
EVANS Samuel	59
FARMER Donald D.	494
FARMER Joseph J.	395
FARQUHARSON Francis E.H.	238
FARRELL John	18
FAULDS William F.	730
FAZAL DIN	1316
FAGEN Edward S.F.	1174
FFRENCH Alfred K.	208
FINCASTLE Viscount	418
FINCH Norman A.	992
FINDLATER George	426
FINDLAY George de C.E.	1143
FINLAY David	614
FIRMAN Humphrey O.B.	700
FIRTH James	463
FISHER Frederick	587
FitzCLARENCE Charles	435
FitzGERALD Richard	190
FITZGIBBON Andrew	302
FITZPATRICK Francis	387
FLAWN Thomas	388
FLEMING-SANDES Arthur J.T.	670
FLINN Thomas	230
FLOWERDEW Gordon M.	974
FOOTE Henry R.B.	1210
FOOTE John W.	1216
FORBES-ROBERTSON James	983
FORREST George	112
FORSHAW William T.	639
FORSYTH Samuel	1044
FOSBERY George V.	311
FOSS Charles C.	579
FOSTER Edward	811
FOWLER Edmund J.	375
FRASER Sir Charles	286
FRASER Ian E.	1338
FREEMAN John	196
FRENCH John A.	1220
FREYBERG Bernard C.	768
FRICKLETON Samuel	837
FRISBY Cyril H.	1090
FULLER Wilfred D.	580
FULLER William C.	539
FURNESS The Hon. Christopher	1167
FYNN James H.	695
GABY Alfred E.	1024
GAJE GHALE	1244
GANJU LAMA	1273
GARDINER George	55
GARDNER Philip J.	1193
GARDNER William	267
GARFORTH Charles E.	524
GARLAND Donald E.	1162
GARVIN Stephen	126
GEARY Benjamin H.	586
GEE Robert	926
GIAN SINGH	1317
GIBSON Guy P.	1243
GILL Albert	737
GILL Peter	117
GLASOCK Horace H.	466
GOAT William	237
GOBAR SING NEGI	571
GOBIND SINGH	933
GODLEY Sidney F.	525
GOOD Herman J.	1025
GOODFELLOW Charles A.	292
GOODLAKE Gerald L.	28
GORDON Bernard S.	1047
GORDON James H.	1188
GORDON William E.	478
GORDON William J.	410
GORLE Robert V.	1105
GORMAN James	35
GORT Viscount	1091
GOSLING William	790
GOUGH Sir Charles	150
GOUGH Sir Hugh	199
GOUGH Sir John	517
GOULD Thomas W.	1201
GOURLEY Cyril E.	927
GRADY Thomas	12
GRAHAM Sir Gerald	79
GRAHAM Sir Reginald	808
GRAHAM Patrick	223
GRANT Charles J.W.	406
GRANT John D.	522
GRANT John G.	1057
GRANT Peter	222
GRANT Robert	169
GRATWICK Percival E.	1222
GRAY Robert H.	1339
GRAY Thomas	1163
GRAYBURN John H.	1290
GREAVES Fred	890
GREEN John L.	716
GREEN Patrick	153
GREENWOOD Harry	1129
GREGG The Hon. Milton	1092
GREGG William	1003
GRENFELL Francis O.	528
GRIBBLE Julian R.	961
GRIEVE John	19
GRIEVE Robert C.	830
GRIFFITHS William	332
GRIMBALDESTON William H.	863
GRIMSHAW John E.	590
GRISTOCK George	1116
GROGAN George W. St. G.	1007
GUISE Sir John	210
GUNN George W.	1190
GURNEY Arthur S.	1215
GUY Basil J.D.	514
HACKETT Thomas B.	226
HACKETT William	709
HAINE Reginald L.	814
HALE Thomas E.	101
HALL Arthur C.	1058
HALL Frederick W.	589
HALL William	211
HALLIDAY Sir Lewis	513
HALLIWELL Joel	1008
HALLOWES Rupert P.	658
HALTON Albert	901
HAMILTON John Brown	883
HAMILTON John Patrick	646
HAMILTON Thomas de C.	64
HAMILTON Walter R.P.	347
HAMMOND Sir Arthur	355
HAMPTON Harry	482
HANCOCK Thomas	123
HANNA Robert H.	869
HANNAH John	1173
HANSEN Percy H.	645
HARDEN Henry E.	1309
HARDHAM William J.	495
HARDING Israel	396
HARDY Theodore B.	998
HARINGTON Hastings E.	203
HARMAN John P.	1262
HARPER John W.	1296
HARRIS Thomas J.	1032
HARRISON Arthur L.	993
HARRISON John	212
HARRISON John	819
HART Sir Reginald	345
HARTIGAN Henry	120

Name	No.
HARTLEY Edmund B.	385
HARVEY Francis J.W.	704
HARVEY Frederick M.W.	787
HARVEY Jack	1065
HARVEY Norman	1133
HARVEY Samuel	671
HAVELOCK-ALLAN Sir Henry	141
HAWKER Lanoe G.	633
HAWKES David	240
HAWTHORNE Robert	157
HAYWARD Reginald F.J.	950
HEAPHY Charles	315
HEATHCOTE Alfred S.	131
HEATON William E.	484
HEAVISIDE Michael W.	821
HEDGES Frederick W.	1131
HENDERSON Arthur	809
HENDERSON Edward E.D.	770
HENDERSON George S.	1156
HENDERSON Herbert S.	413
HENEAGE Clement W.	272
HENRY Andrew	36
HERRING Alfred C.	962
HEWETT Sir William	23
HEWITSON James	999
HEWITT Dennis G.W.	846
HEWITT William H.	880
HILL-WALKER Alan R.	393
HILL Albert	732
HILL Samuel	213
HILLS-JOHNES Sir James	137
HINCKLEY George	306
HINTON John D.	1179
HIRSCH David P.	810
HITCH Frederick	367
HOBSON Frederick	858
HODGE Samuel	328
HOEY Charles F.	1257
HOGAN John	548
HOLBROOK Norman D.	561
HOLLAND Edward J.G.	492
HOLLAND John V.	748
HOLLIS George	273
HOLLIS Stanley E.	1270
HOLLOWELL James	179
HOLMES Frederick W.	535
HOLMES Joel	171
HOLMES Thomas W.	903
HOLMES William E.	1115
HOME Sir Anthony	180
HOME Duncan C.	158
HONEY Samuel L.	1093
HOOK Alfred H.	368
HOPE William	80
HORE-RUTHVEN The Hon. Alexander G.	432
HORLOCK Ernest G.	543
HORNELL David E.	1277
HORSFALL Basil A.	969
HORWOOD Alec G.	1254
HOUSE William	480
HOWELL George J.	822
HOWSE Sir Neville	479
HUDSON Charles E.	1010
HUFFAM James P.	1053
HUGHES Matthew	70
HUGHES Thomas	749
HULL Charles	651
HULME Alfred C.	1182
HUMPSTON Robert	62
HUNTER David F.	1079
HUNTER Thomas P.	1327
HUTCHESON Bellenden S.	1066
HUTCHINSON James	712
HUTT Arthur	891
IND Alfred E.	511
INGOUVILLE George	90
INGRAM George M.	1111
INKSON Edgar T.	462
INNES James J.M.	235
INSALL Gilbert S.M.	678
INWOOD Reginald R.	875
IRWIN Charles	214
ISHAR SINGH	1157
JACKA Albert	620
JACKMAN James J.B.	1194
JACKSON Harold	957
JACKSON Norman C.	1263
JACKSON Thomas N.	1094
JACKSON William	711
JAMES Walter J.	629
JAMES Manley A.	951
JAMIESON David A.	1286
JARRATT George	820
JARRETT Handon C.T.	284
JARVIS Charles A.	527
JEE Joseph	173
JEFFERSON Francis A.	1267
JEFFRIES Clarence S.	902
JENNINGS Edward	202
JENSEN Joergan C.	788
JEROME Henry E.	255
JERRARD Alan	975
JOHNSON Dudley G.	1144
JOHNSON Frederick H.	652
JOHNSON James	1119
JOHNSON William H.	1109
JOHNSTON Robert	436
JOHNSTON William H.	540
JOHNSTONE William	3
JONES Alfred S.	119
JONES David	750
JONES Henry M.	71
JONES Herbert	1349
JONES Loftus W.	705
JONES Richard B.B.	701
JONES Robert	369
JONES Thomas A.	756
JONES William	370
JOTHAM Eustace	568
JOYNT William D.	1041
JUDSON Reginald S.	1048
KAEBLE Joseph	1009
KAMAL RAM	1265
KARAMJEET SINGH JUDGE	1320
KARANBAHADUR RANA	981
KAVANAGH Thomas H.	198
KEATINGE Richard H.	245
KELLAWAY Joseph	106
KELLIHER Richard	1247
KELLS Robert	187
KELLY Henry	762
KENEALLY William	594
KENNA Edward	1334
KENNA Paul A.	429
KENNEALLY John P.	1240
KENNEDY Charles T.	493
KENNY Henry E.	653
KENNY James	209
KENNY Thomas	677
KENNY Thomas J.B.	794
KENNY William	547
KENNY William D.	1155
KER Allan E.	952
KERR George F.	1095
KERR John C.	755
KERR William A.	139
KEYES Geoffrey C.T.	1189
KEYSOR Leonard M.	638
KEYWORTH Leonard J.	623
KHUDADAD KHAN	551
KIBBY William H.	1221
KILBY Arthur F.G.	659
KINGSBURY Bruce S.	1219
KINROSS Cecil J.	907
KIRBY Frank H.	474
KIRK James	1145
KIRK John	118
KNIGHT Alfred J.	881
KNIGHT Arthur G.	1067
KNIGHT Henry J.	483
KNOWLAND George A.	1310
KNOX Cecil L.	958
KNOX John S.	5
KONOWAL Filip	870
KULBIR THAPA	654
LACHHIMAN GURUNG	1332
LAFONE Alexander M.	906
LAIDLAW Daniel	655
LALA	686
LALBAHADUR THAPA	1233
LAMBERT George	143
LANE Thomas	300
LASCELLES Arthur M.	935
LASSEN Anders F.E.V.S.	1328
LAUDER David R.	647
LAUGHNAN Thomas	204
LAURENT Harry J.	1077
LAWRENCE Brian T.T.	481
LAWRENCE Samuel H.	134
LAWSON Edward	423
LEACH Edward P.	346
LEACH James	550
LEAK John	735
LEAKEY Nigel G.	1181
LEARMONTH Okill M.	865
LEAROYD Roderick A.B.	1171
LEET William K.	377
LEITCH Peter	81
LEITH James	250
LENDRIM William J.	53
LENNOX Wilbraham O.	51
LENNON Edmund H.	301
LE PATOUREL Herbert W.	1226
LE QUESNE Ferdinand S.	405
LESTER Frank	1117
LEWIS Herbert W.	1082
LEWIS Leonard A.	764
LIDDELL Ian O.	1326
LIDDELL John A.	635
LINDSAY Robert G.	6
LINTON John W.	1242
LISTER Joseph	898
LLOYD Sir Owen	411
LODGE Issac	470
LOOSEMORE Arnold	856
LORD David S.A.	1293
LOUDON-SHAND Stewart W.	717
LOWERSON Albert D.	1059
LUCAS Charles D.	1
LUCAS John	305
LUKE Frederick	533
LUMLEY Charles	102
LUMSDEN Frederick W.	789
LYALL Graham T.	1096
LYELL The Lord, Charles A.	1237
LYNN John	612
LYONS John	73
LYSONS Henry	378
LYSTER Harry H.	269
McAULAY John	923
McBEAN William	241
McBEATH Robert	917
McCARTHY Lawrence D.	1042
McCORRIE Charles	87
McCREA John F.	389
McCUDDEN James T.B.	942
McDERMOND John	37
MacDONALD Henry	61
McDONELL William F.	146
McDOUGALL John	303
McDOUGALL Stanley R.	972
MacDOWELL Thain W.	798
McFADZEAN William F.	718
McGAW Samuel	339
McGEE Lewis	892
McGOVERN John	127
McGREGOR David S.	1128
MacGREGOR John	1100
McGREGOR Roderick	93
McGUFFIE Louis	1098
McGUIRE James	160
McHALE Patrick	194
McINNES Hugh	205
McINTOSH George I.	848
MacINTYRE David L.	1045
MACINTYRE Donald	336
McIVER Hugh	1043
MACKAY David	215
McKAY Ian J.	1350
MACKAY John F.	473
McKEAN George B.	1000
McKECHNIE James	7
McKENNA Edward	308
McKENZIE Albert E.	994
McKENZIE Hugh McD.	908
MACKENZIE James	565
MACKENZIE John	433
MACKEY John B.	1333
MACKINTOSH Donald	801
MACLEAN Hector L.S.	419
McLEOD Alan A.	970
McMANUS Peter	181
McMASTER Valentine M.	175
McNAIR Eric A.	688
McNALLY William	1135
McNAMARA Frank H.	785
McNAMARA John	1074
McNEILL Sir John	316
McNESS Frederick	754
MACPHERSON Herbert T.	174
McPHERSON Stewart	182

Name	No.	Name	No.	Name	No.
McPHIE James	1120	MURRAY John	320	POULTER Arthur	982
McQUIRT Bernard	232	MYLER Edgar K.	696	PRAKASH SINGH	1311
McREADY-DIARMID Arthur M.C.	931	MYLOTT Patrick	224	PREMINDRA SINGH BHAGAT	1175
MACTIER Robert	1060	MYNARSKI Andrew C.	1274	PRENDERGAST Sir Harry	228
McWHEENEY William	15			PRETTYJOHN John	41
MADDEN Ambrose	26	NAMDEO JADHAV	1330	PRICE-DAVIS Llewellyn A.E.	506
MAGENNIS James J.	1337	NAND SINGH	1259	PRIDE Thomas	323
MAGNER Michael	334	NAPIER William	258	PROBYN Sir Dighton	293
MAHONEY Patrick	168	NASH William	242	PROCTER Arthur H.	707
MAHONY John K.	1268	NEAME Sir Philip	564	PROSSER Joseph	74
MAILLARD William J.	431	NEEDHAM Samuel	1075	PROWSE George	1070
MALCOLM Hugh G.	1227	NEELY Thomas	1097	PRYCE Thomas T.	984
MALCOLMSON John G.	295	NELSON David	538	PURCELL John	124
MALING George A.	656	NESBITT Randolph C.	415	PYE Charles	225
MALLESON Wilfred St. A.	598	NETRABAHADUR THAPA	1278		
MALONE Joseph	20	NETTLETON John D.	1209	QUERIPEL Lionel E.	1294
MANGLES Ross L.	145	NEWELL Robert	247	QUIGG Robert	719
MANLEY William G.N.	317	NEWLAND James E.	791		
MANNOCK Edward	1012	NEWMAN Augustus C.	1206	RABY Henry J.	83
MANSEL-JONES Conwyn	464	NEWTON William E.	1230	RAMAGE Henry	27
MANSER Leslie T.	1211	NGARIMU Moana-Nui-a-Kiwa	1232	RAMBAHADUR LIMBU	1344
MANTLE Jack F.	1169	NICHOLAS Henry J.	936	RAM SARUP SINGH	1300
MARINER William	622	NICHOLLS Harry	1165	RAMSDEN Horace E.	452
MARLING Sir Percival	401	NICKERSON William H.S.	471	RANDLE John N.	1264
MARSHALL James	1146	NICOLSON Eric J.B.	1172	RANKEN Harry S.	544
MARSHALL William T.	399	NOBLE Cecil R.	574	RATCLIFFE William	834
MARTIN Cyril G.	573	NORMAN William	52	RATTEY Reginald R.	1322
MARTINEAU Horace R.	451	NORTON Gerard R.	1289	RAVENHILL George	447
MARTIN-LEAKE Arthur	512 (& after 550)	NORWOOD John	440	RAYFIELD Walter L.	1071
MASTERS Richard G.	978	NUNNEY Claude J.P.	1061	RAYMOND Claud	1321
MASTERSON James E.I.	456	NURSE George E.	450	RAYNES John C.	673
MAUDE Francis C.	170			RAYNOR William	113
MAUDE Sir Frederick	96	OCKENDEN James	893	READ Anketell M.	660
MAUFE Thomas H.B.	828	O'CONNOR Sir Luke	8	READE Herbert T.	164
MAXWELL Francis A.	467	ODGERS William	297	READITT John	779
MAXWELL Joseph	1110	O'HEA Timothy	327	REED Hamilton L.	448
MAY Henry	546	O'KELLY Christopher P.J.	904	REES Ivor	849
MAYGAR Leslie C.	509	O'LEARY Michael J.	569	REES Lionel W.B.	720
MAYO Arthur	229	OLPHERTS Sir William	176	REEVES Thomas	42
MAYSON Tom F.	847	O'MEARA Martin	744	REID Oswald A.	782
MEEKOSHA Samuel	680	O'NEILL John	1122	REID William	1251
MEIKLE John	1018	ONIONS George	1040	RENDLE Thomas E.	557
MEIKLEJOHN Matthew F.M.	437	ORMSBY John W.	804	RENNIE William	167
MELLISH Edward N.	691	O'ROURKE Michael J.	859	RENNY George A.	165
MELLIS Sir Charles	434	OSBORN John R.	1196	REYNOLDS Douglas	534
MELVILL Teignmouth	361	OSBOURNE James	394	REYNOLDS Henry	882
MELVIN Charles	807	O'SULLIVAN Gerald R.	630	REYNOLDS James H.	371
MERRIFIELD William	1106	O'TOOLE Edmund	382	REYNOLDS William	9
MERRITT Charles C.I.	1217	OWENS James	29	RHODES John H.	900
METCALF William H.	1068	OXENHAM William	129	RHODES-MOORHOUSE William B.	604
MEYNELL Godfrey	1158			RICHARDS Alfred J.	592
MIDDLETON Rawdon H.	1225	PALMER Anthony	39	RICHARDSON Arthur H.L.	476
MIERS Sir Anthony	1203	PALMER Frederick W.	775	RICHARDSON George	291
MILBANKE Sir John	453	PALMER Robert A.M.	1305	RICHARDSON James C.	763
MILES Francis G.	1130	PARK James	200	RICHHPAL RAM	1176
MILLAR Duncan	290	PARK John	40	RICKARD William T.	111
MILLER Frederick	38	PARKASH SINGH	1229	RICKETTS Thomas	1123
MILLER James W. (1857)	197	PARKER Charles E.H.	468	RIDGEWAY Richard K.	386
MILLER James (1916)	740	PARKER Walter R.	610	RIGGS Frederick C.	1107
MILLS Walter	939	PARKES Samuel	21	RIPLEY John	613
MILNE William J.	795	PARSLOW Frederick D.	632	RITCHIE Henry P.	560
MINER Harry G.B.	1026	PARSONS Francis N.	460	RITCHIE Walter P.	721
MIR DAST	603	PARSONS Hardy F.	868	RIVERS Jacob	575
MITCHELL Coulson N.	1114	PARTRIDGE Frank J.	1336	ROBARTS John	67
MITCHELL George A.	1255	PATON George H.T.	934	ROBERTS Frank C.	959
MITCHELL Samuel	318	PATON John	218	ROBERTS The Hon. Frederick H.S.	449
MOFFAT Martin	1121	PATTISON John G.	799	ROBERTS F.S. (EARL)	231
MOLYNEUX John	899	PAYNE Keith	1348	ROBERTS James R.	191
MONAGHAN Thomas	282	PEACHMENT George S.	657	ROBERTS Peter S.W.	1202
MONGER George	227	PEARKES The Hon. George	910	ROBERTSON Charles G.	944
MOON Rupert V.	824	PEARSE Samuel G.	1153	ROBERTSON Clement	866
MOOR George R.D.	624	PEARSON James	252	ROBERTSON James P.	913
MOORE Arthur T.	296	PEARSON John	274	ROBERTSON William	439
MOORE Hans G.	343	PECK Cyrus W.	1069	ROBINSON Edward	244
MOORE Montague S.S.	867	PEEL Sir William	13	ROBINSON Eric G.	570
MORLEY Samuel	262	PEELER Walter	894	ROBINSON William L.	746
MORROW Robert	581	PENNELL Henry S.	424	ROBSON Henry H.	562
MOTT Edward J.	772	PERCY Lord Henry	48	RODDY Patrick	280
MOTTERSHEAD Thomas	769	PERIE John	82	RODGERS George	271
MOUAT Sir James	24	PETERS Frederick T.	1224	ROGERS James	502
MOUNTAIN Albert	968	PHILLIPPS Everard A.L.	115	ROGERS Maurice A.W.	1269
MOYNEY John	873	PHILLIPS Robert E.	771	ROGERS Robert M.	304
MOYNIHAN Andrew	103	PHIPPS-HORNBY Edmund J.	469	ROLLAND George M.	518
MUGFORD Harold S.	802	PICKARD Arthur F.	314	ROOM Frederick G.	864
MUIR Kenneth	1340	PITCHER Ernest H.	855	ROOPE Gerard B.	1159
MULLANE Patrick	356	PITCHER Henry W.	312	ROSAMUND Matthew	116
MULLIN George H.	909	PITTS James	457	ROSS John	92
MULLINS Charles H.	438	PLACE Basil C.G.	1248	ROUPELL George R.P.	583
MUNRO James	216	POLLARD Alfred O.	815	ROWLANDS Sir Hugh	43
MURPHY Michael	263	POLLOCK James D.	667	RUSHE David	248
MURPHY Thomas	333	POPE Charles	805	RUSSELL Sir Charles	44
MURRAY Henry W.	773	PORTEOUS Patrick A.	1218	RUSSELL John F.	914
MURRAY James	390	POTTS Frederick W.O.	648	RUTHERFORD Charles S.	1049

Name	No.
RUTHVEN William	1006
RYAN John (1857)	183
RYAN John (1863)	307
RYAN John (1918)	1104
RYAN Miles	161
RYDER Robert E.	758
RYDER Robert E.D.	1207
SADLIER Clifford W.K.	997
SAGE Thomas H.	895
SALKELD Philip	159
SALMON Sir Nowell	219
SAMSON George M.	600
SANDERS George	722
SANDERS William E.	817
SANDFORD Richard D.	995
SARTORIUS Euston H.	350
SARTORIUS Reginald W.	338
SAUNDERS Arthur F.	665
SAVAGE William A.	1208
SAYER John W.	953
SCARF Arthur S.K.	1195
SCHIESS Ferdnand C.	372
SCHOFIELD Harry N.	446
SCHOFIELD John	979
SCHOLEFIELD Mark	45
SCOTT Andrew	342
SCOTT Robert	458
SCOTT Robert G.	384
SCRIMGER Francis A.C.	596
SEAGRIM Derek A.	1231
SEAMAN Ernest	1101
SEELEY William H.H.	322
SELLAR George	353
SEPHTON Alfred E.	1180
SEWELL Cecil H.	1052
SHAHAMAD KHAN	697
SHANKLAND Robert	905
SHARPE Charles R.	615
SHAUL John D.F.	442
SHAW Hugh	324
SHAW Same	270
SHEBBEARE Robert H.	155
SHEPHERD Albert E.	918
SHEPPARD John	91
SHER BAHADUR THAPA	1291
SHERBROOKE Robert St. V.	1228
SHER SHAH	1308
SHERWOOD-KELLY John	919
SHIELDS Robert	104
SHORT William H.	741
SHOUT Alfred J.	644
SIFTON Ellis W.	796
SIMPSON John	265
SIMPSON Rayene S.	1347
SIMS John J.	84
SINNOTT John	195
SINTON John A.	687
SKINNER John K.	866
SLEAVON Michael	256
SMITH Alfred	403
SMITH Alfred V.	684
SMITH Archibald B.	783
SMITH Clement L.	521
SMITH Edward B.	1038
SMITH Ernest A.	1299
SMITH Frederick A.	319
SMITH Henry	163
SMITH Issy	605
SMITH James	421
SMITH James A.	567
SMITH John (Sgt. 1857)	156
SMITH John (Priv. 1857)	206
SMITH John M.	409
SMITH Philip	85
SMYTH The Rt. Hon. Sir John	619
SMYTH Sir Nevill	430
SMYTHE Quentin G.M.	1212
SOMERS James	631
SPACKMAN Charles E.	920
SPALL Robert	1035
SPEAKMAN William	1343
SPENCE David	233
SPENCE Edward	260
STAGPOOLE Dudley	310
STANLAKE William	30
STANNARD Richard B.	1161
STARCEVICH Leslie T.	1335
STATTON Percy C.	1036
STEELE Gordon C.	1152
STEELE Thomas	777
STEWART William G.D.	220
STOKES James	1314
STONE Charles E.	954
STONE Walter N.	928
STORKEY Percy V.	976
STRACHAN Harcus	921
STRINGER George	690
STRONG George	109
STUART Ronald N.	831
STUBBS Frank E.	593
SUKANAIVALU Sefanaia	1275
SULLIVAN Arthur P.	1150
SULLIVAN John	58
SUTTON William	154
SWALES Edwin	1312
SYKES Ernest	806
SYLVESTER William H.T.	105
SYMONS George	14
SYMONS William J.	640
TAIT James E.	1027
TANDEY Henry	1099
TAYLOR John	86
TEESDALE Sir Christopher	108
TEMPLE William	313
THACKERAY Sir Edward	166
THAMAN GURUNG	1301
THOMAS Jacob	184
THOMAS John	929
THOMPSON Alexander	264
THOMPSON George	1306
THOMPSON James	138
THROSSELL Hugo V.H.	649
TILSTON Frederick A.	1315
TISDALL Arthur W. St. C.	597
TOLLERTON Ross	542
TOMBS Sir Henry	136
TOMBS Joseph H.	628
TOPHAM Frederick G.	1323
TOWERS James V.	1112
TOWNER Edgar T.	1062
TOWSE Sir Ernest	443
TOYE Alfred M.	966
TRAIN Charles W.	938
TRAVERS James	132
TRAVIS Richard C.	1019
TRAYNOR William B.	496
TRENT Leonard H.	1241
TREVOR William S.	326
TREWAVAS Joseph	88
TRIGG Lloyd A.	1245
TRIQUET Paul	1253
TUBB Frederick H.	642
TULBAHADUR PUN	1276
TURNBULL James Y.	723
TURNER Alexander B.	668
TURNER Hanson V.	1271
TURNER Sir Richard	491
TURNER Samuel	125
TURNER Victor B.	1223
TURRALL Thomas G.	725
TYTLER John A.	234
UMRAO SINGH	1304
UNWIN Edward	601
UPHAM Charles H.	1183 (& after 1213)
UPTON James	616
VALLENTIN John F.	553
VANN Bernard W.	1102
VEALE Theodore W.H.	733
VICKERS Arthur	661
VICKERS Sir Geoffrey	675
VICKERY Samuel	425
VOUSDEN William J.	354
WADESON Richard	142
WAIN Richard W.L.	922
WAKEFORD Richard	1266
WAKENSHAW Adam H.	1213
WALFORD Garth N.	606
WALKER Sir Mark	46
WALKER William G.	519
WALLACE Samuel T.D.	930
WALLER George	162
WALLER Horace	800
WALLER William F.F.	276
WALTERS George	47
WANKLYN Malcolm D.	1184
WARBURTON-LEE Bernard A.W.	1160
WARD Charles	475
WARD Henry	172
WARD James A.	1187
WARD Joseph	275
WARE Sidney W.	693
WARING William H.	1083
WARK Blair A.	1137
WARNEFORD Reginald A.J.	625
WARNER Edward	611
WASSALL Samuel	362
WATERS Sir Arnold	1147
WATKINS Sir Tasker	1287
WATSON Sir John	201
WATSON Oliver C.S.	973
WATSON Thomas C.	422
WATT Joseph	825
WEALE Henry	1050
WEARNE Frank B.	836
WEATHERS Lawrence C.	1072
WELCH James	816
WELLS Harry	662
WEST Ferdinand M.F.	1028
WEST Richard A.	1039
WESTON William B.	1318
WHEATLEY Francis	10
WHEATLEY Kevin A.	1345
WHEELER George C.	778
WHEELER George G.M.	582
WHIRLPOOL Frederick	253
WHITCHURCH Harry F.	412
WHITE Albert	826
WHITE Archie C.T.	760
WHITE Geoffrey S.	943
WHITE Sir George	349
WHITE Jack	780
WHITE William A.	1084
WHITFIELD Harold	945
WHITHAM Thomas	850
WHITTLE John W.	797
WILCOX Alfred	1078
WILKINSON Alfred R.	1127
WILKINSON Thomas (1855)	72
WILKINSON Thomas (1942)	1200
WILKINSON Thomas O.L.	727
WILLIAMS John (1879)	373
WILLIAMS John H. (1918)	1113
WILLIAMS William (1917)	832
WILLIAMS William C. (1915)	602
WILLIS Richard R.	595
WILMOT Sir Henry	243
WILSON Sir Arthur	400
WILSON Eric C.T.	1170
WILSON George	541
WOOD Harry B.	1118
WOOD Sir Evelyn	285
WOOD John A.	294
WOOD Wilfred	1136
WOODALL Joseph E.	996
WOODCOOK Thomas	874
WOODEN Charles	25
WOODROFFE Sidney C.	634
WOODS James P.	1085
WOOLLEY Geoffrey H.	584
WRIGHT Alexander	54
WRIGHT Peter H.	1250
WRIGHT Theodore	526
WRIGHT Wallace D.	516
WYATT George H.	530
WYLLY Guy G.E.	486
YATE Charles A.L.	531
YESHWANT GHADGE	1281
YOUENS Frederick	838
YOULL John S.	1011
YOUNG Alexander	505
YOUNG Frank E.	1086
YOUNG John F.	1073
YOUNG Thomas	967
YOUNG Thomas J.	221
YOUNG William	683
YOUNGER David R.	477
ZENGEL Raphael L.	1033
THE AMERICAN UNKNOWN WARRIOR	1351

Chapter Eleven
The First World War
1917

No's 769 - 941

The Victoria Cross, Military Medal and campaign medals awarded to Sergeant Harry Cator (793)

The Victoria Cross and campaign medals awarded to Corporal Edward Foster (811)

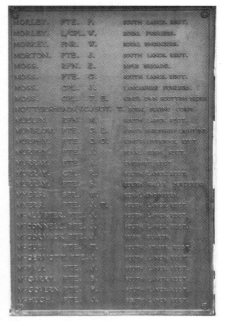

Widnes War Memorial

| 769 | **MOTTERSHEAD Thomas** | **VC DCM** | **Sergeant** | **20 Squadron, Royal Flying Corps** |

Born: 17 January 1892 - 6 Vine Street, Widnes, Lancashire
Died: 12 January 1917 aged 24. Died from severe burns at Bailleul Casualty Clearing Station, France, received during his VC action
Buried: 13 January at Bailleul Communal Cemetery Extension. 8 miles E. of Hazebrouk. Plot III. Row A. Grave 126. Headstone (See Map A - 10)
Deed/Service: 7 January 1917. When on a flying patrol, he was attacked at 9,000 feet and his craft set alight. Unable to subdue the flames, he managed to land behind Allied lines. The undercarriage collapsed, throwing the observer clear of the plane, but he was trapped in the burning cockpit
Commemoration: i) Headstone ii) Name on RAF Memorial in St. Clement Danes Church, Aldwych, London iii) Name on Widnes War Memorial iv) Two roads in Widnes named for him v) The Mottershead Scholarship at Widnes Technical College vi) A VC.10C. Mk 1 named for him

Near Ploegsteert, Belgium
POSTHUMOUS
892

Gazette: 12 February 1917

| 770 | **HENDERSON Edward Elers Delaval** | **VC** | **T/Lt. - Colonel** | **The North Staffordshire Regt. attd. Royal Warwickshire Regt.** |

The North Staffordshire Regt. attd. Royal Warwickshire Regt.
(now The Staffordshire Regt. and The Royal Regt. of Fusiliers)

River Hai, Kut, Mesopotamia
now Iraq
POSTHUMOUS
557

Born: 2 October 1878 - Simla, India
Died: 25 January 1917 aged 38. Died of wounds received in his VC action on the West bank of the River Hai, near Kut, Mesopotamia
Buried: Amara War Cemetery, Iraq. 150 miles S. of Baghdad. Plot XXIV. Row B. Grave 31. Name on wall plaque
Deed/Service: 25 January 1917. When his battalion suffered many casualties during a Turkish attack, the British line was penetrated in several places. Although wounded, he advanced alone ahead of his men, cheering them on under intensive fire over 500 yards of open ground. He was wounded again, but captured the position by bayonet charge, until wounded again and rescued by 771 Phillips
Commemoration: i) Possible headstone ii) Name on wall in Amara War Cemetery iii) Memorial in Garrison Church, Whittington Barracks, Lichfield, Staffs

Gazette: 8 June 1917

771	PHILLIPS Robin Edward VC Captain	13th Bn. Royal Warwickshire Regt. attd. 9th Bn. (now Royal Regt. of Fusiliers)	River Hai, Kut, Mesopotamia now Iraq

Born: 11 April 1895 - 'Hollhead House', Hill Top, West Bromwich, Staffordshire

Died: 23 September 1968 aged 73, in St. Veep, Lostwithiel, Cornwall

Buried: St. Veep Parish Churchyard. Headstone

Deed/Service: 25 January 1917 (T/Lieutenant) Following an attack on the Turkish lines, he went out to rescue 770 Henderson, who was lying mortally wounded in the open. Under heavy fire, he and a comrade succeeded in bringing their commanding officer to the safety of British lines **Gazette: 8 June 1917**

986

Commemoration: i) Headstone ii) Medals at The Royal Warwickshire Regimental Museum

772	MOTT Edward John VC DCM Sergeant	1st Bn. The Border Regiment (now King's Own Royal Border Regiment)	Near Le Transloy, France

Born: 4 July 1893 - Drayton, near Abingdon, Berkshire

Died: 20 October 1967 aged 74, at his home at 38 New Yatt Road, Witney, Oxfordshire

Cremated: 23 October at Oxford Crematorium. Ref: 32633. Ashes in Garden of Remembrance by an oak tree. Plaque in Cloister 3 - Space 1

Deed/Service: 27 January 1917. During an attack, his company were held up by machine-gun fire. Although severely wounded in the eye, he made a rush for the gun and captured both the gunner and gun. Due to his action the left flank of the attack was successful

891

Gazette: 10 March 1917

Commemoration: i) Plaque in Cloisters at Crematorium ii) Medals at The Border Regiment Museum

Pinaroo Cemetery

773	**MURRAY Henry William**	**VC CMG DSO & Bar DCM**	**Lieutenant - Colonel**	**13th Bn. (N.S.W.) Australian Imperial Force**	**Near Gueudecourt, France**

Born: 30 December 1884 - Evandale, Launceston, Tasmania, Australia

905

Died: 7 January 1966 aged 81, at Miles Hospital on the Darling Downs, Queensland, from a heart attack after a motoring accident on the 6th

Cremated: Mount Thompson Crematorium, Brisbane, Queensland. Memorial stone in Crematorium's Garden of Remembrance shows age 85

Deed/Service: 4 - 5 February 1917 (Captain) Led his company in a successful attack on Stormy Trench, repulsing three counter attacks. During the night they suffered heavy casualties, but he saved the situation by encouraging his men, leading bayonet charges and carrying the wounded to safety

Gazette: 10 March 1917

Commemoration: i) Memorial tablet at Crematorium ii) Memorial plaque on Wall 1 in Garden of Remembrance, Pinaroo Cemetery, Albany Creek, Queensland iii) Murray Crescent in Canberra, A.C.T iv) Display at the Australian War Memorial, Canberra

774	**BOOTH Frederick Charles**	**VC DCM**	**Captain**	**British South African Police, attd. Rhodesia Native Infantry**

Songea, German East Africa now Tanzania

104

Born: 6 March 1890 - Upper Holloway, North London

Died: 14 September 1960 aged 70, at St. Anne's, Kemptown, Brighton, Sussex

Buried: 18 September at Bear Road Cemetery, Brighton. Red Cross Plot. ZKZ - 36. Headstone

Deed/Service: 12 February 1917 (Sergeant) During an attack on an enemy position at Johannesbruck, near Songea, he went alone under heavy fire to bring to safety a wounded man. Later he rallied native troops who were badly disorganised and brought them to the firing line

Gazette: 8 June 1917

Commemoration: i) Headstone ii) Name on Roll of Honour, Big Classical, Cheltenham College, Gloucestershire

| 775 | PALMER Frederick William   VC MM   Second Lieutenant   22nd Bn. The Royal Fusiliers (now Royal Regiment of Fusiliers) | Near Courcelette, France |

Born: 11 November 1891 - Hammersmith, West London

957

Died: 10 September 1955 aged 63, at Lymington Hospital, Hampshire

Cremated: 14 September at Bournemouth Crematorium, Dorset. Ref: 17582. Ashes buried in family grave at All Saints Parish Churchyard, Hordle

Deed/Service: 16 - 17 February 1917 (Lance-Sergeant) He assumed command of his company when all officers had become casualties, then went out alone into no-mans-land cutting through wire entanglements under point-blank fire. He dislodged an enemy machine-gun, collected some other men and held the barricade for three hours against seven counter-attacks. When collecting more bombs, an eighth attack was delivered, threatening the advance of the whole flank, and although exhausted he rallied his men and finally drove the enemy back for good

Gazette: 3 April 1917

Commemoration: i) Name on family grave at Hordle

| 776 | CAMPBELL Gordon   VC DSO & 2 Bars   Vice - Admiral   Royal Navy | North Atlantic Ocean |

Born: 6 January 1886 - Croydon, Surrey

178

Died: 3 July 1953 aged 67, at Isleworth, Middlesex

Buried: All Saints Churchyard, Crondall, Hampshire. Headstone

Deed/Service: 17 February 1917 (Commander) While in command of HMS Q.5 (a 'mystery ship'), he sighted a torpedo track and altered course allowing the torpedo to hit Q.5. When the U-Boat surfaced within 100 yards of the ship, he sank it when almost all of the 45 shells fired hit their target

Gazette: 21 April 1917

Commemoration: i) Headstone

4

British troops near Sanna-y-yat

777	STEELE Thomas VC Sergeant 1st Bn. The Seaforth Highlanders (now The Highlanders)

Shumran Bend, Sanna-y-Yat
Mesopotamia, now Iraq
1182

Born: 6 February 1891 - Claytons, Springhead, Oldham, Lancashire
Died: 11 July 1978 aged 87, at his home, 1a Walkers, Springhead
Cremated: 17 July at Hollinwood Crematorium, Oldham. Ashes removed. No memorial tablet
Deed/Service: 22 February 1917. During the British attempt to relieve Kut, the Turks mounted a full-scale attack on their former trenches at Shumran Bend, near Sanna-y-Yat (also Sannaiyat). He kept a machine-gun in action at a critical moment, and was mainly responsible for keeping the entire British Line intact. When the enemy re-took a part of the trench, he led a successful counter-attack although seriously wounded **Gazette: 8 June 1917**
Commemoration:

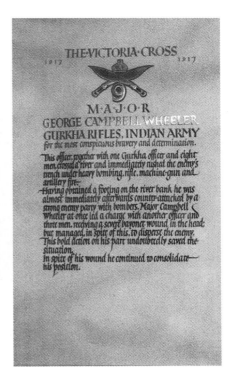

778	WHEELER George Campbell VC Lieutenant - Colonel 2nd Bn. 9th Gurkha Rifles, Indian Army

Shumran, Mesopotamia
now Iraq
1295

Born: 7 April 1880 - Yokohama, Japan
Died: 26 August 1938 aged 58, at Barton-on-Sea, Hampshire
Buried: St. Mary Magdalene Churchyard, New Milton, Hampshire. Headstone
Deed/Service: 23 February 1917 (Major) With a party of nine men he crossed the River Tigris, and under heavy fire captured an enemy trench. Immediately counter-attacked by Turkish bombers, he led a charge dispersing them, consolidating his position but received a bayonet wound to his head **Gazette: 8 June 1917**
Commemoration: i) Headstone ii) Plaque in Memorial Hall, Bedford School, Bedfordshire iii) Medals at the National Army Museum

5

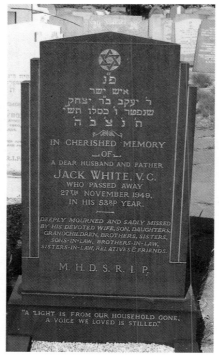

| 779 | READITT John VC Sergeant | 6th Bn. The South Lancashire Regiment (now The Queen's Lancashire Regiment) | Alqayat-al-Gaharbigah Bend, Mesopotamia now Iraq |

Born: 19 January 1897 - 34 Bamford Street, Clayton, Manchester, Lancashire
Died: 9 June 1964 aged 67, at his home in Bury Brow, Clayton
Buried: Gorton Cemetery, Manchester. Section Z. Grave 223. Headstone
Deed/Service: 25 February 1917 (Private) He advanced five times along a water course under heavy machine-gun fire, driving the enemy back and on each occasion was the only survivor. He then made several solo advances, until forced to retire at the enemy barricade, but continued to throw bombs. When support reached him he held a forward bend by bombing, until the position was consolidated
Commemoration: i) Headstone

1030

Gazette: 5 July 1917

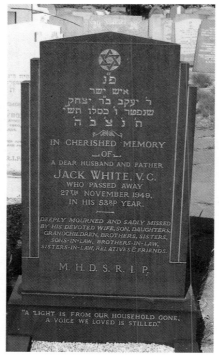

| 780 | WHITE Jack VC Lance - Corporal | 6th Bn. The King's Own (Royal Lancaster) Regt. (now King's Own Royal Border Regt.) | Dialah River, Mesopotamia now Iraq |

Born: 23 December 1896 - Leeds, Yorkshire. Born Jacob WEISS
Died: 27 November 1949 aged 52, at his home at 5 Bentley Road, Higher Broughton, Manchester, Lancashire (now Greater Manchester)
Buried: 28 November at the Jewish Cemetery, Blackley, Manchester. Section F. Grave 341. Headstone
Deed/Service: 7 - 8 March 1917 (Private) During an attempt to cross the river, two pontoons ahead of his came under heavy fire. When every man on his own pontoon was either dead or wounded, he tied a telephone line to it and jumped into the river, towing the wounded and munitions to safety
Commemoration: i) Headstone ii) Plaque outside City Art Gallery, Leeds iii) Memorial plaque in The Priory, Lancaster, Lancashire

1303

Gazette: 27 June 1917

781   **CATES George Edward   VC   Second Lieutenant   9th Bn. The Royal Irish Fusiliers (now disbanded)**

Near Bouchavesnes, France
POSTHUMOUS
195

Gazette: 11 May 1917

Born:	8 May 1892 - 86 Hartfield Road, Wimbledon, South West London
Died:	9 March 1917 aged 24. Died of wounds received during his VC action, near Bouchavesnes, France
Buried:	Hem Military Cemetery, Hem-Monacu, France. 5 miles W. of Peronne. Plot I. Row G. Grave 15. Headstone (See Map A - 30)
Deed/Service:	8 March 1917. When deepening a captured trench, his spade struck a buried bomb which started to burn. Without hesitation he put his foot on it and it exploded mortally wounding him, but by his selfless act he saved the lives of many men around him
Commemoration:	i) Headstone ii) Plaque in St. Mary's Church, Wimbledon iii) Medals at The Royal Green Jackets Museum

Delville Wood Memorial

782   **REID Oswald Austin   VC   Major   1st Bn. The King's (Liverpool) Regiment, attd. The Loyal North Lancashire Regiment**
                                                                (now The King's Regiment and The Queen's Lancashire Regiment)

Dailah River, Mesopotamia
now Iraq
1035

Gazette: 8 June 1917

Born:	2 November 1893 - Johannesburg, South Africa
Died:	27 October 1920 aged 26 in hospital in Johannesburg, from pneumonia brought on by gastro-enteritis
Buried:	Braamfontein Cemetery, Johannesburg. Section E.C. Plot 22932. Headstone
Deed/Service:	8 - 10 March 1917 (Captain) Having consolidated a small post on the opposite side of river to the main body, his lines of communication were cut when the pontoons sank. He held the position for thirty hours against constant heavy attacks, then with his ammunition running low and after repeated attempts to relieve him had failed, he effected a crossing of the river the next night during which he was wounded
Commemoration:	i) Headstone ii) Display in the South African Memorial, Delville Wood, Somme, France iii) Medals and sword at the National Museum of Military History, Johannesburg

Aberdeen War Memorial

| 783 | SMITH Archibald Bissett VC Temporary Lieutenant Royal Naval Reserve | Mid Atlantic Ocean POSTHUMOUS 1154 |

Born: 19 December 1878 - Cults, Aberdeenshire (now Grampian Region)
Died: 10 March 1917 aged 38. Aboard ship 350 miles East of the Azores, Atlantic Ocean, during his VC action
Buried: No known grave - name on the Tower Hill Memorial, City of London. Panel 14
Deed/Service: 10 March 1917. When in command of SS 'Otaki', he sighted a German armed raider who signalled him to stop. A duel ensued when he refused to do so, during which 'Otaki' scored a number of hits, but she was severely damaged and on fire. Smith ordered the crew to abandon ship, but stayed on board and went down with the ship

Gazette: 24 May 1919

Commemoration: i) Name on the Tower Hill Memorial ii) Name on Aberdeen War Memorial iii) Medals at the New Zealand Shipping Company, Auckland

| 784 | COX Christopher VC Private 7th Bn. The Bedfordshire Regiment (now Royal Anglian Regiment) | Achiet-le-Grand, France 267 |

Born: 25 December 1889 - Kings Langley, Hertfordshire
Died: 28 April 1959 aged 69, at the Hill End Hospital, Kings Langley
Buried: Kings Langley Cemetery. Headstone
Deed/Service: 13 March 1917. During an attack by the battalion, the front wave was checked by intense artillery and machine-gun fire and the whole line took cover in shell craters. Going out alone he rescued four wounded men, following this by rescues on the ensuing two days

Gazette: 11 May 1917

Commemoration: i) Headstone

| 785 | McNAMARA Frank Hubert   VC CB CBE   Air Vice - Marshal | 1 Squadron, Australian Flying Corps (now R.A.A.F.) | Near Tel-el-Hesi, Egypt |

Born: 4 April 1896 - Waranga, near Rushworth, Victoria, Australia. Some records show born in 1894

810

Died: 2 November 1961 aged 65, as a result of a fall in the garden at his home in Gerards Cross, Buckinghamshire

Buried: St. Joseph's Priory, Austin Wood, Gerards Cross. Headstone

Deed/Service: 20 March 1917 (Lieutenant) During an bombing raid, a fellow pilot force landed behind enemy lines with hostile cavalry approaching. Although wounded, he landed close to the damaged plane and the downed pilot climbed aboard, but due to his injury he could not keep it straight and it turned over. Both men crawled out, set fire to it and managed to start the damaged craft which he flew them to safety

Gazette: 8 June 1917

Commemoration: i) Headstone ii) Name on RAF Memorial in St. Clement Danes Church, Central London iii) Display at the Australian War Memorial, Canberra, A.C.T. iv) Medals at the R.A.F. Museum

Australian War Memorial

| 786 | CHERRY Percy Herbert   VC MC   Captain   26th Bn. (Q.&T.) Australian Imperial Force | Langnicourt, France |

POSTHUMOUS

Born: 4 June 1895 - Murradoc, Drysdale, Victoria, Australia

208

Died: 27 March 1917 aged 21. Killed in action at Langnicourt, France the day after his VC action

Buried: Queant Road Cemetery, Buissy, France. 13 miles S.E. of Arras. Plot VIII. Row C. Grave 10. Headstone (See Map A - 20)

Deed/Service: 26 March 1917. While in command of a company detailed to clear a village he became the only officer to survive the attack. Despite fierce opposition he took the village and beat off many counter-attacks. Although wounded he remained at his post until killed by a shell

Gazette: 11 May 1917

Commemoration: i) Headstone ii) Medals and display at the Australian War Memorial, Canberra, A.C.T., Australia

| 787 | HARVEY Frederick Maurice Watson   VC MC   Brigadier | Lord Strathcona's Horse, Canadian Expeditionary Force | Guyencourt, France |

Born: 1 September 1888 - Athboy, Co. Meath, Ireland   542
Died: 24 August 1980 aged 91, following a long illness, at Trinity Lodge, Glenmore Trail, Calgary, Alberta, Canada
Buried: Union Cemetery, Fort McLeod, Alberta. Headstone
Deed/Service: 27 March 1917 (Lieutenant) During a mounted attack, the leading troop commanded by Harvey, suffered many casualties from close-range fire. Seeing a wired trench containing a machine-gun, he leapt from his horse over the wire, shot the crew and captured the gun   **Gazette: 8 June 1917**
Commemoration: i) Headstone ii) Mount Harvey in Jasper National Park, Alberta iii) Harvey Barracks, Calgary iv) Medals in Museum of the Regiments, Calgary

| 788 | JENSEN Joergan Christian   VC   Temporary Sergeant   50th Bn. (S.A.) Australian Imperial Force | Noreuil, France |

Born: 15 January 1891 - Loegstoer, Aalborg, Denmark. Many records, including his headstone, show first name as Jorgen   639
Died: 31 May 1922 aged 31, at St. Peters, Adelaide, South Australia, having never fully recovered from his wounds
Buried: West Terrace A.I.F. Cemetery, Adelaide. Light Oval Section - 4 West. Grave 3. Headstone
Deed/Service: 2 April 1917 (Private) With five comrades he attacked a barricade, behind which were 45 of the enemy and a machine-gun. One of his party shot the gunner as he rushed the post and threw in a bomb. He forced the rest to surrender, sending one of them to another group of Germans ordering them to surrender, which they did. When Allied troops fired on them, he stood on the parapet under fire waving until the firing stopped   **Gazette: 8 June 1917**
Commemoration: i) Headstone ii) Medals and display at the Australian War Museum, Canberra, A.C.T.

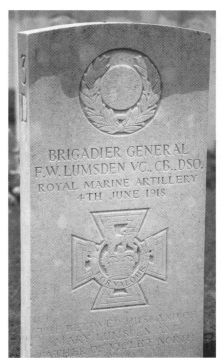

789 **LUMSDEN Frederick William** **VC CB DSO & 3 Bars** **Brigadier - General** **Royal Marine Artillery** **Francilly, France**

Born:	14 December 1872 - Fyzabad, India
Died:	4 June 1918 aged 45. Killed in action by a shot in the head from a sniper while responding to an alarm, at Blairvill, near Arras, France
Buried:	Berles New Military Cemetery, Berles au Bois, France. 10 miles N.E. of Doullens. Plot III. Row D. Grave 1. Headstone (See Map A - 19)
Deed/Service:	3 - 4 April 1917 (Major) Led four artillery teams and a party of infantry to bring in six captured field-guns, which had been left 300 yards in front of British lines. During the entire period the Germans kept the guns under heavy fire, and despite casualties they retrieved all the guns. He made three journeys to the guns and remained there under constant fire until the last gun had been recovered
Commemoration:	i) Headstone ii) Plaque in Garrison Church, Eastney, Hampshire iii) Name on Aberdeen War Memorial iv) Lumsden Road, Gosport, Hampshire v) Portrait in Bristol Grammar School vi) Monument and medals at the Royal Marines Museum

757

Gazette: 8 June 1917

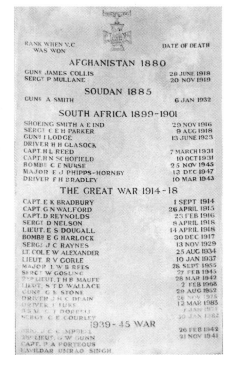

790 **GOSLING William** **VC** **Major** **3rd Wessex Brigade, Royal Field Artillery (now Royal Regiment of Artillery)** **Near Arras, France**

Born:	15 August 1892 - Wanborough, near Swindon, Wiltshire
Died:	12 February 1945 aged 53, at Summerhouse Farm, Wroughton, Wiltshire following a long illness
Buried:	St. John & St. Helen's Churchyard Cemetery Extension, Wroughton. West side. Headstone
Deed/Service:	5 April 1917 (Sergeant) When a faulty bomb fell ten yards from his mortar section, he sprang out quickly unscrewed the fuse and threw it onto the ground where it exploded. His action saved the lives of the whole detachment
Commemoration:	i) Headstone ii) Name on memorial in R.A. Chapel, Woolwich, South East London

467

Gazette: 14 June 1917

| 791 | NEWLAND James Ernest   VC MSM   Major   12th Bn. (S. A., W. A. & Tasmania) Australian Imperial Force | Bapaume and Langnicourt, France 924 |

Born: 22 August 1882 - Highton, Geelong, Victoria, Australia. Shown as John in some records
Died: 19 March 1949 aged 66, at his home 54 Brigg Street, Caulfield, Victoria following a seizure
Buried: East Brighton General Cemetery, Melbourne, Victoria. Methodist Section. Compartment G. Grave 174A. Headstone
Deed/Service: 7 - 9 April 1917 (Captain) Led a bombing attack on an important objective, rallying his men who had suffered heavy casualties. Having captured the position, his company repulsed a heavy counter-attack and succeeded in holding their ground. On 15 April, an adjoining company was overpowered and his own attacked from the rear, his tenacity and courage spurred his men to hold out and repel the attack   **Gazette: 8 June 1917**
Commemoration: i) Headstone ii) Newland Street, Canberra, A.C.T. iii) Medals and display at the Australian War Memorial, Canberra

| 792 | BRYAN Thomas   VC   Lance - Corporal   25th (S) Bn. The Northumberland Fusiliers (now Royal Regiment of Fusiliers) | Near Arras, France 140 |

Born: 21 January 1882 - Bott Lane, Lye, near Stourbridge, Worcestershire
Died: 13 October 1945 aged 63, at his home 44 Askearn Road, Bentley, Doncaster, Yorkshire
Buried: 17 October at Arksey Cemetery, Doncaster. Section J. Grave 237. Headstone
Deed/Service: 9 April 1917. Wounded during an attack which was held up by a machine-gun, he went forward along a communication trench, approached the gun from the rear, killed two of the team and disabled the gun, allowing the advance to continue
Commemoration: i) Headstone ii) Plaque at Castleford Civic Centre, Yorkshire iii) Bryan Close, Castleford   **Gazette: 8 June 1917**

British trench lines, Arras, 1975

| 793 | CATOR Harry VC MM Captain 7th Bn. The East Surrey Regiment (now P.O.W. Royal Regiment) | Near Arras, France |

Born: 24 January 1894 - Drayton, Norwich, Norfolk

197

Died: 7 April 1966 aged 72, in the Norfolk and Norwich Hospital, Norwich from pneumonia

Buried: 13 April in Sprowston Cemetery. Headstone

Deed/Service: 9 April 1917 (Sergeant) After his platoon had suffered many casualties from an enemy machine-gun, he and another advanced across open ground under fire, until his companion was killed. Picking up a Lewis gun, he reached the German trench where he attacked another machine-gun, and killed the entire crew. While holding the end of the trench, a bombing squad captured 100 prisoners and five machine-guns **Gazette: 8 June 1917**

Commemoration: i) Headstone

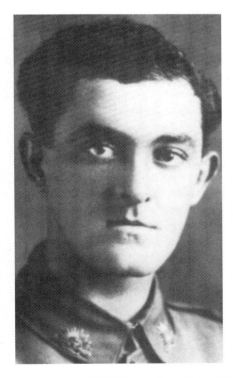

| 794 | KENNY Thomas James Bede VC Corporal 2nd Bn. (N.S.W.) Australian Imperial Force | Hermies, France |

Born: 29 September 1896 - Paddington, Sydney, New South Wales, Australia

683

Died: 15 April 1953 aged 56, at the Concord Repatriation Hospital, Sydney, from a 'combination of illnesses'

Buried: Botany Cemetery, Matraville, Sydney, also known as Eastern Suburbs Cemetery. Roman Catholic Section 3. Grave 441. Headstone

Deed/Service: 9 April 1917 (Private) When his platoon was held up by an enemy strong point, he dashed forward alone killed one man and bombed the position. He captured the gun crew, all of whom had been wounded, killed an officer and seized the gun **Gazette: 8 June 1917**

Commemoration: i) Headstone ii) The Bede Kenny Memorial Ward, Wentworth Private Hospital, Randwick, Sydney (1957) iii) Medals and display at the Australian War Memorial, Canberra, A.C.T.

13

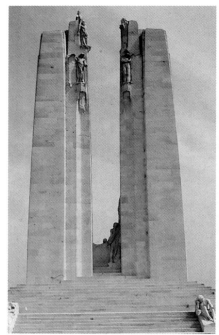

Vimy Memorial

| 795 | MILNE William Johnstone | VC | Private | 16th Bn. Manitoba Regiment (Canadian Scottish), Canadian Expeditionary Force | Near Thelus, France |

795   MILNE William Johnstone   VC   Private   16th Bn. Manitoba Regiment (Canadian Scottish), Canadian Expeditionary Force   Near Thelus, France
                                                                POSTHUMOUS

Born: 21 December 1891 - 8 Anderson Street, Cambusnethan, near Wishaw, Lanarkshire, Scotland   873

Died: 9 April 1917 aged 25. Killed in action near Vimy, France, shortly after his VC action

Buried: Has no known grave - name on the Vimy Memorial, France. 8 miles N. of Arras (See Map A - 20)

Deed/Service: 9 April 1917. Noticing an enemy machine-gun firing on his comrades, he crawled on hands and knees and captured it after killing the crew. Later, he captured another machine-gun in the support line, killing another gun team, but was killed shortly afterwards   **Gazette: 8 June 1917**

Commemoration: i) Name on the Vimy Memorial   ii) Medals at the Canadian War Museum, Ottawa

Menin Gate

796   SIFTON Ellis Welwood   VC   Lance - Sergeant   18th Bn. Western Ontario Regiment, Canadian Expeditionary Force   Neuville-St-Vaast, France
                                                                POSTHUMOUS

Born: 12 October 1891 - Wallacetown, Ontario, Canada

Died: 9 April 1917 aged 25. Killed in action during his VC deed, at Neuville-St-Vaast, France

Buried: Lichfield Crater (Cemetery), Thelus, France. 4 miles N. of Arras. Special wall memorial (See Map A - 20)

Deed/Service: 9 April 1917. When his company were held up by an enemy machine-gun inflicting many casualties, he charged it alone and killed the crew. Later a party of Germans advanced on him, but he held them off with his bayonet until help arrived, but was killed in the ensuing fight   **Gazette: 8 June 1917**

Commemoration: i) Name on plaque in cemetery   ii) Name on Menin Gate, Ypres   iii) Memorial plaque in St.Peter's Cemetery, Tyrconnel, Wallacetown
                  iv) Medal at Elgin County Museum, Ontario

| 797 | WHITTLE John Woods   VC DCM   Sergeant   12th Bn. (S.A., W.A. & Tasmania) Australian Imperial Force | Near Boursies, France |

Born: 3 August 1883 - Huon Island, near Port Cygnet, Tasmania, Australia

1307

Died: 2 March 1946 aged 52, at his home at 27 Avenue Road, Glebe, Sydney, New South Wales, Australia

Buried: Rookwood Cemetery, Sydney. Roman Catholic Section 15. Grave 63. Headstone

Deed/Service: 9 April 1917. When a large enemy force occupied the trench held by his platoon, he led a charge regaining the position. The Germans then broke through the line, enfilading his position with machine-gun fire, he rushed across the fire-swept ground, killed its crew and captured the gun

Gazette: 8 June 1917

Commemoration: i) Headstone ii) Whittle Street, Canberra, A.C.T. iii) Display at the Australian War Museum, Canberra

| 798 | MacDOWELL Thain Wendell   VC DSO   Colonel   38th Ottawa Bn. Eastern Ontario Regiment, Canadian Expeditionary Force | Vimy Ridge, France |

Born: 16 September 1890 - Lachute, Quebec, Canada

776

Died: 27 March 1960 aged 69 in Nassau, Bahamas. Most references show 29 March

Buried: Oakland Cemetery, R.R.3, Brockville, Ontario, Canada. Anglican Section 3. Lot 112. The Richardson family plot. Headstone

Deed/Service: 9 April 1917 (Captain) With the assistance of two men, he captured two machine-guns, two officers and 75 men. Although wounded in the hand, he held the position for five days, in spite of heavy shell fire, until eventually relieved by his battalion

Gazette: 8 June 1917

Commemoration: i) Headstone ii) Memorial plaque at Maitland Road at Highway 2, Maitland, Ontario iii) Medals at the University of Toronto Memorial Trust, Ontario

799	**PATTISON** John George **VC** Private	**50th Bn. Alberta Regiment (Calgary Regiment), Canadian Expeditionary Force**	**Vimy Ridge, France**

799   PATTISON John George **VC** Private   **50th Bn. Alberta Regiment (Calgary Regiment), Canadian Expeditionary Force**

Vimy Ridge, France

971

Born: 8 September 1875 - Woolwich, South East London
Died: 3 June 1917 aged 41. Killed two months after his VC action, during an attack on a generating station at Lieven, near Lens, France
Buried: La Chaudiere Military Cemetery, France. 7 miles N. of Arras. Plot VI. Row C. Grave 14. Headstone shows age 42 (See Map A - 20)
Deed/Service: 10 April 1917. When an advance was held up by an enemy machine-gun inflicting heavy casualties, he ran forward jumping from shell-hole to shell-hole, reaching cover just thirty yards from the gun. Under heavy fire he threw bombs which killed and wounded some of the crew, he then ran forward and bayoneted the surviving gunners. His initiative and valour undoubtedly saved the situation, allowing the advance to continue

Gazette: 2 August 1917

Commemoration: i) Headstone ii) Pattison Mountain, The Victoria Cross Range, Jasper National Park, Alberta iii) Name on Memorial in Lewisham Civic Centre South East London iv) Medals in the Glenbow Museum, Calgary, Alberta

800   WALLER Horace   **VC** Private   **10th (S) Bn. The King's Own Yorkshire Light Infantry (now The Light Infantry)**

**South of Heninel, France
POSTHUMOUS**

1264

Born: 23 September 1897 - 11 Woodhill Terrace, Batley Carr, Dewsbury, Yorkshire
Died: 10 April 1917 aged 19. Killed in action during his VC deed, south of Heninel, France
Buried: Cojeul British Cemetery, St. Martins-sur-Cojeul, France. 5 miles S.E. of Arras. Row C. Grave 55. Headstone shows age 20 (See Map A - 20)
Deed/Service: 10 April 1917. Was with a bombing section forming a block in the enemy line, when the Germans made a violent attack on his position. Five of his section were killed, but the attack was repulsed. He was the sole survivor, but continued to throw bombs for half an hour until he was killed

Gazette: 8 June 1917

Commemoration: i) Headstone ii) Horace Waller VC Parade, Shawcross Business Park, Dewsbury iii) Name on the family grave in Dewsbury Cemetery iv) Name on Dewsbury War Memorial v) Name on Batley Carr War Memorial

801	**MACKINTOSH Donald VC Lieutenant 3rd Bn. The Seaforth Highlanders (now The Highlanders)**	North of Fampoux, France

POSTHUMOUS
803

Born:	7 February 1896 - Partick, Glasgow, Scotland
Died:	11 April 1917 aged 21. Killed in his VC action north of Fampoux, France
Buried:	Brown's Copse Cemetery, France. 5 miles E. of Arras. Plot II. Row C. Grave 49. Headstone (See Map A - 20)
Deed/Service:	11 April 1917. During an advance he was shot through the leg, and although crippled continued to lead his men and captured the trench. Collecting men who had lost their leaders, he drove back a counter-attack, but was wounded again and unable to stand. With fifteen men left, he crawled out of the trench and encouraged them to advance toward their final objective, during which he was mortally wounded

Gazette: 8 June 1917

Commemoration: i) Headstone ii) Medals at The Highlanders Museum

802	**MUGFORD Harold Sandford VC Lance - Corporal 8th Squadron, Machine Gun Corps (now disbanded)**	Monchy-le-Preux, France

897

Born:	31 August 1894 - St. James's, Central London
Died:	16 June 1958 aged 73, at his home in Chignall Road, Chelmsford, Essex. He had been paralysed and in a wheelchair for forty years
Cremated:	19 June at Southend Crematorium, Essex. Ref: 6340. Ashes scattered in June Section, Garden of Remembrance. No memorial tablet
Deed/Service:	11 April 1917. Under intense fire he got his machine-gun into a forward exposed position, from which he dealt very effectively with the enemy Almost immediately his No.2 was killed and he was severely wounded, but refusing to leave his post he continued to inflict severe damage until a shell broke both his legs, but he remained with the gun. He was wounded again while being moved to a dressing station

Gazette: 26 November 1917

Commemoration: i) Medals at the Imperial War Museum

17

| 803 | CUNNINGHAM John VC Corporal 2nd Bn. The Prince of Wales Leinster Regiment (now disbanded) | Bois-en-Hache, France POSTHUMOUS |

Born: 22 October 1890 - Hall Street, Thurles, Co. Tipperary, Ireland

Died: 16 April 1917 aged 26. Died in a field hospital near Barlin, France from wounds received during his VC action

Buried: Barlin Communal Cemetery, France. 5 miles S. of Bethune. Plot II. Row A. Grave 39. Headstone (See Map A - 19)

Deed/Service: 12 April 1917. When in command of a Lewis gun section he came under heavy fire, and although wounded succeeded in reaching his target almost alone. Counter-attacked by twenty Germans, he exhausted his ammunition and began throwing bombs until wounded again. He continued to fight single-handed until his bombs were used up and died four days later from his wounds

Commemoration: i) Headstone ii) Memorial tablet in St. Mary's Church, Thurles

287

Gazette: 8 June 1917

| 804 | ORMSBY John William VC MM Sergeant 2nd Bn. The King's Own Yorkshire Light Infantry (now The Light Infantry) | Favet, France |

Born: 11 January 1881 - Dewsbury, Yorkshire. Several sources state born 1889

Died: 29 July 1952 aged 71, at his home in 28 Low Road, Dewsbury

Buried: Dewsbury Cemetery. Section R. Grave 718. Headstone

Deed/Service: 14 April 1917. When acting as company sergeant-major during operations to capture an important position, he set a fine example by showing complete indifference to heavy machine-gun and rifle fire. After clearing a village of numerous snipers, he took command of the company when all officers had become casualties, and led them forward under heavy fire for 400 yards to a new position, holding it until relieved

Commemoration: i) Headstone ii) John Ormsby VC Way, Shawcross Business Park, Dewsbury iii) Medals at King's Own Yorkshire Light Infantry Museum

948

Gazette: 8 June 1917

805	POPE Charles VC Lieutenant 11th Bn. (W.A.) Australian Imperial Force	Louveral, France

POSTHUMOUS

995

Born: 5 March 1883 - Mile End, East London
Died: 15 April 1917 aged 34. Killed in action during his VC deed at Louveral, France
Buried: Moeuvres Communal Cemetery Extension, France. 8 miles W. of Cambrai. Plot V. Row D. Grave 22. Headstone (See Map A - 20)
Deed/Service: 15 April 1917. When in command of an important picquet post, he was ordered to hold it at all costs. The Germans attacked and surrounded the post with superior numbers and although ammunition was running low, he was seen to charge with his men into the enemy by whom they were overpowered. His body, with many of his men, was found among eighty enemy dead

Gazette: 8 June 1917

Commemoration: i) Headstone ii) Pope Street, Canberra, A.C.T., Australia iii) Medals and display at the Australian War Memorial, Canberra

806	SYKES Ernest VC Private 27th (S) Bn. The Northumberland Fusiliers (now The Royal Regiment of Fusiliers)	Near Arras, France

1198

Born: 4 April 1885 - Quick View, Mossley, Saddleworth, Yorkshire
Died: 3 August 1949 aged 64, at his home 17 Thornfield Avenue, Lockwood, Yorkshire
Buried: Lockwood Cemetery, Meltham, near Huddersfield, Yorkshire. Section F. Grave 227. Headstone
Deed/Service: 19 April 1917. With his battalion held up by intense fire from front and flank, he went forward alone on four occasions bringing back a wounded man each time. He went out a fifth time, in conditions which appeared to mean certain death, until he had tended to all men unable to be moved

Gazette: 8 June 1917

Commemoration: i) Headstone ii) Plaque outside George Lawton Hall, Stamford Street, Ashton-under-Lyne, Manchester iii) Name on memorial outside the Manchester Regimental Museum iv) Patriot Class loco named for him v) Medals and loco nameplate at the Northumberland Fusiliers Museum

807 MELVIN Charles VC Private 2nd Bn. The Black Watch (Royal Highlanders)

Istabulat, Mesopotamia
now Iraq
859

Born:	2 May 1885 - Boddin Craig, Montrose, Scotland
Died:	17 July 1941 aged 56, at Kirriemuir, Tayside Region, Scotland
Buried:	Kirriemuir Cemetery. Headstone
Deed/Service:	21 April 1917. When his company were waiting for reinforcements before attacking a front-line Turkish trench, he rushed forward alone across fire-swept ground. Reaching the trench, he killed several Turks before attacking the rest with his bayonet. Most fled before he killed two more and disarmed nine others, including a wounded man, whose injuries he tended before bringing them to our lines
Commemoration:	i) Headstone ii) Name on the Kirriemuir War Memorial, located in the cemetery iii) Medals at The Black Watch Museum

Gazette: 26 November 1917

808 GRAHAM Sir Reginald VC OBE Lieutenant - Colonel 9th Bn. The Argyll & Sutherland Highlanders (Princess Louise's)
attd.136th Coy. Machine Gun Corps (now disbanded)

Istabulat, Mesopotamia
now Iraq
475

Born:	17 September 1892 - Calcutta, India. Born John Reginald Noble GRAHAM
Died:	6 December 1980 aged 88, in Edinburgh
Cremated:	11 December at Morton Hall Crematorium, Edinburgh. Ashes buried in front of memorial cross in crematorium ground. No memorial tablet
Deed/Service:	22 April 1917 (Lieutenant) Was in command of a machine-gun section under heavy fire. When many of the crew became casualties, he carried ammunition until wounded, then operated one of the guns until forced to retire when the gun was damaged and he was wounded. He brought a Lewis gun into action until wounded again and compelled to retire
Commemoration:	i) Medals at the Argyll & Sutherland Highlanders Museum

Gazette: 14 September 1917

809   HENDERSON Arthur   VC MC   A/Captain   4th Bn. The Argyll & Sutherland Highlanders, attd. 2nd Bn.

Fontaine-les-Croisilles
France
556

Gazette: 5 July 1917

Born: 6 May 1893 - 18 Greenhill Road, Egnal, Paisley, Scotland
Died: 24 April 1917 aged 23. Killed in action the day after his VC action, whilst holding his position at Fontaine-les-Croisilles, France
Buried: Cojeul British Cemetery, St. Martin-sur-Cojeul, France. 5 miles S.E. of Arras. Row B. Grave 61. Headstone (See Map A - 20)
Deed/Service: 23 April 1917. Although wounded in the arm, he led his company through the enemy front line until he gained his objective. Despite heavy bombing and machine-gun fire he consolidated his position, and by his cheerful courage he inspired his men under the most difficult circumstances
Commemoration: i) Headstone ii) Memorial in Paisley Abbey, Glasgow iii) Memorial in Ferguslie Cricket Club, Paisley

Site of his VC action

810   HIRSCH David Philip   VC   A/Captain   4th Bn. The Yorkshire Regiment (now The Green Howards)

Near Wancourt, France
POSTHUMOUS
573

Gazette: 14 June 1917

Born: 28 December 1896 - Weetwood Grove, Leeds, Yorkshire
Died: 23 April 1917 aged 20. Killed during his VC action, near Wancourt, France
Buried: Has no known grave - name on the Arras Memorial, France. W. suburbs of Arras. Bay 5 (See Map A - 20)
Deed/Service: 23 April 1917. During an attack, and having taken his first objective despite being wounded, he returned over the fire-swept slopes to satisfy himself that a defensive flank had been established. He continuously exposed himself to intense enemy machine-gun fire in order to steady and encourage his men, until during a heavy German counter-attack, he was killed standing on the parapet
Commemoration: i) Name on the Arras Memorial ii) Plaque in St. Joseph's Community Home, Nantwich, Cheshire iii) Plaque outside City Art Gallery, Leeds iv) Medals at the Green Howards Museum

811	**FOSTER Edward VC Corporal 13th Bn. The East Surrey Regiment (now P.O.W. Royal Regiment)**	**Villers Plouich, France**

Born:	4 February 1886 - Tooting Grove, Streatham, South West London
Died:	22 January 1946 aged 59, from bronchial pneumonia in St. James's Hospital, Tooting, South West London
Buried:	Streatham Cemetery, Garrett Lane, Tooting. New headstone erected June 1997
Deed/Service:	24 April 1917. During an attack, the advance was held up by two entrenched machine-gun posts. With two Lewis guns he entered the trench and engaged the enemy before bombing them, killing the gunners and capturing the guns
Commemoration:	i) Headstone ii) Foster's Way, King George's Park, Wandswoth, South West London iii) Plaque in Villers Plouich

423

Gazette: 27 June 1917

Pensioners home, Lenton

812	**BALL Albert VC DSO & 2 Bars MC T/Captain 7th Bn. The Sherwood Foresters and Royal Flying Corps**	**Missions over France**
	(now Worcestershire & Sherwood Foresters and Royal Air Force respectively)	**POSTHUMOUS**

Born:	14 August 1896 - Lenton, Nottingham, Nottinghamshire
Died:	7 May 1917 aged 20. Died from wounds received when his S.E.5 crashed following aerial combat, near Seclin, France
Buried:	9 May at Annoeullin Communal Cemetery, German Extension, France. 6 miles N.E. of Lens. Grave 643. Headstone (See Map A - 20)
Deed/Service:	25 April to 6 May 1917. He took part in 26 combats in the course of which he destroyed eleven hostile aircraft, brought down two out of control and forced several others to land. On one occasion when flying solo, he fought six enemy machines, twice he fought five and once four, his craft often being badly damaged. On returning with a damaged plane he had to be restrained from immediately going out in another
Commemoration:	i) Headstone ii) Statue in Nottingham Castle grounds iii) Name on Nottingham War Memorial iv) Pensioners Home in Lenton named for him v) Name on Memorial in St.Clement Danes, Central London vi) A VC.10C Mk 1 named for him vii) Medals at Sherwood Foresters Museum

47

Gazette: 8 June 1917

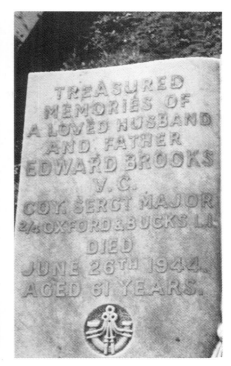

813	**BROOKS Edward** **VC** **Company Sergeant - Major**	**2/4th Bn. The Oxfordshire & Buckinghamshire Light Infantry** **(now The Royal Green Jackets)**	**St. Quentin, France**

Born:	11 April 1883 - Oakley, Buckinghamshire	127
Died:	26 June 1944 aged 61, at his home 42 Morrell Avenue, Oxford from a thrombosis	
Buried:	Rose Hill Cemetery, Oxford. Plot G - 2. Grave 119. Headstone	
Deed/Service:	28 April 1917. During a raid, the front wave was being held up by an enemy machine-gun inflicting many casualties, he ran forward from the second wave, shot one gunner and bayoneted the other and then turned the gun on the retreating enemy. His action preventing many casualties	
		Gazette: 27 June 1917
Commemoration:	i) Headstone ii) Medals at The Royal Green Jackets Museum	

St. Mary's Churchyard

814	**HAINE Reginald Leonard** **VC MC & Bar** **Lieutenant - Colonel** **1st Bn. Honourable Artillery Company**	**Near Gavrelle, France**

Born:	10 July 1896 - Wandsworth, South West London	507
Died:	12 June 1982 aged 85, in St. Thomas's Hospital, Lambeth, South London	
Cremated:	17 June at Chichester Crematorium, Sussex. Ref: 19750. Ashes in Garden of Remembrance. Section J - 60. No memorial plaque	
Deed/Service:	28 - 29 April 1917 (Second Lieutenant) When holding a salient under a heavy enemy attack, he led six bombing parties against a German strong point, capturing it and fifty prisoners. The enemy counter-attacked, regaining some lost ground, but he formed a 'block' in his trench and held the position overnight. The next day he again attacked and recaptured the position, inspiring his men throughout thirty hours of continuous fighting	
		Gazette: 12 June 1917
Commemoration:	i) Plaque on wall of St.Mary's Churchyard, Easebourne-by-Midhurst, Sussex ii) Name on altar rail in St. Mary's iii) H.A.C. plaque at Gavrelle	

815	POLLARD Alfred Oliver	VC MC & Bar DCM	Second Lieutenant	1st Bn. Honourable Artillery Company	Gavrelle, France

Born: 4 May 1893 - Melbourne Road, Wallington, Surrey

Died: 4 December 1960 aged 67, at his home 18 Queen's Park Gardens, Bournemouth, Dorset

Cremated: 7 December at Bournemouth Crematorium. Ref: 29729. Ashes scattered in Garden of Remembrance. No memorial tablet

Deed/Service: 29 April 1917. When men of various units became disorganised following a retirement under heavy fire, he led a four-man counter-attack, pressing it home until the enemy attack broke up. As a result much lost ground was recaptured, his example inspiring courage into his men

Commemoration: i) Medals with The Honourable Artillery Company

992

Gazette: 8 June 1917

816	WELCH James	VC	Sergeant	1st Bn. The Royal Berkshire Regiment (now Royal Gloucester, Berkshire & Wilts Reg.)	Near Oppy, France

Born: 7 July 1889 - Stratfield Saye, north of Basingstoke, Hampshire

Died: 28 June 1978 aged 88, at his home 80 Pinehurst Park, West Moors, Bournemouth, Dorset

Cremated: 4 July at Bournemouth Crematorium. Ref: 99115. Ashes in family grave, North Cemetery, Bournemouth. Section F. 9-18. Headstone

Deed/Service: 29 April 1917 (Lance-Corporal) After entering an enemy trench he engaged in fierce hand-to-hand fighting, chasing and capturing four Germans armed with an empty revolver. He then kept a machine-gun in action for five hours, going out under fire to collect ammunition, until wounded

Commemoration: i) Headstone ii) Portrait and medals at The Duke of Edinburgh's Regimental Museum

1287

Gazette: 27 June 1917

817   **SANDERS William Edward   VC DSO   Lieutenant - Commander   Royal Naval Reserve**   **Eastern Atlantic Ocean**

Born: 7 February 1883 - Auckland, New Zealand   **1104**
Died: 14 August 1917 aged 34. Killed in action when HMS 'Prize' was sunk by another U-Boat off Southern Ireland.
Buried: His body not recovered when the ship went down
Deed/Service: 30 April 1917 (A/Lieutenant) When in command of HMS 'Prize', a three-masted schooner a 'Q' or 'mystery' ship, he was attacked
                    by a German U-Boat 180 miles south of Ireland. When badly damaged, the 'Panic Party' took to the boats as the U-Boat approached to
                    within eighty yards whereupon the White Ensign was hoisted. In spite of damage, 'Prize' opened fire and within minutes the submarine
                    caught fire and sank   **Gazette: 22 June 1917**
Commemoration: i) Name on The Portsmouth Naval Memorial, Panel 23 - Column 1 ii) 'Sanders Cup', New Zealand's premier sailing trophy named for him

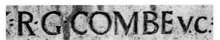

Vimy Memorial

818   **COMBE Robert Grierson   VC   Lieutenant   27th Bn. Manitoba Regiment, Canadian Expeditionary Force**   **South of Acheville, France**
                                                                                                                                                                          POSTHUMOUS
Born: 5 August 1880 - Aberdeen, Scotland   **239**
Died: 3 May 1917 aged 36. Killed during his VC action, south of Acheville, France
Buried: Has no known grave - name on the Vimy Memorial, France. 8 miles N. of Arras (See Map A - 20)
Deed/Service: 3 May 1917. Steadying and leading his company under heavy fire he reached his objective with just five men remaining. He proceeded
                    to bomb the enemy causing heavy casualties, and by collecting small bands of men succeeded in capturing the objective, together with 80
                    prisoners. He repeatedly charged the enemy, driving them before him, but while personally leading his bombers was killed by a sniper   **Gazette: 27 June 1917**
Commemoration: i) Name on Vimy Memorial ii) Name on family headstone, Allen Vale Cemetery, Aberdeen iii) Name on Aberdeen War Memorial
                    iv) Lake in North Saskatchewan named for him v) Medals in the Saskatchewan Archives, Regina, Saskatchewan, Canada

Arras Memorial

| 819 | HARRISON John | VC MC | T/Second Lieutenant | 11th (S) Bn. The East Yorkshire Regt. (now Prince of Wales Regt.) | Oppy, France POSTHUMOUS 536 |

Born: 2 November 1890 - 20 Williamson Street, Drypool, Sculcoates, Kingston-upon-Hull, Yorkshire (now Humberside)

Died: 3 May 1917 aged 26. Reported missing, believed killed following his VC action at Oppy, France

Buried: Has no known grave - name on the Arras Memorial, France. W. suburbs of Arras. Bay 4 - 5 (See Map A-20)

Deed/Service: 3 May 1917. Despite darkness created by smoke from British and German barrages, he twice led his company against an enemy trench sited in a wood under heavy fire, but was repulsed. He then made a solo dash on a machine-gun post, hoping to knock it out, but was never seen again

Commemoration: i) Name on the Arras Memorial ii) Plaque in St. John's College, York iii) Plaque at Hull Rugby Club iv) Medals at P.O.W. Regimental Museum

Gazette: 14 June 1917

V.C. JARRATT G.

| 820 | JARRATT George | VC | Corporal | 8th Bn. The Royal Fusiliers (now The Royal Regiment of Fusiliers) | Near Pelves, France POSTHUMOUS 632 |

Born: 22 July 1891 - Kennington, South East London

Died: 3 May 1917 aged 25. Killed during his VC action near Pelves, France

Buried: Has no known grave - name on the Arras Memorial, France. W. suburbs of Arras. Bay 3 (See Map A-20)

Deed/Service: 3 May 1917. After he had been taken prisoner with some wounded men, he was placed in an dug-out. Later that day the enemy were driven back by a British attack, and a live grenade fell near him. He immediately put both feet on it and the explosion blew off his legs, his action saving the lives of those around him. The wounded were later removed to Allied lines, but he died before he could be moved

Commemoration: i) Name on the Arras Memorial ii) Medals at The Royal Fusiliers Museum

Gazette: 8 June 1917

821	**HEAVISIDE Michael Wilson VC Private 15th Bn. The Durham Light Infantry (now The Light Infantry)**	**Fontaine-les-Croiselles France**

Born: 20 October 1880 - Durham City, Co. Durham
554

Died: 26 April 1939 aged 58, at Bloemfontein Terrace, Craghead, Co. Durham, following a long illness due to effects of gas poisoning from the War

Buried: 30 April at St. Thomas's Churchyard, Craghead, Co. Durham. Grave not marked. Location unknown, church records destroyed in fire

Deed/Service: 6 May 1917. When a wounded man was seen lying some forty yards from the enemy line, he volunteered to take food and water to him. He reached the man despite heavy fire, finding him demented with thirst as he had been there for four days and later brought him to safety   **Gazette: 8 June 1917**

Commemoration: i) Medals at The Durham Light Infantry Museum

822	**HOWELL George Julian VC MM Staff - Sergeant 1st Bn. (N.S.W.) Australian Imperial Force**	**Near Bullecourt, France**

Born: 23 November 1893 - Enfield, Sydney, New South Wales
600

Died: 23 December 1963 aged 71, at the Repatriation General Hospital, Hollywood, Perth, Western Australia

Cremated: 29 December at Karrakatta Crematorium, Hollywood. Ref: 13858. Ashes in Garden of Remembrance. Plaque on Wall 2. Row D. (See Map - F)

Deed/Service: 6 May 1917 (Corporal) Seeing a German party were likely to outflank his battalion, on his own initiative and under heavy bomb and rifle fire, he climbed to the top of the parapet and bombed the enemy. When his stock of bombs was exhausted, he continued the attack with his bayonet, but was severely wounded. His prompt and gallant action was seen by the whole battalion, inspiring them in the later successful counter-attack   **Gazette: 27 June 1917**

Commemoration: i) Plaque at Karrakatta Cemetery ii) Howell Soldiers Club, Randwick, Sydney iii) Howell Place, Canberra, A.C.T. iv) Display at Australian War Memorial, Canberra

823	**DRESSER Tom VC Private 7th Bn. The Yorkshire Regiment (now The Green Howards)**		**Near Roeux, France**
Born:	21 July 1892 - Westgate, Pickering, Yorkshire		**350**
Died:	9 April 1982 aged 89, at his home 63 Errol Street, Middlesbrough, Cleveland		
Buried:	15 April at Thorntree Cemetery, Conway Drive, Middlesbrough. Ref: 26183. R.C. Section. Grave 1901 - Lawn. Not named on family stone		
Deed/Service:	12 May 1917. In spite of being in great pain as result of two wounds, he succeeded in carrying an important message from battalion HQ to the front line trenches, which he reached in an exhausted condition. His courage and determination at a critical time proved vital to his battalion		
			Gazette: 27 June 1917
Commemoration:	i) Medals at The Green Howards Museum		

824	**MOON Rupert Vance VC Captain 58th Bn. (Victoria) Australian Imperial Force**		**Near Bullecourt, France**
Born:	14 August 1892 - Bacchus Marsh, Victoria, Australia		**883**
Died:	28 February 1986 aged 93, at the Bellarine Private Hospital, Whittington, Victoria		
Buried:	4 April at Mount Duneed Cemetery, Victoria. C. of E. Section. Headstone		
Deed/Service:	12 May 1917 (Lieutenant) When given the task of taking a position in front of an enemy trench and also the trench itself, he was wounded while taking the first objective. He was wounded again during the second assault but inspired and encouraged his men in taking it and was wounded a third time when consolidating the position. A fourth wound forced his retirement		
			Gazette: 14 June 1917
Commemoration:	i) Headstone ii) Medals and display at the Australian War Memorial, Canberra, A.C.T.		

825	**WATT Joseph VC Chief Skipper Royal Naval Reserve**	Straits of Otranto, Adriatic

1283

Born: 25 June 1887 - Gardenstown, Gamrie, Banff, Scotland
Died: 13 February 1955 aged 67, at Fraserburgh, Grampian Region, Scotland
Buried: Kirktown Cemetery, Fraserburgh. Headstone
Deed/Service: 15 May 1917 (Skipper) When in command of the Drifter HMS 'Gowan Lea' between Albania and S.E. Italy, he was attacked by an Austrian light cruiser and called on to surrender. He ordered full speed ahead, and called on the crew to fight to the death. The cruiser opened fire and disabled the only gun, causing heavy damage and many casualties. Watt managed to get to partial safety and helped remove the dead and wounded
Commemoration: i) Headstone

Gazette: 29 August 1917

826	**WHITE Albert VC Sergeant 2nd Bn. The South Wales Borderers (now The Royal Regiment of Wales)**	Monchy-le-Preux, France **POSTHUMOUS**

1299

Born: 1889 - 54 Lamb Street, Kirkdale, Liverpool, Lancashire
Died: 19 May 1917 aged 27. Killed during his VC action during the Battle of Arras, at Monchy-le-Preux
Buried: Has no known grave - name on The Arras Memorial, France. West suburbs of town. Bay 6 (See Map A - 20)
Deed/Service: 19 May 1917. During an attack, he realised that a machine-gun would hold-up the whole advance of his company, and dashed ahead to capture it. When within a few yards of it he fell dead riddled with bullets, sacrificing his life trying to ensure the success of the attack
Commemoration: i) Name on Arras Memorial ii) Name on panel in Havard Chapel, Brecon Cathedral, Powys

Gazette: 27 June 1917

  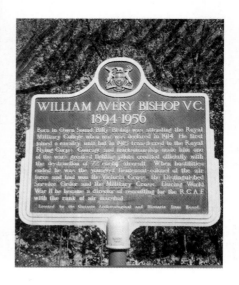

827   **BISHOP William Avery   VC CB DSO & Bar MC DFC   Air - Marshal   Canadian Cavalry & 60 Squadron, Royal Flying Corps**   Near Cambrai, France

Born: 8 February 1894 - Owen Sound, Ontario, Canada   93

Died: 11 September 1956 aged 62, at Palm Beach, Florida, U.S.A.

Cremated: St. James's Crematorium, Toronto, Ontario. Ref: 56199. Ashes buried in Greenwood Cemetery, Owen Sound. Headstone

Deed/Service: 2 June 1917 (Captain) When on a solo flying patrol, he flew to an enemy aerodrome where several planes were standing with their engines running. As one took off he quickly shot it down, then fired at a second causing its pilot to crash into a tree. When two more took off he emptied his Lewis gun into one bringing it down, then fired at the fourth causing it to dive away. Afterwards he flew his damaged aircraft back to the Filescamp base   **Gazette: 11 August 1917**

Commemoration: i) Headstone ii) Memorial plaque at Queen's Park, Owen Sound iii) Plaque and display at his former home in Owen Sound iv) Name on memorial in St. Clement Danes, Strand, Central London v) Medals and display at the Canadian War Museum, Ottawa

  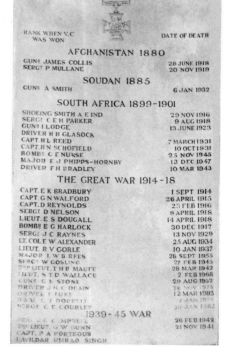

828   **MAUFE Thomas Harold Broadbent   VC Captain   124th Siege Bty. Royal Garrison Artillery (now Royal Regiment of Artillery)**   Feuchy, France

Born: 6 May 1898 - Kings Road, Ilkley, Yorkshire   846

Died: 28 March 1942 aged 43. Accidentally killed during mortar practice at a Home Guard exercise on Manor Farm, Blubberhouses Moor, Ilkley

Buried: Ilkley Cemetery. Row A. Grave 768. Headstone

Deed/Service: 4 June 1917 (Second Lieutenant) Under intense fire and on his own initiative, he repaired unaided a damaged telephone wire between the forward and rear position allowing his battery to open fire with accuracy. He then extinguished a fire in an ammunition dump, regardless of risks involved   **Gazette: 2 August 1917**

Commemoration: i) Headstone ii) Memorial at site of death iii) Memorial at Uppingham School, Leicestershire iv) Memorial in R.A. Chapel, Woolwich, S.E. London

829   **CRAIG John Manson VC Second Lieutenant 1/4th Bn. The Royal Scots Fusiliers, attd. 1/5th (now Royal Highland Fusiliers)**   **Near Suez Canal, Egypt**

Born:	5 March 1896 - Innergeldie, Comrie, near Crieff, Perthshire (now Tayside Region), Scotland	**269**
Died:	19 February 1970 aged 73, at Crieff	
Cremated:	20 February at Perth Crematorium, Crieff Road, Perth. Ref: 4489. Ashes buried in family plot at Comrie Cemetery. Name not on headstone	
Deed/Service:	5 June 1917. When an advanced post had been rushed by the Turks, he organised a counter-attack and drove them back. He then formed a party to rescue the casualties under heavy fire, personally rescuing an NCO and a medical officer, being wounded himself taking the latter to safety	**Gazette: 2 August 1917**

Commemoration:

830   **GRIEVE Robert Cuthbert VC Captain 37th Bn. (Victoria) Australian Imperial Force**   **Messines, Belgium**

Born:	19 June 1889 - Brighton, Melbourne, Victoria, Australia	**495**
Died:	4 October 1957 aged 68, from cardiac failure when at his office in Melbourne	
Buried:	Springvale Cemetery, Melbourne. Presbyterian Section. Headstone	
Deed/Service:	7 June 1917. When his company suffered heavy casualties during an attack, he went on ahead under heavy fire and located two machine-guns responsible. He succeeded in bombing and killing the two gun crews, then reorganized the remnants of his own company and gained his original objective. He had set a splendid example and when he finally fell wounded, the position had been secured	**Gazette: 2 August 1917**
Commemoration:	i) Headstone ii) Display at Australian War Memorial, Canberra, A.C.T. iii) Medals and scholarship in his name at the Wesley College, Melbourne, Victoria, Australia	

831   **STUART Ronald Niel   VC DSO RD   Captain   Royal Naval Reserve**

Atlantic Ocean
ELECTED BY BALLOT
1191

Born: 26 August 1886 - 31 Kelvin Grove, Toxteth Park, Liverpool, Lancashire
Died: 8 February 1954 aged 67, at his home 'Beryl Lodge' in Charing, Kent
Buried: Charing Cemetery. Headstone
Deed/Service: 7 June 1917 (Lieutenant) Was serving on HMS 'Pargust', a 'Q' or 'Mystery Ship', whose task it was to invite attack by U-Boats. When torpedoed by a U-Boat, which caused damage to the engine room, the 'Panic Party' rowed away as the U-Boat surfaced, it's captain believing that a merchant vessel had been hit. The commander of 'Pargust' gave the order to open fire when the submarine was fifty yards away. The U-Boat tried to dive, but had being severely damaged and sank. During the action, 832 Williams was also awarded the VC
Commemoration: i) Headstone ii) Stuart Close in Lee-on-Solent, Hampshire iii) Medals in the National Maritime Museum

Gazette: 20 July 1917

832   **WILLIAMS William   VC DSM & Bar   Seaman   Royal Naval Reserve**

Atlantic Ocean
ELECTED BY BALLOT
1315

Born: 5 October 1890 - 6 Well Street, Amlwch Port, Anglesey, Gwynedd, Wales
Died: 22 October 1965 aged 75, at his home in Station Street, Holyhead, Anglesey
Buried: Amlwch Cemetery, Anglesey. Headstone
Deed/Service: 7 June 1917. With 831 Stuart, was on board HMS 'Pargust' a 'Q' or 'Mystery Ship', when torpedoed by a U-Boat, causing damage to the engine room. As the 'Panic Party' went away, the U-Boat surfaced fifty yards away thinking that 'Pargust' was a merchant vessel. Before 'Pargust' was ready to open fire, one of the gun covers had been loosened by the explosion and Williams physically prevented the heavy covers from falling and betraying the ship to the enemy. He succeeded, and the U-Boat was sunk by numerous hits
Commemoration: i) Headstone ii) Plaque in Amlwch Sailing Club iii) Council School and an Estate named for him at Amlwch Port iv) Medals at National Museum of Wales, Cardiff

Gazette: 20 July 1917

833   CARROLL John   VC   Lance - Corporal   33rd Bn. (N.S.W.) Australian Imperial Force   **St. Yves, France**

Born: 16 August 1892 - Brisbane, Queensland, Australia. References state incorrectly born in 1891   **188**

Died: 4 October 1971 aged 79, at the Repatriation General Hospital, Hollywood, Perth, Western Australia

Buried: Karrakatta Cemetery, Perth. R.C. Section KA. Plot 658. Headstone (See Map - F)

Deed/Service: 7 - 12 June 1917 (Private) During an attack, he rushed the enemy's trench and bayoneted four occupants, then went to the assistance of a wounded comrade, killing another of the enemy. He attacked a machine-gun post single-handed, killing three of the crew and captured the gun. Later when two of his comrades were buried by a shell, he managed to rescue them under heavy fire   **Gazette: 2 August 1917**

Commemoration: i) Headstone ii) Carroll Street, Canberra, A.C.T. iii) Medals and display at the Australian War Memorial, Canberra

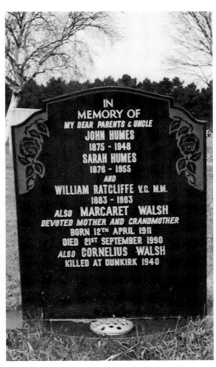

834   RATCLIFFE William   VC MM   Private   2nd Bn. The South Lancashire Regiment (now The Queen's Lancashire Regiment)   **Messines, Belgium**

Born: 21 March 1883 - 5 Linden Street, West Derby, Lancashire   **1021**

Died: 26 March 1963 aged 80, in Liverpool

Buried: Allerton Cemetery, Liverpool. R.C. Section 19. Grave 274. Headstone

Deed/Service: 14 June 1917. After an enemy trench had been captured, he located a machine-gun firing on his comrades from the rear. He rushed the gun and killed the crew single-handed, then brought the gun back into action in the front line. He had displayed similar gallantry on previous occasions   **Gazette: 2 August 1917**

Commemoration: i) Headstone ii) Memorial in the Transport and General Worker's Union Club, South Liverpool. Memorial has apparently now been lost

Priory Churchyard

| 835 | DUNVILLE John Spencer VC Second Lieutenant 1st Royal Dragoons (now The Blues & Royals) | North of St.Quentin, France |

Born: 7 May 1896 - 46 Portland Place, Marylebone, Central London

Died: 26 June 1917 aged 21. Died of wounds received in his VC action in a Casualty Clearing Station near Epehy, France

Buried: Villiers-Faucon Communal Cemetery, France. 6 miles N.E. of Peronne. Row A. Grave 21. Headstone (See Map A - 30)

Deed/Service: 24 - 25 June 1917. In order to demolish a vital enemy section of wire, he placed himself between a Royal Engineer NCO and the enemy, enabling the work to be completed. Although severely wounded in the chest and arm he continued to direct the wire cutting until the raid was over, but died the following day

Commemoration: i) Headstone ii) Name on family headstone in Priory Churchyard, Hollywood Abbey, Co. Down, Northern Ireland. Grave 178/188 iii) Name on Hollywood War Memorial iv) Plaque and memorial window at St. Mary's C. of I. Church, Hollywood v) Medals at the Household Cavalry Museum

POSTHUMOUS
362

Gazette: 2 August 1917

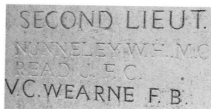

| 836 | WEARNE Frank Bernard VC Second Lieutenant 3rd Bn. The Essex Regiment, attd. 11th Bn. (now Royal Anglian Regiment) | East of Loos, France |

Born: 1 March 1894 - Kensington, West London

Died: 28 June 1917 aged 23. Killed in action during his VC deed, East of Loos, France

Buried: Has no known grave - name on the Loos Memorial, Dud Corner Cemetery, France. 4 miles N.W. of Lens. Panel 85-87 (See Map A - 20)

Deed/Service: 28 June 1917. When commanding a raiding party on the enemy's trenches, he gained his objective and held it against repeated counter-attacks Fearing that if his left flank was lost his men would have to give way, he leapt on the parapet firing and throwing bombs until mortally wounded

Commemoration: i) Name on the Loos Memorial ii) Memorial at Bromsgrove School, Worcestershire

POSTHUMOUS
1285

Gazette: 2 August 1917

34

837	**FRICKLETON Samuel VC Captain 3rd Bn. 3rd New Zealand (Rifle) Brigade, New Zealand Expeditionary Force**	**Messines, Belgium**

Born: 1 April 1891 - Slamannan, Stirlingshire, Scotland

430

Died: 6 September 1971 aged 80, at Hutt Hospital, Naene, near Wellington, New Zealand following a long illness

Buried: Taita Servicemen's Cemetery, Naena, New Zealand. Plot 1188. Headstone

Deed/Service: 7 June 1917 (Lance-Corporal) Although wounded, he dashed forward at the head of his section, pushed into our barrage and personally bombed an enemy machine-gun and crew which was causing heavy casualties. He then attacked a second gun killing the entire crew of twelve. By these actions, he undoubtedly saved his own and other units from severe casualties. Whilst consolidating this position, he received another wound

Gazette: 2 August 1917

Commemoration: i) Headstone ii) Memorial at HQ, Dunedin R.S.A., New Zealand iii) Medals at Queen Elizabeth II Army Museum, Walouru, New Zealand

838	**YOUENS Frederick VC T/ Second Lieutenant 13th Bn. The Durham Light Infantry (now The Light Infantry)**	**Near Hill 60, Belgium** **POSTHUMOUS**

Born: 14 August 1892 - High Wycombe, Buckinghamshire

1341

Died: 7 July 1917 aged 24. Died of wounds at the Casualty Clearing Station, near Hill 60, Ypres, received during his VC action

Buried: Railway Dugouts Burial Ground, Belgium. 2 miles SE of Ypres, Belgium. Plot I. Row O. Grave 3. Headstone (See Map A - 11)

Deed/Service: 7 July 1917. When the enemy were reported to be about to raid our trenches, he rallied a disorganised Lewis gun team although he had been wounded. While doing this an enemy bomb fell on the Lewis gun position without exploding, he picked it up and hurled it over the parapet. A second bomb landed which exploded in his hand, severely wounding him and some men, from which he succumbed

Gazette: 2 August 1917

Commemoration: i) Headstone ii) Name on Wycombe War Memorial, Buckinghamshire iii) Plaque in High Wycombe Church iv) Brass plaque and portrait in the Royal Grammar School, High Wycombe v) Prayer desk at St. Andrew's Chapel, High Wycombe vi) Medals in the Durham Light Infantry Museum

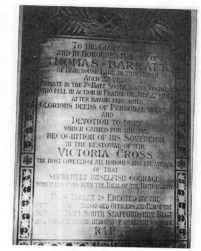

THIS TABLET IS ERECTED
TO THE IMPERISHABLE MEMORY OF
PRIVATE TOM BARRETT, V.C
LATE OF THE 7TH BATTALION
SOUTH STAFFORDSHIRE REGIMENT

Whittington Barracks

Coseley Parish Church

839	BARRATT Thomas VC Private	7th Bn. The South Staffordshire Regiment (now The Staffordshire Regiment)	North of Ypres, Belgium

Born: 5 May 1895 - 9 Foundry Street, Darkhouse, Coseley, near Dudley, Worcestershire

Died: 27 July 1917 aged 22. Killed following his VC action, near Ypres, Belgium

POSTHUMOUS
53

Buried: Essex Farm Cemetery, Boesinghe, Belgium. 2 miles N of Ypres. Plot I. Row Z. Grave 8. Headstone. Original stone named Barrett

Deed/Service: 27 July 1917. When on patrol as a scout under heavy fire, he twice came under fire from snipers whom he stalked and killed. As the Germans began to outflank them, he volunteered to cover the withdrawal which he did, but was killed by a shell on reaching our lines

Commemoration: i) Headstone ii) Memorial in Coseley Parish Church iii) Memorial in Garrison Church, Whittington Barracks, Lichfield, Staffordshire iv) Memorial in Darkhouse Baptist Church v) Barratt Court, Batmans Hill Road, Princes End, Coseley vi) Medals at the Staffordshire Regimental Museum

Gazette: 6 September 1917

840	ANDREW Leslie Wilton VC DSO Brigadier	2nd Bn. Wellington Infantry Regiment, New Zealand Expeditionary Force	La Bassee Ville, France

Born: 23 March 1897 - Ashurst, Palmerston North, New Zealand

Died: 8 January 1969 aged 71, at Palmerston North Hospital following a short illness

30

Buried: 11 January at Levin RSA Cemetery, Tiro Tiro Road, Palmerston North. Returned Servicemen's Section. Row 13. Headstone

Deed/Service: 31 July 1917 (Corporal) Was in charge of a small party during an attack on a machine-gun post located in an isolated building. On leading his men forward, he came across another machine-gun which was holding up another company. He immediately attacked it, capturing the gun and killing several of its crew before taking the original objective

Commemoration: i) Headstone ii) Memorial at HQ, Dunedin Returned Servicemen's Association, New Zealand

Gazette: 6 September 1917

36

841 **BEST - DUNKLEY Bertram   VC   T/Lieutenant - Colonel   2/5th Bn. The Lancashire Fusiliers (now Royal Regt. of Fusiliers)** Wieltje, Belgium
POSTHUMOUS
357

Born: 3 August 1890 - York
Died: 5 August 1917 aged 27, from wounds received in his VC action at a Casualty Clearing Station near Ypres, Belgium
Buried: Mendinghem Military Cemetery, Belgium 12 miles N.W. of Ypres. Plot III. Row D. Grave 1. Headstone (See Map A - 10)
Deed/Service: 31 July 1917. When the leading waves of an attack became disorganised by machine-gun and rifle fire at close range, he dashed forward
and rallied his men then led a counter-attack. He continued to lead his battalion until all objectives had been gained. A later enemy advance
threatened the British line, he collected his battalion HQ and successfully counter-attacked, although seriously wounded in the action   **Gazette: 6 September 1917**
Commemoration: i) Headstone ii) Plaque at Tientsin Grammar School, China, defaced during Cultural Revolution - now No. 20 Tianjin High School

842 **BYE Robert James   VC   Sergeant - Major   1st Bn. Welsh Guards**   Yser Canal, Belgium
161

Born: 12 December 1889 - 13 Maritime Street, Pontypridd, Glamorgan, Wales
Died: 23 August 1962 aged 72 at his daughter's home, 49 Hammerwater Drive, Warsop, Nottinghamshire
Buried: 28 August at Warsop Cemetery. Grave 2129. Headstone
Deed/Service: 31 July 1917 (Sergeant) During an attack he saw the leading waves being stopped by two enemy block-houses. He rushed at one and put
the garrison out of action, then rejoined his company and went forward to the second objective. He volunteered to take charge of a
party to clear a line of block-houses which had been passed and succeeded in taking all the objectives, capturing over seventy prisoners
in the process   **Gazette: 6 September 1917**
Commemoration: i) Headstone ii) Memorial in Guards Chapel, Wellington Barracks, London iii) Medals at Welsh Guards Museum

843 COFFIN Clifford VC CB DSO & BAR Major - General Corps of Royal Engineers, comd. 25th Infantry Brigade Westhoek, Belgium

228

Born: 10 February 1870 - Blackheath, London
Died: 4 February 1959 aged 88 at Torquay, Devon
Buried: Holy Trinity Churchyard, Colemans Hatch, Tunbridge Wells, Kent. Headstone
Deed/Service: 31 July 1917 (T/Brigadier General) When his command was held up due to heavy fire, he went forward to check the forward positions. Under fire and in an exposed position, he calmly walked from shell-hole to shell-hole inspiring his men, and by his courage and example the line was held

Gazette: 14 September 1917

Commemoration: i) Headstone ii) Medals at Royal Engineers Museum

St. Peters Church

844 COLYER - FERGUSSON Thomas Riversdale VC A/Captain 2nd Bn. Northamptonshire Regt. (now Royal Anglian Regt.) Bellewaarde, Belgium
POSTHUMOUS
399

Born: 18 February 1896 - 13 Lower Berkeley Street, Central London
Died: 31 July 1917 aged 21. Shot in the head by a sniper shortly after his VC action at Bellewaarde, Belgium
Buried: Menin Road South Military Cemetery, Belgium. 1 mile E. of Ypres. Plot II. Plot E. Grave 1. Headstone (See Map A - 11)
Deed/Service: 31 July 1917. When he found himself with just six men, he carried out a planned attack and successfully captured an enemy trench. During a counter-attack, assisted only by his orderly, he attacked and captured an enemy machine-gun, turning it on the assailants. Later with the help of a sergeant, he attacked and captured a second enemy gun, but fell soon afterwards from a snipers bullet

Gazette: 6 September 1917

Commemoration: i) Headstone ii) Plaque and memorial window in St. Peters Church, Ightham, Kent iii) Name on Ightham War Memorial iv) Medals at the Northamptonshire Regimental Museum

845 DAVIES James Llewellyn VC Corporal 13th Bn. The Royal Welch Fusiliers Polygon Wood, Belgium
POSTHUMOUS
307

Born:	16 March 1886 - Fronwen, Wyndham, Ogmore Vale, Glamorgan
Died:	31 July 1917 aged 31. Died in a Casualty Clearing Station near Pilckem, Belgium from wounds received in his VC action
Buried:	Canada Farm Cemetery, Belgium. 5 miles N.W. of Ypres. Plot II. Row B. Grave 18. Headstone (See Map A - 11)
Deed/Service:	31 July 1917. During an attack on the enemy line, he single-handed attacked a machine gun emplacement after several men had been killed trying to take it. He bayoneted one of the gun crew and brought in another, together with the captured gun. Then although dangerously wounded, he led a bombing raid on a defended house and killed a sniper who had been harassing his platoon

Gazette: 6 September 1917

Commemoration: i) Headstone ii) Name on Nantymoel War Memorial, Glamorgan iii) Portrait at Berwyn Centre, Nantymoel iv) Medals with Royal Welch Fusiliers

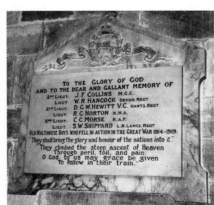

St. George's Church

Hursley Church

846 HEWITT Dennis George Wyldbore VC Second Lieutenant 14th Bn. Hampshire Regt. (now Royal Hampshire Regt.) St. Julien, Belgium
POSTHUMOUS
565

Born:	18 December 1897 - Mayfair, Central London
Died:	31 July 1917 aged 19. Killed after his VC action near St. Julien, N.E. of Ypres, Belgium
Buried:	Has no known grave - name on The Menin Gate Memorial, Ypres, Belgium. Panel 35 (See Map A - 11)
Deed/Service:	31 July 1917. Whilst waiting for a barrage to lift, he was hit by a piece of shrapnel which ignited the signal lights in his haversack and set fire to his equipment and clothes. He extinguished the flames and despite severe pain, he led the remnants of the company under intense machine-gun fire and captured his objective. He was subsequently killed by a sniper while inspecting the consolidation and encouraging his men

Gazette: 14 September 1917

Commemoration: i) Name on Menin Gate Memorial ii) Plaque at St. George's Church, Langton Matravers, Dorset iii) Memorial and his original cross in Hursley Church, near Winchester, Hampshire iv) Name on War Memorial Cloister at Winchester College v) Hewitt Close, Gosport, Hampshire

847	**MAYSON Tom Fletcher**	**VC**	**Lance - Sergeant**	**1/4th Bn. The King's Own Regiment (now King's Own Royal Borderers)**	Wieltje, Belgium

852

Born: 3 November 1893 - 'The John Bull Inn', Silecroft, Cumberland (now Cumbria)

Died: 21 February 1958 aged 68, at the North Lonsdale Hospital, Barrow-in-Furness, Lancashire

Buried: St Mary's Churchyard, Whicham, near Silecroft. Headstone

Deed/Service: 31 July 1917. When his platoon was held up by machine-gun fire, he suddenly attacked and disabled the gun with bombs, wounding four of the team, the remaining three fled to a dug out where he killed them. Later when clearing up a strong-point he tackled a second gun killing all six of the crew and took charge of an isolated post, sucessfully holding it during an attack

Commemoration: i) Headstone ii) Memorial at The Priory, Lancaster iii) Memorial at Millom Museum, Cumbria iv) Medals and memorial at St Mary's Church

Gazette: 14 September 1917

848	**McINTOSH George Imlach**	**VC**	**Private**	**1/6th Bn. The Gordon Highlanders (now The Highlanders)**	Ypres, Belgium

788

Born: 22 April 1897 - 80 Portessie, Rathven, Banffshire, Scotland

Died: 20 June 1960 aged 63, at Woodend Hospital, Aberdeen, Scotland, from a heart disease

Buried: New Cemetery, Buckie, Banff. Headstone

Deed/Service: 31 July 1917 (Private) During the consolidation of a position, his company came under machine-gun fire. He attacked the post with a Mills grenade, killing two of the enemy and wounding a third. Later he found two machine guns which he retrieved. His grasp of the situation and the speed with which he acted allowed the position to be held and saved the live of many of his comrades

Commemoration: i) Headstone ii) McIntosh Avenue, Buckie iii) Medals in The Gordon Highlanders Museum

Gazette: 6 September 1917

CODWYD Y PLAC HWN ER COF AM
SARSIANT IFOR REES
11FED BATALIWN O FFINWYR DE CYMRU
A DDYFARNIWYD Â CHROES VICTORIA AM EI
WEITHREDOEDD YN PILCKEM, GWLAD BELG,
AR 31AIN O ORFFENNAF, 1917

THIS PLAQUE WAS ERECTED
IN MEMORY OF
SERGEANT IFOR REES
11TH BATTALION
THE SOUTH WALES BORDERERS
WHO WAS AWARDED
THE VICTORIA CROSS FOR HIS ACTION
AT PILCKEM, BELGIUM
ON 31ST JULY, 1917.

Llanelly Town Hall

849	REES Ivor	VC	Company Sergeant - Major	11th Bn. The South Wales Borderers (now Royal Regiment of Wales)	Pilckem, Belgium

Born: 18 October 1893 - Union Street, Felinfoel, near Llanelly, Camarthenshire, (now Dyfed) Wales — 1032

Died: 11 March 1967 aged 73, at his home 5 Craddock Street, Llanelly

Cremated: 14 March 1967 at Morriston Crematorium, Swansea. Ref: 17791. Ashes in Garden No.5 in the Garden of Remembrance. No memorial

Deed/Service: 31 July 1917. An enemy machine-gun opened fire at close range inflicting many casualties. He led the platoon forward, working his way round to the rear of the position and single handed killed two of the team and bombed the concrete emplacement. He killed five and captured thirty prisoners together with an undamaged gun

Commemoration: i) Wooden plaque in Brecon Cathedral, Wales ii) Brass tablet in Llanelly Town Hall

Gazette: 14 September 1917

IN LOVING MEMORY OF
Pte. THOMAS WHITHAM V.C.
1st Batt. Coldstream Guards
DIED OCTOBER 22nd 1924,
AGED 36 YEARS.

Erected as a token of esteem,
by the Coldstream Guards.

850	WHITHAM Thomas	VC	Private	1st Bn. Coldstream Guards	Pilckem, Belgium

Born: 11 May 1888 - Worsthorne, near Burnley, Lancashire — 1306

Died: 22 October 1924 aged 36, at Oldham Royal Infirmary, Lancashire, of Peritonitis

Buried: 27 October at Inghamite Burial Ground, Wheatley Lane, Nelson, Lancashire. Section 10. Grave 114. Headstone

Deed/Service: 31 July 1917. During an attack, an enemy machine-gun was seen enfilading the battalion on the right. He worked his way from shell-hole to shell-hole and captured the gun under heavy fire together with an officer and two other ranks

Commemoration: i) Headstone ii) Medals and portrait at Towneley Hall Museum and Art Gallery, Burnley, Lancashire

Gazette: 6 September 1917

Royston War Memorial,

851   **ACKROYD Harold   VC MC   T/Captain**   **Royal Army Medical Corps, attd. The Royal Berkshire Regiment**   **Ypres, Belgium**

                                                                   (the latter now Royal Gloucestershire, Berkshire and Wiltshire Regiment)   **POSTHUMOUS**

Born:	13 July 1877 - Mulcahen, Morley Road, Southport, Lancashire	**4**
Died:	11 August 1917 aged 40. Killed in action at Jargon Trench, Glencourse Wood, Ypres, Belgium	
Buried:	Birr Cross Roads Cemetery at Zillebeke, Belgium. Special Memorial No. 7. Headstone (See Map A-11)	
Deed/Service:	31 July - 1 August 1917. He worked continuously, utterly regardless of danger, saving lives and tending to the wounded men in the front line under heavy fire. Having carried one wounded officer to safety on his back he returned to bring in another under sniper fire	**Gazette: 6 September 1917**
Commemoration:	i) Headstone ii) Name on Royston War Memorial, Hertfordshire iii) Stone memorial in Southport Garden of Remembrance iv) Plaque in Caius College Cambridge v) Memorial in Guy's Hospital, London vi) Plaque at RAMC College, Millbank, London vii) Medals at the RAMC Museum	

852   **EDWARDS Alexander   VC   Acting Company Sergeant - Major   1/6th Bn. The Seaforth Highlanders (now The Highlanders)**   **Pilckem Ridge, Belgium**

Born:	4 November 1885 - Drainie, Morayshire, Scotland	**370**
Died:	24 March 1918 aged 32. Reported as 'wounded and missing in action' near Loupart Wood, Bapaume, Somme France	
Buried:	Has no known grave - name on Arras Memorial, France. Bay 8 (See Map A-20)	
Deed/Service:	31 July 1917. Locating an enemy machine-gun in a wood he attacked it with some men killing the crew and capturing the gun. Although wounded he stalked and killed a sniper causing casualties and continued to lead his men with great daring despite two more wounds	**Gazette: 14 September 1917**
Commemoration:	i) Name on The Arras Memorial ii) Memorial sundial at 18th Green, Lossiemouth Golf Course, Grampian region, Scotland iii) Memorial at the Community Museum, Lossiemouth iv) Medals at The Highlanders Museum	

Chavasse Barracks

See 743	CHAVASSE Noel Godfrey VC & Bar MC Captain	Royal Army Medical Corps attd. The King's (Liverpool) Regiment	Wieltje, Belgium

POSTHUMOUS
207

Born: 9 November 1884 - The Rectory, St. Peter-le-Bailey, Oxfordshire

Died: 4 August 1917 aged 32. Died of wounds two days after his VC Bar action, at Brandhoek Road, Casualty Clearing Station, Ypres, Belgium

Buried: Brandhoek New Military Cemetery, Belgium. 4 miles W. of Ypres. Plot 111. Row E. Grave 15. Headstone (See Map A - 11)

Deed/Service: BAR - From 31 July - 2 August 1917. Although severely wounded early in the action while carrying a wounded officer to a dressing station, he refused to leave his post, and in addition to normal duties went out repeatedly under heavy fire to attend to the wounded. Without food, worn with fatigue and faint from his wound, he helped carry in badly wounded men many who would have died in the dire weather conditions

Bar to VC: Gazette: 14 September 1917

Commemoration: For details of first VC action and location of memorials, see 743

First VC: Gazette: 26 October 1916

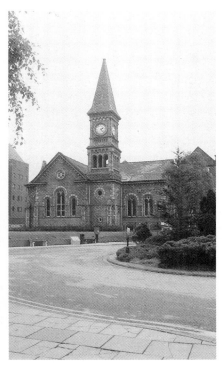

853	BUTLER William Boynton VC Private	17th Bn. The West Yorkshire Regt. attd. 106th T.M. Bty. (now the P.O.W. Regt.)	Near Lempire, France

160

Born: 20 November 1894 - Hunslett Carr, Leeds, Yorkshire.

Died: 25 March 1972 aged 77, at St. James's Hospital, Leeds

Buried: 29 March at Hunslett Cemetery, Leeds. Section 3. Grave 48. Headstone erected 1994

Deed/Service: 6 August 1917. When in charge of a Stokes gun in trenches being heavily shelled, one of the fly-off levers of a Stokes shell came off and fired the shell in the emplacement. He picked up the shell and shouted a warning, then turned and put himself between the party of men and the live shell, which he held until they were out of danger. He then threw it on to the parados and took cover, the resulting explosion only damaged the trench

Gazette: 17 October 1917

Commemoration: i) Headstone ii) Plaque outside City Art Gallery, Leeds

854   **BONNER Charles George**   **VC DSC**   **Captain**   **Royal Naval Reserve**

<table>
<tr><td>**Born:**</td><td>29 December 1884 - Shuttington, Warwickshire</td></tr>
<tr><td>**Died:**</td><td>7 February 1951 aged 66, at his home in Edinburgh</td></tr>
<tr><td>**Cremated:**</td><td>10 February at Warriston Crematorium, Edinburgh. Ashes buried at Aldridge, near Walsall, Staffordshire. Headstone</td></tr>
<tr><td>**Deed/Service:**</td><td>8 August 1917 (Lieutenant) When serving on HMS 'Dunraven' a 'Q' or 'mystery' ship which was shelled by an enemy submarine. He was in the thick of the fighting throughout the action and his pluck and determination had a considerable influence on the crew</td></tr>
<tr><td>**Commemoration:**</td><td>i) Headstone at Aldridge</td></tr>
</table>

Bay of Biscay
Atlantic Ocean
102

Gazette: 2 November 1917

855   **PITCHER Ernest Herbert**   **VC DSM**   **Chief Petty Officer**   **Royal Navy**

<table>
<tr><td>**Born:**</td><td>31 December 1888 - Mullion, Cornwall</td></tr>
<tr><td>**Died:**</td><td>10 February 1946 aged 57, at the Royal Navy Auxiliary Hospital, Sherborne, Dorset</td></tr>
<tr><td>**Buried:**</td><td>Northbrook Cemetery, Swanage, Dorset. Plot F - Unconsecrated. Grave 122. Headstone shows E.J. Pitcher</td></tr>
<tr><td>**Deed/Service:**</td><td>8 August 1917 (Petty Officer) When serving as the 4-inch gun-layer on HMS 'Dunraven' a 'Q' or 'mystery' ship which was shelled by an enemy submarine. He and the rest of crew waited while the battle went on overhead and the magazine below caught fire. They then placed the cartridges on their knees to prevent the heat of the deck igniting them. When the magazine finally exploded they were all blown into the air</td></tr>
<tr><td>**Commemoration:**</td><td>i) Headstone ii) Plaque at Parish Church, Swanage (1963)</td></tr>
</table>

Bay of Biscay
Atlantic Ocean
ELECTED BY BALLOT
988

Gazette: 2 November 1917

| 856 | LOOSEMORE Arnold | VC DCM | Sergeant | 8th Bn. The Duke of Wellington's (West Riding) Regiment (now Duke of Wellington's Regiment) | Near Langemarck, Belgium |

Born: 7 June 1896 - Sharrow, near Sheffield, Yorkshire

750

Died: 10 April 1924 aged 27, at his home in Stannington, Nr. Sheffield, from tuberculosis

Buried: Ecclesall Churchyard, Sheffield. Buried in the Johnson family plot. Headstone

Deed/Service: 11 August 1917 (Private) When his platoon was held up by heavy machine-gun fire during an attack on a strongly held enemy position, he crawled through partially cut wire, dragging his Lewis gun with him and single-handed dealt with a strong party of the enemy, killing about twenty. Immediately afterwards his Lewis gun was destroyed and three Germans rushed at him, but he shot them with his revolver. Later he shot several enemy snipers, and on returning to his original post he brought back a wounded comrade under heavy fire

Gazette: 14 September 1917

Commemoration: i) Headstone ii) Memorial in St. Andrews Church, Sharrow, near Sheffield (1926) iii) Loosemore Drive, Sheffield (1983)

A.J. CORBIN
E. COX
W. COX
F. CRAKE
C.H. CREWS
C. CRISP
F. CRISP
J.F. CRISP
T. CRISP (V.C. D.S.O.)
R.C. CROPLEY
T.S. CROPLEY
N.B. CROSSWELL
E.S. CROUCH
E. CULLING
A.J. CULLINGFORD
F. CULLINGFORD
W. CULLUM
E.E. CURTIS
G. CURTIS

St. Margaret's Church

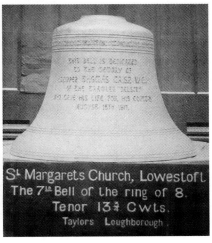

| 857 | CRISP Thomas | VC DSC | Skipper | Royal Naval Reserve | Jim Howe Bank, North Sea POSTHUMOUS |

Born: 28 April 1876 - Stanford Street, Lowestoft, Suffolk

275

Died: 15 August 1917 aged 41. Went down with the ship during his VC action off the Jim Howe Bank, North Sea

Buried: No known grave - name on the Chatham Memorial, Kent. Panel 25

Deed/Service: 15 August 1917. When he was below packing fish on board HM Armed Smack 'Nelson', a German submarine opened fire on them. As he cleared 'Nelson' for action, a shell hit her below the water-line and another passed through the ship, mortally wounding him. Still directing operations, he eventually ordered the ship to be abandoned, but he was too badly injured to be moved and went down with 'Nelson'

Gazette: 2 November 1917

Commemoration: i) Name on the Chatham Memorial ii) Name on War Memorial and on tenor bell at St. Margaret's Church, Lowestoft iii) Crisp Close, Lowestoft iv) Medals at Lowestoft Town Hall

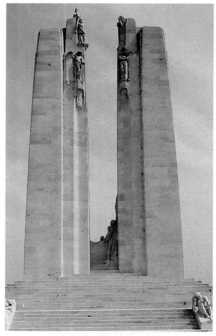

F·HOBSON·V.C.

Vimy Memorial

858	HOBSON Frederick	VC	Sergeant	20th Bn. 1st Central Ontario Regiment, Canadian Expeditionary Force			N.W. of Lens, France

POSTHUMOUS
575

Born: 23 September 1873 - London
Died: 18 August 1917 aged 43. Killed during his VC action near Lens, France
Buried: Has no known grave - name on the Vimy Memorial, France. 8 miles N. of Arras. Inner side wall (See Map A - 20)
Deed/Service: 15 August 1917. During a strong enemy counter-attack a Lewis gun team in a forward position was buried by a shell, and all the crew apart from one man killed. Hobson grasped the importance of the post and rushed from his trench, dug out the gun and got it back into action. The gun jammed and he ran forward at the advancing enemy with bayonet and clubbed rifle, holding them back until he was killed by a rifle shot

Gazette: 17 October 1917

Commemoration: i) Name on Vimy Memorial ii) Medals in Canadian War Museum, Ottawa, Canada

Replacement headstone

859	O'ROURKE Michael James	VC MM	Private	7th Bn. British Columbia Regiment, Canadian Expeditionary Force	Hill 60, Lens, France

949

Born: 19 March 1878 - Limerick, Ireland
Died: 6 December 1957 aged 79, at his sister's home in Vancouver, British Columbia, Canada
Buried: 10 December at Mountain View Cemetery, Vancouver. Abray Section. Grave 6 - 13 - 3. Headstone near flagpole
Deed/Service: 15 - 17 August 1917. When acting as a stretcher-bearer, he worked unceasingly for three days and nights bringing in and tending wounded. During this period the area in which he worked was swept by heavy machine-gun and rifle fire, and on several occasions he was knocked down and half buried by enemy shells. His courage and devotion in rescuing the wounded inspired all ranks, and saved many lives

Gazette: 8 November 1917

Commemoration: i) Headstone ii) Painting in Canadian War Museum, Ottawa iii) Medals in British Columbia Regimental Museum

860   BROWN Harry   VC   Private   10th Bn. Quebec Regiment, Canadian Expeditionary Force

Hill 70, Loos, France
POSTHUMOUS
132

Born:	10 May 1898 - Ganonoque, Ontario, Canada
Died:	17 August 1917 aged 19. Died of wounds received during his VC action, at a Field Dressing Station, near Loos, France
Buried:	Noeux-les-Mines Communal Cemetery, France. 2 miles N.W. of Lens. Plot 11. Row J. Grave 29. Headstone (See Map A - 19)
Deed/Service	16 August 1917. When all signal wires were cut during a counter attack, he and another soldier were given an important message to be delivered. The other messenger was killed and his own arm was shattered, but he struggled through to complete his mission before collapsing
Commemoration:	i) Headstone ii) Medals at The Canadian War Memorial Ottawa, Canada

Gazette: 17 October 1917

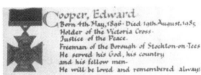

861   COOPER Edward   VC   Major   12th Bn. The King's Royal Rifle Corps (now The Royal Green Jackets)

Langemarck, Belgium
250

Born:	4 May 1896 - Portrack, Stockton-on-Tees, Co. Durham
Died:	19 August 1985 aged 89, at the North Tees Hospital, Stockton-on-Tees, following a heart attack
Cremated:	23 August at Teeside Crematorium, Middlesborough. Ref: 66610. Ashes scattered in August Plot, Garden of Remembrance. No memorial
Deed/Service	16 August 1917 (Sergeant) When enemy machine-guns in a concrete blockhouse were holding up an advance and causing heavy casualties, he rushed towards them with four others. Although they fired at the garrison from close range the guns were not silenced, so he fired his revolver into an opening. The guns ceased firing and the garrison surrendered, a total of forty-five prisoners and seven machine-guns
Commemoration:	i) Name in the Book of Remembrance at the Crematorium ii) Bronze plaque at Stockton Library iii) Name on K.R.R.C. Memorial, Winchester Cathedral, Hampshire iv) Medals at Preston Hall Museum, Teeside

Gazette: 14 September 1917

862	EDWARDS Wilfred VC Major 7th Bn. The King's Own Yorkshire Light Infantry (now The Light Infantry)	Langemarck, Belgium

Born: 16 February 1894 - Norwich, Norfolk
Died: 2 January 1972 aged 77, at his home in Leeds, Yorkshire
Buried: 7 January at Upper and Lower Wortley Cemetery, Leeds. Section M. Grave 42. Headstone
Deed/Service: 16 August 1917 (Private) When all of his officers were lost, he dashed forward under fire towards a concrete fort containing machine-guns. He threw bombs through the loopholes, surmounted the fort then waved his company to advance to assist him with the 33 prisoners he had captured. Later he did valuable work as a runner, guiding most of the battalion through difficult ground regardless of personal danger
Commemoration: i) Headstone ii) Medals at King's Own Yorkshire Light Infantry Museum

374

Gazette: 14 September 1917

863	GRIMBALDESTON William Henry VC A/Company Quartermaster - Sergeant 1st Bn. The King's Own Scottish Borderers	Wijdendrift, Belgium

Born: 19 September 1889 - Hickory Street, Blackburn, Lancashire
Died: 13 August 1959 aged 69, suddenly at his home in Bold Street, Blackburn
Cremated: 17 August at Pleasington Crematorium, Blackburn. Ashes scattered on Plot G. No memorial marker
Deed/Service: 16 August 1917. Noticing that the unit on his left was held up by enemy machine-gun fire from a blockhouse, he armed himself with a rifle and grenades and started to crawl towards his objective. Although wounded he pushed on to the blockhouse, threatened the machine-gun teams with a hand grenade and forced them to surrender. This action resulted in the capture of 36 prisoners, six machine-guns and one trench mortar
Commemoration: i) Memorial in Blackburn Old Town Hall ii) Medals at King's Own Scottish Borderers Museum

497

Gazette: 14 September 1917

864	ROOM Frederick George VC Acting Lance - Corporal 2nd Bn. The Royal Irish Regiment (now disbanded)	Frezenberg, Belgium

Born: 31 May 1895 - Congleton Road, St. George's, Bristol

1080

Died: 19 January 1932 aged 36, at Ham Green Sanatorium, Bristol, from pneumonia

Buried: 25 January at Greenbank Cemetery, Bristol. Ref: 634141. Section 41 - Pink - K. Headstone

Deed/Service: 16 August 1917. When his company were holding a line of shell holes and short trenches and had received many casualties, he was placed in charge of the stretcher-bearers. He worked without regard for himself under intense fire, dressing the wounded and evacuating them to safety

Gazette: 17 October 1917

Commemoration: i) Headstone ii) Medals at National Army Museum

865	LEARMOUTH Okill Massey VC MC A/Major 2nd Bn. Eastern Ontario Regiment, Canadian Expeditionary Force	East of Loos, France POSTHUMOUS

Born: 22 February 1894 - St. Louis Road, Quebec City, Canada

729

Died: 19 August 1917 aged 23. Died of wounds received during his VC action, at a Field Hospital, near Loos, France

Buried: Noeux-les-Mines Communal Cemetery, France. 2 Miles N.W. of Lens. Plot 11. Row K. Grave 9. Headstone (See Map A - 19)

Deed/Service: 18 August 1917. During a heavy counter-attack on his position, he instantly charged and personally disposed of the attackers. Later under intense barrage fire and mortally wounded, he stood on the parapet of the trench bombing the enemy, catching bombs thrown at him and throwing them back. He refused to be evacuated and continued giving instructions and advice before being moved to a hospital where he died

Gazette: 8 November 1917

Commemoration: i) Headstone ii) Memorial and painting in the Canadian War Museum, Ottawa iii) Medals at Governor General's Footguards Museum, Ontario

866 **SKINNER John Kendrick** **VC DCM** **Acting Company Sergeant - Major** **1st Bn. The King's Own Scottish Borderers** Wijdendrift, Belgium

1150

Born:	5 February 1883 - St. Andrew's Road, Pollockshields, Glasgow
Died:	17 March 1918 aged 35. Killed in a later action going to the aid of a wounded man on the Bellevue Spar, near Vlamertinghe, Belgium
Buried:	Vlamertinghe New British Cemetery, Belgium. 3 Miles W. of Ypres. Plot XV1. Row H. Grave 15. Headstone (See Map A - 11)
Deed/Service:	18 August 1917. Although wounded in the head, he collected six men when his company was held up by machine-gun fire and worked his way round the left flank of the three blockhouses from which the fire was coming. He succeeded in bombing and taking the first blockhouse single-handed, then leading his men towards the other two blockhouses he cleared them, taking sixty prisoners, three machine-guns and two trench mortars

Gazette: 14 September 1917

Commemoration: i) Headstone ii) Medals at King's Own Scottish Borderers Museum

867 **MOORE Montague Shadworth Seymour** **VC** **Major** **15th Bn. The Hampshire Regiment (now Royal Hampshire Regiment)** East of Ypres, Belgium

887

Born:	9 October 1896 - Bournemouth, Hampshire (now Dorset)
Died:	12 September 1966 aged 69, at Kiganjo, Nyeri, Kenya
Cremated:	Langata Crematorium, Nairobi, Kenya. Ashes in the Serengeti National Park, Tanzania and the Hyaena Dam, Nairobi National Park
Deed/Service:	20 August 1917 (Second Lieutenant) He volunteered to make a fresh attack on a final objective and went forward with some seventy men, but they met such heavy opposition that when he arrived at his objective he had only five men remaining. He immediately bombed a large dug-out, taking twenty-eight prisoners, two machine-guns and a light field-gun, then when reinforced with more men he held the position for thirty-six hours beating off a number of counter-attacks until his force was reduced to ten men. He eventually withdrew his wounded under cover of a thick mist

Gazette: 8 November 1917

Commemoration: i) Memorial plaque at Bedford School

| 868 | PARSONS Hardy Falconer | VC | T/Second Lieutenant | 14th (S) Bn. The Gloucestershire Regiment
(now Royal Gloucestershire, Berkshire & Wiltshire Regiment) | Near Epehy, France
POSTHUMOUS |

Born: 13 June 1897 - Rishton, Blackburn, Lancashire

967

Died: 21 August 1917 aged 20. Died from wounds following his VC action near Epehy, France

Buried: Villers-Faucon Communal Cemetery, France. 6 miles N.E. of Peronne. Row A. Grave 16. Headstone (See Map A - 30)

Deed/Service: 20 - 21 August 1917. During a night attack by the enemy on a bombing post held by his command, the bombers holding the post were forced back but he remained at his post. Single-handed and although severely burnt by liquid fire, he continued to hold up the enemy with bombs until severely wounded. His gallant action held the enemy long enough for the defence of the position to be consolidated

Gazette: 17 October 1917

Commemoration: i) Headstone ii) Memorial at Kingswood School, Bath iii) Plaque at King Edward VII School, Lytham, Lancashire iv) Medals at the Gloucester Regimental Museum

| 869 | HANNA Robert Hill | VC | Lieutenant | 29th Bn. British Columbia Regiment, Canadian Expeditionary Force | Lens, France |

Born: 6 August 1887 - Aughnahoory, Kilkeel, Co. Down, Northern Ireland

524

Died: 15 June 1967 aged 79, at Mount Lehman, British Columbia, Canada

Buried: The Masonic Cemetery, Burnaby, British Columbia. Plot 49. Section C. Grave 2. Headstone

Deed/Service: 21 August 1917 (Company Sergeant-Major) When his company met with severe resistance at a heavily protected strong point, he collected and led a party against the position under heavy machine-gun fire. He rushed through the wire, killed four of the enemy and took the objective

Gazette: 8 November 1917

Commemoration: i) Headstone

870   **KONOWAL Filip**   **VC**   **Acting Corporal**   **47th Bn. British Columbia Regiment, Canadian Expeditionary Force**   Lens, France

Born: 15 September 1886 - Kedeski, Podolsky, Ukraine, Russia   707

Died: 3 June 1959 aged 72, at The Veterans Pavilion, Ottawa Civic Hospital, Ontario, Canada

Buried: Notre Dame de Lourdes Cemetery, Montreal Road, Ottawa. Section A. Lot 502. Headstone

Deed/Service: 22 - 24 August 1917. Was in charge of a section engaged in mopping up machine-gun emplacements, all resistance was overcome successfully and heavy casualties inflicted on the enemy. He attacked several of the enemy single-handed and on one occasion entered a gun emplacement, killed the crew and captured the gun. The next day he killed another crew, destroyed the gun and the post and was later severely wounded

Commemoration: i) Headstone ii) Bronze plaque at Royal Canadian Legion Building, Ottawa, Ontario iii) Medals and painting in Canadian War Museum, Ottawa, Canada   **Gazette: 26 November 1917**

871   **DAY Sidney James**   **VC**   **Corporal**   **11th Bn. The Suffolk Regiment (now The Royal Anglian Regiment)**   **East of Hargicourt, France**

Born: 3 July 1891 - Norwich, Norfolk   316

Died: 17 July 1959 aged 68, in St. Mary's Hospital, Portsmouth, Hampshire

Buried: Milton Cemetery, Portsmouth. Plot R. Row 11. Grave 6. Headstone

Deed/Service: 26 August 1917. When in command of a bombing section detailed to clear a maze of trenches, he killed two machine-gunners and four prisoners. He returned to his section where a stick bomb fell into a trench occupied by five men. He seized the bomb and threw it over the trench where it exploded. He later cleared the trench and established himself in an advanced position for 66 hours under fire

Commemoration: i) Headstone ii) The Sidney Day Tea Rooms at Landport, Portsmouth   **Gazette: 17 October 1917**

| 872 | CARMICHAEL John VC Sergeant | 9th Bn. The North Staffordshire Regiment (now The Staffordshire Regiment) | Hill 60, Zwarteleen, Belgium |

Born: 1 April 1893 - Hurstmain, Glenmavis, Airdrie, Lanarkshire 185

Died: 20 December 1977 aged 84, at his home at Hurstmain, Glenmavis

Buried: 30 December, at The Landward Cemetery, New Monkland, Airdrie. Headstone

Deed/Service: 8 September 1917. When excavating the Imperial Avenue Trench, he saw a grenade had been unearthed and started to burn. He placed his steel helmet over the grenade and stood on the helmet shouting to his men to get clear. The grenade exploded, seriously injuring and blowing him out of the trench. He could have thrown the grenade clear, but knew it would have killed men working on the parapet   **Gazette: 17 October 1917**

Commemoration: i) Headstone ii) Name on plaque in Garrison Church, Whittington Barracks, Lichfield, Staffordshire iii) Medals at Staffordshire Regiment Museum

| 873 | MOYNEY John VC Sergeant 2nd Battalion, Irish Guards | | Ney Copse, Broenbeek Belgium |

895

Born: 8 January 1895 - Rathdowney, Queen's Co. (now Co. Laoise), Ireland

Died: 10 November 1980 aged 85, at Roscrea, Co. Tipperary, Ireland

Buried: 12 November at Roscrea Roman Catholic Cemetery, Abbey Street, Roscrea. Headstone

Deed/Service: 12 - 13 September 1917 (Lance-Sergeant) When in command of fifteen men forming two advanced posts surrounded by the enemy, he held out for four days with no water and very little food. On the fifth day, with the enemy advancing on his position, he attacked them with bombs and used his Lewis gun with great effect. Finding himself surrounded he led his men in a charge through the enemy, reaching a stream where he and Woodcock (874) covered the party while they crossed unscathed, before crossing themselves under a hail of bullets   **Gazette: 17 October 1917**

Commemoration: i) Headstone ii) Medals at The Irish Guards Museum

CITATION
No. 8367

Private THOMAS WOODCOCK

VICTORIA CROSS, Awarded 13th September, 1917
Gazetted 17th October, 1917

For most conspicuous bravery and determination. He was one of a post commanded by L/Sgt. Moyney which was surrounded. The post held out for ninety-six hours, but after that time was attacked from all sides in overwhelming numbers and was forced to retire.

Private Woodcock covered the retirement with a Lewis Gun, and only retired when the enemy had moved round and up to his post and were only a few yards away. He then crossed the river, but hearing cries for help behind him, returned and waded into the stream amid a shower of bombs from the enemy and rescued another member of the party. The latter he then carried across the open ground in broad daylight towards our front line regardless of machine gun fire that was opened on him.

874　　**WOODCOCK Thomas　VC　Corporal　2nd Battalion, Irish Guards**

Ney Copse, Broenbeek
Belgium
1327

Born:　19 March 1888 - Belvoir Street, Wigan, Lancashire
Died:　27 March 1918 aged 30. Killed in a later action at Bullecourt, France
Buried:　Douchy-les-Ayette British Cemetery, France. 8 miles S.W. of Arras. Plot IV. Row F. Grave 3. Headstone shows age 29 (See Map A - 19)
Deed/Service:　12 - 13 September 1917 (Private) When an advanced post had held out for 96 hours and was forced to retire, he and Moyney (873) covered the retirement. Crossing a stream he heard cries for help and returned, waded into the stream under fire and rescued a wounded man
Commemoration:　i) Headstone ii) Medals at Irish Guards Museum

Gazette: 17 October 1917

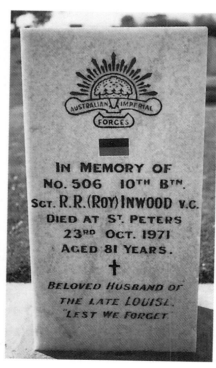

875　　**INWOOD Reginald Roy　VC　Sergeant　10th Bn. (S.A.) Australian Imperial Force**

Polygon Wood, Belgium
620

Born:　14 July 1890 - Renmark, North Adelaide, South Australia
Died:　23 October 1971 aged 81, at The Tara Private Hospital, St. Peter's, Adelaide
Buried:　27 October at the AIF Cemetery, West Terrace, Adelaide. Light Oval. 5-N 1E. Headstone
Deed/Service:　19 - 22 September 1917 (Private) During an attack at Polygon Wood, near Ypres, he moved forward alone through the allied barrage, capturing an enemy strong-point killing several and taking nine prisoners. He later volunteered for a special all-night patrol which went out 600 yards in front of the allied line and succeeded in bringing back valuable information. A third sortie resulted in the capture of a machine-gun and one prisoner
Commemoration:　i) Headstone ii) The Roy Inwood Club, Torrens Parade Ground, Adelaide iii) Medals at the City of Adelaide Museum, Adelaide Town Hall

Gazette: 26 November 1917

1st Australian Division Memorial

876	BIRKS Frederick VC MM Second Lieutenant 6th Bn. (Victoria) Australian Imperial Force		Glencorse Wood, Belgium POSTHUMOUS 91	

Born: 16 August 1894 - Lane End, Buckley, Flintshire, Wales

Died: 21 September 1917 aged 23. Killed by a shell burst the day after his VC action, when trying to rescue wounded men in Glencorse Wood

Buried: Perth Cemetery (China Wall), Belgium. 2 Miles E. of Ypres. Plot I. Row G. Grave 45. Headstone (See Map A - 11)

Deed/Service: 20 September 1917. Accompanied by a corporal he rushed a strong point which was holding up the advance, going on alone when the man was wounded. He killed the remainder of the enemy and captured the machine-gun, then led a small party and attacked another strong point occupied by 25 of the enemy, killing some and capturing an officer and fifteen men

Gazette: 8 November 1917

Commemoration: i) Headstone ii) Name on his parents grave in St. Matthew's Churchyard, Buckley iii) Plaque inside St. Matthew's iv) Obelisk in grounds of St. Mary's Church Hall v) Memorial in Royal British Legion Club, Buckley vi) Medals at the Australian War Memorial, Canberra, Australia

877	BURMAN William Francis VC Sergeant 16th Bn. The Rifle Brigade (now The Royal Green Jackets)		Bulgar Wood, Ypres Belgium 152	

Born: 30 August 1897 - 5 Baker Street, Stepney, East London

Died: 23 October 1974 aged 77 at Halsey House, Cromer, Norfolk

Cremated: 30 October at St. Faith's Crematorium, Norwich, Norfolk. Ashes in Section 2-5, Garden of Remembrance, Golders Green Crematorium, London

Deed/Service: 20 September 1917. When his company was held up by a machine-gun post at point blank range, he ordered his men to wait and went forward alone to what seemed certain death. He killed the enemy gunner and carried the gun to the company's objective, using it with great effect. Within minutes, about forty of the enemy were enfilading the battalion on the right, he and two other men ran behind them, killed six and captured 31.

Gazette: 26 November 1917

Commemoration: i) Name on Rifle Brigade Memorial, Winchester Cathedral, Hampshire ii) Plaque on a bench at Royal British Legion Home, Cromer iii) Medals at the Imperial War Museum

Chester Cathedral

878 **COLVIN Hugh VC Major 9th Bn. The Cheshire Regiment**

Born: 1 February 1887 - Rosegrove, Burnley, Lancashire
Died: 16 September 1962 aged 75, at Bangor, Co. Down, Northern Ireland
Buried: Carnmoney Cemetery, Newtonabbey, Bangor. Headstone
Deed/Service: 20 September 1917 (Second Lieutenant) When all the other officers of his company, and those of the leading company had become casualties, he took command of both companies and led them forward under heavy fire with great success. He then went with two men to a dug-out, and entering it alone brought out fourteen prisoners. He later cleared out other dug-outs single-handed, capturing both guns and many prisoners
Commemoration: i) Headstone ii) Name on War Memorial at Bushmills, Co. Antrim iii) Plaque at Chester Cathedral iv) Medals at Cheshire Regimental Museum

Hessian Wood, Ypres
Belgium
237

Gazette: 8 November 1917

879 **EGERTON Ernest Albert VC Sergeant 16th Bn. The Sherwood Foresters (The Nottinghamshire & Derbyshire Regt.)**
(now The Worcestershire & Sherwood Foresters Regiment)

Born: 10 November 1897 - Mier Lane, Longton, Staffordshire
Died: 14 February 1966 aged 68, at his home 350 Uttoxeter Road, Blythe Bridge, Staffordshire
Buried: St. Peter's Churchyard, Cheadle Road, Blythe Bridge. Headstone
Deed/Service: 20 September 1917 (Corporal) During an attack in poor visibility due to fog and smoke the two leading waves passed over hostile dug-outs without clearing them, resulting in severe casualties as the enemy began firing from the rear. Volunteering to clear the situation, he dashed for the dug-outs under heavy fire from close range, and shot three gunners before support arrived, when another 29 surrendered
Commemoration: i) Headstone ii) Plaque on his home in Uttexeter Road iii) Plaque on the Lodge at Staffordshire Tableware, Mier, Staffordshire iv) Memorial in Bulgar Wood v) Portrait at St. Bartholomew's Church, Burton vi) Medals at Sherwood Foresters Museum

Bulgar Wood, Ypres
Belgium
376

Gazette: 26 November 1917

56

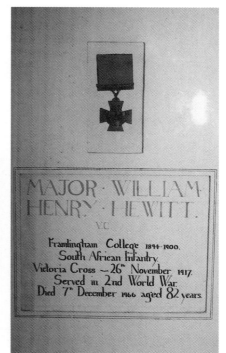

880   **HEWITT William Henry VC Major 2nd South African Light Infantry**   **East of Ypres, Belgium**

Born:	19 June 1884 - Copdock, near Ipswich, Suffolk
Died:	7 December 1966 aged 72 at Cheltenham, Gloucestershire from Parkinson's Disease
Cremated:	10 December at Cheltenham Crematorium. Ref. 25500. Ashes scattered at sea off Hermanus Cliffs, 40 miles E. of Cape Town, South Africa
Deed/Service:	20 September 1917 (Lance-Corporal) Led his section to rush the doorway of an enemy pill-box, but its garrison proved to be very stubborn and he received a severe arm wound. Nevertheless he proceeded to the loophole of the pill-box and tried to insert a bomb, but was again wounded. He finally got the bomb inside and dislodged the occupants who were successfully dealt with by the rest of his section
Commemoration:	i) Display at South African Memorial, Delville Wood, Somme, France ii) Bench in his memory on seafront at Hermanus iii) Medals and memorial at Framlingham College Chapel, Suffolk

566

Gazette: 26 November 1917

881   **KNIGHT Alfred Joseph VC MBE Second Lieutenant 2/8th (City of London) Bn. The London Regt. (Post Office Rifles)**   **Hubner Farm, Ypres Belgium**

Born:	24 August 1888 - Ladywood, Birmingham
Died:	4 December 1960 aged 72, at his home in Elvetham Road, Edgbaston, Birmingham
Buried:	Oscott College Road Cemetery, Sutton Coldfield, Birmingham. Section 2B. Grave 328A. Headstone
Deed/Service:	20 September 1917 (Sergeant) When his platoon came under very heavy fire from an enemy machine-gun, he rushed through our own barrage and captured it single-handed. He performed several other solo acts of conspicuous bravery, all under heavy machine-gun and rifle fire and when all other platoon officers had become casualties, he took command consolidating and reorganising his men
Commemoration:	i) Headstone ii) Painting at the English Barracks, Mill Hill, London iii) Medals at The National Postal Museum, London

701

Gazette: 8 November 1917

882 **REYNOLDS Henry VC MC T/Captain** 12th Bn. The Royal Scots (The Lothian Regiment now The Royal Scots) Near Frezenberg, Belgium

Born: 16 August 1883 - Whilton, near Daventry, Northamptonshire 1041
Died: 26 March 1948 aged 64, at Carshalton, Surrey
Buried: St. Giles' Churchyard, Ashtead, Surrey. Headstone
Deed/Service: 20 September 1917. When his company were suffering heavy casualties from enemy machine-guns and a pill-box, he went out alone, moving from shell-hole to shell-hole under heavy fire. When near the pill-box he threw a grenade which failed to enter, so he crawled to the entrance and forced a phosphorous grenade inside, which set the position on fire killing three, the remainder surrendering along with two machine-guns. Despite being wounded, he later captured another objective, with seventy prisoners and two more machine-guns **Gazette: 8 November 1917**
Commemoration: i) Headstone ii) Medals at Royal Scots Regimental Museum

883 **HAMILTON John Brown VC Sergeant** 1/9th Bn. The Highland Light Infantry (now The Royal Highland Fusiliers) N. of Ypres, Menin Road
Belgium
Born: 26 August 1896 - Dumbarton, Scotland 517
Died: 18 July 1973 aged 76, at Hairmyres Hospital, East Kilbride, Scotland from cancer
Cremated: 21 July at Daldowie Crematorium, Broomhouse, Glasgow. Ashes in the Garden of Remembrance at the Crematorium. No memorial
Deed/Service: 25 - 26 September 1917 (A/Lance-Corporal) During a heavy bombardment, great difficulty was experienced in keeping the front and support lines supplied with small arms ammunition. He volunteered to carry and distribute ammunition on many occasions, in full view of enemy snipers and machine-guns which were close to our front line, greatly inspiring his comrades **Gazette: 26 November 1917**
Commemoration: i) Medals in Scottish United Services Museum, Edinburgh

Vickers machine-gun

884   DWYER John James (later The Hon)   VC   Lieutenant   4th Coy, Machine Gun Corps, Australian Imperial Force   Zonnebeke, Belgium

Born: 9 March 1890 - Lovett, Port Cygnet, Tasmania, Australia   366
Died: 17 January 1962 aged 71, at Bruny Island, Tasmania. Probably as a result of dermatitis, a legacy of mustard gas poisoning
Buried: Allonah Cemetery, Cornelian Bay, Hobart. Catholic Section - ND. Grave 220. Headstone
Deed/Service: 26 September 1917 (Sergeant) During an advance while in charge of a Vickers machine-gun, he rushed the gun forward to within thirty yards of an enemy machine-gun. Firing it at point blank range, he killed the crew, then carried it back to our front line across shell-swept ground. The gun was destroyed the following day during a heavy artillery attack, but he fetched a reserve gun through a heavy barrage, putting it to instant use   Gazette: 26 November 1917
Commemoration: i) Headstone   ii) Dwyer Club at the Tasmania Command Ordnance Depot   iii) Medals at Australian War Memorial, Canberra, A.C.T.

885   BUGDEN Patrick Joseph   VC   Private   31st Bn. (Q.&V.) Australian Imperial Force   Polygon Wood, Belgium

                                                                         POSTHUMOUS
Born: 17 March 1897 - South Gundurimba, New South Wales, Australia   148
Died: 28 September 1917 aged 20. Killed during his VC action at Polygon Wood, Belgium
Buried: i) Glencorse Wood   ii) Hooge Crater Cemetery, Belgium. 2 miles E. of Ypres. Plot VII. Row C. Grave 5. Headstone (See Map A-11)
Deed/Service: 26 - 28 September 1917. When an advance was held up by a heavily defended pill-box, he twice led small parties against it and successfully took the guns and captured the enemy at bayonet point. Later he rescued a corporal from capture, when he rushed up single-handed and shot one of Germans and bayoneted the other two. On four occasions he rescued men under intense fire, and was killed trying to rescue a fifth man   Gazette: 26 November 1917
Commemoration: i) Headstone   ii) Paddy Bugden Memorial, Alstonville, N.S.W.   iii) Bugden Avenue, Canberra, A.C.T.   iv) Display at the Australian War Memorial, Canberra   v) Medals at the Queensland Museum, South Brisbane, Queensland

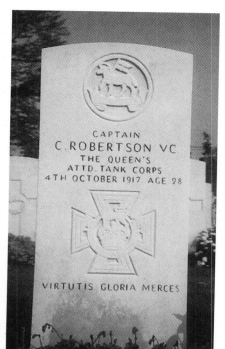

886   **ROBERTSON Clement   VC   A/Captain**   The Queen's Royal West Surrey Regiment, Special Reserve, Tank Corps   Zonnebeke, Belgium
                                                 (now P.O.W. Royal Regiment and Royal Tank Regiment respectively)   **POSTHUMOUS**

Born: 15 December 1890 - Pietermaritzburg, Natal, South Africa   **1065**
Died: 4 October 1917 aged 26. Killed by machine-gun fire near Zonnebeke, Belgium during his VC action
Buried: Oxford Road Cemetery, Belgium. 2 Miles N.E. of Ypres. Plot III. Row F. Grave 7. Headstone shows age 28 (See Map A - 11)
Deed/Service: 4 October 1917. Having spent 72 hours with his batman, reconnoitering ground ploughed up by shell fire, and taping routes for his tanks
to follow, aware of the risks should they lose their way, he led them on foot in an attack. Knowing that his action would almost certainly
cost him his life, he guided them towards their objective. He was shot in the head as the target was reached, but his planning and leadership
ensured success
Commemoration: i)   Headstone   **Gazette: 18 December 1917**

Tyne Cot Memorial

St. Alban's Church, Hindhead

887   **BENT Philip Eric   VC DSO   T/Lt. - Colonel**   Comd. 9th Bn. The Leicestershire Regiment (now Royal Anglian Regt.)   Polygon Wood, Belgium

Born: 3 January 1891 - Halifax, Nova Scotia, Canada   **POSTHUMOUS**
Died: 1 October 1917 aged 26. Killed during his VC action at Polygon Wood, Belgium   **83**
Buried: Has no known grave - name on Tyne Cot Memorial, Belgium. 5 Miles N.E. of Ypres. Panel 50 (See Map A - 11)
Deed/Service: 1 October 1917. During a critical situation caused by an enemy attack and intense artillery fire, he collected a platoon in reserve and with
men from other companies, he organised and led them in a counter-attack. The German attack was checked and a vital portion of the line
was secured essential to subsequent operations. Bent was killed soon afterwards leading another charge
Commemoration: i)   Name on The Tyne Cot Memorial   ii)   Name on War Memorial outside St. Alban's Church, Hindhead, Surrey   iii)   Memorial in the Army   **Gazette: 11 January 1918**
Museum, Halifax   iv)   Memorial at Ashby-de-la-Zouch Grammar School, Leicestershire   v)   Medals at Royal Leicestershire Regimental Museum

888	**COVERDALE Charles Harry**	**VC MM**	**Second Lieutenant**	**11th Bn. The Manchester Regiment (now The King's Regt.)**	**South West of Poelcapelle Belgium**

Born: 21 April 1888 - 53 Clifford Street, Brook's Bar, Manchester, Lancashire

265

Died: 20 November 1955 aged 67 at his home, 37 Ingfield Avenue, Dalton, Huddersfield, Yorkshire

Buried: Edgerton Cemetery, Huddersfield. Section 5G. Grave 105. Headstone

Deed/Service: 4 October 1917 (Sergeant) During an attack on an objective, he disposed of three snipers before rushing two machine-guns, killing or wounding the teams. He subsequently reorganised his platoon in order to capture another position, but was held up by our own barrage and forced to return. As he was going out with five men to try again he saw an large enemy force approaching, and withdrew

Gazette: 18 December 1917

Commemoration: i) Headstone

889	**EVANS Lewis Pugh**	**VC CB CMG DSO & Bar**	**Brigadier - General**	**The Black Watch, comd. 1st Bn. Lincolnshire Regt. (now Royal Anglian Regiment)**	**Near Zonnebeke, Belgium**

Born: 3 January 1881 - Lovesgrove, Abermadd, Dyfed

390

Died: 30 November 1962 aged 81, at Paddington Railway Station, London from a heart attack

Buried: Llanbadarn Churchyard, Cardiganshire. Family Plot. Headstone

Deed/Service: 4 October 1917 (A/Lieutenant Colonel) During an attack he took his battalion through a heavy enemy barrage, then sent troops round the flank of a machine-gun emplacement, rushed at it himself and fired his revolver through the loophole forcing the garrison to surrender. Although severely wounded he refused medical aid and again led his battalion forward and was again wounded. Nevertheless he carried on until the next objective was achieved before collapsing, but due to numerous casualties refused bandaging and reached the dressing station unaided

Gazette: 26 November 1917

Commemoration: i) Headstone ii) Display at Aberystwyth Town Museum iii) Portrait in National Museum of Wales

Book of Remembrance

| 890 | GREAVES Fred VC Sergeant | 9th Bn. The Sherwood Foresters (The Nottinghamshire & Derbyshire Regiment) (now The Worcestershire & Sherwood Foresters Regiment) | Poelcapelle, Belgium |

486

Born: 16 May 1890 - Killamarsh, Derbyshire
Died: 11 June 1973 aged 83, at his home 'Whitelands', Ringwood Road, Brimington, Derbyshire
Cremated: 13 June at Brimington Crematorium, near Chesterfield. Ref: 18186. Ashes scattered on Heath 8 in Garden of Remembrance. No memorial
Deed/Service: 4 October 1917 (A/Corporal) When his platoon was held up by machine-gun fire from a concrete stronghold, he rushed forward with another NCO, and bombed the emplacement, killing or capturing the garrison and machine-gun. Later, during a critical time in the battle, when all the officers of his company became casualties during a German counter-attack, he threw out extra posts on his flank and enfiladed the enemy advance

Commemoration: i) Name in Crematorium Book of Remembrance ii) Medals at Sherwood Foresters Museum

Gazette: 26 November 1917

Tree plaque

Coventry War Memorial Park

| 891 | HUTT Arthur VC Corporal | 1/7th Bn. The Royal Warwickshire Regiment (now Royal Fusiliers Regiment) | Terrier Farm, Poelcapelle Belgium |

613

Born: 12 February 1889 - Earlsden, Coventry, Warwickshire
Died: 14 April 1964 aged 65, at his brothers home 277 Sewall Highway, Coventry, the result of a brain tumour
Cremated: 20 April at Canley Crematorium, London Road, Coventry. Ref: 7935 (L.3). Ashes in Garden of Remembrance. Memorial plaque on a tree
Deed/Service: 4 October 1917 (Private) When all the officers and NCO's of his platoon had become casualties, he took command and led them himself. When held up by a strong post he ran forward alone and shot an officer and three men in the post, with another forty to fifty surrendering. Having pushed too far, he covered a withdrawal by sniping, then carried a wounded man to safety and later brought four more wounded in under heavy fire

Commemoration: i) Plaque on a tree at Crematorium ii) Special memorial stone in Coventry War Memorial Park (1955) iii) Name on the Coventry War Memorial

Gazette: 26 November 1917

892   McGEE Lewis   VC   Acting Company Sergeant - Major   40th Bn. (Tasmania) Australian Imperial Force   Hamburg Redoubt, Ypres
Belgium
POSTHUMOUS
779

Born:	13 May 1888 - 'Verwood', Campbelltown, Tasmania, Australia
Died:	13 October 1917 aged 29. Killed by a shot in the head while attacking a pillbox in Augustus Wood, Passchendaele, Belgium
Buried:	Tyne Cot Cemetery, Belgium. 5 Miles N.E. of Ypres. Plot XX. Row D. Grave 1. Headstone (See Map A - 11)
Deed/Service:	4 October 1917. When the advance of his company was held up by machine-gun fire from a pillbox, he rushed forward armed with a revolver shooting some of the crew and capturing the rest, enabling the advance to proceed. He reorganised remnants of his platoon and consolidated the position, his coolness and bravery contributing largely to his company's successful operation
Commemoration:	i) Headstone ii) Name on War Cenotaph, Ross, Tasmania iii) McGee Soldiers' Club, Anglesea Barracks, Hobart iv) Plaque on RSL Cenotaph, Hobart v) McGee Place, Canberra, A.C.T. vi) Display at Australian War Memorial, Canberra vii) Medals at Launceton Museum, Hobart, Tasmania, Australia

Gazette: 26 November 1917

893   OCKENDEN James   VC MM   Acting Company Sergeant - Major   1st Bn. The Royal Dublin Fusiliers (now disbanded)   't Goed ter Vesten Farm
E. of Langemarck,
Belgium
938

Born:	10 December 1890 - 56 Albert Street, Landport, Portsmouth, Hampshire
Died:	29 August 1966 aged 75, at his home at 5 Yorke Street, Southsea, Hampshire
Cremated:	1 September at Porchester Crematorium, Portsmouth. Ref: C / 18945. Ashes buried at North Border Post - Plot 20 at Crematorium
Deed/Service:	4 October 1917. Seeing the platoon on his right held up by an enemy machine-gun, he rushed the gun and captured it, killing the crew. He then led a section to the attack on a farm, where under heavy fire he went forward calling on the garrison to surrender. As the enemy continued to fire on him he opened fire, killing four, whereupon the remaining sixteen Germans surrendered
Commemoration:	i) Plaque and portrait at the Fratton Bridge British Legion Club, Portsmouth ii) Ockenden Close, Southsea

Gazette: 8 November 1917

| 894 | PEELER Walter VC BEM Sergeant 3rd Pioneer Bn. Australian Imperial Force | Levi Cottages, Ypres Belgium 980 |

Born: 9 August 1887 - Barkers Creek, near Castlemaine, Melbourne, Victoria, Australia
Died: 23 May 1968 aged 80, at his home in Moore Street, South Caulfield, Victoria
Buried: Brighton Cemetery, Melbourne. Lawn Section. Grave 36. Compartment H. Headstone shows age 81
Deed/Service: 20 September 1917 (Lance-Corporal) During the first wave of an attack he encountered an enemy party sniping the advancing troops, and rushing to their position accounted for nine of them, clearing the way for the advance. He repeated this action on two subsequent occasions, each time accounting for the enemy. Later directed to an enemy machine-gun causing casualties, he killed the gunner and bombed the remaining crew

Gazette: 26 November 1917

Commemoration: i) Headstone ii) Memorial in the Victoria Garden of Remembrance, Springvale, Victoria iii) Peeler Soldiers Club, Casula, N.S.W. iv) Peeler Place, Canberra, A.C.T. v) Medals and display at Australian War Memorial, Canberra.

| 895 | SAGE Thomas Henry VC Private 8th Bn. The Somerset Light Infantry (Prince Albert's) (now The Light Infantry) | Tower Hamlets Spur, Ypres Belgium 1099 |

Born: 8 December 1882 - Ham Lane, Tiverton, Devon
Died: 20 July 1945 aged 62, at his home in Council Gardens, Tiverton following a long illness
Buried: Tiverton Cemetery. Section - XB. Obscure additional location reference to '1/36'. Headstone
Deed/Service: 4 October 1917. At Tower Hamlets Spur, he was in a shell-hole with eight other men, one of whom was shot while throwing a bomb which fell into the crater. He threw himself onto it, and saved the lives of several of his comrades, although he was severely wounded

Gazette:18 December 1917

Commemoration: i) Headstone ii) Parchment Memorial at Tiverton Museum

896   **CLAMP William   VC   Corporal   6th Bn. The Yorkshire Regiment (now The Green Howards)**   The Brewery, Poelcapelle
                                                                                                                                               POSTHUMOUS
Born: 28 October 1891 - Bridge Street, Motherwell, Lanarkshire, Scotland   **215**
Died: 9 October 1917 aged 25. Killed by a sniper when encouraging his men, following his VC action at The Brewery, Poelcapelle, Belgium
Buried: Has no known grave - name on The Tyne Cot Memorial, Belgium. 5 Miles N.E. of Ypres. Panel 52/54 (See Map A - 11)
Deed/Service: 9 October 1917. When an advance was checked by intense machine-gun fire from concrete blockhouses and snipers, he attempted to
                    rush the largest block-house. The attempt failed, but collecting more bombs he dashed forward again and hurled his bombs, killing many
                    occupants and capturing a machine-gun and twenty prisoners whom he brought back under heavy fire   **Gazette: 18 December 1917**
Commemoration: i) Name on Tyne Cot Memorial ii) Clamp Prize, Craignenk School, Motherwell iii) Clamp Road, Motherwell iv) Medals at Green
                    Howards Museum

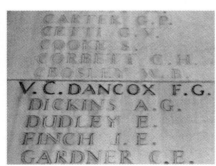

897   **DANCOX Frederick George   VC   Private   4th Bn. The Worcestershire Regiment (now The Worcestershire and   Namur Crossing, Boesinghe
                                                                             Sherwood Foresters Regiment)   Belgium
                                                                                                                                               299**
Born: 1879 - Barbourne, Worcester, Worcestershire
Died: 30 November 1917 aged 38. Struck in head by shrapnel and killed, during a later action near Masnieres, France
Buried: Has no known grave - name on The Cambrai Memorial, Louveral, France. 8 Miles E. of Bapaume. Panel 6 (See Map A - 30)
Deed/Service: 9 October 1917. After an objective had been taken, work was badly hampered by an enemy machine-gun firing from a concrete emplacement.
                    With nine other men he worked his way through the barrage and entered the enemy pill-box from the rear and threatened the garrison with
                    a Mills bomb. He emerged with a machine-gun under his arm and about forty prisoners and later kept the gun in action throughout the day **Gazette: 26 November 1917**
Commemoration: i) Name on The Cambrai Memorial ii) Sheltered housing in Worcester named for him iii) Medals at the Worcestershire Regimental
                    Museum

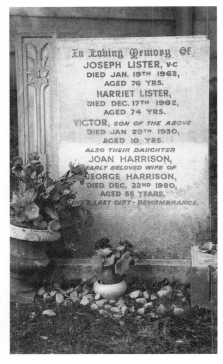

| 898 | LISTER Joseph VC Sergeant 1st Bn. The Lancashire Fusiliers (now The Royal Regiment of Fusiliers) | Olga House, Ypres Belgium 747 |

Born: 19 October 1886 - 65 Fenney Street, Higher Broughton, Salford, Lancashire

Died: 19 January 1963 aged 76, at the Reddish Hospital, Stockport, Cheshire

Buried: Willow Grove Cemetery, Reddish. Section P. Grave 9931. Headstone

Deed/Service: 9 October 1917. When the advance of his company was held up by machine-gun fire from the direction of a pill-box, he rushed ahead of his men, located the gun, killed two of the gunners and the remainder surrendered. Reaching the pill-box, he called on the garrison to surrender, which they did with the exception of one man whom he shot, whereupon almost 100 Germans surrendered as they emerged from nearby shell-holes

Gazette: 26 November 1917

Commemoration: i) Headstone

| 899 | MOLYNEUX John VC Sergeant 2nd Bn. The Royal Fusiliers (now The Royal Regiment of Fusiliers) | Conde House, Langemarck Belgium 880 |

Born: 22 November 1890 - 3 Marshall's Cross Road, Peasley Cross, St. Helens, Lancashire

Died: 25 March 1972 aged 81. Died in Ashtons Green Hostel, Parr, St. Helens, after collapsing in the street on an errand for an elderly neighbour

Cremated: 30 March at St. Helens Crematorium. Ashes scattered in Section 3 in Garden of Remembrance. No memorial tablet

Deed/Service: 9 October 1917. After organising a bombing party to deal with a machine-gun post in a trench in front of a house, which had been holding up an attack and causing many casualties, he captured the gun and killed the crew. Running to the house and calling for reinforcements, he was engaged in hand-to-hand fighting as assistance arrived and the enemy soon surrendered, making a total of some 25 prisoners

Gazette: 26 November 1917

Commemoration: i) Medals at Royal Fusiliers Museum

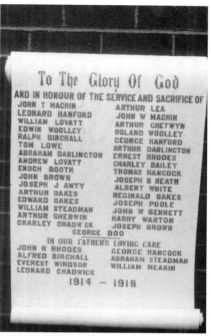

New Chapel Methodist Church

900   **RHODES John Harold   VC DCM & Bar   Lance - Sergeant   3rd Bn. Grenadier Guards**   Houthulst Forest, Belgium

1044

Born:	17 May 1891 - Mellor Street, Packmoor, Stoke-on-Trent, Staffordshire
Died:	27 November 1917 aged 26, of wounds received in later action, at 48 Casualty Clearing Station, near Fontaine Notre Dame, Cambrai, France
Buried:	Rocquigny-Equancourt Road, British Cemetery, France. 7 Miles N. of Peronne. Plot III. Row E. Grave 1. Headstone (See Map A - 30)
Deed/Service:	9 October 1917. When in charge of a Lewis gun section covering the consolidation of the right front company, he accounted for several enemy with his rifle and Lewis gun. Seeing three of the enemy leave a pill-box he went alone through our barrage and machine-gun fire entered the pill-box and captured nine of the enemy, bringing them back to British lines together with valuable information
Commemoration:	i) Headstone ii) Plaque at New Chapel Methodist Church, Stoke-on-Trent iii) Plaque at Packmoor School iv) Road in Tunstall, Staffs planned to be named in his honour v) Medals in Grenadier Guards Museum

Gazette: 26 November 1917

901   **HALTON Albert   VC   Private   1st Bn. The King's Own (Royal Lancaster) Regiment (now King's Own Royal Border Regt.)**   Requete Farm, Poelcapelle Belgium

515

Born:	1 May 1893 - Warton, Carnforth, near Lancaster, Lancashire
Died:	24 July 1971 aged 78, at his home in the Westfield War Memorial Village, Lancaster
Cremated:	Lancaster & Morecombe Crematorium. Ashes in Plot 38/6. Plaque on bench in the Crematorium Garden of Remembrance
Deed/Service:	12 October 1917. After an objective had been reached, he rushed forward some 300 yards under heavy fire, capturing a machine-gun and its crew, which was causing heavy casualties. Showing the greatest disregard for his own safety he later brought in twelve prisoners
Commemoration:	i) Plaque on bench at Crematorium ii) Plaque in Westfield War Memorial Village iii) Medals at the King's Own Regimental Museum

Gazette: 26 November 1917

902	JEFFRIES Clarence Smith VC Captain 34th Bn. (N.S.W.) Australian Imperial Force	Passchendaele, Belgium

Born: 26 October 1894 - Wallsend, Newcastle, New South Wales, Australia

Died: 12 October 1917 aged 22. From wounds received during his VC action at Hillside Farm, Passchendaele, Belgium

Buried: 14 September 1920 in Tyne Cot Cemetery, Belgium. 5 Miles N.E. of Ypres. Plot XL. Row E. Grave 1. Headstone (See Map A - 11)
His body was exhumed from the battle field on 14 September 1920, and re-buried in Tyne Cot Cemetery. Stone shows age 23

Deed/Service: 12 October 1917. Having organised a party of men, he rushed a machine-gun emplacement capturing four machine-guns and 35 prisoners.
He later organised a second attack, capturing two more guns and thirty more prisoners, but was mortally wounded in the stomach

Commemoration: i) Headstone ii) Carved chair to his memory, Holy Trinity Anglican Church, Newcastle iii) Plaque in Newcastle Primary School Library
iv) The Jeffries Memorial Park, Abermain, N.S.W. v) Jefferis (sic) Street, Canberra, A.C.T. vi) Memorial at the Australian War Memorial,
Canberra vii) Medals in Christchurch Cathedral, Newcastle

POSTHUMOUS
637

Gazette: 18 December 1917

903	HOLMES Thomas William VC Private 4th Canadian Mounted Rifles, 2nd Central Ontario Regt., Canadian Expeditionary Force	Wolf Copse, Passchendaele

Born: 14 October 1898 - Montreal, Canada

Died: 4 January 1950 aged 51, in Toronto, Ontario, Canada following a ten year battle with T.B. and cancer

Buried: Greenwood Cemetery, Owen Sound, Ontario, Canada. Headstone

Deed/Service: 26 October 1917. When the right flank of an attack was held up by heavy machine-gun fire from a pill box and heavy casualties were
producing a critical situation, he ran forward alone and threw bombs which killed and wounded the gun crews. He later fetched another
bomb and threw this into the entrance of the pill-box, causing nineteen occupants to surrender

Commemoration: i) Headstone ii) Plaque in Queens Park, Owen Sound iii) Medals at Royal Canadian Legion Post, Owen Sound

Belgium
587

Gazette: 11 January 1918

904	O'KELLY Christopher Patrick John VC MC Major	52nd Bn. Manitoba Regiment, Canadian Expeditionary Force	Passchendaele, Belgium	

Born: 18 November 1895 - Winnipeg, Manitoba, Canada

942

Died: Last seen alive 15 November 1922 when canoeing on Lac Seul, Ontario. Body not recovered

Buried: No known grave. Cairn erected on Goose Island, Lac Seul by brother officers

Deed/Service: 26 October 1917. He led his company with extraordinary skill and determination in capturing six pill-boxes, ten machine-guns and one hundred prisoners. Later his company repelled a strong counter-attack, taking more prisoners, and that night captured a raiding party of eleven men and another gun

Gazette: 11 January 1918

Commemoration: i) Memorial cairn ii) Plaque at the Legion Hall, Red Lake, Ontario iii) Medals at the Canadian War Museum, Ottawa

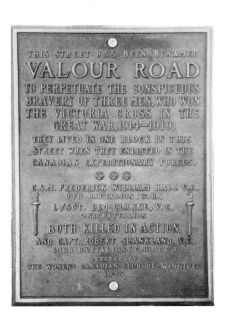

905	SHANKLAND Robert VC DCM Lieutenant - Colonel	43rd Bn. Manitoba Regiment, Canadian Expeditionary Force	Passchendaele, Belgium	

Born: 10 October 1887 - 68 Church Street, Ayr, Scotland

1129

Died: 20 January 1968 aged 80, at the Shaughnessy Hospital, Vancouver, British Columbia, Canada

Cremated: Mountain View Crematorium, Vancouver. Ashes in Mountain View Cemetery. Possible some scattered at sea - unconfirmed

Deed/Service: 26 October 1917 (Lieutenant) Having gained a position on the Bellevue Spur, he rallied the remnants of his own platoon and other companies, disposed them to command the ground and inflicted heavy casualties on the retreating enemy. Later he dispersed a counter-attack and communicated to his H.Q. an accurate report of the brigade frontage. His courage and example inspired all ranks

Gazette: 18 December 1917

Commemoration: i) Bronze plaque on a lamp post in Valour Road, Winnipeg ii) Medals in Winnipeg Rifles Museum, Winnipeg

906	LAFONE Alexander Malins VC Major 1/1st County of London Yeomanry	Beersheba, Palestine now Israel

Born: 19 August 1870 - Cressfield, Crosby Road South, Waterloo, Liverpool

Died: 27 October 1917 aged 47. Killed during his VC action near Beersheba, Palestine

Buried: Beersheba War Cemetery, Israel. N.W. suburbs of town. 25 miles S.E. of Gaza. Row Q. Grave 7. Headstone

Deed/Service: 27 October 1917. He held a position for over seven hours against vastly superior enemy forces, under heavy shell fire and repelled many cavalry charges with heavy losses. When all but three of his men had become casualties he ordered those who could walk to move to a trench in the rear where he maintained a heroic resistance. When finally surrounded he stepped into the open and continued fighting, until mortally wounded

POSTHUMOUS
710

Gazette: 18 December 1917

Commemoration: i) Headstone ii) Name on Regimental Memorial in St. Paul's Cathedral, London iii) Medals at Dulwich College, London

907	KINROSS Cecil John VC Private 49th Bn. Alberta Regiment, Canadian Expeditionary Force	Furst Farm, Passchendaele Belgium

Born: Probably 13 July 1897 although attested - 17 February 1895 - Hillend, Clackmannan, Scotland

Died: 21 June 1957 aged 59 (62), in a hotel room at Lougheed, Alberta, Canada

Buried: Lougheed Cemetery. Soldier's Plot. Headstone shows age 62

Deed/Service: 28 - 29 October and 31 October - 1 November 1917. Shortly after the main attack at Passchendaele was launched, his company was held up by heavy fire from an enemy machine-gun. He studied the situation before divesting himself of all his equipment except rifle and bandolier, then ran alone over open ground. Charging the enemy gun, he killed the crew of six and destroyed the gun, allowing the advance to continue

697

Gazette: 11 January 1918

Commemoration: i) Headstone ii) Playground named for him in Lougheed iii) Kinross Post of R.C.L., Lougheed iv) Mount Kinross, Jasper National Park, Alberta

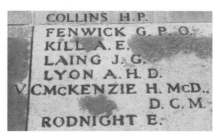

| 908 | McKENZIE Hugh McDonald VC DCM Lieutenant 7th Coy. Canadian Machine Gun Corps, Canadian Expeditionary Force | Meescheele Spur, Belgium POSTHUMOUS 799 |

Born: 5 December 1885 - Liverpool, Lancashire
Died: 30 October 1917 aged 31. Shot in the head during his VC action near Passchendaele, Belgium
Buried: Has no known grave - name on Menin Gate Memorial, Ypres, Belgium. Panel 56 (See Map A - 11)
Deed/Service: 30 October 1917. When in charge of a section of four machine-guns accompanying the infantry in an attack, he saw that all the officers and most of the NCO's of an infantry company had become casualties and the attack was faltering. Handing over his command, he rallied the infantry and captured the strong-point. He then led a successful raid on a pill-box causing the casualties, but was killed in the attempt
Commemoration: i) Name on Menin Gate ii) Mount McKenzie, Jasper National Park, Alberta iii) Medals in the Museum of the Regiments, Calgary, Alberta

Gazette: 13 February 1918

| 909 | MULLIN George Harry VC MM Major | Princess Patricia's Canadian Light Infantry, Eastern Ontario Regiment Canadian Expeditionary Force | Passchendale, Belgium |

Born: 15 August 1892 - Portland, Oregon, United States of America
Died: 5 April 1963 aged 70, at his home in Garnet Street, Regina, Saskatchewan, Canada, from natural causes
Buried: Moosomin South Side Cemetery, Moosomin, Saskatchewan. Legion Plot. Headstone shows age 71
Deed/Service: 30 October 1917 (Sergeant) When an enemy pill-box, was causing heavy casualties and holding up an attack, he crawled close to an enemy post beside the pill-box and killed the occupants before rushing the pill-box. He climbed on top and by firing down on the German gunners inside compelled them to surrender. All this time rapid fire was concentrated on him, his clothing being riddled by bullets, but he never faltered in his purpose and he not only saved the situation, but indirectly saved many lives
Commemoration: i) Headstone ii) Medals in the Museum of the Regiments of the Calgary

Gazette: 11 January 1918

900

910   PEARKES The Hon. George   VC CB DSO MC   Major - General   5th Canadian Mounted Rifles Bn. Quebec Regiment   Vapour Farm, Passchendaele
Canadian Expeditionary Force   Belgium
974

Born:	26 February 1888 - Watford, Hertfordshire. Born George Randolph PEARKES
Died:	30 May 1984 aged 96, in a rest home in Victoria, British Columbia, Canada, following a stroke
Buried:	Holy Trinity Cemetery, West Saanich, Sidney, Victoria. Section 4 - West. Headstone
Deed/Service:	30 - 31 October 1917 (A/Major) Having taken an objective, despite a serious leg wound, he managed to repel many counter-attacks with the few men left at his disposal. His actions throughout showed supreme courage and leadership, with accurate appraisals proving invaluable to his C.O.

Gazette: 11 January 1918

Commemoration: i) Headstone ii) Plaque at R.C.M.P. Museum, Regina, Saskatchewan iii) Two Canadian Legion Posts named for him - Summerside, Prince Edward Island and Princeton, British Columbia iv) Medals at the Canadian War Museum, Ottawa

911   COLLINS John   VC DCM MM   Sergeant   25th Bn. The Royal Welch Fusiliers   Wadi Saba, Beersheba
Palestine, now Israel
233

Born:	10 September 1880 - West Hatch, near Taunton, Somerset. Other references show 1877
Died:	3 September 1951 aged 70, in St. Tydfil's Hospital, Merthyr Tydfil, Mid-Glamorgan, Wales
Buried:	8 September at Pant Cemetery, Merthyr Tydfil. R.C. Section. Plot XE. Grave 44. Headstone
Deed/Service:	31 October 1917 (A/Corporal) When his battalion was forced to lie in the open under heavy shell and machine-gun fire, he went out alone to bring back many wounded to the British lines. He then led the final assault on Wadi Saba with great skill, despite heavy fire at close range and uncut wire, killing fifteen of the enemy. With a Lewis gun section he later effectively covered the reorganisation and consolidation of men under heavy fire

Commemoration: i) Headstone ii) Collins Walk, Wrexham iii) Medals at Royal Welch Fusiliers Museum

Gazette: 18 December 1917

| 912 | BARRON Colin Fraser | VC | Sergeant - Major | 3rd Bn. 1st Central Ontario Regiment, Canadian Expeditionary Force | Vine Cottage Passchendaele, Belgium 55 |

Born: 20 September 1895 - Baldavie, Boyndie, Banff, Alberta, Canada
Died: 15 August 1959 aged 63. Died in Sunnybrook Hospital, Toronto, Ontario, Canada
Buried: Prospect Cemetery, Toronto. Veteran's Section 7. Grave 3562. Headstone
Deed/Service: 6 November 1917 (Corporal) When his unit was held up by three machine-guns posts during an attack, he opened fire on them before rushing the guns, killing four of the crew and capturing the remainder. He then turned one of the guns on the retiring enemy, causing severe casualties
Commemoration: i) Headstone

Gazette: 11 January 1918

| 913 | ROBERTSON James Peter | VC | Private | 27th Bn. Manitoba Regiment (Winnipeg), Canadian Expeditionary Force | Passchendaele, Belgium POSTHUMOUS 1067 |

Born: 26 October 1883 - Albion Mines, Pictou, Nova Scotia, Canada
Died: 6 November 1917 aged 34. Killed by a shell explosion during his VC action in Passchendaele Village, Belgium
Buried: Tyne Cot Cemetery, Passchendaele, Belgium. 5 Miles N.E. of Ypres. Plot LV111. Row D. Grave 26. Headstone (See Map A - 11)
Deed/Service: 6 November 1917. When his platoon was held up by a machine-gun, he rushed the gun, killed four of the crew and then turned the gun on the remainder. He then led his platoon to their final objective and again used the gun to fire on the retreating enemy. Later he went out under heavy fire to bring in two wounded men, carrying the first to safety but was killed as he returned with the second
Commemoration: i) Headstone ii) A memorial park, a swimming pool, a street and a branch of Royal Canadian Legion at Medicine Hat, Alberta all named for him

Gazette: 11 January 1918

MAJOR G.E. MAURICE COWELL.
MAJOR I. PERCY SMITH. D.S.O.
CAPT. J. W. BOWYER.
CAPT. C. W. BRUCE.
CAPT. HENRY FAWCETT GARRETT.
CAPT. PHILIP S. HOUGHTON.
CAPT. C.E.C. JONES.
CAPT. J. FOX RUSSELL. V.C. .M.C.
CAPT. CLAUD GARRETT SALMON.

Aldeburgh Church

| 914 | RUSSELL John Fox VC MC Captain Royal Army Medical Corps attd. 1/6th Bn. The Royal Welch Fusiliers | Tel-el-Khuweilfeh, Palestine now Israel |

Born: 27 January 1893 - Plas Tanalltran, Holyhead, Anglesey, Wales. Name occasionally FOX-RUSSELL
Died: 6 November 1917 aged 24. Fatally wounded in his VC action near Tel-el-Khuweilfeh, Palestine
Buried: i) Where he fell at Tel-el-Khuweilfeh ii) Beersheba War Cemetery, Israel. 25 miles S.E. of Gaza. Row F. Grave 31. Headstone
Deed/Service: 6 November 1917. Under murderous fire from snipers and machine-guns, he repeatedly went out to attend the wounded and although exhausted he carried many casualties to safety until he was fatally wounded
Commemoration: i) Headstone ii) Name on Holyhead War Memorial iii) Plaque in Aldeburgh Church, Suffolk iv) Plaque at St. Bees School, Cumbria v) Plaque in The Middlesex Hospital, London vi) Name on memorial in RAMC HQ, Millbank, London vii) Memorial in Royal British Legion Club, Holyhead viii) Medals in R.A.M.C. Museum

POSTHUMOUS
1088

Gazette: 11 January 1918

| 915 | BORTON Arthur Drummond VC CMG DSO Lieutenant - Colonel 2/22nd (County of London) Bn. The London Regiment | Sheria, Palestine now Israel |

Born: 1 July 1883 - Chevening, Kent
Died: 5 January 1933 aged 50, at Southwold, Suffolk
Buried: Hunton Churchyard, near Maidstone, Kent. Headstone
Deed/Service: 7 November 1917. Under the most difficult conditions he deployed his battalion for attack against a strongly held position in unknown country. As the leading waves were checked by withering fire, he moved along the line under heavy fire before leading them forward and taking their objective. He later led a party of volunteers against a battery of field-guns in action capturing both the guns and their detachments
Commemoration: i) Headstone ii) Plaque in Winchester Cathedral iii) Medals at P.O.W. Royal Regimental Museum

106

Gazette: 18 December 1917

74

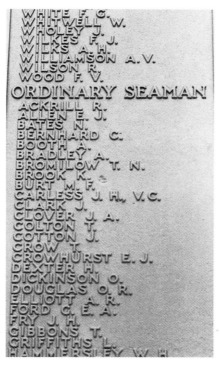

916   **CARLESS John Henry VC Ordinary Seaman Royal Navy**   **Heligoland, North Sea**
POSTHUMOUS

Born:	11 November 1896 - 31 Tasker Street, Walsall, Staffordshire
Died:	17 November 1917 aged 21. Killed in his VC action during the Battle of Heligoland, North Sea
Buried:	At sea, off Heligoland. Name on the Portsmouth Naval Memorial, Hampshire. Column 2. Panel 25
Deed/Service:	17 November 1917. Although mortally wounded in the abdomen early in the battle, he continued serving his gun and helping to clear away casualties, setting an inspirational example. He collapsed but got up again and cheered on the new gun crew before falling dead
Commemoration:	i) Name on Portsmouth Memorial ii) Bust and memorial, Walsall Central Library iii) Carless Street, Walsall iv) Carless Close,Gosport, Hampshire

183

Gazette: 17 May 1918

Jasper National Park

917   **McBEATH Robert Gordon VC Lance - Corporal 1/5th Bn. The Seaforth Highlanders (now The Highlanders)**   **West of Cambrai, France**

Born:	22 December 1898 - Fraserburgh, Caithness, Scotland
Died:	9 October 1922 aged 23. Shot in the chest when making an arrest while serving with the Vancouver Police. He died soon afterwards in St. Paul's Hospital, Vancouver. His killer, Fred Deal, was arrested and received the death sentence, reduced to 21 years prison on appeal
Cremated:	Mountain View Crematorium, Vancouver. Ashes buried in Masonic Section 193. Lot 6. Headstone
Deed/Service:	20 November 1917. When an advance was held up by a nest of machine-guns and heavy casualties resulted, he volunteered to go ahead alone. Finding that several other machine-guns were in action, he attacked them with the assistance of a tank, driving the gun crew to ground in a dug-out. He rushed in after them and shot the first man who opposed him and captured the remaining three officers and thirty men
Commemoration:	i) Headstone ii) Police launch 'R.G. McBeath' iii) Mount McBeath, Jasper National Park, Alberta iv) Medals at the Highlanders Museum

766

Gazette: 11 January 1918

918   **SHEPHERD Albert Edward   VC   Corporal**   12 (S) Bn. The King's Royal Rifle Corps (now Royal Green Jackets)   Villers Plouich, France

Born:	11 January 1897 - Royston, near Barnsley, Yorkshire
Died:	23 October 1966 aged 69, at Royston
Buried:	Royston Cemetery. Headstone
Deed/Service:	20 November 1917 (Rifleman) When his company was held up by a machine-gun at point-blank range, he rushed forward, bombed the team and captured the gun, although ordered not to. The company continued its advance and came under heavy fire losing its last officer and NCO. Taking command, he ordered his men down, went back some seventy yards got the help of a tank and led them to their objective

1135

Gazette: 13 February 1918

Commemoration: i) Headstone   ii) Name on archway to churchyard in Royston   iii) Medals at Royal Green Jackets Museum

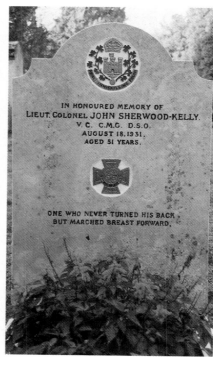
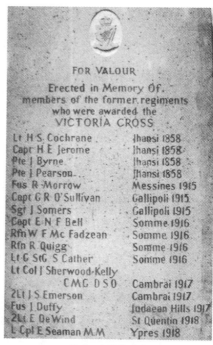

St. Anne's Cathedral

919   **SHERWOOD - KELLY John   VC CMG DSO   A/Lt. - Colonel**   The Norfolk Regiment, comd. 1st Bn. Royal Inniskilling Fusiliers   Marcoing, France
               (now Royal Anglian Regiment and Royal Irish Regiment respectively)

Born:	13 January 1880 - Queenstown, Cape Province, South Africa
Died:	18 August 1931 aged 51, from malaria, in a nursing home in Kensington, West London
Buried:	Brookwood Cemetery, near Woking, Surrey. Block 86. Grave 196296. Headstone (See Map D)
Deed/Service:	20 November 1917. When a party of men were held on the near side of a canal by heavy fire, he led his leading company across the canal then reconnoitred nearby high ground held by the enemy. Forcing his way through obstacles, he took a Lewis gun team and covered the advance of his battalion, who took the position. He later led a charge against some enemy-held pits, capturing five machine-guns and forty-six prisoners

673

Gazette: 11 January 1918

Commemoration: i) Headstone   ii) Plaque at St. Anne's Cathedral, Belfast   iii) Name on South African Memorial, Delville Wood, Somme, France   iv) Medals at the National Museum of Military History, Johannesburg, South Africa

920	SPACKMAN Charles Edward VC MM Sergeant 1st Bn. The Border Regiment (now The King's Own Royal Borderers)	Marcoing, France
Born:	11 January 1891 - Fulham, South West London	1171
Died:	6 May 1969 aged 78, at The General Hospital, Southampton, Hampshire	
Cremated:	9 May at Swaythling Crematorium, Southampton. Ref: 47849. Ashes in Section 7 Sth. Stoneham Garden of Remembrance. No memorial	
Deed/Service:	20 November 1917. During an attack, the leading company was held up by heavy fire from a gun covering the approaches. He went forward alone succeeded in killing all but one of the crew and captured the gun allowing the advance to continue	**Gazette: 11 January 1918**
Commemoration :		

921	STRACHAN Harcus VC MC Lieutenant - Colonel Fort Garry Horse, Canadian Expeditionary Force	Masnieres, France
Born:	7 November 1884 - Borrowstounness, West Lothian, Scotland. Named MARCUS on Birth Certificate	1188
Died:	1 May 1982 aged 97, at the U.B.C. Hospital, Vancouver, Canada	
Cremated:	North Vancouver Crematorium, 1505 Lillooet, Vancouver. Ashes in Rose Garden Columbarium in the Boal vault, under a cedar tree	
Deed/Service:	20 November 1917 (Lieutenant) When his squadron leader was killed while galloping towards the German front line, he led the squadron through a line of enemy machine-gun posts, then with the surviving troopers charged the German battery, killing seven gunners with his sword. When all the gunners had been killed, he rallied the men and fought his way back through enemy lines at night, with the wounded and fifteen prisoners	**Gazette: 18 December 1917**
Commemoration:		

| 922 | WAIN Richard William Leslie | VC | Acting Captain | 'A' Bn. Tank Corps (now Royal Tank Regiment) | Marcoing, France |

Marcoing, France
POSTHUMOUS
1256

Born: 5 December 1896 - 4 Victoria Square, Penarth, Glamorgan, Wales
Died: 20 November 1917 aged 20. Killed during his VC action at Marcoing, near Cambrai
Buried: Where he fell at Marcoing - grave not found. Name on Cambrai Memorial, France. 8 miles E. of Bapaume. Panel 13 (See Map A - 30)
Deed/Service: 20 November 1917. When he and a comrade were the only survivors after his tank was disabled by a direct hit near an enemy strong point, he refused medical aid despite being seriously wounded. He captured the strong point using a Lewis gun, taking half the garrison prisoner and although wounded again he picked up a rifle and continued firing until fatally wounded in the head
Commemoration: i) Name on Cambrai Memorial ii) Plaque at St. Bees School, Cumberland iii) Memorial at Llandaff Cathedral, Cardiff

Gazette: 13 February 1918

| 923 | McAULAY John | VC DCM | Sergeant | 1st Bn. Scots Guards | Fontaine Notre Dame France |

Fontaine Notre Dame
France
764

Born: 27 December 1888 - King Horn, Fife, Scotland
Died: 14 January 1956 aged 67, at his home at 915 Aikenhead Road, Burnside, Glasgow
Buried: 17 January at New Eastwood Cemetery, Glasgow. Section L - V11. Lair 139. Headstone
Deed/Service: 27 November 1917. When all his officers had become casualties, he assumed command of the company and under shell and machine-gun fire successfully held and consolidated the objectives gained. When the Germans counter-attacked, he repulsed them by skilful and bold use of his guns, causing heavy casualties. He then carried his mortally wounded company commander to a place of safety
Commemoration: i) Headstone ii) Medals at the Scots Guards Museum

Gazette: 11 January 1918

Cambrai Memorial

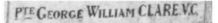

Chatteris War Memorial

924	CLARE George William Burdett VC Private 5th Lancers (Royal Irish now Queen's Royal Lancers)	Bourlon Wood, France

POSTHUMOUS

216

Born: 18 May 1889 - St. Ives, Huntingdonshire

Died: 29 November 1917 aged 28. Killed at conclusion of his VC action, in Bourlon Wood, France

Buried: Has no known grave - name on the Cambrai Memorial, France. 8 Miles E. of Bapaume. Panel 1 (See Map A - 30)

Deed/Service: 28 - 29 November 1917. As a stretcher-bearer he assisted and dressed the wounded under intense fire, and crossed an open area to a detached post when all the occupants had become casualties. Having dressed all the cases, he manned the post single-handed until relieved. He then carried a seriously wounded man through intense fire to a dressing station, before going out to every post to warn them of gas

Gazette: 11 January 1918

Commemoration: i) Name on the Cambrai Memorial   ii) Window at St. Peter's and St. Paul's Church, Chatteris, Cambridgeshire iii) Name on the Chatteris War Memorial iv) Clare Street, Chatteris v) Medals at the Queen's Royal Lancers Museum

St. Mary's War Memorial

925	ELLIOTT - COOPER Neville Bowes VC DSO MC T/Lieutenant - Colonel	Comd. 8th Bn. The Royal Fusiliers (now The Royal Regiment of Fusiliers)	Near Cambrai, France

253

Born: 22 January 1889 - London

Died: 11 February 1918 aged 29. Died of wounds received in his VC action when a prisoner of war in Hanover, Germany

Buried: Hamburg Cemetery, Germany. Plot V. Row A. Grave 16. Headstone

Deed/Service: 30 November 1917. When the Germans broke through an outpost line, east of La Vacquerie, he immediately mounted a parapet calling on the reserve troops to follow him, and although unarmed, he led a counter-attack forcing the enemy back 600 yards. While ahead of his men he was severely wounded, and realising his force was out-numbered he ordered them to withdraw, aware that he would be taken prisoner

Gazette: 13 February 1918

Commemoration: i) Headstone ii) Memorial in Ripon Cathedral, Yorkshire iii) Name on St. Mary's War Memorial, Bentworth, Hampshire iv) Medals in The Royal Fusiliers Museum

926   **GEE Robert   VC MC   T/Captain   2nd Bn. The Royal Fusiliers (now The Royal Regiment of Fusiliers)**   Near Masnieres, France

Born:	7 May 1876 - Leicester	446
Died:	2 August 1960 aged 84, at Perth, Western Australia	
Cremated:	Karrakata Crematorium, Perth. Ashes scattered in Rose Garden P. No memorial tablet/plaque (See Map F)	
Deed/Service:	30 November 1917. Following a German attack which captured the brigade H.Q. and an ammunition dump, he found himself a prisoner	

Escaping immediately, he organised a party of brigade staff and counter-attacked the enemy, closely followed by two companies of infantry.
He saw an enemy machine-gun still in action, and went forward alone although wounded, killed eight of the crew and captured the gun   **Gazette: 11 January 1918**

Commemoration: i) Fountain and Memorial at the War Veterans' House, Perth ii) Medals at The Royal Fusiliers Museum

927   **GOURLEY Cyril Edward   VC MM   Captain**   **'D' Bty. 276th (West Lancashire) Brigade, Royal Field Artillery**   East of Epehy, France
                                                                                                                                  (now The Royal Regiment of Artillery)

Born:	19 January 1893 - 6 Victoria Park, Wavertree, Liverpool, Lancashire	472
Died:	31 January 1982 aged 89 in his sleep, at Grayswood House, Grayswood, Haslemere, Surrey	
Buried:	Grange Cemetery, West Kirby, Wirral, Cheshire. Section F. Plot 17 in family grave. Headstone	
Deed/Service:	30 November 1917 (Sergeant) While manning a section of howitzers, the enemy closed to within 100 yards of him. He pulled the gun out	

of the pit and engaged a machine-gun at 500 yards, knocking it out with a direct hit. He held the Germans in check all day, firing over open
sights, thereby saving his guns which were withdrawn at nightfall   **Gazette: 13 February 1918**

Commemoration: i) Headstone ii) Memorial at Grayswood College, Surrey iii) Plaque at Memorial College, West Kirby, Wirral, Cheshire iv) Plaque in
R.A. Chapel, Woolwich, London

Cambrai Memorial

928   **STONE Walter Napleton   VC DSO MC   A/Captain**   **3rd Bn. The Royal Fusiliers, attd. 17th (S) Battalion**   Cambrai Sector, France
                                                                                       (now The Royal Regiment of Fusiliers)   POSTHUMOUS

Born: 7 December 1891 - Blackheath, South East London   1186
Died: 30 November 1917 aged 25. Killed during his VC action at Moeuvries, near Cambrai, France
Buried: Has no known grave - name on the Cambrai Memorial, France. 8 Miles E. Bapaume. Panel 3/4 (See Map A - 30)
Deed/Service: 30 November 1917. When in command of an isolated company 1,000 yards in front of the British lines, he saw the enemy massing for an
                    attack. Sending the invaluable information back to HQ, he was ordered to withdraw. He sent three platoons back and remained with the
                    rearguard. An unexpected enemy attack developed, and while under heavy bombardment, he stood exposed on the parapet, passing more
                    valuable information back by field telephone until the line was cut. The rearguard was eventually cut to pieces, and he was seen fighting
                    to the last   **Gazette: 13 February 1918**
Commemoration: i) Name on the Cambrai Memorial ii) Name on headstone in the stone wall of Greenwich Cemetery, Well Hall Road, South East London

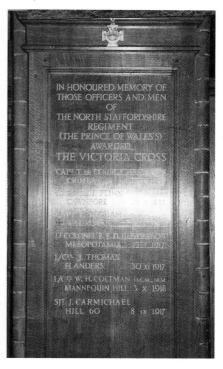

929   **THOMAS John   VC   Sergeant**   **2/5th Bn. The North Staffordshire Regiment (now The Staffordshire Regiment)**   Fontaine, France

Born: 10 May 1886 - Higher Openshaw, Manchester   1210
Died: 28 February 1954 aged 67, at his home in Lowfield Road, Stockport, Cheshire
Buried: Stockport Borough Cemetery, South Buxton Road, Manchester. Section LB. Grave 550. Headstone shows age 68
Deed/Service: 30 November 1917 (Lance-Corporal) Seeing the enemy preparing for a major counter-attack, he and a colleague made a reconnaissance
                    under heavy fire in full view of the Germans. His comrade was hit but he went on alone and reached an empty building. He remained there
                    for an hour, sniping at the enemy, returning with vital information which enabled plans to be made to meet the counter-attack   **Gazette: 13 February 1918**
Commemoration: i) Headstone ii) Plaque at Garrison Church, Whittington Barracks, Lichfield, Staffordshire

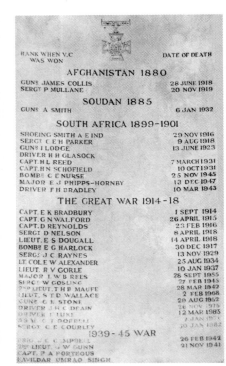

930   **WALLACE Samuel Thomas Dickson   VC   Captain   'C' Bty. 63rd Brigade, Royal Field Artillery (now Royal Regt. of Artillery)**   Gonnelieu, France

Born: 7 March 1892 - Thornhill, Dumfries, Scotland
1262

Died: 2 February 1968 aged 75, at Moffat, Dumfries and Galloway, Scotland

Buried: Moffat Cemetery. On right side of main gate. Headstone

Deed/Service: 30 November 1917 (T/Lieutenant) When surrounded by enemy infantry and his battery reduced to five men, he kept the guns firing by swinging the trails close together, with the men running and loading from gun to gun. He was in action for eight hours firing the whole time and inflicting severe casualties on the Germans. When infantry support finally arrived, he withdrew all his men and disabled the guns

Gazette: 13 February 1918

Commemoration: i) Headstone ii) Name on Memorial in R. A. Chapel, Woolwich, South East London iii) Medals at Royal Artillery Museum

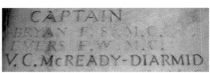

Cambrai Memorial

Middlesex Regiment Memorial, St. Symphorien

931   **McREADY - DIARMID Allastair Malcolm Cluny   VC   A/Captain   17th (S) Bn. The Middlesex Regt. (now P.O.W. Royal Regt.)**   Moeuvres Sector, France
POSTHUMOUS

Born: 21 March 1888 - Southgate, North London. Formerly Allastair Malcolm Cluny DREW, then Arthur Malcolm Cluny McCREADY-DIARMID   327

Died: 1 December 1917 aged 29. Killed by a bomb, during his VC action at Moeuvres, France

Buried: Has no known grave - name on the Cambrai Memorial, France. 8 Miles E. of Bapaume. Panel 9 (See Map A - 30)

Deed/Service: 30 November - 1 December 1917. When the enemy had penetrated our position and the situation was critical, he led his company through a heavy barrage, engaged the Germans and pushed them back 300 yards. The following day the enemy again attacked and pushed back another company, he led a counter-attack and again drove them back. It was entirely due to his accurate bomb throwing that the ground was regained

Gazette: 15 March 1918

Commemoration: i) Name on the Cambrai Memorial ii) Memorial at Victoria College, Jersey iii) Medals at National Army Museum

932 **BOUGHEY Stanley Henry Parry VC Second Lieutenant   1/4th Bn. The Royal Scots Fusiliers (now Royal Highland Fusiliers)** El Burf, Palestine
now Israel
Born: 9 April 1896 - Ayrshire, Scotland   **POSTHUMOUS**
Died: 4 December 1917 aged 21. Mortally wounded during his VC action near Ramleh, Palestine   **107**
Buried: Gaza War Cemetery, Israel. 1 Mile N.E. of Gaza town. 40 Miles S.E. of Tel Aviv. Plot XX. Row A. Grave 1. Headstone
Deed/Service: 1 December 1917. When the enemy attacked in large numbers and closed to within thirty yards of the British line, restricting our machine-gun
fire with bombs and automatic rifles, he rushed forward alone armed with bombs. Reaching the Turkish line, he killed many and caused
another thirty to surrender. As he turned to get more bombs he was mortally wounded at the moment the enemy began to surrender **Gazette: 13 February 1918**
Commemoration: i) Headstone ii) Name on the Blackpool War Memorial

933   **GOBIND Singh   VC   Jemadar (Sergeant - Major)   28th Light Cavalry, attd. 2nd Lancers, Indian Army**   **East of Peizieres, France**
Born: 7 December 1887 - Damoi Village, Jodhpur, India. Named on later records as GOVIND SINGH   **455**
Died: November 1941 aged 53, at Nagaur, Rajputana, India
Cremated: Damoi Village, Naguar Rajasthan
Deed/Service: 1 December 1917 (Lance-Daffadar - Cavalry Corporal) Under heavy fire in open ground, he volunteered on three occasions to carry
messages between the regiment and brigade H.Q., a distance of three miles. He succeeded in delivering the vital communications although
on each occasion his horse was shot, and he was compelled to complete the journey on foot   **Gazette: 11 January 1918**
Commemoration:

934   PATON George Henry Tatham   VC MC   Acting Captain   4th Bn. Grenadier Guards

Gonnelieu, France
POSTHUMOUS
969

Born:	3 October 1895 - Innelllan, Argyllshire, Scotland. Also known as TATHAM-PATON
Died:	1 December 1917 aged 22. Mortally wounded during his VC action, at Gonnelieu, France
Buried:	Metz-en-Couture Cemetery, British Extension, France. 11 miles S.W. of Cambrai. Plot 11. Row E. Grave 24. Headstone (Map A - 30)
Deed/Service:	1 December 1917. When a company on his left was driven back, leaving him practically surrounded, he walked up and down adjusting his line in spite of withering fire from the enemy fifty yards away. Personally removing several wounded, he moved his position from the village and again came under fire organising new lines. During four enemy attacks, he jumped onto the parapet to encourage his men, until mortally wounded
Commemoration:	i) Headstone ii) Name on family headstone in Putney Vale Cemetery, South West London iii) Name on the War Memorial on the promenade at Dunoon, Strathclyde iv) Patons Path, in Putney Vale Cemetery v) Medals at Grenadier Guards Museum

Gazette: 13 February 1918

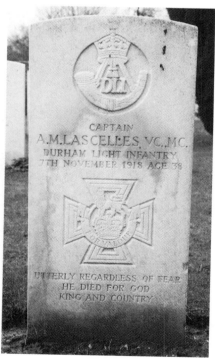

Pennal Cemetery

935   LASCELLES Arthur Moore   VC MC   A/Captain   3rd Bn. The Durham Light Infantry, attd. 14th Bn. (now The Light Infantry)

Masnieres, France
716

Born:	12 October 1880 - Wilby Lodge, Nightingale Lane, Streatham, South West London
Died:	7 November 1918 aged 38. Killed in a later action at Limont, near Fontaine, France
Buried:	Dourlers Communal Cemetery Extension, France. 17 miles S. of Mons. Plot 11. Row C. Grave 24. Headstone (See Map A - 22)
Deed/Service:	3 December 1917. Although wounded during a heavy bombardment, he continued to organize his defences until the enemy were repulsed. When part of his trench was captured, he mounted the parapet with his twelve remaining men, and rushed across machine-gun raked ground and drove sixty of the enemy back. His trench was captured during the next attack, but he escaped despite receiving two further wounds
Commemoration:	i) Headstone ii) Name on family grave, Pennal Cemetery, Gwynedd iii) Name on Pennal War Memorial iv) Name on Tywyn Memorial, Gwynedd v) Name on the Edinburgh University War Memorial vi) Name on University College of North Wales War Memorial vii) Medals at D.L.I. Museum

Gazette: 11 January 1918

936   **NICHOLAS Henry James   VC MM   Sergeant   1st Bn. Canterbury Infantry Regiment, New Zealand Expeditionary Force   Polderhoek, Belgium**

Born:	11 June 1891 - Lincoln, New Zealand	**928**
Died:	23 October 1918 aged 27. Killed in later action near Le Quesnoy, France	
Buried:	Vertigneul Churchyard, Romieres, France. 11 Miles E. of Cambrai. Grave 15. Headstone (See Map A - 21)	
Deed/Service:	3 December 1917 (Private) When his Lewis gun section was checked by heavy machine-gun fire from an enemy strong-point, he went out alone, followed at intervals by his section. He shot the garrison commander and overcame sixteen with bombs and bayonet, capturing the strong-point virtually single-handed and thereby saved many casualties. He later went out collecting ammunition under heavy machine-gun fire	**Gazette: 11 January 1918**
Commemoration:	i) Headstone ii) Memorial at Returned Soldiers Association H.Q., Dunedin, New Zealand iii) Medals at the Canterbury Museum, New Zealand	

Cambrai Memorial

Collon War Memorial

937   **EMERSON James Samuel   VC   T/Second Lieutenant   9th Bn. The Royal Inniskilling Fusiliers (now Royal Irish Regiment)   Near La Vacquerie, France**
POSTHUMOUS

Born:	3 August 1895 - Collon near Drogheda, Co. Louth, Ireland	**382**
Died:	6 December 1917 aged 22. Mortally wounded in his VC action near La Vacquerie, France	
Buried:	Has no known grave - name on Cambrai Memorial, France. 8 Miles E. of Bapaume. Panel 5/6 (See Map A - 30)	
Deed/Service:	6 December 1918. Leading an attack on the Hindenberg Line, he cleared 400 yards of trench before being wounded, then with just eight men left, they were outnumbered by an attack force, but killed many and took six prisoner. For three hours, when all other officers had become casualties, he remained with his men, repelling bombing attacks until mortally wounded when leading his men on another assault	**Gazette: 13 February 1918**
Commemoration:	i) Name on the Cambrai Memorial ii) Name on family headstone in the C. of I. Churchyard, Collon iii) Name on Collon War Memorial iv) Plaque at Mount Temple School, Dublin v) Name on Regt. Memorial, St. Anne's Cathedral, Belfast vi) Name on Ulster Tower, Somme	

938	TRAIN Charles William	VC	Sergeant	2/14th (County of London) Bn. The London Regiment (London Scottish)	Air Karim, Jerusalem

Palestine, now Israel
1225

Born: 21 September 1890 - Finsbury Park, North London
Died: 28 March 1965 aged 74, at Vancouver, British Columbia, Canada
Buried: Forest Lawn Memorial Park, Gilpin Street, Burnaby, B.C. Field of Honour. Normandy Section. Lot 208. Grave 3. Headstone
Deed/Service 8 December 1917 (Corporal) When his company was engaged at close range by the enemy, bringing an attack to a halt, he went forward alone armed with rifle grenades and put out a machine-gun team with a direct hit. He then shot or wounded those of the crew remaining, then went to the assistance of a comrade who was bombing the enemy, and killed a Turk carrying a machine-gun to safety

Gazette: 27 February 1918

Commemoration: i) Headstone   ii) Medals with the London Scottish Regiment

939	MILLS Walter	VC	Private	1/10th Bn. The Manchester Regiment (now The King's Regiment)	Givenchy, France

POSTHUMOUS
872

Born: 20 June 1894 - 4 Wellesley Street, Oldham, Lancashire
Died: 11 December 1917 aged 23. Died from the effects of gas poisoning, during his VC action at Givenchy, France
Buried: Gorre British and Indian Cemetery, France. 4 miles N.E. of Bethune. Plot V. Row C. Grave 2. Headstone (See Map A - 19)
Deed/Service: 10 - 11 December 1918. Following an intense gas attack a strong enemy patrol tried to rush our posts, the garrisons of which had been overcome. Although badly gassed himself, he met the attack single-handed by throwing bombs until reinforcements arrived and the Germans were driven off. He died of gas poisoning as he was carried away, but it was entirely due to him that the enemy had been defeated and the line held

Gazette: 13 February 1918

Commemoration: i) Headstone   ii) His medals were buried with his daughter Ellen

940   **CHRISTIE John Alexander**   **VC**   **Lance - Corporal**   **1/11th (County of London) Bn. The London Regiment (Finsbury Rifles)**   Fejja, Palestine, now Israel

Born:	14 May 1895 - Edmonton, North London
Died:	10 September 1967 aged 72, at St. Thomas's Hospital, Stockport, Greater Manchester
Cremated:	15 September at Stockport Crematorium. Ashes scattered in 'First' Garden of Remembrance. No memorial plaque/tablet
Deed/Service:	21 - 22 December 1918. When a British position had been captured and the enemy were making forays along the communication trenches, he went out alone with a supply of bombs. He began bombing the enemy in spite of heavy opposition, until a block had been established. His prompt action cleared a difficult position at a most critical time, and saved many lives
Commemoration:	i) Patriot Class locomotive named for him

214

Gazette: 27 February 1918

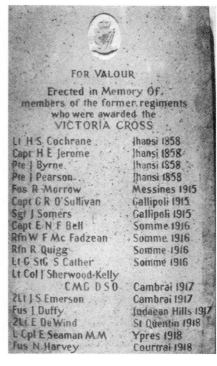

941   **DUFFY James**   **VC**   **Private**   **6th Bn. The Royal Inniskilling Fusiliers (now The Royal Irish Regiment)**   Kereina Peak, Palestine now Israel

Born:	17 November 1889 - Gweedore, Co. Donegal, Ireland
Died:	7 April 1969 aged 79, in Letterkenny, Co. Donegal
Buried:	Conwal Cemetery, Letterkenny. Headstone
Deed/Service:	27 December 1917. He and another stretcher-bearer went to bring in a badly wounded comrade, while his company were holding an exposed position. After his comrade was wounded and a replacement killed, he went out alone under heavy fire and succeeded in getting both the wounded men under cover and attended to their injuries. His gallantry undoubtedly saved both mens lives
Commemoration:	i) Headstone ii) Name on Regimental Plaque at St. Anne's Cathedral, Belfast iii) Medals at Royal Inniskilling Fusiliers Museum

353

Gazette: 28 February 1918

The Victoria Cross, Distinguished Service Medal and campaign medals awarded to Chief Petty Officer Ernest Herbert Pitcher (855)

The Victoria Cross, Order of the British Empire and campaign medals awarded to Sergeant Alfred Joseph Knight (881)

Chapter Twelve
The First World War
1918

No's 942 - 1148

The Victoria Cross and campaign medals awarded to Major Allan Ebenezer Ker (952)

The Victoria Cross and campaign medals awarded to Private Jack Thomas Counter (986)

942	McCUDDEN James Thomas Byford	VC DSO & Bar MC & Bar MM	Major	General List and 56 Squadron		Flying Services over France

Royal Flying Corps (later Royal Air Force)

Born: 28 March 1895 - The Female Hospital, Brompton, Kent

770

Died: 9 July 1918 aged 23. From a fractured skull received in flying accident at No. 21 Casualty Station, Auxi-le-Chateau, Marquise, France.

Buried: 10 July at Wavans British Cemetery, France. 12 Miles S. of Hesdin. Row B. Grave 10. Headstone (See Map A - 18)

Deed/Service: 23 December 1917 - 5 March 1918 (T/Captain) (NB: In line with Sir John Smyth VC, I place McCudden first in 1918. He won his Cross for flying services in latter part of 1917 and early 1918) His deeds are too numerous to list in detail, but during the period shown he accounted for 37 enemy aircraft. He died from injuries received at Auxi-le-Chateau airfield, when his aircraft plunged into trees on takeoff

Gazette: 2 April 1918

Commemoration: i) Headstone ii) Name on family headstone, Chatham Cemetery, Kent. Section CC. Grave 959 iii) Name on Gillingham War Memorial iv) Memorial at Sheerness Parish Church and War Memorial, Kent v) Memorial in St. Clement Dane's, Central London vi) McCudden Row Chatham vii) A VC.10C. Mk.1 XV 104 named for him viii) Medals at the Royal Engineers Museum

943	WHITE Geoffrey Saxton	VC	Lieutenant - Commander	Royal Navy

Dardanelles, Turkey
POSTHUMOUS
1301

Born: 2 July 1886 - Bromley, Kent

Died: 28 January 1918 aged 31. Killed by a shell during his VC action, near Kum Kale

Buried: Has no known grave - name on Portsmouth Naval Memorial, Hampshire. Panel 28. Column 3

Deed/Service: 28 January 1918. When in command of HM Submarine E14 in the Dardanelles, he was ordered to locate the German battle cruiser 'Goeber' reported aground. Unable to locate her, he came across another enemy ship which he torpedoed, there followed a heavy explosion damaging E14 forcing her to surface. When hit again he decided to ground her, giving the crew a chance of safety but was killed during the disembarkation

Gazette: 24 May 1919

Commemoration: i) Name on the Portsmouth Naval Memorial

944   **ROBERTSON** Charles Graham   **VC MM**   Lance - Corporal   **10th Bn. The Royal Fusiliers (now Royal Regt. of Fusiliers)**   Polderhoek Chateau
Belgium
1064

Born: 4 July 1879 - Penrith, Cumberland
Died: 10 May 1954 aged 74, at Garth Nursing Home, Dorking, Surrey
Buried: Dorking Cemetery. Plot 36. Grave 360. Headstone
Deed/Service: 8 - 9 March 1918. Realising that he was being cut off after he had repelled a strong attack, he sent for reinforcements. With only one
other man, he manned a Lewis gun until forced to withdraw when support failed to arrive. Reaching a defended post, he got onto the
parapet and continued firing until severely wounded, but managed to crawl back with the gun, having exhausted his ammunition   **Gazette: 9 April 1918**
Commemoration: i) Headstone ii) Medals at Royal Fusiliers Museum

945   **WHITFIELD** Harold   **VC**   Sergeant   **10th Bn. The King's Shropshire Light Infantry (now The Light Infantry)**   Burj El Lisaneh, Egypt

Born: 11 June 1886 - Oswestry, Shropshire   1305
Died: 19 December 1956 aged 70. Killed in motor accident near Oswestry involving an army Jeep
Buried: Oswestry Cemetery. Plot W. Grave 26. Headstone
Deed/Service: 10 March 1918 (Private) After his battalion had captured a position, they repulsed three strong counter-attacks. Single-handed, he charged
into the enemy, captured a Lewis gun and killed its crew before turning the gun on the Turks and driving them back. He later led a bombing
attack inflicting many casualties then consolidated his position, saving many lives and materially assisting in defeating the counter-attack   **Gazette: 8 May 1918**
Commemoration: i) Headstone

946   BEAL Ernest Frederick   VC   T/Second Lieutenant   13th (S) Bn. The Yorkshire Regiment (now The Green Howards)   St. Leger, France
                                                                                                                                      POSTHUMOUS

Born: 27 January 1885 - East Street, Brighton, Sussex
Died: 22 March 1918 aged 33. Mortally wounded by a shell during his VC action at St. Leger.   67
Buried: Has no known grave - name on the Arras Memorial, France. West side of town. Bay 5 (See Map A - 20)
Deed/Service: 21 - 22 March 1918. When in command of a company occupying a section of trench, he was ordered to work his way along a communication
                   trench to clear a 400 yard gap held by the enemy. Leading a small party, he captured four machine-guns and inflicted heavy casualties. Later
                   in the evening he brought in on his back a wounded man who was lying near enemy lines, but was killed shortly afterwards   **Gazette: 4 June 1918**
Commemoration: i) Name on the Arras Memorial ii) A Boys Brigade Award given annually in his memory iii) Medals at the Green Howards Museum

947   BUCHAN John Crawford   VC   Second Lieutenant   7th Bn. The Argyll & Sutherland Highlanders, attd. 8th Bn.   East of Marteville, France
                                                                                                                                      POSTHUMOUS

Born: 10 October 1892 - Alloa, Clackmannan, Scotland   141
Died: 22 March 1918 aged 25. From wounds received in his VC action while a prisoner of war near Marteville, France
Buried: i) Buried by Germans in Roisel Community Cemetery ii) Later buried in Roisel Communal Cemetery Extension, France. 7 miles E. of
                   Peronne. Plot II. Row I. Grave 6. Headstone (See Map A - 30)
Deed/Service: 21 March 1918. Despite wounds received earlier, he remained with his platoon under severe attack and suffering heavy casualties. He
                   continually encouraged his men, visiting all posts under fire and threat of imminent attack, until called upon to surrender. He fought his way
                   to the support line and held out until dusk, refusing any medical aid. Totally cut off, he was last seen fighting against overwhelming odds   **Gazette: 2 May 1918**
Commemoration: i) Headstone ii) Name on the Alloa War Memorial iii) Plaque in Alloa Museum

948	**DE WIND Edmund VC Second Lieutenant**	**15th Bn. The Royal Irish Rifles (now The Royal Irish Regiment)**	**Near Groagie, France**

POSTHUMOUS
325

Born: 11 December 1883 - 'Kinvara' Comber, Co. Down, Northern Ireland
Died: 21 March 1918 aged 34. Killed in his VC action at the Racecourse Redoubt, South East of Groagie, France
Buried: Has no known grave - name on Pozieres Memorial, France. 3 miles N.E. of Albert. Panel 74/76 (See Map A - 29)
Deed/Service: 21 March 1918. When holding the Racecourse Redoubt, one of fourteen along a defensive line, he spent seven hours almost single-handed under intense fire, being twice wounded whilst waiting for support. On two occasions he got out on top with two NCO's under heavy machine-gun fire, clearing the Germans in the approach trenches. He continued to repel numerous attacks until mortally wounded   **Gazette: 15 May 1919**
Commemoration: i) Name on Pozieres Memorial ii) Plaque in St.Mary's Church, Comber iii) Name on War Memorial, Comber iv) Name-plate on a German gun, Comber v) De Wind Drive, Comber vi) Name on Great West Door, St. Anne's Cathedral, Belfast vii) Name on War Memorial, Campbell College, Belfast viii) Name on Memorial at Ulster Tower, Somme, France ix) Mount De Wind, Jasper National Park, Alberta, Canada

949	**ELSTOB Wilfrith VC DSO & Bar MC T/Lieutenant - Colonel**	**Comd. 16th Bn. The Manchester Regiment (now The King's Regiment)**	**Near St. Quentin, France**

POSTHUMOUS
380

Born: 8 September 1888 - Chichester, Sussex
Died: 21 March 1918 aged 29. Killed during his VC action at the Manchester Redoubt, near St. Quentin, France
Buried: Has no known grave - name on Pozieres Memorial, France. 3 miles N.E. of Albert. Panel 64/67 (See Map A - 29)
Deed/Service: 21 March 1918. Having encouraged his men holding the Manchester Redoubt, which was under a preliminary bombardment, he single-handed repulsed a bombing assault before making several journeys under heavy fire to bring up vital ammunition. Informing his brigade commander that he would hold the position to the last, he inspired his men to do so until he was killed in the final assault   **Gazette: 9 June 1919**
Commemoration: i) Name on Pozieres Memorial ii) Plaque and window, All Saints' Church, Siddington,Cheshire iii) Medals at Manchester Regimental Museum

| 950 | HAYWARD Reginald Frederick Johnson | VC MC & Bar | Lieutenant - Colonel | 1st Bn. The Wiltshire Regiment | Near Frenicourt, France |

(now The Royal Gloucestershire, Berkshire & Wiltshire Regiment)

Born: 17 June 1891 - Beer Mission Station, near Swartberg, East Griqualand, South Africa

550

Died: 17 January 1970 aged 78, from natural causes at his home at 7 Ormonde Gate, Chelsea, South West London

Cremated: 23 January at Putney Vale Crematorium. Ref: 34367. Ashes scattered opposite Panel 13 in the Crematorium's Garden of Remembrance

Deed/Service: 21 - 22 March 1918 (A/Captain) When commanding a company under heavy attack, he displayed supreme courage and endurance until collapsing with exhaustion. During the enemy attack he had been buried, wounded in the head, rendered deaf on the first day and his arm shattered on the third, but he continued to move across open ground from one trench to another with absolute disregard for his own safety **Gazette: 24 April 1918**

Commemoration: i) Hayward Avenue, Putney Vale Cemetery ii) Memorial in St. Mary's Church, Limpley Stoke, Avon iii) Medals with Duke of Edinburgh's Regiment

| 951 | JAMES Manley Angell | VC DSO MC MBE | Brigadier | 8th (S) Bn. The Gloucestershire Regiment | North Velu Wood, France |

(now The Royal Gloucestershire, Berkshire & Wiltshire Regiment)

Born: 12 July 1896 - Odiham, Hampshire

630

Died: 23 September 1975 aged 79, from congestive cardiac failure at his home 101 Passage Road, Westbury on Trym, Bristol

Cremated: Canford Crematorium, Bristol. Ashes spread in 'The Shrubbery' at the Crematorium. No memorial tablet/plaque

Deed/Service: 21 March 1918 (T/Captain) Although wounded he refused to leave his company, leading them forward and capturing two machine-guns and twenty-seven prisoners. The next day he repulsed three enemy assaults, then when the Germans broke through on the 24th, he made a determined stand, not only inflicting heavy losses but gaining time for the withdrawal of his guns. Leading another counter-attack he was again wounded, and last seen working a machine-gun single-handed, being wounded again and eventually being taken prisoner **Gazette: 28 June 1918**

Commemoration:

| 952 | KER Allan Ebenezer   VC   Major   3rd Bn. The Gordon Highlanders (now The Highlanders), attd. 61st Bn. Machine Gun Corps | Near St. Quentin, France |

Born: 5 March 1883 - Edinburgh, Scotland

686

Died: 12 September 1958 aged 75, from a ruptured aneurism, at the New Garden Hospital, Hampstead, North West London

Buried: 17 September at West Hampstead Cemetery, Fortune Green Road, Hampstead. Section Q/4. Grave 7. Headstone

Deed/Service: 21 March 1918 (Lieutenant) After the Germans had broken through our line, he succeeded in stopping an attack by manning a Vickers Gun and inflicting heavy casualties. Staying at his post with several badly wounded men, and fighting with just revolvers, he was finally forced to surrender when totally exhausted, out of food, ammunition and effected by poison gas. He had managed to hold 500 of the enemy off for three hours

Gazette: 4 September 1919

Commemoration: i) Headstone

| 953 | SAYER John William   VC   Lance - Corporal   8th Bn. The Queen's Royal West Surrey Regt. (now P.O.W. Royal Regt.) | Le Verguier, France |

POSTHUMOUS

1111

Born: 12 April 1879 - Ilford, Essex

Died: 18 April 1918 aged 39. From wounds received during his VC action near Le Cateau, France, while a prisoner of war

Buried: Le Cateau Military Cemetery, France. 1 mile W. of Le Cateau. Plot I. Row B. Grave 59. Headstone shows age 38 (See Map A - 31)

Deed/Service: 21 March 1918. On his own initiative and without assistance, he beat off a succession of attacks, inflicting heavy losses when holding an isolated post for two hours. Under heavy fire the small garrison held out until most became casualties, and he was wounded and captured

Gazette: 9 June 1919

Commemoration: i) Headstone

RANK WHEN V.C WAS WON	DATE OF DEATH
AFGHANISTAN 1880	
GUNR JAMES COLLIS	28 JUNE 1918
SERGT P MULLANE	20 NOV 1919
SOUDAN 1885	
GUNR A SMITH	6 JAN 1932
SOUTH AFRICA 1899-1901	
SHOEING SMITH A E IND	29 NOV 1916
SERGT C E H PARKER	9 AUG 1918
GUNR I LODGE	13 JUNE 1923
DRIVER H H GLASOCK	
CAPT. H L REED	7 MARCH 1931
CAPT. H N SCHOFIELD	10 OCT 1931
BOMBR C E NURSE	25 NOV 1945
MAJOR E J PHIPPS-HORNBY	13 DEC 1947
DRIVER F H BRADLEY	10 MAR 1943
THE GREAT WAR 1914-18	
CAPT. E K BRADBURY	1 SEPT 1914
CAPT. G N WALFORD	26 APRIL 1915
CAPT. D REYNOLDS	23 FEB 1916
SERGT D NELSON	8 APRIL 1918
LIEUT. E S DOUGALL	14 APRIL 1918
BOMBR E G HARLOCK	30 DEC 1917
SERGT J C RAYNES	13 NOV 1929
LT COL E W ALEXANDER	25 AUG 1934
LIEUT. R V GORLE	10 JAN 1937
MAJOR L W B REES	28 SEPT 1955
SERGT W GOSLING	27 FEB 1945
2ND LIEUT. T H B MAUFE	28 MAR 1942
LIEUT. S T D WALLACE	2 FEB 1968
GUNR C E STONE	29 AUG 1952
DRIVER J H C DRAIN	26 NOV 1975
DRIVER F LUKE	12 MAR 1983
BSM G T DORRELL	7 JAN 1971
SERGT C E COURTLEY	30 JAN 1982
1939-45 WAR	
BDR J C CAMPBELL	26 FEB 1942
2ND LIEUT. G W GUNN	21 NOV 1941
CAPT. P A PORTEOUS	
HAVILDAR UMRAO SINGH	

954   **STONE Charles Edwin   VC MM   Bombardier   'C' Bty. 83rd Brigade, Royal Field Artillery (now Royal Regiment of Artillery)**   Caponne Farm, France

Born: 4 February 1889 - Street Lane, Ripley, Derbyshire   1185
Died: 29 August 1952 aged 63, at the City Hospital, Derby, from cardiac failure
Buried: 3 September at Belper Cemetery, Derby, in his mother's grave. Headstone
Deed/Service: 21 March 1918 (Gunner) After continually working his gun for six hours under heavy gas and shell fire, he was sent to the rear with an order. He returned under a heavy barrage and immediately assisted in holding up the enemy on a sunken road, first by firing a rifle lying in the open under intense machine-gun fire, then on the right flank. He later was one of a small party who captured a machine-gun and four prisoners   **Gazette: 22 May 1918**
Commemoration: i) Headstone   ii) Name on memorial in the RA Chapel, Woolwich, South East London   iii) Medals at Royal Artillery Institute, Woolwich

All Saint's Church

955   **COLLINGS - WELLS John Stanhope   VC DSO   A/Lieutenant - Colonel   Comd. 4th Bn. The Bedfordshire Regiment**   Marcoing/Albert, France
                                                            (now The Royal Anglian Regiment)   **POSTHUMOUS**

Born: 19 July 1880 - Caddington Hall, Markyate, Befordshire   1289
Died: 27 March 1918 aged 37. Killed during his VC action by a mortar shell, near the railway line west of Albert, France
Buried: Bouzincourt Ridge Cemetery, France. 2 miles N. of Albert. Plot III. Row E. Grave 12. Headstone shows age 38 (See Map A - 29)
Deed/Service: 22 - 27 March 1918. When the rearguard was almost surrounded and in danger of capture, he called for volunteers to remain and cover a withdrawal. For an hour and a half they succeeded until their ammunition expired. He was later ordered to counter-attack, and knowing his men were on the point of exhaustion he personally led them although wounded twice. He was killed the moment the objective was gained   **Gazette: 24 April 1918**
Commemoration: i) Headstone   ii) Name on War Memorial outside, and plaque inside All Saint's Church, Caddington   ii) Name on family grave at Hughenden Manor Church, Buckinghamshire   iv) Memorial at St. Ethelreda's Church, Hatfield, Hertfordshire   v) Memorial window inside Markyate Parish Church   vi) The Collings-Wells VC Memorial Hall and Collings-Wells Close at Caddington   vii) Memorial at Christ's Church, Oxford   viii) Plaque at the Bedford School   ix) Memorial at Uppingham School, Leicestershire   x) Medals at Bedfordshire and Hertfordshire Regimental Museum

956	COLUMBINE Herbert George VC Private 9th Squadron, Machine Gun Corps (now disbanded)

Hervilly Wood, France
POSTHUMOUS
236

Born: 28 November 1893 - Penge, South East, London
Died: 22 March 1918 aged 24. Killed during his VC action at Hervilly Wood, France
Buried: Has no known grave - name on Pozieres Memorial, France. 3 miles N.E. of Albert. Panel 93/94 (See Map A - 29)
Deed/Service: 22 March 1918. When in command of an isolated position he kept a machine-gun firing for four hours, repelling wave after wave of the enemy who failed to get to him. Finally, with the help of a low flying aircraft, the Germans managed to gain a foothold in his trench, when he ordered his two remaining men to get away, and although he was being bombed on either side, he continued to inflict heavy losses until killed by a bomb at his gun position
Commemoration: i) Name on Pozieres Memorial ii) Bronze bust on a pedestal in Memorial Gardens, Parish Church, Walton-on-the-Naze, Essex iii) Columbine Sports Centre and Columbine Gardens, Walton-on-the-Naze iv) Medals with the British Legion, Walton-on-the-Naze

Gazette: 28 June 1918

957	JACKSON Harold VC Sergeant 7th (S) Bn. The East Yorkshire Regiment (now The Prince of Wales Regiment)

Hermies, France
625

Born: 31 May 1892 - Allandales, Kirton, Lincolnshire
Died: 24 August 1918 aged 26. Killed during an attack on the Mouquet Farm, near Thiepval, Somme, France
Buried: i) Buried where he fell near Thiepval ii) In 1927 his body was located and interred in the A.I.F. Burial Ground, Glas Lane, Flers, France. 4 miles S. of Bapaume. Plot XV. Row A. Grave 21/30. Headstone (See Map A - 29)
Deed.Service: 22 March 1918. Having volunteered to go out alone through a heavy barrage, he brought back valuable information regarding enemy movements. He later single-handed bombed out into the open a party of Germans, who had established themselves in our line. When all his officers became casualties, he led his company in an attack, then went repeatedly out under fire to carry the wounded to safety
Commemoration: i) Headstone ii) Name on War Memorial, Kirton iii) Name on War Memorial, Boston, Lincolnshire iv) Name on War Memorial, Wood Green, London

Gazette: 8 May 1918

958   KNOX Cecil Leonard   VC   Major   150th Field Company, Corps of Royal Engineers   Tugny, France

Born: 9 May 1889 - 'The Chase', Nuneaton, Warwickshire   705
Died: 4 February 1943 aged 53, in Nuneaton General Hospital from a fractured skull when his motor cycle skidded on an icy road
Cremated: 8 February at Gilroes Crematorium, Leicester. Ref: 3339. Ashes scattered at his home - Fyves Court, Caldecote, Nuneaton
Deed/Service: 22 March 1918 (T/Second Lieutenant) When entrusted with the demolition of twelve bridges along the Somme Canal, he successfully carried out the task with the exception of a steel girder bridge where the time fuse failed to ignite. As the Germans began to cross, he ran to the bridge under heavy fire and lit an instantaneous fuse, knowing the grave risk to himself, but the bridge was blown and he escaped relatively unscathed   **Gazette: 4 June 1918**
Commemoration: i) Name on the family grave at Oaston Road Cemetery, Nuneaton   ii) Name on the War Memorial, Nuneaton Park   iii) Name on memorial at the Ulster Tower, Somme   iv) Knox Crescent, Nuneaton

959   ROBERTS Frank Crowther   VC DSO MC OBE   Major - General   Comd. 1st Bn. The Worcestershire Regiment   West of Somme/Pargny,
     (now The Worcestershire & Sherwood Foresters Regiment)   France

Born: 2 June 1891 - Highbury, Middlesex (now North London)   1059
Died: 12 January 1982 aged 90, at his home 'Four Winds', Stanhope Bretby, Burton-on-Trent, Staffordshire
Cremated: 18 January at Bretby Crematorium, Derbyshire. Ashes buried in family plot at Bretby Churchyard
Deed/Service: 22 March - 2 April 1918 (A/Lieutenant Colonel) Over a twelve day period, he displayed exceptional military skill and valour in dealing with many difficult situations around Pargny, during a heavy German offensive. On one occasion when the enemy attacked and cleared the village, he led a counter-attack which temporarily drove the enemy back, covering the retirement of troops on their flanks, due entirely to his skillful actions   **Gazette: 8 May 1918**
Commemoration: i) Name on family stone, Bretby Churchyard   ii) Name in Book of Remembrance at Crematorium   iii) Medals at Worcestershire Regiment

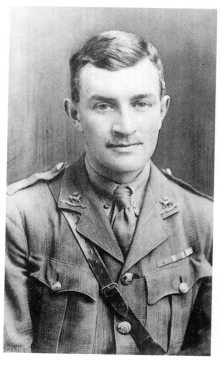

| 960 | BUSHELL Christopher | VC DSO | T/Lieutenant - Colonel | Comd. 7th (S) Bn. The Queen's Royal West Surrey Regiment (now The P.O.W. Royal Regiment (Q & H)) | North of Tergnier, France |

Born: 31 October 1888 - Hinderton Lodge, Neston, The Wirral, Cheshire

Died: 8 August 1918 aged 29. Killed in a later action, leading an attack south of Morlencourt, Somme, France

Buried: Querrieu British Cemetery, France. 9 miles S.W. of Albert. Row E. Grave 6. Headstone (See Map A - 29)

Deed/Service: 23 March 1918. When leading a company of his battalion in a combined Allied counter-attack, he received a severe head wound. Refusing all aid, he continued walking in front of both the English and Allied troops, encouraging them and visiting each portion of the lines in the face of heavy rifle and machine-gun fire. He was finally removed to a dressing station in a fainting condition

Commemoration: i) Headstone ii) Name on Wye Parish Church War Memorial, Kent iii) Name on St.Margaret's-at-Cliffe Parish Church War Memorial, Kent iv) Plaque at St. Mary and St. Helen Church, Neston v) Bushell Road, Neston

157

Gazette: 3 May 1918

| 961 | GRIBBLE Julian Royds | VC | T/Captain | 10th (S) Bn. The Royal Warwickshire Regiment (now Royal Regiment of Fusiliers) | Hermies Ridge, France |

Born: 5 January 1897 - London

Died: 25 November 1918 aged 21. From his wounds complicated by pneumonia, when a prisoner of war near Kessel, Germany

Buried: Niederzwehren Cemetery, Kessel, Hessen State, Germany. Plot III. Row F. Grave 4. Headstone

Deed/Service: 23 March 1918. When ordered to hold Beaumetz, Hermies Ridge at all costs, he and his company were eventually cut off and isolated. Although he could have withdrawn when the battalion on his left were driven back, he obeyed his orders to the letter and when his company were finally surrounded, he was seen fighting to the last

Commemoration: i) Headstone ii) Brass plaque at St. Peter's Church, Long Bredy, Dorset iii) Memorial on a pillar in Chapel Royal Military Academy, Camberley, Surrey iv) Medals at Royal Warwickshire Regimental Museum

493

Gazette: 28 June 1918

100

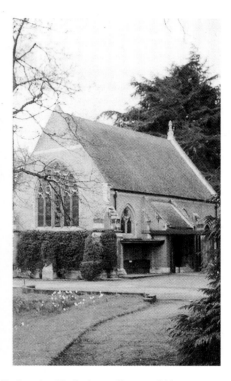

962	HERRING Alfred Cecil VC Major	Royal Army Service Corps. attd. 6th (S) Bn. The Northamptonshire Regiment	Montagne Bridge

962   HERRING Alfred Cecil   VC   Major   Royal Army Service Corps. attd. 6th (S) Bn. The Northamptonshire Regiment   Montagne Bridge
(now The Royal Logistic Corps and The Royal Anglian Regiment respectively)   near Remigny, France
562

Born: 26 October 1888 - Tottenham, North London.
Died: 10 August 1966 aged 77, at his home in Oatlands Park Hotel, Weybridge, Surrey
Cremated: 13 August at Woking Crematorium, Surrey. Ref: 65215. Ashes in Chaucer South area in Garden of Remembrance. No memorial tablet
Deed/Service: 23 - 24 March 1918 (T/Second Lieutenant) From his position close to the St. Quentin Canal bank, he found his post surrounded, but counter-attacked immediately with such dash that the position was quickly recaptured, together with twenty prisoners and six machine-guns. During the night the post was continually attacked, all were repelled due to his bravery and handling of his men, the enemy advance being held for eleven hours

Gazette: 7 June 1918

Commemoration: i) Medals at The Royal Logistic Corps Museum

963   DAVIES John Thomas   VC   Corporal   11th (S) Bn. The South Lancashire Regiment (now Queens Lancashire Regiment)   Near Eppeville, France
308

Born: 29 September 1896 - 19 Railway Road, Tranmere, Birkenhead
Died: 28 October 1955 aged 60, suddenly at his home at 27 Lesley Road, St. Helens, Lancashire
Buried: St. Helens Borough Cemetery. C. of E Section. Area 59. Grave 426. Headstone
Deed/Service: 24 March 1918. During a company withdrawal when almost surrounded, he knew that the only line of escape lay through a stream barricaded with barbed wire. To hold up the enemy as long as possible, he mounted a parapet in full view of the enemy and kept his Lewis gun in action, causing heavy casualties and allowing his company to get away. He was last seen firing his gun, but survived and was taken prisoner soon after

Gazette: 22 May 1918

Commemoration: i) Headstone

964   **ANDERSON William Herbert   VC   A/Lieutenant - Colonel**   Comd. 12th (S) Bn. The Highland Light Infantry   **Bois Favieres, France**
                                                                                  (now Royal Highland Fusiliers)   **POSTHUMOUS**

Born:	29 December 1881 - Glasgow, Scotland.
Died:	25 March 1918 aged 36. Killed during his VC action in Maricourt Wood, on the Albert to Peronne road, Somme
Buried:	Peronne Road Cemetery, France. 6 miles E. of Albert. Plot II. Row G. Grave 36. Headstone (See Map A - 29)
Deed/Service:	25 March 1918. After a heavy barrage followed by a strong frontal attack, the Germans overran a point to the right of his line. Fearing that his flank would be turned, he led a brilliant counter-attack which resulted in driving the enemy back and the capture of 70 prisoners and 12 machine-guns. He was killed shortly afterwards when leading an attack to drive the enemy from their new position in Maricourt Wood, 1,000 yards away
Commemoration:	i) Headstone

29

Gazette: 3 May 1918

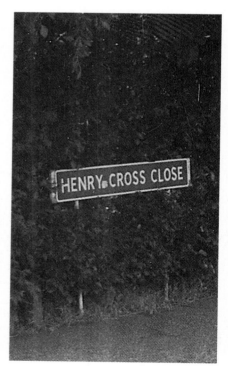

965   **CROSS Arthur Henry   VC MM   A/Lance - Corporal   40th Bn. Machine Gun Corps (now disbanded)**   **Ervillers, France**

Born:	13 December 1884 - Shipdham, Thetford, Norfolk.
Died:	26 November 1965 aged 80, at his home in Marshalsea Road, Lambeth, South East London
Buried:	Streatham Vale Cemetery, South London. Plot E. Square 27. Grave 885. Headstone, name not on stone
Deed/Service:	25 March 1918. After two machine-guns had been captured, he volunteered to reconnoitre the enemy position the following morning. Spotting the two guns in the hands of seven Germans, he forced them to surrender armed with just a service revolver and to carry the guns to British lines. He got the guns in action immediately, annihilating a very heavy enemy attack
Commemoration:	i) Family headstone on his grave ii) Portrait in Shipdham Village Hall iii) Henry Cross Close, Shipdham

277

Gazette: 4 June 1918

966   **TOYE Alfred Maurice   VC MC   Brigadier   2nd Bn. The Middlesex Regiment (now P.O.W. Royal Regiment) (Q & H)**   **Eterpigny Ridge, France**

Born: 15 April 1897 - 'B' Terrace, Stanhope Lines, Aldershot, Hampshire.   **1224**
Died: 6 September 1955 aged 58 from cancer, at the Madame Curie Memorial Foundation, Tidcombe Hall, Tiverton, Devon
Buried: Tiverton Cemetery. Section XF. Grave 36. Headstone
Deeds/Service: 25 March 1918 (A/Captain) By fine leadership and conspicuous bravery, he re-took a post which had been captured on three occasions by the enemy, before fighting his way out with a handful of men. He then counter-attacked with seventy men who were without officers, and took a line which he held until reinforcements arrived, receiving two wounds in doing so. He later covered his battalion's retirement on two occasions   **Gazette: 8 May 1918**
Commemoration: i) Headstone   ii) Medals at the National Army Museum

967   **YOUNG Thomas   VC   Private   9th Bn. The Durham Light Infantry (now The Light Infantry)**   **Bucquoy, France**

Born: 28 January 1895 - Boldon, Co. Durham. Enlisted as YOUNG, his mother's maiden name, but actual name was MORRELL   **1346**
Died: 15 October 1966 aged 71, at the Whickham Council Men's Hostel, The Hermitage, Front Street, Whckham
Buried: St. Patrick's Cemetery, High Spen, Co. Durham. Headstone
Deed/Service: 25 - 31 March 1918. Working as a stretcher-bearer, he saved the lives of nine men. On each occasion he went out under heavy machine-gun and shell fire in open ground and brought the wounded back to safety. With those too badly wounded to be moved before bandaged, he dressed under heavy fire and carried them back unaided. He worked unceasingly to evacuate the wounded from seemingly impossible places   **Gazette: 4 June 1918**
Commemoration: i) Headstone   ii) Medals at the Durham Light Infantry Museum

				Hamelincourt, France
968	MOUNTAIN Albert VC Sergeant	15/17th Bn. The West Yorkshire Regiment (now The Prince of Wales Regiment)		894

Born: 19 April 1895 - Leeds, Yorkshire

Died: 7 January 1967 aged 71, at his home in Aberford Road, Garforth, Leeds, following a long illness

Cremated: Lawnswood Crematorium, Leeds. Ref: 82479. Ashes in New Adel Lane Avenue, Plot K2-380 in Garden of Remembrance. No memorial

Deed/Service: 26 March 1918. When his battalion had been withdrawn having suffered heavy casualties from both artillery and machine-gun fire, he and ten other volunteers staged a counter-attack on an advanced enemy patrol of 200 men, killing half of them with a Lewis gun. With five other men he then held at bay 600 of the enemy to cover the retirement of his company, then held an isolated post for twenty-seven hours before rejoining his company

Commemoration: i) Plaque outside City Art Gallery, Leeds ii) Medals in Prince of Wales Regimental Museum

Gazette: 7 June 1918

				Near Ablainzeville, France
969	HORSFALL Basil Arthur VC Second Lieutenant	3rd Bn. The East Lancashire Regiment, attd. 11th Bn. (now The Queen's Lancashire Regiment)		POSTHUMOUS 597

Born: 4 October 1887 - Colombo, Ceylon now Sri Lanka

Died: 27 March 1918 aged 30. Killed during his VC action when withdrawing to the River Cojeul, near Ayette, France

Buried: Has no known grave - name on the Arras Memorial, France. Western suburbs of town. Bay 6 (See Map A - 20)

Deed/Service: 27 March 1918. During a frontal attack by the Germans, his centre platoon and other sections were driven back and he was wounded in the head. He hastily reorganised his men and made a counter-attack, regaining the original position, then refusing medical aid despite the severity of his wounds, he made a second successful counter-attack. He was killed after being told to withdraw being the last man to leave

Commemoration: i) Name on The Arras Memorial ii) Medals at The Blackburn Museum, Lancashire

Gazette: 22 May 1918

970   **McLEOD Alan Arnett   VC   Second Lieutenant   2 Squadron, Royal Flying Corps (now Royal Air Force)**   Over Albert, France

Born: 20 April 1899 - Stonewall, Winnipeg, Manitoba, Canada   805

Died: 6 November 1918 aged 19, at Winnipeg General Hospital from Spanish Influenza, the world-wide epidemic which claimed 21 million lives

Buried: 9 November 1918 at Winnipeg Presbyterian Cemetery, also known as Old Kildonan Cemetery. Grave 238. Headstone

Deed/Service: 27 March 1918. After destroying an enemy triplane in his FK8 bomber, he and his observer were attacked by eight more, two of which they brought down. Their machine was hit and burst into flames and both men were badly wounded. Crashing in no-mans-land he dragged his observer from the burning wreckage and under heavy fire carried him to safety before collapsing himself   **Gazette: 1 May 1918**

Commemoration: i) Headstone   ii) Memorial tablet in The Highlanders Memorial Church, Glasgow   iii) Name on RAF Memorial in St. Clement Dane's Church, Aldwych, Central London   iv) Medals in Air Command Heritage, Winnipeg

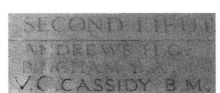

971   **CASSIDY Bernard Matthew   VC   Second Lieutenant   2nd Bn. The Lancashire Fusiliers (now Royal Regiment of Fusiliers)**   Fampoux, Arras, France
POSTHUMOUS

Born: 17 August 1892 - Canning Town, East London. Some references state Manchester   193

Died: 28 March 1918 aged 25. Killed during his VC action, 150 yards north of Fampoux, Arras, France

Buried: Has no known grave - name on The Arras Memorial, France. Western suburbs of town. Bay 5 (See Map A - 24)

Deed/Service: 28 March 1918. On the first day of the Battle of Arras, the Germans launched a massive attack north of the city. When the left flank of the British 26th Division was in danger he was ordered to hold on at all costs. Although the enemy attacked in overwhelming numbers, he continued to rally and encourage his men under terrific bombardment, until they were eventually surrounded and he was killed   **Gazette: 3 May 1918**

Commemoration: i) Name on the Arras Memorial

972	McDOUGALL Stanley Robert VC MM Sergeant 47th Bn. (Queensland) Australian Imperial Force	Dermancourt, France

Born: 23 July 1890 - Recherche, Hobart, Tasmania, Australia

Died: 7 July 1968 aged 77, at the North East Soldiers' Memorial Hospital, Scottsdale, Tasmania

Cremated: Norwood Crematorium, Mitchell, Canberra, A.C.T. Ashes buried in Norwood Cemetery, Mitchell, Canberra. Plaque shows age 78

Deed/Service: 28 March 1918. During a sudden attack by the enemy he charged the German second wave single-handed, killing seven and capturing a machine-gun which he turned on the attackers, routing them and causing many casualties. When his ammunition ran out, he seized a bayonet and charged again, killing four more before using a Lewis gun and killing many more. By his prompt actions 33 prisoners were taken and the enemy halted

775

Gazette: 3 May 1918

Commemoration: i) Plaque at Norwood Crematorium ii) McDougall Street, Canberra iii) Medals and display at Australian War Memorial, Canberra

St. Paul's Cathedral

973	WATSON Oliver Cyril Spencer VC DSC A/Lieutenant - Colonel 1st City of London Yeomanry, comd. 5th Bn. The King's Own Yorkshire Light Infantry (now The Light Infantry)	Rossignol Wood, France POSTHUMOUS

Born: 7 September 1876 - Cavendish Square, London

Died: 28 March 1918 aged 41. Killed during his VC action in Rossignol Wood, France

Buried: Has no known grave - name on The Arras Memorial, France. Western suburbs of town. Bay 7 (See Map A - 20)

Deed/Service: 28 March 1918. During an attack near Hebuterne which had reached its objective, the Germans held two strong points. He led a small bombing party under intense fire to clear them, but heavily outnumbered he was forced to order a withdrawal. He stayed behind to cover the retirement, firing his revolver until killed. His actions without doubt saved the line at a critical time

1281

Gazette: 18 May 1918

Commemoration: i) Name on Arras Memorial ii) Plaque in St. Mary's Church, Wargrave, Berkshire iii) Name on Regimental Memorial, St. Paul's Cathedral, London iv) Medals in Green Howards Museum

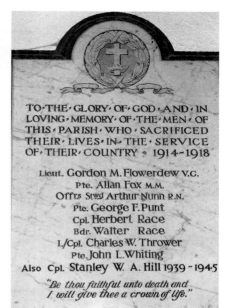

| 974 | FLOWERDEW Gordon Muriel VC Lieutenant Lord Strathcona's Horse, Canadian Expeditionary Force | Bois de Moreuil, France POSTHUMOUS |

Born: 2 January 1885 - Billingford Hall, Scole, Norfolk

Died: 31 March 1918 aged 33. From wounds received during his VC action at a field hospital near Moreuil

Buried: Namps-au-Val British Cemetery, France. 11 miles S.W. of Amiens. Plot I. Row H. Grave 1. Headstone shows age 39 (See Map A - 28)

Deed/Service: 30 March 1918. He led one of three mounted squadrons on a suicidal attack on the German lines armed with machine-guns. Ordering one troop to dismount and engage the enemy, he led the remaining three troops at the charge and successfully reached the objective, before wheeling about and charging them from the rear. He was dangerously wounded, but the enemy fled and left the position

Commemoration: i) Headstone ii) Plaque in Billingford Church, Norfolk iii) His original wooden grave cross at Framlingham College Chapel, Suffolk iv) Painting at the Canadian War Museum, Ottawa v) Medals at the Museum of the Regiments, Calgary, Alberta

415

Gazette: 24 April 1918

| 975 | JERRARD Alan VC Flight - Lieutenant 66 Squadron, Royal Flying Corps (now Royal Air Force) | Near Mansue, Italy |

Born: 3 December 1897 - 13 Vicars Hill, Ladywell, Lewisham, South East London

Died: 14 May 1968 aged 70, at Buckfield Nursing Home, Lyme Regis, Dorset

Cremated: 17 May at Exeter and Devon Crematorium, Exeter. Ref: 8310. Ashes interred in the family grave, Hillingdon Churchyard, Middlesex

Deed/Service: 30 March 1918 (Lieutenant) During an offensive patrol of three Sopwith Camels, he shot down one of five enemy aircraft near Fontane, before attacking an Austro-Hungarian aerodrome at fifty feet. Destroying an Albatross, he was joined by a colleague and took on some nineteen enemy aircraft. He brought down two more before ordered to retire with ten Albatross D111's in pursuit, who forced him to crash land near Gorgo di Molino, with 163 bullet holes in his Camel. He was taken to Austrian HQ at Oderzo, then to a P.o.W. camp

Commemoration: i) Name on family grave at Hillingdon Churchyard ii) Name on RAF Memorial, St. Clement Dane's, Central London iii) Name on Memorial at the Lewisham Civic Centre, South East London iv) Medals at the RAF Museum

641

Gazette: 1 May 1918

976   **STORKEY** Percy Valentine   VC   Captain   19th Bn. (N.S.W.) Australian Imperial Force

Bois de Hangard, France
1187

Born: 9 September 1893 - Napier, Hawks Bay, New Zealand
Died: 3 October 1969 aged 76, at his home at 20 Trowlock Avenue, Teddington, Middlesex
Cremated: 9 October at the South West Middlesex Crematorium, Hanworth. Ref: 32221. Ashes on Lawn 3 - B3 at Crematorium. No memorial
Deed/Service: 7 April 1918 (Lieutenant) With another officer and ten men, he led a charge on an enemy position containing 80-100 Germans holding up an advance. They drove them out of the wood, killing and wounding thirty, and capturing fifty and a machine-gun. His bravery and initiative, together with skilful method of attack against such heavy odds removed a dangerous obstacle, inspired his troops and allowed the advance to continue

Gazette: 7 June 1918

Commemorations: i) Name in Book of Remembrance at Crematorium ii) Portrait in Archives Building, Wellington, New Zealand iii) Storkey Place, Canberra, A.C.T. iv) The captured machine-gun and display at the Australian War Memorial, Canberra v) Medals in Q.E. II Army Memorial Museum, Waloura, N.Z

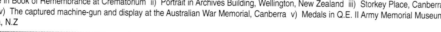

977   **COLLIN** Joseph Henry   VC   Second Lieutenant   1/4th Bn. The King's Own Regiment (now King's Own Royal Borderers)

Givenchy, France
POSTHUMOUS
232

Born: 11 April 1893 - Jarrow, Co. Durham
Died: 9 April 1918 aged 24. Mortally wounded during his VC action in Orchard Keep, Givenchy
Buried: Vielle-Chapelle New Military Cemetery, France. 6 miles N. of Bethune. Plot III. Row A. Grave 11. Headstone (See Map A - 10)
Deed/Service: 9 April 1918. When his platoon of sixteen men was eventually reduced to five by overwhelming odds in Orchard Keep, during the Battle of Estaires, he began to withdraw. Single-handed, he attacked a German machine-gun with a revolver and a Mills grenade, killing and wounding the entire crew before spotting a second machine-gun. Mounting a Lewis gun on an exposed parapet, he held them at bay until mortally wounded

Gazette: 28 June 1918

Commemoration: i) Headstone ii) Brass plaque at The Priory, Lancaster iii) Collin Shield for Carlisle schools race iv) Medals at King's Own Regiment Museum

978   **MASTERS Richard George** **VC** Private Royal Army Service Corps (now Royal Logistic Corps) attd. 141st Field Ambulance Gorre, Bethune, France

Born:	23 March 1877 - 61 Everton Road, Birkdale, Southport, Lancashire	842
Died:	4 April 1963 aged 86 at his home, 35 Palmerston Road, Southport	
Buried:	8 April at St.Cuthbert's Parish Churchyard, Churchtown, Southport. ·Headstone	
Deed/Service:	9 April 1918. Due to an enemy attack during the Battle of Estaires, all communications were cut and the wounded could not be evacuated as a vital road was deemed impassable. He volunteered to try and get through with the wounded and having cleared the debris made many journeys across machine-gun swept open ground. The vast majority of the wounded were evacuated by him	Gazette: 8 May 1918
Commemoration:	i) Headstone ii) A target-towing vessel named for him iii) Name on memorial tablet in Southport Garden of Remembrance iv) Medals at Royal Logistic Corps Museum	

Blackburn Old Town Hall

Arnold House School

979   **SCHOFIELD John** **VC** T/Second Lieutenant   2/5th Bn. The Lancashire Fusiliers (now Royal Regiment of Fusiliers) Givenchy, France
POSTHUMOUS
1115

Born:	4 March 1892 - 16 Wycollar Road, Revidge, Blackburn, Lancashire	
Died:	9 April 1918 aged 26. Killed during his VC action at Givenchy, France	
Buried:	Vielle-Chapelle Military Cemetery, France. 5 miles N. of Bethune. Plot III. Row C. Grave 8. Headstone (See Map A - 10)	
Deed/Service:	9 April 1918. When leading a party of nine men against a strong point, he was attacked by 100 of the enemy. By skillful use of men and arms at his disposal, he took twenty prisoners, then proceeded forward where he again met large numbers of the enemy. Opening fire on them and climbing onto a parapet under heavy fire, he forced another 123 to surrender, but was killed moments later	Gazette: 28 June 1918
Commemoration:	i) Headstone ii) Name on War Memorial, St. Thomas's Church, Blackburn iii) Memorial plaque in Blackburn Old Town Hall iv) Memorial in Arnold House School, Blackburn v) Medals in the Lancashire Fusiliers Museum	

Liverpool Cricket Club

980   **DOUGALL Eric Stuart   VC MC   A/Captain   Spec. Reserve attd. 'A' Bty. Royal Field Artillery (now Royal Regt. of Artillery)   Messines, Belgium**

POSTHUMOUS
339

Born: 13 April 1886 - Brookside, Tunbridge Wells, Kent
Died: 14 April 1918 aged 32. Killed in action when directing the fire of his battery at Kemmel, Belgium
Buried: Westoutre British Cemetery, Belgium. 7 miles S.W. of Ypres. Special Memorial No. 1. His exact location unknown. Headstone (See Map A-11)
Deed/Service: 10 April 1918. During the Battle of Messines, he was forced to move his guns to a ridge during a withdrawal, and began to fire over open sights. When our infantry were pushed back into line with his guns he organised and armed them with Lewis guns and held the line, checking the German advance for twelve hours. When ordered to retire, the guns were man-handled over 800 yards of open ground, under intense enemy fire
Commemoration: i) Headstone ii) Name on War Memorial at Liverpool Cricket Club iii) Brass Plaque in St. Thomas's Cathedral, Bombay, India iv) Medals at Pembroke College, Cambridge

Gazette: 4 June 1918

981   **KARANBAHADUR RANA   VC   Rifleman   2nd Bn. 3rd Q.A.O. Gurkha Rifles, Indian Army**

El Kefr, Egypt
666

Born: 21 December 1898 - Mangalthan Gulmi, Litung, Bag Lung District, Nepal
Died: 25 July 1973 aged 74, at Litung, Nepal
Buried: Bharse Gulmi, Litung. Unknown if Headstone/memorial exists. Both Gurkha Museum and HQ in Nepal certain of location
Deed/Service: 10 April 1918. During an attack, he and a few other men crept forward with a Lewis gun under intense fire to engage an enemy machine-gun. When the leader of the gun team was killed, he took over and quickly knocked out the machine-gun, then silenced enemy bombers and infantry in front of him. Later in the day he assisted with covering fire during a withdrawl, waiting until the enemy were almost upon him before retiring
Commemoration: i) Medals at The Gurkha Museum

Gazette: 21 June 1918

982   POULTER Arthur   VC   Private   1/4th Bn. The Duke of Wellington's (West Riding) Regiment (now D.O.W's Regiment)   Lys Erquinghem, France

Born: 16 December 1893 - Kilgram Bridge, East Witton, Yorkshire   998

Died: 29 August 1956 aged 62, at his home in Florence Road, Wortley, Leeds, Yorkshire

Buried: 1 September at New Wortley Cemetery, Tong Road, Leeds. Grave 2500. Headstone

Deed/Service: 10 April 1918. When acting as stretcher-bearer during the Battle of Lys, he carried badly wounded men on his back through heavy machine-gun and artillery fire on ten separate occasions. During the withdrawal over the River Lys, he ran back under fire and brought in a wounded man who had been left behind. He then bandaged forty men under the same heavy fire and was dangerously wounded when attempting another rescue   **Gazette: 28 June 1918**

Commemoration: i) Headstone ii) Medals in Leeds City Museum

983   FORBES - ROBERTSON James   VC DSO & Bar MC   Brigadier - General   Commanding 1st Bn. The Border Regiment   Near Vieux Bertuin
                                                                  (now The King's Own Royal Borderers)   France
                                                    1066

Born: 7 July 1884 - Strathpeffer, Ross and Cromarty, Scotland

Died: 5 August 1955 aged 71, at his home 'Chardwaw', Bourton-on-the-Water, Gloucestershire

Buried: Cheltenham Borough Cemetery. Section E1. Grave 717. Headstone

Deed/Service: 11 - 12 April 1918 (A/Lieutenant Colonel) On the third day of the Battle of Estaires, he saved the British line from breaking on four occasions, when making a mounted reconnaissance under heavy fire and leading a counter-attack which established our line. After the loss of his horse he continued on foot, steadying and inspiring his men with total disregard for his own personal safety. The next day he rode around to each farm building encouraging his men until his horse was killed, then on foot he organized effective defences to which his men could withdraw   **Gazette: 22 May 1918**

Commemoration: i) Headstone ii) Name on Roll of Honour, Big Classical, Cheltenham College

Ploegsteert Memorial

| 984 | PRYCE Thomas Tannatt   VC MC & Bar   Acting Captain   4th Bn. Grenadier Guards | Vieux Berquin, France |

Born: 17 January 1886, The Hague, Holland

Died: 13 April 1918 aged 32. Last seen alive during his VC action at Vieux Berquin, France

Buried: Has no known grave - name on Ploegsteert Memorial, Belgium. 9 miles S. of Ypres. Panel - 1 (See Map A - 11)

Deed/Service: 11 April 1918. Having led two platoons in a successful attack at Pont Rondin, he occupied a position with just 40 men remaining, from where he beat off four attacks the following day. By evening the enemy were within 60 yards of his trench and he led a bayonet charge pushing them back 100 yards. With few men remaining and out of ammunition, he was last seen engaged in fierce hand-to-hand fighting against overwhelming odds

1009

Gazette: 22 May 1918

Commemoration: i) Name on Ploegsteert Memorial ii) Name on War Memorial, and plaque in church at Llandysilio, Montgomeryshire (now Powys) iii) Name on War Memorial, Maidenhead, Berkshire iv) Name on Stock Exchange War Memorial, City of London v) Plaque at Shrewsbury School, Shropshire vi) Medals at Grenadier Guards Museum

Memorial bench, Woodingdean

| 985 | CROWE John James   VC   Captain   2nd Bn. The Worcestershire Regt. (now Worcestershire & Sherwood Foresters Regt.) | Neuve Eglise, Belgium |

Born: 28 December 1876 - Female Garrison Hospital, Devonport, Devon

Died: 27 February 1965 aged 88, at Brighton General Hospital, Brighton, Sussex

Cremated: 4 March at Downs Crematorium, Bear Road, Brighton. Ref: 55803. Ashes scattered in Section L in Crematorium Garden of Remembrance

Deed/Service: 14 April 1918 (Second Lieutenant) When holding Neuve Eglise, the enemy attacked a post in the village and took a position on the high ground where they established a machine-gun and snipers. Leaving nine men, he engaged the German position forcing them to withdraw, then later he took just two men and attacked two enemy machine-guns, killing both gun crews and capturing the guns

278

Gazette: 28 June 1918

Commemoration: i) Wall Plaque at Crematorium (now missing) ii) Name in Crematorium Book of Remembrance iii) Memorial bench, Woodingdean Community Centre, Brighton iv) Medals at Worcestershire Regimental Museum

St. Andrew's Church

986	COUNTER Jack Thomas VC Private 1st Bn. The King's (Liverpool) Regiment (now The King's Regiment)		Near Boiseux St. Marc

France
263

Born: 3 November 1898 - Blandford Forum, Dorset
Died: 16 September 1970 aged 71, during a visit to relatives in Dorset Street, Blandford Forum
Cremated: 24 September at Bournemouth Crematorium, Dorset. Ashes buried at St. Andrew's Churchyard, First Tower, St. Helier, Jersey
Deed/Service: 16 April 1918. When his battalion HQ were in desperate need of information about the British front line, reports could only be carried across open ground in full view of the enemy. When a small party tried without success, followed by a further six men each being killed, he volunteered and reached HQ under heavy fire and returned with vital orders, repeating the dangerous journey on five subsequent occasions   **Gazette: 22 May 1918**
Commemoration: i) Headstone at St. Andrew's ii) Plaque inside, and plaque on oak tree outside St. Andrew's Church iii) Jack Counter Close, St. Helier
iv) Counter House, St. Saviour's, Jersey v) Medals at Societe Jersiaise, St. Helier

987   BAMFORD Edward   VC DSO   Major   Royal Marine Light Infantry   Zeebrugge, Belgium
ELECTED BY BALLOT
49

Born: 28 May 1897 - 34 Langdon Park Road, Highgate, North London
Died: 30 September 1928 aged 41. On board HMS 'Cumberland' on route for Hong Kong
Buried: Bubbling Road Cemetery, Shanghai, China (also English Cemetery). Now levelled and a shopping centre in Nanjing Rd. - headstone did exist
Deed/Service: 22 - 23 April 1918 (Captain) During the raid on Zeebrugge harbour, he landed on the Mole from HMS 'Vindictive' with three platoons of Royal Marines. Under heavy fire, he commanded his company with total disregard of personal danger and showed a magnificent example to his men. Having established a strong point on the right of the disembarkation, he led an assault on the battery to the left   **Gazette: 23 July 1918**
Commemoration: i) Memorial in Depot Church, Deal, Kent iii) Bamford House, RM Barracks, Eastney, Hampshire iv) Medals in Royal Marines Museum

Zeebrugge Memorial

| 988 | BRADFORD George Nicholson VC Lieutenant - Commander Royal Navy | Zeebrugge, Belgium |
| | | POSTHUMOUS |

Born: 23 April 1887 - Millbanke, Darlington, Co. Durham
115

Died: 23 April 1918 aged 31. Killed during his VC action on the Mole at Zeebrugge, Belgium

Buried: Blankenberge Communal Cemetery, Belgium. 10 miles N.E. of Ostend. Row A. Grave - 5. Headstone

Deed/Service: 22 - 23 April 1918. During the Zeebrugge landing, he commanded the naval storming parties embarked in HMS 'Iris II', encountering difficulties with placing parapet anchors alongside the Mole. Although not part of his duties, he climbed a derrick projecting out over the Mole, and under heavy fire in the violently tossing sea, he jumped with the anchor which he placed when he was killed

Gazette: 17 March 1919

Commemoration: i) Headstone

| 989 | CARPENTER Alfred Francis Blakeney VC Vice - Admiral Royal Navy | Zeebrugge, Belgium |
| | | ELECTED BY BALLOT |

Born: 17 September 1881 - Barnes, Surrey (now South West London)
187

Died: 27 December 1955 aged 74, at his home St. Briavels House, Nr. Lydney, Gloucestershire

Cremated: 29 December at Gloucester Crematorium. Ref: 1184. Ashes scattered in the conifers in Garden of Remembrance at Crematorium, and at sea

Deed/Service: 22 - 23 April 1918 (Captain) When in command of HMS 'Vindictive' during the raid on Zeebrugge, he navigated mined waters to bring the ship alongside the Mole in darkness. When within yards of the Mole, the enemy commenced a heavy fire from batteries, machine-guns and rifles, but he calmly walked the decks supervising the landing, encouraging his men and greatly contributed to the success of the operation

Gazette: 23 July 1918

Commemoration: i) Slate plaque at St. Briavels Church, Lydney ii) Medals at Imperial War Museum

HMS Vindictive bows at Ostend

990	CRUTCHLEY Sir Victor Alexander Charles VC KCB DSC Admiral Royal Navy	Ostend, Belgium

Born: 2 November 1893 - London.

Died: 24 January 1986 aged 92 at Mappercombe, Nettleton, Bridport, Dorset

Buried: St. Mary's Churchyard, Powerstock, Dorset. Headstone

Deed/Service: 22 April and 9 - 10 May 1918 (Lieutenant) Acting with conspicuous gallantry on the first assault to block Ostend harbour, he then took part in the second attempt taking command of HMS 'Vindictive' when its senior officers became casualties. Displaying great bravery in both her and later Motor Launch 254, which rescued 'Vindictive's' crew after charges had sunk her between the piers in the harbour. When 254 was under fire and in a sinking condition, he managed to keep her afloat until HMS 'Warwick' came to the rescue

282

Gazette: 28 August 1918

Commemoration: i) Headstone ii) HMS 'Vindictive' Memorial at Ostend

Blackburn Old Town Hall

991	DEAN Percy Thompson VC Lieutenant - Commander Royal Naval Volunteer Reserve	Zeebrugge, Belgium

Born: 20 July 1877 - Buncer Lane, Blackburn, Lancashire

Died: 20 March 1939 aged 61, at his home in North London

Cremated: 22 March 1939 at Golders Green Crematorium, North West London. Ref: 45215. Ashes on Lawn 2 - B in Garden of Remembrance (2 June)

Deed/Service: 22 - 23 April 1918 (Lieutenant) Commanding ML 282 during the Zeebrugge raid, he took aboard the crews of 'Intrepid' and 'Iphigenia' after they had been scuttled. He embarked over 100 men under constant fire from point-blank range, then as boat was clearing the canal, the steering broke down and he was informed an officer was in the water. He turned back and rescued him before heading for the open sea

319

Gazette: 23 July 1918

Commemoration: i) Plaque at Blackburn Old Town Hall ii) Memorial on the Mole at Zeebrugge iii) Memorial at Bromsgrove School, Worcestershire

992   **FINCH Norman Augustus   VC MSM   Lieutenant and Quartermaster   Royal Marine Artillery**

Zeebrugge, Belgium
402

Born: 26 December 1890 - 42 Minevah Road, Handsworth, Birmingham
Died: 15 March 1966 aged 75 at St. Mary's Hospital, Portsmouth, Hampshire
Cremated: 2 March at Porchester Crematorium, Hampshire. Ashes scattered at South Stoneham Crematorium, Hampshire on Section 3. No memorial
Deed/Service: 22 - 23 April 1918 (Sergeant) As second in command of the pom-poms and Lewis gun aboard HMS 'Vindictive', he and his commander kept up a continuous barrage despite heavy shell fire. When a direct hit killed or wounded all in his position, leaving him seriously wounded, he continued single-handed to harass the enemy on the Mole until a second hit put the guns out of action
Commemoration: i) Memorial at St. Andrew's, Eastney, Hampshire ii) Finch House, Royal Marine Barracks, Eastney iii) Medals at the Royal Marine Museum

Gazette: 23 July 1918

St. Mary's Church

Roehampton War Memorial

993   **HARRISON Arthur Leyland   VC   Lieutenant - Commander   Royal Navy**

Zeebrugge, Belgium
POSTHUMOUS
535

Born: 3 February 1886 - Torquay, Devon
Died: 23 April 1918 aged 32. Killed during his VC action on the Mole at Zeebrugge, Belgium
Buried: Has no known grave - name on Zeebrugge Memorial, Belgium. 10 miles N.E. of Ostend (See Map A - 3)
Deed/Service: 22 - 23 April 1918. When in command of the Naval storming parties during the Zeebrugge raid, which included 994 McKenzie, he was struck on the head by shrapnel as they came alongside the Mole. Regaining consciousness and despite a broken jaw, he led the attack on the seaward batteries, aware that any delay might jeopardise the entire expedition, but was killed almost at once
Commemoration: i) Plaque at St. Mary's Church, Wimbledon, South West London ii) Memorial on the Mole, Zeebrugge iii) Name on Roehampton War Memorial, South West London (now defaced and lead names mostly removed)

Gazette: 17 March 1919

994   **McKENZIE Albert Edward   VC   Able Seaman   Royal Navy**

Zeebrugge, Belgium
ELECTED BY BALLOT
798

Born:	23 October 1898 - Bermondsey, South East London
Died:	3 November 1918 aged 20, at the Royal Naval Hospital, Chatham, Kent from his wounds and influenza
Buried:	9 November at Camberwell Cemetery, Forest Hill Road, South East London. Square 85. Grave 25538. Headstone
Deed/Service:	22 - 23 April 1918. As a member of the storming party at Zeebrugge under the command of 993 Harrison, he landed his machine-gun under intense fire which killed most of his comrades. He managed to account for several of the enemy as he ran seeking shelter by a destroyer alongside the Mole, but was severely wounded whilst working his gun in an exposed position

Gazette: 23 July 1918

Commemoration: i) Headstone ii) Name on the Southwark War Memorial, South London

Submarine Museum

995   **SANDFORD Richard Douglas   VC   Lieutenant   Royal Navy**

Zeebrugge, Belgium
1106

Born:	11 May 1891 - 17 The Becon, Exmouth, Devon. Shown as born 11 July 1891 in other records
Died:	23 November 1918 aged 27, at Evans House, R.N. Auxillary Hospital, Grangetown, Yorkshire (now Cleveland) of typhoid fever and Spanish flu
Buried:	Eston Cemetery, Normanby Road, near Middlesbrough, Cleveland. Section J. Plot U. Grave 709. Headstone
Deed/Service:	22 - 23 April 1918. Commanding HM Submarine C - 3 at Zeebrugge, he skilfully placed the vessel between the piles of the viaduct connecting the Mole to the shore. He refused to use his gyro steering which would enable him and the crew to abandon her at a safe distance, but laid his fuses and left her exactly in position to ensure the mission would be successful

Gazette: 23 July 1918

Commemoration: i) Headstone ii) Plaque at Exeter Cathedral Devon iii) Memorial at the Submarine Museum, Portsmouth, Hampshire iv) Plaque and portrait at HMS 'Dolphin', Gosport, Hampshire v) Sandford Avenue, Gosport

996	WOODALL Joseph Edward VC Captain 1st Bn. The Rifle Brigade (now Royal Green Jackets)	La Pannerie, France

Born: 1 June 1896 - Robinson Street, Salford, Manchester

1326

Died: 2 January 1962 aged 65, at St. Michael's Hospital, Dublin, Ireland. He was found in his flat by his neighbour Joseph King, with burns to his legs and body following a fit. He died of bronchial pneumonia brought on by the burns

Buried: Dean's Grange Cemetery, Dun Laoghaire, Co. Dublin. St. Patrick's Plot. Block H. Grave 173. Plot bought by Joseph King - name not on stone

Deed/Service: 22 April 1918 (Lance-Sergeant) When leading a platoon and held up by machine-gun fire, he rushed forward alone and captured the gun and eight prisoners, then subsequently led ten men and took a farmhouse and thirty more prisoners. When his C.O. was killed, he took command of two platoons, reorganising and placing them skilfully throughout the day and sending back invaluable information

Gazette: 28 June 1918

Commemoration: i) Name on Rifle Brigade Memorial, Winchester Cathedral, Hampshire ii) Medals at Royal Green Jackets Museum

997	SADLIER Clifford William King VC Lieutenant 51st Bn. (Victoria) Australian Imperial Force	Villers-Bretonneux, France

Born: 11 June 1892 - Camberwell, Victoria, Australia

1098

Died: 28 April 1964 aged 71, at Busselton District Hospital, Western Australia

Cremated: Karrakatta Crematorium, Perth, Western Australia. Ashes scattered in Indian Ocean on 17 May 1990

Deed/Service: 24 - 25 April 1918. As his platoon advanced through a wood, they were halted by heavy machine-gun fire. Although wounded, he led his bombing section capturing two guns and killing their crews, by which time all his men had become casualties. He then made a single-handed assault on the third machine-gun armed with a revolver, killing its crew and taking the gun but receiving another serious wound as he did so

Gazette: 11 July 1918

Commemoration: i) Plaque in Karrakatta Cemetery War Grave Gardens, Wall 5, Row D (See Map F) ii) Memorial at Australian War Memorial, Canberra, A.C.T iii) Sadlier Place, Canberra iv) Medals at St. George's Cathedral, Perth

998	HARDY Theodore Bailey VC DSO MC	The Rev. T/Chaplain to the Forces, 4th Class	Army Chaplains' Department	Bucquoy, France
		attd. 9th Bn. The Lincolnshire Regiment (now Royal Anglian Regiment)		

Born:	20 October 1863 - Banfield House, Southernhay, Exeter, Devon
Died:	18 October 1918 aged 54, at No. 2 Red Cross Hospital, Rouen, France, from wounds received in later action at Briastres
Buried:	St. Sever Cemetery Extension, Rouen. Block S. Plot V. Row J. Grave 1. Headstone (See Map A - 37)
Deed/Service:	5, 25 and 27 April 1918. With total disregard for his own safety, he tended many wounded in the open under intense machine-gun fire, helping to bring to safety a wounded officer laying 400 yards from the front line. Later he rushed out into the open to rescue men buried by a shell burst, digging two of them out. He then went out with a sergeant and brought in a wounded man who was lying ten yards from a German pill box
Commemoration:	i) Headstone ii) Plaque in Carlisle Cathedral iii) Memorial stone and plaque at Hutton Roof Church, Cumbria iv) Memorial at Garrison Church, Portsea, Hampshire v) Medals with Royal Army Chaplains' Department

530

Gazette: 11 July 1918

999	HEWITSON James VC Corporal	1/4th Bn. The King's Own Regiment (now The King's Own Royal Borderers)	Givenchy, France

Born:	15 October 1892 - Thwaite Farm, Coniston, Lancashire (now Cumbria)
Died:	2 March 1963 aged 70, in Stanley Hospital, Ulverston, Cumbria, following many years in Stone Mental Hospital
Buried:	6 March in Coniston Churchyard. Headstone
Deed/Service:	26 April 1918 (Lance-Corporal) During a daylight attack on a series of enemy held craters, he led his men and achieved their objective by taking both trenches and dug-out, killing six who would not surrender. Seeing a machine-gun team about to fire on his party he worked his way around the crater single-handed, and killed four of its team. Shortly afterwards he routed a bombing party attacking a Lewis gun, killing six of them
Commemoration:	i) Headstone ii) Name on Coniston War Memorial iii) Memorial plaque and shield inside Coniston Church

564

Gazette: 28 June 1918

1000	McKEAN George Burdon VC MC MM Captain	14th Bn. Quebec Regiment, Canadian Expeditionary Force	Gavrelle Sector, Arras France

Born: 4 July 1888 - Willington, Bishop Auckland, Co. Durham
795

Died: 26 November 1926 aged 38, at Potter's Bar Hospital, Hertfordshire, following a chainsaw accident in his Cuffley workshop

Buried: Brighton Extra-Mural Cemetery, Sussex. Ref: 41624. Headstone shows incorrect date of death and age

Deed/Service: 27 - 28 April 1918 (Lieutenant) When his party was held up at a block by intense fire, he ran into the open and leapt over the block head on top of the enemy. Killing two, he captured the position then sent back for more bombs and until their arrival he engaged the enemy alone. He then rushed a second block, killing two, capturing four and destroying their dug-out

Gazette: 28 June 1918

Commemoration: i) Headstone ii) Wrote several books on scouting iii) Mount McKean, Jasper National Park, Alberta, Canada iv) Medals and display at the Canadian War Museum, Ottawa, Ontario, Canada

1001	CRUICKSHANK Robert Edward VC Major	2/14th (County of London) Bn. The London Regiment (London Scottish)	Jordan, Palestine now Israel

Born: 17 June 1888 - Winnipeg, Manitoba, Canada
281

Died: 30 August 1961 aged 73, at his home in Blaby, Leicestershire

Cremated: 1 September at Gilroes Crematorium, Leicester. Ashes interred at Blaby. No memorial

Deed/Service: 1 May 1918 (Private) He volunteered to take an urgent message to his company HQ from his platoon position at the bottom of a wadi. He was immediately wounded as he rushed up the slope, he tried again and was once more wounded. He made a third attempt when his wounds had been dressed, but was hit again and unable to stand. Rolling himself into a ball amid a hail of bullets, he lay all day in the open and was hit a fifth time

Gazette: 21 June 1918

Commemoration: i) Medals with the London Scottish Regiment

1002	BEESLEY William	VC	Sergeant	13th Bn. The Rifle Brigade (now The Royal Green Jackets)	Bucquoy, France

Born: 5 October 1895 - Gresley, Burton-on-Trent, Staffordshire

72

Died: 23 September 1966 aged 70, in hospital at Abergavenny, Monmouthshire, having been taken ill during a family holiday

Buried: St. Paul's Cemetery, Harbrook Lane, Coventry. Headstone

Deed/Servise: 8 May 1918 (Private) After his section commanders were killed, he took command and single-handed rushed a machine-gun post, shooting four of the enemy and taking six prisoners. He then brought his Lewis gun into action, inflicting many casualties for four hours, until his comrade helping him was wounded. He maintained his position until nightfall, when he brought the wounded man and the gun back to the main line

Gazette: 28 June 1918

Commemoration: i) Headstone ii) Name on the Rifle Brigade Memorial, Winchester Cathedral, Hampshire iii) Road at Bramcote Barracks, Nuneaton, Warwickshire named for him iv) Medals at the Royal Green Jackets Museum

1003	GREGG William	VC DCM MM	Company Sergeant - Major	13th Bn. The Rifle Brigade (now The Royal Green Jackets)	Bucquoy, France

Born: 27 January 1890 - Heanor, Derbyshire

491

Died: 9 August 1969 aged 79, at Heanor Memorial Hospital

Cremated: Heanor Crematorium. Ashes scattered on smaller section in Garden of Remembrance. No memorial

Deed/Service: 8 May 1918 (Sergeant) When all the officers of his company had been hit during an attack he took command, and rushing two enemy posts, he killed some of the gun teams and captured a machine-gun. Driven back by a counter-attack, he consolidated his position until reinforced, then led a charge and personally put a gun crew out of action. Driven back a second time he again counter-attacked, successfully holding the position

Gazette: 28 June 1918

Commemoration: i) Name on Rifle Brigade Memorial, Winchester Cathedral, Hampshire ii) Swimming baths named for him at Heanor Leisure Centre iii) Gregg Street, Heanor named for him iv) Medals at Royal Green Jackets Museum

After the raid

1004 **BOURKE** Rowland Richard Louis   **VC DSO**   **Lieutenant - Commander**   **Royal Naval Volunteer Reserve**

		Ostend, Belgium

Born: 28 November 1885 - London

Died: 29 August 1958 aged 72, at his home at 1253 Lyall Street, Esquimalt, British Columbia, Canada

Buried: Royal Oak Burial Park, Falaise Drive, Victoria, British Columbia. Section O. Plot 10. Grave 16. Headstone

Deed/Service: 9 - 10 May 1918 (Lieutenant) During the first attack on Ostend, when commanding Motor Launch 276, he entered the harbour to ensure that all HMS 'Vindictive's' crew had got away. Hearing cries from the water, he found three men clinging to an up-turned boat and rescued them under intense fire. The launch was hit 55 times, killing two of the crew and causing severe damage but he managed to get it to safety and taken in tow

Commemoration: i) Headstone ii) Medals at the National Archives of Canada, Ottawa, Ontario

111

Gazette: 28 August 1918

1005 **DRUMMOND** Geoffrey Heneage   **VC**   **Lieutenant - Commander**   **Royal Naval Volunteer Reserve**

		Ostend, Belgium

Born: 25 January 1886 - St. James's Place, London

Died: 21 April 1941 aged 55, in hospital in Rotherhithe, South East London

Buried: St. Peter's Church Cemetery, Chalfont St. Peter, Buckinghamshire. Remembrance Gardens. Row J. Grave 13. Headstone

Deed/Service: 9 - 10 May 1918 (Lieutenant) In command of Motor Launch 254, he followed HMS 'Vindictive' into Ostend harbour, and was hit by a shell killing and wounding officers and men including himself. Notwithstanding his wounds, he brought 254 alongside 'Vindictive' and took off two officers and 38 men, remaining conscious long enough to back his vessel away from the piers and into the safety of the open sea before he collapsed

Commemoration: i) Headstone

352

Gazette: 28 August 1918

122

Commemorative Panels at the Australian War Memorial

1006	RUTHVEN William VC Major 22nd Bn. (Victoria) Australian Imperial Force	Ville-Sur-Ancre, France

Born: 21 May 1893 - Collingwood, Melbourne, Victoria, Australia

1091

Died: 12 January 1970 aged 76, at the Heidelberg Repatriation Hospital, Victoria

Cremated: Fawkner Crematorium, New Melbourne Cemetery, Victoria. Ashes interred in Garden of Remembrance. Memorial tablet

Deed/Service: 19 May 1918 (Sergeant) During an attack when his company commander was severely wounded he took charge of company HQ, and rallying the men he captured one machine-gun, wounding two of the enemy and capturing six others in their shelter. Subsequently he rushed a stubborn enemy position, shooting two and then single-handed mopped up the entire post taking 32 prisoners, inspiring and encouraging his men

Gazette: 11 July 1918

Commemoration: i) Plaque at Crematorium ii) Railway Station named for him at Reservoir, Victoria iii) Ruthven Soldiers' Club, Broad Meadows, Victoria iv) Medals and display at the Australian War Memorial, Canberra, A.C.T.

1007	GROGAN George St. George VC CB CMG DSO & Bar T/Brigadier - General	The Worcestershire Regiment	River Aisne, France
	comd. 23rd Infantry Brigade (now The Worcestershire and Sherwood Foresters Regiment)		

Born: 1 September 1875 - St. Andrews, Fifeshire, Scotland

Died: 3 January 1962 aged 86, at his home 'Silverdean', Shrub Hill Lane, Sunningdale, Berkshire

500

Cremated: 8 January at Woking Crematorium, Surrey. Ref: 51565. Ashes scattered in Tennyson Lake Garden in Garden of Remembrance. No memorial

Deed/Service: 27 May 1918. When in command of the remnants of the infantry of a division and attached troops, his utter disregard for personal safety and his tactical ability helped stay the onward thrust of the enemy. Riding up and down the front line, under artillery, mortar, rifle and machine-gun fire he encouraged his men, walking the line when one horse was shot from beneath him. As a result of his courageous actions the line held

Gazette: 25 July 1918

Commemoration:

1008 **HALLIWELL Joel   VC   Lance - Corporal**   **11th Bn. The Lancashire Fusiliers (now Royal Regiment of Fusiliers)** Muscourt, France

Born: 29 December 1881 - 3 Parkfield, Middleton, near Manchester, Lancashire
Died: 14 June 1958 aged 76, from thrombosis at Oldham General Hospital, Lancashire   **513**
Buried: Boarshaw New Cemetery, Middleton. Section 10. Grave 106. Headstone
Deed/Service: 27 May 1918. When the remnants of his batallion were withdrawn, he captured a stray horse and rode out under heavy fire and rescued a man from no-mans-land and carried him to safety. He repeated this action several times successfully rescuing an officer and nine other ranks. His last effort to reach a wounded man was thwarted, being driven back by the very close advance of the enemy   **Gazette: 25 July 1918**

Commemoration: i) Headstone ii) Plaque on side of Cemetery chapel

1009 **KAEBLE Joseph   VC MM   Corporal**   **22nd Bn. Quebec Regiment (Canadien Francais), Canadian Expeditionary Force** Neuville-Vitasse, France

Born: 5 May 1893 - St. Moise, Matane County, Quebec, Canada   **POSTHUMOUS**
Died: 9 June 1918 aged 25. Killed during his VC action at Neuville-Vitasse, France   **663**
Buried: Wanquentin Communal Cemetery Extension, France. 7 miles W. of Arras. Plot II. Row A. Grave 8. Headstone shows age 26 (See Map A-19)
Deed/Service: 8 - 9 June 1918. When in charge of a Lewis gun section during a strong enemy attack, all but one of his crew became casualties. Attacked by 50 of the enemy when the barrage lifted, he jumped over the parapet with his Lewis gun and emptied many magazines into them. Although hit many times he continued to fire, blocking the advance until he fell mortally wounded, firing his last shots at the retreating enemy as he lay in the trench   **Gazette:16 September 1918**

Commemoration: i) Headstone ii) Memorial in Sayabec Parish Church, Quebec iii) Medals and plaque in the Royal 22e Regimental Museum, The Citadel, Quebec

1010   **HUDSON** Charles Edward   **VC CB DSO & Bar MC**   Major - General   Comd. 11th Bn. The Sherwood Foresters Near Asiago, Italy
         (The Nottinghamshire and Derbyshire Regt. now The Worcestershire & Sherwood Foresters Regt.)

Born:	29 May 1892 - Derby
Died:	4 April 1959 aged 66, at St. Mary's, Scilly Isles
Buried:	Denbury Churchyard, near Newton Abbot, Devon. Headstone
Deed/Service:	15 June 1918 (T/Lieutenant Colonel) After the enemy had penetrated our front line during an attack, he collected and personally led various HQ details to the front and shouted for the enemy to surrender some of whom did. He was severely wounded by a bomb which exploded on his foot, and although in great pain he gave directions for the counter-attack which succeeded taking 100 prisoners and six machine-guns
Commemoration:	i) Headstone

602

Gazette: 11 July 1918

1011   **YOULL** John Scott   **VC**   T/Second Lieutenant   1st Bn. The Northumberland Fusiliers, attd. 11th (S) Bn. Near Asiago, Italy
         (now Royal Regiment of Fusiliers)

Born:	6 June 1897 - 'Thorncroft', Thornley, Co. Durham
Died:	27 October 1918 aged 21. Killed in action when struck by a shell during an assault on the River Piave, Italy
Buried:	Giavera British Cemetery, near Treviso, Northern Italy. Plot I. Row H. Grave 2. Headstone
Deed/Service:	15 June 1918. During a patrol which came under heavy fire, he ordered his men back to safety, remaining alone to watch the situation. Unable to rejoin his own company, he took command of men from different units and held the position against enemy attacks, until a machine-gun opened fire behind him. He rushed out and killed its crew and used the gun on the enemy, then led three attacks driving the enemy back each time
Commemoration:	i) Headstone

1342

Gazette: 25 July 1918

1012   **MANNOCK Edward**   **VC DSO & 2 Bars MC & Bar**   **Major**   **85 Squadron, Royal Air Force**

Over France & Flanders

Born:	24 May 1887 - Preston Cavalry Barracks, Brighton, Sussex. Many records show born in Cork, Ireland
Died:	26 July 1918 aged 31. Killed when his plane crashed behind German lines, following combat over Lillers, France
Buried:	i) Has no known grave - name on the Arras Memorial. Western suburbs of town. Bay 1 (See Map A-20) ii) A body was later recovered near Pacaut, France, possibly his and buried in a grave marked 'A British Airman' in Laventie British War Cemetery. Plot III. Row F. Grave 12
Deed/Service:	17 June to 22 July 1918. Although the citation covers one month, his successful career began on 17 May 1917, when he shot down the first of his 73 combat victories. During dates shown, he shot down a Halberstadt on 17 June near Armentieres, destroyed two Fokkers on 7 July near Doulieu, and further two on 14 July near Merville. On 19 July he shot down an Albatross over La Bassee, and two more on 22 July
Commemoration:	i) Name on Arras Memorial ii) Possible grave at Laventie iii) Plaque in the South Aisle of Canterbury Cathedral, Kent iv) Name on War Memorial at Christchurch Gate, Canterbury v) Mannock House, Military Road, Canterbury vi) A VC.10C Mk1 XV103 named for him vii) Name on the RAF Memorial, St. Clement Dane's Church, Central London viii) Display at the RAF Museum

833

Gazette: 18 July 1919

AIF Cemetery, Adelaide

1013   **DAVEY Philip**   **VC MM**   **Corporal**   **10th Bn. (South Australia) Australian Imperial Force**

Merris, France

Born:	10 October 1896 - Near Unley, Goodwood, South Australia
Died:	21 December 1953 aged 57, from coronary occlusion at the Repatriation General Hospital, Springbank, South Australia
Buried:	The AIF Cemetery, Adelaide, South Australia. West Terrace. Headstone
Deed/Service:	28 July 1918. When an enemy machine-gun was causing heavy casualties, he moved forward in the face of point-blank fire and attacked the gun with his grenades, putting half the crew out of action. Replenishing his supply of grenades he again attacked the gun, which had been reinforced, and killed all eight of its crew. He captured the gun and turned it onto the enemy and repelled a counter-attack, but received a severe wound
Commemoration:	i) Headstone ii) Medals and display at the Australian War Memorial, Canberra, A.C.T.

306

Gazette: 17 August 1918

1014	**AXFORD Thomas Leslie**	**VC MM**	**Corporal**	**16th Bn. (S.A. and W.A.) Australian Imperial Force**	Vaire & Hamel Woods France

		41

Born: 18 June 1894 - Carrieton, South Australia
Died: 11 October 1983 aged 89. On a flight between Dubai and Hong Kong having attended the VC Centenary celebrations in London
Cremated: 21 October at Karrakatta Crematorium,Hollywood, Perth, Western Australia. Ashes interred. Portion M. Row C. Niche 1. Memorial
Deed/Service: 4 July 1918 (Lance-Corporal) After his own company commander had become a casualty and the advance of an adjoining platoon had been held up by uncut wire and machine-gun fire, he single-handed charged and threw bombs amongst the enemy gun crews. He then jumped into a trench and charged with his bayonet, killing ten and taking six prisoners, then threw the machine-guns over the parapet allowing the advance to continue
Commemoration: i) Plaque at Karrakatta Remembrance Wall - 19. Row A ii) Axford Place, Canberra, A.C.T. iii) Medals at Australian War Memorial, Canberra

Gazette: 17 August 1918

1015	**DALZIEL Henry**	**VC**	**Sergeant**	**15th Bn. (Q & T) Australian Imperial Force**	Hamel Wood, France

	297

Born: 18 February 1893 - Irvinebank, North Queensland, Australia
Died: 24 July 1965 aged 72, at the Repatriation General Hospital, Greenslopes, Brisbane, Queensland, following a stroke
Cremated: 27 July at Mount Thompson Crematorium, Brisbane. Ashes dispersed in Garden of Remembrance. Memorial plaque
Deed/Service: 4 July 1918 (Driver) When determined resistance came from an enemy strongpoint well protected by wire entanglements, he attacked the position armed only with a revolver. He killed or captured the entire crew and, although severely wounded in the hand, carried on until the final objective was taken. He twice went over open ground under heavy fire to obtain ammunition, continuing to serve his gun until wounded in the head
Commemoration: i) Plaque at Mt. Thompson - Wall 12. Section 16. No. 106 ii) Dalziel Street, Canberra, A.C.T. iii) Display at Australian War Memorial, Canberra

Gazette: 17 August 1918

1016   **BROWN Walter Ernest   VC DCM & Bar   Sergeant   20th Bn. (N.S.W.) Australian Imperial Force**   Villers-Bretonneux, France

Born: 3 July 1885 - New Norfolk, Tasmania, Australia   134

Died: 28 February 1942 aged 56. Killed in action in during Second World War, serving with the Royal Australian Artillery, stating he was born in 1901. As the Japanese entered Singapore, he walked towards them with grenades in his hands, shouting 'No surrender for me'. Body not recovered

Buried: Has no known grave - name on The Singapore Memorial, Kranji War Cemetery, Republic of Singapore. Column 115

Deed/Service: 6 July 1918 (Corporal) On his own initiative, he rushed a machine-gun post which had been causing casualties, and despite being fired on by another post he reached his objective. With a Mills grenade in his hand, he ordered the occupants to surrender and after an initial scuffle, when he knocked down a man with his fist, he took an officer and eleven men prisoner bringing them back under heavy machine-gun fire   **Gazette: 17 August 1918**

Commemoration: i) Name on the Singapore Memorial ii) Plaque at the Leeton Soldiers' Club, New South Wales iii) Brown Street, Canberra, A.C.T. iv) Medals and display at the Australian War Memorial, Canberra

1017   **BORELLA Albert Chalmers (CHALMERS - BORELLA)   VC MM   Captain   26th Bn. (Q.&T.) Australian Imperial Force**   Villers-Bretonneux France

Born: 7 August 1881 - Borung, Victoria, Australia. Changed name by deed poll in 1939 to CHALMERS - BORELLA   105

Died: 7 February 1968 aged 86, at his home at 958 Sylvania Avenue, Albury, Victoria

Buried: 9 February at The Presbyterian Cemetery, North Albury. Headstone

Deed/Service: 17 - 18 July 1918 (Lieutenant) Whilst leading his platoon, he charged and captured an enemy machine-gun, then led his reduced party of ten armed with two Lewis guns against a strongly held trench. Causing many casualties, the trench and two large dug-outs were bombed and thirty prisoners were taken. Later, when outnumbered ten to one, he and his men repulsed the enemy, causing heavy losses   **Gazette: 16 September 1918**

Commemoration: i) Headstone ii) Borella Park, Jingili, Darwin, Northern Territory iii) Borella Club, 31 Supply Bn. Wodonga, New South Wales iv) Borella Road and plaque at Albury v) Borella Street, Canberra, A.C.T. vi) Display at the Australian War Memorial, Canberra

1018   **MEIKLE John**   **VC MM**   **Sergeant**   **4th Bn. The Seaforth Highlanders (now The Highlanders)**   **Near Marfaux, France**
POSTHUMOUS

Born:	11 September 1898 - 34 Freeland Place, Kirkintilloch, Dunbartonshire (now Strathclyde), Scotland
Died:	20 July 1918 aged 19. Killed during his VC action near Marfaux, France
Buried:	Marfaux British Cemetery, France. 8 miles S.W. of Reims. Plot VIII. Row C. Grave 1. Headstone (See Map A - 49)
Deed/Service:	20 July 1918. Single-handed and armed only with a revolver and a stick, he rushed and put out of action a machine-gun which was delaying his company's advance. Shortly afterwards, he seized a rifle and bayonet from a fallen comrade and charged another machine-gun post, but was killed almost on the gun position. His bravery enabled two other men who were following him to put the gun out of action
Commemoration:	i) Headstone ii) Name on Nitshill War Memorial, Glasgow iii) Name on War Memorial, Edinburgh Castle iv) Memorial at St. Enoch's Rail Station, Glasgow v) Plaque at Levern Primary School, Glasgow vi) Memorial in Station Square, Dingwall, Highland Region vii) Medals in Dingwall Museum

854

Gazette: 16 September 1918

1019   **TRAVIS Richard Charles**   **VC DCM MM**   **Sergeant**   **2nd Bn. Otago Infantry Regiment, New Zealand Expeditionary Force**   **Rossignol Wood, France**
POSTHUMOUS

Born:	6 April 1884 - Otara, Opotiki, Southland, Auckland, New Zealand. Birth Certificate shows real name as Dickson Cornelius SAVAGE
Died:	25 July 1918 aged 34. Killed at Rossignol Wood, France
Buried:	Couin New British Cemetery, France. 10 miles N.W. of Albert. Row 9. Grave 5. Headstone (See Map A - 29)
Deed/Service:	24 July 1918. When it was necessary to destroy an impassable wire block, he volunteered to crawl out in broad daylight and successfully bombed the block enabling the attack parties to pass through. Later, when a bombing party was held up by two machine-guns, he rushed the position and killed both crews and four others, allowing the bombers to advance. He was killed the next day, going from post to post encouraging his men
Commemoration:	i) Headstone ii) Memorial at Ryalbush, New Zealand iii) Memorial at R.S.A. H.Q., Dunedin, N.Z. iv) Medals at the Southland Museum, Auckland

1227

Gazette: 27 September 1918

Visitor Centre, Bushkill

1020	AUTEN Harold VC DSC Commander Royal Naval Reserve	English Channel

Born: 22 August 1891 - Leatherhead, Surrey   40

Died: 3 October 1964 aged 73, in the General Hospital, Bushkill, Monroe County, Pennsylvania, U.S.A.

Buried: 6 October at Sandhill Cemetery, Bushkill. Buried in the Steele Family plot. No headstone

Deed/Service: 30 July 1918 (Lieutenant) When in command of HMS 'Stock Force', a 'Q' or mystery ship, she was torpedoed by a U-boat and badly damaged and the 'Panic Party' took to the boats as the U-boat surfaced half a mile away. Fifteen minutes later the 'Panic Party' began to row back, followed by the U-boat. When it lay about 300 yards from 'Stock Force', the guns opened fire, severely damaging the submarine which sank almost immediately. 'Stock Force' sank about four hours later, her crew being taken off by a torpedo boat   **Gazette: 14 September 1918**

Commemoration: i) Name on plaque in Lewisham Civic Centre, South East London ii) St. John's Catholic Church, Bushkill, built by him in 1948, and is now a Visitor Centre iii) Medals at the Royal Naval Museum

Original headstone, Upavon

1021	BEAUCHAMP - PROCTOR Andrew Frederick Weatherby VC DSO MC & Bar DFC A/Captain 84 Squadron, Royal Air Force	Over France

Born: 4 September 1894 - Mossel Bay, East Coast, Cape Province, South Africa. Born PROCTOR, but re-assumed family name during WWI   1006

Died: 21 June 1921 aged 26. Killed during an RAF Display at Enford, near Upavon, Wiltshire

Buried: i) Upavon Cemetery Headstone ii) 8 August 1921 re-interred Mafeking Cemetery, South Africa. European Section. Grave 1050-2. Headstone

Deed/Service: 8 August - 8 October 1918. During this two month period, he was victorious in 26 air combats, but from his first victory in November 1917, he had destroyed 22 aircraft, 16 Kite balloons and drove down a further 16 enemy craft. His work from 8 August in attacking enemy troops on the ground and in reconnaissance during the Allied advance, was almost unsurpassed in its brilliance   **Gazette: 30 November 1918**

Commemoration: i) Headstone at Upavon ii) Headstone at Mafeking iii) Name on RAF Memorial in St. Clement Dane's Church, Central London iv) Plaque inside porch in St. Mary's Church, Droylden, near Manchester

1022   **BRILLANT Jean   VC MC   Lieutenant**   **2nd Bn. Quebec Regiment (Canadien Francais), Canadian Expeditionary Force**   **Near Meharicourt France**
POSTHUMOUS
122

Born: 15 March 1890 - Assametquaghan, Matapadia County, Quebec, Canada
Died: 10 August 1918 aged 28. From three serious wounds received during his VC action near Meharicourt, France
Buried: Villers-Bretonneux Military Cemetery, Fouilloy, France. 10 miles E. of Amiens. Plot VI a. Row B. Grave 20. Headstone (See Map A - 29)
Deed/Service: 8 - 9 August 1918. Although wounded when capturing a machine-gun holding up his company, he refused to leave his command. When later held by heavy machine-gun fire, he led two platoons and attacked the post, capturing 150 prisoners and 15 guns but receiving a second wound. Later he led a 'rushing' party towards a field gun and he was seriously wounded but continued to advance until he collapsed, dying the following day

Gazette: 27 September 1918

Commemoration: i) Headstone   ii) Brillant Street, Rimouski, Quebec   iii) Brillant Street, Montreal, Quebec   iv) Jean Brillant Park, Montreal   v) Royal Canadian Legion Branch named for him in Quebec City   vi) Medals and Plaque in Royal 22nd Regimental Memorial in the Citadel, Quebec

1023   **CROAK John Bernard   VC   Private   13th Bn. Quebec Regt. (Royal Highlanders of Canada), Canadian Expeditionary Force**   **Amiens, France**
POSTHUMOUS
276

Born: 18 May 1892 - Little Bay, Newfoundland, Canada
Died: 8 August 1918 aged 26. Killed during his VC action at Amiens, France
Buried: Hangard Wood British Cemetery, France. 12 miles S.W. of Albert. Plot I. Row A. Grave 9. Headstone (See Map A - 29)
Deed/Service: 8 August 1918. When he became separated from his section, he came upon a machine-gun which he bombed and silenced, taking the gun and crew prisoners. He was severely wounded soon afterwards, but rejoined his platoon and when several more machine-guns were encountered, he ran forward and was first into the enemy trench, bayoneting or capturing the entire garrison. He was again wounded and died almost at once

Gazette: 27 September 1918

Commemoration: i) Headstone   ii) School named for him at St. John's, Newfoundland   iii) Memorial Park in St. John's   iv) Chapter of the Imperial Order of Daughters of Empire named for him at Glace Bay, Nova Scotia   v) Medals at the Army Museum, Halifax, Nova Scotia

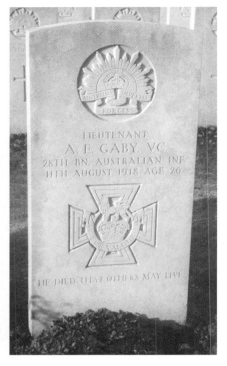
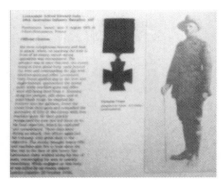

1024 **GABY** Alfred Edward VC Lieutenant 28th Bn. (Western Australia) Australian Imperial Force

Villers-Bretonneux, France
POSTHUMOUS
436

Born: 25 January 1892 - Scottsdale, near Ringarooma, Tasmania, Australia
Died: 11 August 1918 aged 26. Killed by a sniper leading an attack at Villers-Bretonneux, France
Buried: Heath Cemetery, Harbonnieres, France. 11 miles S. of Albert. Plot V. Row E. Grave 14. Headstone (See Map A - 29)
Deed/Service: 8 August 1918. When an advance was checked by a large enemy force forty yards beyond the wire, he found a gap and approached an enemy strong point under heavy machine-gun and rifle fire. Emptying his revolver into the garrison, he drove the crews from their guns and captured fifty prisoners and four machine-guns
Commemoration: i) Headstone ii) Display at Australian War Memorial, Canberra, A.C.T. iii) Medals at Tasmanian Museum and Art Gallery, Hobart, Tasmania

Gazette: 30 October 1918

1025 **GOOD** Herman James VC Corporal 13th Bn. Quebec Regt. (Royal Highlanders of Canada), Canadian Expeditionary Force

Hangard Wood, France

Born: 29 November 1887 - South Bathurst, New Brunswick, Canada
Died: 18 April 1969 aged 81, at his home in Bathurst
Buried: St. Alban's Cemetery, Bathurst. Headstone shows birth as 1888 - all other records show 1887
Deed/Service: 8 August 1918. When his company was held up by heavy fire from three machine-guns, he dashed forward alone and killed several of the crew and capturing the remainder of the garrison. Later, again when alone, he encountered a battery of 5.9-inch guns in action and having collected three men from his section he charged the battery under point-blank fire, and captured the crew members of all three guns
Commemoration: i) Headstone ii) Royal Canadian Legion Branch at Gloucester, New Brunswick named for him (1966)

457

Gazette: 27 September 1918

132

1026   **MINER** Herbert Garnet Bedford   **VC**   Corporal   58th Bn. 2nd Central Ontario Regiment, Canadian Expeditionary Force   Demuin, France
POSTHUMOUS
874

Born: 24 June 1891 - Cedar Springs, Raleigh County, Ontario, Canada
Died: 8 August 1918 aged 27. Killed during his VC action at Demuin, France
Buried: Crouy British Cemetery, Somme, France. 9 miles N.W. of Arras. Plot V. Row B. Grave 11. Headstone (See Map A - 28)
Deed/Service: 8 August 1918. Single-handed, he rushed an enemy machine-gun post holding up an advance, killing the entire crew and turning the gun on the enemy. Later, with two others, he attacked another gun post and put it out of action, before rushing an enemy bombing post alone, killing two and putting the remainder to flight. He was mortally wounded during this action by a German stick-grenade, but refused to withdraw from his position
Gazette: 26 October 1918
Commemoration: i) Headstone ii) Plaque in the United Church, Cedar Springs iii) Medals at the Royal Canadian Legion Post, Clinton, Ontario

Maxwelltown War Memorial

1027   **TAIT** James Edward   **VC MC**   Lieutenant   78th Bn. Manitoba Regt. (Winnipeg Grenadiers), Canadian Expeditionary Force   Amiens, France
POSTHUMOUS
1202

Born: 27 May 1886 - Greenbrae, Dumfries (now Dumfries & Galloway), Scotland
Died: 11 August 1918 aged 32. Killed during his VC action, near Hallu, near Amiens, France
Buried: i) Hallu village ii) Fouquescort British Cemetery, France. 16 miles S. of Albert. Special Memorial. Grave 8. Headstone shows age 31 (Map A-29)
Deed/Service: 8 - 11 August 1918. When an advance had been checked by intense machine-gun fire, he rallied his company and led them forward, going alone to a machine-gun and killing the gunner. This so inspired his men that they rushed the position capturing 12 machine-guns and 20 prisoners. When the enemy attacked under intense artillery fire, he displayed outstanding courage by directing his men, although mortally wounded by a shell blast
Gazette: 27 September 1918
Commemoration: i) Headstone ii) Name on Maxwelltown War Memorial, Dumfries iii) Memorial in Laurieknowe School, Maxwelltown iv) Medals at the Glenbow Museum, Calgary, Alberta, Canada

1028   WEST Ferdinand Maurice Felix   VC CBE MC   Air Commodore   8 Squadron, Royal Air Force   Over Roye, France

Born:	29 January 1896 - Princes Square, Paddington, West London	1290
Died:	7 July 1988 aged 92, at the Princess Margaret Hospital, Windsor, Berkshire	
Buried:	20 July at Holy Trinity Churchyard, Sunningdale, Berkshire. Headstone	
Deed/Service:	10 August 1918 (Captain) Having flown several earlier reconnaissance patrols over enemy positions, he attacked a large concentration of troops and transport at tree level. Noting enemy strengths, he was attacked by several German craft, receiving five bullets in his left leg which was partly severed. Rapidly weakening and in great pain he brought his aircraft back to base, insisting on giving his report before being taken to hospital	

Gazette: 8 November 1918

Commemoration: i) Headstone ii) Name on the RAF Memorial, St. Clement Dane's Church, Aldwych, Central London iii) Medals at the Imperial War Museum

Australian War Memorial

1029   BEATHAM Robert Matthew   VC   Private   8th Bn. (Victoria) Australian Imperial Force   Rosiere, France
POSTHUMOUS

Born:	16 June 1894 - Glassonby, Kirkswald, Penrith, Cumberland (now Cumbria)	68
Died:	11 August 1918 aged 24. Killed during his VC action at Rosiere, East of Amiens, France	
Buried:	Heath Cemetery, Harbonnieres, France. 10 miles S. of Albert. Plot VII. Row J. Grave 13. Headstone (See Map A - 29)	
Deed/Service:	9 August 1918. When an advance at Rosiere, near Villers-Bretonneux was held up by heavy machine-gun fire, he and another man bombed and fought the crews of four enemy machine-guns, killing ten and capturing ten. This helped the advance to continue, and when the final objective was reached, he again dashed forward although wounded and bombed another machine-gun, but was killed while doing so	

Gazette: 14 December 1918

Commemoration: i) Headstone ii) Name on War Memorial, Glassonby, Cumbria iii) Brass plaque at Addingham-with-Gamblesby Church, Yorkshire iv) Display at Australian War Memorial, Canberra, A.C.T.

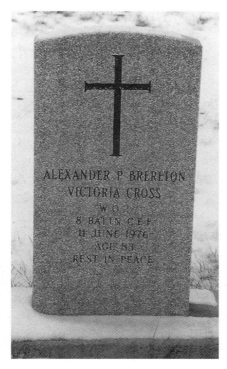

1030   **BRERETON Alexander Picton   VC   Warrant Officer II   8th Bn. Manitoba Regiment, Canadian Expeditionary Force   Aubrecourt, France**

Born:	13 November 1892 - Oak River, Alexander, Manitoba, Canada
Died:	11 June 1976 aged 83, at Golden Hills Lodge, Three Hills, Alberta
Buried:	Elnora Cemetery, Elnora, Alberta. Headstone
Deed/Service:	9 August 1918 (A/Corporal) During an attack, his platoon were caught in an exposed position when a line of machine-guns suddenly opened fire on them. Realising something had to be done or his men would be annihilated, he sprang forward alone and on reaching one of the enemy posts he shot the gunner and bayoneted another, whereupon nine others surrendered. His action inspired his men to charge and capture the other guns
Commemoration:	i) Headstone ii) Royal Canadian Legion Post at Elnora named for him

121

Gazette: 27 September 1918

1031   **COPPINS Frederick George   VC   Corporal   8th Bn. Manitoba Regiment, Canadian Expeditionary Force**   Hackett Woods
Amiens, France

Born:	25 October 1889 - London
Died:	30 March 1963 aged 63, at the United States Administration Hospital, Livermore, California, U.S.A.
Cremated:	Chapel of the Chimes Crematorium, Oakland, California. Name on vault
Deed/Service:	9 August 1918. When his platoon came under unexpected fire from numerous machine-guns in an exposed position with no cover in reach, he called for four volunteers and rushed forward in the face of intense machine-gun fire. The four men with him were killed and he was wounded, but he went on alone and killed the operator of the first gun and three of its crew. Despite his wound, he led his platoon on to their final objective
Commemoration:	i) Name on vault at Crematorium ii) Medals at the Royal Winnipeg Rifles Museum (The Little Black Devils), Winnipeg, Manitoba

254

Gazette: 27 September 1918

HARRIS HOUSE
NAMED IN HONOUR OF
SERGEANT THOMAS JAMES HARRIS V.C.MM.
THE QUEENS OWN ROYAL WEST KENT REGIMENT
BORN IN THIS PARISH OF HALLING 30TH JANUARY 1892
KILLED IN ACTION 9TH AUGUST 1918
A CITATION FOR THE AWARD IS POSTED INSIDE THE
HALLING PARISH CHURCH OF ST. JOHN THE BAPTIST
THIS HOUSE PROVIDED BY THE
STROOD RURAL DISTRICT COUNCIL
OPENED ON THE 30TH JANUARY, 1971

CONTRACTORS   ENGINEER AND SURVEYOR
SELLECK NICHOLLS WILLIAMS (E.C.C.) LTD   -E.L. BOULTER
ST. AUSTELL   C. ENG. M.I.C.E. R.I MUN. E.

1032	HARRIS Thomas James VC MM Sergeant	6th Bn. The Queen's Own Royal West Kent Regt. (now The P.O.W. Royal Regt.)	Morlancourt, France

POSTHUMOUS
534

Born: 30 January 1892 - Manor Terrace, Halling, Kent
Died: 9 August 1918 aged 26. Killed during his VC action at Morlancourt, France
Buried: Dernancourt Communal Cemetery Extension, France. 2 miles S. of Albert. Plot VIII. Row J. Grave 20. Headstone (See Map A - 29)
Deed/Service: 9 August 1918. When an advance was impeded by hostile machine-guns concealed in crops and shell-holes, he led his section against one, killing seven of the enemy. Later, on two separate occasions he attacked two more guns which were inflicting heavy casualties, capturing the first and killing the crew, but was killed when attacking the second. By his courage and initiative, the battalion advance was able to continue

Gazette: 22 October 1918

Commemoration: i) Headstone ii) Memorial stone outside St. John's Church, Harrietsham, Kent iii) Harris House, Halling - block of homes for the aged, named for him in 1996, with a memorial plaque iv) Medals and display at the Queen's Own Royal West Kent Regimental Museum

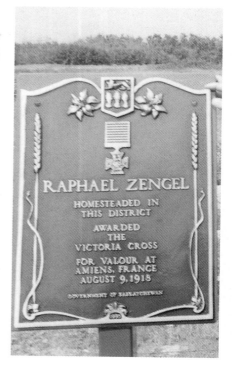

RAPHAEL L ZENGEL
VICTORIA CROSS
MILITARY MEDAL
RSM WO1
5 BATN C.E.F.
27 FEBRUARY 1977
AGE 82
REST IN PEACE

RAPHAEL ZENGEL
HOMESTEADED IN
THIS DISTRICT
AWARDED
THE
VICTORIA CROSS
FOR VALOUR AT
AMIENS, FRANCE
AUGUST 9, 1918
GOVERNMENT OF SASKATCHEWAN

1033	ZENGEL Raphael Louis VC MM Sergeant	5th Bn. Saskatchewan Regiment, Canadian Expeditionary Force	Near Warvillers, France

1350

Born: 11 November 1894 - Faribault, Minnesota, U.S.A.
Died: 27 February 1977 aged 82, in the Nanaimo Regional General Hospital, Victoria Island, British Columbia, Canada
Buried: Pine Cemetery, Rocky Mountain House, Alberta, Canada. Headstone
Deed/Service: 9 August 1918. When leading his platoon forward to the attack, he rushed forward ahead of his men to an enemy machine-gun emplacement, and killed two of the crew, the rest dispersing. Later in the day he was rendered unconscious by an enemy shell, but on recovering continued to direct harassing fire on the enemy. His utter disregard for personal safety and the confidence he inspired, greatly assisted in the success of the attack

Gazette: 27 September 1918

Commemoration: i) Headstone ii) Plaque at his homestead at Rocky Mountain House iii) Name on monument outside Pine Cemetery iv) R.L. Zengel VC Legion Park, Rocky Mountain House v) Mount Zengel, Jasper National Park, Alberta vi) Medals at Royal Canadian Legion Post, Rocky Mountain House

| 1034 | DINESEN Thomas | VC | Lieutenant | 42nd Bn. Quebec Regt. (Royal Highlanders of Canada), Canadian Expeditionary Force | Parvillers, France |

Born: 9 August 1892 - Copenhagen, Denmark

330

Died: 10 March 1979 aged 86, at his home in Leerbaek, Denmark

Buried: i) Hover Cemetery, Denmark ii) Horsholm Cemetery, Ringsted, near Kobenave, Denmark. Family plot. Headstone

Deed/Service: 12 August 1918 (Private) During ten hours of fierce hand-to-hand fighting, which resulted in the capture of over a mile of strongly defended enemy trenches, he displayed conspicuous bravery. Five times in succession he rushed forward alone and put hostile machine-guns out of action, killing and wounding twelve of the enemy with bombs and bayonet. His sustained valour inspired his comrades at a critical stage of the action

Gazette: 26 October 1918

Commemoration: i) Headstone

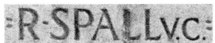

| 1035 | SPALL Robert | VC | Sergeant | Princess Patricia's Canadian Light Infantry, Eastern Ontario Regt., Canadian Expeditionary Force | Parvillers, France |

POSTHUMOUS

Born: 5 March 1890 - Brentford, Middlesex

1172

Died: 13 August 1918 aged 28. Killed during his VC action at Parvillers

Buried: Has no known grave - name on the Vimy Memorial, France. 8 miles N. of Arras (See Map A - 20)

Deed/Service: 12 - 13 August 1918. During an enemy counter-attack his platoon became isolated from the regiment, becoming the focus point of a savage attack. Climbing onto the parapet in full view of the Germans, 200 yards away, he opened fire with his Lewis gun causing many casualties, before directing his men to a sap 75 yards away. He climbed onto the parapet again, and fired into the enemy at point-blank range, but was killed almost at once as he covered the withdrawal of his men

Gazette: 26 October 1918

Commemoration: i) Name on Vimy Memorial ii) Medals at The Museum of the Regiments, Calgary, Alberta

1036   **STATTON Percy Clyde VC MM Sergeant**   40th Bn. (Tasmania) 10th Brigade, 3rd Division, Australian Imperial Force Proyart, France

Born:	21 October 1890 - Beaconsfield, Tasmania, Australia
Died:	7 December 1959 aged 69, in the Repatriation General Hospital, Hobart, Tasmania
Cremated:	Cornelian Bay Crematorium, Hobart. Ashes interred in Garden of Remembrance. Plaque at A.I.F. Arch No. 4. Niche F - 3
Deed/Service:	12 August 1918. When his battalion were assigned an objective, entailing an advance of 1,300 yards over open ground, he engaged two gun posts with his Lewis gun, enabling the advance to reach its target.. As the advance of the 37th Battalion on his left flank became similarly held up by four enemy machine-guns, he worked his way to within 75 yards of their posts and rushed each in succession, putting two out of action and killing five. With a small party he rushed the other two guns, but their crews had retired. That night he went out alone to bring in two men lying in the open

1180

Gazette: 27 September 1918

Commemoration: i) Plaque at Crematorium ii) Two streets in Canberra, A.C.T. named for him iii) Medals and display at Australian War Memorial, Canberra

1037   **BEAK Daniel Marcus William VC DSO MC & Bar Major - General**   Royal Naval Volunteer Reserve Logeast Wood, France
(Drake Battalion, Royal Naval Division)

Born:	27 July 1891 - 42 Kent Road, St. Denys, Southampton, Hampshire
Died:	3 May 1967 aged 75, at the Princess Margaret Hospital, Swindon, Wiltshire, following a long illness
Buried:	9 May at Brookwood Cemetery, near Woking, Surrey. St. Gabriel's Ave. Grave 222960. Unconfirmed if headstone ever existed (See Map-D)
Deed/Service:	21, 25 August & 4 September 1918 (T/Commander) During the entire period he led his men and captured four enemy positions under heavy fire. Four days later, although dazed by a shell fragment, he reorganized the whole brigade under heavy gun fire, and led them towards their objective. When the attack was held up, he and one other man succeeded in knocking out the cause, a nest of machine-guns, taking ten prisoners

66

Gazette: 15 November 1918

Commemoration: i) Name on memorial at New Cemetery, Ayr - Wall Section, Lair 52. Beneath name of wife Matilda - died 1930

1038   **SMITH Edward Benn   VC DCM   Lieutenant & Quartermaster   1/5th Bn. The Lancashire Fusiliers (now Royal Regt. of Fusiliers)**   East of Serre, France

Born: 10 November 1898 - Maryport, Cumberland (now Cumbria)   1156
Died: 12 January 1940 aged 41. Killed in action during the Second World War, serving with the 2nd Bn., Lancashire Fusiliers, near Bucquoy
Buried: Beuvry Communal Cemetery Extension, France. 2 miles S.E. of Bethune. Plot I. Row B. Grave 7. Headstone (See Map A - 19)
Deed/Service: 21 - 23 August 1918 (Lance-Sergeant) When in command of a platoon, he personally took a machine-gun post, rushing the garrison with
                   just rifle and bayonet. The enemy scattered and threw grenades at him, but he continued his rush and shot at least six, heedless of all
                   danger. Later, he led his men to the assistance of a neighbouring platoon, took command and captured their objective, repelling a counter-
                   attack the following day   **Gazette: 22 October 1918**
Commemoration: i) Headstone ii) Name on the Maryport War Memorial

1039   **WEST Richard Annesley   VC DSO & Bar MC   A/Lieutenant - Colonel**   The North Irish Horse (S.R.) seconded to   Courcelles area, France
                                                                                           6th Bn. Tank Corps (now Royal Tank Regiment)   **POSTHUMOUS**

Born: 26 September 1878 - Cheltenham, Gloucestershire   1291
Died: 2 September 1918 aged 39. Killed during his VC action at Vaulx Vracourt, France
Buried: Mory Abbey Military Cemetery, France. 4 miles N. of Bapaume. Plot III. Row G. Grave 4. Headstone shows age 40 (See Map A - 20)
Deed/Service: 21 August 1918. During an attack, the infantry lost their bearings in thick fog, and he collected any men that he could find and led them to
                   their objective in the face of heavy machine-gun fire. Two weeks later at Vaulx Vracourt, he arrived at a crucial time during an enemy attack,
                   many officers had become casualties and the front line was in danger of giving way. He rode his horse up and down in the face of certain death
                   encouraging the men until he fell riddled with bullets, but his magnificent bravery so inspired the infantry that the hostile attack was defeated   **Gazette: 30 October 1918**
Commemoration: i) Headstone ii) Name on family headstone in Coolebrooke Churchyard, Co. Fermanagh, Northern Ireland iii) Memorial in Belfast City Hall
                   iv) Name on War Memorial, Enniskillen, Co. Fermanagh v) Memorial in St. Ronan's Church, Enniskillen vi) Medals and display at The Tank Museum

1040   **ONIONS George VC Major 1st Bn. The Devonshire Regiment (now The Devonshire & Dorset Regiment)**   **Achiet-le-Petit, France**

Born:	2 March 1883 - Bilston, Staffordshire
Died:	2 April 1944 aged 61, at Edgbaston Hospital, Birmingham
Buried:	Quinton Cemetery, Quinton, Birmingham. Section 6. Grave 7364. Headstone
Deed/Service:	22 August 1918 (Lance-Corporal) Having been sent out with another man to contact a battalion on their right flank, he saw the enemy advancing in large numbers. When a German party jumped into the trench and moved towards them, he opened fire and succeeded in causing them to waver with some throwing up their hands, whereupon he rushed forward and the entire party of 242 surrendered and were taken back to the British lines
Commemoration:	i) Headstone ii) Medals and portrait at the Devon and Dorset Regimental Museum

947

Gazette: 14 December 1918

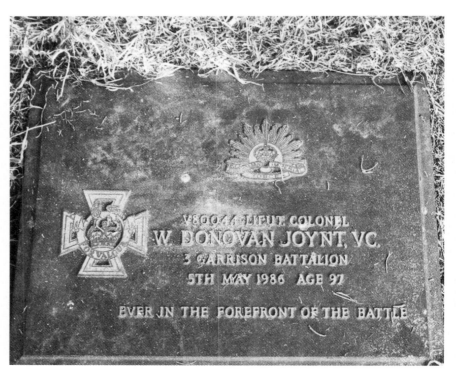

1041   **JOYNT William Donovan VC Lieutenant 8th Bn. (Victoria) 2nd Brigade, 1st Division, Australian Imperial Force**   **Herleville & Plateau Woods Peronne, France**

Born:	19 March 1889 - Elsterwick, Melbourne, Victoria, Australia
Died:	5 May 1986 aged 97, at his home in Windsor, Melbourne
Buried:	Brighton Lawn Cemetery, Victoria. Headstone
Deed/Service:	23 August 1918 (Lieutenant) Taking charge of a company during the Battle of Amiens near Herleville Wood, he rushed forward when the leading battalion in an attack had been demoralised by heavy casualties. Reorganizing the remnants, he led a frontal bayonet charge on Plateau Wood, engaging in severe hand-to-hand fighting, capturing fifty men and forcing the rest of the enemy from the Wood without losing further casualties
Commemoration:	i) Headstone ii) Display at the Australian War Memorial, Canberra, A.C.T.

661

Gazette: 27 November 1918

1042   McCARTHY Lawrence Dominic VC Lieutenant 16th Bn. (S.A. & W.A.) 4th Brigade, 4th Division, Australian Imperial Force   Madame Wood
                                                               Vermandovillers, France

Born: 21 January 1892 - York, Western Australia. Laurence is correct spelling of his forename - Lawrence appears on military records   767

Died: 25 May 1975 aged 83, at the Heidelberg Repatriation Hospital, Heidelberg, Victoria, Australia

Cremated: 28 May at Springvale Crematorium, Melbourne. Ashes interred in Section C. Plot 015 at the Crematorium. Plaque on wall of Necropolis

Deed/Service: 23 August 1918. During the final Allied offensive, his battalion's flank adjoined the British line, and were opposed by two enemy machine-guns. He dashed across the open ground with two other men, and having outpaced them reached the nearest post alone. He put the gun out of action and fought his way down the trench until he made contact with the British, having killed 22 and captured fifty men and five guns during his advance   Gazette: 14 December 1918

Commemoration: i) Wall plaque in Crematorium Necropolis   ii) McCarthy Place, Canberra, A.C.T.   iii) Medals and display at Australian War Museum, Canberra

1043   McIVER Hugh   VC MM & Bar   Private   2nd Bn. The Royal Scots (The Lothian Regiment now The Royal Scots)   Courcelle-le Compte, France
                                                               POSTHUMOUS

Born: 21 June 1890 - Linwood, Kilbarchan, near Johnstone, Renfrewshire (now Strathclyde Region), Scotland   791

Died: 2 September 1918 aged 28. Killed in action near Courcelles, France

Buried: Vracourt Copse Cemetery, France. 10 miles S.E. of Arras. Plot I. Row A. Grave 19. Headstone (See Map A - 20)

Deed/Service: 23 August 1918. When employed as a company runner, he carried many messages under heavy artillery and machine-gun fire, regardless of his own safety. Single-handed he pursued an enemy scout into a machine-gun post, where he killed six of the garrison and captured 20 men and two machine-guns. At great personal risk, he later succeeded in stopping a British tank which was firing inadvertently on our own troops   Gazette: 15 November 1918

Commemoration: i) Headstone   ii) Medals at The Royal Scots Regimental Museum

1044	**FORSYTH Samuel VC Sergeant**	**New Zealand Engineers, attd. 2nd Bn. Auckland Infantry Regiment, N.Z.E.F.**	**Grevillers, France** **POSTHUMOUS** **420**

Born: 3 April 1891 - Wellington, New Zealand
Died: 24 August 1918 aged 27. Killed during his VC action at Grevillers, France
Buried: Adanac Military Cemetery, France. 7 miles N.E. of Albert. Plot I. Row 1. Grave 39. Headstone shows age 25 (See Map A - 29)
Deed/Service: 24 August 1918. As his company neared their objective, they came under heavy machine-gun fire. He immediately led attacks on three gun posts, taking the crews prisoner before they could inflict many casualties. Subsequently, having tried to use a tank to deal with other machine-guns, he led its crew and his own men in an attack, forcing the retirement of the remaining guns. As the advance continued, he was shot by a sniper

Gazette: 22 October 1918

Commemoration: i) Headstone ii) Memorial at the Returned Servicemen's Association HQ, Dunedin, New Zealand

1045	**MacINTYRE David Lowe VC CB Major - General**	**The Argyll & Sutherland Highlanders (Princess Louise's)** **attd. 1/6th Bn. The Highland Light Infantry (now The Royal Highland Fusiliers)**	**Henin and Fontaine** **Croiselles, France** **789**

Born: 18 June 1895 - Portnahaven, near Port Wemyss, Isle of Islay (now Strathclyde Region), Scotland
Died: 31 July 1967 aged 72, in Edinburgh
Cremated: 3 August at Warriston Crematorium, Edinburgh. Ashes scattered in Crematorium Garden of Remembrance. No memorial
Deed/Service: 24 - 27 August 1918 (T/Lieutenant) When acting as adjutant of his battalion, he was constantly in evidence in the firing line under heavy shell and machine-gun fire, inspiring the confidence of all ranks. During one attack, his men encountered extra strong wire entanglements forcing them back, until he organised and led a party to make some gaps in the wire, working under intense fire. Subsequently, when relieved of command in the front line, an enemy machine-gun opened fire close to him, which he rushed single-handed, putting the team to flight and capturing the gun

Gazette: 26 October 1918

Commemoration:

142

1046   **COLLEY Harold John VC MM A/Sergeant**   **10th Bn. The Lancashire Fusiliers (now Royal Regiment of Fusiliers)** **Martinpuich, France**
POSTHUMOUS
231

Born:	26 May 1894 - Winson Street, Smethwick, Birmingham, Staffordshire
Died:	25 August 1918 aged 24. From severe stomach wounds received during his VC action at Martinpuich, France
Buried:	Mailly Wood Cemetery, France. 5 miles N. of Albert. Plot II. Row Q. Grave 4. Headstone shows age 23 (See Map A - 29)
Deed/Service:	25 August 1918. During a strong counter-attack, his company was holding an advanced position with two platoons in advance and two in support. Ordered to hold on at all costs, he went out on his own initiative to assist the forward platoons, rallying them and forming a defensive flank which they held with just three men surviving. Mortally wounded, it was entirely due to his action that prevented the Germans breaking through

Gazette: 22 October 1918

Commemoration: i) Headstone ii) Name on the Smethwick War Memorial iii) Medals at the Lancashire Fusiliers Museum

1047   **GORDON Bernard Sidney VC MM Lance - Corporal**   **41st Bn. (Queensland) 11th Brigade, Australian Imperial Force** **Fargny Wood**
near Bray, France
460

Born:	16 August 1891 - Launceston, Tasmania, Australia
Died:	19 October 1963 aged 72, at his home in Torquay, Queensland
Cremated:	Mount Thompson Crematorium, Queensland. Ashes interred at Pinaroo Lawn Cemetery, Albany, Queensland. Plaque on Wall 10
Deed/Service:	26 - 27 August 1918. During an advance along the Somme River near Fargny Wood, he single-handed attacked an enemy machine-gun post that was persistently enfilading his company's position, killing the gunner and capturing the post with 11 prisoners. Entering the Wood, he then cleared several trenches, taking another 51 prisoners and six machine-guns, allowing his company to take and consolidate over 1,000 yards of ground

Gazette: 26 December 1918

Commemoration: i) Headstone ii) Gordon Soldier's Club, Cabarlah, Toowoomba, Queensland iii) Display at the Australian War Memorial, Canberra, A.C.T.

1048   **JUDSON** Reginald Stanley   **VC DCM MM**   **Major**   **1st Bn. Auckland Infantry Regiment, New Zealand Expeditionary Force**   Near Bapaume, France

Born: 29 September 1881 - Port Albert, Wharehine, New Zealand   662
Died: 26 August 1972 aged 90, of cerebral thrombosis at the Jane Cavenis Private Hospital, Mount Eden, Auckland
Buried: 29 August at Waikumete Cemetery, Auckland. Soldiers Block M. Section 13. Plot 69. Headstone
Deed/Service: 26 August 1918 (Sergeant) During an attack south of Bapaume, he led a small bombing party under heavy fire and captured an enemy
                machine-gun. Proceeding up the sap alone, he bombed another three gun posts before jumping from the trench and running ahead of the
                fleeing Germans. Ordering twelve of the enemy to surrender, they opened fire and he threw a bomb amongst them, killing two and putting
                the rest to flight
Commemoration: i) Headstone ii) Memorial at R.S.A. HQ, Dunedin, New Zealand iii) Medals at the Queen Elizabeth II Army Museum, Walouru, New Zealand   Gazette: 30 October 1918

1049   **RUTHERFORD** Charles Smith   **VC MC MM**   **Captain**   **5th Canadian Mounted Rifles Bn. Quebec Regiment, C.E.F.**   Monchy, France

Born: 9 January 1892 - Near Colbourne, Haldimand County, Ontario, Canada   1089
Died: 11 June 1989 aged 97, at Rideau Veteran's Home, Ottawa, Ontario
Buried: The Union Cemetery, Colbourne. Headstone
Deed/Service: 26 August 1918 (Lieutenant) When commanding an assault party, he found himself a considerable distance ahead of his men at the same
                time he came across a fully armed enemy party of 45 men outside a pill box in front of him. Persuading them that they were totally surrounded,
                they surrendered to him. Joined by his men, he attacked a nearby pill box which was holding up an assault, and captured it and 35 prisoners
Commemoration: i) Headstone ii) Mountain in the VC Range, Jasper National Park, Alberta named for him   Gazette: 15 November 1918

144

1050	WEALE Henry VC Sergeant 14th Bn. The Royal Welch Fusiliers	Bazentin-le-Grand, France

Born: 2 October 1897 - Nine Houses, Shotton, Flintshire (now Clywd), Wales

Died: 13 January 1959 aged 61, at his son's home in Rhyl, Clywd

Buried: Rhyl Cemetery. Headstone shows age 62

Deed/Service: 26 August 1918 (Lance-Corporal) When the advance of an adjacent battalion was held up by enemy machine-guns, he was ordered to put them out of action. When his Lewis gun failed him, he rushed the nearest post and killed the crew, then went for the others, the crews of which fled on his approach. His actions cleared the way for the advance, inspired his comrades and resulted in the capture of all the machine-guns

Commemoration: i) Headstone ii) Weale Hall, Queensferry TA Centre, Clywd iii) Weale Court, Wrexham, Clywd v) Medals at Royal Welch Fusiliers Museum

1284

Gazette: 15 November 1918

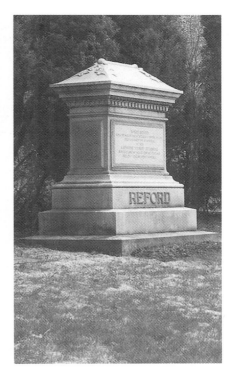

1051	CLARK - KENNEDY William Hew VC CMG DSO & Bar ED Lieutenant - Colonel Comd. 24th Bn. Quebec Regiment (Victoria Rifles), Canadian Expeditionary Force	Wancourt, France

Born: 3 March 1879 - Dunskey, near Castle Douglas, Kirkcudbrightshire, (now Dumfries and Galloway), Scotland

Died: 25 October 1961 aged 82, in Montreal, Quebec, Canada

Buried: Mount Royal Cemetery, Montreal. Pine Hill Section. Reford Family Plot. Lot 258. Headstone

Deed/Service: 27 - 28 August 1918. On the second day of the Arras offensive, he led the centre battalion in an attack which became the focal point of enemy fire and received heavy casualties as a result. As his own and neighbouring lines began to waver, he reorganised and inspired the men, leading from the front and enabling the brigade to meet its objectives. Next day he was severely wounded, but continued to direct operations from a shell hole

Commemoration: i) Headstone

679

Gazette: 14 December 1918

145

1052   **SEWELL Cecil Harold   VC   Lieutenant**   The Royal West Kent Regiment, attd. 3rd (Light) Bn. Tank Corps   **Fremicourt, France**
                                                    (now The P.O.W. Royal Regt. (Q & H) and Royal Tank Regt. respectively)   **POSTHUMOUS**

Born:	27 January 1895 - 26 Crooms Hill, Greenwich, South East London	**1126**
Died:	29 August 1918 aged 23. Killed during his VC action at Fremincourt, France	
Buried:	Vaulx Hill Cemetery, France. 4 miles N.E. of Bapaume. Plot I. Row D. Grave 3. Headstone (See Map A - 20)	
Deed/Service:	29 August 1918. When in command of a section of Whippet light tanks during an attack, he ran from the safety of his own tank across open	

ground under heavy machine-gun fire to rescue the crew of one of his tanks that had side-slipped into a shell-hole, overturned and caught fire. As the door was jammed against the ground, he dug away the earth and released most of the crew, and was trying to free the driver when he was killed   **Gazette: 30 October 1918**

Commemoration: i) Headstone   ii) Name on family grave at Charlton Cemetery, South East London, Section C, Grave 355   iii) Toc-H lamp in his memory at Garrison Church, Bovington Camp, Dorset   iv) Medals, display and plaque at the Tank Museum, Bovington

1053   **HUFFAM James Palmer   VC   Major**   5th Bn. The Duke of Wellington's (West Riding) Regiment, attd. 2nd Bn.   **St. Servin's Farm, France**

Born:	31 March 1897 - Dunblane, Perthshire (now Central Region), Scotland	**603**
Died:	16 February 1968 aged 70, at Edgware General Hospital, Burnt Oak, Middlesex	
Cremated:	21 February at Golders Green Crematorium, North West London. Ref: 19701. Ashes dispersed in Garden of Remembrance. No memorial	
Deed/Service:	31 August 1918 (Second Lieutenant) With three men, he rushed an enemy machine-gun post and put it out of action. When his position	

was then heavily counter-attacked he withdrew, carrying a wounded comrade to safety on his back. Later that night, with two men, he rushed yet another machine-gun post when it was holding his company up, capturing eight prisoners and enabling the advance to continue   **Gazette: 26 December 1918**

Commemoration:

1054   CARTWRIGHT George   VC ED   Captain   33rd Bn. (N.S.W.) 9th Brigade, 3rd Division, Australian Imperial Force   Rood Wood, near Peronne
                                                                                                                                    France
Born: 9 December 1894 - South Kensington, West London   192
Died: 2 February 1978 aged 83, at his home in Epping, Lidcombe, New South Wales
Cremated: Northern Suburbs Crematorium, Sydney. Plaque on War Graves Wall 46, Row B, in the Rookwood Cemetery Garden of Remembrance
Deed/Service: 31 August 1918 (Private) When two companies were held up by withering machine-gun fire during an attack on Rood Wood, near
                     Bouchavesnes, he rushed forward alone and threw a bomb at the post. He then shot three of the crew, captured the gun along with nine
                     prisoners. His gallantry so inspired the battalion, that they stood up and cheered him before renewing their attack with vigour   **Gazette: 14 December 1918**
Commemoration: i) Plaque at Rookwood ii) His medals, the gun he captured and a display at the Australian War Memorial, Canberra. A.C.T

1055   BUCKLEY Alexander Henry   VC   Corporal   54th Bn. (N.S.W.) 14th Brigade, 5th Division, Australian Imperial Force   Peronne, France
                                                                                                                                        POSTHUMOUS
Born: 22 July 1891 - Warren, New South Wales, Australia   144
Died: 1 September 1918 aged 27. Killed during his VC action at Peronne, France
Buried: Peronne Communal Cemetery Extension, St. Radegonde, France. 6 miles E. of Albert. Plot II. Row C. Grave 32. Headstone (See Map A-29)
Deed/Service: 1 September 1918 (T/Corporal) During an advance between the River Somme and Peronne, his battalion was held up by a nest of machine-
                     guns, when he and another man rushed the post, shot four of the enemy and took 22 prisoners. To take their final objective, Peronne, they
                     had to cross by way of a footbridge as the main bridge had been blown by the Germans, he was cut down by machine-gun fire as he tried
                     to rush across   **Gazette: 14 December 1918**
Commemoration: i) Headstone ii) Medals and display at the Australian War Memorial, Canberra, A.C.T.

1056   **CURREY** William Matthew   **VC**   Private   **53rd Bn. (N.S.W.) 14th Brigade, 5th Division, Australian Imperial Force**   Peronne, France

Born:	19 September 1895 - Wallsend, Newcastle, New South Wales, Australia	289
Died:	30 April 1948 aged 52, in hospital in Sydney, N.S.W. of a coronary vascular disease, three days after collapsing in Parliament House	
Cremated:	Woronora Crematorium, Sydney. Ashes interred in Wornora Columbarium. Plaque in Columbarium 15 - C	
Deed/Service:	1 September 1918. During an attack on Peronne, his company were taking heavy casualties early on from a 77mm field gun. He rushed forward despite heavy machine-gun fire, killed the entire crew and captured the gun. He later attacked an enemy strong point single handed, causing many casualties with his Lewis gun. Subsequently, he volunteered and succeeded in taking orders to withdraw to an isolated company under fire	
Commemoration:	i) Plaque on casket ii) Plaque in Rookwood Cemetery Garden of Remembrance, N.S.W. iii) Name on the Leichardt War Memorial, Sydney iv) Currey Memorial Park, Abermain, N.S.W. v) Library named for him, Dudley, N.S.W. vi) Display at Australian War Memorial, Canberra, ACT	Gazette: 14 December 1918

Waikumete Memorial Park

1057   **GRANT** John Gilroy   **VC**   Lieutenant   **1st Bn. Wellington Infantry Regiment, New Zealand Expeditionary Force**   East of Bancourt, France

Born:	26 August 1889 - Hawera, New Zealand	479
Died:	25 November 1970 aged 81, at the Roskill Masonic Village, Auckland, New Zealand	
Buried:	27 November at Golders Cemetery, Waikumete. Block M. Section 9. Plot 95. Headstone shows age 82	
Deed/Service:	1 September 1918 (Sergeant) When in command of a platoon, forming part of the leading wave of a battalion attack on high ground, they were met by a line of five machine-guns on reaching the crest. Leading a charge, he ran ahead when just twenty yards from the guns, entering the centre post, so demoralising the garrison that his platoon mopped up the position. In the same manner he rushed the other posts, until all were taken	
Commemoration:	i) Headstone ii) Plaque on Wall of Remembrance at Waikumete Memorial Park iii) Memorial at RSA HQ, Dunedin iv) Grant Street, Hawera	Gazette: 27 November 1918

| 1058 | HALL Arthur Charles VC Lieutenant | 54th Bn. (N.S.W.) 14th Brigade, 5th Division, Australian Imperial Force | Peronne, France |

Born: 11 August 1896 - Granville, New South Wales, Australia

509

Died: 25 February 1978 aged 81, at Nyngan Hospital, New South Wales

Buried: 28 February at St. Matthew's Anglican Churchyard, West Bogan, Coolabah, New South Wales. Headstone shows rank as Sergeant

Deed/Service: 1 September 1918 (Corporal) When an advance was checked by a machine-gun, he rushed the post single-handed, shooting four and capturing nine of the enemy and two guns. He continued ahead of the main party and located, assaulted and captured many small parties of the enemy and machine-guns. The following day, under a heavy barrage, he carried to safety a dangerously wounded comrade in need of urgent medical care

Gazette: 14 December 1918

Commemoration: i) Headstone ii) Medals and display at the Australian War Memorial, Canberra, A.C.T.

| 1059 | LOWERSON Albert David VC Sergeant | 21st Bn. (Victoria) 6th Brigade, 2nd Division, Australian Imperial Force | Mont St. Quentin, France |

Born: 2 August 1896 - Myrtleford, Bogong, Victoria, Australia

752

Died: 15 December 1945 aged 49, at his home 'St.Quentin', Myrtleford, of leukaemia

Buried: Myrtleford Cemetery. Headstone erected September 1949

Deed/Service: 1 September 1918. When advancing with his company on the right flank during an attack, they were held up by a strong-point manned by twelve machine-guns. Taking seven men, he led a charge which succeeded in capturing all the guns together with thirty prisoners, but received a severe thigh wound, which he refused to have treated until the position had been consolidated. He was finally evacuated to hospital two days later

Gazette: 14 December 1918

Commemoration: i) Headstone ii) Lowerson Place, Canberra, A.C.T. iii) Medals and display at the Australian War Memorial, Canberra

| 1060 | **MACTIER** Robert **VC** Private | 23rd Bn. (Victoria) 6th Brigade, 2nd Divison, Australian Imperial Forces | Mont St. Quentin, France |

POSTHUMOUS
818

Born: 17 May 1890 - 'Reitcam', Tatura, Victoria, Australia
Died: 1 September 1918 aged 28. Killed during his VC action, near Peronne, France
Buried: Hem Farm Cemetery, Hem-Monacu, France. 5 miles W. of Peronne. Plot II. Row J. Grave 3. Headstone (See Map A - 30)
Deed/Service: 1 September 1918. Following the failure of a number of bombing raids in clearing several enemy strong-points which were holding up an attack, he dashed forward alone and killed the eight man crew of one machine-gun. He similarly dealt with a six man team at a second post, then charged and bombed a third position. As he attacked a fourth gun it turned killing him instantly, but his actions enabled the attack to proceed

Gazette: 14 December 1918

Commemoration: i) Headstone ii) Plaque in Club at Watsonia Barracks, Melbourne iii) Mactier Place, Canberra, A.C.T. iv) Medals at Australian War Memorial

| 1061 | **NUNNEY** Claude Joseph Patrick **VC DCM MM** Private | 38th Bn. Eastern Ontario Regiment (Ottawa) Canadian Expeditionary Force | Vitry-en-Artois, France |

POSTHUMOUS
936

Born: 14 December 1892 - Hastings, Sussex
Died: 18 September 1918 aged 25. From wounds received during his VC action, in a casualty clearing station at Vis-en-Artois, France
Buried: Aubigny Communal Cemetery Extension, France. 12 miles E. of St. Pol. Plot IV. Row B. Grave 39. Headstone (See Map A - 19)
Deed/Service: 1 - 2 September 1918. Anticipating a Canadian assault, the Germans launched a heavy counter attack on his battalion. On his own initiative he went forward under a heavy barrage to each of his company's out-posts, encouraging the men by his own fearless example and as a result the attack was repulsed. The next day, his leadership and valour helped carry his company forward to its objective, but he was severely wounded

Gazette: 14 December 1918

Commemoration: i) Headstone ii) Memorial in Glengarry County Municipal Building, North Lancaster, Ontario iii) Medals at the Armouries, Cornwall, Ontario

1062   **TOWNER Edgar Thomas   VC MC   Major**   **2nd Bn. Australian Machine-Gun Corps, Australian Imperial Force**   **Mont St. Quentin, France**

Born:	19 April 1890 - Glencoe Station, near Blackall, Queensland, Australia	**1222**
Died:	18 August 1972 aged 82 at his home, the Kaloola Station, near Longreach, Australia	
Buried:	25 August at Longreach Town Cemetery. Headstone	
Deed/Service:	1 September 1918 (Lieutenant) During the early stages of an attack on the summit of Mont St. Quentin he had single-handed, located and taken an enemy machine-gun and 25 prisoners near Feuillaucourt, turning the gun on the enemy inflicting heavy losses. When the main advance began, he went out alone under heavy fire to reconnoitre prime positions for his guns. Although wounded and short of ammunition he took another enemy gun, using it until the Germans retired and enabling the main advance to continue. He was finally evacuated thirty hours after being wounded	

Gazette: 14 December 1918

Commemoration: i) Headstone   ii) Towner Place, Canberra, A.C.T.   iii) Display at the Australian War Memorial, Canberra

1063   **DOYLE Martin   VC MM   Company Sergeant - Major**   **1st Bn. The Royal Munster Fusiliers (now disbanded)**   **Reincourt, France**

Born:	25 October 1894 - Cloonagh, Gusserane, New Ross, Co. Wexford, Ireland	**347**
Died:	20 November 1940 aged 46, at Sir Patrick Dun's Hospital, Dublin, Ireland	
Buried:	Grangegorman Cemetery, near McKee Barracks, Blackhorse Avenue, Dublin. Also known as Blackhorse Cemetery. Headstone	
Deed/Service:	2 September 1918. Taking command of his company, when all the officers had become casualties, he extricated his men who were had become surrounded by the enemy, carrying a wounded officer to safety on his back. He then went out under fire to the assistance of some wounded men in a tank, and when an enemy machine-gun opened fire on it, making it impossible to get the wounded away, he captured the gun single-handed and took three prisoners. During a later counter-attack, he drove them back, taking many more prisoners	

Gazette: 31 January 1919

Commemoration: i) Headstone

1064   **EVANS Arthur Walter   VC DCM   Sergeant**   6th Bn. The Lincolnshire Regiment (now Royal Anglian Regiment)   **Near Etaing, France**

Born:	8 April 1891 - 33 Caradoc Road, Seaforth, Litherland, Liverpool. Changed name to Walter SIMPSON c.1914	**388**
Died:	1 November 1936 aged 45, at his home in Sydney, New South Wales, Australia	
Cremated:	North Suburbs Crematorium, Sydney. Ashes: i) Sydney Crematorium ii) March 1937, Park Cemetery, Lytham-St.-Annes, Lancashire. Headstone	
Deed/Service:	2 September 1918 (Lance-Sergeant) During a scouting party, he spotted an enemy machine-gun on the opposite (East) bank of a river. Although the river was deep he volunteered to swim across, then crawling to the post he killed two men and captured the gun along with four Germans. When reinforced, they came under heavy fire, and he stayed at the post covering his comrades withdrawal, including a wounded officer	

i):   **Gazette: 30 October 1918**

Commemoration: i) Headstone ii) Evans Crescent, Canberra, A.C.T.   Under name of Evans: ii):   **Gazette: 31 March 1919**

1065   **HARVEY Jack   VC   Sergeant**   1/22nd (County of London) Bn. The London Regiment (The Queen's   **Near Clery, France**
now part of The Territorial & Army Volunteer Reserve)

Born:	24 August 1891 - Peckham, South East London	**543**
Died:	15 August 1940 aged 48, at his home in Redhill, Surrey	
Buried:	Redhill Cemetery. Section C. Grave 2359. Headstone	
Deed/Service:	2 September 1918 (Private) When his company advance was held up by machine-gun fire, he dashed forward alone over fifty yards of open ground through our barrage and heavy enemy fire and reached the gun. Killing three of its crew and destroying the gun, he continued on down the enemy trench, rushing a dug-out where he forced 39 Germans to surrender. His actions saved many casualties and assisted in the success of the attack	

Gazette: 15 November 1918

Commemoration: i) Headstone ii) Memorial 'existed' outside Redhill Town Hall, current location unknown

1066	**HUTCHESON** Bellenden Seymour	**VC MC**	**Captain**	Canadian Army Medical Corps, attd. 75th Bn.	East of Arras, France

1st Central Ontario Regiment, Canadian Expeditionary Force

Born: 16 December 1883 - Mount Carmel, Illinois, U.S.A.
Died: 9 April 1954 aged 70, at Cairo, Illinois
Buried: Rosehill Cemetery, Mount Carmel. Section B. Lot 145. Grave C. Headstone
Deed/Service: 2 September 1918. During his battalion's push along the Queant-Drocourt Support Line, he remained in the open under heavy fire treating every wounded man. Having dressed the wounds of a seriously wounded officer, he succeeded in evacuating him to safety with the help of prisoners and other men. He then rushed out again under a severe barrage to a wounded sergeant, placing him in a shell-hole and dressing his wounds
Commemoration: i) Headstone ii) Memorial in Mount Carmel Court House iii) Medals in The York Armoury, Toronto, Ontario

611

Gazette: 14 December 1918

1067	**KNIGHT** Arthur George	**VC**	**Sergeant**	10th Bn. Alberta Regiment, Canadian Expeditionary Force	Near Cagnicourt, France

POSTHUMOUS

Born: 26 June 1886 - Haywards Heath, Sussex
Died: 3 September 1918 aged 32. From wounds received during his VC action at a Field Hospital near Hendescourt, France
Buried: Dominion Cemetery, France. 10 miles S.E. of Arras. Plot I. Row F. Grave 15. Headstone (See Map A - 20)
Deed/Service: 2 September 1918 (A/Sergeant) Going on alone, after a bombing section he was leading was held up, he bayoneted several machine-gunners and mortar crews, forcing the rest to withdraw by firing on them with a Lewis gun he'd had brought forward. Seeing a number of Germans entering a tunnel, he followed them and captured about twenty. Later he routed another hostile party single-handed before he was fatally wounded
Commemoration: i) Headstone ii) Mount Knight, Jasper National Park, Alberta iii) Knight Crescent, Regina, Saskatchewan iv) Medals at Glenbow Museum, Calgary

702

Gazette: 15 November 1918

Mark V Tanks

| 1068 | METCALF William Henry | VC MM | Lance - Corporal | 16th Bn. Manitoba Regiment (Canadian Scottish) | Arras, France |
| | | | | Canadian Expeditionary Force | |

Born: 29 January 1885 - Waite, Washington County, Maine, USA. Many records show Waite Township, Walsh Co. - these locations do not exist

Died: 8 August 1968 aged 86, at his home in South Portland, Maine. Records show Lewiston, Maine, but correct information from his son

Buried: 12 August at Bayside Cemetery, Eastport, Maine. Section D. Plot 11 - NW. He requested burial at location. Headstone shows MM & Bar

Deed/Service: 2 September 1918. As an attack began, the right flank of his battalion was held up by machine-gun fire and it was decided to wait for a tank before the advance could continue. On its arrival it lost its bearings and was within 100 yards of the German wire, he rushed forward under a hail of fire and using flags he directed it towards the enemy trench, leading it along the line until the strong point had been overcome. Heavy casualties were inflicted and the situation finally relieved, with 17 machine-guns being captured. Despite a severe wound, he continued to advance with his men

Commemoration: i) Headstone ii) Display at the Canadian War Museum, Ottawa, Ontario, Canada

862

Gazette: 15 November 1918

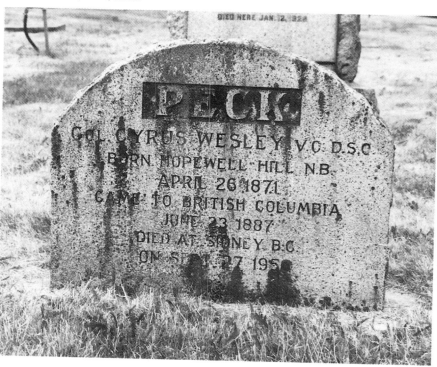

| 1069 | PECK Cyrus Wesley | VC DSO & Bar | Lieutenant - Colonel | Comd. 16th Bn. Manitoba Regiment (Canadian Scottish) | Cagnicourt, France |
| | | | | Canadian Expeditionary Force | |

Born: 26 April 1871 - Hopewell Hill, New Brunswick, Canada

Died: 27 September 1956 aged 85, at his home 'Hopewell', Sidney, Vancouver, British Columbia, Canada

Cremated: New Westminster Crematorium, Vancouver. Ashes buried: i) Crematorium, Range 23. Block 54. Lot B. Headstone ii) At Sea - Rupert Sound

Deed/Service: 2 September 1918. When his command had captured its first objective during the struggle at Drocourt-Queant, they were held up by intense fire. He went out alone under machine-gun and sniper fire to reconnoitre, then reorganized his battalion's flanks and led them forward until he sighted our tanks. From his personal knowledge of the German positions he directed them to fresh targets, paving the way for the infantry to push ahead

Commemoration: i) Headstone ii) Plaque in the Canadian Parliament House of Commons, Ottawa, Ontario iii) Medals at the Canadian War Museum, Ottawa

978

Gazette: 15 November 1918

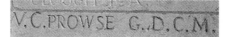

Camerton War Memorial

| 1070 | PROWSE George   VC DCM   Chief Petty Officer   Royal Naval Volunteer Reserve (Drake Battalion, Royal Naval Division) | Pronville, France |

Born: 29 July 1886 - Paulton, Somerset (now Avon)

1008

Died: 27 September 1918 aged 32. Killed in a later action during the Battle for Bapaume, on the Cambrai Road near Arleux, France

Buried: i) Where he fell at Arleux, body not recovered ii) Name on Vis-en-Artois Memorial, France. 7 miles S.E. of Arras. Panel 1-2 (See Map A-20)

Deed/Service: 2 September 1918. During an advance, when his company became disorganized by heavy fire, he led a small party of men against a strong enemy position, capturing it along with 23 men and five machine-guns. On three other occasions he displayed great heroism during the action, at one time dashing forward alone and capturing two gun posts, killing six and taking thirteen prisoners. By his actions, the battalion pushed on in comparative safety

Gazette: 30 October 1918

Commemoration: i) Name on Vis-en-Artois Memorial ii) Name on Camerton Churchyard War Memorial, Avon

| 1071 | RAYFIELD Walter Leigh   VC   Captain | 7th Bn. British Columbia Regiment, Canadian Expeditionary Force | East of Arras, France |

Born: 7 October 1881 - Richmond-upon-Thames, Surrey

1024

Died: 19 February 1949 aged 67, at his home in Toronto, Ontario, Canada

Buried: Prospect Cemetery, Toronto. Soldiers' Plot. Section 7. Grave 4196. Headstone

Deed/Service: 2 - 4 September 1918 (Private) During the struggle for the Drocourt-Queant line, he moved ahead of his company and rushed a trench occupied by a large party of the enemy, bayoneting two and taking ten prisoners. After he had skilfully dealt with a sniper, he rushed the position from which the sniper had been operating and captured another thirty. Subsequently, he ran out into the open under fire and carried a wounded man to safety

Gazette: 14 December 1918

Commemoration: i) Headstone ii) Medals and display at the Canadian War Museum, Ottawa, Ontario

Australian War Memorial

1072　　**WEATHERS Lawrence Carthage　VC　T/Corporal**　　　　43rd Bn. (South Australia) Australian Imperial Force　Allaines, France

Born:	14 May 1890 - Te Koparu, near Whangarei, North Island, New Zealand. Other references incorrectly state North Wairoa, near Napier　**1286**
Died:	29 September 1918 aged 28. Killed in later action by a shell burst, during an attack near Peronne, France
Buried:	Unicorn Cemetery, Vendhuille, France. 12 miles N.E. of Peronne. Plot III. Row C. Grave 5. Headstone (See Map A - 30)
Deed/Service:	2 September 1918. When an attack was held up by two heavily defended trenches - Graz and Scutari, he went forward alone and bombed them, killing the garrison commander. Returning for more bombs, he went out again with three comrades, including a Lewis gunner who covered him as he mounted a parapet and bombed the occupants. With his three comrades he then captured 180 prisoners and three machine-guns
Commemoration:	i) Headstone ii) Display at the Australian War Memorial, Canberra, A.C.T.

Gazette: 26 December 1918

1073　　**YOUNG John Francis　VC　Private**　　87th Bn. Quebec Regt. (Canadian Grenadier Guards), Canadian Expeditionary Force　Dury-Arras Sector France

Born:	14 January 1893 - Kidderminster, Worcestershire　**1345**
Died:	7 November 1929 aged 36, from T.B. at the St. Agathe Sanatorium, St. Agathe-des-Monts, Laurentian Mountains, Quebec, Canada
Buried:	Mount Royal Cemetery, Montreal, Quebec. Section L/2. Plot 2019. Headstone
Deed/Service:	2 September 1918. Following an attack when his company had suffered heavy casualties, he went forward as a stretcher-bearer into open ground swept by machine-gun fire to dress the wounded. He spent over an hour alone at his task, ignoring all danger, returning on several occasions to his company HQ for more dressings. Later in the day he organised and led stretcher-bearers to bring in the wounded he had dressed earlier
Commemoration:	i) Headstone ii) Display at the Canadian War Museum, Ottawa, Ontario

Gazette: 14 December 1918

1074	**McNAMARA John VC Corporal 9th Bn. The East Surrey Regiment (now The P.O.W. Royal Regiment (Q & H)**		**N.W. of Lens, France**
Born:	28 October 1887 - Walton-le-Dale, Preston, Lancashire		**811**
Died:	16 October 1918 aged 30. Killed in a later action near Solesmes, France		
Buried:	Romeries Cemetery Extension, France. 12 miles E. of Cambrai. Plot IV. Row D. Grave 17. Headstone shows age 29 (See Map A-21)		
Deed/Service:	3 September 1918. When operating a telephone in newly taken German trenches, he realised a heavy enemy counter-attack was imminent. He ran to the nearest post as the attack began, and made good use of a revolver he had taken from a wounded officer before using a Lewis gun until it jammed. By then he was the sole survivor in the post, and having destroyed the telephone line he joined another post until reinforcements arrived		**Gazette: 15 November 1918**
Commemoration:	i) Headstone ii) Name on Memorial, All Saint's Church, Kingston-upon-Thames, Surrey iii) Medals at the P.O.W. Royal Regimental Museum		

Turkish Troops

1075	**NEEDHAM Samuel VC Private 1/5th Bn. The Bedfordshire Regiment (now The Royal Anglian Regiment)**		**Kefr Kasim, Palestine now Israel**
Born:	16 August 1885 - Great Limber, North Lincolnshire		**917**
Died:	4 November 1918 aged 33, in Palestine		
Buried:	Kantara War Memorial Cemetery, East Kantara, Egypt. 30 miles S. of Port Said. Row E. Grave 181. Headstone		
Deed/Service:	10 - 11 September 1918. When a member of a fifty man patrol attacked by a large Turkish force at Kefr Kasim, they had been thrown back in some confusion. He ran back alone to confront another enemy party of forty men just thirty yards away, and by firing rapidly, he checked their advance allowing his commander time to organize a withdrawal, which succeeded in getting the patrol and their twenty five casualties back to safety		**Gazette: 30 October 1918**
Commemoration:	i) Headstone ii) Medals at the Bedfordshire and Hertfordshire Regimental Museum		

| 1076 | CALVERT Laurence VC MM Sergeant | 5th Bn. The King's Own Yorkshire Light Infantry (now The Light Infantry) | Havrincourt, France |

Born: 16 February 1892 - Hunslett, Leeds, Yorkshire

173

Died: 7 July 1964 aged 72, at Dagenham, Essex

Cremated: 17 July at South Essex Crematorium, Upminster, Essex. Ref: 9029. Ashes in Garden of Remembrance, Rosebed 32, Path A. No memorial

Deed/Service: 12 September 1918. When his company were held up by heavy machine-gun fire at Boggart's Hole, he rushed forward alone against an enemy gun team, bayoneting three and shooting four. His actions inspired all ranks and enabled the ultimate objective to be taken

Gazette: 15 November 1918

Commemoration: i) Plaque 714 existed in Crematorium Garden of Remembrance; removed due to expiry of contract ii) Plaque outside City Art Gallery, Leeds

| 1077 | LAURENT Harry John VC Lieutenant - Colonel | 2nd Bn. New Zealand (Rifle) Brigade, New Zealand Expeditionary Force | E. of Gouzeaucourt Wood, France |

720

Born: 15 April 1895 - Tarata, Taranaki, New Zealand

Died: 9 December 1987 aged 92, at his home in Hastings, New Zealand

Cremated: Hawera Crematorium, Taraniki. Ashes interred in Memorial Wall at Servicemen's Cemetery, Hawera.

Deed/Service: 12 September 1918 (Sergeant) During an attack, he and a party of twelve men were detailed to exploit an initial success and keep in touch on enemy movements. Coming across a strong German support line he immediately charged them, completely disorganising them by the suddenness of his attack. In the ensuing hand-to-hand fighting thirty of the enemy were killed and 112 captured, with his own party suffering only four casualties

Gazette: 15 November 1918

Commemoration: i) Plaque at Hawera ii) Memorial Wall named for him at Hawera Cemetery iii) Memorial at Returned Servicemen's Association HQ, Dunedin iv) Laurent Street, Hawera v) Medals at the Queen Elizabeth II Army Memorial Museum, New Zealand

| 1078 | **WILCOX Alfred** **VC** Lance - Corporal 2/4th Bn. The Oxfordshire & Buckinghamshire Light Infantry (now Royal Green Jackets) | Near Laventie, France |

Born:	16 December 1884 - Tower Road, Aston, Birmingham	1308
Died:	30 March 1954 aged 69, at his home at 31 Arthur Street, Small Heath, Birmingham (the old 'Prince Arthur Inn'), from a coronary thrombosis	
Buried:	3 April at St. Peter & St. Paul Parish Churchyard, Aston. Burial number 3995. No headstone	
Deed/Service:	12 September 1918. When his company was held up by heavy machine-gun fire at Junction Post, he rushed out alone to the nearest gun, killed the gunner and bombed the post. Attacked by a German bombing party, he led his company to the next gun capturing and destroying it. With one man left, he bombed and captured a third gun before bombing his way up the trench and capturing a fourth gun, then returned to his platoon	
		Gazette: 15 November 1918
Commemoration:	i) Name on War Memorial in St. Peter & St. Paul Churchyard	

Trenches and craters from the air

| 1079 | **HUNTER David Ferguson** **VC** Sergeant | 1/5th Bn. The Highland Light Infantry (now Royal Highland Fusiliers) | Moeuvres, France |

Born:	28 November 1891 - Kingseat, Dunfermline, Scotland	609
Died:	14 February 1965 aged 73, at his home in Dunfermline (now Fife Region)	
Buried:	Dunfermline Cemetery. Division E. Grave 7510. No headstone	
Deed/Service:	16 - 17 September 1918 (Corporal) Having been detailed to take an advanced post in shell craters close to the enemy lines, there was no opportunity for him to reconnoitre the adjacent ground. The following day he found that the Germans had established posts all round him, isolating his command. Determined to hold out, although short of food and water, he repelled many attacks for 48 hours, maintaining his position until relieved	
		Gazette: 23 October 1918
Commemoration:	i) Medals at the Royal Highland Fusilier Regimental Museum	

1080 **BUCKLEY** Maurice Vincent   **VC DCM**   **Sergeant**   **13th Bn. (New South Wales) Australian Imperial Force**   Near Le Verguier, France
Also known as SEXTON Gerald

Born: 13 April 1891 - Upper Hawthorn, Victoria, Australia. Deserted in January 1916, re-enlisted in May using mother's maiden name of SEXTON **147**
Died: 27 January 1921 aged 29, at Fitzroy Hospital, Victoria, from injuries received on 15 January when jumping a young horse over railway gates
Buried: Brighton Cemetery, Melbourne, Victoria. R.C. Section. Grave 114. Compartment B. Headstone shows age 28
Deed/Service: 18 September 1918. As his battalion set off behind a creeping barrage, a field gun was holding up the company. He rushed towards it, shot
the gunner then raced across open ground under machine-gun fire and put a trench mortar out of action. He then fired into an enemy
dug-out, forcing thirty Germans to surrender, subsequently capturing several hostile posts and machine-guns

Original Gazette named to Sexton i): **Gazette: 14 December 1918**
Amended under name of Buckley ii): **Gazette: 8 August 1919**

Commemoration: i) Headstone ii) Buckley Court, Canberra, A.C.T iii) Medals at Australian War Memorial, Canberra

1081 **BURGES** Daniel   **VC DSO**   **T/Lieutenant - Colonel**   **The Gloucestershire Regiment, comd. 7th Bn. South Wales Borderers**   Jumeaux, The Balkans
(now Royal Gloucestershire, Berkshire & Wiltshire Regt. and Royal Regt. of Wales respect.) now Macedonian Region

Born: 1 July 1873 - Central London   **150**
Died: 24 October 1946 aged 73, at his home in Bristol
Cremated: 28 October at Arnos Vale Crematorium, Bristol. No memorial
Deed/Service: 18 September 1918. During the final push on the Bulgarian Army at the Doiran Line (near the 'recent' Yugoslavian - Albanian border), his
battalion came under severe machine-gun fire, despite previous reconnaissance which allowed them to reach an assembly point. Although
wounded, he led his men forward until hit again, when he collapsed and was taken prisoner. Abandoned by his captors he was later found in
a dug-out with his left leg shattered which was later amputated   **Gazette: 14 December 1918**
Commemoration:

Family headstone

Brilley War Memorial

| 1082 | LEWIS Leonard Allan VC Lance - Corporal | 6th Bn. The Northamptonshire Regiment (now Royal Anglian Regiment) | Rossnoy, France POSTHUMOUS |

Born: 28 February 1895 - Wood Villa, Brilley, Whitney-on-Wye, Herefordshire. Recorded incorrectly as Allan LEONARD or Alan E. LEWIS   741
Died: 21 September 1918 aged 23. Killed during his VC action at the Deleful Post, Rossnoy, near Lempire, France
Buried: 30 September at Lempire by Australian troops, grave later lost - name on Vis-en-Artois Memorial. 7 miles S.E. of Arras. Panel 7 (See Map A-20)
Deed/Service: 18 September 1918. When in command of a section on the right flank of an attack, they were held up by intense machine-gun fire from two posts enfilading the line. He crawled forward alone and successfully bombed the position, capturing the crews with rifle fire. Three days later, he rushed his company through an enemy barrage, but was killed by a shrapnel head wound when getting his men under cover from heavy machine-gun fire   **Gazette: 31 January 1919**
Commemoration: i) Name at Vis-en-Artois Memorial ii) Name on War Memorial, St. Mary's Churchyard, Brilley iii) Name on family headstone, Whitney-on-Wye

| 1083 | WARING William Herbert VC MM Lance - Sergeant 25th Bn. The Royal Welch Fusiliers | Ronssby, France POSTHUMOUS |

Born: 13 October 1885 - Rock Terrace, Raven Square, Welshpool, Montgomeryshire (now Powys), Wales   1273
Died: 8 October 1918 aged 32. From wounds received during his VC action at the General Hospital, Le Havre, France
Buried: Ste. Marie Cemetery, Le Havre. Eastern suburbs of town. Division LXII. Row V - 1. Grave 3. Headstone (See Map A - 36)
Deed/Service: 18 September 1918. When leading an attack against enemy machine-guns, he rushed the garrison single-handed under devastating fire, and killed four of the enemy with his bayonet and captured two. He then reorganised his men, inspiring them in another attack, but fell mortally wounded   **Gazette: 31 January 1919**
Commemoration: i) Headstone ii) Name on family grave at Christ Church Welsh Baptist Church Burial Ground iii) Name on Welshpool War Memorial
iv) Waring Court, Hightown, Wrexham v) Waring Court, Alford, Welshpool vi) Medals at the Royal Welch Fusiliers Museum

161

1084	**WHITE William Allison**	**VC TD**	**Captain**	**38th Bn. Machine Gun Corps (now disbanded)**

Gouzeaucourt, France

1304

Born: 19 October 1894 - Mitcham, Surrey

Died: 13 September 1974 aged 83, at his home in Wellington, Shropshire

Cremated: 20 September at Emstrey Crematorium, Shrewsbury, Salop. Ashes buried St. John's Churchyard, Hildenborough, Kent. Grave 506. Headstone

Deed/Service: 18 September 1918 (T/Second Lieutenant) When an advance was held up, he rushed a machine-gun post single-handed and shot three of the crew. With two other men, he later attacked a second gun emplacement, going on alone when his comrades were shot and killed the gunners. He repeated the action a third time, inflicting heavy casualties, before consolidating his position by skillful use of both his own and the captured guns

Gazette: 15 November 1918

Commemoration: i) Headstone

1085	**WOODS James Park**	**VC**	**Private**	**48th Bn. (South Australia) Australian Imperial Force**

Near Le Verguier, France

1330

Born: 2 January 1891 - Gawler, South Australia

Died: 18 January 1963 aged 72, at his home in Claremont, Western Australia

Buried: Karrakatta Cemetery, Perth, Western Australia. Wesleyan Section H-A. Plot 1. Headstone shows age 73 (See Map F)

Deed/Service: 18 September 1918. When on patrol with three other men, during the advance on the Hindenburg Line near Le Verguier, N.W. of St. Quentin, he came across a strongly defended enemy post. As a large force prepared to attack it, he and his small party assaulted it themselves, killing one and putting thirty to flight. When the Germans counter-attacked, he climbed onto the parapet and held them back by throwing bombs until help arrived

Gazette: 26 December 1918

Commemoration: i) Headstone ii) Plaque in Karrakatta Garden of Remembrance, Wall 3, Row C iii) Medals at Australian War Memorial, Canberra, A.C.T

1086   **YOUNG Frank Edward VC Second Lieutenant**   **1st Bn. The Hertfordshire Regiment (now Royal Anglian Regiment)** **Near Havrincourt, France**
POSTHUMOUS
1344

Born:	2 October 1895 - Cherat, North West Province, India now Pakistan
Died:	18 September 1918 aged 22. Killed during his VC action, near Havrincourt, France
Buried:	Hermies Hill British Cemetery, France. 8 miles E. of Bapaume. Plot III. Row B. Grave 5. Headstone shows age 23 (See Map A - 30)
Deed/Service:	18 September 1918. During a heavy enemy counter-attack, he encouraged his men by visiting all his posts under intense fire, rescuing two of them who had been captured and silencing an enemy machine-gun with bombs. Having fought his way back to the main barricade, he inspired his men during four hours of heavy fighting, and was last seen fighting hand-to-hand against a considerable number of the enemy.

Gazette: 14 December 1918

Commemoration: i) Headstone ii) Memorial cross in Garden of Remembrance in St. Mary's Church, Hitchin, Hertfordshire iii) Name on War Memorial outside St. Mary's Church iv) Medals in the Luton Museum, Bedfordshire

1087   **BADLU SINGH VC Ressaidar (Cavalry Troop Commander) 14th Lancers, (Scinde Horse) Indian Army, attd. 29th Lancers** **Khes Samariveh, Palestine**
now Israel
POSTHUMOUS
45

Born:	November 1876 - Dhakla Village, near Jhajjar, Rohtak District, Punjab, India
Died:	23 September 1918 aged 41. From wounds received during his VC action, at Khes Samariveh on west bank of River Jordan
Cremated:	Near where he fell - name inside the Heliopolis Memorial, Heliopolis War Cemetery (Port Tewfik) Egypt
Deed/Service:	23 September 1918. As his squadron were attacking a strong enemy position, they came under fire from machine-guns and infantry from a hill top nearby, causing many casualties. With six men, he charged and captured the position with complete disregard of danger, being mortally wounded when taking one machine-gun single-handed, but all the guns and some 200 infantry surrendered to him before he died

Gazette: 27 November 1918

Commemoration: i) Name on Heliopolis Memorial

| 1088 | BARRETT John Cridlan VC TD Colonel | 1/5th Bn. The Leicestershire Regiment (now Royal Anglian Regiment) | Pontreut, France |

Born: 10 August 1897 - Royal Leamington Spa, Warwickshire

Died: 7 March 1977 aged 79, at his home in Leicester

54

Cremated: 15 March at Gilroes Crematorium, Leicester. Ref: 74560. Ashes laid in: i) 'The Rose Bed' ii) In 'The Glade' at Crematorium. No memorial

Deed/Service: 24 September 1918 (Lieutenant) Due to darkness and a smoke barrage, he found himself heading towards an enemy trench containing numerous machine-guns during an attack. Leading a small party of men he charged the nearest group of guns, and although wounded, he personally inflicted many casualties and took the guns. Wounded again, he ordered his men to cut their way back to the battalion, and was wounded a third time

Gazette: 14 December 1918

Commemoration:

| 1089 | DEAN Donald John VC OBE Colonel | 8th Bn. The Queen's Own Royal West Kent Regt. (now P.O.W. Royal Regt.) | Near Lens, France |

Born: 19 April 1897 - Herne Hill, South East London

Died: 9 December 1985 aged 88, at his home in Sittingbourne, Kent

318

Cremated: 16 December at Charing Crematorium, Kent. Ashes interred in family plot in St. John the Baptist Churchyard, Tunstall, Kent. Headstone

Deed/Service: 24 - 26 September 1918 (T/Lieutenant) Holding a newly captured trench with his platoon, he and his men worked under intense fire to strengthen and consolidate it ready for an assault. The Germans attacked the post five times, and were repulsed on each occasion due to his inspirational and courageous leadership, showing an utter contempt for danger and enabling the post to be held against a much larger German force

Commemoration: i) Name on family headstone ii) Dean Road, Sittingbourne iii) Memorial in Central Avenue, Sittingbourne (May 1995)

Gazette: 14 December 1918

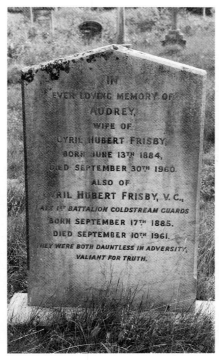

1090 FRISBY Cyril Hubert VC Acting Captain 1st Bn. Coldstream Guards

Canal du Nord
near Graincourt, France
431

Born: 17 September 1885 - New Barnet, Hertfordshire
Died: 10 September 1961 aged 75, at his home in Guildford, Surrey
Buried: Brookwood Cemetery, near Woking, Surrey. Ref: 220173. St. Chad's Avenue. Plot 28. Grave 219662. Headstone (See Map D)
Deed/Service: 27 September 1918. When in command of a company ordered to capture a canal crossing, his leading platoon met with annihilating fire from an enemy post sited under the bridge. With two men, including 1094 Jackson, he climbed down into the canal under intense fire and rushed the post, taking two guns and twelve men. Consolidating the position, he then supported a company which had lost all its officers, beating off a counter-attack
Commemoration: i) Headstone ii) Medals at The Coldstream Guards Museum

Gazette: 27 November 1918

St. Paul's Cathedral

1091 GORT Viscount VC GCB CBE DSO & 2 Bars MVO MC Field - Marshal Comd. 1st Bn. Grenadier Guards

Canal du Nord
near Flesquieres, France
466

Born: 10 July 1886 - 1 Portman Square, Central London. Full given name: John Standish Surtees Prendergast Vereker GORT
Died: 31 March 1946 aged 60 in London, from cancer
Buried: 5 April in the family vault at St. John the Baptist Church, Penshurst, Kent. Headstone
Deed/Service: 27 September 1918 (A/Lieutenant-Colonel) During the attack on the Canal du Nord, he led his battalion under heavy fire until they were forced to a standstill. Although wounded, he went across open ground to obtain assistance from a tank, personally leading it to the best advantage. When wounded again he insisted on staying to direct the attack, resulting in the capture of over 200 prisoners and numerous field and machine-guns
Commemoration: i) Headstone ii) Plaques in the Crypt of St. Paul's Cathedral London iii) Memorial in Garrison Church, Portsea, Hampshire

Gazette: 27 November 1918

165

THIS·COLUMN·MARKS·THE
BATTLEFIELD·WHERE·18,000
CANADIANS·ON·THE·BRITISH
LEFT·WITHSTOOD·THE·FIRST
GERMAN·GAS·ATTACKS·THE
22-24·APRIL·1915·2,000·FELL
AND·LIE·BURIED·NEARBY

Canadian Memorial, Cambrai

1092	**GREGG The Hon Milton VC CBE MC & Bar ED Brigadier**	**Royal Canadian Regiment, Canadian Expeditionary Force**	**Near Cambrai, France**
Born:	10 April 1892 - Mountain Dale, name changed to Snider Mountain, King's County, New Brunswick, Canada. Born Milton Fowler GREGG		**490**
Died:	13 March 1978 aged 85, at his home in Fredericton, New Brunswick		
Buried:	Snider Mountain Baptist Church Cemetery, Fredericton. Headstone		
Deed/Service:	27 September - 1 October 1918 (Lieutenant) During the final Canadian advance to Mons, he was conspicuous throughout a five day period around Cambrai for his gallantry and initiative. Wounded twice, he continued to lead his men against enemy trenches, personally killing or wounding eleven, taking 25 prisoners and twelve machine-guns. In spite of his wounds, he stayed with his men until severely wounded for a third time during an attack		**Gazette: 6 January 1919**
Commemoration:	i) Headstone ii) Mountain named for him in Jasper National Park, Alberta. His medals were stolen from the Regimental Museum, December 1978		

1093	**HONEY Samuel Lewis VC DCM MM Lieutenant**	**78th Bn. Manitoba Regiment (Winnipeg Grenadiers)**	**Bourlon Wood, France**
		Canadian Expeditionary Force	**POSTHUMOUS**
Born:	9 February 1894 - Conn, near Mount Forest, Wellington County, Ontario, Canada		**591**
Died:	30 September 1918 aged 24. From wounds received in his VC action at Bourlon Wood, France		
Buried:	Queant Communal Cemetery, British Extension, France. 12 miles S.E. of Arras. Row C. Grave 36. Headstone (See Map A - 20)		
Deed/Service:	27 September 1918. When all the officers in his company had become casualties he took command, leading an on-going advance to its objective. He then made a personal reconnaissance to locate an enemy machine-gun nest, causing heavy casualties among his men, then rushed it single-handed capturing the guns and ten prisoners. Later he repulsed four enemy counter-attacks, leading his men with great initiative and daring		**Gazette: 6 January 1919**
Commemoration:	i) Headstone ii) Plaque at Westcott United Church, Conn iii) Medals at the Canadian War Memorial, Ottawa, Ontario		

Corporal Thomas Norman Jackson V.C.
COLDSTREAM GUARDS
Killed in action at Graincourt 27th September 1918
Presented to the Township of Swinton by the
Special Constables 31st July 1919
S.C.Ward   F.Jones
Commander   Secretary

1094	JACKSON Thomas Norman VC Lance - Corporal 1st Bn. Coldstream Guards	Near Graincourt, France

POSTHUMOUS

Born: 11 February 1897 - Market Street, Swinton, Rotherham, Yorkshire
Died: 27 September 1918 aged 21. Killed during his VC action at the Canal du Nord, near Graincourt, France
Buried: Sanders Keep Military Cemetery, France. 7 miles W. of Cambrai. Plot II. Row D. Grave 4. Headstone (See Map A - 30)
Deed/Service: 27 September 1918. With another man, he volunteered to follow his company commander (1090 Frisby) across the Canal du Nord and rush an enemy machine-gun post, which resulted in the capture of two guns. Later, when his platoon were ordered to clear an enemy trench, he was the first to enter it, but was killed almost immediately. Throughout the day he had displayed the greatest valour
Commemoration: i) Headstone ii) Painting commissioned by local Special Constabulary, hanging in Swinton Library iii) Medals at the Coldstream Guards Museum

627

Gazette: 27 November 1918

1095	KERR George Fraser VC MC & Bar MM Captain	3rd Bn. 1st Central Ontario Regiment (Toronto Regiment)	Raillencourt, Bourlon Wood
		Canadian Expeditionary Force	France

Born: 8 June 1895 - Deseronto, Ontario, Canada. Records show both 1894 and 1895, the latter is correct
Died: 8 December 1929 aged 34. Asphyxiated by carbon monoxide while running his car engine in the garage at home in Toronto
Buried: Mount Pleasant Cemetery, Toronto, Canada. Plot 14. Section 36. Lot 6 - E 1/2. Headstone
Deed/Service: 27 September 1918 (Lieutenant) During an advance on the outskirts of Raillencourt, he showed conspicuous bravery and leadership by outflanking and taking a machine-gun nest which was impeding the advance. He later rushed another post single-handed, capturing four guns and 31 of the enemy, saving many lives and allowing the advance to continue
Commemoration: i) Headstone ii) Plaque and memorial in Centennial Park, Deseronto

687

Gazette: 6 January 1919

Halfaya Sollum War Cemetery

1096	**LYALL Graham Thomson VC Colonel**	102nd Bn. 2nd Central Ontario Regiment, Canadian Expeditionary Force	Bourlon Wood and Blecourt France

Born: 8 March 1892 - Manchester, Lancashire

758

Died: 28 November 1941 aged 49. Killed in action serving with the R.A.O.C. during the Second War, near Mersa Matruh, Egypt

Buried: Halfaya Sollum War Cemetery, Egypt. 10 miles E. of Libyan border. Plot XIX. Row B. Grave 2. Headstone

Deed/Service: 27 September 1918 (Lieutenant) During the attack on Bourlon Wood and later the advance on Marcoing, he set an 'all-time record' for number of the enemy and equipment captured, a total of two officers, 182 other ranks, 26 machine-guns and a field gun. Leading his platoon, he rushed two strong points single-handed, taking his objectives, the prisoners and the equipment shown, then tended to his wounded when under fire

Gazette: 14 December 1918

Commemoration: i) Headstone

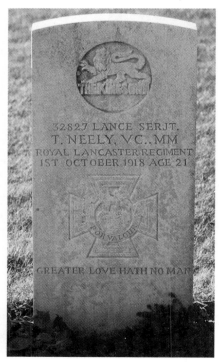

1097	**NEELY Thomas VC MM Lance-Sergeant**	8th Bn. The King's Own Regiment (now King's Own Royal Borderers)	Flesquieres, France

Born: 28 March 1897 - 13 Tabor Street, Poulton-cum-Seacombe, Wallasey, Cheshire. Name appears in many records as NEELEY

918

Died: 1 October 1918 aged 21. Killed in action at Romilly, near Flesquieres France

Buried: Masnieres British Cemetery, Marcoing, France. 4 miles S.W. of Cambrai. Plot II. Row B. Grave 21. Headstone (See Map A - 30)

Deed/Service: 27 September 1918 (Corporal) When his company was held up by heavy machine-gun fire, he dashed out under point-blank range with two men and disposed of the garrisons and captured three machine-guns. He subsequently rushed two more concrete strong points, killing or capturing the occupants, enabling his company to advance over 3,000 yards further along the Hindenberg support line

Gazette: 14 December 1918

Commemoration: i) Headstone ii) Memorial in The Priory, Lancaster

| 1098 | McGUFFIE Louis | VC | Sergeant | 1/5th Bn. The King's Own Scottish Borderers | Near Wytschaete, Belgium POSTHUMOUS 784 |

Born: 15 March 1893 - North Main Street, Wigtown, Galloway (now Dumfries and Galloway Region), Scotland

Died: 4 October 1918 aged 25. Killed in action by a shell during the fighting around Wytschaete, Belgium

Buried: Zantvoorde British Cemetery, Belgium. 6 miles S.E. of Ypres. Plot I. Row D. Grave 12. Headstone shows age 24 (See Map A - 11)

Deed/Service: 28 September 1918 (A/Sergeant) During fighting to gain the crest of the ridge at Wytschaete, he encountered many enemy dug-outs which he entered single-handed, taking numerous prisoners. When consolidating the position, he went out into no-mans-land to re-capture Germans intent on slipping away, coming across a group of British troops in captivity whom he rescued. He continued rounding-up prisoners for the rest of the day

Gazette: 14 December 1918

Commemoration: i) Headstone ii) Bronze plaque, Wigtown Town Hall iii) Name on Wigtown War Memorial iv) Medals at King's Own Scottish Borderers Museum

| 1099 | TANDEY Henry | VC DCM MM | Sergeant | 5th Bn. The Duke of Wellington's (West Riding) Regiment | Marcoing, France 1203 |

Born: 30 August 1891 - Livery Street, Royal Leamington Spa, Warwickshire

Died: 20 December 1977 aged 86, at his home 7 Loudon Avenue, Coundon, Coventry, Warwickshire

Cremated: 23 December at Canley Crematorium, Coventry. Ref: 67160. Ashes scattered on the site of his VC action at Marcoing in France

Deed/Service: 28 September 1918 (Private) When his platoon was held up by machine-gun fire he crawled forward, located the gun and with a Lewis gun team knocked it out. Arriving at a vital crossing in the village, he restored the plank bridge under a hail of bullets, enabling the first crossings to be made. During a later attack, he and eight men were fighting a large enemy force, but he led a bayonet charge, driving 37 into the hands of his company

Gazette: 14 December 1918

Commemoration: i) The Tandey Bar at the Royal Hotel, Royal Leamington Spa ii) Medals 'occasionally' on loan to The Green Howards Museum (owned privately)

| 1100 | McGREGOR John | VC MC & Bar DCM ED | Lieutenant - Colonel | 2nd Canadian Mounted Rifles, 1st Central Ontario Regiment | Cambrai area, France |

Canadian Expeditionary Force

Born: 11 February 1889 - Cawdor, Nairn, near Inverness, Scotland
Died: 9 June 1952 aged 63, at Powell River Hospital, British Columbia, Canada, following a long illness
Buried: Cranberry Lake Cemetery, Powell River. Headstone
Deed/Service: 29 September - 3 October 1918 (T/Captain) During five days continuous fighting, when the Canadian Corps' flanking movement allowed the British to break the Hindenburg Line around Cambrai, he acted with conspicuous gallantry throughout. He led his company under intense fire, putting out machine guns halting progress and constantly reorganising his command under fire against stubborn resistance, particularly the advance to Tilloy

Commemoration: i) Headstone ii) Medals and display at the Canadian War Museum, Ottawa, Ontario

782

Gazette: 6 January 1919

Scole War Memorial

| 1101 | SEAMAN Ernest | VC MM | Lance - Corporal | | 2nd Bn. The Royal Inniskilling Fusiliers (now The Royal Irish Regiment) | Terhand, Belgium |

POSTHUMOUS

Born: 16 August 1893 - Heigham, Norwich, Norfolk
Died: 29 September 1918 aged 25. Killed during his VC action near Terhand, Belgium
Buried: Has no known grave - name on the Tyne Cot Memorial, Belgium. 5 miles N.E. of Ypres. Panel 70 - 72 (See Map A - 11)
Deed/Service: 29 September 1918. Going forward alone with his Lewis gun, he single-handed engaged a machine-gun post, holding up his company during their advance on Terhand. He killed three of the crew and captured two machine-guns and twelve prisoners, then under heavy fire rushed another post and took the position. He was killed immediately afterwards, but it was due to his gallantry that his company were able to take its objective

Commemoration: i) Name on Tyne Cot Memorial ii) Name on War Memorial at Scole, Norfolk iii) Name on Felixstowe War Memorial, Suffolk iv) Name on Ulster Tower Memorial, near Thiepval, France v) Name on Memorial in St. Anne's Cathedral, Belfast vi) Medals at Royal Logistic Corps Museum

1122

Gazette: 15 November 1918

Bellicourt British Cemetery

| 1102 | VANN Bernard William VC MC & Bar A/Lt. - Colonel, The Rev. | 1/8th Bn. The Sherwood Foresters (The Notts & Derby. Regt.) comd. 1/6th Bn. (now The Worcestershire & Sherwood Foresters Regiment) | Canal du Nord, France |

Canal du Nord, France
POSTHUMOUS
1249

Born: 9 July 1887 - Rushden, Northamptonshire
Died: 3 October 1918 aged 31. Killed by a sniper at Rammicourt, France
Buried: 3 October at Bellicourt British Cemetery, France. 12 miles E. of Peronne. Plot II. Row O. Grave 1. Headstone (See Map A - 30)
Deed/Service: 29 September 1918. When leading an attack across the Canal du Nord at Bellenglise and Lehaucourt, through very thick fog and under intense fire from all sides, he realised that the advance depended on keeping-up with the barrage. Moving forward to the firing line and leading from the front, the line swept forward as he encouraged and inspired his men. He then rushed a field gun single-handed, knocking out three of its crew

Gazette: 14 December 1918

Commemoration: i) Headstone

| 1103 | CRICHTON James VC Sergeant | 2nd Bn. Auckland Infantry Regiment, New Zealand Expeditionary Force | Crevecoeur, France |

Crevecoeur, France
273

Born: 15 July 1879 - Carrickfergus, Co. Antrim, Northern Ireland
Died: 22 September 1961 aged 82, at his home 25 Northboro Road, Takapuna, New Zealand
Buried: 25 September at Waikumete Memorial Park Soldiers' Cemetery, Near Auckland. Protestant Section. Block L. Section 4. Plot 9. Headstone
Deed/Service: 30 September 1918 (Private) During an attack he received a wound to his foot, but stayed with the advancing troops despite obstacles in their path. An enemy counter-attack pushed his platoon back and he volunteered to carry a vital message back to HQ, which entailed swimming a river and crossing areas swept by machine-gun fire. Later single-handed he removed live charges laid by the enemy beneath a bridge

Gazette: 15 November 1918

Commemoration: i) Headstone ii) Display at the Returned Serviceman's Association HQ, Dunedin, New Zealand

1104	RYAN Edward John Frances VC Private 55th Bn. (New South Wales) Australian Imperial Force	Hindenberg Defences

Near Bellicourt, France
1093

Born: February 1890 - Tumut, New South Wales, Australia. Usually known as John

Died: 3 June 1941 aged 51, at The Royal Melbourne Hospital, Melbourne, Victoria, Australia from pneumonia

Buried: Springvale Cemetery, Melbourne. Roman Catholic Section. Headstone. Plaque on wall in the Victoria Garden of Remembrance at Cemetery

Deed/Service: 30 September 1918. When the enemy succeeded in establishing a bombing party behind his battalions recently won position, he organized and led a party armed with bombs and bayonets against them. He reached the position with three men remaining and received a severe shoulder wound but succeeded in driving the enemy back into no-mans-land and the trench was re-taken

Gazette: 26 December 1918

Commemoration: i) Headstone ii) Plaque on wall in Cemetery iii) Ryan Street, Canberra, A.C.T. iv) Medals and display at Australian War Memorial, Canberra

1105	GORLE Robert Vaughan VC T/Lieutenant 'A' Bty. 50th Brigade, Royal Field Artillery (now Royal Regiment of Artillery)	Ledeghem, Belgium

464

Born: 6 May 1896 - Southsea, Hampshire

Died: 11 January 1937 aged 40, at Durban, Natal, South Africa, from emphesema and pneumonia

Buried: Stella Wood Cemetery, Durban. Section K. Grave 144. Headstone

Deed/Service: 1 October 1918. When in command of an 18-pounder gun and working in close conjunction with the infantry, he brought the gun into action on four occasions to dispose of enemy machine-guns by firing over open sights under direct fire. Later when the infantry were driven back, he galloped his gun in front of the lead troops and knocked out the machine-guns causing the casualties, enabling the infantry to rally and take their objective

Gazette: 14 December 1918

Commemoration: i) Headstone

1106   **MERRIFIELD William   VC MM   Sergeant**   4th Bn. 1st Central Ontario Regiment, Canadian Expeditionary Force   Abancourt, France

860

Born: 9 October 1890 - Brentwood, Essex
Died: 8 August 1943 aged 52, at Christie Street Military Hospital, Toronto, Ontario, following a stroke
Buried: West Korah Cemetery, Sault Ste. Marie, Ontario.   Headstone
Deed/Service: 1 October 1918. When the advance of his platoon was held up by two machine-gun emplacements, he dashed out alone running from shell-hole to shell-hole and killed the crew of the first post, receiving a wound as he did so. He then approached the second and bombed the occupants. Despite the severity of his wound, he refused to be evacuated and continued to lead his platoon until he was again severely wounded

Gazette: 6 January 1919

Commemoration: i) Headstone

Malmesbury Park School

RIGGS GDNS.

1107   **RIGGS Frederick Charles   VC MM   Sergeant**   6th Bn. The York and Lancaster Regiment (now disbanded)   Near Epinoy, France
POSTHUMOUS
1053

Born: 28 July 1888 - Capstone Road, Bournemouth, Hampshire (now Dorset)
Died: 1 October 1918 aged 30. Killed during his VC action near Epinoy, France
Buried: Has no known grave - name on the Vis-en-Artois Memorial, France. 7 miles S.E. of Arras. Panel 9 (See Map A - 20)
Deed/Service: 1 October 1918. Having led his platoon through strong uncut wire entanglements under heavy fire, he continued forward and reached his objective and captured a machine-gun. Later he handled two captured guns with great effect and caused fifty of the enemy to surrender. When the enemy began to advance in force, he encouraged his men to resist to the last, and was killed in an exposed position as he did so   **Gazette: 6 January 1919**

Commemoration: i) Headstone ii) Plaque in Malmesbury Park School, Bournemouth iii) Riggs Gardens, Bournemouth iv) Medals at the York & Lancaster Museum

| 1108 | COLTMAN William Harold   VC DCM & Bar MM & Bar   Lance - Corporal | 1/6th Bn. The North Staffordshire Regiment
(now The Staffordshire Regiment) | Mannequin Hill, N.E. of
Sequehart, France
235 |

Born: 17 November 1891 - Rangemoor, near Burton-on-Trent, Staffordshire
Died: 29 June 1974 aged 82, at his home in Burton-on-Trent
Buried: St. Peter's Parish Churchyard, also known as Winshill Cemetery, Burton-on-Trent. Headstone
Deed/Service: 3 - 4 October 1918. During a retirement from Mannequin Hill, he was serving as a stretcher-bearer when he heard that some wounded men had been left behind. He went back alone in the face of heavy enfilade fire, found the men and dressed their wounds. Then on three occasions, he retraced his steps under fire and carried some of them on his back to safety, where he tended to them unceasingly for 48 hours

Gazette: 6 January 1919

Commemoration: i) Headstone ii) Name on memorial in Garrison Church, Whittington Barracks, Lichfield, Staffordshire iii) Medals at the Staffordshire's Museum

| 1109 | JOHNSON William Henry VC MM Sergeant   1/5th Bn. The Sherwood Foresters (The Nottinghamshire & Derbyshire Regiment)
(now The Worcestershire and Sherwood Foresters Regiment) | Ramicourt, France
645 |

Born: 15 October 1890 - Worksop, Nottinghamshire
Died: 25 April 1945 aged 54, at his home 33 Nelson Road, Arnold, near Nottingham, Nottinghamshire
Buried: Redhill Cemetery, Nottingham. Section L. Grave 6. Headstone
Deed/Service: 3 October 1918. When his platoon were held up by a nest of machine-guns at very close range, he worked his way forward under intense fire and single-handed charged the post, bayoneting several gunners and capturing two guns. During the ensuing attack, he was severely wounded by a bomb but continued with the attack. Again held up by machine-guns, he once more made a solo attack and succeeded in silencing the guns

Gazette: 14 December 1918

Commemoration: i) Headstone ii) Medals at The Sherwood Foresters Museum

1110   **MAXWELL Joseph**   **VC MC & Bar DCM**   **Lieutenant**   **18th Bn. (New South Wales) Australian Imperial Force**   Near St. Quentin, France

Born:	10 February 1896 - Forest Lodge, Sydney, New South Wales, Australia
Died:	6 July 1967 aged 71, from a heart attack at Matraville, New South Wales
Cremated:	Eastern Suburbs Crematorium, Botany, Sydney. Ashes dispersed at Crematorium Garden of Remembrance. Plaque on Soldiers Wall 9209
Deed/Service:	3 October 1918. Positioned on the Beaurevoir-Fonsomme line near Estrees, his company commander was severely wounded and he immediately took charge. He went out alone on two occasions through heavy wire entanglements, bringing back a number of prisoners and a machine-gun, later skilfully extricating his men from an encounter with a strong enemy force. Throughout the day, he set a high example of personal bravery

848

Gazette: 6 January 1919

Commemoration: i) Wall plaque at Crematorium ii) Plaque in Soldiers Club, Holsworthy Barracks, N.S.W. iii) Display at the Australian War Memorial, Canberra, A.C.T. iv) Medals at the Victoria Barracks, Sydney

1111   **INGRAM George Mawby**   **VC MM**   **Captain**   **24th Bn. (Victoria) Australian Imperial Force**   Montbrehain, France

Born:	18 March 1889 - Bendigo, Victoria, Australia
Died:	30 June 1961 aged 72, from natural causes, at his home in Hastings, Victoria
Buried:	Frankston Cemetery, Victoria. Methodist Section. Grave B - 80. Headstone
Deed/Service:	5 October 1918 (Lieutenant) While leading his men attacking an enemy position, they captured nine machine-guns and killed 42 Germans after stubborn resistance. When his company later suffered heavy casualties, he rushed a machine-gun post single-handed, capturing the gun and shooting six of its team. On two subsequent occasions he attacked enemy posts, inflicting heavy casualties and taking 62 prisoners

616

Gazette: 6 January 1919

Commemoration: i) Headstone ii) Ingram Street, Canberra, A.C.T. iii) Display at the Australian War Memorial, Canberra

1112   TOWERS James V.   VC   Private   2nd Bn. The Cameronians (now disbanded)

Born: 8 September 1897 - Church House Farm, near Broughton, Preston, Lancashire

Died: 24 January 1977 aged 79, at Preston Royal Infirmary

Cremated: 28 January at Preston Crematorium. Ashes dispersed on Crematorium lawns. No memorial

Deed/Service: 6 October 1918. When five runners had been killed or wounded trying to deliver an important message, he volunteered for the duty fully aware of the fate of the previous men. Under heavy fire every step of the way, he dashed from cover to cover and delivered the message

Commemoration: i) James Towers VC Close, Lonsdale Estate, Preston (1997)

Mericourt, France

1221

Gazette: 6 January 1919

John Williams with John Williams (373) c.1928

1113   WILLIAMS John Henry   VC DCM MM & Bar   Warrant Officer Class II   10th Bn. The South Wales Borderers (now The Royal Regiment of Wales)

Villers Outreaux, France

1314

Born: 29 September 1886 - Nantyglo, Monmouthshire (now Gwent), Wales

Died: 7 March 1953 aged 66, at St. Woolo's Hospital, Newport, Gwent

Buried: Ebbw Vale Cemetery, Gwent. Original headstone removed during a cemetery clearance - new headstone erected 21 October 1990

Deed/Service: 7 - 8 October 1918 (Company Sergeant-Major) When his company were suffering heavy casualties from an enemy machine-gun, he went forward alone having ordered a Lewis gun to engage it. Rushing the gun single-handed he captured fifteen Germans, who seeing he was alone tried to overcome him, but he killed five and the rest gave themselves up. His actions enabled his own company and those on their flanks to advance

Commemoration: i) Headstone ii) Memorial at Ebbw Vale Council Chamber iii) Hall named for him at The Centre, Abertillery, Gwent iv) Memorial in Havard Chapel, Brecon Cathedral, Powys v) Medals at the South Wales Borderers Museum

Gazette: 14 December 1918

Field of Honour Cemetery gateway

| 1114 | MITCHELL Coulson Norman VC MC Lieutenant - Colonel | 1st Tunnelling Coy. 4th Canadian Engineers Canadian Expeditionary Force | Near Cambrai, France |

Born: 11 December 1889 - Winnipeg, Manitoba, Canada

876

Died: 17 November 1978 aged 88, at Mount Royal, Quebec, Canada

Buried: Field of Honour Cemetery, Pointe Claire, Mount Royal, Quebec. Section M. Grave 3051. Headstone

Deed/Service: 8 - 9 October 1918 (Captain) He led a small party to examine bridges on the Canal de l'Escaut to prevent their demolition. He managed to cut a number of 'lead' wires on one bridge, then that night he dashed across the heavily charged main bridge, where he and an NCO cut more wires. When the enemy suddenly attacked, he went to assist a wounded sentry before continuing to cut wires and remove charges under heavy fire

Gazette: 31 January 1919

Commemoration: i) Headstone ii) Mount Mitchell, Jasper National Park, Alberta iii) Royal Canadian Legion Post named for him at Montreal iv) Mitchell Street at Mount Royal named for him v) Medals with the Royal Canadian Engineers Museum, Chilliwick, British Columbia

| 1115 | HOLMES William Edgar VC Guardsman 2nd Bn. Grenadier Guards | Cattenieres, France POSTHUMOUS |

588

Born: 26 June 1895 - Wood Stanway, Gloucestershire

Died: 9 October 1918 aged 23. Killed during his VC action at Cattenieres, France

Buried: Carnieres Communal Cemetery Extension, France. 5 miles E. of Cambrai. Plot I. Row B. Grave 3. Headstone (See Map A - 21)

Deed/Service: 9 October 1918. Under the most intense fire, he carried two wounded men to safety, and while attending a third case he was severely wounded. In spite of this he continued to bring in more wounded until falling mortally wounded, but by his self-sacrifice he saved the lives of many comrades

Gazette: 26 December 1918

Commemoration: i) Headstone ii) Memorial at Didbrook Church, Gloucestershire iii) Medals at the Grenadier Guards Museum

| 1116 | ALGIE Wallace Lloyd | VC | Lieutenant | 20th Bn. 1st Central Ontario Regiment, Canadian Expeditionary Force | East of Cambrai, France |

East of Cambrai, France
POSTHUMOUS
18

Born: 10 June 1891 - Alton, Ontario, Canada
Died: 11 October 1918 aged 27. Killed during his VC action north east of Cambrai, France
Buried: Niagara Cemetery, Iwuy, France. 5 miles N.E. of Cambrai. Row C. Grave 7. Headstone (See Map - 21)
Deed/Service: 11 October 1918. During an attack, his men came under heavy enfilading machine-gun fire from a neighbouring village. With nine volunteers he rushed an enemy post, killed the crew and turned the gun on the enemy, enabling his party to reach the village. When clearing the village he ran to another machine-gun, killing its crew and taking eleven prisoners. After going back for reinforcements, he was killed when leading them forward
Commemoration: i) Headstone

Gazette: 21 January 1919

| 1117 | LESTER Frank | VC | Private | 10th Bn. The Lancashire Fusiliers (now The Royal Regiment of Fusiliers) |

Neuvilly, France
POSTHUMOUS
740

Born: 18 February 1896 - West View, Huyton, Liverpool, Lancashire (now Merseyside)
Died: 12 October 1918 aged 22. Killed during his VC action at Neuvilly, France
Buried: Neuvilly Communal Cemetery Extension, France. 3 miles N. of Le Cateau. Row B. Grave 15. Headstone (See Map A - 31)
Deed/Service: 12 October 1918. With a party of seven men and an officer tasked with clearing a village, he was the first to enter a house killing two Germans. The street outside was swept by enemy fire with a sniper covering the exit. On leaving the house he killed the sniper but died doing so

Gazette: 14 December 1918

Commemorations: i) Headstone (No's ii. to x. all Wirral, Cheshire) ii) Name on family grave, Holy Trinity Churchyard, Hoylake iii) Oak plaque at Hoylake Evangelical Church iv) Name on Hoylake War Memorial v) Plaque in Irby Public Library vi) Plaque in Irby Methodist Church vii) Name on the West Kirby War Memorial viii) Name on War Memorial, Holy Cross, Woodchurch ix & x) Plaque inside & War Memorial outside St. Bart's Church, Thutrstaston

1118	WOOD Harry Blanshard VC MM Lance - Sergeant 2nd Bn. Scots Guards	St. Python, France

Born: 21 June 1882 - Pocklington, Newton-on-Derwent, near York, Yorkshire

1322

Died: 15 August 1924 aged 42. In Bristol Mental Hospital, after a six week coma.
He had a seizure after his bride was struck by a truck on honeymoon, she was unhurt

Buried: 20 August at Arnos Vale Cemetery, Bristol. Soldiers Corner. Grave 1738. Headstone.

Deed/Service: 13 October 1918 (Corporal) When ordered to take a bridge over the River Selle, he took command of the leading platoon when they were fiercely opposed, with streets raked with fire and the bridge approach full of snipers. Under fire he carried a large stone into an open space, then lay behind it firing at the snipers, covering his men as they worked their way across to the bridge. He later drove off many enemy counter-attacks

Gazette: 14 December 1918

Commemoration: i) Headstone ii) Name on War Memorial in Bristol Cathedral iii) Medals in The Castle Museum, York

1119	JOHNSON James Bulmer VC Second Lieutenant	2nd Bn. The Northumberland Fusiliers, attd. 36th Bn. (now The Royal Regiment of Fusiliers)	Near Wez Macquart France

644

Born: 31 December 1889 - Widdrington, Northumberland

Died: 23 March 1943 aged 53, at his home 2 Salisbury Road, Plymouth, Devon

Cremated: 26 March at Efford Crematorium, Plymouth. Ref: 2857. Ashes scattered in Garden of Remembrance. No memorial at Crematorium

Deed/Service: 14 October 1918. When in an advanced position and under constant fire, he repelled frequent heavy counter-attacks for over six hours holding the enemy back, until ordered to retire. He was the last to leave the position and when he withdrew carried a wounded man. On three subsequent occasions he returned and brought in badly wounded men across open ground under intense enemy machine-gun fire

Gazette: 26 December 1918

Commemoration: i) Medals at the Royal Northumberland Fusiliers Museum

1120   McPHIE James   VC   Corporal   416th (Edinburgh) Field Co. Corps of Royal Engineers

Aubencheul-au-Bac, France
POSTHUMOUS
816

Born: 18 December 1894 - Rose Street, Edinburgh
Died: 14 October 1918 aged 23. Killed during his VC action at the Canal de la Sensee, near Aubencheul-au-Bac
Buried: Naves Communal Cemetery Extension, France. 3 miles E. of Cambrai. Plot II. Row E. Grave 4. Headstone shows age 24 See Map A-22)
Deed/Service: 14 October 1918. Was with a party of sappers assisting the 2nd Londons to cross a floating bridge in the pre-dawn under shell fire when
                 the bridge broke apart. He swam back to shore and collected materials, aware it was vital the bridge be repaired as half the infantry were
                 now on the enemy bank and it was becoming light. As he began work, he was shot in the face by a sniper and died almost at once

Commemoration: i) Headstone ii) Display at the Royal Engineers Museum iii) Medals in the Imperial War Museum

Gazette: 31 January 1919

1121   MOFFATT Martin Joseph   VC   Private   2nd Bn. The Prince of Wales Leinster Regiment (now disbanded)

Near Ledeghem, Belgium
879

Born: 15 April 1882 - Sligo, Ireland. Records differ with year of birth, 1882 tallies with age at death
Died: 5 January 1946 aged 63. Drowned at sea off the coast of Sligo, a week after he lost his job with the Harbour Police
Buried: Sligo Town Cemetery, Co. Sligo. Headstone. His body was recovered at Rosses Point, opposite Coney Island, Sligo Bay
Deed/Service: 14 October 1918. Advancing with five other men across open ground, they came under heavy rifle fire at close range from a strongly held
                 house. Rushing alone towards the house under a hail of bullets, throwing bombs, he entered by the rear door, killing two and capturing thirty
                 of the enemy

Commemoration: i) Headstone

Gazette: 26 December 1918

1122   O'NEILL John   VC MM   Lieutenant   2nd Bn. The Prince of Wales Leinster Regiment (now disbanded)   **Near Moorseele, Belgium**

Born: 27 January 1897 - 13 Forsyth Street, Airdrie, Lanarkshire, Scotland. Shown incorrectly as O'NIELL on some records   **946**
Died: 16 October 1942 aged 45, from a heart condition whilst serving with The Pioneer Corps at Hoylake, Cheshire during the Second World War
Buried: Holy Trinity Churchyard, Hoylake. Grave No. 8. Headstone
Deed/Service: 14 October 1918 (Sergeant) When the advance of his company was checked by two machine-guns and a field battery firing over open
                   sights, he led eleven men and charged the enemy battery capturing four field guns, two machine-guns and sixteen prisoners. On 20 October
                   he rushed another German machine-gun position with one other man, routing about 100 and causing many casualties   **Gazette: 26 December 1918**
Commemoration: i) Headstone

Pharmacy Memorial

1123   RICKETTS Thomas   VC DCM   Sergeant   1st Bn. Royal Newfoundland Regiment, Canadian Expeditionary Force   **Ledeghem, Belgium**

Born: 15 April 1901 - Middle Arm, White Bay, Newfoundland, Canada   **1051**
Died: 10 February 1967 aged 65, at his home in St. John's, Newfoundland
Buried: Anglican Cemetery, Forest Road, St. John's. Headstone
Deed/Service: 14 October 1918 (Private) In an attempt to out-flank an enemy battery causing heavy casualties from point-blank range, he volunteered
                   to go out with an NCO and a Lewis gun. As they approached, their ammunition ran out and he dashed back under heavy fire for 100 yards,
                   procured more and returned. They then drove the enemy back, allowing the platoon to advance and capture four field guns, four machine-
                   guns and eight prisoners   **Gazette: 6 January 1919**
Commemoration: i) Headstone ii) Stone memorial outside his pharmacy store in St. John's

1124	ELCOCK Roland Edward VC MM Major 11th Bn. The Royal Scots (The Lothian Regiment)	Near Capelle St. Catherine France

Born: 5 June 1899 - 52 Alma Street, Wolverhampton, Staffordshire

Died: 6 October 1944 aged 45 at Dehra Dun, India from 'pslerosis of the liver' (sic), when serving in the Indian Army during the Second World War

Buried: 7 October at St. Thomas's Churchyard, Dehra Dun. Unconfirmed if headstone still exists

Deed/Service: 15 October 1918 (A/Corporal) When in charge of a Lewis gun team, he rushed his gun to within ten yards of two enemy machine-guns which were causing heavy casualties and holding up an advance. He put both their guns out of action and captured five prisoners, enabling the planned attack to advance. Later, near the River Lys, he again attacked an enemy machine-gun and captured both the gun and its crew

Commemoration: i) Headstone   ii) Medals at The Royal Scots Regimental Museum

377

Gazette: 26 December 1918

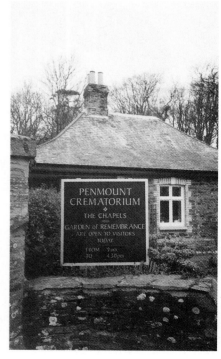

1125	CURTIS Horace Augustus VC Sergeant 2nd Bn. The Royal Dublin Fusiliers (now disbanded)	East of Le Cateau, France

Born: 7 March 1891 - St. Anthony-in-Roseland, Cornwall

Died: 1 July 1968 aged 77 in Redruth Hospital, Cornwall

Cremated: 4 July at Penmount Crematorium, Truro, Cornwall. Ashes scattered in Garden of Remembrance at Crematorium. No memorial

Deed/Service: 18 October 1918. As his platoon were attacking they came under unexpected enemy machine-gun fire, he went forward alone through our own barrage and killed and wounded the crews of two guns. The crews of the remaining four machine-guns immediately surrendered to him and before his men could join him he had succeeded in capturing another 100 enemy troops from a train loaded with reinforcements

Commemoration:

293

Gazette: 6 January 1919

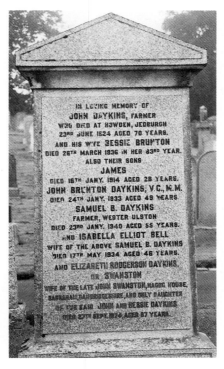

1126 **DAYKINS John Brunton   VC MM   Sergeant   2/4th Bn. The York and Lancaster Regiment (now disbanded)**   Solesmes, France

Born:	26 March 1883 - Ormiston Farm, Hawick, near Roxburgh, Scotland
Died:	24 January 1933 aged 49. In an ambulance on the way to Edinburgh Royal Infirmary, after being found outside his home at Howden Farm with a bullet wound to the head. Recorded that the gun fired accidentally when he had been scaring off animals
Buried:	Castlewood Cemetery, Jedburgh, Borders Region, Scotland. Grave 1431. Headstone
Deed/Service:	20 October 1918 (A/Sergeant) With the twelve remaining men of his platoon, he rushed a machine-gun and during severe hand-to-hand fighting he disposed of many of the enemy. He then located another gun which he approached alone, returning to British lines shortly afterwards with 25 prisoners, enabling his company to advance and take their objective. His spirit and example inspired his men and saved many casualties
Commemoration:	i) Headstone ii) Medals at The York and Lancaster Regimental Museum

317

Gazette: 6 January 1919

1127 **WILKINSON Alfred Robert   VC   Lieutenant**   **1/5th Bn. The Manchester Regiment (now The King's Regiment)**   Marou, France

Born:	5 December 1896 - Leigh, Lancashire (now Greater Manchester)
Died:	18 October 1940 aged 43. Collapsed at work at Bickershaw Colliery, Leigh, from carbon monoxide poisoning due to a blocked ventilator
Buried:	Leigh Borough Cemetery. Plot 1 - U. Grave 99. Headstone
Deed/Service:	20 October 1918 (Private) During an attack at Marou, four runners had been killed attempting to deliver a vital message before he volunteered. Showing supreme courage he succeeded in crossing 600 yards of open ground, swept by both machine-gun and shell fire and delivered it safely
Commemoration:	i) Headstone

1309

Gazette: 6 January 1919

1128	McGREGOR David Stuart	VC	Lieutenant	6th Bn. The Royal Scots (Lothian Regiment) and 29th Bn. Machine Gun Corps (the latter now disbanded)	Near Hoogemolen, Belgium POSTHUMOUS 781

Born: 16 October 1895 - Craigs Road, Corstophine, West Edinburgh, Scotland

Died: 22 October 1918 aged 23. Killed during his VC action near Hill 66, Hoogemolen, Belgium

Buried: Staceghem Communal Cemetery, Belgium. 1 mile E. of Courtrai. Row A. Grave 1. Headstone (See Map A - 12)

Deed/Service: 22 October 1918. When in command of a section attached to an assaulting battalion, he concealed his guns in a sunken road during assembly. During the advance they came under such intense fire that he ordered the teams to take a safer route. He then lay flat on a limber as the driver galloped forward under heavy fire, where the guns were immediately put into action. He was killed when directing fire shortly afterwards

Commemoration: i) Headstone ii) Medals at the Royal Scots Regimental Museum

Gazette: 14 December 1918

1129	GREENWOOD Harry	VC DSO & Bar OBE MC	A/Lt. - Colonel	Comd. 9th Bn. The King's Own Yorkshire Light Infantry (now The Light Infantry)	Ovillers, France 489

Born: 25 November 1881 - Victoria Infantry Barracks, Sheet Street, Windsor, Berkshire. Birth certificate shows HENRY GREENWOOD

Died: 5 May 1948 aged 66, at his home 77 Home Park Road, Wimbledon Park, South West London

Buried: Putney Vale Cemetery, South West London. Block N. Grave 71 - C. Headstone

Deed/Service: 23 - 24 October 1918. When the advance of his battalion was checked by enemy machine-gun fire, he single-handed rushed the position killing the crew. He subsequently took another post, then found that his command was almost surrounded by the enemy who began to attack. He counter-attacked and captured his objective with 150 prisoners and many weapons. The next day he so inspired his men, that they took their final target

Commemoration: i) Headstone ii) Plaque at Victoria Barracks iii) Greenwood Road in Putney Vale Cemetery

Gazette: 26 December 1918

1130   MILES Francis George VC Private 1/5th Bn. The Gloucestershire Regt. (now Royal Gloucestershire, Berkshire & Wiltshire Regt.)   Bois de l'Evique, near
Landrecies, France
867

Born: 9 July 1896 - Clearwell Village, near Coleford, Gloucestershire
Died: 8 November 1961 aged 65, at his cottage in Clearwell
Buried: St. Peter's Parish Churchyard, Clearwell. Headstone
Deed/Service: 23 October 1918. When his company was held up by a line of enemy machine-guns in a sunken road, he went out alone under heavy fire
and shot the first gunner and put the gun out of action. He then shot the second gunner and captured its gun team of eight, then beckoned
his company forward who, acting on his signals, captured a further sixteen machine-guns, one officer and fifty other ranks   **Gazette: 6 January 1919**
Commemoration: i) Headstone ii) Plaque in St. Peter's Church (1973)

1131   HEDGES Frederick William   VC   T/Lieutenant   The Bedfordshire Regt. attd. 6th Bn. The Northamptonshire Regt.   N.E. of Bousies, France
(both now part of The Royal Anglian Regiment)   555

Born: 6 June 1886 - Umballa, India. Recorded as born in 1896, but death and cremation records state died age 67
Died: 29 May 1954 aged 67. Committed suicide at his home in Duchy Road, Harrogate, Yorkshire
Cremated: 2 June at Stonefall Crematorium, Wetherby Road, Harrogate. Ref: 3934. Ashes removed by family, no memorials at Crematorium
Deed/Service: 24 October 1918. Leading his company with great skill towards their final objective, they were abruptly halted by intense fire from a line of
machine-gun posts. With one sergeant and a Lewis gun team some distance behind, he moved forward and captured six machine-guns
and took fourteen enemy prisoners. His gallantry and initiative enabled the whole line to advance, contributing largely to the success of
subsequent operations   **Gazette: 31 January 1919**
Commemoration: i) Name on Roll of Honour at Isleworth County School, Middlesex (currently 'lost') ii) Medals at Bedfordshire & Hertfordshire Regimental
Museum

| 1132 | BISSETT William Davidson VC Major | 1/6th Bn. The Argyll and Sutherland Highlanders (Princess Louise's) | East of Maing, France |

Born: 7 August 1893 - Bauchlands, St. Martin's, Perthshire, Scotland

94

Died: 12 May 1971 aged 77, at Wrexham War Memorial Hospital, Wrexham, Denbighshire (now Clwyd), Wales

Cremated: 17 May at Pentrebychan Crematorium, Wrexham. Ashes interred at Aldershot Military Cemetery, Hampshire. Headstone

Deed/Service: 25 October 1918 (Lieutenant) Due to officer casualties, he was in command of a company when an enemy counter-attack turned his left flank. Realizing the danger, he withdrew to a railway, but the enemy continued to advance until eventually his men ran out of ammunition. Mounting the rail embankment under heavy fire, he organized two bayonet charges which drove the enemy back with heavy losses, saving a critical situation

Gazette: 6 January 1919

Commemoration: i) Headstone at Aldershot ii) Medals at the Argyll and Sutherland Highlanders Regimental Museum

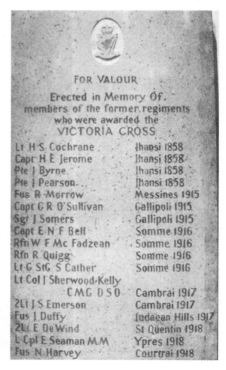

| 1133 | HARVEY Norman VC Company Quartermaster - Sergeant 1st Bn. The Royal Inniskilling Fusiliers (now Royal Irish Regt.) | Ingoyghem, Belgium |

Born: 6 April 1899 - Newton-le-Willows, Lancashire (now Greater Manchester)

544

Died: 16 February 1942 aged 42. Killed when serving with the Royal Engineers near Haifa, Palestine (now Israel) during the Second World War

Buried: Khayat Beach War Cemetery, Haifa (now Sharon), Israel. 2 miles S.W. of town centre. Plot A. Row A. Grave 4. Headstone

Deed/Service: 25 October 1918 (Private) When his battalion was held up and suffering heavy casualties from enemy machine-guns, he rushed forward alone and engaged with the enemy, disposing of twenty of them and capturing their guns. His company were later checked by another enemy strong point which he again charged single-handed, putting them to flight. Subsequently, he went out alone at night on reconnaissance gaining vital information

Gazette: 6 January 1919

Commemoration: i) Headstone ii) Name on plaque in St. Anne's Cathedral, Belfast, Northern Ireland iii) Name on memorial stone at the Ulster Tower, near Thiepval, Somme, France iv) Medals at The Royal Inniskilling Fusiliers Regimental Museum

1134 **BARKER William George** **VC DSO & Bar MC & 2 Bars** **Lieutenant - Colonel** **201 Squadron, Royal Air Force** **Over the Foret de Mormal France 52**

Born:	3 November 1894 - Dauphin, Manitoba, Canada
Died:	12 March 1930 aged 35. Killed when a Fairchild aircraft he was testing crashed at Rockville, Ontario, Canada
Buried:	15 March at Mount Pleasant Cemetery, Inglewood Drive, Toronto, Ontario. Crypt Room B. Crypt B. Large stone tablet
Deed/Service:	27 October 1918 (A/Major) When flying back to Hounslow, he spotted and attacked a German aircraft, causing it to break up in the air. He then shot down a Fokker, and when following it down found himself amid a German formation of fifteen more Fokkers, who immediately attacked him from every angle. Although badly wounded, he managed to shoot down three before landing at an Allied field, unconscious and with a number of severe wounds
Commemoration:	i) Tablet in crypt ii) Name on RAF Memorial, St. Clement Dane's, London iii) Medals and display at Canadian War Museum, Ottawa, Ontario

Gazette: 30 November 1918

1135 **McNALLY William** **VC MM** **Sergeant** **8th (S) Bn. The Yorkshire Regiment (now The Green Howards)** **Piave and Vazzola, Italy 809**

Born:	16 December 1894 - Murton, near Seaham, Co. Durham
Died:	5 January 1976 aged 81, at his home in Bude Square, Murton
Cremated:	9 January at Tyne & Wear Crematorium, Hylton Road, Sunderland. Ashes scattered in Crematorium's Garden of Remembrance. No memorial
Deed/Service:	27 and 29 October 1918. When his company was being hindered by machine-gun fire, he rushed the post single-handed under heavy fire, killed the team and captured the gun. Two days later at Vazzola, he crept to the rear of an enemy post and put the garrison to flight, then while holding a newly captured trench and strongly counter-attacked, he controlled the fire of his men and repelled the attack, inflicting many casualties
Commemoration:	i) Plaque in Murton Park next to the Village War Memorial ii) Medals at The Green Howards Regimental Museum

Gazette: 14 December 1918

Wilfred Wood on the footplate

1136	WOOD Wilfred VC Private 10th Bn. The Northumberland Fusiliers (now Royal Regiment of Fusiliers)	Near Casa Vana, Italy

Born: 2 February 1897 - Adcroft Street, Stockport, Cheshire

1325

Died: 3 January 1982 aged 84, at Stepping Hill Hospital, Stockport

Cremated: 8 January at Stockport Crematorium. Ashes scattered in Crematorium's First Garden of Remembrance. Long entry in Book of Remembrance

Deed/Service: 28 October 1918. When an advance was being held up by hostile machine-gun and sniper fire, he moved forward alone with his Lewis gun and enfiladed the enemy post causing 140 men to surrender. Later, when a hidden machine-gun opened fire at point-blank range, he charged the gun firing his Lewis gun from his hip and killed the crew before advancing on an enemy held ditch, where he captured three officers and 160 men

Gazette: 27 November 1918

Commemoration: i) Name in Book of Remembrance ii) Patriot Class locomotive named for him. Nameplate in the Northumberland Fusiliers Museum

1137	WARK Blair Anderson VC DSO Lieutenant - Colonel 32nd Bn. (S.A. & W.A.) Australian Imperial Force	Bellicourt to Joncourt France

Born: 27 July 1894 - Bathurst, New South Wales, Australia

1274

Died: 13 June 1941 aged 46, at Puckapunyal Military Camp, Victoria, Australia serving with City of Sydney Regiment during the Second World War

Cremated: Eastern Suburbs Crematorium, Sydney, New South Wales. Ashes interred in Worongra Crematorium Columbarium. Shelf D-30. Memorial plaque

Died/Service: 29 September to 1 October 1918 (Major) During an advance from Bellicourt to Joncourt, he moved fearlessly in front of his men, displaying great gallantry. Leading his assault companies, he rushed a battery of 77mm guns, capturing four and ten prisoners, then with two NCO's he captured fifty of the enemy near Magny La Fosse, before silencing several machine-guns which were causing heavy casualties

Gazette: 26 December 1918

Commemoration: i) Plaque in Columbarium ii) Memorial in Rookwood War Cemetery, N.S.W. iii) Medals/display at Australian War Memorial, Canberra, A.C.T.

1138   **CALDWELL Thomas   VC   Company Sergeant - Major   12th Bn. The Royal Scots Fusiliers (now Royal Highland Fusiliers)**   Near Audenarde, Belgium

Born:	10 February 1894 - Carluke, Lanarkshire (now Strathclyde Region), Scotland
Died:	6 June 1969 aged 75 in Adelaide, South Australia
Cremated:	Centennial Park Crematorium, Adelaide. Ashes interred in Wall 104. Row E. Niche 12 at Crematorium. Wall plaque
Deed/Service:	31 October 1918 (Sergeant) When in command of a Lewis gun section engaged in clearing a farmhouse, they came under intense fire. He rushed forward alone and captured the position and eighteen prisoners. By his gallant and determined action, he cleared the way for an advance, leading to the capture by his section of seventy more prisoners, eight machine-guns and a trench mortar
Commemoration:	i) Plaque at Crematorium ii) Medals at the Royal Highland Fusiliers Museum

172

Gazette: 6 January 1919

Valenciennes

1139   **CAIRNS Hugh   VC DCM   Sergeant   46th Bn. (Saskatchewan Dragoons) Saskatchewan Regt., Canadian Expeditionary Force**   Valenciennes, France
POSTHUMOUS

Born:	4 December 1896 - Ashington, Northumberland
Died:	2 November 1918 aged 21. Died from wounds received during his VC action at a Field Hospital in Valenciennes, France
Buried:	Auberchicourt British Cemetery, France. 10 miles N. of Cambrai. Plot I. Row A. Grave 8. Headstone (See Map A - 21)
Deed/Service:	1 November 1918. When a machine-gun opened fire on his platoon, he seized a Lewis gun and rushed the enemy post single-handed, killing the crew of five and capturing the gun. Later, he killed twelve more of the enemy and took two more guns, and although wounded went on to outflank a German position, killing many and capturing the guns. Having forced another sixty to surrender at Marly, he was wounded and died the following day
Commemoration:	i) Headstone ii) 'L'Avenue du Sergent Cairns' and plaque in his memory in Valenciennes iii) Statue erected in his memory in City Park, North Saskatoon, Saskatchewan iv) Medals at the Canadian War Museum, Ottawa, Ontario

171

Gazette: 31 January 1919

1140   **CLARKE James   VC   Sergeant   15th Bn. The Lancashire Fusiliers (now Royal Regiment of Fusiliers)**   **Happegarbes, France**

Born:	6 April 1894 - Greenfield Cottage, High Street, Winsford, Cheshire
Died:	16 June 1947 aged 53, in Birch Hall Hospital, Rochdale, Lancashire from pneumonia
Buried:	Rochdale Cemetery. Section O/P. Grave 14155. Headstone erected November 1994
Deed/Service:	2 November 1918. When his platoon were held up by heavy machine-gun fire, he rushed forward through an enemy held position, capturing four machine-guns and killing the crews. Later, with the remnants of his platoon, he captured three more machine-guns and many prisoners and again when held up personally led a tank against the enemy guns and took the position, showing complete disregard for his own safety throughout
Commemoration:	i) Headstone

217

Gazette: 6 January 1919

1141   **AMEY William   VC MM   Corporal   1/8th Bn. The Royal Warwickshire Regiment (now Royal Regiment of Fusiliers)**   **Landrecies, France**

Born:	5 March 1891 - Duddeston, Birmingham
Died:	28 May 1940 aged 59, at his home in Leamington Spa, Warwickshire
Buried:	All Saint's Churchyard, Leamington Spa. Headstone
Deed/Service:	4 November 1918 (Lance-Corporal) When many hostile machine-gun nests were passed-by during an advance in thick fog, he returned with his section under heavy fire, and drove one garrison into a nearby farmhouse capturing fifty prisoners and several machine-guns. Then single-handed attacked and captured a machine-gun under heavy fire, then rushed another post and captured a further twenty prisoners
Commemoration:	i) Headstone

23

Gazette: 31 January 1919

1142	ARCHIBALD Adam VC Sapper 218th Field Company, Corps of Royal Engineers	Near Ors, France

Born: 14 January 1879 - Leith, Edinburgh, Scotland

36

Died: 10 March 1957 aged 78, at his home in Leith

Cremated: Warriston Crematorium, Edinburgh. Ashes scattered in Garden of Remembrance at the Crematorium. No memorial

Deed/Service: 4 November 1918. During a heavy barrage of artillery and machine-gun fire, he was building a floating bridge across the Sambre-Oise Canal. While positioned in the foremost of the cork floats, most of the machine-gun fire was directed toward him from a few yards distance, but aware of the urgency he persevered, his courage and example being inspirational. He collapsed from gas poisoning soon after completion   **Gazette: 6 January 1919**

Commemoration: i) Display at the Royal Engineers Museum

1143	FINDLAY George de Cardonnel Elmsall VC MC & Bar Colonel 409 (Lowland) Field Company, Corps of Royal Engineers	Sambre-Oise Canal, France

Born: 20 August 1889 - Boturich, Balloch, Dunbartonshire (now Strathclyde), Scotland

404

Died: 26 June 1967 aged 77, at his home Drumfork House, Helensburgh, Renfrewshire (now Strathclyde)

Buried: Kilmaranock Churchyard, near Gartocharn, Helensburgh. Family Plot. Headstone

Deed/Service: 4 November 1918 (A/Major) During the forcing of the Canal at a lock south of Catillon, he was with the leading bridging and assault parties which came under heavy fire. When their advance was halted he began repairing a bridge under fire, and although wounded managed to place it in position across the lock at the third attempt. He was the first man to cross, remaining at this dangerous post until the work was completed   **Gazette: 15 May 1919**

Commemoration: i) Headstone ii) Medals and display at the Royal Engineers Museum

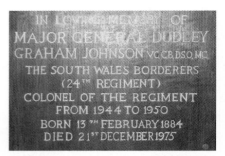

IN LOVING MEMORY OF
MAJOR GENERAL DUDLEY
GRAHAM JOHNSON VC.CB.DSO.MC
THE SOUTH WALES BORDERERS
(24TH REGIMENT)
COLONEL OF THE REGIMENT
FROM 1944 TO 1950
BORN 13TH FEBRUARY 1884
DIED 21ST DECEMBER 1975

1144	JOHNSON Dudley Graham VC CB DSO & Bar MC Major - General The South Wales Borderers (now Royal Regt. of Wales)	Sambre Canal, France

attd. 2nd Bn. The Royal Sussex Regiment (now P.O.W. Royal Regiment)

Born: 13 February 1884 - Rockcliffe, Bourton-on-the-Water, Gloucestershire 642

Died: 21 December 1975 aged 91, at his home in Heathfield Court, Fleet, Hampshire

Buried: Christ Church Churchyard, Church Crookham, Hampshire. Headstone

Deed/Service: 4 November 1918 (A/Lieutenant-Colonel) As part of the 2nd Infantry Brigade, ordered to cross the Sambre-Oise Canal south of Catillon, his men were among those halted by a heavy barrage 100 yards short of the canal. He personally led an assault, but heavy fire broke up the attack, forcing a withdrawal. By his skillful leadership in reorganizing the assaulting and bridging parties, a second attack effected a successful crossing

Gazette: 6 January 1919

Commemoration: i) Headstone ii) Memorial in Brecon Cathedral, Powys iii) Plaque inside Christ Church, Church Crookham iv) The General Johnson Homes, nr. Guildford, Surrey (run by the Royal British Legion) v) Display at Royal Sussex Museum vi) Medals at South Wales Borderers Museum

1145	KIRK James VC Second Lieutenant 10th Bn. The Manchester Regiment, attd. 2nd Bn. (now The King's Regiment)	North of Ors, France

POSTHUMOUS

Born: 27 January 1897 - Willow Bank, Adswood, Cheadle Hulme, Stockport, Cheshire 699

Died: 4 November 1918 aged 21. Killed during his VC action on the Oise Canal, north of Ors, France

Buried: Ors Communal Cemetery, France. 4 miles E. of Le Cateau. Row A. Grave 31. Headstone (See Map A - 31)

Deed/Service: 4 November 1918. When his battalion attempted to bridge the Oise Canal, they came under intense machine-gun fire, and in order to cover the operation he took a Lewis gun, paddled across the canal and opened fire. Further ammunition was brought to him, and he continued to cover the party under heavy fire until he was killed, but his self-sacrifice enabled two platoons to cross and prevented many casualties

Gazette: 6 January 1919

Commemoration: i) Headstone ii) Plaque outside the Manchester Regimental Museum iii) Plaque on previous residence at 530 Edge Lane, Droylsden, Manchester iv) Medals at the Military Medal Museum, San Jose, California, U.S.A.

1146   **MARSHALL James Neville   VC MC & Bar   A/Lieutenant - Colonel   Irish Guards (Special Reserve) attd. The Lancashire**   **Near Catillon, France**
                                                                            Fusilers, comd. 16th Bn. (now Royal Regiment of Fusiliers)   **POSTHUMOUS**

Born:	12 June 1887 - 2 Crosby Place, Steven Street, Stretford, Manchester
Died:	4 November 1918 aged 31. Killed during his VC action at the Sambre-Oise Canal, Catillon, France
Buried:	8 November in Ors Communal Cemetery, France. 4 miles E. of Le Cateau. Headstone in line with A-22 (See Map A-31)
Deed/Service:	4 November 1918. Before his battalion could cross the Sambre-Oise Canal, a partly built and badly damaged bridge needed repair. Under heavy fire the working parties received many casualties, then with a total disregard for his own safety, he stood in the open encouraging and helping his men with the work until the repairs were done and was killed when he began to lead his men across
Commemoration:	i) Headstone ii) Name on War Memorial outside Old Harlow Parish Church, Essex iii) Medals at the Irish Guards Museum

838

Gazette: 13 February 1919

1147   **WATERS Sir Arnold   VC CBE DSO MC   A/Major   218th Field Company, Corps of Royal Engineers**   **North of Ors, France**

Born:	23 September 1886 - Plymouth, Devon. Christened Arnold Horace Santo WATERS
Died:	22 January 1981 aged 94, at his home in Four Oaks, Sutton Coldfield, Warwickshire
Cremated:	Sutton Coldfield Crematorium. Entry in Book of Remembrance. Ashes in Garden of Remembrance, All Saint's Church, Streetly, Warwickshire
Deed/Service:	4 November 1918. During bridging work over the Sambre-Oise Canal, his Field Company were suffering heavy casualties from artillery and close range machine-gun fire. When all his officers had been killed or wounded, he went forward to supervise the completion from a cork float under such intense fire that it seemed impossible anyone could survive, but due to his valour and example the work was finished
Commemoration:	i) Entry in Crematorium Book of Remembrance ii) Medals and display at the Royal Engineers Museum

1278

Gazette: 13 February 1919

| 1148 | **CLOUTMAN Sir Brett** **VC MC** Lieutenant - Colonel 59th Field Company, Corps of Royal Engineers | **Pont-sur-Sambre, France** |

| **Born:** | 7 November 1891 - North London. Christened Brett Mackay CLOUTMAN | **223** |

Died: 15 August 1971 aged 79, at his home in Old Hall, South Grove, Highgate, North London

Cremated: 18 August at Golders Green Crematorium, North West London. Ref: 212774. Ashes beside his brother's grave in France (ii)

Deed/Service: 6 November 1918 (A/Major) When reconnoitring river crossings, he found the Quartres Bridge almost intact but prepared for demolition. Alone, he swam across the river and cut the wires from the charges and returned the same way, despite intense enemy shelling and machine-gun fire which swept the bridge and surrounding area. Although the bridge was blown up later in the day, the abutments remained intact **Gazette: 31 January 1919**

Commemoration: i) Medals at Royal Engineers Museum ii) Lt. Wolfred Cloutman. Died 28 August 1915. Norfolk Cemetery, Somme. Plot I. Row A. Grave14

The Victoria Cross and campaign medals awarded to Lieutenant William Allison White (1084)

Chapter Thirteen
Between the Wars
1919 - 1935

No's 1149 - 1158

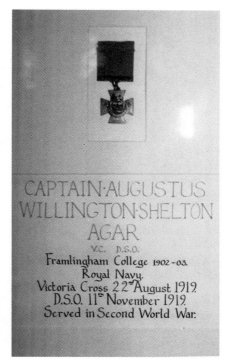

1149	AGAR Augustine William Shelton	VC DSO	Commodore	Royal Navy	Kronstadt Harbour, Russia

Born: 4 January 1890 - Kandy, Ceylon, now Sri Lanka

Died: 30 December 1968 aged 78, at his home in Alton, Hampshire

Buried: Alton Cemetery. Section R. Grave 238. Headstone

Deed/Service: 17 June 1919 (Lieutenant) During an attack on Kronstadt Harbour against the Bolshevik Baltic Fleet, he took HM Coastal Motor Boat 4 through a destroyer screen to engage a warship further inshore, when she broke down. Under heavy fire from the enemy, repairs were made in twenty minutes, then he attacked and sank the cruiser 'Olig' before retiring to the open bay under heavy bombardment from ship and shore

Commemoration: i) Headstone ii) Memorial in Framlingham College, Suffolk iii) Medals at the Imperial War Museum

12

Gazette: 22 August 1919

1150	SULLIVAN Arthur Percy	VC	Corporal	45th Bn. The Royal Fusiliers (now Royal Regt. of Fusiliers) (attd. The North Russia Relief Force)	Shelka River, Russia

Born: 27 November 1896 - Crystal Brook, South Australia

Died: 9 April 1937 aged 40. While in London to attend the Coronation of King George VI, he had brought the ashes of his great friend 1064 Evans 'home' for burial and had slipped, fallen and been struck by a bicycle outside Wellington Barracks, London, dying in Westminster Hospital

Cremated: 13 April at Golders Green Crematorium, North West London. Ref: 38550. Ashes by plaque at Tree 267A, N. Suburbs Crematorium, Sydney

Deed/Service: 10 August 1919. Following a rearguard action, his platoon had to cross a river over a swamp by means of a narrow plank under heavy fire. When four men fell into the river, he immediately jumped in the water and brought all four out one by one. But for his gallant action, all of them would have drowned, as all ranks were totally exhausted and the enemy were less than 100 yards away and closing all the time

Commemoration: i) Plaque in North Suburbs Garden of Remembrance, Sydney, New South Wales, Australia ii) Plaque on railings at Wellington Barracks, Central London iii) Sullivan Crescent, Canberra, A.C.T. iv) Medals and display at the Australian War Memorial, Canberra

1194

Gazette: 29 September 1919

1151   **DOBSON Claude Congreve   VC DSO   Rear - Admiral   Royal Navy**   Kronstadt Harbour, Russia

Born:	1 January 1885 - Barton Regis, Bristol, Somerset, now Avon
Died:	26 June 1940 aged 55, in Chatham, Kent
Buried:	Woodlands Cemetery, Gillingham, Kent. Headstone
Deed/Service:	18 August 1919 (Commander) When in command of the entire Coastal Motor Boat Flotilla attacking Kronstadt, he led them through the chain of forts to the harbour entrance. Aboard CMB 31 he directed general operations, then passed in under heavy machine-gun fire and torpedoed the Bolshevik battleship 'Andrei Pervozanni' before returning to the open sea under intense fire from the forts and shore batteries

333

Commemoration: i) Headstone   ii) Medals at the National Maritime Museum   **Gazette: 11 November 1919**

1152   **STEELE Gordon Charles   VC   Commander   Royal Navy**   Kronstadt, Russia

Born:	1 November 1892 - Exeter, Devon
Died:	4 January 1981 aged 88, at his home in Winkleigh Court, Winkleigh, near Okehampton, Devon
Buried:	All Saint's New Cemetery, Winkleigh. Headstone
Deed/Service:	18 August 1919 (Lieutenant) During an attack on the Russian battleship 'Andrei Pervozanni', he took command of Coastal Motor Boat 88 when her commanding officer had been killed and the boat thrown off course. Taking the wheel he steered into a firing position, and torpedoed the target at 100 yards, then manoeuvred to get a shot at the battleship 'Petropavlosk', before making for the safety of the bay under heavy fire

1181

Commemoration: i) Headstone   ii) Medals at Trinity House, London   **Gazette: 11 November 1919**

Russia Memorial, Brookwood

1153 **PEARSE** Samuel George **VC MM** **Sergeant** **45th Bn. The Royal Fusiliers (now Royal Regiment of Fusiliers)** Emtsa, North Russia
(attd. The North Russia Relief Force) POSTHUMOUS
975

Born: 16 July 1897 - Penarth, Glamorgan, Wales
Died: 29 August 1919 aged 22. Killed during his VC action north of Emtsa, Russia
Buried: i) Obozerskaya Burial Ground, Emtsa ii) Souset Cemetery, a.k.a. Archangel Allied Cemetery, Archangel. Special Memorial B. Grave 107
Deed/Service: 29 August 1919. Under heavy machine-gun fire, he cut his way through enemy barbed wire, clearing a way for his men to approach and
enter an enemy battery. He then made a solo attack on a blockhouse which was harassing the advance and causing many casualties,
killing all of the occupants with bombs. He was killed moments later, but his action ensured that the position was carried with relatively
few casualties **Gazette: 23 October 1919**
Commemoration: i) Believed headstone in Souset Cemetery ii) Name on the Russia Memorial, Brookwood Cemetery, Surrey - Panel 3 (See Map D)
iii) Display at the Australian War Memorial, Canberra, A.C.T. iv) Pearse Place, Canberra

1154 **ANDREWS** Henry John **VC MBE** **Temporary Captain** **Indian Medical Service** Waziristan, North West India
now Pakistan
POSTHUMOUS
32

Born: 1871 - London
Died: 22 October 1919 aged 48. Killed during his VC action near the Khajuri Post, Waziristan
Buried: Bannu Cemetery, south of Peshawar, North West Frontier. Grave 160. Headstone was erected, unconfirmed if still exists
Deed/Service: 22 October 1919. Whilst senior medical officer at Khajuri Post, he heard that a convoy had been attacked nearby and went out immediately.
He set up a Field Aid Post under heavy fire, which gave shelter to the wounded but not himself. When compelled to move the wounded,
he used an old Ford van and was loading it under incessant fire, when he was killed as the task was completed **Gazette: 9 September 1920**
Commemoration: i) Headstone ii) Name on the Delhi Memorial, India, Face 12/18

Family headstone

Donaghadee War Memorial

| 1155 | KENNY William David | VC | Lieutenant | 4th Battery, 39th Garhwal Rifles, Indian Army | Kot Kai, N.W. Frontier, India now Pakistan |

Born: 1 February 1899 - Saintfield, Co. Down, Northern Ireland

POSTHUMOUS

Died: 2 January 1920 aged 20. Killed during his VC action near Kot Kai

685

Buried: Jandola Cemetery, North West Frontier, Pakistan. Grave 5. Unknown if headstone existed/exists

Deed/Service: 2 January 1920. When in command of a company holding an advanced positionm under attack from the Mahsuds, he held his ground for four hours. He was in the foremost of the hand-to-hand fighting during three major attacks and the subsequent withdrawal, he led a handful of men in a counter-attack to cause a diversion, allowing the wounded to be got away, but was killed fighting to the last

Gazette: 9 September 1920

Commemoration: i) Headstone? ii) Name on the Delhi Memorial, India, Face 31 iii) Name on family headstone in Donaghadee Presbyterian Churchyard, Co. Down iv) Name on the Donaghadee War Memorial v) Named on two plaques in Donaghadee Church vi) Plaque in Mount Temple School, Dublin

Jedburgh Memorial

| 1156 | HENDERSON George Stuart | VC DSO & Bar MC | Captain | 2nd Bn. The Manchester Regt. (now The King's Regt.) | Near Hillah, Mesopotamia now Iraq |

Born: 5 December 1893 - East Gordon, Berwickshire

POSTHUMOUS

Died: 24 July 1920 aged 26. Fell mortally wounded during his VC action, 15 miles from Hillah (also Hillahon), Mesopotamia

558

Buried: Has no known grave - name on The Basra Memorial, Iraq. 40 miles N. of Kuwaiti border. Panel 31/64

Deed/Service: 24 July 1920. During the Arab insurrection of 1920, he led his company in three charges against the enemy, who opened fire from his flank during a critical situation in the battle. After steadying his command, he fell mortally wounded during an attack, but refused to leave his men. As his company reached their objective, he was again wounded and died shortly afterwards

Gazette: 29 October 1920

Commemoration: i) Name on the Basra Memorial ii) Name on the Jedburgh Memorial, Berwickshire iii) Name on War Memorial at Gordon, Berwickshire iv) Name on Regimental Memorial, Manchester Cathedral v) Name on Regimental Memorial, Sandhurst, Surrey vi) Plaque in St. Michael's School, Gordon vii) Medals at The King's Regimental Museum (1st Battalion)

1157   **ISHAR SINGH   VC OBI   Hon. Captain (Subadar)**   **28th Punjab Regiment, Indian Army (now part of The Jat Regiment)**   Near Haidari Kach
Waziristan
North West Frontier, India
Born: 30 December 1895 - Nenwan, Hoshiarpur, Punjab, India
Died: 2 December 1963 aged 67, at his home in Nenwan   622
Cremated: Panam Village, Hoshiarpur District, Punjab. No memorial tablet/marker
Deed/Service: 10 April 1921 (Sepoy) During a heavy engagement, he was severely wounded whilst operating a Lewis gun, and all the officers and NCO's
of his company became casualties. Refusing to have his heavily bleeding wound attended to, he continued firing until he assisted the
medical officer by acting as a shield - using his rifle to keep down hostile fire, not submitting to treatment for himself for almost three hours   **Gazette: 25 November 1921**
Commemoration:

1158   **MEYNELL Godfrey   VC MC   Captain**   **5th Bn. Queen Victoria's Own Corps of Guides, 12 Frontier Force, Indian Army**   Point 4080, N.W. Frontier
India, now Pakistan
POSTHUMOUS
Born: 20 May 1904 - Meynell Langley, Derbyshire   863
Died: 29 September 1935 aged 31. Killed in his VC action near Mohmand, India during the Mohmand Campaign
Buried: Guides Cemetery, Mardan, North West Frontier, India. Headstone
Deed/Service: 29 September 1935. During the final phase of an attack, he was sent ahead to establish contact with the forward companies. He found
them in action against a vastly superior number of the enemy, and taking command, inflicted heavy losses on the tribesmen. In the close
hand to hand fighting that ensued he was mortally wounded, but his determined stand prevented the Mohmands from exploiting their success   **Gazette: 24 December 1935**
Commemoration: i) Headstone ii) Memorial in Guides Depot, Mardan iii) Memorial in Kirk Langley Parish Church, Derbyshire iv) Memorial in sanctum
crypt of St. Luke's Church, Chelsea, S.W. London

The Victoria Cross and campaign medals awarded to Lieutenant William David Kenny (1155)

The Victoria Cross and campaign medals awarded to the Hon. Captain Ishar Singh (1157)

Chapter Fourteen

The Second World War
1940

No's 1159 - 1174

The Victoria Cross and campaign medals awarded to Wing Commander Roderick Alastair Brook Learoyd (1171)

The Victoria Cross and campaign medals awarded to Sergeant John Hannah (1173)

In memory of
Lt.Cmdr.G.B.Roope V.C R.N.
and all those of
H.M.S.Glowworm
who lost their lives
April 8th 1940

ROOPE G.B.,V.C.

1159	ROOPE Gerard Broadmead VC Lieutenant - Commander Royal Navy	West Fjord, Norwegian Sea POSTHUMOUS 1081

Born: 13 March 1905 - Hillbrook Trull, near Taunton, Somerset
Died: 8 April 1940 aged 35. Drowned when HMS 'Glowworm' sank during his VC action, off West Fjord, Norway
Buried: Lost at sea off West Fjord. Body not recovered
Deed/Service: 8 April 1940. When in command of the destroyer HMS 'Glowworm' (1,345 tons), he fought an unequal battle with the German cruiser 'Admiral Hipper' (10,000 tons). Firing all ten of her torpedoes without success, 'Glowworm' was badly hit with one gun out of action and her speed much reduced, Roope decided to ram the cruiser. Although some damage was caused, 'Glowworm' stoved in forward, heeled over to starboard and sank, losing 118 out of a complement of 149 men. For such a small ship to ram a cruiser took superb navigational skills and coolness which Roope showed throughout
Commemoration: i) Name on the Portsmouth Naval Memorial, Hampshire. Column 3. Panel 36   ii) Memorial plaque at the Nothe Fort, Weymouth, Dorset

Gazette: 10 July 1945

CAPTAIN
B. A. WARBURTON-LEE
VC RN
H.M.S. HARDY
10TH APRIL 1940 AGE 44

FOR THEIR WORK CONTINUETH
GREATER THAN THEIR KNOWING

1160	WARBURTON - LEE Bernard Armitage Warburton VC Captain Royal Navy	Ofot Fjord, Narvik, Norway POSTHUMOUS 731

Born: 13 September 1895 - Broad Oak, Redbrook, near Whitchurch, Flintshire (now Clwyd), Wales
Died: 10 April 1940 aged 44. From wounds aboard HMS 'Hardy' during his VC action in Ofot Fjord, near Narvik, Norway
Buried: Ballangen New Cemetery, Norway. 20 miles S.W. of Narvik. British Section. Plot IV. Row B. Grave 9. Headstone
Deed/Service: 10 April 1940. On board HMS 'Hardy', he led a flotilla of five destroyers in a blinding snowstorm on a surprise attack against German warships in the fjord. Following a successful attack on five destroyers, he engaged five more during which he was mortally wounded by a shell
Commemoration: i) Headstone   ii) Memorial in Whitewell Church, Maelor, Clywd   iii) Name on Iscoed War Memorial, Clywd

Gazette: 7 June 1940

Namsos Wharf, Norway
1178

1161   STANNARD Richard Been   VC DSO   Captain   Royal Naval Reserve

Born: 21 August 1902 - Blyth, Northumberland
Died: 22 July 1977 aged 74, in Sydney, New South Wales, Australia
Cremated: Rookwood Crematorium, Rookwood, Sydney. Ashes scattered in Garden of Remembrance. Wall plaque
Deed/Service: 28 April - 2 May 1940 (Lieutenant) Commanding HMS 'Arab' during Operation Maurice, the landing at Namsos, he survived 31 hours bombing in five days. At one point he rammed the wharf to try and extinguish many fires caused by enemy bombers next to a large ammunition store Part of the jetty was saved and proved invaluable during later evacuations. Finally, when leaving the Namsen Fjord, he was attacked by an enemy bomber whose pilot directed him to steer east. Refusing, he headed west and held fire before bringing the aircraft down
Commemoration: i) Wall plaque at Rookwood Crematorium, War Grave Section, Wall 47, Row J. - shows age 75 ii) Medals at RNPS, Lowestoft, Suffolk

Gazette: 16 August 1940

Over Albert Canal, Belgium
POSTHUMOUS
443

1162   GARLAND Donald Edward   VC   Flying Officer   12 Squadron, Royal Air Force

Born: 28 June 1918 - Ballinacor, Co. Wiclow, Ireland
Died: 12 May 1940 aged 21. Killed during his VC action, when his Fairey Battle bomber was shot down in the Maastricht region, Holland
Buried: i) Secretly by local citizens (see 1163) ii) Re-interred by Allies in 1945 in Lanaken Cemetery, 20 miles N. of Liege iii) Heverlee War Cemetery, near Louvain, Belgium. Collective Grave. Plot VI. Row F. Grave 14 - 16. Headstone (See Map A - 15)
Deed/Service: 12 May 1940. When the RAF were ordered to demolish a vital bridge, he led five bombers on the attack. Despite an inferno of anti-aircraft fire, the mission was accomplished due to his expert leadership and the coolness of his navigator Gray (See 1163). Only one bomber returned to base. Due to the dangerous nature of the mission all crew members were volunteers
Commemoration: i) Headstone ii) Memorial headstone to him and his three brothers, all killed serving with the RAF during the Second World War, in Midhurst Cemetery, Sussex iii) Name on RAF Memorial, St. Clement Dane's, London iv) VC.10C Mk 1 named for him v) Medals in RAF Museum

Gazette: 11 June 1940

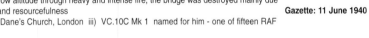

| 1163 | GRAY Thomas VC Sergeant 12 Squadron, Royal Air Force | Over Albert Canal, Belgium |

1163   GRAY Thomas   VC   Sergeant   12 Squadron, Royal Air Force

Over Albert Canal, Belgium
POSTHUMOUS
484

Born: 17 May 1914 - Urchfont, near Devizes, Wiltshire
Died: 12 May 1940 aged 24. Killed when the bomber he was navigating was shot down during his VC action, near Maastricht, Holland
Buried: i) Buried in secret location with his two comrades, near crash site, by local citizens ii) Re-interred in Lanaken Cemetery, 20 miles N. of Liege
ii) Heverlee War Cemetery, near Louvain, Belgium. Collective Grave. Plot VI. Row F. Grave 14 - 16. Headstone shows age 25 (See Map A - 15)
Deed/Service: 12 May 1940. As one of the volunteers who undertook a bombing mission on a vital bridge, used by the Germans invading Belgium, he
was navigator on 1162 Garland's lead bomber. Flying at low altitude through heavy and intense fire, the bridge was destroyed mainly due
to the formation leader (Garland) and his own coolness and resourcefulness

Gazette: 11 June 1940

Commemoration: i) Headstone ii) Name on RAF Memorial, St. Clement Dane's Church, London iii) VC.10C Mk 1 named for him - one of fifteen RAF
VC's so honoured

1164   ANNAND Richard Wallace   VC   Captain   2nd Bn. The Durham Light Infantry (now The Light Infantry)

River Dyle, Belgium
34

Born: 5 November 1914 - South Shields, Co. Durham
Deed/Service: 15 - 16 May 1940 (Second Lieutenant) Prior to the Dunkirk evacuation of the B.E.F., as the massed German armies began entering France,
he and his platoon were holding a bridge astride the River Dyle. Armed with hand grenades, he inflicted over twenty casualties under heavy
fire before being wounded. Later that night, he made another attack before being ordered to withdraw, but noticing that his batman was
wounded and missing, he returned to the position bringing the man back in a wheelbarrow before fainting from loss of blood

Gazette: 23 August 1940

Commemoration:

1165   NICHOLLS Harry   VC   Corporal   3rd Bn. The Grenadier Guards

Near River Scheldt, Belgium
929

Born: 21 April 1918 - Hope Street, The Meadows, Nottingham. Some records show born 1915 confirming age on headstone
Died: 11 September 1975 aged 57, in a Grenadier Guards Association flat in Leeds, Yorkshire, following a long illness
Buried: Southern Cemetery, Wilford Hill, Nottingham. Section L. Grave 34. Headstone shows age 60
Deed/Service: 21 May 1940 (Lance-Corporal) During the B.E.F. withdrawal, he continued to lead his section forward despite being wounded by shrapnel. When advancing over a ridge they met heavy machine-gun fire, he seized a Bren gun and put three out of action. He then attacked massed infantry until running out of ammunition and taken prisoner. He was awarded the VC posthumously as he was believed to be missing presumed dead. Later notified of the award by the Camp Commandant of Stalag XXA, on the orders of Adolf Hitler

Commemoration: i) Headstone ii) Plaque at Bosworth Junior School, Nottingham iii) Medals at the Grenadier Guards Museum

Gazette: 30 June 1940

1166   GRISTOCK George   VC   Company Sergeant - Major   The Royal Norfolk Regiment (now The Royal Anglian Regiment)

South of Tournai, France
Nr. River Escaut/Scheldt
499

Born: 14 January 1905 - Pretoria, Transvaal, South Africa
Died: 16 June 1940 aged 35, in Brighton Hospital, Sussex from wounds received during his VC action
Buried: Bear Road Cemetery, Brighton. War Graves Section. Plot Z.G.L. Grave 28. Headstone
Deed/Service: 21 May 1940. Having organised eight riflemen holding a position near the River Escault, he noticed the company's right flank was being threatened. He went out with one man to try to put an enemy machine-gun out of action, but came under fire and was severely wounded in both legs. He silenced the gun, and dragged himself back to the right flank, refusing aid until contact with the battalion had been made

Commemoration: i) Headstone ii) Memorial at Britannia Court, Norwich, Norfolk iii) Gristock Place, Norwich iv) Medals at Royal Norfolk Regimental Museum

Gazette: 23 August 1940

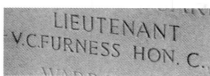

1167   **FURNESS Christopher (The Hon.)**   **VC**   **Lieutenant**   **1st Bn. Welsh Guards**

Near Arras, France
POSTHUMOUS
434

Born:	17 May 1912 - 5 Cambridge Gate, N.W. London
Died:	24 May 1940 aged 28. Killed during his VC action near Arras, France
Buried:	Has no known grave - name on the Dunkirk Memorial, France. Column 34 (See Map A - 1)
Deed/Service:	17 - 24 May 1940. When in command of a Carrier Platoon, he was ordered to cover the withdrawal of over forty vehicles en route to Douai. On 24 May, the enemy advanced towards the retiring convoy and he decided to attack, reaching their position under heavy fire. When the carriers and crews become casualties, he engaged them in hand-to-hand combat until he was killed, but his action enabled the convoy to get clear
Commemoration:	i) Name on Dunkirk Memorial ii) Memorial in Guards Chapel, Wellington Barracks iii) Plaque in Eton College iv) Medals in Welsh Guards Museum

Gazette: 7 February 1946

1168   **ERVINE - ANDREWS Harold Marcus**   **VC**   **Lieutenant - Colonel**   **The East Lancashire Regiment (now Queen's Lancs. Regt.)**   Canal de Bergues, France

Born:	29 July 1911 - Keadue, Co. Cavan, Ireland
Died:	30 March 1995 aged 83, at his home 'Trevor Cottage', Gorran, Cornwall
Cremated:	7 April at Glynn Valley Crematorium, Bodmin, Cornwall. Ashes scattered in his garden at Gorran
Deed/Service:	31 May 1940 (Captain) During the evacuation to Dunkirk, he was in command of a company heavily outnumbered under intense fire along a canal on outskirts of the town. When the Germans attacked, he and a party of volunteers rushed to a barn and from the roof inflicted casualties on the enemy for over ten hours. Finally, he led his surviving men to safety, having gained valuable time at a critical time during the embarkation
Commemoration:	i) Name on War Memorial at Stonyhurst College, Lancashire ii) Painting in Officer's Mess, 1st Bn. East Lancashire Regiment, Plymouth, Devon iii) Medals in the Blackburn Museum, Lancashire

31

Gazette: 30 July 1940

W.O.'s Mess, HMS 'Osprey'

1169   **MANTLE** Jack Foreman   VC   Acting Leading Seaman   Royal Navy

Portland Harbour, Dorset
POSTHUMOUS
835

Born:	12 April 1917 - Wandsworth, S.W. London
Died:	4 July 1940 aged 23. From numerous wounds received during his VC action, on HMS 'Foylebank', Portland Harbour, Dorset, England
Buried:	Portland Royal Naval Cemetery, Portland Bill, Dorset. C. of E. Section. Grave 672. Headstone
Deed/Service:	4 July 1940. During an air raid on Portland Naval Base, he manned his 20 mm pom-pom gun despite having his left leg shattered by a bomb blast earlier in the action. As more than twenty Stukas dived in on 'Foylebank', he continued firing until the ship's electric power failed, when he was again wounded in many places and fell beside his gun. His gallantry was noted as 'Foylebank' sank, by the merchant cruiser's captain
Commemoration:	i) Headstone ii) Name on 'Foylebank' Memorial, St. Paul's Cathedral, London iii) Memorial in W.O.'s Mess, HMS 'Osprey', Portland iv) Memorial at the Nothe Fort, Weymouth, Dorset v) Mantle Close, Gosport, Hampshire

Gazette: 3 September 1940

1170   **WILSON** Eric Charles Twelves   VC   Lt. - Colonel   The East Surrey Regiment, attd. Somaliland Camel Corps

Tug Argan Gap, Somaliland
1320

Born:	2 October 1912 - Sandown, Isle of Wight, Hampshire
	The citation stated that he had been killed in his VC action, but he not only survived his wounds and acute malaria from which he was suffering, but was freed from capture when British forces took Eritrea from the Italians. A fellow prisoner informed him of his 'posthumous' award
Deed/Service:	11 - 15 August 1940 (A/Captain) When in command of machine-gun posts manned by Somali soldiers on Observation Hill, a key position, his men first beat off an attack on nearby Mill Hill inflicting heavy casualties. He was severely wounded when his position came under heavy fire and his guns damaged, but he managed to effect repairs. They came under artillery fire on 12th,14th and 15th, and despite his untended wounds and a bout of malaria, kept his guns in action before being over-run by the enemy, fighting to the last until 'killed in action'

Gazette: 14 October 1940

1171   LEAROYD Roderick Alastair Brook   VC   Wing Commander   49 Squadron, Royal Air Force

North of Munster, Germany

730

Born:	5 February 1913 - Folkestone, Kent
Died:	24 January 1996 aged 82, following a heart attack at his home in Rustington, Littlehampton, Sussex
Cremated:	2 February at Worthing Crematorium, Sussex. Ashes interred in Plot 35/34 in Garden of Remembrance at Crematorium. No memorial tablet
Deed/Service:	12 August 1940 (Flight Lieutenant) Was the pilot of the last of five Hampden bombers ordered to destroy an aqueduct carrying the Dortmund - Ems Canal supplying munitions. Of the other Hampdens, two were destroyed and two badly hit, but he took his plane in at 150 feet, dropping his bombs on target despite severe damage to the aircraft. He subsequently brought the crippled plane back to England, and with great skill landed without causing injury to his crew or further damage to the aircraft
Commemoration:	i) Name on R.A.F. Memorial in St. Clement Dane's Church, Aldwych, Central London

Gazette: 20 August 1940

1172   NICOLSON Eric James Brindley   VC DFC   Wing Commander   249 Squadron, Royal Air Force

Over Southampton, England

931

Born:	29 April 1917 - Hampstead, N.W. London
Died:	2 May 1945 aged 28. Whilst serving in the Far East, he died when a Liberator in which he was flying, crashed into the sea off Calcutta, India
Buried:	Has no known grave - name on the Singapore Memorial at Kranji War Cemetery. Column 445
Deed/Service:	16 August 1940 (Flight Lieutenant) During an engagement near Southampton, his Hurricane was severely damaged and he was badly wounded when fired on by a Messerschmitt 110. Struggling with the controls and about to bale out, he sighted another 110 which he attacked and brought down despite his severe injuries. He then baled out, landing in a field but was unable to release his parachute due to his badly burned hands
Commemoration:	i) Name on Singapore Memorial ii) Name on Memorial in St. Clement Dane's Church, Central London iii) Plaque at Boscombe Down RAF Station, Wiltshire iv) VC.10C Mk 1 XV107 named for him v) Memorial at Mullards Industrial Estate, Southampton vi) Medals at R.A.F. Museum

Gazette: 15 November 1940

1173	HANNAH John VC Sergeant 83 Squadron, Royal Air Force	Over Antwerp, Belgium

Born: 27 November 1921 - Paisley, Renfrewshire, Scotland

Died: 9 June 1947 aged 25, from T.B. at Markfield Sanatorium, Leicestershire

Buried: St. James's Churchyard, Birstall, Leicestershire. East side of churchyard. Headstone

Deed/Service: 15 September 1940. Following a successful attack on enemy barge concentrations at Antwerp, the Hampden in which he was radio operator/air gunner, was subjected to intense anti-aircraft incendiary fire and received a direct hit. The resulting fire spread quickly and as he fought the fire alone, thousands of rounds of ammunition exploded in all directions causing two men to bale out. He continued to fight the fire with his bare hands sustaining severe injuries, but he put out the fire and the pilot was able to land the badly crippled aircraft back at RAF Scampton

Commemoration: i) Headstone ii) Name on Memorial in St. Clement Dane's Church, Central London iii) Name on War Memorial at Birstall iv) Name on Roll of Achievement, RAF West Freugh, Stranraer, Scotland v) Ranger Safety Boat at Drummer, Stranraer named for him vi) Medals at RAF Museum **Gazette: 1 October 1940**

525

1174	FEGEN Edward Stephen Fogarty VC SGM Acting Captain Royal Navy	Mid Atlantic Ocean POSTHUMOUS

Born: 8 October 1891 - Southsea, Portsmouth, Hampshire

Died: 5 November 1940 aged 49. Last seen on the bridge and assumed drowned when HM AMC 'Jervis Bay' sank during his VC action

Buried: Lost at sea. Body not recovered. Name on the Chatham Naval Memorial, Kent. Column 1. Panel 34

Deed/Service: 5 November 1940. When in command of HM Armed Merchant Cruiser 'Jervis Bay', was escorting 38 merchantmen en route to Canada in high seas, when he sighted the German pocket battleship 'Admiral Scheer'. He drew clear of the convoy and brought his ship between the raider and her prey so they could scatter and escape. Out-gunned, crippled, on fire and unable to reply, 'Jervis Bay' held the German's fire, although his arm was shattered and the bridge shot from beneath him. Due to his heroic action, all but five of the convoy escaped

Commemoration: i) Name on the Chatham Naval Memorial ii) Column at St.John's Hospital, New Brunswick, Canada iii) Sundial to his memory in Hamilton, Bermuda iv) Memorial at Seamans Institute, Wellington, New Zealand v) Medals at the Royal Naval Museum **Gazette: 22 November 1940**

398

Chapter Fifteen

The Second World War
1941

No's 1175 - 1196

The Victoria Cross and campaign medals attributed to Sergeant Nigel Gray Leakey (1181)

The Victoria Cross, Military Cross and campaign medals awarded to T/Lt. Colonel Geoffrey Charles Tasker Keyes (1189)

1175   **PREMINDRA SINGH BHAGAT   PVSM VC   Lt. - General   Corps of Indian Engineers, attd. Royal Bombay Sappers & Miners**   Gallabat - Metemma Region
Abyssinia, now Ethiopia
1000

Born: 14 October 1918 - Bhagat Kot, Mussourie, India
Died: 23 May 1975 aged 56, at Eastern Command Hospital, Calcutta, India
Cremated: 24 May at Keoratola Crematorium, India. Ashes confined to various rivers of India. No memorial tablet/plaque at Crematorium
Deed/Service: 31 January to 1 February 1941 (Second Lieutenant) Following the capture of Gallabat, he combined his pursuit of the enemy with clearing fifteen Italian minefields over a distance of 55 miles. His carrier was blown up with casualties to his men on two occasions, then a third time during an enemy ambush his eardrum was punctured. His gallantry over 96 hours ensured the safety of the Column, relying on both his speed and effort

Gazette: 10 June 1941

Commemoration: i) Medals and memorabilia at the Bhagat Memorial Hall, Bombay Engineers Group Museum, Kirkee, Poona, India

1176   **RICHHPAL RAM   VC   Subadar (Captain)   6th Rajputana Rifles, Indian Army**   Keren, Abyssinia
now Ethiopia
POSTHUMOUS
1049

Born: 20 August 1899 - Barda, Patiala State, Rajputana, India. Also recorded as RICHPAL RAM.
Died: 12 February 1941 aged 41. Killed five days after his VC action, when leading another attack near Keren
Cremated: Near Keren, Abyssinia. Name on the Keren Cremation Memorial. Western suburbs of Keren, 60 miles W. of Asmara. Column 5
Deed/Service: 7 February 1941. Having led a successful attack and subsequently repelled six counter-attacks, he brought the survivors of his company back to safety when ammunition ran out. On 12 February his right foot was blown off when leading another attack, but he encouraged his men until he died

Gazette: 4 July 1941

Commemoration: i) Name on the Keren Memorial

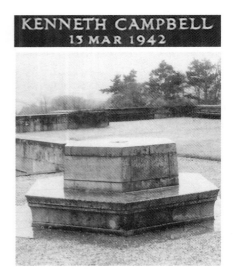

KENNETH CAMPBELL
13 MAR 1942

1177	CAMPBELL Kenneth VC Flying Officer 22 Squadron, Royal Air Force Volunteer Reserve	Over Brest Harbour, France

POSTHUMOUS
181

Born: 21 April 1917 - Saltcoats, Ayr, Scotland
Died: 6 April 1941 aged 23. Killed when his aircraft crashed into Brest Harbour during his VC action
Buried: Brest (Kerfautras) Cemetery, Lambezellec, France. N.W. suburbs of Brest. Plot XL. Row I. Grave 10. Headstone
Deed/Service: 6 April 1941. When both German battle-cruisers 'Gneisnau' and 'Scharnhorst' were seen in Brest Harbour, a raid was quickly arranged. Leading a flight of three Beauforts he arrived over Brest alone due to atrocious weather conditions. Making his torpedo run at fifty feet, he succeeded in severely damaging 'Gneisau' before the whole defence system erupted, hitting his Beaufort almost immediately, killing the crew of four

Gazette: 13 March 1942

Commemoration: i) Headstone ii) Memorial stone seat at Sedburgh Schoool, Yorkshire iii) Name on RAF Memorial in St. Clement Dane's Church, Central London iv)) VC.10C Mk 1 XR 808 named for him

1178	EDMONDSON John Hurst VC Corporal 2/17th New South Wales Battalion, Australian Military Forces	Tobruk, Libya

POSTHUMOUS
369

Born: 8 October 1914 - Wagga Wagga, New South Wales, Australia
Died: 14 April 1942 aged 26. From wounds received during his VC action at Post R. 33, Tobruk, Libya
Buried: Tobruk War Cemetery, Libya. On the coast road, W. of Tobruk. Plot III. Row J. Grave 8. Headstone
Deed/Service: 13 - 14 April 1941. Although severely wounded when counter-attacking an enemy force which had broken through Allied defences, he continued to advance. Seeing an officer in difficulties he immediately went to his assistance, killing two Germans in the rescue, but died soon afterwards

Gazette: 4 July 1941

Commemoration: i) Headstone ii) Memorial Clubhouse, wall plaque and clock at Liverpool, N.S.W. iii) Edmonson Street, Canberra, A.C.T. iv) Medals and display at Australian War Memorial, Canberra

1179	HINTON John Daniel VC Sergeant 20th Bn. 2nd New Zealand Expeditionary Force (The Canterbury Regiment)	Kalamai, Greece

Born: 17 September 1909 - Colac Bay, Riverton, Southland Province, New Zealand

572

Died: 28 June 1997 aged 87, at Princess Margaret's Hospital, Christchurch, New Zealand, following a fall at his home

Buried: 2 July at Ruru Lawn Cemetery, Christchurch. Returned Servicemen's League Section. Headstone

Deed/Service: 28 - 29 April 1941. When New Zealand troops were heading to the port for evacuation, they came under heavy attack from enemy machine-guns and 6 inch guns. Although ordered to retire, he rushed the nearest gun and killed it's crew with two grenades before clearing two other gun posts and the garrison of a house where the enemy were sheltering near the quay. When the main enemy force attacked, he was finally subdued and captured after being severely wounded

Gazette: 17 October 1941

Commemoration: i) Headstone ii) Display at the HQ of the Returned Servicemen's Association, Dunedin, New Zealand

1180	SEPHTON Alfred Edward VC Petty Officer Royal Navy	S. of Crete. Mediterranean

POSTHUMOUS

Born: 19 April 1911 - 30 Collier Street, Warrington, Lancashire

1125

Died: 19 May 1941 aged 30. From wounds received during his VC action in the sick bay of HMS 'Coventry', north of Alexandria, Egypt

Buried: 19 May, at sea off the coast of Alexandria. Name on the Portsmouth Naval Memorial, Hampshire. Panel 46. Column 2

Deed/Service: 18 May 1941. As he stood at his post as director layer on HMS 'Coventry', she responded to a call for assistance from the hospital ship 'Aba' which was under attack from squadrons of Stukas while heading for Alexandria. When two Stukas attacked 'Coventry', a bullet passed through his body, but he remained at his instrument panel carrying out his duties until the attack was over, dying of wounds the following day

Gazette: 2 December 1941

Commemoration: i) Name on the Portsmouth Naval Memorial ii) Red granite memorial at St. John's Church, Wolverhampton iii) Sephton Close, Gosport, Hampshire iv) Medals and memorabilia at Coventry Cathedral. The VC was reported stolen in May 1982

VC.LEAKEY N.G.

1181   **LEAKEY Nigel Gray**   **VC**   **Sergeant**   **1st/6th Bn. The King's African Rifles**

Born:	1 January 1913 - Kiganjo, Kenya
Died:	19 May 1941 aged 28. Killed during his VC action near the Billate River, Colito, Abyssinia
Buried:	Has no known grave - name on The East African Memorial, Nairobi, Kenya. Column 37 - 2nd West
Deed/Service:	19 May 1941. After his company had established a bridgehead against strong Italian opposition, the enemy counter-attacked with tanks. He leapt on top of one tank, wrenched open the turret and killed the crew, before stalking the rest of the tanks. He again leapt onto one of them and killed a crew member before he was killed, but his deed resulted ultimately in an Italian defeat
Commemoration:	i) Name on The East African Memorial ii) Plaque in Old Nyeri Church, Kenya iii) Memorial in The Kenya Regiment Association Club, Nairobi iv) Memorial in Bromsgrove School, Worcestershire

Colito, Abyssinia
now Ethiopia
POSTHUMOUS
728

Gazette: 15 November 1945

1182   **HULME Alfred Clive**   **VC**   **Sergeant**   **23rd Bn. 2nd New Zealand Expeditionary Force (Canterbury Regiment)**

Born:	24 January 1911 - Dunedin, South Island, New Zealand
Died:	2 September 1982 aged 71, at Tauranga, New Zealand
Buried:	The Dudley Cemetery, Vercre Drive, Te Puke. 20 miles from Tauranga. Civilian Section. Headstone
Deed/Service:	20 - 28 May 1941. During the entire period he displayed outstanding leadership and courage, leading his men in action at Maleme against a strong enemy position and at Galatos where he drove the enemy from a school building with hand grenades. He later killed five snipers at Suda Bay and at Stylos he wiped out a mortar crew and three more snipers
Commemoration:	i) Headstone ii) Display at the Returned Servicemen's Association HQ, Dunedin

Maleme, Crete
607

Gazette: 14 October 1941

1183   **UPHAM Charles Hazlitt   VC & BAR   Captain   20th Bn. 2nd New Zealand Expeditionary Force (Canterbury Regiment)**   Maleme, Crete
1246

Born: 21 September 1908 - Gloucester Street, Christchurch, South Island, New Zealand
Died: 22 November 1994 aged 86, at a retirement home in Christchurch
Cremated: 25 November at Harewood Crematorium, Christchurch. Ref: 22339. Ashes in family plot at St. Paul's Churchyard, Papanui. Headstone
Deed/Service: i) 22 - 30 May 1941 (Second Lieutenant) He displayed outstanding gallantry in close-quarter fighting, when blown up by two mortar shells and badly wounded. In spite of this and an attack of dysentry which reduced him to skeletal appearance, he refused hospital treatment and carried a wounded man to safety when forced to retire. Eight days later he beat off an attack at Sphakia, 22 Germans falling to his accurate fire   **Gazette: 14 October 1941**
ii) BAR to VC from 14 - 15 July 1942, in Western Desert. See entry following 1213   **Gazette: 26 September 1945**
Commemoration: i) Name on family headstone ii) Statue at Amberley, Christchurch (1998) iii) Bronze relief on Bridge of Remembrance, Christchurch
iv) Royal NZ Navy Supply Ship named for him v) Display at RSA HQ, Dunedin vi) Medals in Queen Elizabeth II Army Memorial Museum, Walouru

1184   **WANKLYN Malcom David   VC DSO & 2 Bars   Lieutenant - Commander   Royal Navy**   Off Sicily, Mediterranean
1267

Born: 28 June 1911 - Calcutta, India
Died: 14 April 1942 aged 30. Aboard HMS 'Upholder' in the Gulf of Tripoli on her 25th patrol, after landing agents on the North African coast
Buried: Has no known grave. Name on The Portsmouth Naval Memorial, Hampshire. Panel 61. Column 3
Deed/Service: 24 May 1941. When in command of HM Submarine 'Upholder', he torpedoed a strongly protected Italian troopship south of the Sicilian coast and survived a strong counter-attack in which 37 depth charges were dropped in twenty minutes. By the end of 1941, he had sunk nearly 140,000 tons of enemy shipping, including warships and supply vessels   **Gazette: 16 December 1941**
Commemoration: i) Name on Portsmouth Naval Memorial ii) Portraits in both the Wardroom of HMS 'Dolphin' and the Senior Ratings Mess, Gosport, Hampshire

1185   **CUTLER Sir Roden   VC AK KCMG KCVO CBE   Lieutenant   2nd/5th Field Artillery, Australian Military Forces**   Mergjayoun, Syria

Born: 24 May 1916 - Darley Road, Manly, Sydney, New South Wales, Australia. Born: ARTHUR RODEN CUTLER   **295**

Deed/Service: 19 June to 6 July 1941. During the entire period in the Megjayoun (also Merdayoun) - Damour area, his many outstanding exploits included the repair of a vital telephone line when under heavy fire, the repulse of enemy tanks with an anti-tank rifle, setting-up an outpost to bring under fire a road used by enemy transport and demolishing a post holding up a British advance. When laying a line at Damour he was seriously wounded, and by the time that he had been rescued 26 hours later, his leg had to be amputated   **Gazette: 28 November 1941**

Commemoration: i) Portrait in Officer's Mess at the School of Artillery, North Head, New South Wales ii) Display at the Australian War Memorial, Canberra, A.C.T.

1186   **EDWARDS Sir Hughie   VC KCMG CB DSO OBE DFC   Air Commodore   105 Squadron, Royal Air Force**   Over Bremen, Germany

Born: 1 August 1914 - Masmen Park, Perth, Western Australia. Born: HUGHIE IDWAL EDWARDS   **372**

Died: 5 August 1982 aged 68, at his home at Darling Point, New South Wales

Cremated: North Suburbs Crematorium, Sydney. Ashes placed in Karrakatta Cemetery, Perth, in his parent's grave - Welsh Free Church Portion Wall AA Niche 74. Headstone. (Official commemoration also in Karrakatta Cemetery - see Map - F for both)

Deed/Service: 4 July 1941 (Wing Commander) Following several unsuccessful attacks on Bremen, he led a daring daylight raid of fifteen Blenheim bombers on the vital port, flying at fifty feet through telephone wires and cables. To reach their objective, they penetrated fierce anti-aircraft fire and a dense balloon barrage, losing four aircraft en route. He skilfully withdrew the surviving Blenheims without further loss   **Gazette: 22 July 1941**

Commemoration: i) Name on parent's headstone ii) Official plaque on Wall 27, Row F. at Karrakatta Garden of Remembrance iii) Name on the RAF Memorial in St. Clement Dane's Church, Central London iv) Medals and display at Australian War Memorial, Canberra, A.C.T.

HUGHIE IDWAL EDWARDS
22 JULY 1941
JAMES ALLEN WARD
5 AUG 1941
KENNETH CAMPBELL
13 MAR 1942
JOHN DERING NETTLETON
28 APRIL 1942
LESLIE THOMAS MANSER
23 OCT 1942
RAWDON HUME MIDDLETON
15 JAN 1943

1187	WARD James Allen VC Sergeant Royal New Zealand Air Force, attd. 75 Squadron, Royal Air Force	Zuider Zee, Holland
Born:	14 June 1919 - Wanganui, Wellington, New Zealand	1270
Died:	15 September 1941 aged 22. When his Wellington bomber was shot down on a raid on Hamburg, Germany - his eleventh mission	
Buried:	Ohlsdorf Cemetery, Hamburg. Plot V - A. Row A - 1. Grave 9. Headstone	
Deed/Service:	7 July 1941. Following an attack on Munster, fire broke out in the Wellington bomber in which he was second pilot after they had been attacked by a Messerschmidt Bf 110 over the Zuider Zee. He crawled through a thirty inch hatch to reach the burning engine being lashed by the 100 mph slipstream and tried to extinguish the flames with a cockpit cover. Despite injuries, he managed to get back into the aircraft and the temporary repairs were sufficient to allow the pilot to fly back to their Newmarket base	Gazette: 5 August 1941
Commemoration:	i) Headstone ii) Name on RAF Memorial, St. Clement Dane's Church, Central London iii) Memorial at HQ Dunedin RSA, New Zealand	

1188	GORDON James Heather VC Warrant Officer Class II 2nd/31st Bn. (Q & V) Australian Military Forces	Greenhill, Djezzine, Syria
Born:	7 March 1909 - Rockingham, Western Australia	461
Died:	24 July 1986 aged 77, at Perth, Western Australia	
Cremated:	Karrakatta Crematorium, Hollywood, Perth. Ashes interred in Anglican Section. Plaque on Wall VC. No. 7 - 26. Shows age 79 (See Map - F)	
Deed/Service:	10 July 1941 (Private) When his company was pinned down by intense machine-gun fire at Djezzine (also Jezzine), he crept forward alone toward the post, then charged it and killed the crew of four. His action completely demoralizing the enemy in this sector and allowing the company to advance	Gazette: 28 October 1941
Commemoration:	i) Plaque at Karrakatta Crematorium ii) Display at the Australian War Memorial, Canberra, A.C.T.	

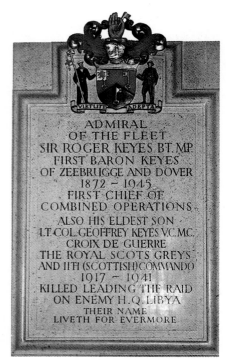

1189	**KEYES Geoffrey Charles Tasker VC MC T/Lt. - Colonel**	**Royal Scots Greys, Royal Armoured Corps** **(11th Scottish Commando)**	**Beda Littoria, Libya** **POSTHUMOUS** 690

Born: 18 May 1917 - Aberdour, Fifeshire, Scotland
Died: 18 November 1941 aged 24. Killed during his VC action at Sidi Rafa, Libya
Buried: Benghazi War Cemetery, Libya. Plot VII. Row D. Grave 5. Headstone
Deed/Service: 17 - 18 November 1941. When leading a raid 250 miles behind enemy lines on a house being used as Rommel's HQ, the surprise was lost by having to shoot an alert sentry. With Keyes leading, followed by an officer and an NCO, a number of Germans were killed before it transpired that Rommel was absent. He was killed inside the house and the survivors reached British lines 41 days after setting out
Commemoration: i) Headstone ii) His original cross and plaque at St. Mary's Church, Tingewick, Buckinghamshire iii) Name on War Memorial and special plaque at Aberdour iv) Name on family grave at St. James's Cemetery, Dover, Kent v) Plaque in St. Paul"s Cathedral, London vi) Keyes Road, Gosport

Gazette: 19 June 1942

1190	**GUNN George Ward VC MC Second Lieutenant 3rd Regt. Royal Horse Artillery (now Royal Regiment of Artillery)**	**Sidi Rezegh, Libya** **POSTHUMOUS** 502

Born: 26 July 1912 - Muggleswick, Co. Durham
Died: 21 November 1941 aged 29. Killed during his VC action near Sidi Rezegh Airfield, Libya
Buried: Knightsbridge War Cemetery, Acroma, Libya. 15 miles W. of Tobruk on the Benghazi Road. Plot IV. Row F. Grave 1. Headstone
Deed/Service: 21 November 1941. During an attack by the Germans, sixty of their tanks were met by four anti-tank guns under his command. He drove from gun to gun encouraging his men until all but one were destroyed and when that was hit with only its sergeant surviving, he ran to it and continued to fire. The portee (ammunition container) was alight, and despite the danger of it exploding he managed to fire fifty rounds before dying of a head wound
Commemoration: i) Headstone ii) Memorial stone seat at Sedbergh School, Yorkshire iii) Plaque at St. Mary's & St. Helen's Church, Neston, Wirrall iv) Plaque in Neston Memorial Cottage Hospital v) Gunn Road, Neston vi) Memorial at Royal Artillery Chapel, Woolwich vii) Medals at Royal Artillery Museum

Gazette: 21 April 1942

Original grave at Sidi Rezegh

| 1191 | BEELEY John VC Rifleman The King's Royal Rifle Corps. (now The Royal Green Jackets) | Sidi Rezegh, Libya
POSTHUMOUS
70 |

Born: 8 February 1918 - 9 Pendle Street, Lower Openshaw, Manchester, Lancashire

Died: 21 November 1941 aged 23. Killed during his VC action at Sidi Rezegh Airfield, Libya. Stone shows age 24

Buried: i) Sidi Rezegh ii) Knightsbridge War Cemetery, Acroma, Libya. 15 miles W. of Tobruk on Benghazi Road. Plot X. Row E. Grave 4. Headstone

Deed/Service: 21 November 1941. During the battalion attack on Sidi Rezegh Airfield, his company were held up by heavy point-blank fire from both the front and flank. On his own initiative, he ran forward over open ground firing his Bren gun and put an anti-tank gun and two machine-guns out of action. Finally falling dead over his gun, his bravery inspired his comrades to further efforts and their objectives were taken, along with 700 prisoners

Gazette: 21 April 1942

Commemoration: i) Headstone ii) Medals in Royal Green Jackets Museum

Memorial seat at Thurso

| 1192 | CAMPBELL John Charles (Jock) VC DSO & Bar MC Major - General Royal Horse Artillery, comd. 7th Armoured Div. | Sidi Rezegh, Libya
179 |

Born: 10 January 1894 - Thurso, Caithness, Scotland (now Highland Region)

Died: 26 February 1942 aged 48. Killed in a car accident near Halfaya Pass, Libya

Buried: Cairo War Memorial Cemetery, Egypt. Row K. Grave 171. Headstone

Deed/Service: 21 November 1941 (A/Brigadier General) During the Battle of Sidi Rezegh his small force was holding a position between the aerodrome and the ridge, and was repeatedly under heavy attack. Wherever the fighting was the hardest he was seen with his forward troops, either on foot or in an open car. The next day the enemy attacks were intensified, again he was at the front - twice manning a gun to replace casualties. Although wounded in the final assault he stayed with his men, his leadership being the direct cause of inflicting heavy casualties on the enemy

Gazette: 3 February 1942

Commemoration: i) Headstone ii) Plaque in All Saints' Cathedral, Cairo iii) Memorial seat at Thurso iv) Memorial stone seat at Sedbergh School, Yorkshire v) Name on memorial at Royal Artillery Chapel, Woolwich vi) Medals at Royal Artillery Museum

1193	GARDNER Philip John VC MC Acting Captain Royal Tank Regiment, Royal Armoured Corps	Tobruk, Libya

Born: 25 December 1914 - Sydenham, S.E. London

440

Deed/Service: 23 November 1941. When ordered to take two tanks to the rescue of two disabled armoured cars of the King's Dragoon Guards and under heavy attack, he ordered one tank to give him covering fire as he closed up to the foremost. He then dismounted and hitched a tow rope to it before lifting an officer, whose legs had been blown off. The tow rope broke so he returned to the car but was twice wounded, despite this he carried the wounded man to the second tank and returned to British lines through intense shell-fire

Gazette: 10 February 1942

Commemoration: i) Name on Memorial in Lewisham Civic Centre, South East London

1194	JACKMAN James Joseph Bernard VC T/Captain	1st Bn. The Royal Northumberland Fusiliers (now Royal Regt. of Fusiliers)	El Duda Ridge, Tobruk, Libya POSTHUMOUS

Born: 19 March 1916 - 'Alverno', Glenageary, Dun Laoghaire, Co. Dublin

624

Died: 25 November 1941 aged 25. Killed by a mortar splinter in the neck the day after his VC action at El Duda, S.E.of Tobruk

Buried: Tobruk War Cemetery, Libya. Plot VII. Row H. Grave 9. Headstone

Deed/Service: 25 November 1941. During a tank attack on a vital ridge, the advance was slowed by intense fire of all descriptions. He calmly led his machine-gun company as if on manoeuvres, getting them into action and securing the right flank. Then standing up in his vehicle, drove between the two sides to get his guns into action on the left flank. By his exemplary courage and bearing, he inspired not only his own men, but also the tank crews

Gazette: 31 March 1942

Commemoration: i) Headstone ii) Portrait in Stonyhurst College, Lancashire iii) Memorial and display at the Royal Northumberland Regimental Museum

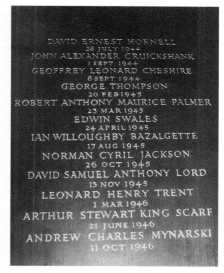

1195   SCARF Arthur Stewart King   VC   Squadron Leader   62 Squadron, Royal Air Force

<table>
<tr><td>Born:</td><td>14 June 1913 - Wimbledon, S.W. London</td></tr>
<tr><td>Died:</td><td>9 December 1941 aged 29. From wounds received during his VC action at the Alor Star Hospital, Malaya</td></tr>
<tr><td>Buried:</td><td>Taiping War Cemetery, Malaysia (Perkuburan Peperangan Cemetery). 60 miles S.E. of Penang. Plot II. Row G. Grave 14. Headstone</td></tr>
<tr><td>Deed/Service:</td><td>9 December 1941. When the Japanese overran Siam (now Thailand), Allied aircraft were prepared to make a raid on Singora. As leader, he took off first in his Blenheim, when enemy aircraft suddenly swept in destroying or disabling the rest of the force. He opted to fly alone to Singora and despite attacks from roving fighters completed his bombing run and turned for home, when twelve enemy fighters bore down on him, damaging the aircraft and severely wounding him. He managed to crash-land at Alor Star base without injuring his crew but died several hours later</td></tr>
<tr><td>Commemoration:</td><td>i) Headstone ii) Name on RAF Memorial, St. Clement Dane's Church, Central London iii) VC.10C Mk 1 XV 109 named for him iii) 'Scarf Trophy' - annual award for Far East Air Force weaponry skills iv) Medals in RAF Museum</td></tr>
</table>

Over Malaya and Siam now Malaysia
POSTHUMOUS
1112

Gazette: 21 June 1946

1196   OSBORN John Robert   VC   Company Sergeant-Major   1st Bn. The Winnipeg Grenadiers, Canadian Infantry Corps

<table>
<tr><td>Born:</td><td>2 January 1899 - Foulden, near Thetford, Norfolk</td></tr>
<tr><td>Died:</td><td>19 December 1941 aged 42. Killed during his VC action on Mount Butler, Hong Kong</td></tr>
<tr><td>Buried:</td><td>Has no known grave - name on The Sai Wan Bay Memorial, Hong Kong. Column 23</td></tr>
<tr><td>Deed/Service:</td><td>19 December 1941 (Warrant Officer Class II) During the attack on Mount Butler, his company captured and held the hill until the position became untenable. He then helped stragglers to the new company position, exposing himself to heavy fire, and when the enemy began hurling grenades he picked them up and threw them back. One live grenade was impossible to return, whereupon he threw himself on it to save his comrades</td></tr>
<tr><td>Commemoration:</td><td>i) Name on Sai Wan Bay Memorial ii) Bronze statue outside Flagstaff House Museum, Hong Kong iii) Osborn Barracks in old Victoria Barracks, Hong Kong named for him iv) Plaque in Trail Legion Hall, British Columbia, Canada v) Medals in Canadian War Museum, Ottawa</td></tr>
</table>

Mount Butler, Hong Kong
POSTHUMOUS
950

Gazette: 2 April 1946

The Victoria Cross, Military Cross and campaign medals awarded to Second Lieutenant George Ward Gunn (1190)

The Victoria Cross, Military Cross and campaign medals awarded to Acting Captain Philip John Gardner (1193)

Chapter Sixteen
The Second World War
1942

No's 1197 - 1228

The Victoria Cross and campaign medals awarded to Petty Officer Thomas William Gould (1201)

The Victoria Cross and campaign medals awarded to Captain Stephen Halden Beattie (1204)

| 1197 | CUMMING Arthur Edward VC OBE MC Brigadier Comd. 2/12th Frontier Force Regiment, Indian Army | Near Kuantan, Malaya
now Malaysia
284 |

Born: 18 June 1896 - Karachi, India (now Pakistan)
Died: 10 April 1971 aged 74, at Edinburgh, Scotland
Cremated: 14 April at Warriston Crematorium, Edinburgh. Ashes in Garden of Remembrance. Area C. 20. No memorial tablet/marker
Deed/Service: 3 January 1942 (Lieutenant-Colonel) When a strong Japanese force penetrated British lines, he led a small counter-attack allowing HQ and part of a brigade to withdraw. Although all his men became casualties and he received two bayonet wounds in the stomach, his covering action was successful. He later drove a carrier under heavy fire collecting isolated groups of men and was again wounded, but managed to get to safety

Gazette: 20 February 1942

Commemoration: i) Name on chair in Chapel of St. Luke's Church, Chelsea, S.W. London ii) Plaque at Lewisham Civic Centre, S.E. London iii) Medals at the National Army Museum

| 1198 | ANDERSON Charles Groves Wright VC MC Lieutenant - Colonel Comd. 2/19th Bn. (N.S.W.) Australian Military Forces | Battle of Muar River, Malaya
now Malaysia
25 |

Born: 12 February 1897 - Cape Town, South Africa
Died: 11 November 1988 aged 91, at Redhill, Canberra, A.C.T., Australia
Cremated: Norwood Crematorium, Mitchell, Canberra. Ashes interred in Wall 61. Panel A. Name on family stone monument - Grave 2 at Crematorium
Deed/Service: 18 - 22 January 1942. When in command of a small force near the River Muar, he destroyed ten enemy tanks before finding himself cut off. He led his men out through fifteen miles of enemy lines, being attacked by air and ground forces until again surrounded and receiving many casualties. To fight his way out was impossible, so destroying his equipment and carrying the wounded he made his way around the enemy to safety

Gazette: 13 February 1942

Commemoration: i) Name on stone memorial and plaque on wall at Crematorium ii) Plaque at Rookwood Garden of Remembrance, N.S.W. iii) Medals and display at the Australian War Memorial, Canberra

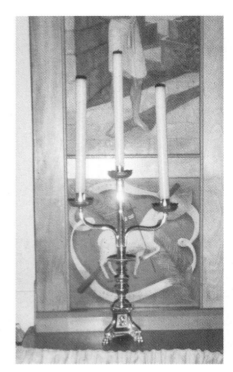

1199   ESMONDE Eugene Kingsmill   **VC DSO**   Lieutenant - Commander   Royal Navy (825 Squadron, Fleet Air Arm)

Straits of Dover
POSTHUMOUS
386

Born:	1 March 1909 - Huthwaite House, Thurgoland, Wortley, Yorkshire
Died:	12 February 1942 aged 32. Killed during his VC action in the Straits of Dover. Body recovered 26 April
Buried:	30 April at Woodlands Cemetery, Gillingham, Kent. Naval Reservation Section A. R C Plot. Grave 187. Headstone
Deed/Service:	12 February 1942. When two German battle cruisers and the cruiser 'Prinz Eugen' entered the Straits with a strong escort, he led a squadron of six Swordfish and escort fighters in an attack. Ten miles east of Ramsgate they were met by enemy fighters, sustaining damage before sighting the fleet, where Esmonde targeted the 'Scharnhorst' and began his torpedo run. Hit by a shell, his Swordfish burst into flames but he continued the attack until the aircraft curved steeply and crashed into the sea. None of the six aircraft returned, but five crew members survived

Gazette: 3 March 1942

Commemoration: i) Headstone ii) Missionary Church at Musoli, Kenya named for him iii) Memorial in St. Michael's, HMS 'Daedalus', Lee-on-Solent, Hampshire

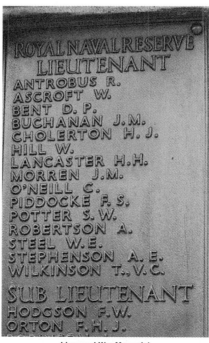

Liverpool War Memorial

1200   WILKINSON Thomas   **VC**   Temporary Lieutenant   Royal Naval Reserve

Malayan Straits, Java Sea
POSTHUMOUS
1311

Born:	1 August 1898 - 96 Mersey Road, West Bank, Widnes, Lancashire
Died:	14 February 1942 aged 43. Went down with the ship during his VC action. Body not recovered
Buried:	Lost at sea. Name on the Liverpool Naval Memorial. Panel 1. Column 2
Deed/Service:	14 February 1942. When commanding HMS 'Li Wo', a patrol vessel of 1,000 tons, he sighted two enemy convoys escorted by Japanese warships en route between Singapore and Batavia and decided to attack. With the support of the ship's company of 84 men, he set one troopship on fire before being hit at point blank range. Ordering the crew to abandon ship, he remained on board

Gazette: 17 December 1946

Commemoration: i) Name on Liverpool War Memorial ii) Name on Widnes War Memorial iii) Name on family headstone at Widnes Cemetery iv) Road in Widnes

1201 **GOULD Thomas William** **VC** **Petty Officer** **Royal Navy** **Sea of Crete, Mediterranean**

Born: 28 December 1914 - Dover, Kent

471

Deed/Service: 16 February 1942. After attacking and sinking a heavily escorted supply ship in daylight, HM Submarine 'Thrasher', in which he was serving, was attacked by depth charges and bombed by aircraft. Surfacing soon afterwards, two unexploded bombs were discovered in the gun-casing, and with 1201 Roberts he volunteered to extract them. The first came out fairly easily, but the second was lying in a confined space and to reach it meant lying full length. With the bomb in his arms and lying on his back, he was dragged twenty feet by Roberts until forty minutes later the bomb was put overboard. An additional danger was the possibility of having to crash dive when both men would have drowned

Gazette: 9 June 1942

Commemoration: i) Silver punch bowl in Senior Ratings Mess, HMS 'Dolphin', Gosport, Hampshire ii) Gould Close, Rowner, Gosport

1202 **ROBERTS Peter Scawen Watkinson** **VC DSC** **Lieutenant** **Royal Navy** **Sea of Crete, Mediterranean**

Born: 28 July 1917 - Chesham Bois, Buckinghamshire

1063

Died: 8 December 1979 aged 62, at Newton Ferrers, Devon

Cremated: 13 December at Efford Crematorium, Plymouth, Devon. Ref: 57912. Ashes buried in Newton Ferrers Churchyard

Deed/Service: 16 February 1942. Following an attack and sinking of an enemy supply ship north of Crete by HM Submarine 'Thrasher', it was discovered that two unexploded bombs from an attack on the submarine had lodged in the gun-casing. 'Thrasher' surfaced after dark and began to roll, with 1201 Gould he removed the first without too much difficulty, but the second had to be approached by lying full length in a very confined space. Gould lay on his back with the bomb in his arms while he dragged him by the shoulders. Forty minutes later the bomb was clear and dropped overboard

Gazette: 9 June 1942

Commemoration: i) Headstone

1203	MIERS Sir Anthony Cecil Capel VC KBE CB DSO & Bar Rear - Admiral Royal Navy	Corfu Harbour, Ionian Sea

Born: 11 November 1906 - Birchwood, Inverness, Scotland

865

Died: 30 June 1985 aged 78, in Inverness

Buried: Tomnahurich Cemetery, Inverness. Roman Catholic Section. Headstone

Deed/Service: 4 March 1942 (Commander) When commanding HM Submarine 'Torbay', he followed an enemy convoy into Corfu Harbour at night, and waited to attack at dawn, surfacing to re-charge his batteries to allow for a hasty withdrawal. At first light he scored direct hits on two supply ships before they came under attack from both sea and air, enduring forty depth-charges and 17 hours of close pursuit during his hazardous return to the open sea

Commemoration: i) Headstone ii) Medals in the Imperial War Museum

Gazette: 7 July 1942

1204	BEATTIE Stephen Halden VC Captain Royal Navy	St. Nazaire, France

Born: 29 March 1908 - The Vicarage, Leighton, Montgomery (now Powys), Wales

69

Died: 24 April 1975 aged 66, at his home 'Salt House' Mullion, Cornwall

Buried: 28 April at Ruan Minor Churchyard, Helston, Cornwall. Headstone

Deed/Service: 27 March 1942 (Lieutenant-Commander) During the attack on St. Nazaire, the only dock capable of holding the great German battleships on the French Atlantic coast, he was in command of HMS 'Campbeltown', an ageing destroyer selected to ram the lock gates packed with explosives. At 100 yards the bridge came under intense fire and blinding glare from many searchlights, but he struck the lock gates and scuttled her exactly on target. The VC was awarded not only for his own valour but that of the un-named officers and men of the ship's company

Commemoration: i) Headstone ii) Medals in the Imperial War Museum

Gazette: 21 May 1942

1205   DURRANT Thomas Frank   VC   Sergeant   Corps of Royal Engineers, attd. No.1 Commando

St. Nazaire, France
POSTHUMOUS
364

Born:	17 October 1918 - Green Street Green, Farnborough, Kent
Died:	28 March 1942 aged 23. From numerous wounds at a German military hospital at St. Nazaire, following his VC action
Buried:	Escoublac-la-Baule War Cemetery, near St. Nazaire. Plot I. Row D. Grave 11. Headstone
Deed/Service:	27 March 1942. When in charge of a Lewis gun in an exposed position on HM Motor Launch 306, they came under heavy fire when entering the River Loire. Severely wounded from shore fire as they entered the port, he remained at his post despite further wounds from a German destroyer having fired on it's bridge. Refusing to surrender when called upon to do so, he kept up continuous fire until the destroyer came alongside, with those still alive being taken prisoner. The German boarding party dressed his wounds, but he died the following day

Gazette: 19 June 1945

Commemoration: i) Headstone ii) Name on the St. Nazaire Memorial, France iii) Durrant Bridge over Vrvas River, Jajce, Bosnia - erected 1996 by Royal Engineers when on U.N. duty iv) Plaques in Vine Street School and Scout HQ at Green Street Green iv) Medals in Corps of Royal Engineers Museum

1206   NEWMAN Augustus Charles   VC OBE TD   Lieutenant - Colonel

The Essex Regt. (now Royal Anglian Regt.)   St. Nazaire, France
attd. No.2 Commando
925

Born:	19 August 1904 - Buckhurst Hill, Chigwell, Essex
Died:	26 April 1972 aged 62, at Sandwich, Kent
Cremated:	2 May at Barham Crematorium, Kent. Ref: 29764. Ashes by beech tree in Garden of Remembrance - tree lost in the 1987 gale. No memorial
Deed/Service:	27 March 1942. Was in overall command of the 44 officers and 224 men to land at St. Nazaire. Although he need not have landed, he was one of the first ashore, directing operations in the open and under fire for five hours. When the demolition parties had done their work, evacuation by landing craft was out of the question, so he fought his way inland until all ammunition was expended and he and his men were taken prisoner

Gazette: 19 June 1945

Commemoration:

MERTON & MORDEN
MEMBERS OF PARLIAMENT
...
1950 .. CAPT. R.E.D. RYDER. V.C. R.N.
1951 .. CAPT. R.E.D. RYDER. V.C. R.N.

1207	RYDER Robert Edward Dudley VC Captain Royal Navy	St. Nazaire, France

Born: 16 February 1908 - India

Died: 29 June 1986 aged 78, of a heart attack on board the yacht 'Watchdog', fifteen miles off Guernsey, Channel Islands en route to Brittany

Cremated: 10 July at Headington Crematorium, Oxford. Ref: 85765. Ashes interred at Inkpen, Berkshire and at Flower Bed North - J at Crematorium

Deed/Service: 27 March 1942 (Commander) Commanding the 18 vessels in the raid, leading HMS 'Campbeltown' in and getting her successfully beached, he remained on the spot under heavy fire for over an hour, ensuring all the men from 'Campbeltown' were evacuated. When he saw he could do no more for the Commandos still on the shore, he began to withdraw. By some miracle his gun boat, full of dead and wounded and under constant fire had survived sinking and he completed the retirement under a continuous barrage of fire from shore

Commemoration: i) Name on Roll of Honour, Cheltenham College, Glos. ii) Name on plaque at Crown House, Morden, Surrey iii) Medals at Imperial War Museum

1097

Gazette: 21 May 1942

W A SAVAGE VC

Smethwick

1208	SAVAGE William Alfred VC Able Seaman Royal Navy	St. Nazaire, France

POSTHUMOUS
1110

Born: 30 October 1912 - 7 Raglan Avenue, Smethwick, Staffordshire (now Birmingham)

Died: 28 March 1942 aged 29. Killed on board Motor Gun Boat 314, during his VC action in St. Nazaire Harbour

Buried: Town Cemetery, Falmouth, Cornwall. Section K. Row C. Grave 15. Headstone

Deed/Service: 27 March 1942. When acting as a gun-layer of a pom-pom in MGB 314 in St. Nazaire Harbour, he was shooting with great accuracy at the shore positions from a completely exposed position. He kept up the fire until the withdrawal began and he was killed at his gun. This VC was awarded not only for his gallantry, but for other un-named men in the Launches, MGB's and MTB's who carried out their duties in an exposed position

Commemoration: i) Headstone ii) Name on the St. Nazaire Memorial, France iii) Memorial in vestibule of 'a Smethwick Council House' iv) Savage Close, Rowner, Gosport, Hampshire v) Medals in the National Maritime Museum

Gazette: 21 May 1942

Runnymede Memorial

KENNETH CAMPBELL
13 MAR 1942
JOHN DERING NETTLETON
28 APRIL 1942
LESLIE THOMAS MANSER
23 OCT 1942

Runnymede Memorial

1209   **NETTLETON John Dering   VC   Wing Commander   44 Squadron, Royal Air Force**   Over Augsberg, Germany

Born:	28 June 1917 - Nongoma, Natal, South Africa	922
Died:	13 July 1943 aged 26. Following a bombing raid on Turin, his plane was shot down in the Bay of Biscay by three German fighters	
Buried:	Has no known grave - name on The Runnymede Memorial, near Egham, Surrey. Panel 118. Death presumed on 23 February 1944	
Deed/Service:	17 April 1942 (Squadron Leader) Leading one of two formations of six of the then relatively new Lancaster bombers, on a 1,200 mile round trip daylight raid on the vital M.A.N. diesel engine factory, they were attacked soon after take-off. Four were shot down, but he held course through heavy fire, bombing the objective at roof top level. Nettleton, the only survivor managed to bring his damaged aircraft safely back	Gazette: 28 April 1942
Commemoration:	i) Name on Runnymede Memorial ii) Nettleton School, Harare, Zimbabwe iii) Name on RAF Memorial, St. Clement Dane's Church, London	

IN LOVING MEMORY OF
MAJ. GENERAL H.R.B. FOOTE
(BOB)
VC. CB. DSO.
ROYAL TANK REGT.
1904 - 1993

1210   **FOOTE Henry Robert Bowreman   VC CB DSO   Major - General   Commanding 7th Royal Tank Regiment**   Battle of Knightsbridge Libya

Born:	5 December 1904 - Ishapur, Bengal, India. Raised in Birmingham. Several records show incorrectly he was born there	416
Died:	22 November 1993 aged 88, at Pulborough Hospital, Sussex	
Buried:	St. Mary's Churchyard, West Chiltington, Sussex. Headstone - left side of churchyard, adjacent to 584 Woolley's headstone	
Deed/Service:	27 May to 15 June 1942 (T/Lieutenant-Colonel) For a three week period he displayed outstanding courage during continual fighting in the Knightsbridge, Gazala and Bir Hacheim area, always being in the right spot at the right time. On 6 June, although wounded, he led his battalion in defeating an enemy force attempting to encircle two British divisions. On the 13th, he went around on foot to encourage each of his men who were under intense artillery fire, and by his example the corridor was kept open for the brigade to march through	Gazette: 18 May 1944
Commemoration:	i) Headstone ii) Memorial plaque at Bedford School	

JOHN DERING NETTLETON
28 APRIL 1942
LESLIE THOMAS MANSER
23 OCT 1942
RAWDON HUME MIDDLETON
15 JAN 1943

| 1211 | MANSER Leslie Thomas   VC   Flying Officer   50 Squadron, Royal Air Force Volunteer Reserve | Cologne Raid, Germany
POSTHUMOUS
834 |

Born: 11 May 1922 - New Delhi, India
Died: 31 May 1942 aged 20. Killed during his VC action 3 miles east of Bree, Belgium, close to the Dutch border
Buried: Heverlee War Cemetery, Belgium. Plot VII. Row G. Grave 1. Headstone (See Map - 15)
Deed/Service: 30 - 31 May 1942. During the massive attack on Cologne, he was captain and first pilot of a Manchester bomber, one of 1,046 despatched on the raid. Having dropped his 1,260 four pound incendiary bombs on target, the craft was hit repeatedly and his rear gunner wounded. As the plane filled with smoke, he set course at 2,000 feet for Manston, Kent, but losing more height and in danger of stalling, he ordered the crew to bale out. By remaining at the controls those extra seconds, he preserved the lives of his crew but sacrificed his only chance of survival

Commemoration: i) Headstone ii) Memorial in Christ Church, Radlett, Hertfordshire iii) Name on RAF Memorial, St. Clement Dane's Church, Central London

Gazette: 23 October 1942

| 1212 | SMYTHE Quentin George Murray   VC   Captain   Royal Natal Carabineers, South African Force | Alem Hamza area. Libya
1169 |

Born: 6 August 1916 - Nottingham Road, Natal, South Africa
Died: 22 October 1997 aged 81, in Durban Hospital, South Africa from terminal cancer
Cremated: Durban Crematorium. Ashes buried on his farm in Nottingham Road
Deed/Service: 5 June 1942 (Sergeant) When on patrol fifteen miles north of the Cauldron, he took command of a platoon when his officer was severely wounded in an attack on an Italian strong point. Although wounded himself, he attacked a machine-gun nest with hand grenades, capturing the crew, before leading another attack. Weak from loss of blood he again attacked, taking an anti-tank position single-handed, killing several of the enemy

Commemoration: i) Painting in S.A. Museum of Military History, Johannesburg ii) Painting in Estcourt High School, Nottingham Road

Gazette: 11 September 1942

| 1213 | WAKENSHAW Adam Herbert VC Private 9th Bn. The Durham Light Infantry (now The Light Infantry) | Mersa Matruh, Egypt POSTHUMOUS 1258 |

Born: 9 June 1914 - Duke Street, Newcastle upon Tyne, Northumberland (now Tyne and Wear)
Died: 27 June 1942 aged 28. Killed during his VC action south of Mersa Matruh, Egypt
Buried: i) Where he fell ii) On 7 February 1943 - El Alamein War Cemetery, Egypt. 80 miles W. of Alexandria. Plot XXXII. Row D. Grave 9. Headstone
Deed/Service: 27 June 1942. After the Afrika Korps and the Italians had inflicted 80,000 casualties and the Eighth Army were withdrawing to Egypt, he crewed a 2-pounder gun as part of the rearguard. During an enemy attack his gun was hit, causing many casualties and he had his left arm blown off, but he managed to fire five more rounds until hit again. He prepared to fire again, but a direct hit on his ammunition killed him and destroyed the gun
Commemoration: i) Headstone ii) Memorial in St. Aloysius School, Newcastle on Tyne iii) Medals in Durham Light Infantry Museum

Gazette: 11 September 1942

| (See 1183) | UPHAM Charles Hazlitt VC & BAR Captain 20th Bn. 2nd New Zealand Expeditionary Force (Canterbury Regiment) | El Ruweisat Ridge, Egypt 1246 |

Born: 21 September 1908 - Gloucester Street, Christchurch, South Island, New Zealand
Died: 22 November 1994 aged 86, at a retirement home in Christchurch, New Zealand
Cremated: 25 November at Harewood Crematorium, Christchurch. Ref: 22339. Ashes in family plot, St. Paul's Churchyard, Papanui
Deed/Service: i) 22 - 30 May 1941 (Second Lieutenant) Awarded for action at Maleme, Crete (See entry 1183 for details)
ii) BAR: 14 - 15 July 1942. When leading his company attacking an enemy held ridge overlooking El Alamein battlefield, he was wounded twice but took the objective after fierce fighting. He personally destroyed a German tank, several guns and vehicles with grenades, despite a broken arm. After his wounds were dressed, he returned to his men but was again severely wounded and unable to move
Commemoration: See entry 1183 for details of six known memorials

Gazette: 14 October 1941

BAR: Gazette: 26 September 1945

1214	ELLIOTT Keith VC Second Lieutenant 22nd Bn. 2nd New Zealand Expeditionary Force	Ruweisat, Egypt

Born: 25 April 1916 - Apiti, New Zealand. Later The Rev.

Died: 7 October 1989 aged 73, of cancer at Te Omanga Hospice, Lower Hutt, North Island, New Zealand

Buried: 12 October at Paraparaumu Cemetery, Lower Hutt. Returned Servicemans' Lawn Section. Headstone

Deed/Service: 15 July 1942 (Sergeant) While leading his platoon in an attack under heavy machine-gun fire, he was wounded in the chest. Despite the wound he carried on and led a bayonet charge which resulted in the capture of four enemy machine-gun posts, an anti-tank gun and fifty prisoners. He refused medical aid until he had reformed his men and handed over the prisoners, which amounted to over 130

Commemoration: i) Headstone ii) Display at the RSA HQ, Dunedin, S. Island iii) Medals at the Fielding Agricultural High School, Auckland, N. Island New Zealand

378

Gazette: 24 September 1942

1215	GURNEY Arthur Stanley VC Private 2nd/48th Bn. (South Australia) Australian Military Forces	Tel-el-Eisa, Egypt POSTHUMOUS

Born: 15 December 1908 - Dayawn, Murchison Goldfields, Western Australia

Died: 22 July 1942 aged 33. Killed in his VC action at Tel-el-Eisa, Tripolitania, Egypt

Buried: El Alamein War Cemetery, Egypt. 80 miles W. of Alexandria on the coast road. Plot XVI. Row H. Grave 21. Headstone

Deed/Service: 22 July 1942. When his company received numerous casualties and their advance held up, he single-handed charged the nearest machine-gun post and put it out of action. After he had silenced a second machine-gun, he was knocked down by a grenade but picked himself up and charged a third. Nothing more was seen of him until his body was found by his comrades, whose advance he had made possible

Commemoration: i) Headstone ii) Memorial at Gurney Soldiers Club, Karrakatta Camp, Perth iii) Medals and display at Australian War Memorial, Canberra, A.C.T.

503

Gazette: 14 September 1942

1216   **FOOTE John Weir VC Major, The Rev.**   Canadian Chaplains' Service, attd. The Royal Hamilton Light Infantry **Dieppe, France**
                                                                 Canadian Infantry

Born:	5 May 1904 - Madoc, Ontario, Canada
Died:	2 May 1988 aged 83, from influenza aggravated by a heart condition, at Norwood, Ontario
Buried:	St. Andrew's Presbyterian Churchyard (Union Cemetery), Coburg, Ontario. Headstone
Deed/Service:	19 August 1942 (Hon. Captain) During the Allied amphibious assault on Dieppe to partly test the 'Atlantic Wall', he calmly walked about collecting wounded for the entire eight hour operation. Having saved many lives he declined to be taken away by landing craft and to safety, deliberately being taken prisoner so that he could help the men being taken into captivity until the end of the war
Commemoration:	i) Headstone ii) Plaque at Westerleigh School, Hastings, Sussex iii) Plaque at Trail Canadian Legion Post, British Columbia iv) Medals and display at The Hamilton Light Infantry Heritage Museum, Ontario

417

Gazette: 14 February 1945

1217   **MERRITT Charles Cecil Ingersoll VC Lt. - Colonel Comd. The South Saskatchewan Regiment, Canadian Infantry Corps** **Dieppe, France**

Born:	10 November 1908 - Vancouver, British Columbia, Canada
Deed/Service:	19 August 1942. At Dieppe his regiment made up part of the 5,100 Canadians and 1,000 British Commandos engaged in the raid, his unit being ordered to advance across a bridge. During an attack on German pill-boxes, the first units were destroyed by heavy machine-gun artillery and mortar fire, he rushed forward and led the survivors in successful attacks, receiving two wounds, then continued to direct the units operations. He organised the collection of all Bren and Tommy - guns and prepared a defensive position to cover the withdrawal from the beach
Commemoration:	i) Plaque in Royal Canadian Legion Post at Trail, British Columbia

861

Gazette: 2 October 1942

1218 **PORTEOUS Patrick Anthony   VC   Colonel   Royal Regiment of Artillery**   Dieppe, France

Born: 1 January 1918 - Abbotabad, North West Frontier, India (now Pakistan)   996
Deed/Service: 19 August 1942 (T/Major) When acting as Liaison Officer between two detachments, during the attack on the heavy coast defence guns he was wounded in the hand, but bayoneted his assailant as he was about to kill a British NCO. In the meantime two officers of the second detachment were killed, and he rushed across open ground under withering fire to take command, leading the men in a successful charge to take an objective. Despite receiving another wound he continued to the second target, eventually collapsing when the last of the guns had been destroyed   **Gazette: 2 October 1942**
Commemoration: i) Avenue Captain Porteous, Belleville-sur-mer, Dieppe ii) Name on Memorial in Royal Artillery Chapel, Woolwich, South East London

1219 **KINGSBURY Bruce Steel   VC   Private   2nd/14th Bn. (Victoria) Australian Military Forces**   Isurava, New Guinea
now Papua New Guinea
POSTHUMOUS

Born: 8 January 1918 - Armadale, Melbourne, Victoria, Australia   696
Died: 29 August 1942 aged 24. Killed during his VC action at Isurava, New Guinea
Buried: Port Moresby War Cemetery, Papua New Guinea, also called Bomana War Cemetery. On south coast. Plot C-6. Row E. Grave 1. Headstone
Deed/Service: 29 August 1942. When the Japanese had broken through his battalions flank, he volunteered to join a platoon to counter-attack. Rushing forward, he cleared a path through the enemy by firing his Bren gun from his hip and inflicting a large number of casualties. He was shot dead by a sniper, but his superb courage made possible the recapture of a position which saved the Battalion Headquarters   **Gazette: 9 February 1943**
Commemoration: i) Headstone ii) Kingsbury Street, Canberra, A.C.T. iii) Display at the Australian War Memorial, Canberra

240

1220   **FRENCH John Alexander   VC   Corporal   2nd/9th Bn. (Queensland) Australian Military Forces**

**Milne Bay, New Guinea
now Papua New Guinea
POSTHUMOUS
428**

Born: 15 July 1914 - Crows Nest, near Toowoomba, Queensland, Australia
Died: 4 September 1942 aged 28. Killed during his VC action at Milne Bay, New Guinea
Buried: Port Moresby War Cemetery, Papua New Guinea, also called Bomana War Cemetery. On south coast. Plot A-2. Row E. Grave 16   Headstone
Deed/Service: 4 September 1942. When the advance of his section was held up by three enemy machine-gun posts, he ordered his men to take cover. He then advanced and silenced the first two posts with grenades, before attacking the third when obviously seriously wounded. When all firing ceased, his men pushed forward finding all gun-crews dead and his body lying by the third. His supreme courage enabled the section to complete its mission

Gazette: 14 January 1943

Commemoration: i) Headstone   ii) French Memorial Library, Crows Nest   iii) French Street, Canberra, A.C.T.   iv) Display at the Australian War Memorial, Canberra

1221   **KIBBY William Henry   VC   Sergeant   2nd/28th Bn. (South Australia) Australian Miltary Forces**

**Miteiriya Ridge, Egypt
POSTHUMOUS
694**

Born: 15 April 1903 - Winlaton, Co. Durham (now Tyne and Wear)
Died: 31 October 1942 aged 39. Killed during his VC actions around Miteiriya Ridge, El Alamein, Egypt
Buried: El Alamein War Cemetery, Egypt. 80 miles W. of Alexandria. Plot XVI. Row A. Grave 18. Headstone
Deed/Service: 23 - 31 October 1942. During the entire period beginning with the initial attack on the Ridge, he repeatedly distinguished himself leading a platoon when his commander had been killed. On 23 October he silenced a machine-gun post and captured twelve of the enemy. In the following days he was constantly cheering his men, several times going out alone under heavy fire to repair damaged communication lines. On 31 October he advanced alone, throwing grenades to destroy the enemy a few yards away, but as success appeared certain he was cut down by machine-gun fire

Gazette: 28 January 1943

Commemoration: i) Headstone   ii) Kibby Place, Canberra, A.C.T.   iii) Medals and display at the Australian War Memorial, Canberra

| 1222 | GRATWICK Percival Eric   VC   Private   2nd/48th Bn. (South Australia) Australian Military Forces | Miteiriya Ridge, Egypt POSTHUMOUS |

Born: 19 October 1902 - Katanning, Western Australia

482

Died: 25 / 26 October 1942 aged 40. Killed during his VC action at Miteiriya Ridge, El Alamein, Egypt

Buried: i) 27 October at Tel-el-Eisa Cemetery, Libya ii) El Alamein War Cemetery, Egypt. 80 miles W. of Alexandria. Plot XXII. Row A.Grave 6. Headstone

Deed/Service: 25 - 26 October 1942. When his platoon suffered heavy casualties during the attack on Miteiriya Ridge, he charged on alone with hand grenades. He killed the crew of an enemy machine-gun post and an entire mortar team, before pushing on under heavy machine-gun fire and charging with a rifle and bayonet toward another post. As he inflicted more casualties he was killed by machine-gun fire, but his actions allowed the company to gain their objective

Gazette: 28 January 1943

Commemoration: i) Headstone ii) Gratwick Club Room, Campbell Barracks, Swanbourne, Western Australia iii) Display at the Australian War Memorial Canberra, A.C.T. iv) Medals at the Army Museum of Western Australia, Perth

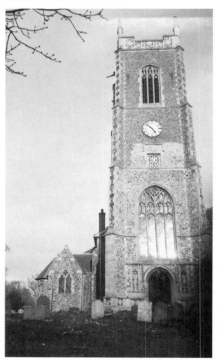

| 1223 | TURNER Victor Buller   VC CVO   T/Lieutenant - Colonel | The Rifle Brigade (Prince Consort's Own) (now Royal Green Jackets) | El Alamein, Egypt |

Born: 17 January 1900 - Thatcham, Berkshire

1241

Died: 7 August 1972 aged 72, at Ditchingham, near Bungay, Suffolk

Cremated: St. Faith's Crematorium, Norwich, Norfolk. Ashes interred at St. Mary's Churchyard, Ditchingham. No memorial marker/tablet

Deed/Service: 27 October 1942. During the Second Battle of El Alamein, he was sent with his battalion to capture a strategic objective, code named 'Snipe' at El Aqqaqir. Having taken their target they were isolated for fourteen hours, fighting off continuous attacks by 90 tanks. Over thirty were set alight and twenty more immobilised. At one point he acted as loader of a 6-pounder anti-tank gun, when the crew had become casualties, and put five more tanks out of action. He was then wounded in the head, but refused medical aid until the last tank had been repulsed

Gazette: 20 November 1942

Commemoration: i) Rifle Brigade Memorial, Winchester Cathedral, Hampshire ii) Memorial on Ditchingham Town Clock iii) Medals at Royal Green Jackets Museum

1224	**PETERS Frederick Thornton**	**VC DSO DSC & Bar Acting Captain Royal Navy**	Oran Harbour, Algeria

Born: 17 September 1889 - Charlottetown, Prince Edward Island, Canada

984

Died: 13 November 1942 aged 53. Killed aboard a Sunderland flying boat that crashed on landing near the Plymouth Harbour breakwater

Buried: No known grave, no bodies were recovered after the crash. Name on Portsmouth Naval Memorial, Hampshire. Panel 61. Column 3

Deed/Service: 8 November 1942. When commanding HMS 'Walney' during the raid on Vichy held Oran Harbour, he led his force through the boom towards the jetty under intense fire from ship and shore. Blinded in one eye, he was the sole survivor of the seventeen men on 'Walney's' bridge, but she reached the shore disabled and ablaze before sinking when her boilers blew. The second ship in the raid, HMS 'Hartland' was also blown up, and with just ten men, including US Rangers, they got ashore and were taken prisoner. Interrogated by a Vichy Admiral, all were released soon afterwards

Gazette: 18 May 1943

Commemoration: i) Name on Portsmouth Naval Memorial ii) Name on plaque at Trail Royal Canadian Legion Post, British Columbia, Canada

1225	**MIDDLETON Rawdon Hume**	**VC Pilot Officer Royal Australian Air Force, attd. 149 Squadron Royal Air Force**	Raid on Turin, Italy

POSTHUMOUS

Born: 22 July 1916 - Waverley, Sydney, New South Wales, Australia. Promotion to P.O. with effect from 14 November 1942 notified posthumously

864

Died: 29 November 1942 aged 26. Killed during his VC action when his Stirling bomber crashed at sea, 3 miles from Dymchurch, Kent

Buried: 5 February 1943 at St. John's Churchyard, Beck Row, Mildenhall, Suffolk. Service Section. Row D. Grave 1. Headstone

Deed/Service: 28 - 29 November 1942. Flying one of 182 bombers on a raid on the Fiat factories at Turin, his Stirling was badly damaged by A.A. fire on his final approach, grievously wounding him and two of his crew of seven. Having released his bombs, he re-crossed the Alps and set course for England, weakening quickly from blood loss and pain. To give the crew a chance, he flew inland over Kent where four baled out, then turned back to avoid civilian casualties. Two bodies were recovered by naval rescue on 30th, his body being washed ashore 1 February 1943 near Dover

Gazette: 15 January 1943

Commemoration: i) Headstone ii) Name on RAF Memorial, St. Clement Dane's Church, Central London iii) Middleton Close, RAF Uxbridge, Middlesex iv) Room at Air Force Club, Sydney v) Middleton Court, Canberra, A.C.T. vi) Medals and display at Australian War Memorial, Canberra

1226   **LE PATOUREL Herbert Wallace   VC   Brigadier   2nd Bn. The Hampshire Regiment (now The Royal Hampshire Regiment)**   Tebourba, Tunisia

Born:	20 June 1916 - Guernsey, Channel Islands
Died:	4 September 1979 aged 63, at his home in Chewton Mendip, Somerset
Cremated:	South Bristol Crematorium, Bridgewater Road, Bristol. Ref: 7593. Ashes scattered in the fields at the rear of his home in Chewton Mendip
Deed/Service:	3 December 1942 (T/Major) When the Eighth Army pushed the Afrika Corps back into Tunisia, he was ordered to take high ground twelve miles from Tunis, essential for an attack on the city. Initial assaults had been repulsed and he called for four volunteers to silence several machine-gun posts. When his men became casualties, he went on alone using his pistol and hurling grenades until 'killed' by the enemy. He had in fact been badly wounded and taken prisoner of war, but his citation recorded that it was a posthumous award.

738

Gazette: 9 March 1943

Commemoration: i) Memorial plaque beneath tree at The Royal Hampshire Regimental Museum ii) Medals on display inside The Royal Hampshire's Museum

  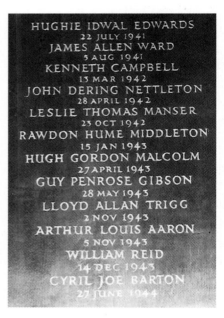

1227   **MALCOLM Hugh Gordon   VC   Wing Commander   18 Squadron, Royal Air Force**   Over North Africa
POSTHUMOUS

Born:	2 May 1917 - Broughty Ferry, Dundee, Scotland
Died:	4 December 1942 aged 25. Shot down during his VC action near Chouigui, Tunisia
Buried:	Beja War Cemetery, Tunisia. Northern suburbs of town. 60 miles from Tunis. Plot II. Row E. Collective Grave 6. Headstone shows age 26
Deed/Service:	17 November to 4 December 1942. His squadron of Blenheims were engaged on many raids on the enemy airfields along the 'Mareth Line', and on three occasions he acted with conspicuous bravery. On 17 November he led a successful attack on Bizerte in atrocious weather conditions, a later low altitude raid on the same airfield on 28 November resulted in considerable ground damage. On 4 December he led an attack on an enemy fighter base at Chouigui, but was intercepted by an overwhelming force resulting in the loss of eight of the eleven Blenheims, including his own

826

Gazette: 27 April 1943

Commemoration: i) Headstone ii) Name on RAF Memorial, St.Clement Dane's, Central London iii) A VC.10C Mk 1 XV809 named for him

1228	SHERBROOKE Robert St. Vincent VC CB DSO Rear Admiral Royal Navy	Off North Cape, Norway

Born: 8 January 1901 - Oxton Hall, Oxton, Newark, Nottinghamshire

1138

Died: 13 June 1972 aged 71, at his home in Oxton

Buried: St. Peter and St. Paul Churchyard, Oxton. Headstone

Deed/Service: 31 December 1942 (Captain) As senior officer in command of five destroyers, on board HMS 'Onslow' escorting a vital supply convoy en-route to Murmansk, Russia, he spotted a vastly superior force when in the Barents Sea. Four times the enemy attacked, but were repelled He was seriously wounded in the face and temporarily blinded, but continued to direct the ships under his command, until further hits on 'Onslow' compelled him to disengage and seek aid. He insisted on seeing all reports until the convoy reached its destination

Gazette: 12 January 1943

Commemoration: i) Headstone ii) Memorial plaque to him and the ensign from HMS 'Onslow' in St.Peter and St. Paul, Oxton

The Victoria Cross, Order of the British Empire and campaign medals awarded to Lt. Colonel Augustus Charles Newman (1206)

The Victoria Cross and campaign medals awarded to Able Seaman William Alfred Savage (1208)

The Victoria Cross and campaign medals attributed to Flying Officer Leslie Thomas Manser (1211)

Chapter Seventeen
The Second World War
1943

No's 1229 - 1253

The Victoria Cross and campaign medals awarded to Company - Quartermaster - Sergeant John Patrick Kenneally (1240)

The Victoria Cross, Distinguished Service Order, Distinguished Service Cross and campaign medals awarded to Commander John Wallace Linton (1242)

NIAZ MUHAMMAD
V.C.PARKASH SINGH
SADHU SINGH

1229   **PARKASH SINGH   VC   Major   8th Punjab Regiment, Indian Army**

Born: 31 March 1913 - Chak 266 RB Village, Sharikar, Jaranevala Tehsil, Lyallpur District, India (now Pakistan)
Died: 23 March 1991 aged 77, at Old Court Hospital, Ealing, West London, following an operation
Cremated: 28 March at Golders Green Crematorium, N.W. London. Ref: 281043. Ashes returned to his home village near Jullundur, Punjab, India
Deed/Service: 6 January 1943 (Havildar/Sergeant) Under heavy Japanese fire, he drove his carrier forward to rescue the crews of two disabled carriers. In the same area, he rescued two more carriers on 19 January knocked-out by anti-tank fire, repeating the act again under heavy fire he drove to a damaged carrier containing two wounded men and brought them to safety
Commemoration: i) Name on the Rangoon Memorial, Burma (Myanmar) ii) Medals at the Imperial War Museum

Donbaik, Mayu Peninsula
Burma, now Myanmar
961

Gazette: 13 May 1943

1230   **NEWTON William Ellis   VC   Flight Lieutenant   22 Squadron, Royal Australian Air Force**

Born: 8 June 1919 - St. Kilda, Melbourne, Victoria, Australia
Died: 29 March 1943 aged 23. Following his VC action at Kila Point, New Guinea
Buried: i) Bomb crater at Kila Point ii) c. October 1943 at Salamaua War Cemetery, near Lae iii) 1946 in Lae War Cemetery, Papua New Guinea. Next to Lae Zoo, on the East coast overlooking the Huon Gulf. Section S. Row A. Grave 4. Headstone
Deed/Service: 16 March 1943. With a two man crew in a Boston aircraft, he led a raid on fuel dumps on the Salamaua Isthmus. Flying through heavy fire the plane was hit repeatedly, but he dropped his bombs and flew the crippled aircraft back to base at Wards Field. Ordered to repeat the raid on the 18th, he swept in at fifty feet but the Boston was hit and burst into flames. He headed out to sea to give the crew a better chance, but only Newton and his Flight Sergeant made it to shore, where both were captured, interrogated and beheaded
Commemoration: i) Headstone ii) Plaques in the Presbyterian Church and cricket pavilion in St. Kilda iii) Plaque at Victoria Golf Club, Melbourne iv) Newton Field Airstrip, Nadzab Airfield, Philippines v) Medals and display at The Australian War Memorial, Canberra, A.C.T.

Salamaua, New Guinea
POSTHUMOUS
926

Gazette: 19 October 1943

| 1231 | SEAGRIM Derek Anthony   VC   T/Lieutenant - Colonel   Comd. 7th Bn. The Green Howards (Alexandra, P.O.W. Own York Reg.) | Mareth Line, Tunisia POSTHUMOUS |

Born: 24 September 1903 - Bournemouth, Hampshire (now Dorset)
1121

Died: 6 April 1943 aged 39. From wounds received in his VC action, at a Military Hospital near Sfax, Tunisia

Buried: Sfax War Cemetery, Tunisia. 150 miles S. of Tunis. Plot XIV. Row C. Grave 21. Headstone

Deed/Service: 20 - 21 March 1943. Ordered to attack and capture an important objective on the left flank of the forty mile long Mareth Line, the initial attack faltered due to intense fire. The following day he led his battalion in a counter-attack and was first across a scaling ladder over an anti-tank ditch. He continued to lead until mortally wounded

Gazette: 13 May 1943

Commemoration: i) Headstone ii) Name on War Memorial in Whissonsett Churchyard, Norfolk iii) Plaque in St. Mary's Church, Whissonsett iv) Name in St.Mary's Churchyard on family grave v) His name, and that of his twin brother Hugh (a GC holder) on plaque below the village sign at Whissonsett

| 1232 | NGARIMU Moana-Nui-a-Kiwa   VC   Second Lieutenant   28th (Maori) Bn. 2nd New Zealand Expeditionary Force | Tobago Gap, Tunisia POSTHUMOUS |

Born: 7 April 1918 - Sir Apiraia Nata's Village, Ruatoria, New Zealand
927

Died: 27 March 1943 aged 24. Killed during his VC action at Tobaga Gap, Tunisia

Buried: Sfax War Cemetery, Tunisia. 150 miles S. of Tunis. Plot X. Row E. Grave 14. Headstone shows first name as Moana-nui-a-Kiwa

Deed/Service: 26 - 27 March 1943. Led his platoon up the face of a strongly defended hill, being the first to reach the top. He personally destroyed two machine-gun posts then inspired his men to beat off several counter-attacks. When all but two of his men were casualties and he was shot in the shoulder and wounded in the leg by shrapnel, the Germans attacked again. At the same time reinforcements arrived, he was killed

Gazette: 4 June 1943

Commemoration: i) Headstone ii) Memorial at HQ, Dunedin RSA, N.Z. iii) Full size bust and his medals in Queen Elizabeth II Army Memorial Museum Walouru

1233   **LALBAHADUR THAPA VC OBI   Subadar - Major   1st Bn. 2nd Gurkha Rifles, Indian Army**   **Rass-es-Zouai, Tunisia**

Born:	February 1906 - Somsa Village, Thum Thant Hup, Baghlung, Parbat District, Western Nepal. Some records show born 1907
Died:	20 October 1968 aged 62, at the Gurkha Depot at Paklihawa, Nepal
Buried:	Paklihawa Camp Cemetery. Grave unmarked outside north perimeter fence on a patch of waste ground. Accurate location not recorded
Deed/Service:	5 - 6 April 1943 (Subadar/Captain) In command of two sections during a silent attack, he came into enemy company at the foot of a pathway winding up a narrow cleft studded with enemy posts. Killing the garrison of each outpost and the machine-gun crews by means of kukri or bayonet, he fought his way up the bullet-swept approaches to the crest, clearing the enemy and allowing the advance of a division below
Commemoration:	i) Medals with the 1st Royal Gurkha Rifles

713

Gazette: 15 June 1943

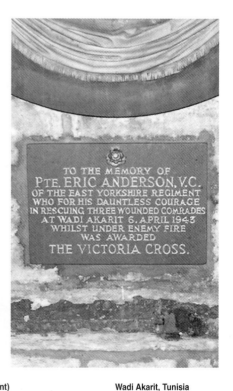

1234   **ANDERSON Eric VC Private   5th Bn. The East Yorkshire Regiment (now the P.O.W. Regiment)**   **Wadi Akarit, Tunisia**
POSTHUMOUS

Born:	15 September 1915 - Fagley, Eccleshill, Bradford, Yorkshire
Died:	6 April 1943 aged 27. Killed during his VC action at Akarit on the Wadi, Tunisia
Buried:	Sfax War Cemetery, Tunisia. 150 miles S. of Tunis. Plot II. Row C. Grave 14. Headstone
Deed/Service:	6 April 1943. During the attack on Wadi Akarit, his Regiment had to withdraw behind the crest of a hill. As a stretcher-bearer, he knew wounded men were lying in 'No Man's Land'. On his own initiative he went out alone under heavy fire to tend and bring to safety wounded comrades on three separate occasions. He was mortally wounded on the fourth occasion as he prepared to bring in another wounded man
Commemoration:	i) Headstone ii) Plaque in Bradford Cathedral iii) Memorial in Beverley Minster, Yorkshire iv) Memorial in Thornbury Boys School, Bradford v) Plaque in St. John's United Reform Church, Bradford vi) Medals at the P.O.W. Regimental Museum

26

Gazette: 29 July 1943

1235   **CAMPBELL Lorne MacLaine** **VC DSO & Bar OBE TD** **Brigadier**   Comd. 7th Bn. The Argyll & Sutherland Highlanders Wadi Akarit, Tunisia

Born:	22 July 1902 - The Airds, Argyllshire, Scotland
Died:	25 May 1991 aged 88, at his home at The Airds
Buried:	Warriston Cemetery, Edinburgh. Section B.1. Headstone
Deed/Service:	6 April 1943 (T/Lieutenant-Colonel) During the Battle of Wadi Akarit, his battalion was given the task of crossing an enemy minefield and anti-tank ditch in order to form a bridgehead. Forming up in darkness and traversing the off-shoot of the Wadi in order to attack, he accomplished his objective and took 600 prisoners. The following day his position was under constant heavy bombardment and although wounded in the neck by shrapnel, he inspired his men to such an extent that all attacks were repulsed and the bridgehead held
Commemoration:	i) Headstone ii) Medals at The Argyll & Sutherland Highlanders Regimental Museum

182

Gazette: 8 June 1943

1236   **CHHELU RAM** **VC** Company-Havildar-Major (Company Sergeant-Major) 4th Rajputana Rifles, Indian Army   Djebel Garli, Tunisia

POSTHUMOUS

Born:	10 May 1905 - Dhenod Village, Bhiwani Hissar District, Punjab, India
Died:	20 April 1943 aged 37. From numerous wounds received during his VC action near Enfidaville, Tunisia
Buried:	Sfax War Cemetery, Tunisia. 150 miles S. of Tunis. Plot H. Row C. Grave 5. Headstone shows age 38
Deed/Service:	19 - 20 April 1943. When the 5th Indian Infantry Brigade's advance was held up by machine-gun and mortar fire, he dashed forward with a tommy-gun and killed the post's occupants. He then went to the aid of his wounded company commander and was wounded but took over command and led his men in hand-to-hand fighting. Despite receiving a mortal wound, he continued rallying the men until he died
Commemoration:	i) Headstone

210

Gazette: 27 July 1943

1237   **LYELL The Lord, Charles Anthony   VC   Temporary Captain   1st Bn. Scots Guards**   Djebel Bou Aoukaz, Tunisia
POSTHUMOUS

Born:	14 June 1913 - Cadogan Gardens, S.W. London	**759**
Died:	27 April 1943 aged 29. Killed during his VC action at Dj Bou Arada, Tunisia	
Buried:	i) Bou Arada ii) Massicault War Cemetery, Tunisia. Near Borj-el-Amri, S.W. of Tunis. Plot V. Row H. Grave 5. Headstone	
Deed/Service:	22 - 27 April 1943. Throughout the period he led his company with great gallantry, leading charges under heavy fire on 22 and 23 April. On the 27th with four men, he led an attack on an enemy post consisting of an 88mm gun and two separate machine-gun pits. Having destroyed the crew of one gun, he leapt into the second pit with one man giving him covering fire, killing several of the crew before being killed himself	**Gazette: 12 August 1943**
Commemoration:	i) Headstone ii) Plaque in St. George's Church, Langton Matravers, Dorset iii) Plaque in St. Columbus Episcopal Church, Largs, Strathclyde iv) Name on Kirriemuir War Memorial, Kirriemuir Cemetery, Angus v) Plaque in St. Mary's Church, Kirriemuir	

1238   **ANDERSON John Thompson McKellar   VC DSO   Major   8th Bn. The Argyll & Sutherland Highlanders**   Longstop Hill, Tunisia

Born:	12 January 1918 - Hampstead, N.W. London	**27**
Died:	5 October 1943 aged 25. Killed in action six months after his VC action, leading his men near Termoli, Italy	
Buried:	Sangro River War Cemetery, Italy. 25 miles S. of Pescara, Abrizzi Province. Plot VIII. Row A. Grave 44. Headstone	
Deed/Service:	23 April 1943 (Acting Major) During the Eighth Army's second attempt to take Hill 290, known as Longstop or Christmas Hill, overlooking the vital Medjerda Valley, he led his men for five hours under intense enemy fire on the open sloping approach. With just 44 men left, he finally took the hill despite being wounded earlier, being the first man into three enemy machine-gun posts during the assault and taking 200 prisoners	**Gazette: 29 June 1943**
Commemoration:	i) Headstone ii) Name on War Memorial outside, and plaque inside Bagshot Parish Church, Surrey iii) Medals in Argyll & Sutherland Museum	

1239	SANDYS - CLARKE Wilwood Alexander VC Lieutenant The Loyal North Lancashire Regiment (now Queen's Lancashire Regt.)	Guirat el Atach, Tunisia

POSTHUMOUS

219

Born: 8 June 1919 - 3 Saunders Street, Southport, Lancashire. Some records show first name as WILLWARD

Died: 23 April 1943 aged 23. Killed during his VC action near the small settlement at Guirat el Atach, Tunisia

Buried: Massicault War Cemetery, Tunisia. S.W. of Tunis near Borj-el-Amri. Plot V. Row B. Grave 1. Headstone

Deed/Service: 23 April 1943. After his company were counter-attacked and almost wiped out, he was the sole remaining officer. Although wounded in the head he gathered a composite platoon and volunteered to attack a machine-gun post causing heavy casualties. Ordering his men to give him cover, he single-handed knocked-out the gun and two other posts, then led his platoon forward, but was killed within a few feet of the enemy

Gazette: 29 June 1943

Commemoration: i) Headstone ii) Name on family grave at Little Bollington Churchyard, Lymm, Cheshire iii) Name on lectern in Preston Parish Church Lancashire iv) Name on memorial in Southport Garden of Remembrance

1240	KENNEALLY John Patrick VC Company - Quartermaster - Sergeant Irish Guards	The Bou, Dj Arada, Tunisia

677

Born: 15 March 1921 - Alexandra Road, Balsall Heath, Birmingham

Deed/Service: 28 April 1943 (Lance-Corporal) During an attack on The Bou, a point of tactical importance that had to be taken for the final assault on Tunis, he charged alone down an open slope straight into the main German force, firing his Bren from his hip, unbalancing an enemy company which broke up in disorder. He repeated the act the next day and inflicted many casualties before being wounded, but refused to give up and kept up his fire

Gazette: 17 August 1943

Commemoration: i) Medals at The Irish Guards Museum

| 1241 | TRENT Leonard Henry | VC DFC | Group Captain | Royal New Zealand Air Force, attd. 48 Squadron, Royal Air Force | Over Amsterdam, Holland |

Born: 14 April 1915 - Nelson, South Island, New Zealand

1229

Died: 19 May 1986 aged 71, at the North Shore Hospital, Auckland, North Island, New Zealand

Cremated: 26 May at North Shore Crematorium. Ref: 42104/9005. No memorial plaque/tablet at Crematorium

Deed/Service: 3 May 1943 (Squadron Leader) Leading twelve Ventura bombers on a daylight raid on Amsterdam power station, they were attacked by large numbers of enemy fighters, reducing their force to just three aircraft by the time the target was in sight Trent's Ventura was the sole survivor Releasing his bombs, the plane was hit and all control was lost, sending it spinning to the ground near the Fokker Works, throwing Trent and his navigator clear. After interrogation he was sent to Stalag Luft III, where on the night of 24 March 1944 Trent was one of the 76 men in 'The Great Escape'

Gazette: 1 March 1946

Commemoration: i) Name on RAF Memorial in St. Clement Dane's Church, Central London ii) Memorial at HQ, Dunedin RSA, New Zealand

| 1242 | LINTON John Wallace | VC DSO DSC | Commander | Royal Navy | Service in HMS 'Turbulent'
POSTHUMOUS |

Born: 15 October 1905 - Claremont, Malpas, near Newport, Monmouthshire (now Gwent), Wales

746

Died: 23 March 1943 aged 37. Aboard HM Submarine 'Turbulent' with all hands, after striking a mine off Maddelina Harbour, Sardinia, Italy

Buried: Body not recovered. Name on The Portsmouth Naval Memorial, Hampshire. Panel 72. Column 3

Deed/Service: 1939 - March 1943. From the outbreak of the war until 'Turbulent's final patrol in the Mediterranean, he was responsible for sinking a cruiser, a destroyer, a U-Boat and 28 supply ships, some 100,000 tons in all and destroying three trains by gun fire. In his last year he spent 254 days at sea, half submerged. His ship was hunted thirteen times and had 250 depth charges aimed at her. The public death announcement was 4 May 1943

Gazette: 25 May 1943

Commemoration: i) Name on Portsmouth Naval Memorial ii) Portrait in Wardroom HMS 'Dolphin', Gosport, Hampshire iii) Name on memorial Newport (unconfirmed)

| 1243 | GIBSON Guy Penrose | VC DSO & Bar DFC & Bar | Wing Commander | 617 Squadron, Royal Air Force | Mohne and Eder Dams Germany |

Born: 12 August 1918 - Simla, India

Died: 19 September 1944 aged 26. Killed after a raid on Rheydt, Germany, when his Mosquito crashed at Bergen-op-Zoom, Holland, his 177th mission

448

Buried: Steenbergen-en-Kruisland R.C. Churchyard, Holland. 25 miles S. of Rotterdam. Headstone

Deed/Service: 16 - 17 May 1943. With nineteen Lancaster bombers, eight of which took part and returned from the raid, he led the famous 'Dam Busters Raid' on the Mohne and Eder Dams. Delivering the Barnes-Wallis designed rotating bombs from a few feet above the water and drawing enemy fire upon himself, the Mohne Dam was breached. Leading the remainder of his force to the Eder Dam and repeating the tactics, that too was destroyed

Gazette: 28 May 1943

Commemoration: i) Headstone ii) Propeller Memorial, Steenbergen Park iii) Gibsonstraat, Steenbergen iv) Memorial window, St. Edward's School, Oxford v) Name on RAF Memorial, St. Clement Dane's Church, Central London vi) A VC.10C Mk 1 XV102 named for him vii) Medals in Royal Air Force Museum

Hon. Captain Ganju Lama VC and Hon. Captain Gaje Ghale VC - 1995

| 1244 | GAJE GHALE | VC | Hon. Captain | 2nd Bn. 5th Royal Gurkha Rifles, Indian Army | Basha East Hill, Burma |

Born: 1 August 1918 - Barabak Village, Gorkha District, Nepal. Given name GYANTSO - misheard by recruiting officer

437

Deed/Service: 24 - 27 May 1943 (Havildar/Sergeant) When in charge of a platoon of young soldiers, he was tasked with taking a strong Japanese position in the Chin Hills. Leading assault after assault shouting the Gurkha's battle-cry despite being wounded in the chest, arm and leg, he spurred his men on and captured the position, then held and consolidated it under heavy fire. Only then did he follow orders and seek medical aid

Gazette: 30 September 1943

1245	**TRIGG Lloyd Allan** **VC DFC** **Flying Officer** Royal New Zealand Air Force, attd. 200 Squadron, Royal Air Force

Atlantic Ocean, off W. Africa
POSTHUMOUS
1232

Born: 6 June 1914 - Houhora, North Auckland, North Island, New Zealand
Died: 11 August 1943 aged 29. Killed during his VC action some 240 miles S.W. of Dakar, Senegal
Buried: Body not recovered. Name on the RAF Memorial, Valetta, Malta. Mem. G. Panel 12. Column 1
Deed/Service: 11 August 1943. When on a routine patrol in a Liberator with a crew of seven he sighted the surfaced U-Boat 468 and prepared to attack. During the approach the aircraft was hit many times and caught fire but he continued his bombing run-in without deviation. At fifty feet he released six depth charges before crashing into the sea 300 yards beyond the U-Boat which sank . The only survivors were seven Germans one of whom, Oberleutnant Schamong, was in the unique position of filing the only report detailing Trigg's outstanding courage
Commemoration: i) Name on RAF Memorial, Malta ii) Memorial at HQ, Dunedin RSA, New Zealand

Gazette: 2 November 1943

1246	**AARON Arthur Louis** **VC DFM** **Acting Flight Sergeant** 218 Squadron, Royal Air Force Volunteer Reserve

Over Turin, Italy
POSTHUMOUS
1

Born: 5 March 1922 - Gledhow, Leeds, Yorkshire
Died: 13 August 1943 aged 21. From wounds received in his VC action, at Bone Airfield Hospital, Tunisia
Buried: Bone War Cemetery, Tunisia (now Annaba). c.150 miles W. of Tunis on N. coast. Plot II. Row B. Grave 3. Headstone shows 14 August
Deed/Service: 12 August 1943. With a crew of six, his Stirling bomber was sent on a raid over Turin. After the bombs were dropped, they were attacked badly damaging the plane and severely wounding Aaron and several of the crew. He had a broken jaw and part of his face torn away with a punctured lung and his right arm useless and limp. Despite these injuries he managed to level the plane and flew to an Allied base at Bone, where he died in the hospital nine hours later. It transpired that they had been fired on by another Stirling from the same flight
Commemoration: i) Headstone ii) Display outside St. Mary's Church, Bexwell, Norfolk iii) Name on RAF Memorial, St. Clement Dane's, Central London
iv) Plaque in RAF Association Club, Salford, Lancashire v) Plaque outside and medals inside the City Art Gallery, Leeds

Gazette: 5 November 1943

1247   KELLIHER Richard   VC   Private   2nd/25th Bn. (Queensland) Australian Military Forces

North Nadzab, New Guinea now Papua New Guinea 670

Born:	1 September 1910 - Ballybeggan, Tralee, Co. Kerry, Ireland
Died:	28 January 1963 aged 52, at Heidelberg Repatriation Hospital, Melbourne, Victoria, Australia, following a stroke on 16 January
Buried:	Springvale Lawn Cemetery, Melbourne. Headstone
Deed/Service:	13 September 1943. When his platoon was under heavy fire from a concealed machine-gun post, inflicting heavy casualties and preventing their advance, he dashed forward and hurled two grenades at the crew. He returned to his section, seized a Bren gun and ran back to the post and killed-off the gunners. He then went out under heavy fire from another position to rescue a wounded comrade, bringing him to safety

Gazette: 30 December 1943

Commemoration: i) Headstone   ii) Kelliher Drive, Canberra, A.C.T.   iii) Medals and display at the Australian War Memorial, Canberra

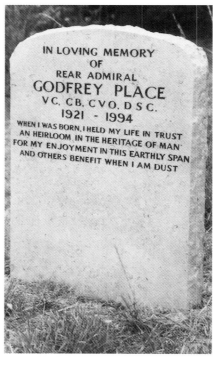

1248   PLACE Basil Charles Godfrey   VC CB CVO DSC   Rear Admiral   Royal Navy

Kaafiord, North Norway 991

Born:	19 July 1921 - Little Malvern, Worcestershire
Died:	27 December 1994 aged 73, at St. Bartholomew's Hospital, Holborn, Central London
Buried:	2 January 1995 at Corton Denham Churchyard, Dorset. Headstone
Deed/Service:	22 September 1943 (Lieutenant) Following numerous attempts to sink the German Battleship 'Tirpitz', six midget submarines were sent to attack her in Kaafiord. Travelling 1,000 miles from their base, Midget Submarines XE 6 and XE 7, commanded by 1249 Cameron and Place respectively, successfully negotiated a mine field, dodged nets, gun defences and enemy listening posts closing on 'Tirpitz'. Place's craft became entangled in 'Tirpitz's' net at 75 feet, but freed itself, dived and placed his charges. When the Amatol blew three minutes early, XE 7 became uncontrollable and under fire he ordered abandon ship. He was taken prisoner, but the damage to 'Tirpitz' was immense. She was later sunk by the RAF in 1944

Gazette: 22 February 1944

Commemoration: i) Headstone   ii) Portrait in RNSS 'MacKenzie', HMS 'Dolphin', Gosport, Hampshire   iii) Medals in The Imperial War Museum

1249 **CAMERON** Donald **VC** **Commander** **Royal Naval Reserve**

Born: 18 March 1916 - Carluke, Lanarkshire, Scotland
Died: 10 April 1961 aged 45, at the Royal Naval Hospital, Haslar, Hampshire
Cremated: Portchester Crematorium, Hampshire. Ashes scattered at sea off the Nab Tower, from HM Submarine 'Thule'
Deed/Service: 22 September 1943 (Lieutenant) With 1248 Place, carried out a daring raid on the German Battleship 'Tirpitz'. Commanding Midget Submarine XE 6 he also negotiated the mine fields, dodged nets, gun defences and listening posts in Kaafiord. After XE 6 had run aground, broken surface and became entangled in nets, the alarmed crew of 'Tirpitz' opened a tremendous fire on her, but he managed to release his 2 ton Amatol charges before scuttling XE 6. He and his crew were picked up by a picket boat from 'Tirpitz' and taken on board, where they waited to be interrogated trying to keep cool, aware of the charges below. Place was later captured and unusually but not uniquely they were given a joint VC citation **Gazette: 22 February 1944**
Commemoration: i) Cameron Close, Gosport, Hampshire

1250 **WRIGHT** Peter Harold **VC** **Company Sergeant - Major (Warrant Officer Class II)** **3rd Bn. Coldstream Guards**

Born: 10 August 1916 - Mettingham, near Bungay, Suffolk
Died: 5 April 1990 aged 73, at Ipswich, Suffolk
Buried: All Saint's Churchyard, Ashbocking, Suffolk. Grave No. 136 - 5.A. Headstone
Deed/Service: 25 September 1943. When his company attacked a steep hill, they were held up near the crest by heavy Spandau and mortar fire, killing most of its officers. He took charge and single handed silenced with grenades and bayonet three Spandau posts, then led his men to consolidate the position. He then beat off a counter-attack before bringing up much needed ammunition, disregarding the heavy fire and distributed it to the company **Gazette: 7 September 1944**
Commemoration: i) Headstone ii) Memorial in Helmingham Parish Church, Suffolk iii) Painting of his action in the Coldstream Guards Regimental HQ

| 1251 | REID William   VC   Acting Flight Lieutenant   61 Squadron, Royal Air Force Volunteer Reserve | Raid on Dusseldorf Germany 1036 |

Born: 21 December 1921 - 43 Main Street, Baillieston, Glasgow, Scotland

Deed/Service: 3 November 1943. Captaining a Lancaster bomber en-route to Dusseldorf, they were attacked as they crossed the Dutch coast damaging the plane and seriously wounding him in the head, shoulders and hands. He continued the mission and was attacked again, causing more damage to the aircraft, killing and badly wounding crew members and himself. He flew on without radio or navigational aids, dropping bombs on the target before turning for home. Weak from loss of blood and vitually without instruments, he landed the crippled plane safely

Gazette: 14 December 1943

Commemoration: i) Name on RAF Memorial, St. Clement Dane's Church, Aldwych, Central London

| 1252 | DERRICK Thomas Currie   VC DCM   Lieutenant   2nd/48th Bn. (South Australia) Australian Military Forces | Sattelberg, New Guinea now Papua new Guinea 324 |

Born: 20 March 1914 - Berri, Murray River, South Australia

Died: 23 May 1945 aged 31. From stomach wounds received in later action on 'Freda' Knoll, at a field hospital on Tarakan Island, Borneo

Buried: Labuan War Cemetery, Borneo. On a small island in Brunei Bay, N.W. Borneo, 2 miles from Victoria. Plot XXIV. Row A. Grave 9. Headstone

Deed/Service: 24 November 1943 (Sergeant) When his platoon was ordered to take a position near Sattelberg by storm, they were held up by intense fire from enemy posts. He volunteered to go out alone and silence the guns armed with grenades and so effective were his actions that the Japanese fled leaving their weapons, allowing his entire battalion to move forward capturing Sattelberg the following day. He had knocked-out ten posts in all

Gazette: 23 March 1944

Commemoration: i) Headstone ii) Memorial in the Garden of Remembrance, Centennial Park Crematorium, Adelaide, South Australia iii) Derrick Street Campbell, Canberra, A.C.T. iv) Medals and display at the Australian War Memorial, Canberra

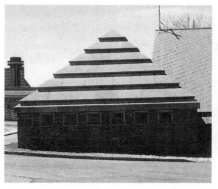

1253	TRIQUET Paul VC CD Major Royal 22nd Regiment, Canadian Army	Casa Beradi, Italy

Born: 2 April 1910 - Cabano, Quebec, Canada

Died: 8 August 1980 aged 70 in Quebec City. His health had deteriorated following three heart attacks, diabetes, gout, arthritis and near blindness

Cremated: Mount Royal Crematorium, Quebec. Ashes interred in the Royal 22nd Regimental Memorial, The Citadel, Quebec. Plaque

Deed/Service: 14 December 1943 (Captain) During the attack on Casa Beradi, all the other officers and half the men of his company had become casualties. He dashed forward and led his reduced force through all enemy resistance, until left with just seventeen men on the outskirts of the town. They then repulsed attack after attack due to his inspirational leadership and courage, holding on until relieved the following day by the remainder of the battalion

Commemoration: i) Plaque at The Citadel ii) Name on plaque at Trail Royal Canadian Legion Post, British Columbia iii) Medals with Royal 22nd Regiment Quebec

1233

Gazette: 6 March 1944

The Victoria Cross, Distinguished Service Order, Distinguished Flying Cross and campaign medals awarded to Wing Commander Guy Penrose Gibson (1243)

The Victoria Cross, Distinguished Flying Cross and campaign medals awarded to Flying Officer Lloyd Allan Trigg (1245)

The Victoria Cross and campaign medals awarded to Acting Flight Lieutenant William Reid (1251)

Chapter Eighteen

The Second World War 1944

No's 1254 - 1305

The Victoria Cross and campaign medals awarded to Corporal Richard Henry Burton (1297)

The Victoria Cross, Military Medal and campaign medals awarded to Company Sergeant - Major George Harold Eardley (1298)

1254　　HORWOOD Alec George　　VC DCM　　Lieutenant　　1st/6th Bn. Queen's Royal Regt. attd. 1st Bn. Northamptonshire Regt.　　Kyauchaw, Arakan, Burma
　　　　　　　　　　　　　　　　　　　　　　　　　　　　　　　　　　(now P.O.W. Royal Regt. and Royal Anglian Regt. respectively)　　now Myanmar

Born:	6 January 1914 - Deptford, South London	**POSTHUMOUS**
Died:	20 January 1944 aged 30. Mortally wounded during his VC action, leading an attack on a ridge near Kyauchaw, Burma	**598**
Buried:	Body not recovered. Name on the Rangoon Memorial, Burma. 20 miles N. of Rangoon (now Yangon). Face 4	
Deed/Service:	18 January 1944. Over a three day period, he performed gallantly during a three-pronged attack on a heavily defended Japanese position. On the	
	18th, he went to a forward observation post under heavy fire, bringing back valuable information. On the 19th, he established a forward post and	
	directed fire to support two attacks. The third day he volunteered to lead an attack, and was mortally wounded as they reached the enemy wire	**Gazette: 30 March 1944**
Commemoration:	i) Name on Rangoon Memorial ii) Memorial at Imphal War Cemetery, Assam	

1255　　MITCHELL George Allan　　VC　　Private　　The London Scottish (Gordon Highlanders)　　Damiano Ridge, Italy

		POSTHUMOUS
Born:	30 August 1911 - Highgate, North London	**877**
Died:	24 January 1944 aged 32. Killed in his VC action at Damiano Ridge, Italy	
Buried:	Minturno War Cemetery, Italy, also called Sessa Arunca New Military Cemetery. 40 miles N. of Naples. Plot III. Row H. Grave 19. Headstone	
Deed/Service:	23 - 24 January 1944. After the Allied landing at Anzio, his company were ordered to take a German position to get a foothold on the hills around	
	the town. When their advance was held up, he charged alone through heavy Spandau fire and killed the crew. He repeated this action at a second	
	post, killing six and taking twelve prisoner. A few moments later, one of the prisoners picked up a rifle and shot Mitchell through the head	**Gazette: 10 August 1944**
Commemoration:	i) Headstone ii) Medals and memorial at the George Mitchell School, Leyton, East London	

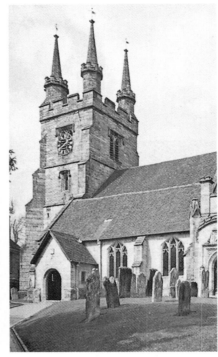

1256   **DE L'ISLE Viscount   (SIDNEY William Philip)   VC KG GCMG GCVO   Temporary Major**   **5th Bn. Grenadier Guards**   **Carroceto, Anzio, Italy**

1143

Born: 23 May 1909 - Chelsea, South West London

Died: 5 April 1991 aged 81, at the Kent and Sussex Hospital, Tunbridge Wells, Kent, after he collapsed at home at Penshurst Place, Kent

Buried: 11 April, in the family tomb at St. John The Baptist Church, Penshurst. Memorial over tomb

Deed/Service: 7 - 8 February 1944. Following the Allied landings at the Anzio Beach Head, the Germans held the high ground ringing the Beach, he successfully led an attack to clear a gully. He then led a second attack, when dashing forward he engaged the enemy with his Tommy-gun at point-blank range forcing a withdrawal. He was later wounded but refused treatment, encouraging his men until the newly taken position had been consolidated   **Gazette: 30 March 1944**

Commemoration: i) Memorial on tomb ii) Plaque inside St. John The Baptist's Church

1257   **HOEY Charles Ferguson   VC MC   Temporary Major**   **1st Bn. The Lincolnshire Regiment (now Royal Anglian Regiment)**   **Ngakkyedauk Pass, Burma now Myanmar**

POSTHUMOUS

577

Born: 29 March 1914 - Duncan, Vancouver Island, British Columbia, Canada

Died: 17 February 1944 aged 29. From wounds received during his VC action in the Mayu Range, near Arakan, Burma

Buried: i) On hill where he fell ii) Taukkyan War Cemetery, Burma. 20 miles N. of Rangoon (Yangon). Plot XII. Row H. Grave 2. Headstone (See Map - G)

Deed/Service: 16 February 1944. When his company came under intense machine-gun fire, he led his men forward to silence it, despite wounds to the head and leg. Firing a Bren gun from the hip, he was first to enter the strong point where he killed all the occupants before falling mortally wounded   **Gazette: 18 May 1944**

Commemoration: i) Headstone ii) Name on War Memorial, Cowichigan, Vancouver iii) Primary School and Memorial Park named for him in Duncan iv) Memorial in Soldiers' Chapel, Lincoln Cathedral v) Plaque in Trail Royal Canadian Legion Post, British Columbia vi) Medals in Lincolnshire Regimental Museum

1258	CAIRNS George Albert VC Lieutenant	The Somerset Light Infantry, attd. The South Staffordshire Regiment (now The Light Infantry and The Staffordshire Regiment respectively)	Henu Block, Burma now Myanmar POSTHUMOUS 170

Born: 12 December 1913 - Sidcup, Kent

Died: 19 March 1944 aged 30. Died from wounds received during his VC action, after a sword had severed his arm at Henu Block, Burma

Buried: Taukkyan War Cemetery, Burma. 20 miles N. of Rangoon (now Yangon). Plot VI. Row A. Grave 5. Headstone (See Map - G)

Deed/Service: 13 March 1944. As part of Orde Wingate's Chindit force, he and his men were landed by glider at 'Broadway', near Henu Block. Attacking a hill top position, his left arm was hacked off by a Japanese officer, but he killed the man and picking up the sword continued to lead his men, killing and wounding many of the enemy before he collapsed. His action so inspired his men, that the enemy were routed, a rare occurrence at that time

Gazette: 20 May 1949

Commemoration: i) Headstone ii) Name on memorial in Garrison Church, Whittington Barracks, Lichfield, Staffordshire iii) Memorial headstone outside and plaque inside, St. Mary The Virgin's, Brighstone, Isle of Wight, Hampshire iv) Name on Chindit Memorial, Victoria Embankment, London v) Memorial at the Somerset Light Infantry Museum, Taunton, Somerset vi) Medals in The Staffordshire Regimental Museum

Destroyed bridge on the Maungdaw to Buthidaung road

1259	NAND SINGH VC Jemadar (First Lieutenant) 1st/11th Sikh Regiment, Indian Army	Buthidaung, Arakan, Burma now Myanmar 912

Born: 24 September 1914 - Bahadur Village, Patiala State, Punjab, India

Died: 12 December 1947 aged 32, at Uri, Jammu and Kashmir, India

Cremated: 12 December at Uri. Indian High Commission unable to confirm if memorial exists

Deed/Service: 11 - 12 March 1944 (Acting Naik/Corporal) When ordered to recapture a position gained by the enemy, he led his section up a steep knife-edge ridge, on the Maungdaw to Buthidaung Road. Under very heavy machine-gun and rifle fire, he was wounded in the thigh, but led his men on and captured the first trench, he then went forward alone capturing the second and third trenches, despite further wounds to face and shoulder

Gazette: 6 June 1944

Commemoration:

1260　　BARTON Cyril Joe　VC　Pilot Officer　578 Squadron, Royal Air Force Volunteer Reserve

Nuremburg Raid, Germany
POSTHUMOUS
58

Born: 　　5 June 1921 - Elveden, Suffolk

Died: 　　31 March 1944 aged 22. From injuries received during his VC action after his plane crashed at Ryhope, Co. Durham

Buried: 　　6 April at Bonner Hill Road Cemetery, Kingston-upon-Thames, Surrey. Class C Consecrated Section. Grave 6700. Headstone

Deed/Service: 　30 March 1944. When his Halifax bomber was severely damaged en-route to Nuremburg, a mistaken message resulted in three of his crew baling out including the navigator and wireless operator. Despite the damage, he bombed the target before heading home, but reaching the English coast low on fuel, he ordered his crew to take-up crash positions as he narrowly avoided hitting a village before crash landing nearby

Gazette: 27 June 1944

Commemoration: i) Headstone ii) Name on Ryhope War Memorial iii) Name on RAF Memorial, St. Clement Dane's Church, Central London iv) Barton Green and Barton Hall, New Malden, Surrey v) Portrait in New Malden Library vi) Plaque in New Malden Parish Church vii) Medals in RAF Museum

1261　　ABDUL HAFIZ　VC　Jemadar (First Lieutenant)　9th Jat Infantry, Indian Army

Waken Hill, Imphal, India
POSTHUMOUS
2

Born: 　　4 September 1915 - Kalanaur Village, Rohtak District, Punjab, India.

Died: 　　6 April 1944 aged 28. Killed during his VC action at Waken Hill, near Imphal, India

Buried: 　　Imphal Indian Army War Cemetery, Manipur State, India. One mile from main Imphal War Cemetery. Plot III. Row Q. Grave 2. Headstone

Deed/Service: 　6 April 1944. When ordered to lead his platoon and attack a prominent enemy position, the only approach was across a bare slope and then up a steep cliff, both swept by fire. Leading the way he killed several Japanese, pressing on regardless of the intense fire which finally cut him down. By his action he routed a vastly superior numerical force and captured a most important position

Gazette: 27 July 1944

Commemoration: i) Headstone

1262 **HARMAN John Pennington   VC   Lance - Corporal   4th Bn. The Queen's Own Royal West Kent Regt. (now P.O.W. Royal Regt.)**   Kohima, Assam, India
POSTHUMOUS

Born:	20 July 1914 - Beckenham, Kent
Died:	9 April 1944 aged 29. Killed during his VC action at Kohima, India
Buried:	Kohima War Cemetery, India. 60 miles N. of Imphal. Plot VIII. Row E. Grave 3. Headstone
Deed/Service:	8 - 9 April 1944. When the 3,500 men of the Kohima garrison were surrounded and under heavy attack from 15,000 Japanese, his platoon came under fire from a machine-gun post fifty yards away. Going forward alone, he threw a grenade into the position which annihilated it. On the 9th, he again went out alone, and charged a party of Japanese who were digging in nearby and wiped them out, but was killed by a burst of machine-gun fire returning to our lines
Commemoration:	i) Headstone ii) Memorial in St. Peter and St. Paul's Church, Chaldon, Surrey iii) Memorial on cliffs of Lundy Island, Bristol Channel iv) Medals at Queen's Own Royal West Kent Regimental Museum

532

Gazette: 22 June 1944

1263 **JACKSON Norman Cyril   VC   Warrant Officer   106 Squadron, Royal Air Force Volunteer Reserve**   Schweinfurt Raid, Germany

Born:	8 April 1919 - Ealing, West London
Died:	26 March 1994 aged 74, at his home in Burton's Road, Hampton Hill, Middlesex
Buried:	6 April at Percy Road Cemetery, Twickenham, Middlesex. Section O. Grave 181. Headstone
Deed/Service:	26 April 1944 (Sergeant) Following a successful bombing raid on Schweinfurt, his Lancaster was attacked by an enemy fighter and fire broke out. With the plane flying at 200 mph at 20,000 feet, he clipped on a parachute and climbed out onto the wing. Holding on with one hand, he tried to extinguish the fire and as the flames died down he turned to crawl back but felt a searing pain in his legs and back as the fighter returned and opened fire. With both hands burnt he lost his grip and was swept from the wing, his damaged chute trailing behind. Breaking an ankle on landing, he was paraded through a village and stoned by the inhabitants before receiving treatment to his many wounds
Commemoration:	i) Headstone ii) Name on RAF Memorial, St. Clement Dane's Church, Central London

626

Gazette: 26 October 1945

| 1264 | RANDLE John Neil VC Temporary Captain | 2nd Bn. The Royal Norfolk Regiment (now Royal Anglian Regiment) | Kohima Ridge, India POSTHUMOUS 1019 |

Born: 22 December 1917 - Benares, India
Died: 6 May 1944 aged 26. Killed during his VC action at Kohima, India
Buried: Kohima War Cemetery, India. 60 miles N. of Imphal. Plot II. Row C. Grave 8. Headstone
Deed/Service: 4 - 6 May 1944. During an attack on a Japanese position on Kohima Ridge, he took command of a company despite being wounded, inspiring his men with his leadership. Leading another attack on an enemy bunker on the 6th, he realised its importance and charged ahead single-handed, being mortally wounded just as he reached it. He threw a grenade through the bunker slit then sealed it with his body
Commemoration: i) Headstone ii) Name on the Regimental Memorial, Norwich Cathedral, Norfolk iii) Memorial plaque in St. Peter's Church, Petersham, Surrey iv) British 2nd Division Monument on Jail Hill, Kohima v) Plaque in Britannia Court, Norwich vi) Randle Green, Norwich

Gazette: 12 December 1944

| 1265 | KAMAL RAM VC Hon. Major 8th Punjab Regiment, Indian Army (later The Rajpur Regiment) | Near Monte Cassino, Italy 664 |

Born: 17 December 1924 - Bhalupura Village, Karauli State, India
Died: 1 July 1982 aged 57, at his home in Bholupura
Cremated: 1 July at Sawai Madhopur, Rajasthan, India. Indian High Commission unable to verify if memorial exists
Deed/Service: 12 May 1944 (Sepoy/Private) During the advance on Monte Cassino his company were being held up by four enemy machine-gun posts near the River Gari on the Gustav Line. As their objective was essential, he volunteered to silence them and under heavy fire he attacked the first two and put them out of action. With a havildar he then went on and destroyed the third, his bravery unquestionably saving a critical situation
Commemoration:

Gazette: 27 July 1944

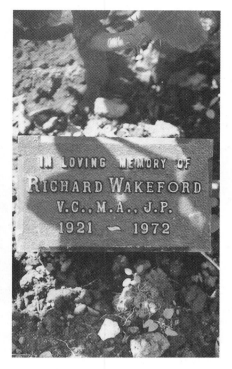

1266	WAKEFORD Richard VC Major 2nd/4th Bn. The Hampshire Regiment (now The Royal Hampshire Regiment)	Rapido River, Cassino, Italy

Born: 23 July 1921 - Kensington, West London — **1257**

Died: 27 August 1972 aged 51, at Leatherhead, Surrey

Cremated: 1 September at Randall's Park Crematorium, Leatherhead. Ref: 12584. Ashes and plaque in Crematorium's Garden of Remembrance

Deed/Service: 13 May 1944 (T/Captain) When held up during an attack on high ground, accompanied by his orderly and armed with a revolver, he went forward and killed several of the enemy and took twenty prisoners. The following day his company came under heavy fire when attacking a hill, but he pressed home the attack despite wounds to his face and arms. He was then wounded in both legs, but reached and consolidated the position **Gazette: 13 July 1944**

Commemoration: i) Plaque at Crematorium, with a smaller one on the site of ashes ii) Medals with the Haberdashers Company

1267	JEFFERSON Francis Arthur VC Lance - Corporal 2nd Bn. The Lancashire Fusiliers (now Royal Regiment of Fusiliers)	Monte Cassino, Italy

Born: 18 August 1921 - Sunderland Terrace, Ulverston, Lancashire — **636**

Died: 4 September 1982 aged 61. When in deep depression after his VC had been stolen, he threw himself under a train, dying in Bolton Infirmary

Cremated: Overdale Crematorium, Bolton, Lancashire. Ashes scattered in the Memorial Garden at Wellington Barracks, Bury. Memorial plaque

Deed/Service: 16 May 1944 (Fusilier) During the attack on the Gustav Line, the leading company of his battalion had to dig in without protection when the enemy counter-attacked with infantry and tanks. On his own initiative he seized a PIAT gun and, running forward under a hail of bullets, destroyed the leading tank. As he reloaded to attack a second tank the enemy withdrew, at which time our own tanks arrived and the Germans were thrown back **Gazette: 13 July 1944**

Commemoration: i) Plaque at Wellington Barracks ii) Plaque in Coronation Hall, Ulverston iii) Jefferson Street, Ulverston

1268   **MAHONY** John Keefer   **VC**   **Major**   **The Westmister Regiment (Motor), Canadian Infantry Corps**   Melfa Bridgehead, Italy

Born: 30 June 1911 - New Westminster, British Columbia, Canada   824

Died: 16 December 1990 aged 79, at St. Mary's Hospital, London, Ontario, after a long battle with Parkinson's disease

Cremated: Mount Pleasant Crematorium, London. No memorial plaque at Crematorium

Deed/Service: 24 May 1944. During the Battle of the Liri Valley, he and his company were ordered to establish a bridgehead over the River Melfa, which he accomplished and held for five hours under heavy fire. Refusing medical aid after receiving wounds to the head and legs, he continued to direct the defence, despite being the target of enemy gunners who were aware of his conspicuous leadership and inspiration   **Gazette: 13 July 1944**

Commemoration: i) Plaque at the Trail Royal Canadian Legion Post, British Columbia

1269   **ROGERS** Maurice Albert Windham   **VC MM**   **Sergeant**   **2nd Bn. The Wiltshire Regiment**   Anzio, Italy

    (now Royal Gloucestershire, Berkshire and Wiltshire Regiment)   **POSTHUMOUS**

Born: 17 July 1919 - Bristol, Avon   1077

Died: 3 June 1944 aged 24. Killed in his VC action near Anzio, Italy

Buried: Beach Head War Cemetery, Anzio, Italy. 30 miles S. of Rome. Plot X. Row D. Grave 8. Headstone

Deed/Service: 3 June 1944. A carrier platoon was held up by barbed wire and intense machine-gun fire 70 yards from its objective, when he jumped down with a Thompson gun and crashed through the wire. He then ran across a mine-field and accounted for two of the enemy posts and so inspired his men, now 100 yards behind, that they joined in the assault. Although wounded in the leg, he continued to advance until killed at point blank range   **Gazette: 10 August 1944**

Commemoration: i) Headstone ii) Plaque at the Rogers Estate, Bethnal Green, East London iii) Medals/display at The Duke of Wellington's Regimental Museum

1270   **HOLLIS Stanley Elton**   **VC**   **Company Sergeant - Major**   **6th Bn. The Green Howards (Alexandra Princess of Wales's Own)**   **Normandy Beaches, France**
D-Day Landings
583

Born:	21 September 1912 - Middlesbrough, Yorkshire (now Cleveland)
Died:	8 February 1972 aged 59, at Liverton Mines, near Loftus, Cleveland
Buried:	Acklam Cemetery, Middlesbrough. Grave 260 on Lawn Section. Headstone
Deed/Service:	6 June 1944. Following the D-Day landings, he went with his company commander to check two pill-boxes. When twenty yards away a machine-gun opened fire from one of them. He rushed at it with his Sten gun and threw a grenade taking all but five Germans inside prisoner. He then took the second box along with 26 prisoners saving his company from being fired on from the rear. Later at Crepon, he put a field gun and its crew out of action before going out under heavy fire to rescue two of his men, among many he saved by his actions throughout the day
Commemoration:	i) Headstone ii) Bronze statue of him at Crepon iii) 'Hollis VC' pub in Middlesbrough (since demolished) iv) Medals at Green Howards Museum

Gazette: 17 August 1944

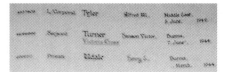

1271   **TURNER Hanson Victor**   **VC**   **A/Sergeant**   **1st Bn. The West Yorkshire Regiment (now The P.O.W. Regiment)**   **Ningthoutong, Burma**
now Myanmar
POSTHUMOUS
1238

Born:	17 July 1910 - Andover, Hampshire
Died:	7 June 1944 aged 34. Killed during his VC action at Ningthoutong Kha Khunog, Burma
Buried:	Imphal War Cemetery, Imphal, Manipur State, North East India. Plot VI. Row B. Grave 7. Headstone shows age 33
Deed/Service:	6 - 7 June 1944. After the Kohima siege was broken, the Japanese moved south to reinforce Imphal, but were held up by his Regiment. Forced to give ground, Turner's platoon pulled back and reformed, where the enemy tried repeatedly to dislodge them. On his own initiative he went forward alone armed with grenades using them to great effect. He was killed throwing a grenade
Commemoration:	i) Headstone ii) Name in Roll of Honour Book, York Minster iii) Medals at The Duke of Wellington's Regimental Museum

Gazette: 17 August 1944

1272 **ALLMAND Michael   VC   A/Captain   Indian Armoured Corps, attd. 6th Gurkha Rifles, Indian Army**

Near Myitkyina, Burma
now Myanmar
POSTHUMOUS
22

Born:	22 August 1923 - Golders Green, North West London
Died:	24 June 1944 aged 20. From wounds received in his VC action at Mogaung Railway Bridge, Burma
Buried:	Taukkyan War Cemetery, Burma. 20 miles North of Rangoon (now Yangon). Plot XIII. Row A. Grave 4. Headstone (See Map G)
Deed/Service:	11 - 23 June 1944. During operations in the Kachin Hills, near the Chinese border, his platoon came under fire attacking the Pin Hmi Road Bridge. He charged forward alone and killed three of the enemy inspiring his men to capture the position. On 13 June he again rushed ahead of his men and captured an enemy machine-gun on a ridge near Myitkyina. He was wounded on 23 June charging an enemy gun near Mogaung
Commemoration:	i) Headstone ii) Name on Chindit Memorial, Victoria Embankment, Central London iii) Old stone building rebuilt to his memory on a hill above Oldstead, Yorkshire, between Kilburn and Ampleforth College iv) Display at Gurkha Museum v) Medals with 1st Royal Gurkha Rifles

Gazette: 26 October 1944

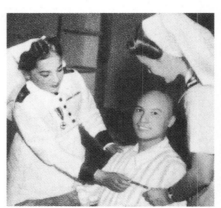

1273 **GANJU LAMA   VC MM   Subadar (Captain)   1st Bn. 7th Gurkha Rifles, Indian Army**

Ninthoukhong, Burma
now Myanmar
438

Born:	22 July 1924 - Sangmo, Busty, Sikkim, India
Deed/Service:	12 June 1944 (Rifleman) As his company were attempting to check an enemy advance, they came under heavy machine-gun and tank fire. Taking his PIAT gun, he crawled forward to within thirty yards of the enemy tanks and knocked out two of them. Despite a broken wrist and serious wounds to both hands he engaged a third tank crew who were trying to escape. Only when he had accounted for them all did he seek medical aid
Commemoration:	i) Display at the Gurkha Museum

Gazette: 7 September 1944

1274   **MYNARSKI Andrew Charles   VC   Pilot Officer   419 Squadron, Royal Canadian Air Force**

Over Cambrai, France
POSTHUMOUSLY
910

Born: 14 October 1916 - Winnipeg, Manitoba, Canada
Died: 13 June 1944 aged 27. From burns and injuries received during his VC action, near Cambrai, France
Buried: Meharicourt Communal Cemetery Extension, near Cambrai, France. British Plot. Grave 20. Headstone (See Map A - 29)
Deed/Service: 12 June 1944 (Warrant Officer II) During a rare low-level attack by Lancaster bombers on the marshalling yards at Cambrai, he was mid-upper gunner on the seven man crew. Before the target was reached, a Junkers 88 fighter attacked their bomber setting it alight. Ordered to bale out, he saw the rear gunner was trapped and made his way through the flames to try and free his comrade, but his efforts were in vain. With his own clothing ablaze he jumped from the escape hatch and fell to earth like a human torch and died soon after from his horrific injuries   **Gazette: 11 October 1946**
Commemoration: i) Headstone ii) Mynarski Lakes, Manitoba (Lat.56.10'/Long.99.12') iii) Mynarski High School, Winnipeg iv) Name on RAF Memorial, St.Clement Dane's Church, London v) Plaque at Royal Canadian Legion Post, Trail, British Columbia vi) Medals at Air Command Heritage Museum, Winnipeg

1275   **SUKANAIVALU Sefanaia   VC   Corporal   3rd Bn. Fijian Infantry Regiment**

Bougainville, Solomons
POSTHUMOUS
1193

Born: 1918 - Yathata Island, Fiji
Died: 23 June 1944 aged 26. Killed during his VC action at Bougainville, Solomon Islands, South West Pacific Ocean
Buried: Rabual War Cemetery, Bita Paka, New Britain, Papua New Guinea. 30 miles S. of Rabual. Plot V. Row B. Grave 13. Headstone
Deed/Service: 23 June 1944. Following an engagement with the Japanese, he crawled out under fire and rescued two wounded men and was about to rescue a third when he was seriously wounded in the groin and thigh and unable to move his lower body. Attempts to rescue him resulted in failure and as his men would not leave him as long as he was still alive, he deliberately raised himself in full view of the enemy and was riddled with bullets   **Gazette: 2 November 1944**
Commemoration: i) Headstone ii) Memorial in Suva Civic Buildings, Fiji

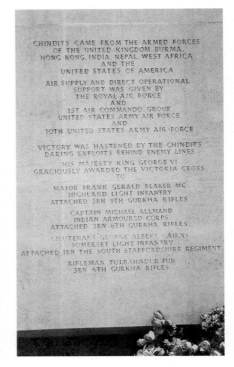

1276   **TULBAHADUR PUN**   **VC**   **Warrant Officer Class I**   **3rd Bn. 6th Gurkha Rifles, Indian Army**

Mogaung, Burma
now Myanmar
1235

Born: 23 March 1923 - Banduk Village, Gulmi Tehsal, W. of Katmandu, Parbat District, Nepal

Deed/Service: 23 June 1944 (Rifleman) During an attack on a rail bridge at Mogaung, his section was wiped out with the exception of three men, soon to be just himself when the other two were wounded. Armed with a Bren gun he charged an enemy position alone, killing three, putting five to flight and capturing two light machine-guns with ammunition. He then gave accurate support fire, enabling the rest of his platoon to gain their objective

Gazette: 9 November 1944

Commemoration: i) Name on the Chindit Memorial, Victoria Embankment, Central London   ii) Medals with the 1st Royal Gurkha Rifles

1277   **HORNELL David Ernest**   **VC**   **Flight Lieutenant**   **162 Squadron, Royal Canadian Air Force**

North Atlantic patrol
POSTHUMOUS
596

Born: 26 January 1910 - Mimico, Ontario, Canada

Died: 24 June 1944 aged 34. Died in a dinghy, north of the Shetland Islands, North Atlantic, following his VC action

Buried: Lerwick New Cemetery (in hospital grounds), Knab Road, Shetland Islands. Upper Ground 17. RP Terrace 7B. Grave 17. Headstone

Dee/Service: 24 June 1944. During a sea patrol with a seven man crew aboard a Catalina aircraft, a German submarine U-1225 was sighted following a ten hour patrol. Badly damaged as they flew into attack, Hornell roared in at fifty feet and released his depth charges, sinking the U-Boat almost immediately. With superhuman effort he managed to land the blazing aircraft in the heavy swell, the crew taking it in turns in the sea as the four-man dinghy could not hold them all. When rescued 21 hours later, Hornell was blinded and weak from exposure and died soon after

Gazette: 28 July 1944

Commemoration: i) Headstone   ii) Name on the RAF Memorial, St. Clement Dane's Church, Central London   iii) Plaque at Royal Canadian Legion Post Trail, British Columbia, Canada   iv) Medals at Air Command Heritage Museum, Winnipeg, Manitoba

1278	NETRABAHADUR THAPA VC Acting Subadar (Captain) 2nd Bn. 5th Royal Gurkha Rifles, Indian Army	Bishenpur, Burma now Myanmar

Born: 8 January 1916 - Rahu Village, Lamjung, Nepal. Name also recorded as NETRA BAHADUR THAPA

Died: 26 June 1944 aged 28. Killed during his VC action on a small hill post near Bishenpur, Burma

POSTHUMOUS
921

Buried: Has no known grave - name on The Rangoon Memorial, Burma. 20 miles N. of Rangoon (now Yangon). Face 63

Deed/Service: 25 - 26 June 1944. Was in command of a small isolated hill post when the enemy attacked in force. The men, inspired by his example, held their ground and beat the enemy off, but casualties were heavy. When reinforced, these men too became casualties, but he retrieved the ammunition and took the offensive with grenades and kukris, until he was killed. His body was recovered the following day

Gazette: 12 October 1944

Commemoration: i) Name on The Rangoon Memorial

1279	AGANSING RAI VC MM Hon. Lieutenant 2nd Bn. 5th Royal Gurkha Rifles, Indian Army	Bishenpur, Burma now Myanmar

Born: 24 April 1920 - Amsara Village, Chisankkhu, Okhaldunga District, Nepal

11

Deed/Service: 26 June 1944 (Naik - Corporal) Led his section in an attack on one of two posts recently taken by the Japanese, threatening communication lines. Under withering fire they charged a gun post where he killed three of the crew, before rushing a second machine-gun post, where he killed three. He then took a bunker single-handed, killing all four occupants, by which time the enemy were totally demoralized and fled the area

Gazette: 5 October 1944

Commemoration:

| 1280 | BLAKER Frank Gerald | VC MC | T/Major | The Highland Light Infantry, attd. 3rd Bn. 9th Gurkha Rifles, Indian Army | Taunghi, Burma |
| | | | | (now Royal Highland Fusiliers) | now Myanmar |

POSTHUMOUS
98

Born: 8 May 1920 - Kasauli, Punjab, India. Some records state he was born in Meiktila, Burma
Died: 9 July 1944 aged 24. From wounds when being evacuated following his VC action, above Taunghi (Taunggyi), Burma
Buried: Taukkyan War Cemetery, Burma. 20 miles North of Rangoon (now Yangon). Plot VI. Row E. Grave 2. Headstone (See Map G)
Deed/Service: 9 July 1944. During an advance on a vital hill top position overlooking a major Japanese base at Taunghi, his company were held up by machine-gun fire. In spite of being severely wounded in his arm, he went ahead of his men and charged the machine-gun posts single-handed. He was hit by three rounds through his body, but continued to cheer on his men while lying on the ground, inspiring them to storm and capture the objective **Gazette: 26 September 1944**
Commemoration: i) Headstone ii) Name on Chindit Memorial, Victoria Embankment

| 1281 | YESHWANT GHADGE | VC | Naik (Corporal) | 5th Mahratta Light Infantry, Indian Army | Upper Tiber Valley, Italy |

POSTHUMOUS
1340

Born: 16 November 1921 - Palasgaon Village, near Amnechiwadi, Kolaba District, Bombay, India
Died: 10 July 1944 aged 22. From wounds following his VC action in the Upper Tiber Valley, Italy
Buried: Has no known grave - name on The Cassino Memorial, Italy. 75 miles S.E. of Rome. Panel 17. Name shown as YASHWANT GHATGE
Deed/Service: 10 July 1944. When a rifle section under his command came under heavy machine-gun fire at close range, he was the only man not to be killed or wounded. Throwing a grenade at the enemy gun position, which knocked out the gun and the firer, he rushed it and shot another crew member, then with no time to re-load he clubbed to death the two remaining crew. As he finished his task, he was mortally wounded by a sniper **Gazette: 2 November 1944**
Commemoration: i) Name on The Cassino Memorial

1282   CRUICKSHANK John Alexander   VC   Flight Lieutenant   210 Squadron, Royal Air Force Volunteer Reserve

Northern Waters, near
Arctic Circle 68.21N - 05.56E
280

Born: 20 May 1920 - Aberdeen, Scotland

Deed/Service: 17 - 18 July 1944 (Flying Officer) During his 48th mission, flying with a ten man crew aboard a Catalina flying boat, a German submarine, U-347, from the Arctic flotilla was sighted. Nosing toward his target at fifty feet, the Catalina's depth charges failed to release, causing him to turn for a second attack. As he did so the plane was hit by flak, killing one of the crew and wounding others, but he released a stick of six depth charges which sank U-347 immediately. It was then discovered that Cruickshank had received 72 wounds as he made the attack, without telling his crew. After treatment, he survived the six hour flight to their base in Sullum Floe, Shetland Islands and helped to land the damaged aircraft

Gazette: 1 September 1944

Commemoration: i) Name on RAF Memorial, St. Clement Dane's Church, Aldwych, Central London

1283   CHESHIRE Geoffrey Leonard   VC OM DSO & 2 Bars DFC   Group Captain   Royal Air Force Volunteer Reserve

Flying Duties 1940 - 1944
LORD CHESHIRE
209

Born: 7 September 1917 - Chester, Cheshire

Died: 31 July 1992 aged 74, at the Sue Ryder Home, Cavendish, Suffolk from motor neurone disease

Buried: Cavendish Churchyard, opposite Cavendish Parish Church, near Sudbury, Suffolk. Headstone

Deed/Service: June 1940 to July 1944. From his first operational sortie on 9 June 1940 with 102 Squadron, through to his 100th mission at the conclusion of his fourth tour, he displayed the courage and determination of an exceptional leader. In four years of fighting against a bitter enemy, he maintained a standard of outstanding achievement, the result of superb planning and execution together with a total contempt for danger

Gazette: 8 September 1944

Commemoration: i) Headstone ii) Established the Cheshire Foundation Homes for the incurably sick iii) Name on the RAF Memorial, St. Clement Dane's Church, Central London iv) Plaque in Horndean Brewery, Hampshire v) Subject of many books on his life and works vi) Medals in Imperial War Museum

1284   **BAZALGETTE Ian Willoughby   VC DFC   A/Squadron Leader   635 Squadron, Royal Air Force Volunteer Reserve**   **Trossy St. Maximin, France**

Born:	19 October 1918 - Calgary General Hospital, Alberta, Canada	**POSTHUMOUS**
Died:	4 August 1944 aged 25. Killed during his VC action at Senantes, France	**64**
Buried:	i) By local Resistance near crash site ii) 8 October 1944 in Senantes Churchyard. 13 miles N.W. of Beauvais. Military Grave No.1. Headstone	
Deed/Service:	4 August 1944. Was the pilot of a Lancaster bomber on a daylight raid on a V1 storage depot. Nearing the target his aircraft came under heavy anti-aircraft fire, setting the fuselage alight and both starboard engines out of action. In spite of this, he marked the target before the severely burning aircraft turned away in a slow spin. Gaining some control, he flew for thirty miles before ordering the crew to bale out. Landing in a field, the plane immediately exploded killing him and two other crew members	**Gazette: 17 August 1945**
Commemoration:	i) Headstone ii) Marker stone at crash site iii) Memorial at St. Mary's Church, Bexwell, Suffolk iv) Bazalgette Mountain, Jasper National Park, Alberta v) Name on RAF Memorial, St. Clement Dane's Church, Central London vi) Plaque at Trial Canadian Legion Post, British Columbia vii) Painting at New Malden Library, Surrey viii) Avro Lancaster FM 159 named for him ix) Medals at the Royal Air Force Museum	

1285   **BATES Sidney   VC   Corporal   The Royal Norfolk Regiment (now The Royal Anglian Regiment)**   **Near Sourdeval, France**

		POSTHUMOUS
Born:	14 June 1921 - Camberwell, South East London	**61**
Died:	8 August 1944 aged 23. From wounds received during his VC action near Sourdeval, France	
Buried:	Bayeux War Cemetery, Normandy, France. 1 mile S. of Bayeux. Plot XX. Row E. Grave 19. Headstone	
Deed/Service:	6 August 1944. When his regiment were holding a position near Sourdeval village, they were attacked in strength by the German 10th SS Panzer Division. Moving his section to an advantageous position, they were halted by mortar and machine-gun fire, seizing a light machine-gun he rushed forward, forcing the Germans to withdraw. Already wounded twice, a third mortar wound proved fatal, but his actions saved a critical situation	**Gazette: 2 November 1944**
Commemoration:	i) Headstone ii) Bates Green and Bates Green Health Centre in Norwich, Norfolk iii) Medals with The Royal Norfolk Regiment	

1286   JAMIESON David Auldgo   VC CVO   Major   The Royal Norfolk Regiment (now The Royal Anglian Regiment)   River Orne Bridgehead
Grimbosq, France
631

Born: 1 October 1920 - Thornham, near King's Lynn, Norfolk

Deed/Service: 7 - 8 August 1944 (Captain) Was in command of a company of less than 100 men which had established a bridgehead over the River Orne. As Panzer units struggled to take the position, he held out for 36 hours of bitter and close fighting, repulsing seven counter-attacks and inflicticting heavy casualties. He was wounded in the eye and left arm, but refused to be evacuated, reorganising his men when all other officers had become casualties. Often in the open, he showed superb leadership and great personal bravery and was largely responsible for the position being held   **Gazette: 26 October 1944**

Commemoration: i) Name on plaque in Britannia Court, Norwich, Norfolk ii) Jamieson Place, Norwich iii) High Sheriff of Norfolk 1980

1287   WATKINS The Rt. Hon. Sir Tasker   VC GBE   Major   1/5th Bn. The Welch Regiment (now Royal Regiment of Wales)   Barfour, Battle of Falaise
Normandy, France
1279

Born: 18 November 1918 - 19 Shinrig Road, Nelson, Glamorgan , Wales

Deed/Service: 16 August 1944 (Lieutenant) When ordered to cut rail lines at Barfour, part of the Allied plan to close the 'Falaise Gap' through which German units were withdrawing, his company came under murderous machine-gun fire when crossing a booby trapped corn field to reach their objective. As the only officer left, he led a bayonet charge of thirty men and wiped out fifty of Hitler's prestigious 12th SS Youth Division. Cut-off and without radio contact, he did not receive the order to withdraw and decided to order his men to scatter. Crossing the same corn field, he personally charged and silenced an enemy machine-gun post before leading his men back to safety, his superb leadership influencing the course of the battle   **Gazette: 2 November 1944**

Commemoration: i) Tasker Watkins House at Morfa T.A. Centre, Swansea ii) Deputy Chief Justice of England 1988-1993 iii) Privy Councillor 1980

1288	CURRIE David Vivian VC CD Lieutenant - Colonel	29th Canadian Armoured Reconnaissance Regiment	St. Lambert-sur-Dives
		(The South Alberta Regiment) Canadian Armoured Corps	Battle of Falaise, France

Born: 8 July 1912 - Sutherland, Saskatchewan, Canada

290

Died: 24 June 1986 aged 73, in hospital in Ottawa, Ontario, Canada following a heart attack

Buried: Greenwood Cemetery, Owen Sound, Ontario. Headstone

Deed/Service: 18 - 20 August 1944 (Major) When in command of a small mixed force of tanks, self-propelled anti-tank guns and infantry, he was ordered to cut one of the German escape routes through the 'Falaise Gap'. After attacking, capturing and consolidating his position at St. Lambert, he repulsed many heavy enemy attacks. Throughout three days and nights of continuous fighting, he was seen everywhere, both fighting and encouraging his men. Finally routed, the Germans lost seven tanks, twelve heavy guns and forty vehicles, with over 1,000 casualties and 11,000 taken prisoner   **Gazette: 27 November 1944**

Commemoration: i) Headstone ii) Plaque at Owen Sound Municipal Park iii) Plaque in Royal Canadian Legion Post, Trail, British Columbia

1289	NORTON Gerard Ross VC MM Captain	Kaffrarian Rifles, South African Forces, attd. 1/4th Bn. The Hampshire Regt.	Monte Gridolfo, Italy
		(now The Royal Hampshire Regiment)	The Gothic Line

934

Born: 7 September 1915 - Herschel, Cape Province, South Africa

Deed/Service: 31 August 1944 (Lieutenant) During the advance on the western side of the 200 mile long Gothic Line, his platoon were pinned down by heavy fire. He went forward alone, attacked a machine-gun post killing the three man crew, before going on to a second position containing two guns and fifteen riflemen. Under constant fire he wiped out both killing or capturing the occupants, then calmly went on to lead his men in the main attack   **Gazette: 26 October 1944**

Commemoration: i) Painting and 'Toys Norton' hostel at Selbourne College, East London, South Africa ii) Painting in South African Military Museum Johannesburg

1290 GRAYBURN John Hollington VC Lieutenant The Parachute Regiment (Army Air Corps)

Arnhem, Holland
POSTHUMOUS
485

Born: 30 January 1918 - Manora Island, Karachi Harbour, India (now Pakistan)
Died: 20 September 1944 aged 26. Killed during his VC action at the Lek Bridge, Arnhem, Holland
Buried: Arnhem Oosterbeek War Cemetery, Holland. N. suburbs of Oosterbeek, 4 miles W. of Arnhem. Plot XIII. Row C. Grave 11. Headstone
Deed/Service: 17 - 20 September 1944. From his position at the North end of Lek Bridge, he was ordered to lead his platoon on an assault to capture the South end. Although wounded early in the action, he led his men with supreme gallantry and determination for the entire period, without food and sleep. Finally his position became untenable, and he ordered a withdrawal, covering his men until they reached safety. He was killed later that night
Commemoration: i) Headstone ii) Name on Chalfont St. Giles War Memorial, Buckinghamshire iii) Memorial at the Hong Kong and Shanghai Bank Gracechurch Street, City of London iv) Medals at the Airborne Forces Museum

Gazette: 25 January 1945

His mother with the Victoria Cross

1291 SHERBAHADUR THAPA VC Rifleman 1st Bn. 9th Gurkha Rifles, Indian Army

San Marino, Italy
POSTHUMOUS
1137

Born: 20 November 1921 - Ghalechhap Village, Jyamruk, No. 3 West, Nepal. Also shown as SHER BAHADAR THAPA in records
Died: 19 September 1944 aged 22. Killed during his VC action on a ridge above San Marino, Italy
Buried: Rimini Gurkha War Cemetery, Italy. 10 miles N. of San Marino. Plot VI. Row E. Grave 7. Headstone shows 18th September age 23
Deed/Service: 18 - 19 September 1944. During an attack on a strong German position, he and his section commander charged and silenced a machine-gun, he then went on alone, ignoring a hail of bullets in an exposed part of a ridge. He put two more machine-guns out of action, covered a withdrawal and rescued two wounded men before he was killed
Commemoration: i) Headstone ii) Medals at the 9th Gurkha Rifles Regimental HQ, Varanasi, India

Gazette: 28 December 1944

1292   **CAIN Robert Henry   VC   T/Major   Royal Northumberland Fusiliers, attd. The S. Staffordshire Regiment - 1st Airborne Division**   **Arnhem, Holland**
(now Royal Regiment of Fusiliers and The Staffordshire Regiment respectively)

Born:	2 January 1909 - Shanghai, China	**169**
Died:	2 May 1974 aged 65, at his home in Crowborough, Sussex	
Cremated:	10 May at Worth Crematorium, Crawley, Sussex. Ashes buried in family grave in Braddan Cemetery, Isle of Man. Name not on headstones	
Deed/Service:	19 - 25 September 1944. For the entire six day period his company were cut off from the battalion and engaged with self-propelled guns, tanks and infantry. He was constantly under fire and in positions where the fighting was at its thickest, on several occasions using his PIAT when alone and knocking out tanks. Despite multiple wounds and a perforated ear-drum, he refused all medical aid until the Germans withdrew	**Gazette: 2 November 1944**
Commemoration:	i) Memorial in St. Brigit's Hospice, Douglas, Isle of Man ii) Plaque in Bedford School, Bedfordshire iii) Plaque in the Garrison Church Whittingdon Barracks, Lichfield, Staffordshire iv) Medals at The Staffordshire Regimental Museum	

1293   **LORD David Samuel Anthony   VC DFC   Flight Lieutenant   271 Squadron, Royal Air Force**   **Over Arnhem, Holland**

Born:	18 October 1913 - St. Mary's Avenue, Cork, Ireland	**POSTHUMOUS**
Died:	19 September 1944 aged 30. Killed during his VC action north west of Arnhem, Holland	**751**
Buried:	Arnhem Oosterbeek War Cemetery, Holland. N. suburbs of Oosterbeek. 4 miles W. of Arnhem. Plot IV. Row B. Grave 5. Headstone	
Deed/Service:	19 September 1944. On his third flight to Arnhem, he carried much needed ammunition to the besieged 1st Airborne in a Dakota III with seven others aboard. Hit twice when flying through intense enemy AA fire, one engine caught fire but he managed to drop the supplies, finding at the end of the run that two containers had failed to drop. He made a second run even though the starboard wing was about to collapse and the aircraft in flames. Making the drop, he ordered his crew out, but a few moments later the Dakota crashed killing all on board	**Gazette: 13 November 1945**
Commemoration:	i) Headstone ii) Memorial in St. Mary's R.C. Cathedral, Wrexham iii) Memorial window at Down Ampney Church, Gloucestershire iv) A VC.10C Mk1 of 10 Squadron, RAF named for him v) Name on Memorial, St. Clement Dane's Church, Central London vi) Lord Trophy RAF Transport Command	

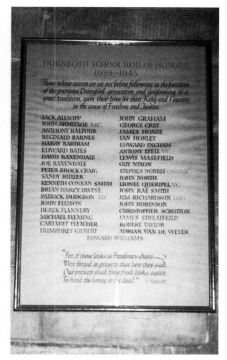

1294   **QUERIPEL Lionel Ernest   VC   Captain**   **The Royal Sussex Regiment, attd. 10th Parachute Regiment (Army Air Corps)**   Arnhem, Holland
(the former now The P.O.W. Royal Regiment (Q & H))

Born:	13 July 1920 - Winterbourne Monkton, Dorset
Died:	19 September 1944 aged 24. From wounds received during his VC action at Arnhem, Holland. Initially reported as 'wounded and missing'
Buried:	Arnhem Oosterbeek War Cemetery, Holland. N. suburbs of Oosterbeek. 4 miles W. of Arnhem. Plot V. Row D. Grave 8. Headstone
Deed/Service:	19 September 1944. During nine hours of confused and bitter fighting, he led a composite company from three Parachute Battalions advancing on an embankment. Coming under heavy fire, he carried a wounded NCO to an aid post although wounded in the face. He then led his men against a strong enemy point which had been holding up the advance, killing two machine-gun crews and recapturing an anti-tank gun. Despite protests, he remained behind to cover a withdrawal, armed with a pistol and a few grenades, this being the last time he was seen alive
Commemoration:	i) Headstone ii) Name on Regimental Memorial, Chichester Cathedral, Sussex iii) Plaque in Langton Matravers Parish Church, Dorset iv) Display at Royal Sussex Regimental Museum v) Memorial Book at Winchester Cathedral, Hampshire vi) Medals at Airborne Forces Museum

1012

Gazette: 1 February 1945

1295   **BASKEYFIELD John Daniel   VC   Lance - Sergeant**   **The South Staffordshire Regiment, 1st Airborne Division**   Arnhem, Holland
(the former now The Staffordshire Regiment)   POSTHUMOUS
59

Born:	18 November 1922 - Burslem, Staffordshire
Died:	20 September 1944 aged 21. Killed during his VC action at 'Station Oosterbeek', a suburb of Arnhem, Holland
Buried:	Has no known grave - name on The Groesbeek Memorial, Holland. 10 miles S. of Arnhem. Panel 5. A body found in 1981 by Dutch workmen at the site of his death 'may' possibly be his and was interred as 'Unknown' in Arnhem Oosterbeek Military Cemetery
Deed/Service:	20 September 1944. When in charge of a 6-pounder anti-tank gun at Station Oosterbeek, the enemy attacked his sector. He destroyed two Tiger tanks and a self-propelled gun (SPG). He was badly wounded and all his crew killed or wounded, but he stayed at his gun until it was destroyed. He crawled to another gun putting another SPG out of action. As he was preparing another round, he was killed by a shell from a supporting enemy tank
Commemoration:	i) Name on Groesbeek Memorial ii) 12 ft. high statue on a roundabout near Festival Park, Burslem iii) Memorial Plaque at Burslem War Memorial iv) Plaque in Garrison Church, Whittington Barracks, Lichfield, Staffordshire v) Jack Baskeyfield Tree, on the site where he died in a suburban garden at Oosterbeek vi) Plaque in Burslem Museum vii) Baskeyfield Close, Lichfield viii) Medals at Staffordshire Regimental Museum

Gazette: 23 November 1944

| 1296 | HARPER John William VC Corporal | 4th Bn. (Hallamshire) The York and Lancaster Regiment (now disbanded) | Antwerp, Belgium |

1296   **HARPER John William**   **VC**   **Corporal**   **4th Bn. (Hallamshire) The York and Lancaster Regiment (now disbanded)**   Antwerp, Belgium
POSTHUMOUS
533

Born: 6 August 1915 - Doncaster, Yorkshire
Died: 29 September 1944 aged 28. Killed during his VC action, on an embankment at the Depot de Mendicite, Antwerp, Belgium
Buried: Leopoldsburg War Cemetery, Belgium. 12 miles N. of Hasselt. Plot V. Row B. Grave 15. Headstone (See Map A - 7)
Deed/Service: 29 September 1944. During an assault on the Depot de Mendicite, a natural defensive position surrounded by an earthen wall and a waterway, he led his section across 300 yards of completely exposed ground under a hail of mortar bombs and small arms fire. Capturing the Germans holding one side, he then climbed a wall alone and throwing grenades at the enemy on the far side, forced them to flee. He continued to ignore heavy fire as he crossed open ground once more, but was killed when directing his company commander to a crossing point in the dykes   **Gazette: 2 January 1945**
Commemoration: i) Headstone ii) Name on War Memorial, Hatfield Woodhouse, Doncaster iii) Memorial in Thorne Parish Church, near Doncaster iv) Medals at The York and Lancaster Regimental Museum

1297   **BURTON Richard Henry**   **VC**   **Corporal**   **1st Bn. The Duke of Wellington's (West Riding) Regiment**   Monte Ceco, near Bologna
Italy
156

Born: 29 January 1923 - Melton Mowbray, Leicestershire
Died: 11 July 1993 aged 70, at the Stracathro Hospital, Kirriemuir, Angus, Scotland
Buried: 14 July at Kirriemuir Cemetery, Brechin Road, Kirriemuir. Section N.E. Lair 103. Headstone
Deed/Service: 8 October 1944 (Private) When an attack was held up on one of many vital and well-fortified German positions at 2,200 feet, he rushed forward alone and engaged a Spandau position with his Tommy - gun, killing three of the crew. He then attacked two machine-gun posts and disposed of their crews, allowing his company to consolidate their position on the slopes. The Germans then launched two counter-attacks and despite most of his comrades being casualties, his accurate fire secured the position and the enemy withdrew   **Gazette: 4 January 1945**
Commemoration: i) Headstone ii) Memorial in St. Mary's Church, Kirriemuir

1298	**EARDLEY George Harold VC MM Company Sergeant - Major**		**4th Bn. The King's Shropshire Light Infantry** **(now The Light Infantry)**	**Near Overloon, Holland**

Born: 6 May 1912 - Congleton, Cheshire

Died: 11 September 1991 aged 79, at his home in Congleton

368

Cremated: 18 September at Macclesfield Crematorium, Cheshire. Ashes scattered on a hill in the Garden of Remembrance on 30 September. No plaque

Deed/Service: 16 October 1944 (A/Sergeant) When units of the British Second Army were advancing towards Venlo, they were held up by strong opposition at Overloon, where Eardley's platoon were ordered to clear some orchards. When halted by fire from machine-gun posts, he moved forward alone and killed the officer at one post with a grenade, then went on to destroy two more posts single-handed. His actions were carried out under fire so intense that it daunted all who were with him, but he enabled the platoon to achieve its objective and ensured the success of the whole attack **Gazette: 2 January 1945**

Commemoration: i) Name in Book of Remembrance at the Crematorium - 11 September 1991

1299	**SMITH Ernest Alvia VC Sergeant The Seaforth Highlanders of Canada, Canadian Infantry Corps**		**Savio River, Italy**

Born: 3 May 1914 - New Westminster, British Columbia, Canada

1157

Deed/Service: 21- 22 October 1944 (Private) When in the spearhead of an attack to establish a bridgehead at the River Savio, North Italy, his company were in the process of consolidating a position at Pievesestina when attacked by three tanks, two self-propelled guns and infantry. With a PIAT gun he put one tank out of action single-handed, then another when protecting a wounded comrade, finally routing the infantry using his Tommy-gun **Gazette: 20 December 1944**

Commemoration: i) Name on plaque at Trail Royal Canadian Legion Post, British Columbia

1300	RAM SARUP SINGH VC Acting Subadar (Captain) 1st Punjab Regiment, Indian Army	Tiddim Area, Burma now Myanmar POSTHUMOUS 1017

Born: 12 April 1919 - Kheri, Patiala, India

Died: 25 October 1944 aged 25. Killed during his VC action at Kennedy Peak, Tiddim Area, Burma

Buried: Has no known grave - name on The Rangoon Memorial, Burma. 20 miles S. of Rangoon (Yangon). Face 30. Shown as RAM SWARUP SINGH

Deed/Service: 25 October 1944. Leading one of two platoons during an attack against a strong Japanese position, he not only gained his objective but routed the enemy despite being wounded in both legs. He later led a charge to thwart a fierce counter-attack, killing four of the enemy himself and was again wounded in the leg. Refusing medical aid, he led yet another attack and killed two more of the enemy until he fell mortally wounded

Gazette: 8 February 1945

Commemoration: i) Name on The Rangoon Memorial

1301	THAMAN GURUNG VC Rifleman 1st Bn. 5th Royal Gurkha Rifles, Indian Army	Monte San Bartolo, Italy POSTHUMOUS 1208

Born: 2 October 1924 - Singla Village, Barbak No. 2 West, Gorkha District, West Nepal

Died: 11 November 1944 aged 20. Killed in his VC action on a hill near Monte San Bartolo, Italy

Buried: Rimini Gurkha War Cemetery, Italy. 10 miles S. of San Marino. Plot III. Row B. Grave 5. Headstone shows name as THAMMAN GURUNG

Deed/Service: 10 November 1944. With another scout, he was detailed to reconnoitre German positions on a crest, prior to an attack. Coming across an enemy party about to throw grenades, he attacked them in the open under a hail of fire, allowing his section to reach the summit. Noting many German gun placements he retired under fire, destroying several posts with Tommy-gun and grenades as he did so. To ensure the safe withdrawal of his section, he covered them by standing in the open drawing enemy fire, until he was killed. The hill was taken three days later due to his efforts

Gazette: 22 February 1945

Commemoration:

1302	BHANDARI RAM VC Subadar (Captain) 10th Baluchi Regiment, Indian Army	East Mayu, Arakan, Burma now Myanmar

Born: 24 July 1919 - Pargna Gugeda Village, Bilaspur State, Simla Hills, India. Also shown as BANDARI RAM
89
Deed/Service: 22 November 1944 (Sepoy/Private) Although wounded, he crawled up to a Japanese machine-gun post in full view of the enemy when his platoon had been pinned down. He got to within five yards of his objective, despite being wounded again, then threw a grenade into the position killing three crew. His actions inspired his platoon to rush and capture the position, after which he allowed his wounds to be dressed
Gazette: 8 February 1945
Commemoration:

1303	BRUNT John Henry Cound VC MC T/Captain The Sherwood Foresters (The Nottinghamshire & Derbyshire Regt.) attd. 6th Bn., The Lincolnshire Regt. (now Worcestershire & Sherwood Foresters and Royal Anglian Regt. respect.)	Near Faenza, Italy

Born: 6 December 1922 - Paddock Wood, Kent
139
Died: 10 December 1944 aged 22. Killed by a shell the day after his VC action, at platoon HQ, near Faenza, Italy (also Fienza)
Buried: Faenza War Cemetery, Italy. 30 miles S. E. of Bologna. Plot III. Row A. Grave 8. Headstone
Deed/Service: 9 December 1944. When holding a position in atrocious muddy conditions, he rallied his men after the house around which they were dug-in was destroyed. Heavily outnumbered, they held another position from which he personally killed fourteen with his Bren, then used a PIAT and 2-inch mortar to good effect. This aggressive defence enabled him to re-occupy his old position and get his wounded away. During a later enemy counter-attack, he rallied his men, seized a Bren and leapt onto a Sherman tank, directing fire under a hail of bullets until the enemy withdrew in great haste
Gazette: 8 February 1945
Commemoration: i) Headstone ii) War Memorial, and pub named for him (closed 1997) at Paddock Wood iii) Name on altar rail Soldiers' Chapel, Lincoln Cathedral

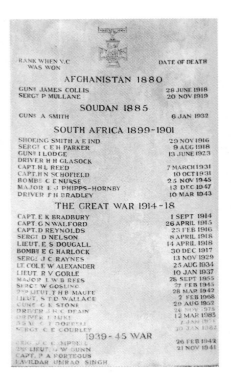

1304   **UMRAO SINGH   VC   Subadar - Major (Captain)   Royal Indian Artillery**   Kaladan Valley, Burma
now Myanmar
1244

Born: 21 November 1920 - Palra Village, Jrajur, Rhotak, Punjab, India
Deed/Service: 15 - 16 December 1944 (Havildar/Sergeant) When in charge of a gun in an advanced section of his battery, he repeatedly beat off heavy enemy attacks. In the final assault on the objective, he struck down three Japanese in hand-to-hand fighting and when found wounded and exhausted beside his gun, there were ten enemy dead lying around him. The gun was still working and was in action again later that day   **Gazette: 31 May 1945**
Commemoration: i) Name on plaque in Royal Artillery Chapel, Woolwich, South East London

1305   **PALMER Robert Anthony Maurice   VC DFC & Bar   Squadron Leader   109 Squadron, Royal Air Force Volunteer Reserve**   Over Cologne, Germany
POSTHUMOUS
958

Born: 7 July 1920 - Gillingham, Kent
Died: 23 December 1944 aged 24. Killed during his VC action near Hoffnungsthal, near Cologne, Germany
Buried: i) Hoffnungsthal Village Cemetery ii) 18 December 1945 in Rheinberg War Cemetery, Germany. Plot XIV. Row C. Joint Grave 13-14. Headstone
Deed/Service: 23 December 1944. Seconded from his normal duties flying Mosquitos with the Path Finder Force, he led three formations of Lancasters on a raid against the Gremburg marshalling yards at Cologne, a major transport centre. Tasked to mark the target, the bomber was hit by flak during his run-in setting two engines on fire, but aware that the following bombers were awaiting his own bomb release, he kept the damaged craft on a straight course and hit his target. The bomber immediately spiralled to earth and crashed in flames, with just one man parachuting to safety   **Gazette: 23 March 1945**
Commemoration: i) Headstone ii) Name on the RAF Memorial, St. Clement Dane's Church, Aldwych, Central London

Chapter Nineteen
The Second World War
1945

No's 1306 - 1339

The Victoria Cross and campaign medals awarded to Lance - Corporal Henry Eric Harden (1309)

The Victoria Cross, British Empire Medal and campaign medals awarded to Company Sergeant - Major Edward Thomas Chapman (1325)

1306   **THOMPSON George   VC   Flight Sergeant   9 Squadron, Royal Air Force Volunteer Reserve**   Dortmund-Ems Canal
Germany
POSTHUMOUS

Born: 23 October 1920 - Borestone Cottage, Trinity Gask, Perthshire, Scotland   **1212**
Died: 23 January 1945 aged 24. From wounds and pneumonia at Number 50 Field Military Hospital, Eindhoven, Holland, a result of his VC actions
Buried: Brussels Town Cemetery, Evere-les-Brizelles, Belgium. Plot X. Row 27. Grave 45. Headstone (See Map A - 14)
Deed/Service: 1 January 1945. Following a dawn raid on the Dortmund-Ems Canal, when his Lancaster released twelve 1,000lb bombs on target, the plane
was hit by two 88mm shells setting the bomber ablaze. He went to the assistance of two gunners, extinguishing their burning clothing with his bare
hands. His own clothing was now on fire and he had received severe burns to his face, hands and legs. The pilot managed to crash-land the
aircraft in a field near Heesch, but Thompson was burned black and unrecognisable, dying three weeks later from his dreadful injuries   **Gazette: 20 February 1945**
Commemoration: i) Headstone ii) 'Sgt. Thompsonstraat' in Heesch iii) A VC.10C Mk 1 XV806 named for him iv) Name on RAF Memorial, St. Clement Dane's
Church, Aldwych, Central London v) Medals at The Scottish United Services Museum, Edinburgh

1307   **DONNINI Dennis   VC   Fusilier   4/5th Bn. The Royal Scots Fusiliers (now The Royal Highland Fusiliers)**   Rivers Roer and Maas
Holland
POSTHUMOUS

Born: 17 November 1925 - Easington Colliery, Co. Durham   **335**
Died: 18 January 1945 aged 19. Killed during his VC action near Roermond, Holland
Buried: Sittard War Cemetery, Limburg, Holland. 20 miles N.W. of Aachen, Germany. Row H. Grave 10. Headstone
Deed/Service: 18 January 1945. When his platoon were ordered to eliminate a German pocket of resistance near Roermond, they were met by heavy fire
from a house as they left their trench and he was wounded in the head. He then dashed forward thirty yards and hurled a grenade through a
window in the house, causing the occupants to flee. Although wounded a second time, he continued firing his Bren gun in the open until he
was killed when a bullet struck a grenade that he was carrying   **Gazette: 20 March 1945**
Commemoration: i) Headstone

1308		**SHER SHAH** VC Lance - Naik (Lance - Corporal) 16th Punjab Regiment, Indian Army			**Kyeyebyin, Burma now Myanmar POSTHUMOUS 1139**

Born: 14 February 1917 - Chakrala Village, near Mianwali, North Punjab, India (now North West Frontier, Pakistan)

Died: 20 January 1945 aged 27. Killed during his VC action at Kyeyebyin, near Kaladan, Burma

Buried: Has no known grave - name on The Rangoon Memorial, Burma. 20 miles N. of Rangoon (Yangon). Face 48

Deed/Service: 19 - 20 January 1945. While commanding a section of his platoon that was attacked by an overwhelming enemy force, he crawled into the middle of their position and opened fire at point blank range breaking up two attacks. His leg was shattered but he maintained the injury was slight and when a third attack came, he again crawled forward to engage the enemy until killed by a shot through the head

Commemoration: i) Name on The Rangoon Memorial

Gazette: 8 May 1945

1309		**HARDEN Henry Eric** VC Lance - Corporal Royal Army Medical Corps, attd. 45 Royal Marine Commando	**Brachterbeek, Holland POSTHUMOUS 527**

Born: 23 February 1912 - Northfleet, Kent

Died: 23 January 1945 aged 32. Killed during his VC action near Brachterbeek, Holland

Buried: Nederweert War Cemetery, Holland. Plot IV. Row E. Grave 13. Headstone

Deed/Service: 23 January 1945. When attached to 45 Commando, whose task it was to clear pockets of Germans in blockhouses under heavy fire, he ran across 100 yards of open ground to tend to three wounded men. Giving first aid to two of them, he carried the third back to safety being wounded as he did so, then insisted on going out again to rescue the others. As he prepared to carry another man back, he was killed by enemy fire

Commemoration: i) Headstone ii) Memorial plaque on the bridge where he died, over the Montforterbeek River, Brachterbeek iii) Name on the family headstone in Northfleet Cemetery iv) 'Henry Hardenstraat', Neederweert v) Harden Barracks at Catterick Camp, Yorkshire vi) Medals at R.A.M.C. Museum

Gazette: 8 March 1945

1310	KNOWLAND George Arthur	VC	Lieutenant	The Royal Norfolk Regt. (now Royal Anglian Regt.) attd. No.1 Commando	Near Kangaw, Burma

now Myanmar

Born: 16 August 1922 - Catford, Kent (now South East London)

Died: 31 January 1945 aged 22. Killed in his VC action near Kangaw (Gangaw),120 m. W. of Mandalay, Burma

Buried: Taukkyan War Cemetery, Burma. 20 miles N. of Rangoon (Yangon). Plot XI. Row J. Grave 1. Headstone (See Map G)

Deed/Service: 31 January 1945. When in command of a forward platoon of 24 men positioned on a hill top, they were attacked by a force of 300 Japanese. He encouraged his men constantly and when the crew of a Bren gun team had all been wounded, he manned it himself, firing at the enemy from ten yards until all the casualties had been evacuated. During a fresh attack he stood up, and firing a mortar from his hip he killed many of the enemy, before snatching up a Tommy-gun inflicting even more casualties. He was mortally wounded after twelve hours fighting, but the position was held

Commemoration: i) Headstone ii) Brass plaque at Elmwood School, Croydon, Surrey iii) Knowland Grove, Norwich, Norfolk iv) Memorial in Lewisham Civic Centre

POSTHUMOUS
704

Gazette: 12 April 1945

NIAZ MUHAMMAD
V.C.PARKASH SINGH
SADHU SINGH

1311	PRAKASH SINGH	VC	Jemadar (First Lieutenant)	4/13th Frontier Force Rifles, Indian Army	Kanlan Ywatkit, Burma

now Myanmar

Born: 1 April 1913 - Kanachak Village, Kathua District, Kashmir, India

Died: 17 February 1945 aged 31. Died from a third wound received during his VC action at Kanlan Ywatkit (also Ywathit), Burma

Buried: Has no known grave - name on The Rangoon Memorial, Burma. 20 miles N. of Rangoon (now Yangon). Face 43 (See below)

Deed/Service: 16 - 17 February 1945. When commanding a platoon taking the brunt of an enemy attack, he was wounded in both ankles. When his subordinate was wounded, he crawled forward to encourage and direct his men, before being wounded again in both legs. Dragging himself by his hands from one position to another, he received a mortal wound and lay shouting the Dogra war-cry, inspiring his men to eventually drive the enemy back

Commemoration: i) Name on The Rangoon War Memorial shown as PARKASH SINGH

POSTHUMOUS
999

Gazette: 1 May 1945

| 1312 | SWALES Edwin | VC DFC | Major | South African Air Force, serving with 582 Squadron, Royal Air Force | Over Pforzheim, Germany |

Over Pforzheim, Germany
POSTHUMOUS
1197

Born: 3 July 1915 - Inanda, Natal, South Africa
Died: 23 February 1945 aged 29. Killed during his VC action 2 miles S.E. of Denam, near Valenciennes, France
Buried: Leopoldsburg War Cemetery, Limburg, Belgium. Plot VIII. Row C. Grave 5. Headstone shows rank as Major - see below
Deed/Service: 23 February 1945 (Captain - his promotion to Major was in 'the channels') Leading a 374 aircraft raid on the vital rail junction at Pforzheim, he was attacked by a Messerschmitt night fighter as he reached the target. Although his Lancaster was badly damaged he carried on, but was again hit when circling Pforzheim having released his target indicators. Hoping to get the crippled aircraft back to base, he reached Allied-occupied territory before ordering the crew to bail out, then hitting high tension cables the Lancaster plunged to earth with Swales still at the controls
Commemoration: i) Headstone ii) Edwin Swales Drive, Durban, South Africa iii) Name on RAF Memorial, St. Clement Dane's Church, Aldwych, Central London iv) His medals and other memorabilia on display at The National Museum of Military History, Johannesburg, South Africa

Gazette: 24 April 1945

| 1313 | COSENS Aubrey | VC | Sergeant | The Queen's Own Rifles of Canada, Canadian Infantry Corps | Mooshof, Holland |

Mooshof, Holland
POSTHUMOUS
257

Born: 21 May 1921 - Latchford, Ontario, Canada
Died: 26 February 1945 aged 23. Killed during his VC action at Mooshof, Holland
Buried: Groesbeek Canadian War Cemetery, Nijmegen, Holland. 10 miles S. of Arnhem. Plot VIII. Row H. Grave 2. Headstone shows age 24
Deed/Service: 25 - 26 February 1945. Having assumed command of the four surviving members of his platoon, he positioned them to give him cover as he ran forward alone to a tank. Sitting in an exposed position in front of the turret, he directed its fire on the enemy before ordering it to ram some farm buildings, which he entered alone killing several defenders and taking the rest prisoner. He was shot by a sniper when entering another house
Commemoration: i) Headstone ii) The 'Sgt. Aubrey Cosens VC Memorial Bridge', with plaque, over the Montreal River, Latchford iii) Memorial plaque at Porquis Junction, Ontario iv) Name on plaque at Trail Royal Canadian Legion Post, British Columbia v) Tourist steamer plying Lake Temagami, Ontario named for him vi) Memorial at Latchford Legion Post vii) Medals at The Queen's Own Rifles of Canada Museum, Ottawa, Ontario

Gazette: 22 May 1945

				Kervenheim, Germany
1314	STOKES James VC Private 2nd Bn. The King's Shropshire Light Infantry (now The Light Infantry)			POSTHUMOUS

1314   STOKES James   VC   Private   2nd Bn. The King's Shropshire Light Infantry (now The Light Infantry)

Kervenheim, Germany
POSTHUMOUS
1184

Born: 6 February 1915 - Hutchesontown, Lanark (now Strathclyde), Scotland

Died: 1 March 1945 aged 30. Killed in his VC action at Kervenheim, Germany

Buried: Reichswald Forest War Cemetery, Germany. 3 miles S.W. of Kleve and 8 miles E. of Dutch border. Plot LXII. Row E. Grave 14. Headstone

Deed/Service: 1 March 1945. During the final push into the Rhineland, his platoon were pinned down by intense fire from a German held farm building, which he attacked single-handed, emerging with twelve prisoners. Although wounded, he rejoined his platoon as the advance continued, then rushed a second house and took five more prisoners. He fell mortally wounded when firing his rifle just twenty yards from their final objective

Gazette: 17 April 1945

Commemoration: i) Headstone ii) Medals at Strawberry Farm, Jersey, Channel Islands

1315   TILSTON Frederick Albert   VC   Hon. Colonel   The Essex - Scottish Regiment, Canadian Infantry Corps

Hochwald Forest
near Xanten, Germany
1215

Born: 11 June 1906 - Toronto, Ontario, Canada

Died: 23 September 1992 aged 86, at his home in Kettleby, near Toronto, Ontario

Buried: Mount Hope Cemetery, Erskine Avenue, Toronto. R.C. Section. Plot 23 - N.W. Corner. Headstone

Deed/Service: 1 March 1945 (A/Major) When his Regiment was tasked with breaking the German defences at Udem and clearing the northern half of Hochwald Forest, he led his company through a belt of wire ten feet deep to the enemy line. He was first in the trenches and personally silenced a machine-gun, before pressing on to the second line where he was badly wounded in the hip. He then made six trips under heavy fire bringing ammunition to the front, until one of his legs was blown off and the other shattered. He refused medical aid until he had given instructions for holding the position

Gazette: 22 May 1945

Commemoration: i) Headstone ii) Tilston Legion Post, Aurora, Ontario iii) Plaque at Trail Legion Post, B.C. iv) Medals at Royal Canadian Military Institute, Ontario

| 1316 | FAZAL DIN | VC | Acting Naik (Corporal) | 7th Bn. 10th Baluch Regiment, Indian Army | Near Meiktila, Burma now Myanmar |

Born: 1 July 1921 - Husain Pur, Hoshiarpur District, Punjab (now Himachal Pradesh), India

POSTHUMOUS
397

Died: 2 March 1945 aged 23. From wounds received during his VC action near Pakokku, Meiktila, Burma

Buried: Has no known grave - name on The Rangoon Memorial, Burma. 20 miles N. of Rangoon (now Yangon). Face 39. Name shown as FAZL DIN

Deed/Service: 2 March 1945. During an attack, his section was held up by fire from enemy bunkers. He personally attacked the first and silenced it, then led his men against the other. Suddenly six Japanese wielding swords rushed out, and he was run through the chest by one of them. As the sword was withdrawn, he wrested it from its owner and killed him and another with it. Waving the sword aloft, he continued to encourage his men before he staggered back to make his report. He collapsed and died from his wound shortly afterwards

Gazette: 24 May 1945

Commemoration: i) Name on The Rangoon Memorial

| 1317 | GIAN SINGH | VC | Hon. Subadar-Major (Captain) | 4th Bn. 15th Punjab Regiment (later Sikh Regiment), Indian Army | Kamye - Myingyan Road Burma, now Myanmar |

Born: 5 October 1920 - Sahabpur Village, Nawashahr, Jullundur, Northern Punjab, India

447

Died: 6 October 1996 aged 76, at his family farm in Nawashahr, near Jullundur

Cremated: Jalandhar Cantt, near Jullundur. Ashes scattered 'to the rivers'. No memorial

Deed/Service: 2 March 1945 (Naik/Corporal) When in charge of the leading section of his platoon, in a strong Japanese position on the road between Kamye and Myingyan, he rushed forward alone firing his Tommy-gun at enemy foxholes. He then began hurling grenades, despite an arm wound, before locating a hidden anti-tank gun which he attacked, killing the entire crew. Leading his men again, he cleared all enemy positions in his sector

Gazette: 22 May 1945

Commemoration:

1318   WESTON William Basil   VC   Lieutenant   The Green Howards attd. 1st Bn. The West Yorkshire Regiment   Meiktila, Burma
                                                    (the latter now The P.O.W. Regiment)   now Myanmar

Born:	3 January 1924 - Ulverston, Lancashire	**POSTHUMOUS**
Died:	3 March 1945 aged 21. Killed in his VC action during attack on Meiktila, Burma	**1292**
Buried:	Taukkyan War Cemetery, Burma. 20 miles N. of Rangoon (Yangon). Plot XX. Row A. Grave 7. Headstone (See Map - G)	
Deed/Service:	3 March 1945. During the ten day struggle to capture Meiktila, he led his platoon in operations to clear 1,600 yards of jungle held by the Japanese ensconced in a labyrinth of bunkers. Encouraging his men from one position to another, they approached the last where he fell wounded in the entrance. Knowing his men would not be able to capture it without heavy casualties, he pulled the pin out of one of his grenades as he lay on the ground and deliberately blew himself up along with the enemy in the bunker. His bravery throughout four hours of heavy fighting was inspirational	**Gazette: 15 May 1945**
Commemoration:	i) Headstone ii) Plaque and window in St. Mary's RC Church, Ulverston iii) Plaque in Ulverston Royal British Legion iv) Weston Avenue, Ulverston	

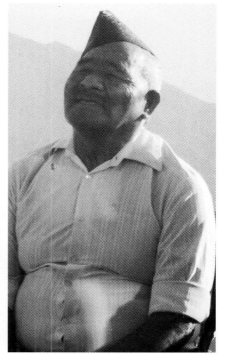

1319   BHANBHAGTA GURUNG   VC   Lance - Naik (Lance - Corporal)   3rd Bn. 2nd Gurkha Rifles, Indian Army   Snowdon East, Tamandu
                                                                        Burma, now Myanmar

Born:	September 1921 - Phalbu Village, Gorkha District, Nepal. Shown in records as BHANUBAKTA GURUNG, his preferred spelling	**88**
Deed/Service:	5 March 1945 (Rifleman) When his section was pinned down by heavy fire and a sniper, he killed the sniper, then dashed forward alone when the section was attacked, clearing four enemy foxholes and silencing a machine-gun. With the help of three other men, he then repelled a Japanese counter-attack on a captured bunker and caused heavy losses. His action in clearing these positions was decisive in capturing the objective	**Gazette: 5 June 1945**
Commemoration:	i) Medals with the 1st Royal Gurkha Rifles	

| 1320 | KARAMJEET SINGH JUDGE | VC | Lieutenant | 4th Bn. 15th Punjab Regiment, Indian Army | Myingyan, Burma now Myanmar |

Myingyan, Burma now Myanmar
POSTHUMOUS
665

Born: 25 May 1923 - Kapurthala, Kapurthala State, India
Died: 18 March 1945 aged 21. Killed during his VC action at Myingyan, near Meiktila, Burma
Cremated: Place unknown - name on The Taukkyan Cremation Memorial, Burma. 20 miles N. of Rangoon (Yangon). Column 25 (See Map - G)
Deed/Service: 18 March 1945. Commanding a company ordered to capture a heavily defended cotton mill at Myingyan, his numerous acts of gallantry dominated the battlefield. After eliminating ten enemy bunkers he directed one tank to within twenty yards of another requesting the tank to cease fire while he entered the bunker where he was killed

Gazette: 3 July 1945

Commemoration: i) Name on Taukkyan Cremation Memorial

| 1321 | RAYMOND Claud | VC | Lieutenant | Corps of Royal Engineers | Taluka Village, Burma now Myanmar |

Taluka Village, Burma now Myanmar
POSTHUMOUS
1025

Born: 2 October 1923 - Mottistone, Isle of Wight, Hampshire
Died: 22 March 1945 aged 21. From wounds received during his VC action aboard a landing craft on the Thinganet Chaung River, Burma
Buried: Taukkyan War Cemetery, Burma. 20 miles N. of Rangoon (Yangon). Plot XII. Row G. Grave 9. Headstone (See Map - G)
Deed/Service: 21 March 1945. When ordered to create a diversion in the Taungup area forty miles ahead of the Indian Infantry Brigade, his patrol came under fire from a fortified Japanese position at Taluka. Seriously wounded in the shoulder and face by a grenade and later a shattered wrist, he led his men and took the position after a fierce fight, then refused aid until the other wounded had been treated. He died from his wounds the next day

Gazette: 28 June 1945

Commemoration: i) Headstone ii) Name on Seaford War Memorial, Sussex iii) Medals and display at the Royal Engineers Museum

1322 RATTEY Reginald Roy VC Sergeant 25th Infantry Bn. 7th Brigade, 3rd Division, Australian Military Forces

Tokinotu, Bougainville
Solomon Islands, Pacific
1022

Born: 28 March 1918 - Barmedman, New South Wales, Australia
Died: 10 January 1986 aged 67, at his home in West Wyalong, New South Wales
Buried: West Wyalong Lawn Cemetery, Shire Street. Headstone shows age 68
Deed/Service: 22 March 1945 (Corporal) When his company was held up by heavy fire from enemy pill-boxes, causing many casualties during their advance on Tokinotu, he dashed forward firing his Bren gun and put three bunkers out of action. Having neutralized their fire, he hurled a grenade in each, enabling his company to continue. He later rushed and put to flight an enemy machine-gun crew, capturing the gun and its ammunition   **Gazette: 26 August 1945**
Commemoration: i) Headstone ii) Display at the Australian War Memorial, Canberra, A.C.T.

1323 TOPHAM Frederick George VC Corporal 1st Canadian Parachute Battalion, Canadian Army

Weser, near Diersfordter
Germany
1220

Born: 10 August 1917 - Toronto, Ontario, Canada
Died: 31 May 1974 aged 56, suddenly at his home in Etobicoke, Ontario
Buried: Sanctuary Park Cemetery, Etobicoke. Headstone
Deed/Service: 24 March 1945. During 'Operation Varsity', the final major European undertaking, he was dropped from one of 2,900 carriers and gliders near Wesel, east of the Rhine. When tending to a wounded man under heavy fire he was shot through the nose, but carried the man to safety, refusing any aid. He later rescued three men from a gun carrier which was ablaze and under fire with exploding ammunition all around him   **Gazette: 3 August 1945**
Commemoration: i) Headstone ii) Plaque in Etobicoke Civic Center iii) Plaque in the Royal Canadian Legion Post, Trail, British Columbia

1324   **CHOWNE Albert   VC MM   Lieutenant   2/2nd Infantry Bn. (N.S.W.) 16th Brigade, 6th Division, Australian Military Forces**   **Near Dagua, New Guinea now Papua New Guinea**

Born: 19 July 1920 - Sydney, New South Wales, Australia   **POSTHUMOUS**
Died: 25 March 1945 aged 24. Killed during his VC action between Dagua and Wewak, New Guinea   **212**
Buried: Lae War Cemetery, New Guinea. Near Lae Zoo, on the East coast of Huon Gulf. Plot QQ. Row A. Grave 8. Headstone
Deed/Service: 25 March 1945. When attacking a position holding up the advance to Wewak with his leading platoon suffering heavy casualties, he rushed ahead and knocked-out two light machine-guns with grenades. Calling for support and firing his sub-machine-gun, he charged further ahead and received two wounds in the chest, but his impetus carried him forward another fifty yards under fire, killing two more enemy before he was killed   **Gazette: 6 September 1945**
Commemoration: i) Headstone ii) Chowne Memorial Hall, Willoughby, Sydney iii) Chowne Street,Canberra, A.C.T. iv) Medals at Australian War Memorial, Canberra

1325   **CHAPMAN Edward Thomas   VC BEM   Company Sergeant - Major   3rd Bn. The Monmouthshire Regiment**   **Teutoburger Wald ermany**

Born: 13 January 1920 - Pen-y-graig, Pontlottyn, Glamorgan, Wales   **202**
Deed/Service: 2 April 1945 (Corporal) As the Germans fell back in the West, their fierce resistance astonished the Allies. When his Battalion faced one of the most fanatical Nazi units left at the Dortmund-Ems Canal, his section received heavy casualties. Using his Bren gun he went forward alone, mowing down the enemy at point-blank range, forcing their withdrawal. His section were by now isolated, but he halted an enemy attack virtually single-handed, before going out fifty yards under heavy fire to carry his wounded C.O. to safety, but was hit in the hip and his C.O. killed by a sniper   **Gazette: 13 July 1945**
Commemoration: i) Chapman House at the T.A. Centre, Cwmbran, Gwent

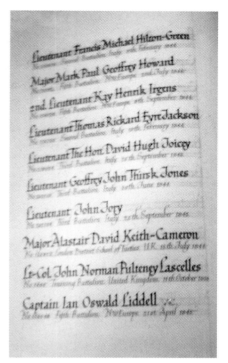

1326   **LIDDELL Ian Oswald   VC   T/Captain   5th Bn. Coldstream Guards**   Near Lingen, Germany

Born:	19 October 1919 - Shanghai, China	743
Died:	21 April 1945 aged 25. Killed in a later action by a sniper near Rothenburg, Germany	
Buried:	Becklingen War Cemetery, Soltau, Germany. 30 miles S.W. of Hamburg. R.C. Plot. Plot III. Row D. Grave 13. Headstone	
Deed/Service:	3 April 1945. When in command of a company ordered to capture a bridge intact over the River Ems, he found the position covered by an enemy strong point and the bridge set for demolition with 500lb bombs. He ran forward alone under intense fire, scaled a ten foot road block, crossed the bridge and disconnected the charges. Still under fire he climbed the block again and signalled for the leading platoon to advance	**Gazette: 7 June 1945**
Commemoration:	i) Headstone ii) Name in Book of Remembrance, Guards Chapel, Wellington Barracks, London iii) Plaque in the Speech Room, Harrow School, Middlesex iv) Memorial in Mounton Church, Chepstow, Monmouthshire v) Memorial in St. Thomas's Church, Shirenewton, Monmouthshire vi) Medals in Coldstream Guards Museum	

1327   **HUNTER Thomas Peck   VC   Corporal   No. 43 Royal Marine Commando, attd. Special Service Troops**   Argenta Gap, Italy
      POSTHUMOUS

Born:	6 October 1923 - Aldershot, Hampshire. Records show Stenhouse, Edinburgh - this is where he was brought up	610
Died:	3 April 1945 aged 21. Killed during his VC action at Argenta Gap, near Ravenna Ferrara, Italy	
Buried:	Argenta Gap War Cemetery, Ravenna Ferrara, Italy. 30 miles E. of Bologna. Plot III. Row G. Grave 20. Headstone	
Deed/Service:	3 April 1945. During the Battle of Lake Comacchio, on the German Gothic Line defences, he was in charge of a Bren gun section advancing in the open. Realising his men were devoid of cover, he charged alone across 200 yards of fire-swept ground towards three machine gun positions in some houses, attracting their fire but putting the crews to flight as he approached. As his men advanced, they came under fire from six Spandaus by a canal, and he again made himself a target to enable his men to take cover in the houses. He wa hit in the head and died instantly	**Gazette: 12 June 1945**
Commemoration:	i) Headstone ii) Ship's bell and plaque at the R.M. Depot, Lympstone, Devon iii) Plaque in Tyne Castle School, Edinburgh iv) Eight cottages built in his memory, Stenhouse Street West, Edinburgh v) Hunter Close, Gosport, Hampshire vi) Medals in the Royal Marines Museum	

Resistance Museum, Copenhagen

| 1328 | LASSEN Anders Frederik Emil Victor Schau | VC MC & 2 Bars | T/Major | General List, attd. Special Boat Service | Lake Comacchio, Italy |
| | | | | No. 1 Special Air Service Regiment | POSTHUMOUS |

Born: 22 September 1920 - 'Hovdingsgard' Mern, South Zealand, Denmark
717

Died: 9 April 1945 aged 24. Killed during his VC action on the north shore of Lake Comacchio, Italy

Buried: i) 9 April by local partisans, behind a stone wall at the S.B.S. Island Base, Lake Comacchio. Temporary cross erected ii) Re-interred 1945/46 in the Argenta Gap War Cemetery, Ravenna Ferrara, Italy. 30 miles E. of Bologna. Plot II. Row E. Grave 11. Headstone

Deed/Service: 8 - 9 April 1945. Tasked with causing many casualties and confusion around fortified enemy pill boxes along the north shore of Lake Comacchio, to give the impression of a major landing, he led a ninteen man patrol. In the face of overwhelming numbers he fulfilled his mission and wiped out three positions until mortally wounded. He refused medical aid, so the withdrawal would not be hindered and his men could be safely evacuated

Gazette: 7 September 1945

Commemoration: Denmark iv) Memorial at St. Peter's Chapel, Praesto Fjord, Norway v) Lassen Memorial Grove in the Danish Forest, Hills of Galilee, Israel

| 1329 | ALI HAIDAR | VC | Havildar (Sergeant) | 13th Frontier Force Rifles, Indian Army | Near Fusignano, Italy |

Born: 21 August 1913 - Shahu Village, Kohat, North West Frontier, India (now Pakistan)
19

Deed/Service: 9 April 1945 (Sepoy/Rifleman) In order to establish a position on far side of the Senio River, his company were ordered to cross under machine-gun fire. When only three of his section reached the opposite bank, two covered him while he, although wounded put an enemy strong point out of action. He took a second position and was again wounded, but his actions enabled the company to cross safely, and establish a bridgehead

Gazette: 3 July 1945

Commemoration:

1330	**NAMDEO JADHAV VC Havildar (Sergeant) 5th Maratha Light Infantry, Indian Army**	Senio River, Italy
Born:	10 November 1921 - Nimai Village, Admednagar District, Bombay, India. Also shown as NAMDEO JADHAO on many records	911
Died:	2 August 1984 aged 62, at Pune, Maharashtra State, India	
Cremated:	Pune. Ashes scattered. No memorial known	
Deed/Service:	9 April 1945 (Sepoy/Private) During an assault on the east floodbank of the Senio River, he carried two wounded men under heavy fire through deep water, up a steep bank and through a minefield to safety. Then to avenge his dead comrades he re-crossed the river alone, and wiped-out three enemy machine-gun posts, before calling for other companies to cross. By his actions, the battalion were able to secure a vital bridgehead	Gazette: 19 June 1945
Commemoration:	i) No memorials known, but was awarded the PVSM (India) - Param Visassa Seva Medal, a 'special' form of Long Service Good Conduct Medal	

St.John's Church

Manchester Abattoir Memorial

1331	**CHARLTON Edward Colquhoun VC Guardsman 2nd Bn. Irish Guards**	Wistedt, Germany
Born:	15 June 1920 - 11 Cowan Terrace, Rowlands Mill, near Gateshead, Co. Durham	POSTHUMOUS
Died:	21 April 1945 aged 24. From three serious wounds received during his VC action in a German Prison Camp at Bremervorde, Germany	204
Buried:	i) By Germans at Elsdorf, Germany ii) Re-interred by the Germans in January 1947 in Wistedt Cemetery, Rhade, Germany iii) Exhumed by Allies in February 1947 and buried in Becklingen War Cemetery, Soltau, Germany. 30 miles S. of Hamburg. Plot VII. Row F. Grave 13. Headstone	
Deed/Service:	21 April 1945. With tanks and an infantry platoon, the town of Wistedt had been captured by the Allies, but were counter-attacked and in danger of being over-run. He seized a Browning, and firing it from the hip, advanced alone, inflicting many casualties before halting the enemy. Despite an arm wound, he mounted his gun on a fence and caused more casualties until receiving two more wounds, collapsing and being taken prisoner	Gazette: 2 May 1945
Commemoration:	i) Headstone ii) Plaque and desk at St.John's Church, Old Trafford, Manchester iii) Name on the Manchester Abattoir Memorial, Phillip's Park Cemetery, Manchester iv) Name in Book of Remembrance, Guards Chapel, Wellington Barracks, London v) Plaque in Old Trafford Boys School,Manchester vi) Charlton Road, Stretford, Manchester named for him vii) Medals in The Irish Guards Museum	

1332   **LACHHIMAN GURUNG   VC   Hon. Havildar (Sergeant)   8th Gurkha Rifles, Indian Army**

Taungdaw, Burma
now Myanmar
709

Born: 30 December 1916 - Dawakhani Village, Chitwan District, Western Nepal

Deed/Service: 12 - 13 May 1945 (Rifleman) When manning the most forward post of his platoon with two other men, they bore the brunt of an attack by over 200 Japanese troops. Twice he hurled back grenades that had fallen in his trench, but the third exploded in his hand, blowing off his fingers, shattering his arm and causing other severe wounds. His two comrades were also badly wounded and so alone he loaded and fired his rifle with his left hand for over four hours, calmly waiting for each attack which he met with fire at point blank range against vastly superior numerical odds

Gazette: 27 July 1945

Commemoration: i) 'Lachhiman VC House' - erected from monies donated by Daily Express readers, at Bharatpur ii) Medals with the 8th Gurkha Rifles, India

1333   **MACKEY John Bernard   VC   Corporal   2/3rd Pioneer Bn. Australian Military Forces**

Tarakan Island, Borneo
POSTHUMOUS
802

Born: 16 May 1922 - Leichhardt, Sydney, New South Wales, Australia

Died: 12 May 1945 aged 24. Killed in his VC action on Tarakan Island, Sulawesi Sea, off the coast of North Borneo

Buried: Labuan War Cemetery, Borneo (now Sabah, Malaysia). 5 miles from Victoria Township, Brunei Bay. Plot XXVII. Row C. Grave 9. Headstone

Deed/Service: 12 May 1945. When leading his section along a narrow spur, they came under fire from three enemy positions. Single-handed he charged the first position and killed one of the enemy, then rushed a heavy machine-gun post and killed its crew. He then attacked the third position further along the spur and was killed, but not before he had killed two more of the enemy. His courageous and inspiring actions allowed his men to advance

Gazette: 8 November 1945

Commemoration: i) Headstone shows age 25 ii) Large memorial obelisk outside the R.S.L. Building, Portland, N.S.W. iii) Plaque in front of the War Memorial in Pioneer's Park, Leichhardt iv) Mackey Place, Canberra, A.C.T. v) Medals and display at the Australian War Memorial, Canberra

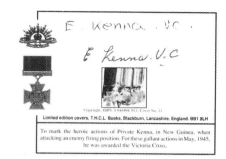

1334   **KENNA Edward   VC   Private   2/4th Infantry Bn. (New South Wales) Australian Military Forces**   **Wewak, New Guinea**
Born: 6 July 1919 - Hamilton, Western Victoria, Australia   **675**
Deed/Service: 15 May 1945. When fire from a bunker was holding up his company's advance, he stood up in full view of the enemy fifty yards away. Under a hail
                   of bullets he fired his Bren gun then when he had exhausted his ammunition he continued to fire with a rifle. During the entire period he
                   totally ignored his own safety and as a result of his gallantry the enemy bunker was captured without further casualties to his comrades   **Gazette: 6 September 1945**
Commemoration: i) Display at the Australian War Memorial, Canberra, Australian Capital Territory, Australia

1335   **STARCEVICH Leslie Thomas   VC   Private   2/43rd Infantry Bn. (South Australia) Australian Military Forces**   **Beaufort, North Borneo**
Born: 5 September 1918 - Subiaco, Western Australia   **117**
Died: 17 November 1989 aged 71, at his home in Carnamah, Western Australia
Buried: Esperance Public Lawn Cemetery, Western Australia. 500 miles E.S.E. of Perth, on S. coast. War Graves Section. Grave 1366. Headstone
Deed/Service: 25 May 1945. During the capture of Beaufort, the leading troops in his section came under fire from two machine-gun posts, suffering casualties.
                   He moved forward alone and attacked each post in turn, killing five of the enemy with his Bren gun and putting the rest to flight. He later adopted
                   similar tactics and single-handed captured two more posts, killing seven of the enemy when they came under intense fire   **Gazette: 8 November 1945**
Commemoration: i) Headstone ii) Statue of him, with plaque, on Grass Patch War Memorial, Carnamah iii) Tablet at scene of his action at Beaufort (now Sabah,
                   Malaysia) iv) Display at Australian War Memorial, Canberra, A.C.T. v) Medals at the Army Museum of Western Australia, Perth

1336 **PARTRIDGE Frank John VC Private 8th Infantry Bn. (Victoria) Australian Military Forces**

Bougainville, Solomon
Islands, S.W. Pacific
968

Born: 29 November 1924 - Grafton, New South Wales, Australia
Died: 23 March 1964 aged 39. Killed in a road traffic accident near Bellinger, New South Wales
Buried: Macksville Cemetery, New South Wales. Headstone
Deed/Service: 24 July 1945. When his section came under heavy machine-gun fire on the Bonis Peninsula, near Bougainville, he rushed a bunker under covering
fire from a Bren gun. He silenced the machine-gun with a grenade, killing the only occupant and attacked another bunker, but loss of blood from
a severe wound halted him. Later rejoining the fight, he remained in action while the platoon withdrew from an untenable situation

Gazette: 22 January 1946

Commemoration: i) Headstone ii) Memorial stone in Macksville iii) Plaque in Nambucca Heads R.S.L., Bellinger iv) Display at Australian War Memorial,
Canberra

Bradford Cathedral

Belfast City Hall

1337 **MAGENNIS James Joseph VC Acting Leading Seaman Royal Navy**

Johore Straits, Singapore
821

Born: 27 October 1919 - Belfast, Northern Ireland
Died: 11 February 1986 aged 66, in 'needy circumstances' at his home in Halifax, Yorkshire
Cremated: 18 February at Nab Wood Crematorium, Scholemoor Cemetery, Shipley, Yorkshire. Ref: 34776. Ashes scattered in Garden of Remembrance
Deed/Service: 31 July 1945. Serving as a diver in HMS Midget Submarine XE 3 under command of 1338 FRASER, he attached limpet mines to the Japanese
cruiser 'Takao'. As XE 3 was tightly jammed under the target, he had great difficulty in squeezing through the hatch, then had to scrape barnacles
off the bottom of 'Takao' to fix mines, all with faulty breathing apparatus. He returned in an exhausted state, but volunteered to go out again
to free one of the jettisoned limpet carriers which had jammed next to XE 3. He cleared it after seven minutes nerve-racking work

Gazette: 13 November1945

Commemoration: i) Plaque in Bradford Cathedral, Yorkshire ii) Plaque and painting in Belfast City Hall iii) Painting in the War Memorial Building, Belfast iv) Plaque
in Garrison Church, Portsea, Hampshire v) Magennis Close, Gosport, Hampshire vi) Punch Bowl in Senior Mess, HMS 'Dolphin', Medway, Kent

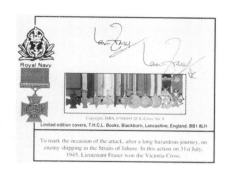

To mark the occasion of the attack, after a long hazardous journey, on enemy shipping in the Straits of Jahore. In this action on 31st July, 1945, Lieutenant Fraser won the Victoria Cross.

1338	**FRASER Ian Edward VC DSC RD & Bar Lieutenant - Commander Royal Naval Reserve**	**Johore Straits, Singapore**
Born:	18 December 1920 - 79 Uxbridge Road, Ealing, West London	**426**
Deed/Service:	31 July 1945 (Lieutenant) Commanding HMS Midget Submarine XE 3, he negotiated a long difficult approach up the Singapore Straits by leaving the believed safe channel and entering mined waters to avoid detection. Sliding XE 3 beneath the Japanese cruiser 'Takao', 1337 Magennis went out to fix limpet mines, then problems occurred when a jettisoned charge became stuck. Great difficulties were experienced inextricating the craft after the attack had been completed, until finally XE 3 was clear and commenced her forty mile journey out to sea	
Commemoration:	i) Plaque at the Conway Centre, Llanfairpwll, North Wales ii) Portrait at The Royal Grammar School, High Wycombe, Buckinghamshire	**Gazette: 13 November1945**

1339	**GRAY Robert Hampton VC DSC T/Lieutenant Royal Canadian Naval Volunteer Reserve, with 1841 Squadron, Fleet Air Arm**	**Onagawa Wan, Japan**
Born:	2 November 1917 - Trail, British Columbia, Canada	**POSTHUMOUS**
Died:	9 August 1945 aged 27. Killed during his VC action in Onagawa Bay, Honshu, Japan	**483**
Buried:	Body not recovered. Name on The Halifax Memorial, Nova Scotia, Canada. Panel 13.	
Deed/Service:	9 August 1945. Leading eight Corsair fighter bombers from HM Aircraft Carrier 'Formidable', ordered to attack prime Japanese airfields. On reaching the target he saw the fields had already been attacked and headed back to Onagawa Bay, where enemy warships had been seen. Targeting the destroyer 'Amakusa', he pressed home his attack under heavy fire from shore and ship batteries and dropped his bombs from just forty feet. The direct hit sank the 'Amakusa', but wounded and with the plane on fire, he plunged straight into the bay	
Commemoration:	i) Name on Halifax Memorial ii) Memorial in Sakiyama Peace Park, overlooking Onagawa Bay iii) Plaque in the Legion Post at Trail iv) Plaque in R.C. Church, HMS 'Daedulus', Lee-on-Solent, Hampshire v) Memorial in Point Pleasant Park, Halifax vi) Memorial in Garrison Church, Portsea, Hampshire vii) Numerous lakes, mountains and buildings named for him in British Columbia viii) Medals in Canadian War Museum, Ottawa	**Gazette: 13 November 1945**

The Victoria Cross and campaign medals awarded to Acting Leading Seaman James Joseph Magennis (1337)

The Victoria Cross, Distinguished Service Cross and campaign medals awarded to Lieutenant - Commander Ian Edward Fraser (1338)

Chapter Twenty
The Closing Episode
1951 - 1982

No's 1340 - 1351

The Victoria Cross and campaign medals attributed to Lieutenant Philip Kenneth Edward Curtis (1342)

The Victoria Cross and campaign medals awarded to Sergeant William Speakman (1343)

| 1340 | MUIR Kenneth VC Major 1st Bn. The Argyll and Sutherland Highlanders (Princess Louise) | Hill 282, Sonju, Korea POSTHUMOUS 898 |

Born: 6 March 1912 - Chester, Cheshire
Died: 23 September 1950 aged 38. Mortally wounded during his VC action on the crest of Hill 282
Buried: United Nations Memorial Cemetery, Pusan, Korea. Headstone
Deed/Service: 23 September 1951. When difficulties arose in evacuating wounded men, his arrival with a stretcher party eased the situation. When the enemy launched further attacks he took command, leading a counter-attack until the crest of the position was regained. He was determined to hold it until all the wounded had been taken to safety and moved about encouraging his men, firing a mortar himself until falling mortally wounded **Gazette: 5 January 1951**
Commemoration: i) Headstone ii) Name on father's headstone at St. Peter's Churchyard, Frimley, Surrey iii) Medals at Argyll & Sutherland Highlanders Museum

| 1341 | CARNE James Power VC DSO Colonel 1st Bn. The Gloucestershire Regiment (now Royal Glos. Berks & Wilts Regiment) | Imjin River, Korea 186 |

Born: 11 April 1906 - Falmouth, Cornwall
Died: 19 April 1986 aged 80, in Cheltenham Hospital, Gloucestershire following a fall on the 17th
Cremated: 25 April at Cheltenham Crematorium. Ashes buried at Cranham Churchyard, Gloucestershire
Deed/Service: 22-23 April 1951 (Lieutenant-Colonel) When his battalion was under heavy attack by vastly superior numbers of the enemy, he moved about the men under heavy machine-gun fire, inspiring confidence and the will to resist. He personally led two assault parties to drive back the enemy armed with rifle and grenades and his courage, coolness and leadership was felt throughout the entire brigade **Gazette: 27 October 1953**
Commemoration: i) Headstone at Cranham ii) The Carne Cross at Gloucester Cathedral iii) Medals at The Gloucestershire Regimental Museum

1342   **CURTIS Philip Kenneth Edward   VC   Lieutenant   The Duke of Cornwall's Light Infantry, attd. 1st Bn. The Gloucestershire Regt.**   Castle Hill, Imjin River, Korea
POSTHUMOUS

Born:	7 July 1926 - Devonport, Devon
Died:	23 April 1951 aged 24. Killed in his VC action on Castle Hill
Buried:	June 1951 at the United Nations Memorial Cemetery, Pusan, Korea. Headstone
Deed/Service:	22 - 23 April 1951. During a heavy enemy attack, his platoon was ordered to carry out a counter-attack which was held up by heavy fire and grenades. Ordering his men to give him covering fire, he rushed the main position of resistance but was severely wounded. He insisted on making a second attempt, but was killed within a few yards of his objective
Commemoration:	i) Headstone ii) Curtis Street Flats, Devonport iii) Medals in The Duke of Cornwall's Light Infantry Museum

294

Gazette: 1 December 1953

1343   **SPEAKMAN William   VC   Sergeant   The Black Watch (Royal Highlanders), attd. 1st Bn. The King's Own Scottish Borderers**   'United' Hilltop, Korea

Born:	21 September 1927 - 17 Moss Lane, Altrincham, Cheshire. Name recently changed to SPEAKMAN-PITT
Deed/Service:	4 November 1951 (Private) When a section holding the left flank of the company position had been seriously depleted by casualties and being over-run by the Chinese, on his own initiative he gathered six men and a supply of grenades. He then led at least ten charges towards the enemy, breaking up their attacks and causing heavy casualties until wounded by mortar fragments in the leg. Despite the wounds, he continued to throw in excess of 100 grenades and lead charge after charge, keeping the enemy at bay long enough to allow the withdrawal of his company
Commemoration:	i) Street in Slough named for him ii) Medals at the Scottish United Services Museum

1173

Gazette: 28 December 1951

1344   **RAMBAHADUR LIMBU   VC MVO   Captain   2nd/10th Gurkha Rifles (Princess Mary's) (now Brigade of Gurkhas)**   **Gunong Tepoi, Indonesia**
East of Sarawak border
1016

Born: July 1939 - Chyangthapu Village, Yangrop Thum, East Nepal
Deed/Service: 21 November 1965 (Lance-Corporal) When in an advance party of sixteen Gurkhas, they encountered some thirty Indonesians holding a strong position
on the peak of a jungle hill. With two men he went forward toward a machine-gun post and when just yards away a sentry opened fire. He
rush forward and killed the man with a grenade, whereupon the enemy opened fire on the party from all sides, wounding his two comrades.
He stood up in full view of the enemy under heavy fire and made two journeys dragging each man to safety over some sixty yards   **Gazette: 21 April 1966**
Commemoration: i) Display at the Gurkha Museum

1345   **WHEATLEY Kevin Arthur   VC   Warrant Officer Class II   Australian Army Training Team, Vietnam**   **Binh Hoa Village, Vietnam**
POSTHUMOUS
1294

Born: 13 March 1937 - Sydney, New South Wales, Australia
Died: 13 November 1965 aged 28. Killed during his VC action in the Tra Bong Valley, Vietnam
Buried: i) 15 November in Saigon, South Vietnam ii) 26 November in Lawn Cemetery, Pine Grove Memorial Park, Blacktown, N.S.W. Headstone
Deed/Service: 13 November 1965. During a search and clear operation his company were ambushed, resulting in many casualties. He insisted on staying with
a badly wounded fellow Australian, although he had ample chance to escape. He was killed trying to drag him to the safety of the jungle   **Gazette: 13 December1966**
Commemoration: i) Headstone ii) Memorial in the Hall of Heroes, JFK Center, Fort Bragg, North Carolina, USA iii) Memorial in the New South Wales Garden of

| 1346 | BADCOE Peter John   VC   Major   Australian Army Training Team, Vietnam | Thua Thien Province Vietnam |

Thua Thien Province
Vietnam
POSTHUMOUS
44

Born: 11 January 1934 - Adelaide, South Australia

Died: 7 April 1967 aged 33. Killed during the third 'part' of his VC action, near An Thuan Village, N.W. of Hue, South Vietnam

Buried: Terendak Garrison Camp Cemetery, Malaysia. 13 miles north of Malacca, on the Masjid Tanah Road. Headstone

Deed/Service: i) 23 February 1967. Near Phu Tu hamlets, he rescued a wounded U.S. officer under a hail of bullets ii) 7 March. At Qaing Dien he led his men in an attack, turning almost certain defeat into a victory iii) 7 April. In trying to stem a determined ARVN attack, he and a US NCO went forward alone under heavy fire, throwing grenades and firing at overwhelming numbers until shot through the head

Gazette: 13 October 1967

Commemoration: i) Headstone ii) Badcoe Hall, Officer Cadet School, Portsea, Victoria iii) Peter Badcoe ANZAC Club, Saigon iv) Streets in Canberra, Sydney and Adelaide v) Badcoe Park, Sydney vi) Medals and display at Australian War Memorial, Canberra

| 1347 | SIMPSON Rayene Stewart   VC DCM   Warrant Officer Class II   Australian Army Training Team, Vietnam | Ben Het, Kontum Province, South Vietnam |

Ben Het, Kontum Province,
South Vietnam
1146

Born: 26 February 1926 - Chippenden, New South Wales, Australia

Died: 18 October 1978 aged 52, from pneumonia brought on by cancer of lymph glands, in Tokyo, Japan

Cremated: 20 October in Tokyo. Half ashes buried in Yokohama War Cemetery, Japan and half returned to Australia 18 months later. Headstone (Japan)

Deed/Service: i) 6 May 1969. When on patrol near the Cambodian border, his company were ambushed by regular NVA troops and one of the platoon NCO's fell dangerously wounded. Rushing into the open under heavy enemy fire he brought the man to safety before reluctantly ordering a withdrawal. ii) 11 May. Following another ambush, he covered the evacuation of the wounded against vastly superior numbers and fire-power

Gazette: 29 August 1969

Commemoration: i) Headstone ii) Memorial in Hall of Heroes, JFK Center, Fort Bragg, North Carolina, USA iii) Simpson Street, Canberra, A.C.T. iv) Display and medals at the Australian War Memorial, Canberra

1348   PAYNE Keith   VC   Warrant Officer Class II   Australian Army Training Team, Vietnam

Ben Het, Kontum Province,
South Vietnam
972

Born: 30 August 1933 - Ingham, Queensland, Australia

Deed/Service: 24 May 1969. When ordered to seek out the position of a large NVA attack force, his own small force of under 100 ill-trained men arrived at the same jungle ridge as the force they were seeking. Having called in American aerial strafing of the NVA position, they were surprised to find that the enemy suddenly attacked them from all sides. Despite a serious head wound, he volunteered to go solo into the now enemy held position to seek the wounded. He made four return journeys leading the wounded to safety and organising a defensive base

Gazette: 19September1969

Commemoration: i) Keith Payne Park, Brisbane, Queensland ii) Display in Hall of Heroes, Fort Bragg, North Carolina, USA iii) Display at Australian War Memorial

1349   JONES Herbert (Known as 'H')   VC OBE   Lieutenant - Colonel   Comd. 2nd Bn. The Parachute Regiment

Darwin Hill, East Falklands
POSTHUMOUS
653

Born: 14 May 1940 - Putney, S.W. London

Died: 28 May 1982 aged 42. Killed during his VC action on the slopes of Darwin Hill

Buried: i) 30 May at Ajax Bay, near where he fell ii) 25 October at Blue Beach War Cemetery, Port San Carlos, Falkland Islands. Headstone

Deed/Service: 28 May 1982. When his battalion was held up during an attack on an Argentine position, and a called for Harrier strike was rejected due to poor conditions, he moved to a forward position. When the next assault went to ground he charged alone up the slope, but fell under heavy fire

Gazette: 11 October 1982

Commemoration: i) Headstone ii) Memorial cairn where he fell iii) Name on South Atlantic Task Force Memorial, St. Paul's Cathedral, London iv) Memorial in Eton College, Berkshire v) 'The Colonel H' pub, Lowestoft, Suffolk vi) Plaque on footpath, Kingswear, Devon vii) Name on the Parachute Regiment Memorial, Aldershot Military Cemetery, Hampshire viii) Medals in National Army Museum

1350 **McKAY Ian John VC Sergeant 3rd Bn. The Parachute Regiment**

Mt. Longdon, East Falklands
POSTHUMOUS
793

Born: 7 May 1953 - Wortley, near Sheffield, Yorkshire
Died: 12 June 1982 aged 29. Killed in his VC action on the slopes of Mount Longdon
Buried: 26 November at Aldershot Military Cemetery, Hampshire. Lower Section. Row A. Grave 101. Headstone
Deed/Service: 12 June 1982. When his immediate commander had been wounded, he took charge of the platoon during the assault on a strong Argentinian post near the top of the rocky eastern slope. When they were pinned down, he charged up the slope with four comrades who all fell wounded, but he continued alone until killed. His action enabled the rest of his comrades to extricate themselves from a dangerous position

Gazette: 11 October 1982

Commemoration: i) Headstone ii) Name on South Atlantic Task Force Memorial, St.Paul's Cathedral, London iii) Memorial in Garrison Church, Aldershot iv) Plaque at Rotherham Grammar School, Yorkshire v) McKay Memorial Cottages, Barnsley, Yorks vi) McKay Trophy for 3 PARA inter-platoon competition vii) Name on Parachute Regiment Memorial, Aldershot Military Cemetery

1351 **THE UNKNOWN WARRIOR OF THE UNITED STATES**

First World War
POSTHUMOUS
1351

Buried: Arlington National Cemetery, Arlington, Virginia, U.S.A.
Circumstances: Although it is generally believed that the Unknown British Warrior buried in Westminster Abbey was bestowed with the Victoria Cross, it is without foundation. The United States had awarded the Congressional Medal of Honor to the 'unknown, unidentified British soldier' by Act of Congress approved on 4 March 1921, and in the same spirit of comradeship a Cabinet meeting of 26 October 1921 approved the award of the Victoria Cross upon the Unknown Warrior of the United States. It arrived by diplomatic bag aboard HMS 'Eurydice' on 31 October, and was presented on behalf of King George V by Admiral of the Fleet Lord Beatty on 11 November 1921 at Arlington National Cemetery. (PRO, WO 32/4996)

318

Images
1857 - 1997

The first investiture at Hyde Park, 26 June 1857. Henry Raby (83) received the first award

William Allen (363) receiving his Victoria Cross from Queen Victoria, 9 December 1879 at Windsor Castle

320

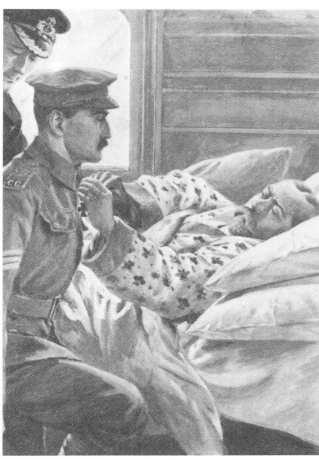

Oliver Brooks (672) receiving his VC from King George V, 1 November 1915 at Aire, France

Angus Buchanan (692) after receiving his VC from King George V, 8 November 1917

Daniel Beak (1037) receiving his VC from King George V, Autumn 1918

321

Cecil Knox (958) receiving his VC from King George V, Summer 1918

Theodore Hardy (998) receiving his VC from King George V, 9 August 1918

John Kenneally (1240) receiving his VC from General Alexander 28 April 1943

An investiture by King George VI at Buckingham Palace, 1945

Captain Hugh Burgoyne (66) c. 1860's

Colonel Francis Maude (170) (seated) an early portrait

Private Timothy O'Hea (327)

Colonel Mark Bell (340)

Lieutenant Walter Hamilton (347)

General Sir Redvers Buller (376)

Brigadier - General Edmond Costello (416)

Lieutenant - Colonel Frank Kirby (474) c.1910

VC's of the 24th Regiment c.1895
Back Row - Robert Jones (369), Alfred Hook (368), William Jones (370)
Front Row - David Bell (329), Colonel Edward Browne (379), Frederick Hitch (367), John Williams (373)

Instructors and visitors including the regiments three Boer War V.C.'s at the depot of the King's (Liverpool) Regiment c.1903
Colour - Sergeant Harry Hampton (482) - Backrow 2nd left, Corporal Henry Knight (483) - Backrow 4th left, Sergeant William Heaton (484) - Middle row 3rd left

A VC group at Chelsea Royal Hospital, 6 July 1910
Left to Right - Lieutenant - General Sir James Hills - Johnes (137), Major - General Sir Luke O'Connor (8), Field - Marshal Sir Evelyn Wood (285)
Field - Marshal Sir George White (349), Field - Marshal Rt. Hon. Earl Roberts (231), Colonel Sir Edward Thackeray (166)

A First World War VC group
(L-R) Michael O'Rourke (859), James Ockenden (893), William Butler (853), Ernest Egerton (879)

Francis Grenfell (528) with his twin brother Riversdale

Frederick Edwards (757) with his mother and brother at their home in Woolwich c.1916

Norman Holbrook (561) with the crew of the submarine B.11 c.1915

Wilfred Malleson (598) (centre) with fellow Midshipmen at Gallipoli

Ernest Pitcher (855) with King George V, Queen Mary and Queen Alexandra, 27 July 1918 at the Naval Exhibition, Piccadilly

A Western Front group John Crowe (985), Cecil Knox (958), Charles Train (938)

A naval VC group (L-R) Percy Dean (991), Gordon Steele (1152), Augustine Agar (1149), Sir Arthur Wilson (400), Edward Unwin (601)

Sgt. Alfred Ablett (95) and Head Constable Anthony Palmer (39) in the Millwall Docks Police c.1885

The Prince of Wales meets George Evans (739), John Readitt (779), George Stringer (690) and Charles Coverdale (888) outside the Town Hall in Albert Square, Manchester, July 1921

Armistice Day parade, Hyde Park c.1920's

A New Zealand VC group, 1929
Back row (L-R) Reginald Judson (1048), John Grant (1057), James Crichton (1103), Harry Laurent (1077)
Front row (L-R) Leslie Andrew (840), Samuel Frickleton (837), Cyril Bassett (637)

The VC Reunion Dinner, 9 November 1929 in the Royal Gallery, House of Lords, London

Armistice Day parade, 11 November 1929
Earl Jellicoe leades the VC procession

VC group, 1934
(L-R) Robert Downie (765), Martin Moffat (1121), John Ormsby (804), John Caffry (679), John O'Neill (1122)

John Smyth (619) c.1930

Augustine Agar (1149) leaving St. James Palace, 9 February 1937

Edward Foster (811) with his father c.1917

Edward Foster (811), Wandsworth c.1935

Quentin Smythe (1212) cheered by his comrades c.1942

Agansing Rai (1279) (right) c.November 1944

Naik Gian Singh (1319) and Rifleman Bhanbhagta Gurung (1317), 1945

Buckingham Palace investiture, 22 June 1945
(L-R) Basil Place (1248), Stephen Beattie (1204), Harry Nicholls (1165),
Donald Cameron (1249), Frederick Tilston (1315) (seated)

VC group, 1944
(L-R) Henry Foote (1210), Richard Wakeford (1266), Francis Jefferson (1267)

New Zealand VC Group
Back row (L-R) Leslie Andrew (840), Reginald Judson (1048), James Crichton (1103), Harry Laurent (1077), Cyril Bassett (637)
Front row (L-R) John Hinton (1179), Keith Elliot (1214), Charles Upham (1183), Alfred Hulme (1182), Samuel Frickleton (837), John Grant (1057)

A VC group at the grave of John Edmondson (1178)
(L-R) John Hinton (1179), Edward Kenna (1334), Richard Kelliher (1247), Frank Partridge (1336), Reginald Rattey (1322)

Ivor Rees (849) and Leonard Lewis (764) c.1958

Frederick Edwards (757) and Robert Ryder (758) at the Horse Guards, Whitehall, 1963

John Williams (1113), Edward Chapman (1325) and Major General Dudley Johnson (1144) c.1945

337

Arthur Proctor (707), Robert Ryder (758), James Hutchinson (712), Archie White (760)
Tom Adlam (759) and Theodore Veale (733) at the Thiepval Memorial, Somme, 1 July 1966

Back row (L-R) Ernest Frost (GC), David Currie (1288) Alexander Brereton (1030), Charles Rutherford (1049), Charles Merritt (1217)
John Mahony (1268), Coulson Mitchell (1114), Frederick Tilston (1315), Arthur Ross (GC), Thomas Dineson (1034), John Foote (1216), John Pattan (GC)
Front row (L-R) Raphael Zengel (1033), William Bishop (827), George Pearkes (910)
Gov. Gen. Roland Michener, Paul Triquet (1253), Ernest Smith (1299), Benjamin Geary (586)

John Moyney (873) and Tom Dresser (823) outside St. Clement Dane's Church, London c.1975

Double VC winner Charles Upham (1183) and John Hinton (1179), 1993

Agansing Rai (1279), Lalbahadur Thapa (1233) Ganju Lama (1273), Tulbahadur Pun (1276), Bhanbhagta Gurung (1319), Gaje Ghale (1244) c.late 1960's

339

Keith Payne (1348), Sir Roden Cutler (1185) and Edward Kenna (1334), 1995

Charles Merritt (1217) and Ernest Smith (1299) at a Royal Canadian Legion meeting 1994

Back row (L-R) Eric Wilson (1170), John Cruickshank (1282), Umrao Singh (1304), Roderick Learoyd (1171), William Reid (1251)
Middle row (L-R) Thomas Gould (1201), Ian Fraser (1338), Edward Chapman (1325), Richard Annand (1164), Pat Porteous (1218)
Agan Singh Rai (1279), Gian Singh (1317), Ernest Smith (1229), Bhanbhagta Gurung (1319), Ganju Lama (1273)
Front row (L-R) Gaje Ghale (1244), Sir Roden Cutler (1185), Bhandari Ram (1302), David Jamieson (1286), Ali Haidar (1329), John Hinton (1179) - May 1995

Agansing Rai (1279), Ganju Lama (1273), Gaje Ghale (1244), Bhanbhagta Gurung (1319) - 1995

341

The Victoria Cross, campaign medals and Scout badges awarded to Jack Cornwell (703)

Twenty four VC's at the Royal Army Medical Corps Museum
Top (L-R) Martin-Leake (512), Manley (317), Babtie (444), Ranken (544), Bradshaw (177), Douglas (441), Crean (510), Farmer (395)
Middle (L-R) Jee (173), Harden (1309), Green (716), Hale (101), Inkson (462), Lloyd (411), Sylvester (105), Allen (747)
Bottom (L-R) Home (180), Reynolds (371), Fox-Russell (914), Ackroyd (851), Hartley (385), Sinton (687), Mouat (24), Marling (401)

Memorial Window to Hamilton (347), St. Canice's Cathedral, Kilkenny, Ireland

Memorial Window to Bromhead (364), St. Germain's Church, Thurlby, Lincolnshire

Memorial Gates to Buchanan (692), Coleford, Gloucestershire

Memorial Stone near Noccundra Station, Queensland, Australia
Commemorating the Andrew Hume Expedition and O'Hea (327)

The statue of Albert Ball (812) at Nottingham

Village sign at Whissonsett, Norfolk in memory of
Derek Seagrim (1231) and his brother Hugh awarded the George Cross

Memorial Plaque at Salisbury British Legion Club commemorating twelve VC's with Wiltshire associations

"COBBERS" The Fromelles Australian Memorial Park, Bullecourt, France

The entrance to the British Cemetery and Memorial at Pozieres, Somme, France

Keren Cremation Memorial, Eritrea

Kohima Memorial, India

Taukkyan Memorial, Burma (now Myanmar)

East African Memorial, Nairobi, Kenya

Port Moresby Memorial, Papua New Guinea

Merchant Seamen Memorial, Tower Hill, London

Cassino Memorial, Italy

St. Nazaire Memorial, France

Tyne Cot Memorial and Cemetery, Belgium

Cairo War Cemetery, Egypt

Heliopolis War Cemetery, Egypt

El Alamein War Cemetery, Egypt

Nakuru European Cemetery, Kenya

Knightsbridge War Cemetery, Acroma, Libya

Beja War Cemetery, Tunisia

Gwelo Cemetery, Zimbabwe

350

Labuan War Cemetery, North Borneo

Rabaul War Cemetery, Papua New Guinea

Taiping War Cemetery, Malaysia

Yokohama War Cemetery, Japan

Arnhem Oosterbeek War Cemetery, Holland

Berlin South Western Military Cemetery, Stahnsdorf, Germany

San Carlos War Cemetery, Falkland Islands

The original grave of Corporal Leonard Keyworth (623)

The original grave of Sergeant John Rhodes (900)

The original grave of Corporal John Edmondson (1178)

The original grave of T/Captain The Lord Lyell (1237)

The funeral cortege of Private William Young (683), 31 August 1916 at Preston

The funeral cortege of Boy, First Class Jack Cornwell (703), 29 July 1916 at Manor Park

The funeral cortege of Walter Congreve (445), 4 March 1927 at Valetta, Malta

The reburial of Adam Wakenshaw (1213), 7 February 1943 at El Alamein War Cemetery

The funeral of Rawdon Middleton (1225), 5 February 1943 at Beck Row, Suffolk

The funeral of Ferdinand West (1028), 20 July 1988 at Sunningdale, Berkshire

357

The funeral of John Hinton (1179), 2 July 1997 at Christchurch, New Zealand

Appendices

INDEX TO APPENDICES

Gazetteer	-	361
Map - A (Western Front)	-	371
Map - B (Gallipoli)	-	372
Map - C (Brompton)	-	373
Map - D (Brookwood)	-	374
Map - E (Kensal Green)	-	376
Map - F (Karrakatta)	-	377
Map - G (Taukkyan)	-	378
Awards by Theatre of War	-	379
Family Ties/Posthumous etc	-	380
VC's by Mother Regiment	-	385
Birth Places of VC's - UK	-	395
Birth Places of VC's - Overseas	-	397
Average Age, Won/Died	-	398
VC's by Service/Country	-	398
Awards by Rank - Naval	-	399
Awards by Rank - Marine	-	399
Awards by Rank - Army	-	399
Awards by Rank - RAF	-	400
Living Recipients - March 1999	-	401
Museum Locations	-	402
Bibliography	-	409
Glossary of terms used	-	412
Main Acknowledgments	-	414
Photograph Acknowledgments	-	419
Special Thanks	-	431

AVON

BATH
Bath Abbey Cemetery (2)
Lansdown Cemetery (255)
Locksbrook Cemetery (164) (165) (276)
St Mary's Cemetery (311)
WESTON-SUPER-MARE
Weston-Super-Mare Cemetery ((107)
WOOLVERTON
St Lawrence's Churchyard (710)

BEDFORDSHIRE

SHARNBROOK
St Peter's Churchyard (515)

BERKSHIRE

BRAY
Touchen End Cemetery (639)
FINCHAMPSTEAD
St James Churchyard (119) (201)
INKPEN
Inkpen Churchyard (1207)
MAIDENHEAD
All Saints Churchyard (304)
READING
Reading Crematorium (648)
SONNING
St Andrews Churchyard (469) (506)
SOUTH ASCOT
All Souls Churchyard (340)
STUBBING
St James the Less Churchyard (269)
SUNNINGDALE
Holy Trinity Churchyard (1028)
SWALLOWFIELD
All Saints Churchyard (44)
WINDSOR
St Peter & St Andrew Churchy'd Old Windsor (244)
Town Cemetery (170)
Windsor Borough Cemetery (672)

BIRMINGHAM

ASTON
St Peter & St Paul Churchyard (1078)
HOCKLEY
Warstone Lane Cemetery (330)
QUINTON
Quinton Cemetery (1040)
SOLIHULL
Robin Hood Cemetery (725)
SUTTON COLDFIELD
Oscott College Road Cemetery (881)
Sutton Coldfield Crematorium (1147)
WITTON
Witton Cemetery (447) (661)

BRISTOL

Arnos Vale Cemetery (100) (1118)
Arnos Vale Crematorium (1081)
Canford Cemetery (500)
Canford Crematorium (951)
Greenbank Cemetery (864)
Redland Green Chapel Churchyard (192)
South Bristol Crematorium (1226)
Westbury-on-Trym Cemetery (405)

BUCKINGHAMSHIRE

CHALFONT ST PETER
St Peter Church Cemetery (1005)
GERARDS CROSS
St Josephs Priory Burial Ground (785)
MARLOW
Parish Churchyard (248)

CAMBRIDGESHIRE

CAMBRIDGE
City Cemetery (235) (489)
CHESTERTON
Parish Churchyard (126)

CHESHIRE

ACTON
Acton Parish (101)
ECCLESTON
St Mary the Virgin Churchyard (511)
HOYLAKE
Holy Trinity Churchyard (1122)
MACCLESFIELD
Macclesfield Crematorium (1298)
REDDISH
Willow Grove Cemetery (898)
RUNCORN
Runcorn Cemetery (756)
STOCKPORT
Stockport Crematorium (1136)
WEST KIRBY
Grange Cemetery (927)

CLEVELAND

MIDDLESBROUGH
Acklam Cemetery (1270)
Acklam Crematorium (567)
Eston Cemetery (995)
Teeside Crematoriuym (861)
Thorntree Cemetery (823)

CORNWALL

BODMIN
Glynn Valley Crematorium (1168)
FALMOUTH
Town Cemetery (1208)
HELSTON
Ruan Manor Churchyard (1204)
MOUSEHOLE
Old School Cemetery, Paul Village (88)
PADSTOW
Padstow Parish Churchyard (91)
PENZANCE
St Clare's Churchyard (152)
ST ERTH
St Ercus Churchyard (520)
ST VEEP
St Veep Parish Churchyard (771)
SALTASH
St Stephen's Churchyard (297)
TORPOINT
Anthony Cemetery (68)
TRURO
Penmount Crematorium (598) (1125)

CUMBRIA

BARROW-IN-FURNESS
Barrow-in-Furness Cemetery (362)
CONISTON
Coniston Churchyard (999)
WHICHAM
St Mary's Churchyard (847)
WHITEHAVEN
Egremont Cemetery (676)

DERBYSHIRE

BELPER
Belper Cemetery (954)
BRETBY
Bretby Crematorium (959)
CHADDESDON
St Mary's Churchyard (243)

CHESTERFIELD
Brimington Crematorium (890)
Spittal Cemetery (56)
HEANOR
Heanor Crematorium (1003)

DEVON

BIDEFORD
East-the-Water Cemetery (79) (341)
CHUDLEIGH
Ugbrooke House (Private) (33)
CREDITON
Holy Cross Churchyard (376)
DAWLISH
St Gregory's Churchyard (424)
DENBURY
Denbury Parish Churchyard (1010)
EXETER
Exeter & Devon Crematorium (975)
Exwick Cemetery (273)
Higher Cemetery (129)
HARBERTON
Harberton Parish Churchyard (238)
NEWTON FERRERS
Parish Church (1202)
PAIGNTON
Paignton Cemetery (105)
PLYMOUTH
Efford Crematorium (1119) (1202)
Ford Park Cemetery (36) (306)
Plymouth Naval Memorial (817)
SIDMOUTH
Temple Road Cemetery (406)
TIVERTON
Tiverton Cemetery (895) (966)
TORQUAY
Torquay Crematorium (670) (696) (712)

DORSET

BOSCOMBE
East Cemetery (229)
BOURNEMOUTH
Bournemouth Crematorium (483) (618)(731) (754)
(775) (815) (816) (986)
North Cemetery (816)
BRANKSOME
All Saints Cemetery (323)
CHRISTCHURCH
Christchurch Cemetery (281)
St Marks Churchyard (249)
CORTON DENHAM
Corton Denham Churchyard (1248)
LANSDOWNE
Wimbourne Road Cemetery (431)
NETHERBURY
Netherbury Churchyard (345)
PARNHAM
Parnham House Grounds (Private) (604)
POOLE
Evening Hill (731)
PORTLAND BILL
Portland Royal Naval Cemetery (1169)
POWERSTOCK
St Mary's Churchyard (990)
SWANAGE
Northbrook Cemetery (855)
WEYMOUTH
Weymouth Crematorium (691)

CO. DURHAM

CRAGHEAD
St Thomas's Churchyard (821)

DARLINGTON
North Road Municipal Cemetery (263)
EASINGTON
Wheatley Hill Cemetery (677)
HIGH SPEN
St Patrick's Cemetery (967)
RYTON
Ryton and Crawcrook Cemetery (545)
SEAHAM HARBOUR
Princess Road Cemetery (283)
SUNDERLAND
Tyne & Wear Crematorium (1135)

EDINBURGH
Grange Cemetery (241
Morningside Cemetery (59)
Morton Hall Crematorium (808)
North Merchiston Cemetery (261) (493)
Old Calton Cemetery (303)
Piershill Cemetery (541)
Tranent Parish Churchyard (122)
Warriston Crematorium (560) (721) (854) (1045)
(1142) (1197) (1235)

ESSEX
BARKING
Rippleside Cemetery (532)
BRENTWOOD
Christchurch Cemetery (29)
CHIGWELL
St Mary's Churchyard (402)
COLCHESTER
Colchester Cemetery (375)
GREAT DUNMOW
St Mary's Churchyard (691)
LOUGHTON
St John's Churchyard (525)
MALDON
London Road Cemetery (397)
SOUTHEND-ON-SEA
Southend Crematorium (802)
UPMINSTER
South Essex Crematorium (1076)

GLASGOW
Daldowie Crematorium (647) (883)
Eastern Necropolis (7)
Linn Crematorium (533)
Maryhill Crematorium (417)
New Eastwood Cemetery (923)
Riddrie Park Cemetery (546)
St Kentigern's Cemetery (290) (387) (765)
St Peter's Roman Catholic Cemetery (205)
Southern Necropolis (271)
Western Necropolis (61)
Woodside Cemetery (Paisley Old Cemetery) (37)

GLOUCESTERSHIRE
CHELTENHAM
Cheltenham Cemetery (5) (64) (317) (983)
Cheltenham Crematorium (595) (753) (880) (1341)
CHURCHAM
St Andrew's Churchyard (368)
CLEARWELL
St Peter's Churchyard (1130)
COLEFORD
Coleford Churchyard (692)
GLOUCESTER
Gloucester Crematorium (989)
LECKHAMPTON
St Peter's Churchyard (146)
LONGBOROUGH
Longborough Churchyard (499)

RODMARTIN
St Peter's Churchyard (378)
SELSEY
All Saints Churchyard (401)
SHIPTON MOYNE
St John's Churchyard (432)

HAMPSHIRE
ALDERSHOT
Aldershot Military Cemetery (285) (1132) (1350)
BASINGSTOKE
Basingstoke Old Cemetery (635)
BLACKMOOR
St Mark's Churchyard (759)
BROCKENHURST
St Nicholas's Churchyard (464)
BROOK (I.O.W.)
St Mary the Virgin Churchyard (151)
CARISBROOKE (I.O.W.)
Carisbrooke Cemetery (136)
CHURCH CROOKHAM
Christs Church Cemetery (1144)
CRONDLE
All Saints Churchyard (776)
CURDRIDGE
St Peter's Churchyard (219)
HORDLE
All Saints Churchyard (775)
PORCHESTER
Porchester Crematorium (893) (992) (1249)
PORTSMOUTH
Highland Road Cemetery (23) (67) (83)
(237) (251) (313)
(324) (396)
Kingston Cemetery, Portsea (76)
Milton Cemetery (391) (871)
St Mary Magdalene Churchyard, New Milton (778)
Portsea General Cemetery (42*)
Portsmouth Naval Monument (602) (916) (943)
(1224) (1242)
RYDE (I.O.W.)
Town Cemetery (111) (277)
SOUTHAMPTON
Swaythling Crematorium (681)
SOUTH BADDESLEY
St Mary's Churchyard (338)
WATERLOOVILLE
Hulbert Road Cemetery (456)
WINCHESTER
West Hill Cemetery (207) (579)
(*Site now a P & O Ferry Terminal car park)

HEREFORDSHIRE
PETERCHURCH
St Peters Churchyard (369)

HERTFORDSHIRE
CHIPPING BARNET
Bells Hill Cemetery (461)
ENFIELD
Enfield Crematorium (512*) (733)
KINGS LANGLEY
Kings Langley Cemetery (784)
WATFORD
West Hertfordshire Crematorium (666)
WIGGINGTON
St Bartholomews Churchyard (394)
(* also after 550 - Double award recipient)

HUMBERSIDE
KINGSTON UPON HULL
Western Cemetery (767)

KENT
BARHAM
Barham Crematorium (1206)
CANTERBURY
West Gate Cemetery (427)
CHARING
Charing Cemetery (831)
Charing Crematorium (1089)
CHATHAM
Chatham Naval Memorial (704) (857)
Maidstone Road Cemetery (106)
CHISLEHURST
Chislehurst Cemetery (656)
COLEMANS HATCH
Holy Trinity Churchyard (843)
DARTFORD
Watling Street Burial Ground (421)
DOVER
Charlton Cemetery (496)
St James's Cemetery (15) (25) (480)
FOLKESTONE
Cheriton Road Cemetery (46) (110) (139)
GILLINGHAM
Woodlands Cemetery (329) (1151) (1199)
GREAT CHART
St Mary the Virgin Churchyard (377)
HILDENBOROUGH
St John's Churchyard (1084)
HUNTON
Hunton Parish Churchyard (915)
IGHTHAM
St Peter's Churchyard (154)
MEREWORTH
St Lawrence's Churchyard (1)
PENSHURST
St John the Baptist Church (1091) (1256)
SELLING
St Mary the Virgin Churchyard (564)
SHORNCLIFFE
Shorncliffe Military Cemetery (194) (254) (392)
TUNBRIDGE WELLS
Tunbridge Wells Crematorium (522)
TUNSTALL
St John the Baptist Churchyard (1089)

LANCASHIRE
(See also Manchester & Liverpool)
BLACKBURN
Pleasington Crematorium (863)
Whalley Road Cemetery (457)
BOLTON
Overdale Crematorium (1267)
LANCASTER
Lancaster & Morecombe Crematorium (901)
LYTHAM ST ANNES
Park Cemetery (1064)
MIDDLETON
Boarshaw New Cemetery (1008)
NELSON
Inghamite Burial Ground (850)
OLDHAM
Chatterton Cemetery (548)
Hollinswood Crematorium (777)
ORMSKIRK
Ormskirk Parish Churchyard (484)
PRESTON
New Hall Cemetery (683)
Preston Crematorium (1112)
ROCHDALE
Haywood Cemetery (39)
Rochdale Cemetery (1140)
ST HELENS
St Helens Borough Cemetery (963)
St Helens Crematorium (899)

SOUTHPORT
St Cuthbert's Parish Churchyard (978)

LEICESTERSHIRE
BIRSTALL
St James's Churchyard (1173)
COALVILLE
London Road Cemetery (508)
KIBWORTH HARCOURT
Kibworth Harcourt Parish Churchyard (299)
LEICESTER
Gilroes Crematorium (958) (1001) (1088)
QUENIBOROUGH
Ratcliffe Roman Catholic College Cemetery (173)
WHITWICK
Whitwick Cemetery (359)

LINCOLNSHIRE
SLEAFORD
Newport Cemetery (615)

LIVERPOOL
ALLERTON
Allerton (450) (834)
ANFIELD
Anfield Cemetery (74) (118) (224)
Anfield Crematorium (494)
CROSBY
St Peter & St Paul Churchyard (742)
KIRKDALE
Kirkdale Cemetery (135)
LITHERLAND
Ford Cemetery (133)
LIVERPOOL
St James's Cemetery (476)

LONDON
BECKENHAM (SE)
Elmers End Cemetery (739)
BOW (E)
Tower Hamlets Cemetery, Southern Grove (114)
BROMPTON (SW)   (* = Memorial stone)
Brompton Cemetery (10) (21) (66*) (80) (96) (123)
                (142) (208) (212) (266) (286)
                (395) (625)
CAMBERWELL (SE)
Camberwell Cemetery (994)
Camberwell Old Cemetery (30)
CHISWICK (W)
St Nicholas's Churchyard (367)
ELTHAM (SE)
Eltham Cemetery (573)
FINCHLEY (N)
St Pancras & Islington Cemetery (92) (268)
City of Westminster Cemetery (47)
GOLDERS GREEN (NW)
Golders Green Crematorium (407) (418) (422) (488)
                (616) (619) (638) (640) (702)
                (877) (991) (1053) (1148) (1229)
HACKNEY (E)
St John's Churchyard (242)
HAMMERSMITH (W)
Margravine Road Cemetery (81) (275)
HENDON (NW)
Hendon Park Cemetery (310) (470)
HIGHGATE (N)
Highgate Cemetery (169) (180)
KENSAL GREEN (W)
Kensal Green Cemetery   (11) (24) (60) (199) (236)
                (293) (295) (301) (326)
                (408) (409) (411) (479)
Kensal Green Crematorium (West London) (629)
KENSAL RISE (W)
St Mary's R.C.Cemetery (8) (371) (510)

LEYTONSTONE (E)
St Patrick's Roman Catholic Cemetery (356)
MANOR PARK (E)
City of London Cemetery (84) (599)
Manor Park Cemetery (703)
MILL HILL (NW)
Mill Hill Cemetery (569)
PADDINGTON (W)
Old Paddington Cemetery (191)
PLUMSTEAD (SE)
Plumstead Cemetery (388) (403)
St Nicholas Parish Churchyard (98)
PUTNEY VALE (SW)
Putney Vale Cemetery (446) (592) (1129)
Putney Vale Crematorium (529) (728) (950)
ST PAULS (City)
St Pauls Cathedral (231)
STOKE NEWINGTON (N)
Abney Park Cemetery (196)
STREATHAM (SW)
Streatham Vale Cemetery (965)
Streatham Vale Crematorium (474)
TOTTENHAM (N)
Tottenham Cemetery (485)
TOWER HILL (City)
Tower Hill Memorial (783)
WANDSWORTH (SW)
Lambeth Cemetery, Blackshaw Road (187) (233)
Magdalene Road Cemetery (357)
Streatham Cemetery, Garratt Lane (811)
WEST HAMPSTEAD (NW)
West Hampstead Cemetery (952)
WESTMINSTER (SW)
Westminster Abbey, St Nicholas Chapel (48)
WEST NORWOOD (SW)
West Norwood Crematorium (552)
WOOLWICH (SE)
Woolwich Cemetery (86) (282)

MANCHESTER
Ardwick Cemetery (157)
Blackley Jewish Cemetery (780)
Gorton Cemetery (779)
Leigh Borough Cemetery (1127)
Phillips Park Cemetery (370) (690)
Southern Cemetery (41) (762)
Stockport Borough Cemetery (929) (940)
Swinton Cemetery (504)
Weaste Cemetery (Salford) (52)

MIDDLESEX
ENFIELD
Enfield Crematorium (512) (733)
HANWORTH
South West Middlesex Crematorium (590) (976)
HAREFIELD
St Mary the Virgin Churchyard (28) (758)
HARROW WEALD
All Saints Church Cemetery (746)
HILLINGDON
Hillingdon Churchyard (975)
TWICKENHAM
Percy Road Cemetery (1263)

NORFOLK
BUXTON
St Andrew's Churchyard (49)
DITCHINGHAM
St Mary's Churchyard (1223)
HARDINGHAM
St George's Churchyard (398)
NORWICH
St Faith's Crematorium (877) (1223)
Sprowston Cemetery (793)

SWAFFHAM
St Peter & St Paul's Churchyard (400)

NORTHERN IRELAND
CO. ANTRIM
BILLY
Parish Churchyard (719)
BROUGHSHANE
Presbyterian Churchyard (349)
BELFAST
Belfast City Cemetery (175) (232)
Friars Bush Roman Catholic Cemetery (259)
CO. DOWN
KILKEEL
Christchurch Cemetery (458)
NEWTONABBEY
Carnmoney Cemetery (878)
CO. FERMANAGH
LINASKEA
Donagh Cemetery (160)
MAGHERAVEELY
Agfhadrumsee St Mary's C of I Churchyard (214)
TUBRID
Bannagh Roman Catholic Churchyard (256)
CO. TYRONE
CREGGAN
Presbyterian Churchyard (687)

NOTTINGHAMSHIRE
NOTTINGHAM
Nottingham General Cemetery (62) (262)
Redhill Cemetery (1109)
Southern Cemetery (1165)
Wilford Hill Cemetery (679)
Wilford Hill Crematorium (524)
OXTON
St Peter & St Paul Churchyard (1228)
STAPLEFORD
Stapleford Cemetery (610)
WARSOP
Warsop Cemetery (842)

OXFORDSHIRE
ARDINGTON
Ardington Churchyard (6)
GORING
St Thomas of Canterbury Churchyard (443)
OXFORD
Oxford Crematorium (675) (772) (1207)
Rosehill Cemetery (813)

RUTLAND
ASHWELL
Ashwell Parish Churchyard (351)

SCOTLAND
ABERDEEN
St Peter's Cemetery (82)
AIRDRIE
Landward Cemetery, New Monkland (872)
AYR
Ayr Cemetery (667)
Kirkmichael Churchyard (50)
BOTHWELL
Bothwell Park Cemetery (267)
BUCKIE
New Cemetery (848)
CARLUKE
Wilton Cemetery (626)
COUR
*Private grounds (471)
CRAIGDUNIN
Craigdunin Cemetery (829)

CUPAR
St Monance Cemetery (527)
DRUMNADROCHIT
St Mary's Churchyard (93)
DRYNACHAN
Banchor Bridge (Site of ashes) (753)
DUNDEE
Eastern Necropolis (31) (222)
DUNFERMLINE
Culross Abbey Cemetery (182)
Dunfermline Cemetery (1079)
***EDINBURGH** (See separate entry)
ELGIN
Elgin Cemetery (167)
Holy Trinity Churchyard (621)
FORGLEN
Forglen Cemetery (426)
FORTROSE
Rosemarkie Cemetery (336)
FRASERBURGH
Kirktown Cemetery (825)
GLENKINDIE
Towie Churchyard (250)
***GLASGOW** (See separate entry)
GRANDTULLY
St Mary's Churchyard (220)
INVERESK
St Michael's Churchyard (19)
INVERNESS
Tomnahurich Cemetery (1203)
IRVINE
Knadgerhill Cemetery (542)
ISLE of ORONSAY
Oronsay Priory (316)
JEDBURGH
Castlewood Cemetery (1126)
KILMARANOCK (nr. Helensburgh)
Kilmaranock Cemetery (1143)
KIRKCALDY
Bannochy Road Cemetery (399)
KIRRIEMUIR
Kirriemuir Cemetery (807) (1297)
LAIRG
Lairg Cemetery (353)
LERWICK (Shetlands)
Lerwick New Cemetery (1277)
LESMAHAGOW
Lesmahagow (215)
MELROSE
Trinity Churchyard (149)
MOFFAT
Moffat Cemetery (930)
MUSSELBURGH
Portobello Cemetery (439)
NORHAM
Norham Churchyard (655)
PERTH
Perth Crematorium (829)
Wellshill Cemetery (264)
ST ANDREWS
Eastern Cemetery (130)
Upper Largo Cemetery (613)
ST MARTINS
Balbeggie Churchyard (265)

SHROPSHIRE
OSWESTRY
Oswestry Cemetery (945)
SHREWSBURY
Emstrey Crematorium (1084)

SOMERSET
FROME
Christchurch Churchyard (580)

HATCH BEAUCHAMP
St John the Baptist Churchyard (365)
WELLS
Wells Cemetery (331) (404)
WHITESTAUNTON
St Andrew's Parish Churchyard (57)

STAFFORDSHIRE
ALDRIDGE
Aldridge Churchyard (854)
BLYTHE BRIDGE
St Peter's Churchyard (879)
BRIERLEY HILL
St Michael's Roman Catholic Churchyard (374)
BURTON UPON TRENT
St Peter's Churchyard (1108)
WALSALL
Queen Street Cemetery (138)

SUFFOLK
ASBOCKING
All Saints Churchyard (1250)
BARDWELL
Bardwell Parish Church (287)
CAVENDISH
Cavendish Churchyard (1283)
IPSWICH
Ipswich Crematorium (420) (665)
Ipswich Old Cemetery (671)
MILDENHALL
St John's Churchyard, Beck Row (1225)
WEYBREAD
St Andrew's Parish Churchyard (95)

SURREY
ASHTEAD
St Giles Churchyard (882)
BROOKWOOD
Brookwood Cemetery (9) (145) (179) (385) (437)
(462) (516) (547) (658) (694)
(919) (1037) (1090) (1153)
CAMBERLEY
Royal Military Academy Cemetery (53)
St Michael's Churchyard (239) (355)
CHILWORTH
St Martha's Churchyard (768)
CLAYGATE
 ·· ly Trinity Churchyard (617)
DORKING
Reigate Road Cemetery (944)
EAST SHEEN
East Sheen Cemetery (348) (448)
Ashley Road Cemetery (441)
EWHURST
St Peter & St Paul Churchyard (350)
FRIMLEY
St Peter's Churchyard (128) (434)
GRAYSHOTT
St Luke's Churchyard (601)
GUILDFORD
Guildford Crematorium (583)
Stoke Cemeterty (444)
HERSHAM
St Mark's Churchyard, Whiteley Village (653)
HINDHEAD
St Alban's Churchyard (478)
KINGSTON-UPON-THAMES
Bonner Hill Road Cemetery (1260)
LEATHERHEAD
Randall's Park Crematorium (513) (536) (1266)
MORDEN
Battersea Cemetery (195)
NORTH SHEEN
Mortlake Crematorium (550)

PIRBRIGHT
St Michael & All Angel's Churchyard (514)
REDHILL
Hawthorn Way Cemetery (1065)
RICHMOND UPON THAMES
Richmond Cemetery (176) (228) (482) (757)
WOKING
Woking Crematorium (144) (277) (462) (465)
(486) (609) (653) (760)
(962) (1007)
WOLDINGHAM
St Agatha's Churchyard (16)

SUSSEX (East & West)
BOGNOR REGIS
St Mary Magdalene Churchyard, S.Bersted (108)
BOSHAM
Fairfield Road Cemetery (337)
BRACKLESHAM BAY
Earnley Cemetery (747)
BRIGHTON
Bear Road Cemetery (774) (1166)
Downs Crematorium (985)
Extra Mural Cemetery (1000)
Lewes Road Cemetery (51)
Woodvale Crematorium (519)
CHICHESTER
Chichester Crematorium (814)
CRAWLEY
Worth Crematorium (1171)
EASTBOURNE
Eastbourne Crematorium (674)
Ocklynge Old Cemetery (71)
HADLOW DOWN
St Marks Churchyard (416)
HASTINGS
Hastings Borough Cemetery (227)
HORSHAM
Hill Street Cemetery (245)
HURSTPIERPOINT
Holy Trinity Churchyard (162)
LANGRISH
St John's Churchyard (570)
MIDHURST
St James's Churchyard (561)
WEST CHILTINGTON
St Mary's Churchyard (584) (1210)
WORTHING
Worthing Crematorium (1171)

TYNE & WEAR
NEWCASTLE
Heaton Cemetery (423)
NORTH SHIELDS
Preston Cemetery (202)

WALES
(All counties)
ABERYSTWYTH
Llanbadarn Churchyard (889)
ANGLESEY
Amlwch Cemetery (832)
BRECON
Brecon Cathedral Burial Ground (102)
CAIO
Caio Churchyard (137)
EBBW VALE
Ebbw Vale Cemetery (1113)
LLANFIHANGEL
St Michael's Churchyard (373)
LLANRUG
St Michael's Churchyard (43)
MERTHYR TYDFIL
Pant Cemetery (911)

MILFORD HAVEN
St Katherine's Cemetery (764)
MONMOUTH
Monmouth Cemetery (363)
MUMBLES
Oystermouth Cemetery (539)
NEWPORT
St Woolo's Cemetery (32)
PONTYPRIDD
Glyntaff Crematorium (425) (680)
RHYL
Rhyl Cemetery (1050)
SWANSEA
Morriston Crematorium (849)
WHITCHURCH
St Mary's Churchyard (475)
WREXHAM
Pentrebychan Crematorium (1132)

WARWICKSHIRE
COVENTRY
Canley Crematorium (891) (1099)
London Road Cemetery (468)
St Paul's Cemetery (1002)
ROYAL LEAMINGTON SPA
All Saint's Churchyard (1141)
Royal Leamington Spa Cemetery (292)
STREETLY
All Saint's Churchyard (1147)

WILTSHIRE
COMPTON BASSETT
St Swithin's Parish Church (272)
SAVERNAKE
Cadley Churchyard (69)
SHERSTON
Church of the Holy Cross Churchyard (109)
UPAVON
Upavon Cemetery (1021) (Later interred in S.Africa)
WROUGHTON
St John & St Helen's Churchyard (790)

WORCESTERSHIRE
GREAT MALVERN
Great Malvern Cemetery (172)
KEMPSEY
St Mary's Churchyard (4)

YORKSHIRE
BRADFORD
Undercliffe Cemetery (70)
BURLINGTON
Burlington Priory Churchyard (14)
DEWSBURY
Dewsbury Cemetery (804)
DONCASTER
Arksey Cemetery (792)
Cadeby Churchyard (530)
Rose Hill Crematorium (678)
HALIFAX
All Souls Cemetery (171)
HARROGATE
Stonefall Crematorium (1131)
HUDDERSFIELD
Edgerton Cemetery (888)
ILKLEY
Ilkley Cemetery (828)
LEEDS
Cottingley Crematorium (772)
Harehills Cemetery, Chapeltown (673)
Hunslett Cemetery (853)
Lawnswood Crematorium (386) (578) (968)
New Wortley Cemetery (982)
Upper & Lower Wortley Cemetery (862)
Woodhouse Lane Cemetery (651)

MELTHAM
Lockwood Cemetery (806)
ROTHERHAM
Rotherham Crematorium (706)
ROYSTON
Royston Cemetery (918)
SHEFFIELD
Burngreave Cemetery (463)
City Crematorium (707)
Ecclesall Churchyard (856)
Sheffield Cathedral (707)
Wardsend Cemetery, Hillsborough (143)
SHIPLEY
Nab Wood Crematorium (1337)
THIRSK
Maunby Churchyard (393)
YORK
York Cemetery (72)

CHANNEL ISLANDS
JERSEY
ST HELIER
Mount L'Abbe Cemetery (280)
St Andrews Churchyard (986)

****
OVERSEAS

AFGHANISTAN

KABUL
Garden near the old Embassy (347)
SHERPUR
Sean Sang Cemetery (325)
Sherpur Cantonment Cemetery (344)

AUSTRALIA

AUSTRALIAN CAPITAL TERRITORY
CANBERRA
Norwood Crematorium, Mitchell (972) (1198)
NEW SOUTH WALES
BLACKTOWN
Blacktown Lawn Cemetery (1345)
MACKSVILLE
Macksville Cemetery (1336)
McGRATHS HILL
General Presbyterian Cemetery (253)
SYDNEY
Botany Cemetery, Matraville (794)
Eastern Suburbs Crematorium, Botany (1110) (1137)
Northern Suburbs Crematorium (1054) (1064)(1186)
Pioneers Memorial Park, Leichhardt (35)
Rookwood Cemetery, Strathfield (218) (797)
Rookwood Crematorium, Strathfield (1161)
St James's Churchyard (131)
Woronora Cemetery (646)
Woronora Crematorium (1056)
WEST BOGAN
St Matthews Anglican Churchyard, Coolabah (1058)
WEST WYALONG
West Wyalong Lawn Cemetery (1322)

QUEENSLAND
ALBANY
Pinaroo Lawn Cemetery (1047)
BRISBANE
Mount Thompson Crematorium (773) (1015) (1047
Toowong Cemetery (315)
LONGREACH
Longreach Town Cemetery (1062)
NOCCUNDRA
Noccundra Station - Hume's Creek, area fringing on Simpson's Desert (Memorial) (327)

SOUTH AUSTRALIA
ADELAIDE
West Terrace A.I.F. Cemetery (734) (788)
(875) (1013)
Centennial Park Crematorium (1138)
Stirling District Cemetery (735)
Stirling North Garden Crematorium (535)
TASMANIA
HOBART
Allonah Cemetery (884)
Cornelian Bay Cemetery (748)
Cornelian Bay Crematorium (1036)
TRANQUILITY
St James's Churchyard (487)
VICTORIA
BALMORAL
Balmoral Cemetery (430)
BOGONG
Myrtleford Cemetery (1059)
CASTLEFORD
St Kilda Cemetery (620)
FRANKSTON
Frankston Cemetery (1111)
KOROIT
Tower Hill Cemetery (225)
MELBOURNE
Brighton Cemetery (894) (1041) (1080)
East Brighton Cemetery (791)
Fawkner Cemetery (605)
Fawkner Crematorium (1006)
Melbourne General Cemetery (12) (334)
Springvale Cemetery (1104) (1247)
Springvale Crematorium (502) (643) (711)
(830) (1042)
MOUNT DUNEED
Mount Duneed Cemetery (824)
NORTH ALBURY
Presbyterian Cemetery (1017)
ROCHESTER
Bendigo General Cemetery (258)
WESTERN AUSTRALIA
ESPERANCE
Esperance Public Lawn Cemetery (1335)
PERTH
Karrakatta Cemetery (649) (744) (1085)
Karrakatta Crematorium (822) (833) (926) (997)
(1014) (1186) (1188)

THE BAHAMAS

NASSAU
Nassau War Cemetery (720)

BELGIUM

(Pre First World War)
BRUGES
Town Cemetery (78)

*First World War British Cemeteries
and Memorials - the names of nearest
village or town shown in bold type*

Bedford House **Zillebeke** *(658)*
Birr Crossroads **Zillebeke** *(851)*
Blankenberghe *Communal Cemetery Exten. (988)*
Brandhoek New **Vlamertinghe** *(743 & after 852)*
Canada Farm **Elverdinghe** *(845)*
Essex Farm **Boesinghe** *(839)*
Grootebeek **Reninghelst** *(612)*
Hooge Crater **Zillebeke** *(885)*
La Brique **St Jean-les-Ypres** *(682)*
Lijssenthoek **Poperinghe** *(642)*
Mendinghem **Proven** *(841)*

Menin Gate Memorial **Ypres** (435) (553) (587) (589)
(611) (634) (846) (908)
Menin Road South **Ypres** (844)
Oxford Road **Ypres** (886)
Perth (China Wall) **Zillebeke** (540) (876)
Ploegsteert Memorial (565) (709) (984)
Railway Dugouts **Zillebeke** (838)
Staceghem Communal **Courtrai** (1128)
St Symphorien **Mons** (523)
Tynecot Cemetery **Passchendaele** (892) (902) (913)
Tynecot Memorial **Passchendaele**(887) (896) (1101)
Vlamertinghe Military (528)
Vlamertinghe New (866)
Westoutre (980)
White House **St Jean-les-Ypres** (581)
Ypres Reservoir **Ypres** (467)
Zantvoorde (549) (1098)
Zeebrugge Memorial (993)

Second World War British Cemeteries

BRUSSELS
Brussels Town Cemetery (1306)
HEVERLEE
Heverlee War Cem., **Louvain** (1162) (1163) (1211)
LEOPOLDSBURG
Leopoldsburg War Cemetery (1296) (1312)

BELIZE
BELIZE CITY
Belize City Military Cemetery, Yarborough (328)

BERMUDA
ST DAVIDS ISLAND
St George's Methodist Cemetery (600)

BURMA (now MYANMAR)
NOKA
Yay Way Cemetery (174)
RANGOON (now Yangon)
Rangoon Memorial (1254) (1278) (1300)
(1308) (1311) (1316)
Taukkyan War Cemetery (1257) (1258) (1272)
(1280) (1310) (1318) (1321)
Taukkyan Cremation Memorial (1320)

CANADA

ALBERTA
ELNORA
Elnora Cemetery (1030)
FORT McLEOD
Union Cemetery (787)
LOUGHEED
Lougheed Cemetery (907)
ROCKY MOUNTAIN HOUSE
Pine Cemetery (1033)

BRITISH COLUMBIA
BURNABY
Forest Lawn Memorial Park (938)
Masonic Cemetery (869)
KAMLOOPS
Hillside Cemetery (588)
POWELL RIVER
Cranberry Lake Cemetery (1100)
VANCOUVER
Mountain View Cemetery (472)(755)(859)(905)(917)
Mountain View Crematorium (905) (917)
New Westminster Crematorium (1069)
North Vancouver Crematorium (921)
VICTORIA
Holy Trinity Cemetery, West Saanich (910)
Royal Oak Burial Park (1004)

MANITOBA
WINNIPEG
Winnipeg Presbyterian Cemetery (970)

NEW BRUNSWICK
BATHURST
St Alban's Cemetery (1025)
FREDERICTON
Snider Mountain Baptist Church Cemetery (1092)

NEWFOUNDLAND
ST JOHN'S
Anglican Cemetery (1123)

NOVA SCOTIA
HANTSPORT
Hantsport Church Cemetery (211)

ONTARIO
BROCKVILLE
Oakland Cemetery (798)
COBURG
St Andrew's Churchyard (1216)
COLBOURNE
Union Cemetery (1049)
ETOBICOKE
Sanctuary Park Cemetery (1323)
HAMILTON
Holy Sepulchre Cemetery (127)
LAC SEUL
Goose Island (Memorial cairn) (904)
LIONS HEAD
Eastnor Township Cemetery (274)
LONDON
Mount Pleasant Crematorium (1268)
NIAGARA-on-the-LAKE
St Mark's Church Cemetery (586)
OTTAWA
Notre Dame de Lourdes Cemetery (870)
OWEN SOUND
Greenwood Cemetery (827) (903) (1288)
SAULTE STE. MARIE
West Korah Cemetery (1106)
TORONTO
Mount Hope Cemetery (1315)
Mount Pleasant Cemetery (1095) (1134)
Pine Hill Cemetery (628)
Prospect Cemetery (291) (912) (1071)
St James Cemetery (490)
St James Crematorium (492) (827)
St Michael's Cemetery (147)
York Cemetery (562)

QUEBEC
MONTREAL
Field of Honour Cemetery, Mount Royal (1114)
Mount Royal Cemetery (596) (1051) (1073)
QUEBEC CITY
Mount Hermon Cemetery (491)
Mount Royal Crematorium (1253)

SASKATCHEWAN
MOOSOMIN
South Side Cemetery (909)

CHINA
SHANGHAI
Bubbling Road Cemetery (987)

CORFU
CORFU TOWN
Corfu British Cemetery (99)

CYPRUS
KYRENIA
British Cemetery (St Andrew's) (339)

DENMARK
COPENHAGEN
Garnisons Kirkegaard (Garrison Churchy'd) (645)
RINGSTED
Horsholm Cemetery (1034)

EGYPT
ALEXANDRIA
Hadra War Cemetery (543)
CAIRO
Cairo War Cemetery (1192)
EAST KANTARA
Kantara War Cemetery (1075)
EL ALAMEIN
El Alamein War Cemetery (1213) (1215)
(1221) (1222)
HALFAYA
Halfaya Sollum War Cemetery (1096)
PORT TEWFIK
Heliopolis Memorial (1087)

ERITREA
KEREN
Keren Cremation Memorial (1176)
SENAFE
Military Cemetery (17)

FALKLAND ISLANDS
PORT SAN CARLOS
Blue Beach War Cemetery (1349)

FRANCE

(Pre First World War)
CAEN
Protestant Cemetery (221)
CANNES
Cimitiere Protestant du Grand Jus (185) (314)
NICE
Cimitiere de Caucade (473)

First World War British Cemeteries and
Memorials - the names of nearest
village or town shown in **bold** type
Abbeville Communal Cemetery (623)
Adanac Military, **Miraumont-Pys** (1044) (763)
A.I.F. Burial Ground, **Flers** (957)
Annoeullin Communal, German Extension (812)
Arras Road Cemetery, **Roclincourt** (659)
Arras Memorial (633) (701) (708) (810) (819)
(820) (826) (852) (946) (969)
(971) (973) (1012)
Arras Road Cemetery, **Roclincourt** (659)
Auberchicourt British Cemetery (1139)
Aubigny Communal Extension (1061)
Bailleul Communal Cemetery Extension (769)
Bancourt British Cemetery (750)
Barlin Communal Cemetery (803)
Bellicourt British Cemetery (1102)
Berles New Military, **Berles-au-Bois** (789)
Bethune Town Cemetery (559)
Beuvry Communal Extension (1038)
Bienvillers Military Cemetery (554)
Boulogne Eastern Cemetery (627)
Bouzincourt Ridge Cemetery, **Albert** (955)
Braine Communal Cemetery (544)
Browns Copse Cemetery, **Roeux** (801)
Cambrai Memorial, **Doignies** (652) (897) (922)
(924) (928) (931) (937)
Carnieres Communal Extension (1115)

Chocques *Military Cemetery (668)*
Cojeul British Cem.,**St Martin-sur-Cojeul**(800)(809)
Contalmaison *Chateau Cemetery (741)*
Corbie *Communal Extension (729)*
Couin *New British Cemetery (1019)*
Crouy British Cemetery, **Hangest** *(1026)*
Dartmoor Cemetery, **Becordel-Becourt** *(740)*
Delville Wood Cemetery, **Longueval** *(737)*
Dernancourt *Communal Extension (1032)*
Dominion Cem., **Hendecourt-les-Cagnicourt** *(1067)*
Douchy-les-Ayette *British Cemetery (874)*
Dourlers *Communal Extension (935)*
Dud Corner Cemetery, **Loos** *(660) (662)*
Estaires *Communal Cemetery (517)*
Etaples *Military Cemetery (534)*
Etretat *Churchyard (715)*
Fillievres *British Cemetery (698)*
Flatiron Copse Cemetery, **Mametz** *(585)*
Foncquevillers *Military Cemetery (716)*
Fouquescourt *British Cemetery (1027)*
Gordon Dump Cemetery, **Mametz** *(726)*
Gorre British Cemetery, **Beuvry** *(939)*
Guards (Windy Corner) Cemetery, **Cuinchy** *(433)*
Hangard Wood British Cemetery, **Hangard** *(1023)*
Heath Cemetery, **Harbonnieres** *(1024) (1029)*
Hem Farm Military Cem.,**Hem-Monacu** *(781)(1060)*
Hermies *British Cemetery (761)*
Hermies Hill British cemetery, **Bertincourt** *(1086)*
La Chaudiere Military Cemetery, **Vimy** *(799)*
Le Cateau *Military Cemetery (953)*
Le Touret Memorial, **Richebourg L'Avoue** *(566)*
                                    (575) (576) (577)
Lichfield Crater Cemetery, **Thelus** *(796)*
Lillers *Communal Cemetery (538) (689)*
Longuenesse Souvenir Cemetery, **St Omer** *(574)*
Lonsdale Cemetery, **Aveluy** *(723)*
Loos *Memorial (657) (659) (663) (836)*
Marcoing *(1099 - ashes site)*
Mailly Wood, **Mailly-Maillet** *(1046)*
Marfaux British Cemetery, **Chambrecy** *(1018)*
Masnieres British Cemetery, **Marcoing** *(1097)*
Mazingarbe Communal, **Mazingarbe-Halte** *(664)*
Metz-en-Couture Communal Cem., **Fins** *(934)*
Moeuvres *Communal Cemetery Extension (805)*
Mory Abbey Military Cemetery, **St Leger** *(1039)*
Namps-au-Val Cem., **Namps-Quevauvillers** *(974)*
Naves Communal Extension, **Naves-Halte** *(1120)*
Nery *Communal Cemetery (537)*
Neuve-Chapelle Memorial, **Laventie** *(563) (571)*
Neuvilly *Communal Extension (1117)*
Niagara Cemetery, **Iwuy** *(1116)*
Noeux-les-Mines *Communal Cemetery (855) (860)*
Norfolk Cem., **Becordel-Becourt** *(717) (1148-ashes)*
Ors *Communal Cemetery (1145) (1146)*
Peronne Communal Ext.Cem., **Ste Radegonde**(1055)
Peronne Road Cemetery, **Maricourt** *(964)*
Pozieres British Cemetery **Ovillers-la-Boiselle** *(738)*
Pozieres Memorial, **Ovillers-la-Boiselle** *(948) (949)*
                                            (956)
Queant *Communal Cemetery (1093)*
Queant Road Cemetery, **Buissy** *(786)*
Querrieu British Cemetery, **Daours Halte** *(960)*
R.I. Rifles Churchyard, **Laventie** *(713)*
Rocquigny-Equancourt Rd. Cem., **Manancourt**(900)
Roisel *Communal Extension Cemetery (947)*
Romieres Communal Extension, **Solesmes** *(1074)*
Sablonnieres *New Communal Cemetery (440)*
Sanders Keep Military Cemetery, **Graincourt** *(1094)*
St Sever Extension Cemetery, **Rouen** *(998)*
Ste Marie Cemetery, **Le Havre** *(1083)*
Thiepval *Memorial, Somme (505) (572) (622) (714)*
                            (715) (718) (727)
Unicorn Cemetery, **Vendhuile** *(1072)*
Vadencourt British Cemetery, **Maissemy** *(555)*

Vailly British Cemetery, **Vailly-sur-Somme** *(526)*
Vaulx Hill Cemetery, **Vaulx-Vracourt** *(1052)*
Vertigneul Churchyard, **Romieres** *(936)*
Vielle-Chapelle New Mil.Cem., **Lacoutre** *(977) (979)*
Villers-Bretonneux *Memorial (736)*
Villers-Bretonneux *Military Cemetery (1022)*
Villers-Faucon *Communal Cemetery (835) (868)*
Vimy Memorial,**Vimy Ridge** *(795) (818) (858)(1035)*
Vis-en-Artois Mem., **Haucourt** *(1070) (1082) (1107)*
Vraucourt Copse Cemetery, **Vaulx-Vraucourt**(1043)
Wanquentin Com.Cem Ext **Beaumetz-Riviere** *(1009)*
Warlencourt British Cemetery, **Bapaume** *(752)*
Wavans British Cemetery, **Auxile-Chateau** *(942)*
Y Farm Military Cemetery, **Bois-Grenier** *(624)*

Second World War Cemeteries & Memorials

Bayeux *War Cemetery (1285)*
Brest *Cemetery (1172)*
Dunkirk *Memorial (1167)*
Escoublac-le-Baule War Cem., **St.Nazaire** *(1205)*
Meharicourt *British Cemetery (1274)*
Senantes *Churchyard (1284)*

GERMANY

HAMBURG
Hamburg Cemetery (925)
Ohlsdorf Cemetery (1187)
KESSEL
Niederzwehren Cemetery (961)
KLEVE
Reichswald Forest War Cemetery (1314)
SOLTAU
Becklingen War Cemetery (1326) (1331)
STAHNSDORF
Berlin South West Cemetery (531)
WESEL
Reichswald Forest War Cemetery (1314)

GIBRALTAR

North Front Cemetery (198)

HOLLAND

GROESBEEK
Groesbeek Memorial (1295)
LIMBURG
Sittard War Cemetery (1307)
NEDERWEERT
Nederweert War Cemetery (1309)
NIJMEGEN
Groesbeek Canadian War Cemetery (1313)
OOSTERBEEK
Arnhem-Oosterbeek War Cem., (1290) (1293) (1294)
ROOSENDAAL
Steenbergen-en-Kruisland Churchyard (1243)

HONG KONG

Sai Wan Bay Memorial (1196)

INDIA

(Place names are invariably old spellings)

AGRA
Agra Cemetery (203)
ALIGARTH
Bolandsarth Cemetery (158)
ALLAHABAD
Allahabad Cemetery (40) (181 - probable)
New Cantonment Cemetery (364)

BENGAL
Exact location unknown (161)
BOMBAY
St Thomas's Cathedral (104)
CALCUTTA
Barrackpore New Cemetery (120)
Exact location in city unknown (54)
CAWNPORE
Old British Cemetery (13) (183) (186)
DAMOI
Damoi Village (cremation), Rajputana (933)
DEHRA DUN
Dehra Dun Cemetery (112)
St Thomas's Churchyard (1124)
DELHI
Old Delhi Military Cemetery(115)(124)(159)(302)
DHARMSALA
Dharmsala Churchyard (412)
FEROZEPORE
Ferozepore Cemetery (113) (240 - probable)
GHAZIABAD
Exact location unknown (190)
GWALIOR
Artillery Lines Cemetery (117)
Gwalior Cemetery (163)
HOOGHLY
Bandel Churchyard, Darjeeling (184)
IMPHAL
Indian Army War Cemetery, Manipur (1261)(1271)
JALANDHAR
Jalandhar Cantt (cremation) (1317)
JULLUNDAR
Artillery Lines Cemetery (156)
KARFARTEER
Karfarteer Village (cremation), U.P. (558)
KASHMIR
Kashmir Cemetery (342)
KEORATOLA
Keoratola Crematorium (1175)
KOHAL
Kohal Cemetery (234)
KOHAT
Dehra Ismail Khan Cemetery (312)
KOHIMA
Kohima War Cemetery (1262) (1264)
LUCKNOW
Alumbagh (where he fell) (75)
Exact location unknown - (94) (168) (200) (246)
MADRAS
Exact location in city unknown (252) (289)
MEERUT
St John's Cantonment Cemetery (125) (213)
MOOLTAN
Mooltan Cemetery (209)
NAGPUR
Takli Cemetery (518)
OUDE
Fort Ruhya Cemetery (260)
PANAM
Panam Village (cremation) Punjab (1157)
PAROL
Parol Village (cremation) near Jullundar (686)
POONA
Cremated in Poona (now Pune) (1330)
St Mary's Churchyard (294)
St Patrick's Churchyard (335)
RAWALPINDI
Harley Street Cemetery (141)
RIVER RAVI
Believed drowned (288)
SANGOR
New Cemetery Sangor (284)
SAWAI MADHOPUR
Sawai Madhopur (cremation), Rajasthan (1265)

SECUNDERABAD
Secunderabad Cemetery (18)
SIMLA
Simla Cemetery (197)
TILSARA
Tilsara Village (cremation), near Kanpur (685)
TRICHINOPOLY
Taujore Cemetery (206)
UMBALLA
Umballa Cemetery (247)
URI
Uri Village (cremated), Kashmir (1259)

IRAQ

AMARA
Amara War Cemetery (669) (693) (770)
BASRA
Basra Memorial (582) (614) (695) (699) (700)
(1156)

IRELAND.

CO.CORK
Aghada Cemetery (153)
Cobh (Cork) Old Church Cemetery (632)
Cork City - exact location unknown (217)
Killinardish Churchyard (724)
Upper Aghada Cemetery (608)

CO. DUBLIN
DUBLIN
Arbour Hill Cemetery (223)
Fullamore District - exact location unknown (193)
Glasnevin Cemetery (58) (85) (178) (257) (390)
Grangegorman Cemetery (1063)
Mount Jerome Cemetery (22) (296) (343)
St James's Churchyard (305)
DUN LAOGHAIRE
Dean's Grange Cemetery (996)

CO. DONEGAL
LETTERKENNY
Conwal Cemetery (941)
LIFFORD
Clonleigh Churchyard (55)

CO. GALWAY
GORT
Believed to be buried in Gort area (204)

CO. KILDARE
BALLYMORE
Ballymore Roman Catholic Churchyard (140)
NAAS
Believed to be buried in Naas (73)
NEWBRIDGE
Newbridge Cemetery (27)

CO. KILKENNY
INISTIOGNE
St Mary's Churchyard (436)

CO. LIMERICK
LIMERICK
St John's Churchyard - 'probable' site (63)

CO. LONGFORD
LONGFORD
St John's Church of Ireland Churchyard (275)

CO. MAYO
WESTPORT
Westport Old Cemetery (121)

CO. MEATH
ASHBOURNE
Donaghmore Roman Catholic Churchyard (189)
DULEEK
Duleek Churchyard (319)

CO. MONAGHAN
CARRICKMACROSS
Old Bloomfield Cemetery (749)

CO. OFFALY
DERRINLOUGH
Eglish Churchyard (320)

CO. ROSCOMMON
ATHLONE
Cornamagh R.C. Cemetery (a.k.a.Athlone Old) (230)

CO. SLIGO
SLIGO
Sligo Town Cemetery (1121)

CO. TIPPERARY
CLONMEL
St Patrick's Cemetery (150)
MODREENY
St Kiernan's Churchyard
RIVERSTOWN
Lockeen Churchyard (226)
ROSCREA
Roscrea Roman Catholic Cemetery (873)
THURLES
St Mary's Church of Ireland Churchyard (177)

CO. WATERFORD
CLONAGEM
Clonagem Churchyard (380)

CO. WESTMEATH
CASTLETOWN
Castletown Church of Ireland Old Churchyard (636)

CO. WEXFORD
GOREY
Gorey Churchyard (210)

ISRAEL

BEERSHEBA
Beersheba War Cemetery (509) (906) (914)
GAZA
Gaza War Cemetery (932)
HAIFA
Khayat Beach War Cemetery (1133)

ITALY

ALASSIO
English Cemetery (521)
ANZIO
Beach Head War Cemetery (1269)
ARGENTA
Argenta Gap War Cemetery (1327) (1328)
BORDIGHERA
Old English Cemetery (166)
CADDENABIA
Grienze Churchyard (346)
CASSINO
The Cassino Memorial (1281)
FAENZA
Faenza War Cemetery (1303)
GENOA
Staglieno War Cemetery (688)
MINTURNO
Minturno War Cemetery (1255)

PAGLIETA
Sangro River War Cemetery (1238)
PALLANZA
Municipal Ossuary (132)
RIMINI
Rimini Gurkha War Cemetery (1291) (1301)
TREVISO
Giavera British Cemetery (1011)
VICENZA
Vicenza Cemetery (766)

JAMAICA

UP PARK
Up Park Military Camp Cemetery (26) (410)

JAPAN

YOKOHAMA
Yokohama War Cemetery (1347)

KENYA

NAIROBI
East African Memorial (1181)
Langata Crematorium (867)
NAKURU
Nakuru Crematorium (481)
VOI
Voi Cemetery (650)

KOREA

PUSAN
United Nations Memorial Cemetery (1340) (1342)

LIBYA

ACROMA
Knightsbridge War Cemetery (1190) (1191)
BENGHAZI
Benghazi War Cemetery (1189)
TOBRUK
Tobruk War Cemetery (1178) (1194)

MADEIRA

FUNCHAL
English Cemetery (65)

MALAYSIA

MALACCA
Terrendak Garrison Camp Cemetery (1346)
PENANG
Taiping War Cemetery (1195)
SABAH
Labuan War Cemetery (1252) (1333)

MALTA

TA BRAXIA
International Cemetery (103)
VALETTA
Msida Bastion Cemetery (Probable) (87)

NEPAL

LITUNG
Bharse Gulmi (981)
PAKILHAWA
Gurkha HQ Camp Cemetery (1233)
PALPA DISTRICT
Nagalpani (654)

NEW ZEALAND

AUCKLAND
North Shore Crematorium, Albany (637) (1241)
Otahuhu Old Cemetery (309)
Papaparaumu Crematorium (1214)
Purewa Cemetery, St John's (89)
Golders Cemetery, Waikumete (1057)
Waikumete Cemetery (1048) (1103)
Waihou at junction with River Thames (298)
CHRISTCHURCH
Harewood Crematorium (1183)
Ruru Lawn Cemetery (1179)
DUNEDIN
Andersons Bay Soldiers Cemetery (451)
Southern Cemetery (321)
HOKTIKA
Hoktika Municipal Cemetery (34)
MASTERTON
Masterton Cemetery (188)
NAENA
Taita Servicemen's Cemetery (837)
PALMERSTON
Levin R.S.A. Cemetery (840)
Terrace End Cemetery (308)
PAPANUI
St Paul's Anglican Church (Ashes) (1183)
ROSS
Isloated grave on hillside near town (318)
TARANIKI
Hawera Crematorium (1077)
TAUKAN
Alexandra Redoubt Commem. Park Cemetery (307)
TE PUKE
Dudley Cemetery (1182)
WELLINGTON
Karori Soldiers Cemetery (495)

NORWAY

NARVIK
Ballangen New Cemetery (1160)

PAKISTAN

BANNU
Bannu Cemetery, N.W.F. (1154)
BASALI
Takhti Village Burial Ground (697)
CHAKAWL
Rukhan Village Cemetery (551)
JANDOLA
Jandola Cemetery, N.W.F. (1155)
LAHORE
Lahore Cemetery (354)
MARDAN
Guides Cemetery, N.W.F. (419) (1158)
MIRANSHAR
Miranshar Cemetery, N.W.F. (568)
QUETTA
The English Cemetery (358)
SHAGI LANDI KYAN
Warsak Road Cemetery (603)

RUSSIA

ARCHANGEL
Souset Cemetery (1153)
(also known as Archangel Allied Cemetery)

SINGAPORE

SINGAPORE
Singapore Memorial, Kranji War Cemetery (1016)
(1172)

SOUTH AFRICA

CAPE PROVINCE
CAPE TOWN
Maitland Crematorium, Woltemade (415) (452)
Maitland Road No.1 Cemetery (557)
Maitland Road No.4 Cemetery (466)
St Peter's Cemetery (38)
Woltemade Cemetery (383)
GRAHAMSTOWN
Grahamstown Old Cemetery (438)
HERMANUS CLIFFS
(Near Cape Town - ashes) (880)
KING WILLIAM'S TOWN
King William's Town Old Cemetery (381)
KOKSTAD
Kokstad Cemetery (389)
MAFEKING
Mafeking Cemetery (1021)
MOLTENO
Molteno Cemetery (near Dordrecht) (428)
PINETOWN
St Andrew's Churchyard (20)
PORT ELIZABETH
Russell Road Roman Catholic Cemetery (366)
St Mary's Cemetery (97)
UITENHAGE
Old Anglican Cemetery (148) (reinterment)
WYNBERG
Plumstead Cemetery (384)

NATAL
CHIEVELY
Chievely War Cemetery (449)
DUNDEE (nearby)
Isandhlwana Battlefield (332)
DURBAN
Durban Crematorium (1212)
Stella Wood Cemetery (1105)
HELPMAKAAR (nearby)
Fugitive's Drift, Buffalo River (360) (361)
LADYSMITH
Ladysmith Cemetery (352) (455)
Wagon Hill Cemetery (454)
NEWCASTLE
Town Cemetery (498)

ORANGE FREE STATE
BOTHAVILLE
Lambrechfontein Farm (501)
DRIEFONTEIN
Driefontein Cemetery (460)
KIMBERLEY
Gladstone Cemetery (300)

TRANSVAAL PROVINCE
ERMELO
Ermelo Cemetery (745)
JOHANNESBURG
Belfast Cemetery (497)
Bramfontein Cemetery (782)
KRUGERSDORP
Krugersdorp Cemetery (477)
PAARDEBERG
Gruisbank British Cemetery (459)

SWEDEN

GOTHENBURG
Kviberg Cemetery (705)

SWITZERLAND

MONTREAUX (nearby)
Clarens Cemetery, Chemin de Muraz (379)

TANZANIA

MOROGORO
Morogoro Cemetery (556)

TUNISIA

ANNABA
Bone War Cemetery (1246)
BEJA
Beja War Cemetery (1227)
MASSICAULT
Massicault War Cemetery (1237) (1239)
SFAX
Sfax War Cemetery (1231) (1232) (1234) (1236)

TURKEY

Helles *Memorial (453) (591) (593) (597) (630)*
Lala Baba *Cemetery (429)*
Lancashire Landing *Cemetery (594)*
Lone Pine *Memorial (641) (644)*
Twelve Trees Copse *Cemetery (684)*
V Beach *Cemetery (606)*
Seddul Bahr *(isolated grave near V Beach) (607)*

UNITED STATES of AMERICA

CALIFORNIA
OAKLAND *Chapel of Chimes Crematorium(1031)*
ILLINOIS
MOUNT CARMEL *Rosehill Cemetery (1066)*
MAINE
EASTPORT *Bayside Cemetery (1068)*
MASSACHUSETTS
STOUGHTON *Evergreen Cemetery (322)*
PENNSYLVANIA
BUSHKILL *Sandhill Cemetery (1020)*
PHILADELPHIA *Laurel Hill Cemetery (333)*
RHODE ISLAND
JOHNSTON *Highland Memorial Park (732)*
VIRGINIA
ARLINGTON *National Cemetery (1351)*

URUGUAY

MONTEVIDEO
British Cemetery, Ave General Rivera (134)

YEMEN

ADEN
Maala Christian Cemetery (503)

ZIMBABWE

BULAWAYO
Bulawayo Cemetery (442)
Bulawayo Town Cemetery (413) (414)
GWELO
Gwelo Cemetery (507)
HARARE (Salisbury)
Harare Cathedral (415)
Harare Cemetery (382)
Pioneer Cemetery (730)

LOST AT SEA

AEGEAN SEA
Off Gallipoli (644)
ATLANTIC OCEAN
(EAST) Bay of Biscay, off Ushant (77)
(EAST) Bay of Biscay (1209)
(EAST) Exact position unknown (90)
(EAST) Off Angola (372)
(EAST) Off Azores (783)

(EAST) Off West Africa (1245)
(EAST) Off Ireland (817)
(EAST) Off West Fjiord, Norway (1159)
(MID) Exact position unknown (1174)
(WEST) Off St Vincent (3)
BAY OF BENGAL
Bay of Bengal (66) (277)
JAVA SEA
Java Sea (1200)

MEDITERRANEAN SEA
Off Gibraltar (1224)
Off Malta (445)
Off Sardinia (1242)
Mediterannean (1180) (1184)
NORTH SEA
Off Denmark (916)
Off Jim Howe Bank (857)
Off Jutland (704)

PACIFIC OCEAN
Off China (155)
Onagawa Bay, off Japan (1339)
RED SEA
Red Sea (116)
UNKNOWN
Between India and Great Britain (270)
Unknown (45)
(Most lost at sea recorded on memorial see entry)

*********************************** *********************************** ***********************************

All cemeteries referred to in the book located on the Western Front are within the coded boxes, with the distance and direction from a nearby town/city. Readers intending to visit cemeteries are advised to purchase large scale maps of the area as there are up to a hundred or more close together particularly around Albert and Ypres. These can be obtained from the Commonwealth War Graves Commission, 2 Marlow Road, Maidenhead, Berkshire SL6 7DX (Telephone 01628 - 634221   Fax: 01628 - 771208.

Allied Cemetery (now levelled) outside Sebastopol, Crimea, 1855

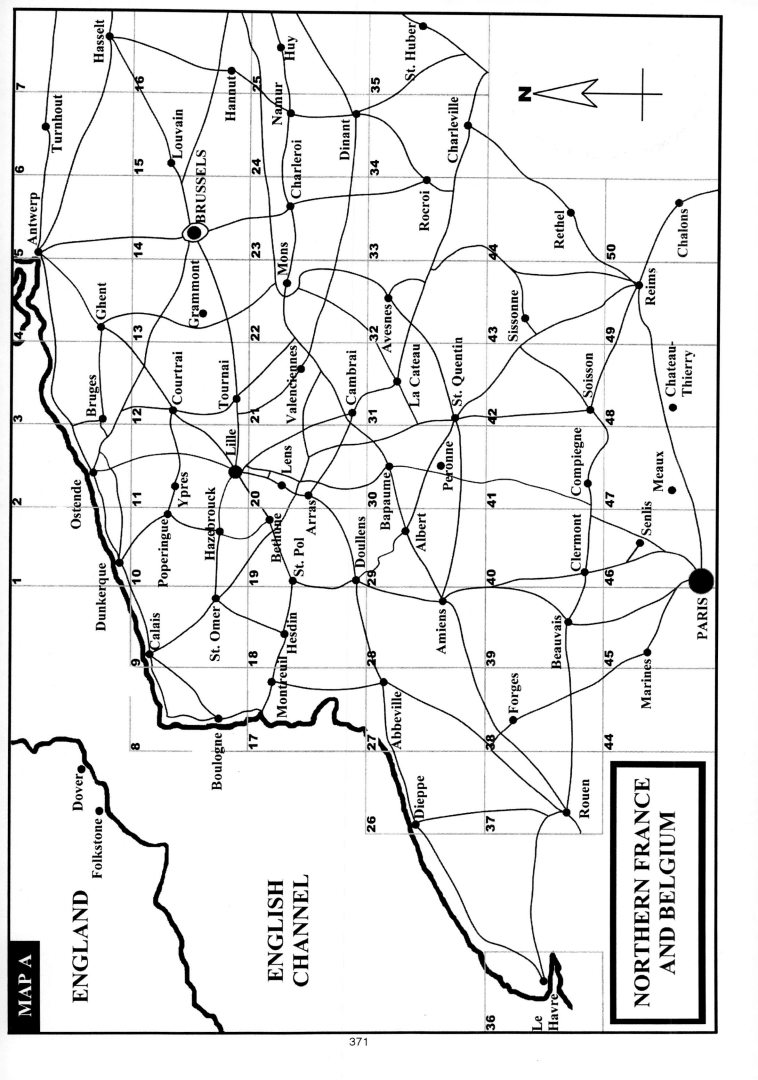

THE GALLIPOLI PENINSULA

MAP 'B'

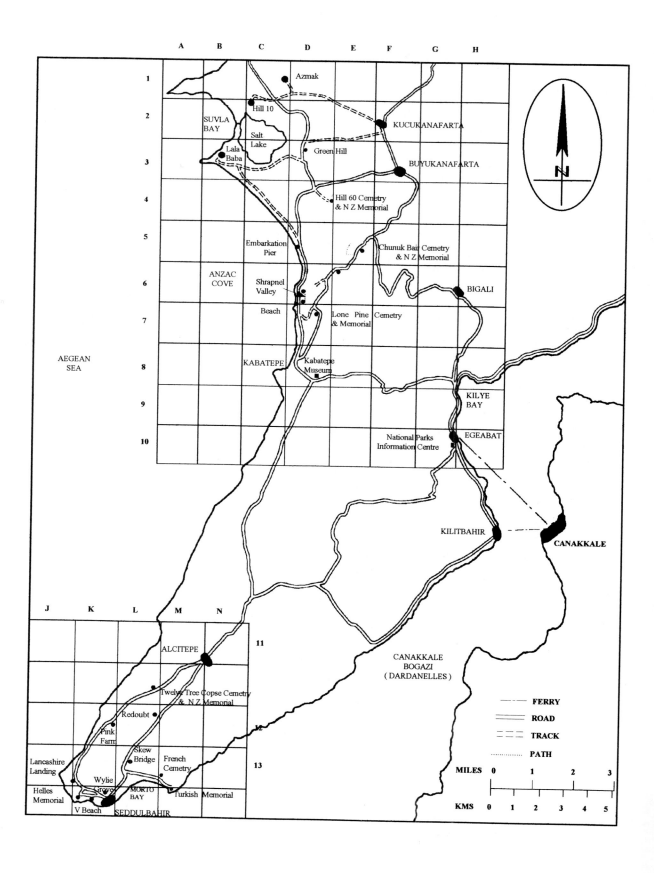

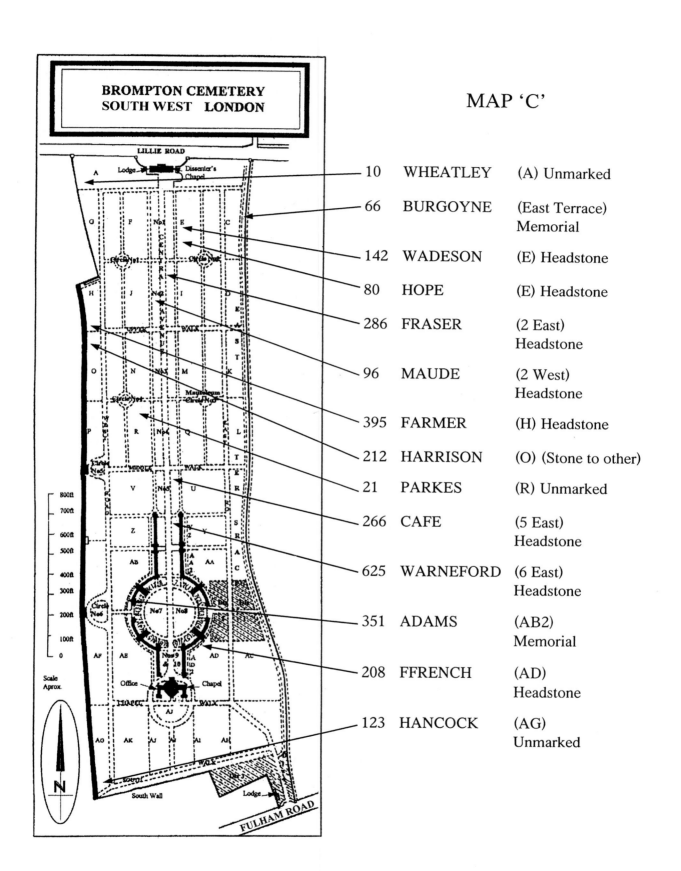

MAP 'C'

10	WHEATLEY	(A) Unmarked
66	BURGOYNE	(East Terrace) Memorial
142	WADESON	(E) Headstone
80	HOPE	(E) Headstone
286	FRASER	(2 East) Headstone
96	MAUDE	(2 West) Headstone
395	FARMER	(H) Headstone
212	HARRISON	(O) (Stone to other)
21	PARKES	(R) Unmarked
266	CAFE	(5 East) Headstone
625	WARNEFORD	(6 East) Headstone
351	ADAMS	(AB2) Memorial
208	FFRENCH	(AD) Headstone
123	HANCOCK	(AG) Unmarked

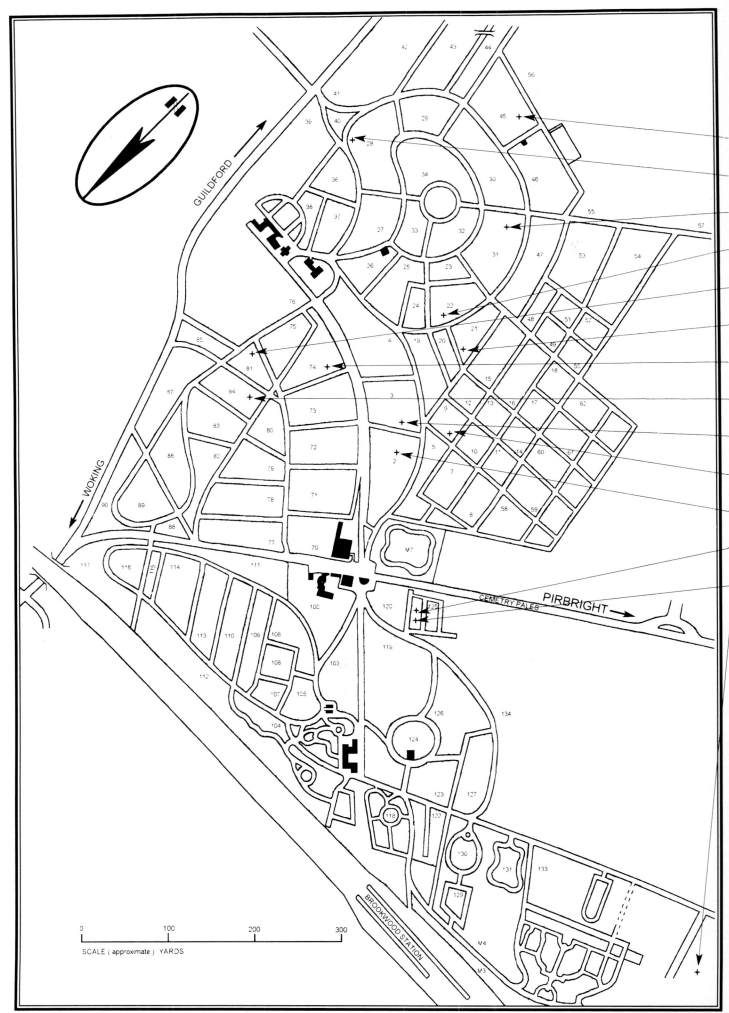

SCALE (approximate) YARDS

0   100   200   300

GUILDFORD →

← WOKING

CEMETRY PALES

PIRBRIGHT →

BROOKWOOD STATION

374

BROOKWOOD CEMETERY, SURREY.
MAP 'D'

9 **REYNOLDS** (Bloomsbury Plot) Unmarked

1090 **FRISBY** (28) Headstone

145 **MANGLES** (31) Headstone

694 **ADDISON** (22) Headstone

919 **SHERWOOD-KELLY** (81) Headstone

1037 **BEAK** (St Gabriel's Avenue) Unmarked

462 **INKSON** (74) Headstone

658 **HALLOWES** (84) Memorial

437 **MEIKLEJOHN** (3) Headstone

516 **WRIGHT** (9) Headstone

385 **HARTLEY** (2) Headstone

179 **HALLOWELL** (Corps of Commissionaires
Plot - both Unmarked)

547 **KENNY**

1153 **PEARSE** (Russia Memorial) Memorial

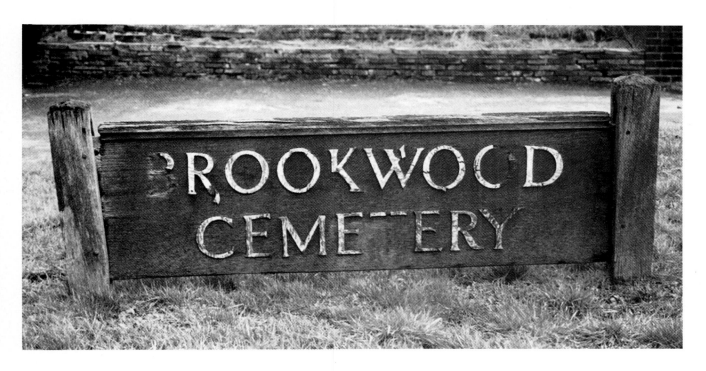

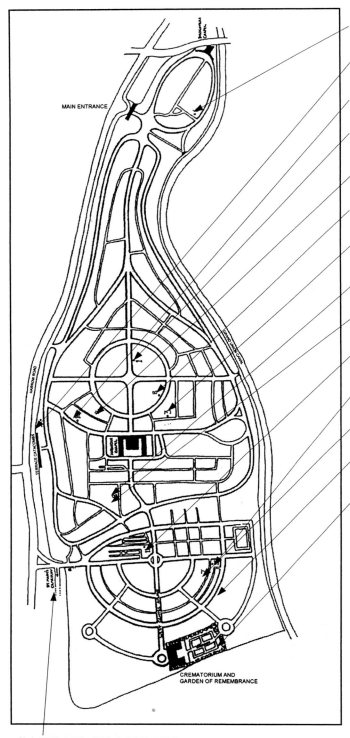

479   HOWSE (14) Headstone

408   BOISRAGEN (119) Headstone

293   PROBYN (117) Headstone

236   AIKMAN (76) Headstone

60   DIXON (103) Headstone

295   MALCOLMSON (99)
                  Headstone

11   DICKSON (112) Headstone

301   LENON (154) Unmarked

24   MOUAT (154) Headstone

326   TREVOR (179) Headstone

199   GOUGH (175) Headstone

411   LLOYD (188) Headstone

409   SMITH (187) Headstone

629   JAMES Cremated - ashes in
garden of memorial (No Memorial)

GATE TO ST MARY'S
8   O'CONNOR (1100)
371   REYNOLDS (504)
510   CREAN (896)

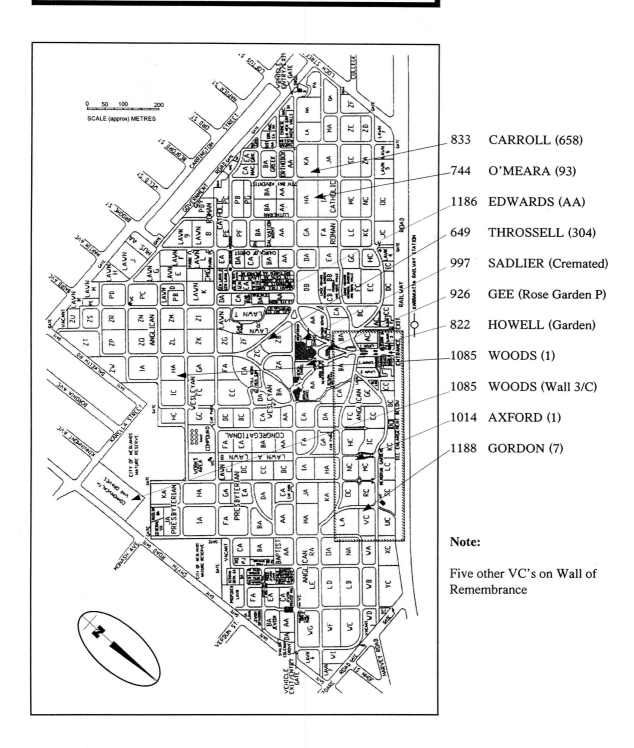

KARRAKATTA CEMETERY, PERTH, WESTERN AUSTRALIA

MAP 'F'

833   CARROLL (658)

744   O'MEARA (93)

1186   EDWARDS (AA)

649   THROSSELL (304)

997   SADLIER (Cremated)

926   GEE (Rose Garden P)

822   HOWELL (Garden)

1085   WOODS (1)

1085   WOODS (Wall 3/C)

1014   AXFORD (1)

1188   GORDON (7)

Note:

Five other VC's on Wall of Remembrance

377

TAUKKYAN WAR CEMETERY, CREMATION MEMORIAL AND THE RANGOON MEMORIAL

MAP 'G'

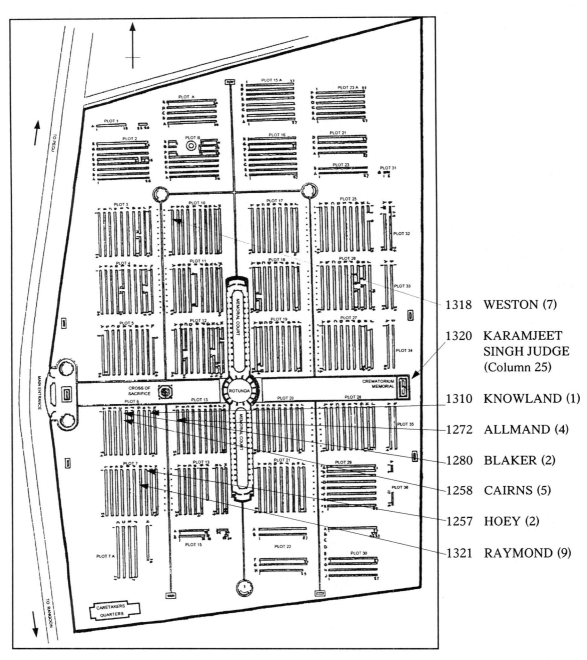

1318 WESTON (7)

1320 KARAMJEET SINGH JUDGE (Column 25)

1310 KNOWLAND (1)

1272 ALLMAND (4)

1280 BLAKER (2)

1258 CAIRNS (5)

1257 HOEY (2)

1321 RAYMOND (9)

NAMES ON THE RANGOON MEMORIAL

1254 HORWOOD (Face 4)
1278 NETRABAHADUR THAPA (Face 63)
1300 RAM SARUP SINGH (Face 30)
1308 SHER SHAH (Face 48)
1311 PRAKASH SINGH (Face 43)
1316 FAZIL DIN (Face 39)

VICTORIA CROSSES AWARDED BY CAMPAIGNS (57)

A detailed breakdown of Campaigns, enlarging on those shown in the twenty chapters

Crimean War, 1854 - 56	**(111)**	Hunza-Naga Campaign, India, 1891	**(3)**
Persian War, 1856 - 57	**(3)**	The Gambia, 1892	**(1)**
Indian Mutiny, 1857 - 59	**(182)**	Kachin Hills Expedition, Burma, 1892 - 93	**(1)**
Taranaki Maori War, 1860 - 61	**(2)**	North West Frontier, India, 1895	**(1)**
Third China War, 1860	**(7)**	Matabele Rebellion, Rhodesia, 1896	**(2)**
T'ai P'ing Rebellion, 1851 - 64	**(1)**	Mashona Rebellion, Rhodesia, 1896 - 97	**(1)**
Waikato-Hauhau Maori War, 1863 - 66	**(13)**	Malakand Frontier War, India, 1897 - 98	**(4)**
Umbeyla Expedition, NWF, India, 1863	**(2)**	Mohmand Campaign, India, 1897 - 98	**(3)**
Shimonoseki Expedition, 1864	**(3)**	Tirah Campaign, India, 1897 - 98	**(4)**
Bhutan War, 1864 - 65	**(2)**	Sudan Campaign Campaign, 1896 - 1900	**(5)**
Canada, 1866	**(1)**	Crete, 1898	**(1)**
The Gambia, 1866	**(1)**	South African War, 1899 - 1902	**(78)**
Andaman Islands Expedition, 1867	**(5)**	Third Ashanti Expedition, 1900 - 01	**(2)**
Abyssinia Expedition, 1867 - 68	**(2)**	Boxer Rising, China, 1900	**(2)**
Lushai Expedition, India, 1872	**(1)**	Second Somaliland Expedition, 1902	**(1)**
First Ashanti Expedition, 1873 - 74	**(4)**	Kano-Sokoto Expedition, Nigeria, 1903	**(1)**
Malaya, 1875 - 76	**(1)**	Third Somaliland Expedition, 1902 - 03	**(3)**
Baluchistan, 1877	**(1)**	Fourth Somaliland Expedition, 1903 - 05	**(2)**
Ninth Kaffir War, 1877 - 1878	**(1)**	Armed Mission to Tibet, 1903 - 04	**(1)**
Second Kaffir War, Afghanistan, 1878 - 80	**(16)**	First World War, 1914 - 18	**(628)**
Zulu War, 1879	**(23)**	North Russia Relief Force, 1919	**(5)**
Basuto War, 1879 - 82	**(6)**	Waziristan Campaign, India, 1919- 21	**(3)**
Second Naga Hills Expedition, 1879 - 80	**(1)**	Arab Revolt, Mesopotamia, 1920	**(1)**
First Boer War, 1880 - 81	**(6)**	Mohmand Campaign, India, 1935	**(1)**
Occupation of Egypt, 1882	**(3)**	Second World War, 1939 - 45	**(182)**
Sudan, 1881 - 85	**(5)**	Korean War, 1950 - 53	**(4)**
Karen-Ni Expedition, Burma, 1888 - 89	**(1)**	Vietnam War, 1962 - 75	**(4)**
Chin Field Force, 1889	**(1)**	Malaysia-Indonesia Confrontation 1963 - 66	**(1)**
Manipur Expedition, India, 1891	**(1)**	Falkland Islands War, 1982	**(2)**
	The Unknown American Warrior - First World War **(1)**		

TOTAL NUMBER OF AWARDS (Including Bars) 1,354

BARS - FAMILY TIES - CIVILIANS - FORFEITURES - NOT IN FACE OF ENEMY - ELECTED and POSTHUMOUS VC's

THREE MEN AWARDED BARS

Surgeon Captain Arthur **MARTIN-LEAKE (512)** of the South African Constabulary, awarded VC for action during South African (Second Boer) War on 8 February 1902; received Bar when a Lieutenant in Royal Army Medical Corps in the First World War on 8 November 1914.
Captain Noel **CHAVASSE (743)** of the Royal Army Medical Corps, attached to the 1/10 Bn. Liverpool Regiment (T.F.), awarded VC for action at Guillemont, France on 9 August 1916; received Bar at Wieltje, Belgium on 31 July and 2 August 1917.
Second Lieutenant Charles **UPHAM (1183)** of the 20th Battalion, New Zealand Military Forces, awarded VC for action in Crete on 22 - 30 May 1941; received Bar in the Western Desert on 14 - 15 July 1942, having been promoted to Captain.

FAMILY AWARDS

There are three instances of the VC being awarded to father and son:
445 Walter CONGREVE father of **729** Walter CONGREVE
150 Charles GOUGH father of **517** Sir John GOUGH
231 Earl ROBERTS father of **449** Frederick ROBERTS, with
1091 Viscount GORT being the father-in-law of **1256** Viscount De Le'Isle
In four instances the VC has been won by brothers:
761 Roland BRADFORD and **988** George BRADFORD
150 Charles GOUGH and **199** Hugh GOUGH
350 Euston SARTORIUS and **338** Reginald SARTORIUS
668 Alexandet TURNER and **1223** Victor TURNER, with
221 Thomas YOUNG and **321** Duncan BOYES being brothers-in-law, as were
128 William CUBITT and **137** Sir James HILLS-JOHNES and
1211 Leslie MANSER and **1264** John RANDLE.
1231 Derek SEAGRIM was the brother of **George Cross** recipient Hugh SEAGRIM
Four uncles and nephews have received the award:
19 John GRIEVE and **830** Robert GRIEVE
128 William CUBITT and **889** Lewis EVANS
269 Harry LYSTER and **448** Hamilton REED and
337 Lord Edric GIFFORD and **556** John BUTLER, with
78 Thomas ESMONDE being the great-uncle of **1199** Eugene ESMONDE
Four pairs of cousins have similarly received the award:
96 Frederick MAUDE and **170** Francis MAUDE
122 Thomas CADELL and **134** Samuel LAWRENCE
149 James BLAIR and **186** Robert BLAIR and
674 James DAWSON and **667** James POLLOCK

FIVE CIVILIAN AWARDS

Mr Ross **MANGLES (145)** of the Bengal Civil Service, awarded VC for action at Arrah during the Indian Mutiny on 30 July 1857
Mr William **McDONNELL (146)** of the Bengal Civil Service, awarded VC during the retreat from Arrah in the Indian Mutiny on 30 July 1857
Mr Thomas **KAVANAGH (198)** of the Bengal Civil Service, awarded VC at Lucknow, during the Indian Mutiny on 9 November 1857
Mr George **CHICKEN (279)** a volunteer with the Indian Naval Brigade, awarded the VC for action near Peroo during the Indian Mutiny, on 27 September 1858
The Reverend James **ADAMS (351)** of the Bengal Ecclesiastical Department, for action at Killa Kazi during the Afghan (Second Kaffir) War, on 11 December 1879

EIGHT FORFEITURES

The date in each case shown, is that of the forfeiture. The Cross itself is legally the recipient's personal property, and cannot be confiscated (Clause 15/1856 Warrant)

4 September 1861 - Midshipman Edward DANIEL **(34)** - Desertion
22 December 1862 - Sergeant James McGUIRE **(160)** - Felony
3 December 1863 - Private Valentine BAMBRICK **(268)** - Theft and assault
5 March 1872 - Private Michael MURPHY **(263)** - Theft
7 April 1881 - Private Thomas LANE **(300)** - Desertion and theft
30 July 1884 - Private Frederick CORBETT **(397)** - Embezzlement and theft
18 November 1895 - Gunner James COLLIS **(357)** - Bigamy
24 August 1908 - Private George RAVENHILL **(447)** - Theft.

SIX AWARDS MADE WHEN NOT IN FACE OF ENEMY

19 June 1866 - Private Timothy O'HEA **(327)** - locomotive incident, Canada
7 May 1867 - Assistant Surgeon Campbell DOUGLAS, Privates David BELL, James COOPER, William GRIFFITHS and Thomas MURPHY - at sea off the Little Andaman Islands. **(329 to 333)**
(Debatable seventh - 26 July 1877 - Captain Andrew SCOTT **(342)** - Quetta barracks)

ELECTED BY BALLOT

Forty seven awards have been made following ballots under Clause 13 of the original 1856 Royal Warrant. The number of VC's that could be granted by election was later modified, but the principal remained, distribution as follows:

Thirty during the Indian Mutiny in four 'incidents' - four awarded during the Siege of Delhi, **131** Heathcote, **152** Divane, **154** Sutton and **162** Waller all between June and September 1857; two during the Siege of Lucknow, **138** Thompson and **195** Sinnott, July to November 1857; twenty during the Relief of Lucknow **176** Olpherts, **200** Park, **202** Jennings, **203** Harrington, **204** Laughnan, **205** McInnes, **206** Smith, **208** Ffrench, **209** Kenny, **210** Guise, **213** Hill, **214** Irwin, **215** Mackay, **217** Dunley, **218** Paton, **220** Stewart, **222** Grant, **223** Graham, **224** Mylott and **225** Pye, all from September to November 1857; four awards for the charge at Gwalior on 17 June 1858 - **272** Heneage, **273** Hollis, **274** Pearson and **275** Ward.

Four were made during the South African (Second Boer) War - **466** Glasock **468** Parker, **469** Phipps-Hornby and **470** Lodge, all for the action at Korn Spruit on 31 March 1900.

The final thirteen were all awarded for actions during the First World War, the first for the 'six before breakfast' Lancashire Fusiliers, during the Gallipoli landings at Cape Helles on 25 April 1915 - **590** Grimshaw, **591** Bromley, **592** Richards, **593** Stubbs, **594** Keneally and **595** Willis. Two men from HMS *"Pargust"*, one of the 'Q' or 'Mystery Ships' **831** Stuart and **832** Williams were chosen by ballot for their action on 7 June 1917, followed two months later by **855** Pitcher's election aboard another 'Q' ship, HMS *"Dunraven"* on 8 August. The final four awards were for the Zeebrugge raid on 22 - 23 April 1918, **987** Bamford, **989** Carpenter, **992** Finch and **994** McKenzie.

POSTHUMOUS AWARDS (298*)

*I stress again, that the figures below are my own interpretation of warrants and the qualification for posthumous awards. With my contemporaries still unable to agree about an exact number, I have been on the generous side and consider 298 (plus the United States Unknown Warrior) to be the figure. I think that I have made a strong case for including such men as 947 Buchan, missing from many lists. During his VC action on 21 March 1918 he was severely wounded, surrounded and last seen fighting against overwhelming odds, leading to his capture and dying from his wounds the following day whilst a prisoner of the Germans. His award was announced in the London Gazette of 22 May 1918, two months following his action, yet his name is not included in most posthumous lists. I am sure that others will debate his inclusion below, perhaps with two or three others, as the current consensus is that the number of posthumous awards total 295.

2. Indian Mutiny (2)

115 Phillips E A L   260 Spence E

4. Zulu War (2)

360 Coghill N J A   361 Melvill T

5. Kipling's Soldiers (2)

414 Baxter F W   419 MacLean H L S

6. South African War (6)

449 Roberts F H S	454 Albrecht H	455 Digby-Jones R J T
477 Younger D R	497 Barry J	501 Coulson G H B

8. First World War 1914 (13)

523 Dease M J	531 Yate C A L	544 Ranken H S	559 De Pass
526 Wright T	537 Bradbury E K	549 Brooke J A O	563 Bruce W A McC
528 Grenfell F O	540 Johnston W H	553 Vallentin J F	565 Mackenzie J
	566 Acton A		

9. First World War 1915 (39)

568 Jotham E	591 Bromley C	627 Campbell F W	659 Kilby A F G
571 Gobar Singh Negi	593 Stubbs F E	630 O'Sullivan G R	660 Read A M
574 Noble C R	594 Keneally W	632 Parslow F	662 Wells H
575 Rivers J	597 Tisdall A W St. C	634 Woodroffe S C	663 Douglas-Hamilton
576 Anderson W	602 Williams W C	635 Liddell J A	668 Turner A B
577 Barber E	604 RhodesMoorhouse	641 Burton A S	669 Cookson E C
581 Morrow R	606 Walford G N	644 Shout A J	682 Drake A G
582 Wheeler G G M	607 Doughty-Wylie C	650 Dartnell W	683 Young W
587 Fisher F	611 Warner E	657 Peachment G	684 Smith A V
589 Hall F W	612 Lynn J	658 Hallowes R P	

10. First World War 1916 (28)

693 Ware S W	704 Harvey F J W	717 Loudon-Shand S	737 Gill A
695 Fynn J H	705 Jones L W	718 McFadzean W F	738 Castleton C C
698 Baxter E F	709 Hackett W	723 Turnbull J Y	740 Miller J
699 Cowley C H	713 Carter N V	726 Bell D S	741 Short W
700 Firman H O B	714 Bell E N F	727 Wilkinson T O L	750 Jones D
701 Jones R B B	715 Cather G St. G S	729 Congreve W La T	752 Brown D F
703 Cornwell J T	716 Green J L	736 Cooke T	763 Richardson J

11. First World War 1917 (52)

769 Mottershead T	818 Combe R G	(743) Chavasse N G	906 Lafone A M
770 Henderson E E D	819 Harrison J	857 Crisp T	908 McKenzie H
781 Cates G E	820 Jarratt G	858 Hobson F	913 Robertson J P
783 Smith A B	826 White A	860 Brown H	914 Russell J F
786 Cherry P H	835 Dunville J S	865 Learmouth O M	916 Carless J H
795 Milne W J	836 Wearne F B	868 Parsons H F	922 Wain R W L
796 Sifton E W	838 Youens F	876 Birks F	924 Clare G W
800 Waller H	839 Barratt T	885 Bugden P	928 Stone W N
801 Mackintosh D	841 Best-Dunkley B	886 Robertson C	931 McReady-Diarmid
803 Cunningham J	844 Colyer-Fergusson	887 Bent P E	932 Boughey S H P
805 Pope C	845 Davies J L	892 McGee L	934 Paton G H T
810 Hirsch D P	846 Hewitt D G W	896 Clamp W	937 Emerson J S
812 Ball A	851 Ackroyd H	902 Jeffries C S	939 Mills W

12. First World War 1918 (56)

943 White G S	979 Schofield J	1035 Spall R	1093 Honey S L
946 Beal E F	980 Dougall E S	1039 West R A	1094 Jackson T N
947 Buchan J C	988 Bradford G N	1043 McIver H	1098 McGuffie L
948 De Wind E	993 Harrison A L	1044 Forsyth S	1101 Seaman E
949 Elstob W	1009 Kaeble J	1046 Colley H J	1102 Vann B
953 Sayer J W	1018 Meikle J	1052 Sewell C H	1107 Riggs F
955 Collings-Wells J	1019 Travis R C	1055 Buckley A H	1115 Holmes W E

956 Columbine H G	1022 Brillant J	1060 Mactier R	1116 Algie W L
964 Anderson W H	1023 Croak J B	1061 Nunney C J P	1117 Lester F
969 Horsfall B A	1024 Gaby A E	1067 Knight A G	1120 McPhie J
971 Cassidy B M	1026 Miner H G B	1082 Lewis A L	1128 McGregor D S
973 Watson O C S	1027 Tait J E	1083 Waring W	1139 Cairns H
974 Flowerdew G M	1029 Beatham R M	1086 Young F E	1145 Kirk J
977 Collin J H	1032 Harris T J	1087 Badlu Singh	1146 Marshall J N

13. Between the Wars (5)

1153 Pearse S G 　　　　1154 Andrews H J 　　　　1155 Kenny W D

1156 Henderson G S 　　　1158 Meynell G

14. Second War 1940 (7)

1159 Roope G B 　　1160 Warburton-Lee B 　　1162 Garland D E 　　1163 Gray T

1167 Furness Hon. C 　　　1169 Mantle J F 　　　1174 Fegen E S F

15. Second War 1941 (11)

1176 Richpal Ram	1180 Sephton A E	1190 Gunn G W	1195 Scarf A
1177 Campbell K	1181 Leakey N	1191 Beeley J	1196 Osborn J R
1178 Edmondson J H	1189 Keyes G C T	1194 Jackman J J B	

16. Second War 1942 (13)

1199 Esmonde E	1208 Savage W A	1215 Gurney A S	1221 Kibby W H
1200 Wilkinson T	1211 Manser L T	1219 Kingsbury B S	1222 Gratwick P E
1205 Durrant T F	1213 Wakenshaw A H	1220 French J A	1225 Middleton R H
	1227 Malcolm H G		

17. Second War 1943 (10)

1230 Newton W E	1234 Anderson E	1242 Linton J W
1231 Seagrim D A	1236 Chhelu Ram	1245 Trigg L A
1232 Ngarimu M-N-A-K	1237 Lyell The Lord	1246 Aaron A L
	1239 Clarke W A S	

18. Second War 1944 (27)

1254 Horwood A G	1264 Randle J N	1278 Netrabahadur T	1293 Lord D S A
1255 Mitchell G A	1269 Rogers M A W	1280 Blaker F G	1295 Baskeyfield J D
1257 Hoey C F	1271 Turner H V	1281 YeshwantGhadge	1296 Harper J W
1258 Cairns G A	1272 Allmand M	1284 Bazalgette I W	1300 Ram Sarup Singh
1260 Barton C J	1274 Mynarski A C	1285 Bates S	1301 Thaman Gurung
1261 Abdul Hafiz	1275 Sukanaivalu S	1290 Grayburn J H	1305 Palmer R A M
1262 Harman J P	1277 Hornell D E	1291 Sherbahadur T	

19. Second War 1945 (19)

1306 Thompson G	1311 Prakash Singh	1318 Weston W B	1328 Lassen A F E V S
1307 Donnini D	1312 Swales E	1320 Karamjeet Singh	1331 Charlton E C
1308 Sher Shah	1313 Cosens A	1321 Raymond C	1333 Mackey J B
1309 Harden H E	1314 Stokes J	1324 Chowne A	1339 Gray R H
1310 Knowland G A	1316 Fazal Din	1327 Hunter T P	

20. The Closing Episode (6)

1340 Muir K	1342 Curtis P K E	1345 Wheatley K A	1346 Badcoe P J
	1349 Jones H	1350 McKay I J	

UNTIMELY DEATHS

Rather then dwell and identify each of the recipients who met 'untimely' deaths, I merely note the numbers and leave it to the reader to research further, having noted the cause of death with each entry, where known. I merely record here the fact that seventeen recipients committed suicide; five died whilst in mental asylums; eleven spent their final years in workhouses; two were murdered (a possible third is a matter of conjecture) and forty one were killed as a result of road, rail or riding accidents. The brief facts given obviously do not tell the full story, and I have applied the same maxim with the eight forfeitures, as it is not the purpose of 'Monuments to Courage' to delve into private lives in any great depth.

Victoria Cross holders were 'ordinary' men after all, and subject to the same problems and the highs and lows as any other man. If one were to dig for skeletons they would probably be found, the reasons for seventeen suicides, for instance, probably being the only one of these categories where being a VC recipient brought on extra pressures, and I would recommend Dennis Winter's book "Death's Men" to anyone who has not experienced warfare themselves, revealing the many kinds of strains and illnesses brought about by exposure to combat - particularly during and immediately following the First World War, where almost half of the awards were won.

SUMMARY

During the First World War, 188 of the 626 Victoria Crosses were awarded posthumously (30%), compared to the 87 out of 181 (48%) during the Second World War. It is impossible to draw parallels with other conflicts due to fact that the warrants had not been fully clarified until shortly before the First World War. Those awarded since have, in general, been awarded in smaller conflicts, the exception being Vietnam where Australian involvement had been small.

As can be seen from the percentages, it became increasingly difficult to survive the action in which recipient took part, and a comparison with the United States Congressional Medal of Honor reveals a similar survival rate, out of their 119 First War recipients, 25 awards were posthumous (20%), of the 433 from the Second War, 191 (44%) were killed or mortally wounded during their action, and to give their posthumous numbers during their involvement in Vietnam possibly reflects the ever decreasing survival rate for both our nation's highest award for bravery in the face of the enemy, with 150 (62%) of the 239 awards being made posthumously. Although comparisons with the American award can be misleading, due to fact that 1,527 awards were made during their Civil War, almost half the current total of 3,416, when standards were somewhat lower, a tightening of legislation relating to entitlement prior to the First War makes correlation in terms of figures a good deal more accurate

It is sometimes an overlooked fact that of the 3,416 Medal of Honor recipients, 436 were born in the United Kingdom, most being awarded during the Civil and Indian Wars when a large percentage of the U. S. Armed Forces were made up from first generation immigrants.

It would be impossible to compare Victoria Cross holders who were born 'abroad' to the Medal of Honor, as the vast majority of the 465 VC's born overseas came from the old Commonwealth countries (322) or from India (94), where the recipients were either native troops or were born of British parents serving in various capacities in the Raj. Of the 322 (24%) from the the Commonwealth, 134 were born in Ireland, all prior to the 1921 Anglo-Irish Treaty which resulted in the creation of the Irish Free State, and final independence from Britain in 1937. Twelve years later, Eire left the Commonwealth becoming the Republic of Ireland and so in terms of it being shown in tables as an 'overseas' country, it should be kept in mind that each one of Ireland's recipients were born there when it was 'part' of Great Britain.

Statistics can be misleading, and can be shaped to suit the writer's need to highlight any particular subject to prove his or her point of view, and with this in mind I have endeavoured to stick solely to basic facts. If a man was born in Manchester in 1865, was awarded the VC for an action in August 1900, and died in Brighton in 1930 and all the facts are indisputable, then there is little problem including those details in the various graphs and percentages without fear of later dispute. As I have stated above, there are discrepancies interpreting the posthumous awards and whilst I bow to current authorities, particularly John Tamplin MBE TD, who states categorically that there were 295 plus the Unknown American Warrior, I offer 'my' 298 as an analysis based on my own reading of the warrants, and leave the reader to research the subject for himself/herself for their own satisfaction and clarification.

BREAKDOWN OF VICTORIA CROSSES BY 'MOTHER' SERVICE, REGIMENT, UNIT AND COUNTRY

In order to give an idea to which service, regiment or unit each Victoria Cross was awarded, the list below shows each recipient along with the 'unit' the man was either commissioned in, or enlisted in IRRESPECTIVE OF any other 'unit' to which he was attached at the time he was awarded the VC. One notable example of this would be Albert BALL (812), who is naturally known as having received the award for flying services with the Royal Flying Corps, but was in fact commissioned in, and attached from The Sherwood Foresters, now The Worcestershire & Sherwood Foresters Regiment, under which you will find his name below. For the knowledgeable and purists the list may cause some consternation, but I include it merely as a guide in the hope that it may prove useful to many researchers

BRITISH RECIPIENTS ARE LISTED IN THE PRESENT ORDER OF SERVICE AND REGIMENTAL PRECEDENCE

ROYAL NAVY

ROYAL NAVY (104)

AGAR A W	1149	GORMAN J	35	ROBARTS J	67
AUTEN H	1020	GOULD T W	1201	ROBERTS P S W	1202
BEAK D M W	1037	GUY B J	514	ROBINSON E	244
BEATTIE S H	1204	HALL W	211	ROBINSON E G	570
BINGHAM E B	702	HARDING I	396	ROOPE G B	1159
BONNER C G	854	HARRISON A L	993	RYDER R E D	1207
BOURKE R R L	1004	HARRISON J	212	SALMON N	219
BOYES D G	321	HEWETT W	23	SAMSON G M	600
BOYLE E C	609	HINCKLEY G	306	SANDERS W E	817
BRADFORD G N	988	HOLBROOK N D	561	SANDFORD R D	995
BUCKLEY C W	65	INGOUVILLE G	90	SAVAGE W A	1208
BURGOYNE H T	66	JOHNSTONE W	3	SCHOLEFIELD M	45
BYTHESEA J	2	JONES L W	705	SEELEY W H H	322
CAMERON D	1249	KELLAWAY J	106	SEPHTON A E	1180
CAMPBELL G	776	LINTON J W	1242	SHEPPARD J	91
CARLESS J H	916	LUCAS C D	1	SHERBROOKE R St V	1228
CARPENTER A F B	989	MAGENNIS J J	1337	SMITH A B	783
COMMERELL J E	110	MAILLARD W J	431	STANNARD R B	1161
COOKSON E C	669	MALLESON W St A	598	STEELE G C	1152
COOPER H	68	MANTLE J F	1169	STUART R N	831
CORNWELL J T	703	McKENZIE A E	994	SULLIVAN J	58
COWLEY C H	699	MIERS A	1203	TAYLOR J	86
CRISP T	857	MITCHELL S	318	TISDALL A W St C	597
CRUTCHLEY V	990	ODGERS W	297	TREWAVAS J	88
CURTIS H	76	PARSLOW F D	632	UNWIN E	601
DANIEL E St J	34	PEEL W	13	WANKLYN M D	1184
DAY G F	107	PETERS F T	1224	WARBURTON-LEE B A	1160
DEAN P T	991	PITCHER E H	855	WATT J	825
DOBSON C C	1151	PLACE B S G	1248	WHITE G S	943
DREWRY G L	599	PRIDE T	323	WILKINSON T	1200
DRUMMOND G H	1005	PROWSE G	1070	WILLIAMS W	832
DUNBAR-NASMITH M	621	RABY H J	83	WILLIAMS W C	602
FEGEN E S F	1174	REEVES T	42	WILSON A K	400
FIRMAN H O B	700	RICKARD W T	111	YOUNG T J	221
FRASER I E	1338	RITCHIE H P	560		

ROYAL MARINES (10)

BAMFORD E	987	HALLIDAY L	513	PARKER W R	610
DOWELL G D	89	HARVEY F J W	704	PRETTYJOHN J	41
FINCH N A	992	HUNTER T P	1327	WILKINSON T	72
		LUMSDEN F W	789		

FLEET AIR ARM (1)
ESMONDE E   1199

ROYAL NAVAL AIR SERVICE (2)
DAVIES R B   681
WARNEFORD R A J   625

HOUSEHOLD CAVALRY

BLUES AND ROYALS
1st (Royal) Dragoon Guards (1)
DUNVILLE J S   835

ROYAL ARMOURED CORPS

QUEEN'S DRAGOON GUARDS (5)
1st Dragoon Guards (1)

DOOGAN J	392

2nd Dragoon Guards (4)

ANDERSON C	283	BLAIR R	186
MONAGHAN T	282	SMYTH N	430

ROYAL DRAGOON GUARDS (3)

4th Dragoon Guards (1)	5th Dragoon Guards (1)	6th Dragoons (1)
CARTON de WIART A 724	NORWOOD J 440	MOUAT J 24

385

ROYAL SCOT DRAGOON GUARDS
Royal Scot Greys (3)

GRIEVE J 19	KEYES G 1189	RAMAGE H 27

QUEEN'S ROYAL HUSSARS (8)

7th Hussars (2)	4th Light Dragoons (1)		8th Hussars (5)	
BANKES W G H 246	PARKES S 21	CHAMPION J 278	PEARSON J 274	
FRASER C 286		HENEAGE C W 272	WARD J 275	
		HOLLIS G 273		

9/12th ROYAL LANCERS
9th Lancers (14)

BERESFORD W 380	HANCOCK T 123	PURCELL J 124
DONOHUE P 336	HARTIGAN H 120	ROBERTS J R 191
FREEMAN J 196	JONES A S 119	RUSHE D 248
GOAT W 237	KELLS R 187	SPENCE D 233
GRENFELL F O 528	NEWELL R 247	

KING'S ROYAL HUSSARS (5)

10th Hussars (2)	11th Hussars (1)	14th Hussars (2)
ENGLEHEART H W 465	DUNNE A R 17	BROWNE E D 488
MILBANKE J 453		LEITH J 250

LIGHT DRAGOONS (4)

13th/18th Royal Hussars (2)	15th/19th King's Royal Hussars (2)
CRANDON H G 504	GARFORTH C E 524
MALONE J 20	MARSHALL W T 399

QUEEN'S ROYAL LANCERS (12)

16th Lancers (1)	17th Lancers (5)	21st Lancers (4)	
FINCASTLE Viscount 418	BERRYMAN J 16	BYRNE T	42?
5th Lancers (2)	FARRELL J 18	De MONTMORENCY R H	42?
CLARE G W B 216	LAWRENCE B T 481	HULL C	65?
DUGDALE F B 499	WOOD E 285	KENNA P A	429
	WOODEN C 25		

ROYAL TANK REGIMENT (3)

FOOTE H R B 1210	GARDNER P J 1193	WAIN R W L 922

ROYAL REGIMENT OF ARTILLERY
(47)

ALEXANDER E W	529	GOSLING W	790	PHIPPS - HORNBY E J	46?
ARTHUR T	69	GOURLEY C E	927	PICKARD A F	314
BRADBURY E K	537	GUNN G W	1190	PORTEOUS P A	121?
BRADLEY F H	507	HENRY A	36	RAYNES J C	67?
BRENNAN J C	254	HORLOCK E G	543	REED H L	448
CAMBRIDGE D	98	IND A E	511	REES L W B	72?
CAMPBELL J C	1192	LODGE I	470	REYNOLDS D	534
COLLIS J	357	LUKE F	533	SCHOFIELD H N	44?
DAVIS G	100	MANLEY W G N	317	SMITH A	403
DICKSON C	11	MAUDE F C	170	STONE C E	954
DIXON M C	60	MAUFE T H B	828	SYMONS G	1?
DORRELL G T	536	MILLER F	38	TEESDALE C	10?
DOUGALL E S	980	MULLANE P	356	TEMPLE W	313
DRAIN J H C	532	NELSON D	538	WALFORD G N	60?
GLASOCK H H	466	NURSE G E	450	WALLACE S T D	93?
GORLE R V	1105	PARKER C E H	468		

CORPS OF ROYAL ENGINEERS
(36)

ARCHIBALD A	1142	GRAHAM G	79	LENNOX W O	5?
AYLMER F	407	HACKETT W	709	MARTIN C G	57?
BELL M S	340	HART R C	345	McDONALD H	6?
CHARD J R M	365	HAWKER L G	633	McPHIE J	112?
CLOUTMAN B	1148	JARVIS C A	527	NEAME P	564
COFFIN C	843	JOHNSON F H	652	PERIE J	82
COLVIN J M C	420	JOHNSTON W H	540	RAYMOND C	132?
DAWSON J L	674	KIRBY F H	474	ROSS J	92
DIGBY - JONES R J	455	KNOX C L	958	SLEAVON M	256
DURRANT T F	1205	LEACH E P	346	WATERS A	1147
ELPHINSTONE H C	77	LEITCH P	81	WATSON T C	422
FINDLAY G de C E	1143	LENDRIM W J	53	WRIGHT T	526

FOOT GUARDS (44)

GRENADIER GUARDS (13)

ABLETT A	95	HOLMES W E	1115	PRYCE T T	984
BARBER E	577	NICHOLLS H	1163	RHODES J H	900
DE L'ISLE The Viscount	1256	PALMER A	39	RUSSELL C	44
FULLER W D	580	PATON G H T	934		
GORT Viscount	1091	PERCY H H M	48		

COLDSTREAM GUARDS (12)

BROOKS O	672	GOODLAKE G L	28	STRONG G	109
CAMPBELL J V	753	JACKSON T N	1094	WHITHAM T	850
DOBSON F W	545	LIDDELL I O	1326	WRIGHT P H	1250
FRISBY C H	1090	STANLACK W	30	WYATT G H	530

SCOTS GUARDS (11)

BOYD - ROCHFORT G A	636	LYELL The Lord	1237	McNESS F	754
CRAIG J	97	MACKENZIE J	56	REYNOLDS W	9
KNOX J S	5	McAULAY J	923	WOOD H B	1118
LINDSAY R J	6	McKECHNIE J	7		

IRISH GUARDS (6)

CHARLTON E C	1331	MARSHALL J N	1146	O'LEARY M	569
KENNEALLY J P	1240	MOYNEY J	873	WOODCOCK T	874

WELSH GUARDS (2)

BYE R J	842
FURNESS Hon. C	1167

INFANTRY REGIMENTS

ROYAL SCOTS (7)

DUNSIRE R	664	McGREGOR D S	1128	REYNOLDS H	882
ELCOCK R E	1124	McIVER H	1043	ROBSON H H	562
		PROSSER J	74		

POW ROYAL REGIMENT (Q&H) (41)

The Royal West Surrey Regiment (6)

BUSHELL C	960	HORWOOD A G	1254	SAYER J W	953
FREYBURG	768	ROBERTSON C	886	WRIGHT W D	516

The Buffs (4)

CONNORS J	99	COTTER W R	689	SMITH J	421
		MAUDE F	96		

The East Surrey Regiment (9)

CATOR H	793	FLEMING - SANDES A	670	McNAMARA J	1074
CURTIS A E	461	FOSTER E	811	ROUPELL G R P	583
DWYER E	585	GEARY B H	586	WILSON E C T	1170

The Royal Sussex Regiment (5)

CARTER N V	713	QUERIPEL L E	1294	
McNAIR E A	688	WELLS H	662	
	McNEILL J C	316		

The Queen's Own Royal West Kent Regiment (6)

COLEMAN J	94	HARMAN J P	1262	LUMLEY C	102
DEAN D J	1089	HARRIS T J	1032	SEWELL C H	1052

The Middlesex Regiment (11)

DOWN J T	309	McCORRIE C	87	STAGPOOLE D	310
EDWARDS F J	757	McREADY - DIARMID A M	931	TOYE A M	966
GARDINER G	55	PARK J	40	WRIGHT A	54
HALLOWES R P	658	RYDER R E	758		

KING'S OWN ROYAL BORDER REG. (19)

The King's Own (9)

CHRISTIAN H	676	HALTON A	901	MILLER J	740
COLLIN J H	977	HEWITSON J	999	NEELY T	1097
GRADY T	12	MAYSON T F	847	WHITE J	780

The Border Regiment (10)

ACTON A	566	ELTON F C	57	SIMS J J	84
BEACH T	31	FORBES - ROBERTSON J	983	SMITH J	567
COFFEY W	56	MOTT E J	772	SPACKMAN C E	920
		RICHARDSON G	291		

THE ROYAL REGIMENT OF FUSILIERS (52)

Royal Northumberland Fusiliers (10)

BRYAN T	792	JACKMAN J J B	1194	SYKES E	806
CAIN R H	1292	JOHNSON J	1119	WOOD W	1136
GRANT R	169	McHALE P	194	YOULL J S	1011
		McMANUS P	181		

Royal Warwickshire Regiment (5)

AMEY W	1141	GRIBBLE J R	961	HUTT A	891	PHILLIPS R E	771	VICKERS A	675

The Royal Fusiliers (19)

AHFORD T E	359	GODLEY S F	525	NORMAN W	52
DARTNELL W T	650	HALE T E	101	PALMER F W	775
DEASE M J	523	HOPE W	80	PEARSE S G	1153
ELLIOTT - COOPER N B	925	HUGHES M	70	ROBERTSON C G	944
FITZCLARENCE C	435	JARRATT G	820	STONE W N	928
GEE R	926	JONES H M	71	SULLIVAN A P	115
		MOLYNEUX J	899		

The Lancashire Fusiliers (18)

BEST - DUNKLEY B	841	HALLIWELL J	1008	LYNN J	612
BROMLEY C	591	HUTCHINSON J	712	RICHARDS A J	592
CASSIDY B M	971	JEFFERSON F A	1267	SCHOFIELD J	979
CLARKE J	1140	KENEALLY W	594	SMITH E	1038
COLLEY H J	1046	LESTER F	117	STUBBS F E	593
GRIMSHAW J E	590	LISTER J	898	WILLIS R R	595

THE KING'S REGIMENT (23)
The King's (Liverpool) Regiment (9)

BAXTER E F	698	HEATON W	484	PROCTOR A H	707
COUNTER J T	986	JONES W	750	REID O A	782
HAMPTON H	482	KNIGHT H J	483	TOMBS J H	628

The Manchester Regiment (14)

COVERDALE C H	888	HOGAN J	548	SCOTT R	458
ELSTOB W	949	KIRK J	1145	SMITH I	605
EVANS G	739	LEACH J	550	STRINGER G	690
FORSHAW W T	639	MILLS W	939	WILKINSON A R	1127
HENDERSON G S	1156	PITTS J	457		

ROYAL ANGLIAN REGIMENT (38)
Royal Norfolk Regiment (6)

BATES S	1285	JAMIESON D A	1286	RANDLE J N	1264
GRISTOCK G	1166	KNOWLAND G A	1310	SHERWOOD - KELLY J	919

Lincolnshire Regiment (7)

DEMPSEY D	147	HANSEN P H	645	KIRK J	118
EVANS A	1064	HAVELOCK H	141	SHARPE C R	615
		HOEY C F	1257		

Suffolk Regiment (2)

DAY S J	871	SAUNDERS A F	665

Bedfordshire Regiment (7)

ADLAM T E	759	COLLINGS-WELLS	955	COX C A	784	FOSS C A	579	HEDGES F W	1131
		NEEDHAM S	1075	WARNER E	611				

Royal Leicestershire Regiment (4)

BARRETT J C	1088	BENT P E	887	BUCKINGHAM W	572	SMITH P	85

Essex Regiment (6)

McDOUGALL W	303	NEWMAN A C	1206	ROGERS R M	304
McWHEENEY W	15	PARSONS F N	460	WEARNE F B	836

Northamptonshire Regiment (6)

BOULTER W E	728	HILL A R	393	OSBORNE J	394
COLYER - FERGUSSON T	844	LEWIS A L	1082	READ A M	660

DEVONSHIRE & DORSET REGIMENT (4)

Devonshire Regiment (3)		Dorset Regiment (1)	
MASTERSON J E	456	VICKERY S	425
ONIONS G	1040		
VEALE T W A	733		

THE LIGHT INFANTRY (39)

Somerset Light Infantry (5)		Duke of Cornwall's Light Infantry (7)		King's Own Yorkshire Light Infantry (8)	
CAIRNS G A	1258	CURTIS P K E	1342	CALVERT L	1076
CARLIN P	259	DOWLING W	133	EDWARDS W	862
LEET W K	377	GORE - BROWNE H G	151	GREENWOOD H	1129
NAPIER W	258	LAWRENCE S H	134	HOLMES F W	535
SAGE T H	895	OXENHAM W	129	ORMSBY J W	804
		RENDLE T E	557	WALLER H	800
		SMITH C L	521	WARD C	475
				YATE C A L	531

King's Shropshire Light Infantry (8)				Durham Light Infantry (11)			
DYNON D	193	KENNY J	209	ANNAND R W	1164	LASCELLES A M	935
EARDLEY G H	1298	PYE C C	225	BRADFORD R B	761	MURRAY J	320
FFRENCH A K	208	STOKES J	1314	BYRNE J	32	WAKENSHAW A H	1213
IRWIN C	214	WHITFIELD H	945	HAMILTON T de C	64	YOUENS F	838
				HEAVISIDE M	821	YOUNG T	967
				KENNY T	677		

PRINCE OF WALES'S REGIMENT (12)

The West Yorkshire Regiment (7)
BUTLER W B	853
MANSEL - JONES C	464
MEEKOSHA S	680
MOUNTAIN A	968
SANDERS G	722
TRAYNOR W B	496
TURNER H V	1271

The East Yorkshire Regiment (5)
ANDERSON E	1234
CHAFER G W	706
CUNNINGHAM J	767
HARRISON J	819
JACKSON H	957

THE GREEN HOWARDS (16)

ANDERSON W	576	CLAMP W	896	HOLLIS S E	1270	SEAGRIM D A	1231
ATKINSON A	459	DRESSER T	823	LOUDON-SHAND S W	717	SHORT D A	741
BEAL E F	946	EVANS S	59	LYONS J	73	WESTON W B	1318
BELL D S	726	HIRSCH D P	810	McNALLY W	1135	WHITE A C T	760

THE ROYAL HIGHLAND FUSILIERS (19)

Royal Scots Fusiliers (6)

Highland Light Infantry (13)

BOUGHEY S H P	932	ANDERSON W H	964	HUNTER D F	1079
CALDWELL T	1138	ANGUS W	626	KENNEDY C T	493
CRAIG J M	829	BLAKER F G	1280	RODGERS G	271
DONNINI D	1307	BRODIE W L	554	SHAUL J D F	442
LAUDER D R	647	EDWARDS W M M	398	TURNBULL J Y	723
RAVENHILL G	447	HORE - RUTHVEN A G	432	WILSON G	541

THE CHESHIRE REGIMENT (2)
COLVIN H	878
JONES T A	756

THE ROYAL WELCH FUSILIERS (14)

BARTER F	618	DOUGHTY - WYLIE C H	607	SHIELDS R	104
BELL E W D	4	HACKETT T B	226	SYLVESTER W H T	105
COLLINS J	911	HILL A	732	WARING W H	1083
DAVIES J L	845	MONGER G	227	WEALE H	1050
DAVIES J J	731	O'CONNOR L	8		

THE ROYAL REGIMENT OF WALES (28)

South Wales Borderers (22)

ALLAN W W	363	DOUGLAS C M	331	JONES W	370
BELL D	329	FYNN J H	695	MELVILL T	361
BROMHEAD G	364	GIFFORD E F	337	MURPHY T	333
BROWNE E S	379	GRIFFITHS W	332	REES I	849
BUCHANAN A	692	HITCH F	367	WHITE A	826
COGHILL N J A	360	HOOK A H	368	WILLIAMS J	373
COOPER J	330	JOHNSON D G	1144	WILLIAMS J H	1113
		JONES R	369		

The Welch Regiment (6)
FULLER W C	539	MYLES E K	696
LEWIS H W	764	ROWLANDS H	43
MADDEN A	26	WATKINS T	1287

KING'S OWN SCOTTISH BORDERERS (5)

COULSON G H 501	GRIMBALDESTON W 863	LAIDLAW D 655	McGUFFIE L 1098	SKINNER J 866

THE ROYAL IRISH REGIMENT (16)

The Royal Innniskilling Fusiliers (7)
BELL E W F	714	HARVEY N	1133
DUFFY J	941	O'SULLIVAN G R	630
EMERSON J S	937	SEAMAN E	1101
SOMERS J	631		

The Royal Irish Fusiliers (2)
CATHER G St G S	715
MORROW R	581

The Royal Irish Rangers (7)
BYRNE J	257	JEROME H E	255
COCHRANE H S	251	McFADZEAN W F	718
DE WIND E	948	PEARSON J	252
QUIGG R	719		

THE ROYAL GLOUCESTERSHIRE, BERKSHIRE & WILTSHIRE REGIMENT (14)

The Gloucestershire Regiment (6)
BURGES D	1081
CARNE J P	1341
JAMES M A	951
MILES F G	1130
PARSONS H F	868
READE H T	164

The Royal Berkshire Regiment (6)
CONNOLLY J A	2
HOUSE W	480
OWENS J	29
TURNER A B	668
WALTERS G	47
WELCH J	816

The Wiltshire Regiment (2)
HAYWARD R F	950
ROGERS M A W	1269

THE WORCESTERSHIRE & SHERWOOD FORESTERS (22)
The Worcestershire Regiment (8)

BENNETT E P	766	DANCOX F G	897	JAMES H	629	ROBINSON W L	746
CROWE J J	985	GROGAN G W St G	1007	ROBERTS F C	959	TURRALL T G	725

The Sherwood Foresters (14)

BALL A	812	BRUNT J H C	1303	JOHNSON W H	1109	UPTON J	616
BEES W	508	EGERTON E A	879	McQUIRT B	232	VANN B W	1102
BEET H C	472	GREAVES F	890	PENNELL H S	424	VICKERS G	675
		HUDSON C E	1010	RIVERS J	575		

THE QUEEN'S LANCASHIRE REGIMENT (17)

The East Lancashire Regiment (7)		The South Lancashire Regiment (5)		The Loyal (North Lancashire) Regiment (5)	
BENT S J	552	COURY G G	742	CLARKE W A S	1239
ERVINE - ANDREWS H M	1168	DAVIES J T	963	JONES R B B	701
HORSFALL B A	969	LUCAS J	305	KENNY H E	653
SARTORIUS E A	350	RATCLIFFE W	834	McDERMOND J	37
SMITH A V	684	READITT J	779	WILKINSON T O L	727
WALKER M	46				
YOUNG W	683				

THE DUKE OF WELLINGTON'S REGIMENT (9)

BERGIN J	335	HUFFAM J P	1053	MAGNER M	334
BURTON R H	1297	KELLY H	762	POULTER A	982
FIRTH J	463	LOOSEMORE A	856	TANDEY H	1099

THE ROYAL HAMPSHIRE REGIMENT (9)

BURSLEM N	298	LANE T	300	MOOR G R D	624
CHAPLIN J W	299	LE PATOUREL H W	1226	MOORE M S S	867
HEWITT D G W	846	LENON E H	301	WAKEFORD R	1266

THE STAFFORDSHIRE REGIMENT (11)

South Staffordshire Regiment (6)		North Staffordshire Regiment (5)	
BARRATT T	839	CARMICHAEL J	872
BASKEYFIELD J D	1295	COLTMAN W H	1108
BOOTH A C	374	FLINN T	230
KILBY A F G	659	HENDERSON E E D	770
VALLENTIN J F	553	THOMAS J	929
WASSALL S	362		

THE BLACK WATCH (15)

COOK W	288	FINLAY D	614	RIPLEY J	613
DAVIS J	261	GARDNER W	267	SIMPSON J	265
EDWARDS T	402	McGAW S	339	SPEAKMAN W	1343
EVANS L P	889	MELVIN C	807	SPENCE E	260
FARQUHARSON F E H	238	MILLAR D	290	THOMPSON A	264

THE HIGHLANDERS (39)
The Seaforth Highlanders (18)

BOGLE A C	144	McBEATH R	917	MEIKLE J	1018
CAMERON A S	249	McMASTER V M	175	RITCHIE W P	721
CROWE J P H	148	McPHERSON S	182	SELLAR G	353
EDWARDS A	852	MACKENZIE J	433	STEELE T	777
HOLLOWELL J	179	MACKINTOSH D	801	WARD H	172
JEE J	173	MACPHERSON H T	174	WARE S W	693

The Gordon Highlanders (17)

BROOKE J A O	549	KENNY W	547	ROBERTSON W	439
COUGHLAN C	121	KER A E	952	TOWSE E	443
DICK - CUNYNGHAM W H	352	LAWSON E	423	WADESON R	142
FINDLATER G	426	McINTOSH G I	848	WHITE G S	349
GORDON W E	478	McKAY J F	473	YOUNGER D R	477
GREEN P	153	MEIKLEJOHN M F M	437		

The Cameron Highlanders (4)

DOUGLAS - HAMILTON A	663
FARMER D D	494
POLLOCK J D	667
TOLLERTON R	542

ARGYLL & SUTHERLAND HIGHLANDERS (16)

ANDERSON J T Mc	1238	DUNLAY J	217	LIDDELL J A	635	MUIR K	1340
BISSETT W D	1132	GRAHAM J R V	808	McBEAN W	241	MUNRO J	216
BUCHAN J C	947	GRANT P	222	MacINTYRE D L	1045	PATON J	218
CAMPBELL L M	1235	HENDERSON A	809	MACKAY D	215	STEWART W G D	220

THE PARACHUTE REGIMENT (3)

GRAYBURN J H	1290	JONES H	1349	McKAY I J	1350

THE ROYAL GREEN JACKETS (53)
The Oxfordshire & Buckinghamshire Light Infantry (6)

ADDISON H	287	SMITH F A	319
BROOKS E	813	SMITH H	163
HAWTHORNE R	157	WILCOX A	1078

The King's Royal Rifle Corps (21)

BAMBRICK V	268	DIVANE J	152	PRICE - DAVIES L A	506
BEELEY J	1191	GARVIN S	126	ROBERTS F H S	449
BULLER R H	376	GILL A	737	SHEPHERD A E	918
BUTLER J F P	556	HEATHCOTE A S	131	SUTTON W	154
COOPER E	861	MARINER W	622	THOMPSON J	138
CORBETT F	397	MARLING P	401	TURNER S	125
DIMMER J H S	555	PEACHMENT G S	657	WALLER G	162

The Rifle Brigade (26)

BEESLEY W	1002	DANIELS H	578	NOBLE C R	574
BOURCHIER C T	49	DRAKE A G	682	O'HEA T	327
BRADSHAW J	63	DURRANT A E	485	SHAW S	270
BURMAN W F	877	GOUGH J E	517	TURNER V B	1223
CATES G E	781	GREGG W	1003	WHEATLEY F	10
CLIFFORD H H	33	HAWKES D	240	WILMOT H	243
CONGREVE W N	445	HUMPSTON R	62	WOODALL J E	996
CONGREVE W La T	729	McGREGOR R	93	WOODRUFFE S C	634
CUNNINGHAME W J M	50	NASH W	242		

BRIGADE OF GURKHAS (1)

RAMBAHADUR LIMBU	1344

DISBANDED REGIMENTS (32)
(Plus 31 Disbanded Irish = 63)
CAMERONIANS (SCOTTISH RIFLES) (13)

ALEXANDER J	75	GRAHAM P	223	MAY H	546
BRADSHAW W	177	GUISE J	210	MOYNIHAN A	103
ERSKINE J	708	HILL S	213	RENNIE W	167
FOWLER E J	375	HOME A D	180	TOWERS J	1112
		LYSONS H	378		

YORK AND LANCASTER REGIMENT (13)

ANSON A H	185	HARPER J W	1296	MYLOTT P	224
BOULGER A	140	HARVEY S	671	RIGGS F C	1107
CAFFREY J	679	HOLMES J	171	RYAN J	307
DAYKINS J B	1126	LAMBERT G	143	SINNOTT J	195
		McKENNA E	308		

WEST INDIA REGIMENT (2)

GORDON W J	410
HODGE S	328

MACHINE GUN CORPS (4)

COLUMBINE H G	956
CROSS A H	965
MUGFORD H S	802
WHITE W A	1084

DISBANDED IRISH REGIMENTS (31)

ROYAL IRISH REGIMENT (4)

BARRY J	497
ESMONDE T	79
ROOM F G	864
SHAW H	324

CONNAUGHT RANGERS (5)

FITZPATRICK F	387
FLAWN T	388
HUGHES T	749
MOORE H G	343
MURRAY J	390

LEINSTER REGIMENT (5)

CUNNINGHAM J	803
HOLLAND J V	748
MOFFATT M	1121
O'NEILL J	1122
WHIRLPOOL F	253

ROYAL MUNSTER FUSILIERS (9)

BATTEN - POOLL A H H	710
BROWN F D M	207
BUTLER T A	239
CADELL T	122
COSGROVE W	608
DOYLE M	1063
McGOVERN J	127
McGUIRE J	160
RYAN M	161

ROYAL DUBLIN FUSILIERS (7)

CURTIS H A	1125
DOWNIE R	765
DUFFY T	178
MAHONEY P	168
OCKENDEN J	893
RYAN J	183
SMITH J	206

NORTH IRISH HORSE (S.R.) (1)

WEST R A	1039

SPECIAL AIR SERVICE REGIMENT (1)		ROYAL ARMY CHAPLAINS DEPARTMENT (3)		ROYAL LOGISTIC CORPS (6)	
LASSEN A F	1328	ADDISON W R	694	**ROYAL LOGISTIC CORPS (1)**	
		HARDY T B	998	**Royal Army Ordnance Corps (1)**	
		MELLISH E N	691	BUCKLEY J	114
				Royal Army Service Corps (5)	
				DALTON J L	366
				HERRING A C	962
				MASTERS R G	978
				MORLEY S	262
				MURPHY M	263

ROYAL ARMY MEDICAL CORPS (16)

ACKROYD H	851	DOUGLAS H E M	441	INKSON E T	462	NICKERSON W H S	471
ALLEN W B	747	FARMER J J	395	LE QUESNE F	405	RANKEN H S	544
BABTIE W	444	GREEN J L	716	LLOYD O E P	411	REYNOLDS J H	371
CHAVASSE N G	743	HARDEN H E	1309	MALING G A	656	RUSSELL J F	914

HONOURABLE ARTILLERY COMPANY (2)

HAINE R L	814	POLLARD A O	815

TERRITORIAL and ARMY VOLUNTEER RESERVE (17)

Berkshire Yeomanry (1)		**Hertfordshire Regiment (2)**		**The London Regiment (9)**	
POTTS F W O	648	BURT A A	666	BELCHER D W	617
City of London Yeomanry (1)		YOUNG F E	1086	BORTON A D	915
LAFONE A M	906	**London Scottish (1)**		CHRISTIE J A	214
County of London Yeomanry (1)		MITCHELL G A	1255	CRUICKSHANK R E	1001
WATSON O C S	973	**Monmouthshire Regiment (1)**		HARVEY J	1065
Imperial Yeomanry (1)		CHAPMAN E T	1325	KEYWORTH L J	623
DOXAT A C	489			KNIGHT A J	881
				TRAIN C W	938
				WOOLLEY G H	584

ROYAL AIR FORCE (32)

Royal Flying Corps (6)

INSALL G S M	678
JERRARD A	975
McCUDDEN J T B	942
McLEOD A A	970
MOTTERSHEAD T	769
RHODES - MOORHOUSE W	604

Royal Air Force (26)

AARON A L	1246	JACKSON N C	1263
BARKER W G	1134	LEAROYD R A B	1171
BARTON C J	1260	LORD D S A	1293
BAZALGETTE I W	1284	MALCOLM H G	1227
BEAUCHAMP-PROCTOR A F	1021	MANNOCK E	1012
CAMPBELL K	1177	MANSER L T	1211
CHESHIRE G L	1283	NETTLETON J D	1209
CRUICKSHANK J A	1282	NICOLSON E J B	1172
EDWARDS H I	1186	PALMER R A M	1305
GARLAND D E	1162	REID W	1251
GIBSON G P	1243	SCARF A S K	1195
GRAY T	1163	THOMPSON G	1306
HANNAH J	1173	WEST F M F	1028

CIVILIANS (4)

CHICKEN G B	279
KAVANAGH T H	198
MANGLES R L	145
McDONNELL W F	146

(There is a case for the Reverend J W ADAMS (351) to be included, but he is listed with the Indian Army)

OVERSEAS FORCES (360)

AUSTRALIAN FORCES (91)

Name	No.	Name	No.	Name	No.
ANDERSON C G W	1198	GORDON B S	1047	MAYGAR L C	509
AXFORD T L	1014	GORDON J H	1188	MIDDLETON R H	1225
BADCOE P J	1346	GRATWICK P E	1222	MOON R V	824
BEATHAM R M	1089	GRIEVE R C	830	MURRAY H W	773
BELL F W	500	GURNEY A S	1215	NEWLAND J E	791
BIRKS F	876	HALL A C	1058	NEWTON W E	1230
BISDEE J H	487	HAMILTON J P	646	O'MEARA M	744
BLACKBURN A S	734	HOWELL G J	822	PARTRIDGE F J	1336
BORELLA A C	1017	HOWSE N	479	PAYNE K	1348
BROWN W E	1016	INGRAM G M	1111	PEELER W	894
BUCKLEY A H	1055	INWOOD R R	875	POPE C	805
BUCKLEY M V	1080	JACKA A	620	RATTEY R R	1322
BUGDEN P J	885	JACKSON W	711	RUTHVEN W	1006
BURTON A S	641	JEFFRIES C S	902	RYAN J	1104
CARROLL J	833	JENSEN J C	788	SADLIER C W K	997
CARTWRIGHT G	1054	JOYNT W D	1041	SHOUT A J	644
CASTLETON C C	738	KELLIHER R	1247	SIMPSON R S	1347
CHERRY P H	786	KENNA E	1334	STARCEVICH L T	1335
CHOWNE A	1324	KENNY T J B	794	STATTON P C	1036
COOKE T	736	KEYSOR L	638	STORKEY P V	976
CURREY W M	1056	KIBBY W H	1221	SYMONS W J	640
CUTLER A R	1185	KINGSBURY B S	1219	THROSSELL H V H	649
DALZIEL H	1015	LEAK J	735	TOWNER E T	1062
DAVEY P	1013	LOWERSON A D	1059	TUBB F H	642
DERRICK T C	1252	McCARTHY L D	1042	WARK B A	1137
DUNSTAN W	643	McDOUGALL S R	972	WEATHERS L C	1072
DWYER J J	884	McGEE L	892	WHEATLEY K A	1345
EDMONDSON J H	1178	McNAMARA F H	785	WHITTLE J W	797
FRENCH J A	1220	MACKEY J B	1333	WOODS J P	1085
GABY A E	1024	MACTIER R	1060	WYLLY G G	486
		MAXWELL J	1110		

CANADA (80)

Name	No.	Name	No.	Name	No.	Name	No.
AGIE W L	1116	FOOTE J W	1216	LYALL G T	1096	PECK C W	1069
BARRON C F	912	GOOD H J	1025	MacDOWELL T W	798	RAYFIELD W L	1071
BELLEW E D	588	GRAY R H	1339	MacGREGOR J	1100	RICHARDSON A H L	476
BISHOP W A	827	GREGG M F	1049	McKEAN G B	1000	RICHARDSON J C	763
BRERETON A P	1030	HALL F W	589	McKENZIE H M	908	RICKETTS T	1123
BRILLANT J	1022	HANNA R H	869	MAHONY J K	1286	ROBERTSON J P	913
BROWN H	860	HARVEY F M W	787	MERRIFIELD W	1106	RUTHERFORD C S	1049
CAIRNS H	1139	HOBSON F	858	MERRITT C C I	1217	SCRIMGER F A C	596
CAMPBELL F W	627	HOLLAND E J G	492	METCALF W H	1068	SHANKLAND R	905
CLARK - KENNEDY W H	1051	HOLMES T W	903	MILNE W J	795	SIFTON E W	796
CLARKE L	751	HONEY S L	1093	MINER H G	1026	SMITH E A	1299
COCKBURN H Z	490	HORNELL D E	1277	MITCHELL C N	1114	SPALL R	1035
COMBE R G	818	HUTCHESON B S	1066	MULLIN G H	909	STRACHAN H	921
COPPINS F	1031	KAEBLE J	1009	MYNARSKI A C	1274	TAIT J E	1027
COSENS A	1313	KERR G F	1095	NUNNEY C J	1061	TILSTON F A	1315
CROAK J B	1023	KERR J C	755	O'KELLY C P	904	TOPHAM F G	1323
CURRIE D V	1288	KINROSS C J	907	O'ROURKE M J	859	TRIQUET P	1253
DINESON T	1034	KNIGHT A G	1067	OSBORN J R	1196	TURNER R E W	491
FISHER F	587	KONOWAL F	870	PATTISON J G	799	YOUNG J F	1073
FLOWERDEW G M	974	LEARMOUTH O M	865	PEARKES G R	910	ZENGEL R L	1033

FIJI (1)

Name	No.
SUKANAIVALU S	1275

KING'S AFRICAN RIFLES (1)

Name	No.
LEAKEY N G	1181

NEW ZEALAND (21)

Name	No.	Name	No.	Name	No.
ANDREW L W	840	GRANT J G	1057	NGARIMU M-N-a-K	1232
BASSETT C R G	637	HARDHAM W J	495	NICHOLAS H J	936
BROWN D F	752	HEAPHY C	315	TRAVIS R C	1019
CRICHTON J	1103	HINTON J D	1179	TRENT L H	1241
ELLIOTT K	1214	HULME A C	1182	TRIGG L A	1245
FORSYTH S	1044	JUDSON R S	1048	UPHAM C H	1246
FRICKLETON S	837	LAURENT H J	1077	WARD J A	1187

HEIC and INDIAN ARMY (137)

Name	No.	Name	No.	Name	No.
ABDUL HAFIZ	1261	GOBAR SING NEGI	571	PARK J	200
ADAMS J W	351	GOBIND SINGH	933	PARKASH SINGH	1229
ADAMS R B	417	GOODFELLOW C A	292	PHILLIPS E A L	115
AGANSING RAI	1279	GOUGH C J S	150	PITCHER H W	312
AIKMAN F R	236	GOUGH H H	199	PRAKASH SINGH	1311
AITKEN R H M	130	GRANT C J W	406	PREMINDRA SINGH BHAGAT	1175
ALI HAIDAR	1329	GRANT J D	522	PRENDERGAST H N D	228
ALLMAND M	1272	HAMILTON W R P	347	PROBYN D M	293
ANDREWS H J	1154	HAMMOND A G	355	RAM SARUP SINGH	1300
BADLU SINGH	1087	HARINGTON H E	203	RAYNOR W	113
BAKER C G	281	HILLS J	137	RENNY G A	165
BHANBHAGTA GURUNG	1319	HOME D C	158	RICHHPAL RAM	1176
BHANDARI RAM	1302	INNES J J M	235	RIDGEWAY R K	386
BLAIR J	149	ISHAR SINGH	1157	ROBERTS Earl	231
BOISRAGON G H	408	JARRETT H C T	284	RODDY P	280
BROWNE S J	277	JENNINGS E	202	ROLLAND G M	518
BRUCE W A M	563	JOTHAM E	568	ROSAMUND M	116
CAFE W M	266	KAMAL RAM	1265	SALKELD P	159
CARTER H A	520	KARAMJEET SINGH JUDGE	1320	SARTORIUS R W	338
CHANNER G N	341	KARANBAHADUR RANA	981	SCOTT A	342
CHASE W St L	358	KEATINGE R H	245	SHAHAMAD KHAN	697
CHATTA SINGH	685	KENNY W D	1155	SHEBBEARE R H	155
CHHELU RAM	1236	KERR W A	139	SHER SHAH	1308
CLOGSTOUN H M	289	KHUDADAD KHAN	551	SHERBAHADUR THAPA	1291
COBBE A	515	KULBIR THAPA	654	SINTON J A	687
CONNOLLY W	135	LACHIMAN GURUNG	1332	SMITH John	156
COOK J	344	LALA	686	SMITH J M	409
COSTELLO E W	416	LALBAHADUR THAPA	1233	SMYTH J G	619
CREAGH O'M	348	LAUGHNAN T	204	THACKERAY E	166
CRIMMIN J	404	LYSTER H H	269	THAMAN GURUNG	1301
CUBITT W G	128	McINNES H	205	THOMAS J	184
CUMMING A E	1197	MacINTYRE D	336	TOMBS H	136
DARWAN SING NEGI	558	MACLEAN H L S	419	TRAVERS J	132
DAUNT J C C	192	MALCOLMSON J G	295	TREVOR W S	326
De PASS F A	559	MAXWELL F A	467	TULBAHADUR PUN	1276
DIAMOND B	188	MAYO A	229	TYTLER J A	234
DUNDAS J	325	MELLISS C J	434	UMRAO SINGH	1304
FAZAL DIN	1316	MEYNELL G	1158	VOUSDEN W J	354
FITZGERALD R	190	MILLER J	197	WALKER W G	519
FITZGIBBON A	302	MIR DAST	603	WALLER W F F	276
FORREST G	112	MOORE A T	296	WATSON J	201
FOSBERY G V	311	NAMDEO JADHAO	1330	WHEELER G C	778
GAJE GHALE	1244	NAND SINGH	1259	WHEELER G G M	582
GANJU LAMA	1273	NETRABAHADUR THAPA	1278	WHITCHURCH H F	412
GIAN SINGH	1317	OLPHERTS W	176	WOOD J A	294
GILL P	117			YESHWANT GHADGE	1281

SOUTH AFRICA (29)

Name	No.	Name	No.
ALBRECHT H	454	MARTIN - LEAKE A	512
BAXTER F W	414	MARTINEAU H R	451
BLOOMFIELD W	745	McCREA J F	389
BOOTH F C	774	MULLINS C H	438
BROWN P	383	NESBITT R C	415
CLEMENTS J J	498	NORTON G R	1289
CREAN T J	510	O'TOOLE E	382
D'ARCY H C D	381	RAMSDEN H E	452
DANAHER J	391	ROGERS J	502
ENGLISH W J	503	SCHEISS F C	372
FAULDS W F	730	SCOTT R G	384
HARTLEY E B	385	SMYTHE Q G M	1212
HENDERSON H S	413	SWALES E	1312
HEWITT W H	880	YOUNG A	505
JOHNSTON R	436		

UNITED STATES UNKNOWN WARRIOR - 1351

TOTAL NUMBER OF VICTORIA CROSSES AWARDED TO MEN OF BRITISH REGIMENTS (Including 63 from disbanded Regiments) = 990
TOTAL NUMBER OF VICTORIA CROSSES AWARDED TO MEN OF OVERSEAS REGIMENTS (Including one to the Unknown US Warrior) = 361 = 135
*NB: These numbers do NOT include the three Bars - if included, see below:

MARTIN - LEAKE A   512 (and following 550) First award with South African Forces. Bar awarded with RAMC; Totals change to 991 and 360 respectively
CHAVASSE N G   743 (and following 852) Both awards whilst serving with RAMC
UPHAM C H   1183 (and following 1213) Both awards whilst serving with New Zealand Forces. With three Bars, total awards amount to 1354

WHERE RECIPIENTS BORN (A) - UNITED KINGDOM (BY COUNTY/LARGER CITIES & 'NEW' REGIONS ie Avon)

A TOTAL OF 885 OF THE 1350 RECIPIENTS WERE BORN IN THE U.K (65%)

CHAPTER	1	2	3	4	5	6	7	8	9	10	11	12	13	14	15	16	17	18	19	20	Total
Avon	3	-	-	-	-	-	-	2	-	-	-	-	-	-	-	-	-	1	-	-	6
Beds	-	1	1	-	-	-	-	-	-	-	-	1	-	-	-	-	-	-	-	-	3
Berkshire	2	-	-	-	1	1	-	-	2	-	1	1	-	-	-	1	-	-	-	-	9
Birmingham	-	-	1	1	-	1	-	-	2	2	1	5	-	-	-	-	1	-	-	-	14
Bristol	-	-	-	-	-	-	-	-	-	-	1	-	-	-	-	-	-	-	-	-	1
Bucks	1	-	-	-	1	-	-	-	-	-	2	-	-	-	-	1	-	-	-	-	5
Cambs	-	-	1	1	1	-	-	-	-	-	-	-	-	-	-	-	-	-	-	-	3
Cheshire	2	-	-	-	2	-	-	-	1	2	-	6	-	-	-	-	-	2	-	2	17
Channel Isles	1	-	-	-	2	-	-	-	-	-	-	-	-	-	-	1	-	-	-	-	4
Cleveland	-	-	-	-	-	-	-	-	-	1	-	-	-	-	-	-	-	-	-	-	1
Cornwall	3	-	1	-	-	-	-	2	2	-	-	-	-	-	-	-	-	-	-	1	9
Cumbria	-	2	-	-	-	-	-	2	-	-	1	3	-	-	-	-	-	-	-	-	8
Derbyshire	1	2	-	-	-	-	-	-	1	-	1	3	1	-	-	-	-	-	-	-	9
Devon	6	1	2	2	2	-	1	-	3	1	1	5	1	-	-	-	-	1	-	-	26
Dorset	1	2	1	-	-	-	1	-	-	-	-	1	1	-	-	-	-	1	-	-	7
Co.Durham	2	2	-	-	-	-	1	1	2	1	2	6	-	1	1	1	-	-	-	-	20
Edinburgh	-	3	-	-	-	4	-	4	-	1	2	4	-	-	-	-	-	-	2	-	18
Essex	1	4	-	-	-	1	-	1	1	1	-	2	-	1	-	1	-	-	-	-	11
Glasgow	2	5	-	-	1	1	-	2	1	3	-	4	-	-	1	-	1	-	-	-	17
Glos.	-	3	1	1	1	1	-	-	1	2	1	1	-	1	-	1	-	1	-	-	15
Hampshire	3	5	-	-	2	2	2	2	3	2	4	5	-	2	-	-	1	1	2	-	36
Hereford.	-	-	-	-	-	1	-	-	-	-	-	-	-	-	-	-	-	-	-	-	1
Herts	-	1	-	-	1	1	-	(*)	3	1	2	1	-	-	-	-	-	-	-	-	10*
Humberside	-	-	-	-	-	-	-	-	-	-	1	-	-	-	-	-	-	-	-	-	1
Hunts	-	1	-	-	-	-	-	-	-	1	1	-	-	-	-	-	-	-	-	-	3
Kent	2	2	-	-	1	4	-	1	1	2	1	4	-	1	-	2	1	4	2	-	27
Lancashire	1	4	-	-	-	5	-	1	4	5	16	8	-	-	2	1	1	1	1	-	50
Leic.	-	1	-	-	-	1	-	-	1	1	1	-	-	-	-	-	-	1	1	-	6
Lincolnshire	1	-	-	-	-	-	-	-	3	1	-	2	-	-	-	-	-	-	-	-	7

Continued

('Chapters')	1	2	3	4	5	6	7	8	9	10	11	12	13	14	15	16	17	18	19	20	344
Liverpool	-	2	1	-	1	-	-	1	-	2	3	2	-	-	-	-	-	-	-	-	12
London	7	12	2	3	6	9	-	6	15	8	23	20	1	3	2	-	2	7	1	1	128
Manchester	1	1	-	-	-	1	-	-	-	1	2	3	-	-	-	-	-	-	-	-	9
Middlesex	-	-	-	-	-	-	-	-	-	1	-	2	-	-	-	-	-	-	-	-	3
Norfolk	-	2	-	-	2	1	-	-	1	-	3	3	-	-	1	-	-	1	-	-	14
Northants	-	-	1	-	1	-	-	-	-	-	1	1	-	-	-	-	-	-	-	-	4
N.IRELAND	9	12	4	1	1	-	-	2	1	4	1	2	1	-	-	-	-	-	1	-	36
Northumb.	-	-	-	1	1	1	-	2	2	-	-	2	-	1	-	1	-	-	-	-	10
Notts	1	2	-	1	1	1	-	-	4	1	1	1	-	1	-	1	-	-	-	-	15
Oxfordshire	-	1	-	-	-	1	-	-	-	1	(*)	-	-	-	-	-	-	-	-	-	3*
SCOTLAND	15	21	11	-	3	4	-	5	9	2	22	17	1	1	3	2	2	1	2	-	121
Shropshire	-	-	-	-	-	1	-	1	1	1	-	1	-	-	-	-	-	-	-	-	5
Somerset	3	-	1	-	2	3	-	-	1	1	1	1	1	1	-	1	-	-	-	-	14
Staffordshire	1	2	-	-	-	-	-	-	-	1	4	4	-	1	-	1	1	1	-	-	14
Suffolk	1	2	1	1	-	-	-	1	2	1	2	-	-	-	-	-	1	-	-	-	12
Surrey	1	2	1	1	-	6	-	1	5	1	2	4	-	-	-	-	-	-	-	-	24
Sussex	3	-	-	-	1	-	-	3	3	1	-	5	-	-	-	-	-	-	-	-	16
WALES	2	3	-	2	1	-	-	-	1	2	8	3	1	1	-	1	1	-	1	-	27
Warwicks.	1	1	-	-	-	-	-	1	-	-	2	3	-	-	-	-	-	-	-	-	8
Wiltshire	1	2	2	-	-	-	-	-	-	1	1	-	-	1	-	-	-	-	-	-	8
Worc.	1	-	-	1	-	1	-	1	1	1	3	1	-	-	-	-	1	-	-	-	11
Yorkshire	4	4	1	-	1	4	-	-	3	6	11	5	-	-	-	1	2	2	-	1	45
Unknown	-	1	-	-	-	1	-	-	-	-	-	-	-	-	-	-	-	-	-	-	2
TOTALS	83	108	34	15	32	54	4	40*	79	64	128*	144	7	13	9	15	13	25	12	6	885

(* = Birthplace of Bar recipients listed in previous 'chapter(s)')

United Kingdom totals – England (666); Scotland (156); Wales (27); Northern Ireland (36 – to which can be added many from Ireland pre-1921)
Early 'chapters' covering the Crimea (1) through to South African War (6) give a rough idea of recruitment areas when matched with regiments

WHERE RECIPIENTS BORN (B) - OVERSEAS

A TOTAL OF 465 OF THE RECIPIENTS WERE BORN OVERSEAS (35%)

CHAPTER	1	2	3	4	5	6	7	8	9	10	11	12	13	14	15	16	17	18	19	20	Total
Australia	-	-	1	-	-	5	-	-	10	2	16	25	1	-	4	5	2	-	6	4	81
Belgium	-	-	-	-	-	-	-	-	-	1	-	-	-	-	-	-	-	-	-	-	1
Canada	1	2	1	-	1	4	-	-	3	3	10	17	-	-	-	3	1	7	4	-	57
China	-	-	-	-	-	-	-	-	1	-	-	-	-	-	-	-	-	1	1	-	3
Denmark	-	-	-	-	-	-	-	-	-	-	1	-	-	-	-	-	-	1	1	-	3
Egypt	-	-	-	-	-	-	-	-	1	-	-	-	-	-	-	-	-	-	-	-	1
Fiji	-	-	-	-	-	-	-	-	1	-	-	-	-	-	-	-	-	-	-	-	1
France	3	1	-	1	-	-	-	-	-	-	-	-	-	-	-	-	-	1	-	-	6
Germany	2	-	-	-	-	-	-	-	-	-	-	-	-	-	-	-	-	-	-	-	2
Gibraltar	-	-	-	-	-	-	1	-	-	-	-	-	-	-	-	-	-	-	-	-	1
Holland	-	-	-	-	1	-	-	-	-	-	-	1	-	-	-	-	-	-	-	-	2
India	-	22	5	-	7	3	5	2	8	5	4	3	1	-	3	5	3	11	7	-	94
Iraq	-	-	-	-	-	-	-	-	-	1	-	-	-	-	-	-	-	-	-	-	1
Ireland	20	45	20	4	8	8	-	3	9	4	6	2	-	2	1	1	1	-	-	-	134
Japan	-	-	-	-	-	-	-	-	1	-	-	-	-	-	-	-	-	-	-	-	1
Kenya	-	-	-	-	-	-	-	-	-	-	-	-	-	-	1	-	-	-	-	-	1
Nepal	-	-	-	-	-	-	-	-	1	-	-	2	-	-	-	-	2	5	2	-	12
NewZealand	-	-	-	1	-	1	-	-	2	2	3	7	-	-	4	1*	3	-	-	-	24*
Portugal	-	-	2	-	-	-	-	-	-	-	-	-	-	-	-	-	-	-	-	-	2
Russia	1	1	-	-	-	-	-	-	-	-	1	-	-	-	-	-	-	-	-	-	3
SouthAfrica	1	1	-	1	1	3	-	-	1	1	3	2	-	1	-	3	-	1	1	-	20
Sri Lanka	-	-	-	-	-	-	-	-	-	1	-	1	1	-	-	-	-	-	-	-	3
Sweden	-	-	-	-	1	-	-	-	-	-	-	-	-	-	-	-	-	-	-	-	1
Switzerland	-	-	-	1	-	-	-	-	-	-	-	-	-	-	-	-	-	-	-	-	1
U.S.A.	-	-	1	-	-	-	-	-	-	-	1	3	-	-	-	-	-	-	-	(x)	5(x)
West Indies	-	2	2	-	1	-	-	-	-	-	-	-	-	-	-	-	-	-	-	-	5
TOTALS	28	74	32	8	20	24	6	5	38	20	45	63	3	3	13	17*	12	27	22	5x	465(x)

(* = Birthplace of Bar recipient - awarded later 'chapter'/ (x) = the Unknown U.S. Warrior)

AGE BREAKDOWN: *Average age when Victoria Cross awarded and when died (Allowing for 29 living recipients as at 1st April 1999)*																					
CHAPTER	1	2	3	4	5	6	7	8	9	10	11	12	13	14	15	16	17	18	19	20	Av. Age
AGE WON	27·2	28·8	28·2	29·7	30·4	25·0	29·1	28·7	27·7	27·0	26·7	27·6	28·4	33·3	29·2	32·4	28·8	23·9	25·0	33·3	27·8
AGE DIED	56·3	56·8	56·9	52·1	67·4	59·3	64·2	54·5	50·4	50·4	53·4	55·6	47·5	43·4	43·2	55·9	44·6	38·1	36·0	40·7	53·8
ALIVE	-	-	-	-	-	-	-	-	-	-	-	-	-	2	2	3	3	10	6	3	79·6

The higher proportion of posthumous awards during both the First & Second World Wars (8 to 12 and 14 to 19) reflect in the average age at death

The table below is a basic guide to awards by service and country, rather than those which show the ranks by service. The three numbers shown underlined, relate to the three bars which brings the total number of awards to 1,353 - the Unknown United States Warrior takes the final total to 1,354. The figures for the Honourable East India Company (HEIC) and the Indian Army will always arouse debate for the period 1856 - 1914, considering that up until 1861 all Army units in India were technically under the HEIC. Similar disputes concern the awards for civilians, the three for the Indian Mutiny were designated "Mr" and worked for the Bengal Civil Service - a case could be made for The Rev James ADAMS (351) during the Afghan War in 1879, but as he was a member of the Bengal Ecclesiastical Department of the Indian Army, I have incorporated him there.

VICTORIA CROSS AWARDS BY SERVICE AND COUNTRY																					
CHAPTER	1	2	3	4	5	6	7	8	9	10	11	12	13	14	15	16	17	18	19	20	Total
ROYAL NAVY/RESERVE/VOLUNT.RESERVE	24	6	6	-	3	-	1	2	11	5	10	13	3	5	2	10	3	-	2	-	106
ROYAL MARINE/ROYAL MARINE ARTILL.	3	-	-	-	-	-	1	-	1	1	1	2	-	-	-	-	-	-	1	-	10
ARMY	84	111	38	20	40	57	3	39	78	60	111	116	3	6	6	7	8	23	12	6	828
HEIC/ INDIAN ARMY/GURKHA FORCES	-	62	20	-	-	1	5	4	6	4	2	2	4	-	2	1	4	15	7	1	140
ROYAL FLYING CORPS & R.A.F.	-	-	-	-	-	-	-	-	6	2	3	7	-	5	4	4	3	7	1	-	42
AUSTRALIAN FORCES	-	-	-	-	-	5	-	-	9	6	19	29	-	-	3	6	3	-	6	4	90
CANADIAN FORCES	-	-	-	-	-	4	-	-	5	3	22	32	-	-	1	2	1	5	4	-	79
NEW ZEALAND FORCES	-	-	1	-	-	1	-	-	1	1	3	6	-	-	3	-	3	-	-	-	20
SOUTH AFRICAN FORCES	-	-	-	3	8	10	-	-	-	2	2	-	-	-	-	1	-	1	1	-	28
FIJI MILITARY FORCES	-	-	-	-	-	-	-	-	-	-	-	-	-	-	-	-	-	1	-	-	1
KING'S AFRICAN RIFLES	-	-	-	-	-	-	-	-	-	-	-	-	-	-	1	-	-	-	-	-	1
WEST INDIAN FORCES	-	-	1	-	1	-	-	-	-	-	-	-	-	-	-	-	-	-	-	-	2
CIVILIANS	-	3	-	-	-	-	-	-	-	-	-	-	-	-	-	-	-	-	-	-	3
TOTALS	111	182	66	23	52	78	10	45	117	84	173	207	10	16	22	32	25	52	34	11	1350

BREAKDOWN OF AWARDS - by SERVICE, COUNTRY and RANKS

Royal Navy/Royal Naval Reserve/Royal Naval Volunteer Reserve/(Including overseas forces)
(NB - Royal Naval Air Service included with RFC/RAF) *A volunteer with the Indian Naval Brigade

CHAPTER	1	2	3	4	5	6	7	8	9	10	11	12	13	14	15	16	17	18	19	20	TOTAL
Seaman	6	3	3	-	1	-	-	-	2	1	2	1	-	1	-	1	-	-	1	-	22
'NCO'	8	-	2	-	-	-	-	-	-	-	1	1	-	-	1	1	-	-	-	-	14
Midship.	2	1	1	-	-	-	1	-	2	-	-	-	-	-	-	-	-	-	-	-	7
Lieuten't	6	2	-	-	-	-	-	1	2	1	4	6	2	1	-	2	2	-	1	-	30
Lt.Comd	-	-	-	-	-	-	-	-	4	1	-	3	-	-	1	2	-	-	-	-	11
Commdr	1	-	-	-	-	-	-	1	1	2	1	1	1	1	-	2	1	-	-	-	12
Captain	1	-	-	-	1	-	-	-	-	-	-	1	-	2	-	2	-	-	-	-	7
Skipper	-	-	-	-	-	-	-	-	-	-	2	-	-	-	-	-	-	-	-	-	2
Surgeon	-	-	-	-	1	-	-	-	-	-	-	-	-	-	-	-	-	-	-	-	1
Mr.	-	1*	-	-	-	-	-	-	-	-	-	-	-	-	-	-	-	-	-	-	1
TOTAL	24	7	6	-	3	-	1	2	11	5	10	13	3	5	2	10	3	-	2	-	107

Royal Marines/Royal Marine Artillery

CHAPTER	1	7	9	10	11	12	19	TOTAL
Bombardier	1	-	-	-	-	-	-	1
Corporal	1	-	1	-	-	-	1	3
Sergeant	-	-	-	-	-	1	-	1
Lieutenant	1	-	-	-	-	-	-	1
Captain	-	1	-	-	-	1	-	2
Major	-	-	-	1	1	-	-	2
TOTAL	3	1	1	1	1	2	1	10

Army
(Including HEIC, Indian Army and overseas forces) - The three underlined numbers indicate Bar to be added

CHAPTER	1	2	3	4	5	6	7	8	9	10	11	12	13	14	15	16	17	18	19	29	TOTAL
Private	27	62	13	7	15	19	-	16	26	28	37	37	1	-	2	4	2	10	10	1	317
Corporal	5	11	3	2	4	7	-	6	24	7	26	33	1	1	1	1	1	7	8	1	149
Sergeant	21	22	4	2	3	15	-	3	11	11	35	37	1	1	4	4	5	6	1	4	190
Lieuten't	12	52	16	6	13	20	4	_8_	23	14	27	45	1	2	4	_=_	2	6	6	1	262
Captain	10	13	11	2	7	12	3	8	11	9	_20_	10	3	2	3	1	3	8	1	-	137
Major	3	5	7	1	-	3	1	2	2	2	5	4	-	-	-	2	1	6	2	2	48
Lt. Col	2	-	1	1	1	-	-	-	2	4	7	17	-	-	1	6	2	-	-	2	46
Colonel	1	1	-	-	-	-	-	-	-	-	-	-	-	-	-	-	-	-	-	-	2
Brig Gen	-	-	-	-	-	-	-	-	-	-	1	1	-	-	1	-	-	-	-	-	3
HospAp	-	-	1	-	-	-	-	-	-	-	-	-	-	-	-	-	-	-	-	-	1
Ass Surg	2	2	3	-	-	-	-	-	-	-	-	-	-	-	-	-	-	-	-	-	7
Surgeon	1	3	-	-	3	-	-	-	-	-	-	-	-	-	-	-	-	-	-	-	7
SurgCap	-	-	-	-	1	2	-	-	-	-	-	-	-	-	-	-	-	-	-	-	3
SurgMaj	-	-	-	1	2	-	-	-	-	-	-	-	-	-	-	-	-	-	-	-	3
Commiss	-	1	-	1	-	-	-	-	-	-	-	-	-	-	-	-	-	-	-	-	2
Mr		3	-	-	-	-	-	-	-	-	-	-	-	-	-	-	-	-	-	-	3
Chaplain	-	-	1	-	-	-	-	-	-	1	-	1	-	-	-	-	-	-	-	-	3
TOTAL	84	175	60	23	49	78	8	_43_	99	76	_158_	185	7	6	16	_18_	16	43	28	11	1183

Royal Flying Corps/Royal Air Force/Fleet Air Arm*/Royal Naval Air Service* (Including overseas forces) (NB: The latter two(*) 'technically' under Royal Navy) Ranks include those prior to 1 April 1918													
CHAPTER	9	10	11	12	13	14	15	16	17	18	19	20	TOTAL
Sergeant	-	-	1	-	-	2	1	-	-	2	-	-	6
Flight Sergeant	-	-	-	-	-	-	-	-	1	-	1	-	2
FlightSub.Lieut*	1	-	-	-	-	-	-	-	-	-	-	-	1
Lieutenant	2	1	1	2	-	-	-	-	-	-	1	-	7
Captain	2	-	2	3	-	-	-	-	-	-	1	-	8
Major	-	1	-	2	-	-	-	-	-	-	-	-	3
Pilot Officer	-	-	-	-	-	-	-	1	1	1	-	-	3
Flying Officer	-	-	-	-	-	1	1	1	2	1	-	-	6
FlightLieutenant	-	-	-	-	-	2	-	-	-	2	-	-	4
SquadronLeader	-	-	-	-	-	-	1	1	1	2	-	-	5
Wing Command.	-	-	-	-	-	-	-	1	1	1	-	-	3
Group Captain	-	-	-	-	-	-	-	-	-	1	-	-	1
Squad Commd*	1	-	-	-	-	-	-	-	-	-	-	-	1
TOTAL	6	2	4	7	-	5	4	4	6	9	3	-	50

AWARDS SHOWN BY RANK AT TIME OF ACTION

The four tables show a basic breakdown of the ranks of all 1,350 recipients at the time of their award. For convenience, Royal Naval 'NCO's' covers 'ranks' such as Petty Officer, Boatswain etc; the Army rank of Private embraces Sappers, Drummers, Pipers, Sepoys etc; Lance-Corporal is incorporated with Corporal; Sergeant comprises of the ranks of T.S.M., C.S.M. etc; I have listed every flying award under RFC/RAF, including two Royal Naval Air Service awards from 1915, an inclusion bound to upset the purists! Bearing in mind that each table includes all overseas forces, a hypothetical Temp/Major from a New Zealand Infantry Regiment who served with the RFC during 1916, and awarded the Victoria Cross for flying services, will be shown in the RFC/RAF table under Major rather than under Army. The tables are intended as a guide only, and open to interpretation.

The British Unknown Soldier is laid to rest, Westminister Abbey, London

LIVING VICTORIA CROSS RECIPIENTS (29) *(As of 1st April 1999)*

NAME	DATE & PLACE OF ACTION	BORN
SECOND WORLD WAR (26)		
1164 ANNAND Richard W (Captain)	15 May 1940, near River Dyle, Belgium	Co. Durham on 5 November 1914
1170 WILSON Eric C T (Lt. Colonel)	11 - 15 August 1940, Somaliland	Isle of Wight on 2 October 1912
1185 CUTLER Sir Roden (Lieutenant)	19 June to 6 July 1941, Syria	N.S.W., Australia on 24 May 1916
1193 GARDNER Philip J (A/Captain)	23 November 1941, Tobruk, Libya	South East London on 25 December 1914
1201 GOULD Thomas W (Petty Officer)	16 February 1942, Mediterranean Sea	Dover, Kent on 28 December 1914
1217 MERRITT Charles C I (Lt. Colonel)	19 August 1942, Dieppe, France	Vancouver, Canada on 10 November 1908
1218 PORTEOUS Patrick A (Colonel)	19 August 1942, Dieppe, France	N.W.F., India on 1 January 1918
1240 KENNEALLY John P (C.Q.M.S.)	28 April 1943, Dj Arada, Tunisia	Birmingham on 15 March 1921
1244 GAJE GHALE (Hon. Captain)	24 - 27 May 1943, Chin Hills, Burma	Nepal on 1 August 1918
1251 REID William (A/Flight Lieutenant)	3 November 1943, over Germany	Glasgow on 21 December 1921
1273 GANJU LAMA (Captain)	12 June 1944, Ninthoukhong, Burma	Sikkim, India on 22 July 1922
1276 TULBAHADUR PUN (WO I)	23 June 1944, Mogaung, Burma	Nepal on 23 March 1923
1279 AGANSING RAI (Sergeant)	26 June 1944, Bishenpur, Burma	Nepal on 24 April 1920
1282 CRUICKSHANK John A (Fl. Lieut.)	17 - 18 July 1944, over Arctic Circle	Aberdeen on 20 May 1920
1286 JAMIESON David A (Major)	7 - 8 August 1944, Normandy, France	Norfolk on 1 October 1920
1287 WATKINS Sir Tasker (Major)	16 August 1944, Normandy, France	Glamorgan, Wales on 18 November 1918
1289 NORTON Gerard R (Captain)	31 August 1944, Monte Gridolfo, Italy	Hershel, South Africa on 7 September 1915
1299 SMITH Ernest A (Sergeant)	21 - 22 October 1944, River Savio, Italy	British Columbia, Canada on 3 May 1914
1302 BHANDARI RAM (Captain)	22 November 1944, Arakan, Burma	Simla Hills, India on 24 July 1919
1304 UMRAO SINGH (Captain)	15 - 16 December 1944, Kaladan, Burma	Punjab, India on 11 July 1920
1319 BHANBHAGTA GURUNG (Captain)	5 March 1945, Tamandu, Burma	Nepal in September 1921
1325 CHAPMAN Edward T (C.S.M.)	2 April 1945, near Dortmund, Germany	Glamorgan, Wales on 13 January 1920
1329 ALI HAIDAR (Sergeant)	9 April 1945, Fusignano, Italy	N.W.F., India on 21 August 1913
1332 LACHHIMAN GURUNG (Hon. Sgt.)	12 - 13 May 1945, Taungdaw, Burma	Nepal on 30 December 1916
1334 KENNA Edward (Private)	15 May 1945, Wewak, New Guinea	Victoria, Australia on 6 July 1919
1338 FRASER Ian E (Lt. Commander)	31 July 1945, off Singapore	West London on 18 December 1920
KOREAN WAR (1)		
1343 SPEAKMAN William (Sergeant)	4 November 1951, United Hilltop, Korea	Cheshire on 21 September 1927
BORNEO/SARAWAK INCIDENT (1)		
1344 RAMBAHADUR LIMBU (Captain)	21 November 1965, Gunong Tepoi, Indonesia	Nepal in July 1939
VIETNAM WAR (1)		
1348 PAYNE Keith (WO II)	24 May 1969, Kontum Province, Vietnam	Queensland, Australia on 30 August 1933

****

The average age of the above men, when they performed the deed leading to the award of their Victoria Cross, was 23.6 months, compared to the 27.8 months overall average of all 1,350 recipients. The average age of the 29 men above is 78.11 months, compared to the overall average of 53.7 months, but it should be taken into account that 298 received their awards posthumously, bringing the average down considerably, with many other men killed in later actions or theatres, or dying of disease in tropical areas whilst still serving with the forces. Add to this a number of men who died some years later as a result of their wounds or from illnesses now easily curable, and the average age increases to the mid-eighties. Figures, percentages and statistics can be arranged in any way to prove a point, as has been said elsewhere, thus these ages are included merely as a guide for general interest.

MUSEUMS WHERE MANY OF THE VICTORIA CROSSES CAN BE SEEN

The museums listed below are referred to in the **Commemoration** *section in most entries in the text, as the current repository where the actual Victoria Crosses may be seen. Not all of the museums shown possess Crosses, but may be useful as a general guide as to the location of the various regimental museums. With the numerous amalgamations of regiments since the inauguration of the Victoria Cross, it may be just as well to telephone before any planned visit to check on which Crosses are on display, as well as establishing opening times. Many are on 'permanent' loan, whilst others are replica's, due to the actual cost of insuring the groups (that may reach in excess of £100,000 at auction) which would make it financially impossible for the smaller museums running on a limited budget to pay the insurance premiums of the groups in their possession. The locations shown in the text are accurate as of January 1998, thanks to the efforts of Dennis Pillinger and Anthony Staunton, their book on the subject - "Victoria Cross Locator" - being an invaluable guide to anyone interested in the history of the Cross at auctions, showing not only prices realised, but the 'final resting place' of the actual medal where known.*

MUSEUMS OF THE BRITISH ARMY

The Life Guards: Household Cavalry Museum, Combermere Barracks, St.Leonard's Road, Windsor, Berkshire. 01753-868222 ext.203
PREDECESSOR'S: **The 1st Life Guards** and **The 2nd Life Guards** (as above)

The Blues and Royals (Royal Horse Guards and 1st Dragoons): (as above)
PREDECESSOR's: **The Royal Horse Guards (The Blues)** and **The Royal Dragoons (1st Dragoons)** (as above)

1st The Queen's Dragoon Guards: Cardiff Castle, Cardiff, South Glamorgan. 01222-229367
PREDECESSOR's: **1st King's Dragoon Guards** and **The Queens bays (2nd Dragoon Guards)** (as above)

The Royal Scots Dragoon Guards (Carabiniers and Greys): The Castle, Edinburgh. 0131-225-7534
PREDECESSOR's: **The Royal Scots Greys (2nd Dragoons):** The Royal Scots Greys Room, United Services Museum (as above); **3rd Carabiniers (P.O.W's Dragoon Guards):** The Castle, Chester, Cheshire. 01244-327617; **(P.O.W's Dragoon Guards) 3rd Dragoon Guards (P.O.W's):** (as 3rd); **The Carabiniers (6th Dragoon Guards):** (as 3rd)

4th/7th Royal Dragoon Guards: 3 Tower Street, York. 01904-642036
PREDECESSOR's: **4th Royal Irish Dragoon Guards** and **7th Dragoon Guards(Princess Royal's)** (as above)

5th Royal Inniskilling Dragoon Guards: The Chester Military Museum, The Castle, Chester, Cheshire. 01224-347203.

PREDECESSOR's: **5th Dragoon Guards (Princess Charlotte of Wales's)** and **The Inniskilling (6th Dragoons)** (as above)

The Queen's Own Hussars: Lord Leycester Hospital, High Street, Warwick, Warwickshire. 01926-492755
PREDECESSOR's: **3rd The King's Own Hussars** and **7th Queen's Own Hussars** (as above)

The Queen's Royal Irish Hussars: Museum of Irish Cavalry Regiments, Carrickfergus, C.Antrim, Northern Ireland. 0123-83-62273, AND Sussex Combined Services Museum, The Redoubt Fortress, Royal Parade, Eastbourne, East Sussex. 01323-460300
PREDECESSOR's: **4th Queen's Own Hussars** and **8th (King's Royal Irish) Hussars** (as above)

9th/12th Royal Lancers (Prince of Wales's): Derby Museum and Art Gallery, The Strand, Derby, Derbyshire. 01332-255581
PREDECESSOR's: **9th Queen's Royal Lancers** and **12th Royal Lancers (P.O.W's)** (as above)

The Royal Hussars (Prince of Wales's Own): Peninsula Barracks, Winchester, Hampshire. 01962-863751
PREDECESSOR's: **10th Royal Hussars (P.O.W's Own)** and **11th Hussars (Prince Albert's Own)** (as above)

13th/18th Royal Hussars (Queen Mary's Own): Cannon Hall, Barnsley, South Yorkshire. 01226-790270
PREDECESSOR's: **13th Hussars** and **18th Royal Hussars (Queen Mary's Own)** (as above)

14th/20th King's Hussars: County and Regimental Museum, Stanley Street, Preston, Lancashire. 01772-264075
PREDECESSOR's: **14th King's Hussars** and **20th Hussars** (as above)

15th/19th The King's Royal Hussars: The John George Joicey Museum, City Road, Newcastle-upon-Tyne. 0191-232-4562. AND Fenham Barracks, Newcastle-upon-Tyne. 0191-261-1046 ext. 3142.
PREDECESSOR's: **15th The King's Hussars** and **19th (Queen Alexandra's Own Royal) Hussars** (as above)

16th/5th The Queen's Royal Lancers: Kitchener House, Lammascote Road, Stafford, Staffordshire. 01785-45840 ext. 4519
PREDECESSOR's:**16th The Queen's Lancers** and **5th Royal Irish Lancers** (above)

17th/21st Lancers: Belvoir Castle, near Grantham, Lincolnshire. 01476-870262
PREDECESSOR's: **17th Lancers (Duke of Cambridge's Own)** and **21st Lancers (Empress of India's)** (as above)

The Royal Tank Regiment: The Tank Museum, Bovington Camp, Wareham, Dorset, Dorsetshire. 01929-462721 ext. 3329 & 3463

The Royal Regiment of Artillery: Royal Artillery Regimental Museum, Old Royal Military Academy, Woolwich, London. 0181-316-5402

Corps of Royal Engineers: Brompton Barracks, Chatham, Kent. 01634-406397

Royal Corps of Signals: Blandford Camp, Blandford Forum, Dorset. 01258-452581 ext. 2248

The Guards: Wellington Barracks, Birdcage Walk, London SW1. 0171- 4466 ext. 3271
Grenadier Guards, Coldstream Guards, Scots Guards, Irish Guards and **Welsh Guards** (all as above)

The Royal Scots (The Royal Regiment): The Castle, Edinburgh. 0131-336-1761 ext. 4265

The Queen's Regiment: Dover Castle, Dover, Kent. 01304-240121
PREDECESSOR's: **The Queen's Royal Surrey Regiment, The Queen's Royal regiment (West Surrey), The East Surrey Regiment:** all at Clandon Park, West Clandon, Guildford, Surrey. 01483-223419: **The Queen's Own Buffs, The Royal Kent Regiment, The Buffs (Royal East Kent Regiment):** The Royal Museum and Art Gallery, High Street, Canterbury, Kent. 01227-763434/452747: **The Queen's Own Royal West Kent Regiment:** Maidstone Museum and Art Gallery, St. Faith's Street, Maidstone, Kent. 01622-754497: **The Royal Sussex Regiment:** Sussex Combined Services Museum, The Redoubt Fortress, Royal Parade, Eastbourne, East Sussex. 01323-410300: **The Middlesex regiment (Duke of Cambridge's Own):** Bruce Castle, Lordship Lane, Tottenham, London N. 0181-808-8772.

The King's Own Royal Border Regiment: Queen Mary's Tower, The Castle, Carlisle, Cumbria. 01228-32774.
PREDECESSOR's: **The King's Own Royal Regiment (Lancaster)** and **The Border Regiment** (as above)

The Royal Regiment of Fusiliers: HM Tower of London, London EC. 0171-709-0765 ext.295
PREDECESSOR's: **The Royal Northumberland Fusiliers:** The Abbot's Tower, Alnwick Castle, Alnwick, Northumberland. 01665-602152: **The Royal Warwickshire Fusiliers:** St. John's House, Coten End, Warwick, Warwickshire. 01926-491653: **The Royal Fusiliers (City of London Regiment):** HM Tower of London (as above): **The Lancashire Fusiliers:** Wellington Barracks, Bury, Lancashire. 0161-764-2208.

The King's Regiment: County Museum, William Brown Street, Liverpool. 0151-207-0001/5451.

PREDECESSOR's: **The King's Regiment (Liverpool)** (as above) and **The Manchester Regiment:** The Museum of the Manchesters, Ashton Town Hall, The Market Place, Ashton-under-Lyne, Lancashire. 0161-344-3078.

The Royal Anglian Regiment:
PREDECESSOR's: **The Norfolk Regiment:** Cameron House, Britannia Barracks, Norwich, Norfolk. 01603-628455. **The Suffolk Regiment:** The Keep, Gibraltar Barracks, Bury St. Edmunds, Suffolk. 01284-2394. **The Royal Lincolnshire Regiment:** Museum of Lincolnshire Life, Old Barracks, Burton Road, Lincoln, Lincolnshire. 01522-528448. **The Northamptonshire Regiment:** Abington Park Museum, Abington, Northampton. 01604-31454. **The Bedfordshire & Hertfordshire Regiment:** Luton Museum, Wardown Park, Luton, Bedfordshire. 01582-36941/36492. **The Essex Regiment:** Essex regiment Museum, Oaklands Park, Moulsham Street, Chelmsford, Essex. 01245-260614. **The Royal Leicestershire Regiment:** The Mgazine, Oxford Street, Leicester. 01533-555839.

The Devonshire and Dorset Regiment: The Keep, Bridport Road, Dorchester, Dorset. 013052-64066.

The Light Infantry: Peninsula Barracks, Winchester, Hampshire. 01962-885222. PREDECESSOR's: **The Somerset Light Infantry (Prince Albert's):** Somerset Military Museum, The Castle, Taunton, Somerset. 01823-255504. **The Duke of Cornwall's Light Infantry:** The Keep, Bodmin, Cornwall. 01208-2810. **The King's Own Yorkshire Light Infantry:** Chequer Road, Doncaster, South Yorkshire. 01302-734287. **The King's Shropshire Light Infantry:** The Castle, Shrewsbury, Shropshire. 01743-58516. **The Durham Light Infantry:** Aykley Heads, Durham City, Co. Durham. 0191-384-2214.

The Prince of Wales's Own Regiment of Yorkshire: The Museum, Tower Street, York. 01904-642038.
PREDECESSOR's: **The West Yorkshire Regiment (The Prince of Wales's Own):** (as above): **The East Yorkshire regiment (The Duke of York's):** (as above).

The Green Howards (Alexandra, Princess of Wales's Own Yorkshire Regiment): Trinity Church Square, The Market Place, Richmond, North Yorkshire. 01748-2133.

The Royal Highland Fusiliers (Princess Margaret's Own Glasgow & Ayrshire Regiment): 518 Sauchiehall Street, Glasgow. 0141-332-0961.
PREDECESSOR's: **The Royal Scots Fusiliers:** (as above). **The Highland Light Infantry (City of Glasgow Regiment):** (as above).

The Cheshire Regiment: The Castle, Chester, Cheshire. 01244-37617.

The Royal Welch Fusiliers: The Queen's Tower, Caernarfon Castle, Caernarfon, Gwynnedd. 01286-673362.

The Royal Regiment of Wales (24th/41st Foot): The Barracks, Brecon, Powys. 01874-3111 ext. 2310.

PREDECESSOR's: **The South Wales Borderers:** (as above). **The Welch Regiment:** Black and Barbican Towers, Cardiff Castle, Cardiff. 01222-229367.

The King's Own Scottish Borderers: The Barracks, Berwick-on-Tweed, Northumberland. 01289-307426.

The Royal Irish Rangers (27th (Inniskilling) 83rd and 87th): 5, Waring Street, Belfast. 01232-232086.
PREDECESSOR's: **The Royal Ulster Rifles:** (as above). **The Royal Inniskilling Fusiliers:** The Castle, Enniskillen, Co. Fermanagh, Northern Ireland. 01365-323142. **The Royal Irish Fusiliers (Princess Victoria's):** Sovereign's House, The Mall, Armagh, Co. Armagh, Northern Ireland. 01861-522911.

The Gloucestershire Regiment: Custom House, Commercial Road, Gloucester. 01452- 22682

The Worcestershire and Sherwood Foresters Regiment:
PREDECESSOR's: **The Worcestershire Regiment:** Worcester City Museum and Art Gallery, Foregate Street, Worcester. 01905-25371. **The Sherwood Forsters (Nottinghamshire and Derbyshire Regiment):** The Castle, Nottingham. 01602-483504, and Derby Museum and Art Gallery, The Strand, Derby, Derbyshire. 01332-255586.

The Queen's Lancashire Regiment: County and Regimental Museum, Stanley Street, Preston, Lancashire. 01772-264075.
PREDECESSOR's: **The Lancashire Regiment (P.O.W's Volunteers):** Peninsula Barracks, Orford, Warrington, Lancashire. 01925-335363.
PREDECESSOR's: **The East Lancashire Regiment:** Blackburn Museum and Art Gallery, Museum Street, Blackburn, Lancashire. 01254-667130. **The South Lancashire Regiment (The P.O.W's Volunteers):** (same as Lancashire Regiment). **The Loyal Regiment (North Lancashire):** Fulwood Barracks, Preston, Lancashire. 01772-716543 ext. 2362.

The Duke of Wellington's Regiment (West Riding): Bankfield Museum, Akroyd Park, Halifax, West Yorkshire. 01422-54823.

The Royal Hampshire Regiment: Serle's House, Southgate Street, Winchester, Hampshire. 01962-863658.

The Staffordshire Regiment (The Prince of Wales's): Whittington Barracks, Lichfield, Staffordshire. 01543-433333.
PREDECESSOR's: **The South Staffordshire Regiment:** (as above). **The North Staffordshire Regiment (The P.O.W's):** (as above)

The Black Watch (Royal Highland Regiment): Balhousie Castle, Perth. 01738-21281 ext. 8530.

The Duke of Edinburgh's Royal Regiment (Berkshire and Wiltshire): The Wardrobe, 58 The Close, Salisbury, Wiltshire. 01722-336222.
PREDECESSOR's: **The Royal Berkshire Regiment (Princess Charlotte of Wales's):** (as above - ext. 2683). **The Wiltshire Regiment (Duke of Edinburgh's):** (as above - ext. 2683)

Queen's Own Highlanders (Seaforth and Camerons): Fort George, Ardersier, By Inverness, Highland Region. 01463-224380.
PREDECESSOR's: **Seaforth Highlanders (Ross-Shire Buffs, The Duke of Albany's):** (as above). **The Queens Own Cameron Highlanders:** (as above)

The Gordon Highlanders: St. Luke's, Viewfield Road, Aberdeen. 01224-318174

The Argyll and Sutherland Highlanders: The Castle, Stirling. 01786-75165.

The Parachute Regiment: Airborne Forces Museum, Browning Barracks, Aldershot, Hampshire. 01252-24431 ext. 4619.
The Brigade of Gurkhas: Peninsular Barracks, Romsey Road, Winchester, Hampshire. 01962-842832.

The Royal Green Jackets: Peninsular Barracks, Romsey Road, Winchester, Hampshire. 01962-63846
PREDECESSOR's: **The Oxfordshire and Buckinghamshire Light Infantry:** The TAVR Centre, Slade Park, Headington, Oxford. 01865-716060. **The King's Royal Rifle Corps:** (as Royal Green Jackets). **The Rifle Brigade (The Prince Consort's Own):** (as above)

Special Air Services Regiment: 21st SAS Regiment (Artists') Museum, B Block, Duke of York's Headquarters, Chelsea, London, SW.

Army Air Corps: Museum of Army Flying, Army Air Corps Centre, Middle Wallop, Hampshire. 01264-62121 ext. 421/428.

Royal Army Chaplains' Department: Bagshot Park, Bagshot, Surrey. 01276-71717 ext. 2845

Royal Corps of Transport: Buller Barracks, Aldershot, Hampshire. 01252-24431 ext. 3834/3857
PREDECESSOR: **Royal Army Service Corps:** (as above)

Royal Army Medical Corps: Keogh Barracks, Ash Vale, Aldershot, Hampshire. 01252-24431. ext. Keogh 5212.

Royal Army Ordnance Corps: Blackdown Barracks, Deepcut, camberley, Surrey. 01252-24431 ext. 515/516.

Corps of Royal Electrical and Mechanical Engineers: Isaac Newton Road, Arborfield Cross, Reading, Berkshire. 01734-760421 ext. 2567.

Corps of Royal Military Police: Red Cap Museum, Roussillon Barracks, Broyle Road, Chichester, West Sussex. 01243-786311 ext. 237

Royal Army Veterinary Corps: RAVC Support Group, Gallwey Road, Aldershot, Hampshire. 01252-24431. ext. 3527

Royal Pioneer Corps: Simpson Barracks, Northampton. 01604-762742 ext. 4705

MUSEUMS OF THE ROYAL NAVY

Royal Navy Museum: HM Naval Base, Portsmouth, Hampshire. 01705-733060

National Maritime Museum: Greenwich, London, SE10 9NF. 0181-858-4422

Royal Navy Volunteer Reserve: Sussex Combined Services Museum, Redoubt Fortress, Royal Parade, Eastbourne, Sussex. 01323-410300

Royal Naval Air Service: Display at the Royal Air Force Museum, Grahame Park Way, Hendon, London, NW9 5LL. 0181-205-2266

MUSEUMS OF THE ROYAL AIR FORCE

Royal Air Force Museum: Grahame Park Way, Hendon, London, NW9 5LL. 0181-205-2266

Royal Air Force Regiment Museum: RAF Regiment Depot, RAF Catterick, Yorkshire. 01748-811441 ext. 7202

MAJOR NATIONAL MILITARY MUSEUMS

Imperial War Museum: Lambeth Road, Kennington, London, SE1 6HZ 0171-416-5000

National Army Museum: Royal Hospital Road, Chelsea, London SW3 4HT 0171-730-0717

Australian War Memorial: GPO Box 345, Canberra, ACT 2601, Australia. (06) 243-4211

National Archives of Canada: 395 rue Wellington, Ottawa, Ontario K1A 0N3, Canada. (613) 943-0891

National Library of New Zealand: Alexander Turnbull Library, Cnr Molesworth & Aitken Street, PO Box 12349, Wellington 6001, New Zealand. 66-4-474-3063

BIBLIOGRAPHY

Adkin Mark. The Last Eleven Winners of the Victoria Cross since the Second World War. Lee Cooper, London, 1991

Agar, Capt. Augustine, V.C., D.S.O. Footprints in the Sea:The Autobiography of Capt. Augustine Agar. Evans Brothers, London, 1959

Asbury - Bailey, Jock, B.H.Geary V.C. Parkers. Canterbury. 1997

Auten Harold, V.C. Q-Boat Adventures. Herbert Jenkins, London, n.d.

Bancroft, James W. Deed of Valour. The House of Heroes, 1994

Bancroft, James W. The Zulu War V.C.s. J W Bancroft, 1992

Bancroft, James W. The Victoria Cross Roll of Honour. Aim High Publications, Manchester, 1990.

Bancroft, James W. Devotion to Duty: Tributes to a Region's V.C. Aim High Publications, Manchester, 1990

Barber, Laurie-Tonkin-Covell, John. Freyberg; Churchill's Salamander; Lt.Gen. Bernard Cyril Freyberg, V.C. Century Hutchinson, Auckland 1989.

Barthorp, Michael. The Anglo Boer Wars, 1815 - 1902. Blanford, London, 1987.

Barthrop, Michael. Heroes of the Crimea. Blanford, London, 1991.

Barthrop, Michael. The Zulu War. Blanford, London, 1980.

Barthrop, Michael & Anderson, Douglas. British Troops in the Indian Mutiny, 1857-59. Osprey, 1994.

Batchelor, Peter F & Matson, Christopher. The Western Front 1915. Allan Sutton, Stroud, 1997.

Beckett, Ian W. Johnnie Gough, V.C.: A Biography of Brigadier-General Sir John Emund Gough, V.C., K.C.B., C.M.G. Tom Donovan, London 1989.

Beeton, Samuel Orchart. Our Soldiers and the Victoria Cross. Ward, Lock and Tyler, London, Circa 1867.

Bills, Leslie William. A Medal For Life: Lt. W.L. Robinson, V.C. Spellmount Ltd., Tunbridge Wells, Kent, 1990.

Bingham, V.C., Edward Barry Stewart Falklands. Jutland and the Bight. John Murray, London, 1919.

Birrell, Dave. BAZ : Biography of Squadron Leader Bazalgette, V.C., D.F.C. National Lancaster Society 1996.

Bishop, William Avery. Winged Warfare. McLelland, Goodchild, Stewart, Toronto, 1918.

Bishop, William Arthur. The Courage of the Early Morning: The Story of Billy Bishop, V.C.. Mclelland, Stewart Inc., Toronto, 1965.

Boden, A. F.W. Harvey: Soldier Poet. Allen Sutton, Gloucestershire, 1988.

Boorman, Derek. At the Going Down of The Sun. The Ebor Press 1988.

Borg, Alan. War Memorials. Leo Cooper, London. 1991.

Bowyer, Chaz. Albert Ball, V.C., William Kimber, London, 1977.

Bowyer, Chaz. For Valour: The Air V.C.s. William Kimber, London, 1978.

Bowyer, Chaz. Eugene Esmonde, V.C., D.S.O. William Kimber, London, 1983.

Boyle, Vice Admiral, W.H.D. Gallant Deeds. Gieves Ltd., Portsmouth, England, n.d.

Braddon, Russell. Cheshire V.C.: A Story of War and Peace. Evans Brothers Ltd., London, 1954.

Branch, Newton. The Boys Book of V.C. Heroes. Publicity Products, London, n.d.

British Photographers Liaison Committee. Photographic Copyright. London, 1994.

Burns, Rose. The World War One Album. Saturn Books, 1991.

Bryant, George. Where the Prize is Highest: The Stories of the New Zealanders who Won the Victoria Cross. Collins Brothers, Auckland, 1972.

Campbell, Vice Admiral, V.C., D.S.O. My Mystery Ships. Hodder, Stoughton Ltd., London, 1928.

Campbell, Vice Admiral, Gordon, V.C., D.S.O., M.P. Brave Men All: Tales of Great Courage. Hodder, Stoughton Ltd., London, 1935.

Campbell, Vice Admiral Gordon, V.C., D.S.O. Captain James Cook, R.N., F.R.S. Hodder, Stoughton Ltd., London, 1936.

Carpenter, Captain Alfred F.B., V.C., R.N.. The Blocking of the Zeebrugge. Herbert, Jenkins Ltd., London, 1921.

Carton, De Wiart, Sir Adrian, V.C. Happy Odyssey: The Memoirs. Jonathan Cape, London, 1950.

Chamberlain, W.M. Victoria Cross Winners of New Zealand. Military Historical Society of Australia, 1967.

Cheshire, Squadron Leader Leonard, V.C., D.S.O., D.F.C. Bomber Pilot. Hutchison & Co., London, n.d.

Chesney, Kellow. A Crimean War Reader. Frederick Muller, London, 1960.

Civil and Military Gazette Ltd.. The V.C. : India's V.C.s in Two World Wars. Lahore, 1950

Clayton, Ann. Chavasse Double V.C. Lee Cooper, London, 1992.

Clayton, Ann. Martin-Leake Double, V.C. Lee Cooper, London 1994.

Clifford, Henry, V.C.: His Letters and Sketches from The Crimea. Michael Joseph, London, 1956.

Cole, Christopher. McCudden, V.C.. William Kimber, London, 1967.

Cole, Jean. & Church, Rosen,. In and Around Record Repositories. Family Tree Magazine. Ramsey, 1991.

Collier, Richard. The Great Indian Mutiny. E.P.Dutton and Co. Inc., U.S.A., 1964.

Collister, Peter. Hellfire Jack, V.C.: General Sir William Olpherts 1822 - 1902. British Association for Cemeteries in South East Asia , London 1989.

Colville, J.R. Man of Valour: Field Marshall Lord Gort, V.C. Collins, London, 1972.

Cooksley, Peter G. The Air V.C.s. V.C.s of the First World War. Sutton Publishing, 1996.

Cooms, Rose E B,. Before Endeavours Fade. Battle of Britain Prints International Ltd. 1976.

Cornwell, Jack. The Story of John Travers Cornwell, V.C., Boy 1st Class. Hodder, Stoughton, London, 1917.

Creagh, Sir O'Moore, V.C. and Humphris, E.M., Editors. The V.C. and D.S.O. Vol.1 - The Victoria Cross. The Standard Art Book Co. Ltd., London 1920

Crook, M.J. The Evolution of the Victoria Cross. The Ogilby Trust, London, 1975.

Daily Express Publications. The First World War, 1933.

D'Arcy, Patricia. What Happened to a V.C.. 1973

Dudgeon, James M. "Mick" , The Story of Major Edward Mannock, V.C., D.S.O., M.C. Robert Hale, London, 1981.

Elder, John F. The Last Heroes. Vantage Press, New York, U.S.A. 1980.

Fabb, John and Carman, W.Y. The Victorian and Edwardian Army. Purnell Books. n.d.

Farrar-Hockley, General Sir A. The Somme. Batsford, London. 1964.

Farwell, Byron. The Gurkha's. Allen Lane, London. 1984.

Featherstone, Donald. Weapons and Equipment of the Victorian Soldier. Blanford Press Ltd. 1978.

Fincastle, Viscount, V.C. and Elliot-Lockhart, P.C. A Frontier Campaign. R.J. Leach Co., London, 1990 reprinted.

Foxley, Norris, Air Chief Marshal Sir C. The Royal Air Force at War. Ian Allen, London. 1983.

Freyberg, Paul. Bernard Freyberg, V.C. - Soldier of Two Nations. Hodder, Stoughton, London, 1991.

Fuller, Major General J.F.C. The Second World War. Eyre & Spollisworde, London. 1948.

Gaylor, John. Military Badge Collecting. Seeley Service & Company. 1971.

Gerard, Maurice. The Victoria Cross: A Story for the Young T. Nelson, 1891, 1893

Gibson, Jeremy. Record Offices. Federation of Family History Society. Birmingham, 1993.

Gibson, Jeremy. Local Newspapers, 1750 - 1920. Federation of Family History Society. Birmingham, 1991

Gibson, T A and Kingsley, Ward. Courage Remembered. H.M.S.O. 1989

Gibson, Mary. Warneford, V.C.. Fleet Air Arm Museum, Somerset, 1991.

Gleichen, Major General. Lord E. Chronology of The Great War. Greenhill, London, 1998.

Glidden, Gerald. V.C.s of the First World War - 1914. Allan Sutton, Gloustershire 1994.

BIBLIOGRAPHY

Glidden, Gerald. V.C.s of the Somme - A Biographical Portrait. Glidden Books, Norwich, Norfolk. 1991

Glidden, Gerald. The Western Front - 1915. Allan Sutton, Stroud, Gloucestershire. 1997.

Glidden, Gerald. Arras & Messines - 1917. Allan Sutton, Stroud, Gloustershire. 1998.

Glidden, Gerald. Spring Offensive - 1918. Allan Sutton, Stroud, Gloustershire. 1997.

Gordon, Brian and Stupples, Peter. Charles Heaphy V.C. - Master of New Zealand Painting. Pitman, Wellington, 1987.

Gough, General Sir Hugh, V.C. . Old Memories. William Blackwood, London, 1917..Grant, Ian. Jacka, V.C. MacMillan, Melbourne, 1989

Grant, Ian. JACKA, V.C. MacMillan, Melbourne, 1989.

Gray Elizabeth. The Noise of Drums and Trumpets. Longman, n.d.

Groser, Horace G. Field Marshal Lord Roberts V.C., K.P., G.C.B. Andrew Melrose, nd.

Guildhall Library. Greater London Parish Records. Guildhall Library, London. 1990

Gummer, Conon Selwyn. The Chevasse Twins. Hodder and Staughton, 1963.

Gurkha Museum. The Story of the Gurkha V.C.s, 1993

Hallows, Ian S. Regiments and Corps of the British Army. New Orchard Editions, 1994.

Hare- Scott, Kenneth. For Valour. Peter Garnett, London, 1985.

Harris, Barry. Black Country V.C.s. Black Country Society, 1985.

Hastings, Max. Battle for the Falklands. Michael Joseph , London, 1983.

Haydon, A.L. The Book of the V.C. Andrew Melrose, London, 1906.

Haythornthwaite, Philip,J. A Photo History of World War One. Sterling Publishing, New York, U.S.A. 1994.

Haythornthwaite, Philip J. The Colonial Wars Source Book. Sterling Publishing, New York, U.S.A. 1994.

Hawker, T.M. Hawker, V.C.: The Biography of the Late Major L.G. Hawker. Mitre, London, 1965.

Hayward, P.H.C. Brigadier. Janes Dictionary of Military Terms. Purnell Books, 1975.

Her Majesty's Stationary Office. Victoria Cross Centenary Exhibition 1856 - 1956.

Hilton, Major General Richard. The Indian Mutiny. London. 1957.

HMSO. Record Repositories in Great Britain. HMSO. London, 1979.

Holt, Tonie and Valmai. Battlefields of the First Woirld War. Pavilion Books Ltd. 1995

Home, Sir A.D., V.C. Surgeon. Service Memories. Arnold, London, 1912.

Horan, Bill. Military Modelling Master Class. Windrow and Green Ltd.

Hurst, Sidney C. The Silent Cities. The Naval and Military Press, 1993.

Hutchinson, Co., Wonderful Stories Winning the V.C. in the Great War., London, n.d.

Indian Army, G.H.Q. India V.C.s in Two World Wars. Civil and Military Gazette. Lahore, circa 1950.

Imperial War Museum. The Victoria Cross and George Cross Handbook, 1970.

Indian Command. Inter Service Public Relation Directory, Officers and Men of the Indian Army Awarded the V.C. Civil and Military Gazette.

Jameson, Rear Admiral Sir William. Submariners V.C. Peter Davies, London, 1962.

Jerold, Walter. Field Marshal Lord Roberts, V.C. - The Story of a Great Soldier. W.A.Hammond, London, 1911.

Johnson, Barry C. King of Air Fighters: The Biography of Major Mick Mannock, V.C. Ivor Nicholson Watson,1934: Reprint Greenhill Books, 1989.

Johnson, Barry C. Rorkes Drift and The British   The Life of Henry Hook V.C., 1988.

Keegan, John. The Face of Battle. John Cape. 1982.

Kenneally, John Patrick, V.C. Kenneally V.C. - The Autobiography of John Patrick Kenneally, V.C. Kenwood, Huddersfield, England, 1991.

Keown-Boyd, Henry. A Good Dusting; The Sudan Campaigns. Lee Cooper, 1986.

Keown-Boyd, Henry. Fists of Righteous Harmony,: The Boxer Rebellion. Leo Copper, 1991.

Keys, Elizabeth. Geoffrey Keyes, V.C. of the Rommel Raid. George Newnes, London, 1956.

Kiernan, R.H. Captain Albert Ball, V.C. - A Historical Record. John Hamilton, London, 1933.

Kipling, Arthur L.and King, Hugh L. Head-Dress Badges of the British Army. Frederick Muller Ltd, London, 1972.

Kirby, H.l and R.R. Walsh. The Four Blackburn V.C.s. THCL Books, Blackburn, England, 1986.

Kirby, HL and R.R. Walsh. Drummer Spencer John Bent, V.C. THCL Books, Blackburn, England, 1986.

Kirby, H.L. and R.R. Walsh. The Seven V.C.s of Stonyhurst College. THCL Books, Blackburn, England, 1987.

Kirby, H.L. Private William Young, V.C. THCL Books, Blackburn, England, 1985.

Kirby, H.L. and R.R. Walsh. Andrew Moynihan, V.C. THCL Books, Blackburn, England, 1993.

Kirby, H.L. & Walsh, R.R. The Four Blackburn V.C.s. THCL Books, Blackburn. 1986.

Kirby, H.L. & Walsh, R.R. Andrew Moynihan V.C.

Knight, Ian and Castle, Ian. The Zulu War: Then and Now . Battle of Britain Prints International, 1993.

Knight, Ian. Brave Men's Blood : The Epic of the Zulu War, 1879. Guild Publishing, 1990.

Kohen, George, C. Dictionary of Wars. Fact on File, New York. 1986.

Laffin, John. The Western Front Illustrations, 1914-1918. Allan Sutton, 1991.

Laffin, John. British V.C.s of World War Two. Allan Sutton, 1997.

La Rousse. The Second World War : Photographic Record in Clour. Guild Publishing, 1984.

Leyland, Eric. For Valour - The Story of the Victoria Cross. E. Ward, London, 1960.

Limbu, Lt. Rambahadur, V.C. My Life Story. Gurkha Welfare Trust, London, n.d.

Lindsay, Sid. Merseyside Heroes. Private edition.

Litherland, A.R. and Simpkin, B.T. British Orders, Decorations and Medals. Spink & Son Ltd. 1990.

Little, Matthew G. The Royal Marine Victoria Cross. Royal Marine Museum, n.d.

Little, M.G. The Royal Marine Victoria Crosses. Holbrook and Son. Portsmouth.

Lloyd, W.G. John Williams, V.C.: A Biography. W.G. Lloyd, Gwent, 1993.

Longworth Philip. The Unending Vigil.: History of C.W.G.C. Constables, London. 1967.

Lummis, Lt. W.M. The Roll of the V.C. Belgaum, India, n.d.

Lummis, W.M. Padre George Smith of Rorkes Drift. Wynmondham Press, n.d.

Lummis, W.M. & Wynn, K.G. Honour The Light Brigade. Hayward & Son, London. 1973.

Macdonald, Lyn. 1914. Mick Joseph. London, 1987.

Macdonald, Lyn. 1915. Headline Books. London, 1993.

Macdonald, W..J. A Bibliography of the Victoria Cross. W.J.D. Nova Scotia. 1994.

Mannock, V.C., D.S.O. + Bar, M.C. + Bar. The Personal Diary of Mick Mannok. Frederick Oughton, 1966.

Manson, James A. Valour for Victoria : Stirring Deeds that Won the Victoria Cross. George Newnes, London, 1901.

Mason, P. A Matter of Honour. Jonathan Cape. London, 1974.

Marling, Col. Sir Percival, V.C. Rifleman and Hussar. John Murray, London, 1931.

Mason, Peter D. Nicolson V.C.: The Full and Authorised Biography of James Brindley Nicolson. Geerings of Ashford, Kent, England, 1991.

Mason, Philip. A Matter of Honour : Account of Indian Army Officers and Men. Purnell Book Service, 1974.

BIBLIOGRAPHY

Maxwell, Lt. Col., F.A., V.C. I Am Ready. Hazell, Watson, Viney, London, 1955.

McClintock, Mary Howard. The Queen Thanks Sir Howard : The Life of Maj.Gen. Sir Howard Elphinstone, V.C.,K.C.B., C.M.G. John Murray, London, 1945

McCrery, Nigel. For Conspicuous Gallantry. J.H. Hall, Derby, England.

McCudden, James, V.C. Flying Fury : Five Years in the Royal Flying Corps (First published in 1918, reprinted 1933. Greenhill Books, Hertfordshire.

Melville, Douglas A. Canadians and the Victoria Cross. The Vanwell History Project Series, St. Catherines, Canada, 1986.

Menzies, Mrs. Stewart. Lord William Beresford, V.C. Herbert Jenkins, London, 1917.

Middlebrook, Martin. The First Day on the Somme. Allen Lane. London, 1971.

Mollo, Boris. The Indian Army. Blanford Press, 1981.

Morris, Donald. Washing of The Spears. Simon & Schuster, New York, 1965.

Morris, Richard. Guy Gibson. Viking Books, London, 1994.

Muddock, J.E. For Valour. Hutchinson, London, 1895.

Mundell, Frank. Stories of the Victoria Cross. The Sunday School Union, England, n.d. circa 1895.

Murphy, Micheal. Newspapers and Local History. Phillimore, Chichester. 1991.

Napier, Gerald. The Sapper V.C.'s HMSO. 1998.

Narbeth Colin. Taku Forts. Picton Publishing, 1980

National Army Museum. The V.C. and G.Cs of the H.E.I.C..& Indian Army 1856-1945. National Army Museum Publications 1962

National Postal Museum. The Victoria Cross 1856- 1881.   1981.

Neaeme. Lt. Gen. Sir Phillip, V.C. Playing with Strife: The Autobiography of a Soldier. George G. Harrap, London, 1982.

Nolan, E.H. History of War Against Russia (8 Volumes).   London, 1955 - 57.

Norman, Terry, Editor. Armageddon Road: a V.C.s diary 1914-1916, Billy Congreve, V.C. William Kimber, London, 1982.

Paget, Lord George. Light Cavalry Brigade in the Crimea. London, 1881.

Parry, D.H. Britains Roll of Glory of The Victoria Cross, 1906. Its Heroes and Their Valour, 1913. Cassell, London, Printed in 1895,1898,1899,1906.

Peacock, A.J., Editor. Reluctant Hero: Harry Blanshard Wood of York (and Bristol), A Great War V.C. Gun Fire Journal, No.28, v.2. 126 Holgate Rd. York

Pearce, Sgt. L. A Short History of the Regiment's Victoria Cross Holders. Coldstream Guards, 1988.

Percival, John. For Valour: The Victoria Cross, Courage in Action. Thames Methuen, London, 1985.

Perkins, Roger. The Kashmir Gate: Lt. Home and the Delhi V.C.s. Picton Publishing, Chippenham, England, 1983.

Phillips, C.E. Lucas. Victoria Cross Battles of the Second World War. Heinemann, London, 1973.

Pillinger, Dennis and Staunton, Anthony. Victoria Cross Locator, High Press, Australia, 1997.

Powell Geoffrey. Buller: A Scapegoat. Lee Cooper, London, 1994.

Raw, David. It's Only Me: A Life of the Rev.Theodore Bailey Hardy, V.C., D.S.O., M.C., 1863-1918. Frank Peters Publishing, Gatebeck, Cumbria,1988

RAMC. The Medical Victoria Crosses. Arrow Press. Aldershot, 1983.

Reid, P.R. Winged Diplomat: The Story of Air Commodore, Freddie West, V.C. Chatto & Windus, London, 1962.

Revel, Alex. James McCudden, V.C. Albatros Productions Ltd., England, 1987.

Rimell, Raymond Lawrence. The Airship V.C. - The Life of Captain William Leefe Robinson. Aston Publications, Bourne End, England, 1989.

Roe, Gordon F. The Bronze Cross. P R. Gawthorn, London, 1945.

Ross, Graham. Scotland's Forgotten Valour.

Royal Army Medical Corps Historical Museum Publication. The Medical Victoria Crosses. 1988.

Rule , E.J. Jacka's Mob - Victoria Cross. Angus Robertson, Sydney, 1933.

Sanders, Jim. New Zealand V.C. Winners. Wilson Horton, Auckland, 1974.

Sanford, Kenneth. Mark of a Lion: The Story of Captain Charles Upham, V.C. and Bar. Hutchinson, London, 1962.

Scott, K.B.H. For Valour. Peter Garnett, London, 1949.

Shankland, P. and Hunter, A. Dardenelles Patrol (Martin Dunbar- Nasmith.). Charles Scribner's, New York, 1964.

Slater, Guy: Editor. My Warrior Sons: The Borton Family Diary 1914 - 1918 (Arthur Drummond Borton, V.C.). Peter Davies, London, 1973.

Smith, Peter C. Victoria's Victories. Spellmount Ltd. 1987.

Smyth, John Sir, V.C. The Story of the Victoria Cross, 1856-1963. Frederick Muller, London, 1963.

Smyth, John Sir, V.C. Milestones A Memoir. Sidgwick and Jackson, 1979.

Smyth, John Sir, V.C. Great Stories of the Victoria Cross. Arthur Barker, London, 1977.

Snelling, Stephen. Gallilpoli, VC's of the First World War. Alan Sutton, Stroud, 1995.

Snelling, Stephen. Passchendale 1917, V.C.s of the First World War. Alan Sutton, Stroud, 1998.

Stanistreet, Allan. Gainst All Disaster. Picton Press, 1986.

Stanway, Kate. Sons of Valour: A Complete Record of Victoria Cross Heroes. Drand, H.J., n.d. circa 1904.

Stevens,W.G. Major General Freyberg V.C.: The Man. A.H.& A.W. Reed, Auckland, New Zealand, 1965.

Stewart, Charles H. Victoria Cross and the Medal of Honour. Toronto, 1987.

Stewart, Major Rupert. The Book of the Victoria Cross. Hugh Rees, London, 1916.

Stewart, Major Rupert. The Victoria Cross: The Empire's Roll. Hutchinson, London, 1928.

Swettenham, John. Valiant Men: Canada's Victoria Cross and George Cross. Hakkert, Toronto, 1973.

Tameside Metropolitan Borough. Tribute to Tameside V.C.s. Tameside Leisure Services. 1995.

Taylor, A.J.P. The First World War. Hamish Hamilton, London. 1963

This England Magazine. Register of the Victoria Cross, Cheltenham, England, 1988.

Thompson, R.W.   Battle for the Rhineland. Hutchinson, London, 1958.

Thornton, Lt. Col. L.H. and Fraser, Pamela. The Congreves: Father and Son V.C.s. John Murray, London, 1930.

Tisdall, Sub Lt. Arthur, W: Verses, Letters and Remembrances. Naval and Military Press, 1992.

Toomey, T.E. Heroes of the Victoria Cross. George Newnes, London, 1895.

Turner, John Frayn. V.C..s of the Air. George G. Harrap, London, 1960.

Turner, John Frayn. V.C..s of the Army 1939-1951. George G. Harrap, London, 1962.

Turner, John Frayn. V.C.s of the Royal Navy. George G. Harrap, London, 1956.

Uys, Ian S. For Valour: The History of Southern Africa's Victoria Cross Heroes. Published by the Author, Johannesburg, 1973.

Wantage, Harriet S. Lord Wantage, V.C., K.C.B. - A Mmemoir by His Wife. Smith, Elder, London, 1907

Westlake, Ray, Publisher. Brigadier General R.B. Bradford. V.C., M.C. and his Brothers. Reprint 1994, first published after the Great War.

Who Was Who Volume 1-7. A.&C. Black, London.

Wigmore, Lionel, Editor. They Dared Mightily: Australia Victoria Cross Winners. Australia War Memorial, Canberra, 1963.

Wiggins, Roy. St.Catherine's House Districts. J.R. Wiggins, Northwood, 1990

Wilkins, Philip Aueling. The History of the Victoria Cross. A, Constable, London, 1904.

Williams, Charles. The Life of Lt. Gen. Sir Henry Evelyn Wood, V.C. London, 1892.

Williams, W.A. The V.C.s of Wales and the Welsh Regiment. Bridge Books, Wrexham, England, 1984.

Williams, W.A. Against The Odds: The Life of Group Captain Lionel Rees, V.C. Bridge Books, Wrexham, England, 1989.

BIBLIOGRAPHY

Williams, W.A. Rowlands, V.C. V.C. Books, Wrexham, England, 1992.
Winter, Denis. Deaths Men. Allen Lane. London, 1978.
Winton, John. The Victoria Cross at Sea. Joseph, London, 1978.
Wolfston, Patricia, S. Great Land Cemeteries and Crematoria. Society of Genealogists. London, 1994.
Woodham - Smith, Cecil. The Reason Why. London 1953.
Wood, Field Marshal Sir Evelyn, V.C. The Crimea in 1854 - 94. London, 1895.
Wood, Field Marshal Sir Evelyn, V.C. : From Midshipman to Field Marshall. Methuen, London, 1906.
Woods, Rex. One Man's Desert: The Story of Captain Phillip Gardner, V.C., M.C. William Kimber, London, 1986.
Woolley, Reverend G.H., V.C. Sometimes a Soldier. Ernest Benn, London, 1963.

NEWSPAPERS , PERIODICALS & JOURNALS

After The Battle	Military History Magazine
BACSA Chowkidar	OMRS Journal
Best of British	Soldier Magazine
CWRS The War Correspondent	This England
Daily Telegraph	Trail Times (BC)
Family Tree	The Times
London Gazette	VMS Soldiers of the Queen
Medal News	Western Daily Post

The Lummis Files
PRO WO/Series
List of Recipients of the Victoria Cross (War Office) 1953

GLOSSARY OF SOME MILITARY TERMS AND ABBREVIATIONS USED

AAG	Assistant Adjutant-General
Abattis	Defensive work made by binding tree trunks and branches
Ack-Ack	Anti-Aircraft
ADC	Aide-de-Camp, commissioned rank attending senior officer
Adj.	Adjutant, commanding officer's principal staff officer
AG	Adjutant General
A I F	Australian Imperial Force
ANZAC	Australian and New Zealand Army Corps (First World War)
Bagh	Indian walled garden, occasionally fortified
Barghir	Indian cavalryman
Barrage	Curtain of heavy fire brought down upon an enemy position
Battery	Artillery unit corrsponding to a company
Bazooka	Anti-tank rocket launcher (slang)
B E F	British Expeditionary Force
Bivouac	Temporary encampment, usually without tents
Bmdr.	Bombardier - lowest NCO in the artillery
Bn.	Battalion - approx.700-900 men under a Lieutenant Colonel
Bren	A light machine-gun, now obsolete
Brevet	Rank usually awarded for distinguished service, above that for which paid. Confers seniority in Army, not his regiment
Brigade	Formation of three or four battalions with ancillary arms
Browning	Machine-gun used by Cavalry instead of the Infantry Bren
CB	Companion of the Order of Bath
Cadre	A small body of troops assembled for various purposes
Calibre	Internal diameter of a gun barrel
Cantonment	Section or area of an Indian town occupied by the garrison

CBE	Commander of the Order of the British Empire
C E F	Canadian Expeditionary Force
CGM	Conspicuous Gallantry Medal
CGS	Chief of the General Staff
Chowkidar	Indian caretaker or watchman, employed by cemeteries etc
Chokra	Indian officer's page, generally a young recruit
C-in-C	Commander in Chief
Claymore	Type of mine/ sword used by officers in Scottish regiments
Cluster	Group of bombs released together, fragmentation/incendiary
CO	Commanding Officer
Col.	Colonel
Cooloie	Indian term for labourer, generally Indian or Chinese natives
Cornet	Former junior commissioned cavalry rank - now 2nd-Lieut.
Cpl.	Corporal
CSI	Companion of the Star of India
CSM	Company Sergeant-Major
Daffadar	Indian cavalry sergeant (also Duffadar)
DCM	Distinguished Conduct Medal
Defilade	Protection from hostile file/observation by hill, ridge etc
Detachment	Part of unit separated from main organization for other duty
Detail	Small party assigned to special duty - firing party, fatigues..
Diversion	Feint drawing enemy attention away from principal operatio
Donga	A river bed, usually dried-up
DSC	Distinguished Service Cross
DSM	Distinguished Service Medal
DSO	Distinguished Service Order

Dud	Explosive munition, intentionally unarmed or faulty	**NCO**	Non-commissioned Officer
Earthworks	Defensive work of which earth movement main ingredient	**No-mans-land**	Area between opposing forces - not physically occupied
Emplacement	Prepared position for one or more weapons with protection	**Nullah**	Indian dry ravine or water-course
Enfilade	Fire usually from a flank, sweeping a line from end to end	**NZEF**	New Zealand Expeditionary Force
Ensign	Former junior commissioned rank - now Second-Lieutenant	**OBE**	Officer of the Order of the British Empire
Fascine	Brushwood bundles used to fill ditches etc, as protection	**OC**	Officer Cammanding
Field Defence	Temporary protection, capable of fast and easy construction	**Ordnance**	Collective noun for guns, also denoting military stores
Field of fire	Area covered effectively by weapon(s) from given position	**OS**	Ordinary Seaman
Flank	Extreme left or right of body of troops on military position	**OTC**	Officer Training Corps
Fl. Sgt.	Flight Sergeant	**Outflank**	To move a force to oppose enemy to side, rather than frontal
FO	Flying Officer (or Foreign Office)	**Palisade**	Barrier of wooden posts set in the ground
Foss(e)	Ditch, moat trench or canal capable of being defended	**Palliasse**	Rough straw mattress issued to soldiers
Gabion	Hollow cylinder filled with earth to revet a trench	**Parados**	Excavated earth from trench placed behind it for protection
Gasht	An Indian military patrol	**Parapet**	Excavated earth from trench placed in front for protection
Gazette	Official newspaper to announce/confirm promotion, award..	**PIAT**	Projectile Infantry Anti-Tank
GBE	Knight Grand Cross of the Order of the British Empire	**Pillbox**	Small fortification housing machine-guns etc., reinforced
GC	George Cross	**Platoon**	Infantry unit of c30 men, commanded by Second-Lieutenant
GCB	Knight Grand Cross of the Order of Bath	**Pom-Pom**	Rapid firing 20mm cannon/also 37mm Vickers-Maxim gun
GCIE	Knight Grand Commander of the Order of Indian Empire	**POW**	Prisoner of War
GCMG	Knight Grand Cross of the Order of St Michael & St George	**PRO**	Public Record Office
GHQ	General Headquarters	**Pte.**	Private - lowest non-commissioned rank
GOC	General Officer Commanding	**PVSM**	Param Vashist Seva Medal
Grp. Capt.	Group Captain	**QMS**	Quartermaster-Sergeant
GSCI	Knight Grand Commander of the Order of the Star of India	**RA**	Royal Artillery
Guerilla	Member of irregular force, often operating behind lines	**RAF**	Royal Air Force
Halvildar	Indian infantry sergeant	**RAMC**	Royal Army Medical Corps.
HE	High explosive, intended to burst opposed to solid shot	**RE**	Corps of Royal Engineers
HMS	Her/His Majesty's Ship	**Reg.**	Regiment
Howitzer	An artillery ordnance with high trajectory	**RFC**	Royal Flying Corps.
HQ	Headquarters	**Risaldar**	Indian Cavalry Lieutenant
ILH	Imperial Light Horse	**RNVR**	Royal Naval Volunteer Reserve
ILN	Illustrated London News	**RSM**	Regimental Sergeant-Major
IMA	Indian Military Academy	**Sally**	A sortie, sudden rush of troops to attack besiegers
Impi	Zulu body of armed men, from army down to contingent	**Salvo**	A number of rounds of artillery fired at the same moment
Jemadar	Indian second-lieutenant	**Sap**	Extension to a trench, undertaken to facilitate offensives
KAR	King's African Rifles	**2nd. Lieut**	Second-Lieutenant, lowest commissioned rank
KCB	Knight Commander of the Order of Bath	**Sector**	Defence area designated by boundaries for unit operations
KCMG	Knight Commander of the Order of St Michael & St George	**Sepoy**	Indian private soldier (Plural = Indian troops in general)
KCIE	Knight Commander of the Order of the Indian Empire	**Sgt.**	Sergeant
KCSI	Knight Commander of the Order of the Star of India	**Sgt. Maj.**	Sergeant-Major
KCVO	Knight Commander of the Royal Victorian Order	**Sowar**	Indian cavalry trooper
KG	Knight of the Order of the Garter	**Spandau**	German type of machine-gun
Kot-daffadar	Indian cavalry trroop sergeant-major	**Spr.**	Sapper - Royal Engineers equivalent of private
KT	Knight of the Order of the Thistle	**Spruit**	South African steam or small river
Laager	South African encampment with fortified perimeter	**Sqd. Ldr.**	Squadron Leader
LAC	Leading Aircraft(s)man	**SS**	Steamship
L/Cpl.	Lance-Corporal	**Subadar**	Indian Captain of Infantry
L/Daff.	Lance-Daffadar	**Subaltern**	A Second-Lieuteant or a Lieuteant
L/Naik	Lance-Naik	**Surg.**	Surgeon
LSGC	Long Service Good Conduct (medal)	**Syce**	Indian grrom or mounted attendant
L/Sgt.	Lance-Sergeant	**TA**	Territorial Army
Lt.	Lieutenant	**Tahsil**	Officer in charge of an Indian district
Lt. Col.	Lietenant-Colonel	**TAVR**	Territorial and Army Volunteer Reserve
Lt. Gen.	Lieutenant-General	**TD**	Territorial Decoration
Magazine	Any store authorized for storage of explosives	**Tpr.**	Trooper - lowest non-commissioned cavalry rank
Maj.	Major	**Traverse (i)**	Turning a weapon to the right or left on its mount
Maj. Gen.	Major-General	**Traverse (ii)**	Passageway between fire trenches, set back as protection
MC	Military Cross	**Troop**	Mounted equivalent of an infantry platoon
Middy	Midshipman	**TSM**	Troop Sergeant-Major
Militia	Able bodied men enrolled as soldiers for home defence	**Vedette**	Mounted sentry stationed to watch the enemy
MM	Military Medal	**VC**	Victoria Cross
Mortar	High elevation ordnance, usually throwing light projectiles	**Wing Cmdr.**	Wing Commander
MVO	Member of the Royal Victorian Order	**WO**	Warrant Officer (also War Office)
Naik	Indian infantry corporal	**Zillah**	Indian administration district

There are many spelling variations on some of the above, particularly those of Indian extraction, and I have used those most commonly used. A good example would be 'Naik', where 'naick, naique and naigue' are acceptable alternatives as all are/have been commonly used. The same principle has been used with place names both in the text and in the Gazetteer, major changes such as Rangoon, Burma - now being known as Yangon, Myanmar, have been noted where appropriate in the text.

ACKNOWLEDGEMENTS

(For fear of omitting orders or decorations, I have excluded all except the VC)

From the very outset, I have endeavoured to try and keep an accurate record of every person who has made a contribution to this work, not easy when I have moved home on seventeen occasions and my records have taken several forms. Friends and colleagues around the world spent a lot of their time and energy in following-up leads, but a large number of people previously unknown to me responded to articles, advertisements and following the occasional media attention my research attracted. The list grew longer each week, with enquiries to museums, libraries, recipient's families, cemeteries and local history groups often leading to many follow-up letters. A number of researchers who were working in related fields sent countless cuttings and photographs enabling me to enter extra data on the subjects within. The following five pages list all these people and institutions who have helped, and I have taken an unusual step of listing six 'special' people - Pat Doak, David Rushmer, Bob Fuller, Kevin and Kay Patience and Pat Mendes da Costa in a section at the rear.

It is difficult to know where to start for fear of upsetting someone, and I have tried to separate my regular collaborator's and the individuals who have made themselves available to do 'odd' tasks at a moments notice with those that have occasionally assisted, even the 'one-offs'. I was aware that several others were working on similar lines of research to my own, the actual number turned out to be almost fifty world-wide, most being happy to share their knowledge. Uppermost was being able to assist the late Canon William Lummis for so many years, who allowed me full access to all his files, giving me hundreds of photographs and setting me off on the right foot by demanding accuracy.

As Victoria Cross holders are the subject of the work, then it is only right and proper to begin with the contributions they have made, resulting in valued friendships. Sir Roden Cutler VC readily agreed to write the Foreword, the result of a conversation at St Martins-in-the-Field in 1995 following the memorial service for Charles Upham VC & Bar. Later the same year I received a call from Lt.Col. Eric Wilson VC, who wished to arrange a meeting to discuss the project, having heard of its existence at a regimental luncheon. Following several lengthy and enjoyable visits to each others homes, he has written a short item covering two sensitive subjects that I wished to address, feeling it rather presumptious to cover myself, but right and proper coming from a recipient whom I felt had the necessary credentials to mention the issues. Later conversations and correspondence with Tommy Gould VC, Colonel Pat Porteous VC, Major David Jamieson VC and John Kenneally VC were very encouraging, and resulted in some historical corrections and valued messages of support. The late Norman Jackson VC visited me in hospital, lifting my spirits enormously - one has only to read his citation to realise just how much I valued his time. Being aware of the heavy workload of the Secretary of the VC & GC Association, I was reluctant to write with questions she must get asked on a regular basis. I was saved the problem when I managed to speak to her at a ceremony early in 1995. Didy Grahame was not only helpful with answers to the questions I had wanted to pose, but has since frequently gone out of her way to assist and provide wonderful moral support. Since then I have been fortunate in enjoying Didy's delightful company on many occasions, becoming the envy of every red-blooded male with whom we came into contact. I loathed intruding on the families and descendants of over one hundred recipients, but all took the time and trouble to respond to questions, and sent family photographs. Of the many, Lord Clifford, Robert Salkeld, Mrs Theo Bradford, Sylvia Manners-Smith, Lord De L'Isle, Robert McBeath and Peter James could not have been kinder, and I offer my sincere gratitude for their help.

I was honoured that HRH Princess Alexandra found the time in her busy schedule to pen a short message in her capacity as President of the Royal Star & Garter Home, and I am grateful to its Governor, Vice-Admiral Sir David Dobson for the item on its history, whilst Patsy Willis, head of fund raising has helped immensely after I had decided that proceeds should go to the Home.

Dennis Pillinger, the keeper of the Lummis Files, has always been just a 'phone call away from answering any questions, and I trust that it has been reciprocal and that he received useful answers from myself - at least our telephone conversations have kept BT in profit for several years now. For the past five years Dennis has been an enthusiastic supporter, and I am indebted to him for the amount of time he has spent looking for small clues in the Files. It seems that I bump into Dennis and his charming wife Mary every time I make a rare sortie to the outside world, a welcome sight knowing that we can have longer chats and share the latest medal news without the 'phone bills! Tom Miles and his son Tom Junior, have photographed memorials in every corner of the globe, and during the final months of collating, Tom has usually found last minute needs. Tom has organised several memorials for VC's to be erected in recent years without the attendant publicity sought by a few fellows, who seem more concerned with personal glory than interest in the matter in hand. Following my final 'escape' from hospital, I was surprised to find I was living within a mile of an

414

ex-colleague, Ron Biddle. *By coincidence Ron is also a keen VC researcher and has not only loaned many rare photographs obtained over a number of years, but has assisted in some of the more mundane tasks in the latter months. With the able help of his wife* Margaret, *the final grave to be confirmed in the UK was down to their doggedness, and found with just weeks to go before deadline!*
*Five other men who have been working on similar lines for a number of years, Dave Nash, Steve Bench, Brad Smith, Alan Jordan *and* Stan Applin, *have all made available items and photographs from their own files. With just a matter of weeks to go before publication,* Stan *sadly died following a short but brave fight against cancer, a quick glance through the photo acknowledgements will show how much* Stan *and his wife* Iris *have contributed on their many military trips around the world - the last being the North West Frontier. They were an inseperable couple, and my deepest sympathies go to* Iris, *I just wish* Stan *could have seen the finished book and note his enormous input.* Alan *has gone out of his way on many occasions to re-take photo's of memorials, resulting in excellent new images.* Steve's *knowledge of the Western Front and the Royal Navy,* Brad's *years of research of VC's with South Coast connections and a 30 year naval career recently behind him, together with* Dave's *many photo trips around the country, have all been put to good use, and I am indebted to them for sharing their knowledge and expertise.*
*The thought of having to learn computer skills was daunting, my years of claiming that the only things I knew about were horses and cemeteries had served me well for many years, and I had survived on it until having to accept the inevitable. Fortunately another old colleague came to my rescue after I had made several disastrous starts. Robin Elks *is one of the very few knowledgeable computer experts who are able to teach computer skills using the English language, and how he must regret saying "call me anytime if you have a problem". I have probably taken him up on the offer one hundred times in the past year, but I have to say that the man has the patience of a saint, either explaining what I had done wrong over the telephone or by making the long drive over to my home, touching one key and sorting out the problem. I can honestly say that but for his help the book would have been in notebook form long after I'd been pushing up the daisies! Know-how also came from* Roger Firth *who drew the cemetery maps and the monuments in the appendix. I had known exactly what I wanted for the cover design, with the need to keep a 'generic feel', and I am grateful to* Keith Allen's *professional flair in putting it together using my basic sketches. I cannot thank* David Cook *enough for his superb last minute work on 'Map-A' after the original was 'lost'.*
*I received help in myriad ways from researchers and people who just happened to see one of my advertisements, and I have established friendships with a number of them with whom I am now in regular contact, John Manock, Doreen Naylor, Pat Batty, Frank Long, Biny Dureeka *and* Hal Egerton, *with their welcome and regular letters of encouragement, along with photographs and cuttings galore have been a real bonus.* John *has covered many a mile 'up North' for me, not only supplying me with requested photographs, but finding new plaques and memorials by taking that one extra step, when others would have given up.* Doreen *has scoured Liverpool for memorials,and both* Pat *and* Frank *have covered the South East.* Biny *had sent MANY images from India, from a large collection of Mutiny images gathered over forty years, but unfortunately passed away in 1997 at the grand age of 91. I had first met* Hal *during a trip to the Somme in 1988, and did not hear from him again until a letter out of the blue seven years later, since when he has ensured that I receive a weekly parcel of cuttings, photographs and useful articles. It never ceases to amaze me just how fortunate I have been with friends, willing to assist in so many ways. Personal thanks naturally go to my 'carers' and minders -* Linda Hamer *and* Maureen Juckes *who somehow get my body jump-started each day,* Wendy Nelham *for household needs, the secretarial skills of* Jean Gander *who is also assisting with distribution, and I can even add the support and friendship with my bank manager* Karen Bell! *Returning to research, the following have all written frequently and sent important items:* Adrian Bay, Betty Collar, David Cairns, Norah Sanders, Eve Logan, John Chidzey, 'Clive' Dunn, Muriel Monk, David McLeish, Mike Wade, Gerard Conway, *and his late wife* Maureen, Norman Gordon, Pat Blackett-Barber, Bert Gedin, Derek Hunt, Helen Smith, Wanda Williams, Sid Lindsey, John Lester, Brian Cornelius, W. Gordon Hornsby, Bill Cable, Gus Dawson, Tom Story, Geoffrey Clouder, David Tomlins *and* Major Alf Flatow - *the number of times their names can be seen in the photo acknowledgements are testimony to their help.*
*The following ex-work colleagues I burdened with doing just 'odd little jobs' which at times took them weeks to complete, and I now offer my apologies! Stewart *and* Vivian Smith *have driven all over Scotland following a request for just one item near their Dundee home, and even asked if there was anything else they could do.* Mick Kelsey *used his famous nose for tracking down records in Devon and Cornwall;* Reg Plant, Clive Roberts, Steve Peters, Chris Forester, David Tatlock, Roger Webster, Peter Briggs *and* Jim Hingle *have all furnished important items. The latter was*

one of several people who not only undertook to go out on research himself, but formed a group to collate even more information - Jim's contribution has been enormous and I hope he is now proud of all that he has done. A call to a dear friend in Dorset, Steve Smith, *proved a materstroke - not only did he undertake to take check record offices for memorials within a fifty mile radius of his home, but by renewing our friendship after 15 years, he has provided much needed moral support during my long hospital stay, and has been just a 'phone call away when I have needed a chat.*

*The last few years has seen the untimely passing of three other good friends, in addition to Stan *and* Biny *- all were enthusiastic supporters, and I am saddened that they were not to see the final product.* Rose Coombs, *a name familiar to all involved in military research was a one-off lady, eager to help anyone with a genuine interest in the Great War in particular, but whose knowledge was extensive in many other fields. Having had the joy of meeting her in the mid-60's at the* Canon's *home, she immediately offered help once my own project began in earnest. Every time I was on the Western Front I was sure to bump into* Rose, *whether it be emerging from a wood she had been investigating or in cemeteries from Albert to Ypres. Two fellow First War enthusiasts who were of immense help, as well as dear friends, have also died before they could see the fruits of their labour - both* Bob Puffett *and* Gordon Smith *died at tragically early ages in the prime of life. The great help rendered by friends whose field of research does not centre around the VC was very much appreciated, particularly* Jim Boys *and* Ken Horton, *both being Crimean specialists.* Ken *spent much time in the Balaclava area in late 1998 at the behest of the Russian authorities, overseeing the restoration of the Balaclava Obelisk and the 'courtyard' at Cathcart's Hill, but has always found time to check on my Midland 'problems'.* Jim's *name is linked with his superb in-depth studies on the Light Brigade, scouring his files for VC related material and sending many useful items.*

*Authorities from the medal world could not have been kinder, with expert assistance from such notables as David Erskine-Hill *of* Spink & Son, *who has sent some superb images of many recipients. Despite a busy schedule,* David *is involved in a new 'VC Book Initiative' being set-up by Spinks, beginning with 'Monuments to Courage' and to be followed by a VC Bibliography due out later in 1999. (I also take this opportunity of thanking* David *for obtaining a very good result when handling my collection last year!)* Edward Playfair *from* Sotheby's *answered my prayers by locating a particular item I was seeking when deadline was fast approaching, whilst* Chris Dixon *of* C.J & A.J. Dixon Ltd *and* Philip Matthew's *of* DMD Services *both very kindly lent original and rare medals to be computer enhanced.* Mark Cline *of* M.C. Miniatures *has been a solid prop for the past three years, quitely offering advice on many related subjects, and helping in numerous ways 'behind the scenes'. Through my friendship with* Mark, Dr. Llew Lloyd *and* Tony Sabell *made timely contributions, one particular favour entailed the good Doctor performing a mammoth cleaning-up job on a headstone attired in full evening dress, which I think one could say was well above the call of duty!* John Sly, *the editor of the "Medal News" and a near neighbour is another who has been supportive since his days as editor of the OMRS 'Journal', and its current editor* John Tamplin *has answered many questions and readily offered his expert advice.* John Elliott, *editor of 'Soldier' magazine, has regularly up-dated his readers and helped immensely. A long-time Spinks' associate* Terry Duncan *has kindly provided me some magnificent photographs of medal groups.*

*With illustrations forming a vital part of this work, the Imperial War Museum have been particularly helpful, originally Rose Coombs *was my kind 'provider', and I have lost count of the number of superb images she gave me.* Diana Condell's *extensive knowledge of medals and friendly advice, coupled with photo archivist* John Delaney's *hours of effort locating several hundred perfect images, are very much appreciated and will not be forgotten The IWM also very kindly waived all reproduction fess, knowing that all proceeds from sales are going to the Royal Star & Garter, a gesture their near neighbours across the Thames should well note, requesting over £30 for every image I wanted to use from their superb archives, an unreasonable sum in my humble opinion!*

*A chance letter from a complete stranger, followed by a meeting some weeks later caused me to almost jump for joy. Adrian Channing *had a beautiful old family photograph album with portraits taken by an ancestor, a senior Royal Engineer officer who had served during the latter half of the 19th Century. A section of the album contained a dozen unique photographs of VC's, some being named, with the wonderful discovery that Sapper* John PERIE (82) *was among them. It had been believed that his likeness had never been captured on film, so one can imagine my delight. John Perie's grave had been extremely difficult to locate, despite a correspondence 'blitz' I had targeted in the Aberdeen area. However, armed with several clues,* Bob Fuller's *many hours foot work resulted in its discovery in a paupers' plot in St Peters Cemetery, Aberdeen. During this time I had been corresponding with* Colonel Gerald Napier, *assisting him with grave locations of RE recipients for his 1998 book "The Sapper VC's", thankfully the information on Perie was in time for inclusion,*

and was a typical example of the teamwork required to complete many entries. Gerald was in turn extremely generous in supplying photographs of RE personnel, in tandem with the staff of the Royal Engineers Museum at Chatham, where he had been its curator for many years.

*Having mentioned authors I am indebted for the help given by the following, many of whom were kind enough to allow me to use photographs from their own collections: Dr. John Laffin, Henry Keown-Boyd, Stephen Snelling, Ian Knight, Tim Day, Lyn Macdonald, Theon Wilkinson, Dr. Rosie Llewellyn-Jones, Ann Clayton, Susan Farrington, Raymond Walsh, Les Perrin *and the late* Zoe Yalland. *I have corresponded with* Lt. Col. Paul Oldfield *for a number of years, exchanging information on First War recipients, and look forward to reading* Paul's *forthcoming thoroughly researched book on all Western Front VC's - a mammoth task and likely to be 'must have' volume!*

*The drawings of headstones used on the opening pages are by kind permission of the artist, Don Bianco, *whilst the technical names for each style of the various memorial stones were supplied by monumental craftsman* Cliff Palmer *of The Kingston Masonry Company, who spent many hours going through the photographs to correctly identify each type. Unable to visit the PRO and other major repositories as often as I would have liked, I had no choice but to try some 'professionals' listed in family history magazines. After three disasters I contacted* David Annal, *who was both thorough and interested in the project, and resulted in many helpful leads. As a member of some two dozen military societies around the world, both my fellow members and journal editors have assisted greatly, including the distribution of early flyers.* Major Colin Robins *of the Crimean War Research Society has been a keen supporter, updating the membership of progress and inserting the odd item when I have needed some facts verified. As a life member of British Association of Cemeteries South Asia (BACSA), many members of which dwelt in the sub-continent during the Raj, I was contacted by a variety of people with both long memories and information about VC graves in India. I also belong to ten 'Cemetery Friend' work-groups, and again their newsletters carried regular items listing current needs, and my thanks go to the many who responded with leads.*

*To part-conclude the major UK contributors, a colleague from many years ago - Steve Rouse, *called to volunteer the services of his son* Daniel *to re-take ANY memorial or grave in London, the latter concluding a university degree in photography, and wished to try his hand at monuments. Most of the resulting forty photographs are included, together with my grateful thanks for not only the time and trouble involved, but for the wonderful support that both have constantly given me.*

*More British help came from the following: Lorna Alexander, Cliff Bond, Alan Barnett, George Bell, Richard Baldwin, David Bews, David Barker, Mick Barnbrook, Eric Black, Edward Burns, Phil Crooks, Pat Clarke, John Chambers, Malcolm Cook, Michael Caine, Tony Cotes, Leopold de Coutere, Alasdair Dewar, Idris Davies, Jill Dudman, Graham Evans, Daniel Eggleshaw, Frank Franklin, Philip Freear, Valerie Foster, John Flower, Bob Flanagan, June Green, Ron Gould, Jason Horne, Michael Hickey, A. J. Henderson, Tony James, J. A. Johnston, Androulla Kafetzis, Neil Kew, David Lambeth, Graham Lee, Raymond Law, Ade Lanigan, Anthony Montan, Paul Mallatrat, Graeme Murdoch, Marie Murphy, Donald Martin, Dr. Lisa Miller, John Moore, Major R Moore, Hughina MacDonald, Anna MacDonald, Rosemary Noakes, Les Owen, Charles Ogston, Robert Pirie, Len Parkes, John Pearson, Roy Page, Mark Roberts, Ann Rowell, Sylvia Ross, Dr. D. K. L. Sladden, Albert Saunders, John Tamplin, David Tomlins, Alan Virgo, Tony Venables, Ron Woollacott, Vicky Webster, David Williams, Sonia Yates *and* Ron Clark.

*From overseas I have received help from a variety of people and institutions, the British Embassy's, Consulates and High Commissions have usually turned up trumps, with Julia Billingsly *in Milan and* Michael Gluckstern *in Venice being a tremendous help in Italy;* Jason Smith *and* Jacqui Booker *in Dar-es-Salaam, Tanzania;* Dennis Carter *in Montevideo, Uruguay;* Bob Colby *in Copenhagen, Denmark;* Andrew Noble *in Cape Town;* Colonel Tony Moorby *and* Colonel J J Dumas *in Kingston, Jamaica;* Colin Gedge *in Funchal, Madeira and* Sandra Darra *in St Legier, Switzerland have all checked records and sent the occasional photograph. The following diplomats have also gone out of their way to oblige with much needed information:* Brigadier Rakesh Dhir (India), Colonel Mukhtar Ahmed (Pakistan) *and* Colonel Angelo Pacifici (Italy) *in particular spent many days finding the answers to 'unusual' questions. Prominent amongst other overseas diplomats/military attaches were* Colonel Xaing-Dhi (China); Colonel Andre Pittoire (Burma) Major Hector Vedovatti (Uruguay); Major Gonen Gucuk (Turkey); Dr. Helena Peterssen (Norway); Colonel J-P Rochefort (France); Eka Vissen (Belgium); Colonel Ari Bromberg (Israel); Colonel A Rossan (Egypt), Dr Pieter Moone (Zimbabwe) *and* Major 'Scooter' Burns (Malaysia).

*From Australia, Judith 'Butter' McClymont *of Queensland toured Australia on two occasions on my behalf, supplying the great percentage of photographs from that country and many from surrounding countries. A dear friend since her teenage days, when touring Europe in the late 70's,*

417

Butter spent many months sorting through years of loose notes, then putting them in some semblance of order complete with an index which I still use to this day. David Hewson *of Perth has scoured many record offices for extra information in Australia and enlisted his contacts in Kenya;* Anthony Staunton *and I have corresponded for many years, and his own VC files have provided the answers to some difficult questions. I struck gold in New Zealand following a letter from* Joyce Major, *who not only travelled around the Islands personally, but recruited her own network to supply material. My sincere thanks to all of her 'crew', particularly* Laurie Trubshoe *who was kind enough to share his own research on Kiwi recipients.* Dolores Grant *from Vancouver also took a lot of time to organise her own team to assist, and provided many photographs and news cuttings from the Pacific North West. Fortunately, both she and her New Zealand counterpart,* Joyce, *have been able to visit me in the past few years, and I was able to thank them both personally. Other generous Canadian's -* Etta Walker *from Alberta,* Rod Travers-Griffin *of Toronto and* R Stanley Goat *have all given much time to the project, covering many miles to check records and take photographs. From a variety of countries, the following have been of inestimable help:* David Redl *(Germany);* Jean Attard *(Malta);* Colonel Langlands *and* Lt. Col. J B Smart *(Nepal);* Lars Meyering, Lt. Col. J M Plant, Major Peter Scholes *and* Maurice Gough-Palmer *(South Africa);* Superintendent Andy Bermingham *(Bermuda);* Rani Advani *and* Biny Dureeka *(India)* Terry Sentance *and* Mike Webley *(Kenya);* Erik Cipriano, Arthur Gaynor *and* Mauro Sequi *(Italy);* Owain Raw-Rees *(Saudi Arabia);* Rani Alcan *(Turkey);* Lynn Martin *(Tanzania) and* Ivan Goraschkov *(Russia).*

*There are a large number of researchers in the United States who study aspects of the Victoria Cross, many in conjunction with Medal of Honor studies. Donald Jennings *of Florida has been the provider of photographs of Western Front graves to illustrate several VC publications, and he has very kindly allowed me permission to use half a dozen others in this book. Others from the States that have shared their own research are:* Daniel Zepeda *(CA);* Paul Doty *(GA);* Colonel Paul Wimert *(VA);* Ed Murphy *(AZ);* Major General Pony Scherrer *(SC) the late* Jack Brown *(OH) who had files on over 80,000 famous American's, including the VC's;* John Fital *(PA);* C.Pat Tate *(FL);* Colonel Billy Greear *(TX);* Captain Wilbur Martin *(NY) and* Brigadier Zeb Anderson *(CO), who between them knew six of the seven Victoria Cross recipients personally.*

Two Congressional Medal of Honor recipients wrote letters of support in the 1980's - Army Colonel William Barber *(Korea) and Marine* Brigadier Jay Vargas *(Vietnam), the latter opening many new research doors for me in both the US and Canada. A good friend and soul mate* Timothy Lowry *from Colorado, a four-term Vietnam Marine vet and the author of two fine books on the Vietnam recipients of the Congressional Medal of Honor, ensured I kept my VC work going despite the temptations of US research, as did a close friend* Judith Burk, *who accompanied me on many cross country trips.* Jim *and* Richard Owen *are publishers from South Carolina, producing the excellent quarterly magazine 'USA Yesterday', and frequently updated readers of my project, resulting in one 'find' in Ireland, when readers/VC descendants in New Orleans, LA and Flagstaff, AZ sent me vital clues - to all these friends across the ocean, my sincere gratitude for help and comradeship.*

*Nearer to home in Ireland, two good friends have performed wonders in areas where records are notoriously difficult to locate. Roger White *and* Bob Cudmore, *the former the grandson of a Light Brigade charger - Captain (later General) Robert White of the 17th Lancers, supplied many leads and photographs having toiled through many overgrown cemeteries, whilst* Maire Bacon, Sven A-Persson, Harry Irwin, Norman Irvine *and* Martin O'Dwyer *from both sides of the border, have added wonderful material, and pointed the way to the location of elusive records.*

*Regimental museums of the British Army have been especially helpful, and to all curators I offer sincere thanks for help over many years. The following assisted far above the call of duty - Major Martin Everett *and* Colonel John Grundy *of the South Wales Borderers,* Martin *constantly supplying new material up until the last possible moment;* Lt.Col. Alexander Scott-Elliott *of the Argyll & Sutherland Highlanders;* Colonel Michael Cooper *of the Royal Engineers;* Major Hugo White *from the DCLI's;* Lt. Col. Angus Fairrie *of The Highlanders,* Captain P A Starling *of the R.A.M.C.;* Douglas Hill *of 14th/20th Hussars;* Major Ron Cassidy *of the Royal Green Jackets; yet another old workmate -* Dr Michel Fopp, *now the Director of the Royal Air Force Museum Hendon;* Angela Kelsall *of the Derby County Museum left no stone unturned;* Frances Dimond *of the Royal Archives, Windsor; and both* Rebecca Barnett *of the Australian War Memorial and* Heather Matthie *of the Alexander Turnbull Library in New Zealand were both supportive and friendly.*

*To ALL of the above I give my heartfelt thanks, no matter how small you may have felt the odd item you provided, I assure you that without such items I would have been unable to put the story of the monuments together. I apologise profusely to anyone I have omitted from this list, if I have then it is entirely down to my failing memory over 36 years of endeavour, I can offer no other defence.

PHOTOGRAPH ACKNOWLEDGEMENTS

With any large collection of photographs accumulated over almost four decades of research, the necessity to faithfully record the source of each one that had been sent or given, on the grounds that they may one day appear in booklet or other form of publication was essential. Having regularly responded to requests from authors to supply images to illustrate their own proposed book, I have often been annoyed that the source of the photograph(s) has not been acknowledged - not because I was eager to see my name in print, but on the grounds of courtesy and copyright. As a result, the following list of acknowledgements is rather long due to the fact that so many images have been used in 'Monuments to Courage'. With regard to the graves on the Western Front, or other well-recorded headstones around this country, I have many pictures of the same grave sent by perhaps half a dozen people, in such cases I have used the most suitable which may disconcert a contributor who has sent an almost identical image, I offer my apologies and thanks for your time and trouble.

The many people who have provided numerous images are acknowledged elsewhere, but I must mention a few here, predominanly those that have gone out of their way to ensure that my requests were fulfilled. Apart from several thousand I had taken myself prior to 1992, the late Canon William Lummis MC (WML) gave me many portraits together with numerous artistic impressions of recipients deeds, most of which bore no mention of the source. He was also to give me copies of portraits that he had given by other collectors in the 1930's, and I have shown them as L/WML. Miss Jane Priestley kindly gave me carte-blanche to use any that have appeared in 'This England' publications, and military museums have responded willingly since the project began, with one notable exception I will not mention by name, but discerning readers will note its omission! I am indebted to John Delaney, the late Rose Coombs MBE and the Board of the Imperial War Museum,(IWM) who not only waived publication fees but supplied hundreds of images for a nominal sum per print. Two regimental museum curators, Major Martin Everett of the South Wales Borderers and Major Ron Cassidy of the Royal Green Jackets have been magnificent, supplying both quantity and quality in photographs of the many recipients from their respective regiments, whilst Colonel Gerald Napier and the current staff at the Royal Engineers Museum have responded to every request. Rebecca Barnett of the Australian War Memorial (AWM) was able to supply many prints, as was Heather Mathie of the Alexander Turnbull Library in Wellington, New Zealand, whilst the photo archivists at the University of Texas in Austin were able to supply and allow me to use many Crimean images from their large collection.

Of many individuals who have provided material, Tom Miles and his much-travelled son Tom Jr. and the late Stan Applin were just a 'phone call away from having exactly the 'right' photo when needed, and David Erskine-Hill of Spinks has made available several rare images in addition to passing-on the names of associates who were able to help. Jim Hingle of Wakefield, Joyce Major in New Zealand, Judith McClymont in Australia, B.S. Dureeka in India and Dolores Grant in Canada not only took many images themselves,but set-up their own 'networks' to record remote memorials.

To avoid repetition, the following initials (plus those indicated above) are used to record sources: SAFE refers to a large collection of portraits I purchased at auction in Santa Fe in 1984, most in the form of clippings: RF - Robert Fuller; DH - David Harvey; NMM - National Maritime Museum; The enhanced photograph of the single Victoria Cross and other medals are from the Kevin Patience Collection (KP) and wherever they appear his name has at times been omitted. Where three images appear with an entry and two credits are shown, the third came from the source immediately above.

(I have consulted the many provisions of the Copyright Acts of 1911, 1956 and all sections of the 1988 Act, relating to reproducing photographs, and have taken legal advice regarding images originating overseas. Any errors or omissions are my own)

Chapter 1 - The Crimean War

1. NMM-C 3398
   RF
   Ron Biddle
2. IWM-Q80484
   DH
   Steve Smith
3. KP
   Peter Briggs
4. IWM-Q80470
   Alan Jordan
   WML

5. Royal Green Jackets
   DH
6. WML
   DH
7. SAFE
   Stewart Smith
8. Ken Horton
   Dave Nash
   WML
9. L/WML
   RF

10. Royal Green Jackets
    RF
    DH
11. SAFE
    DH
    Tom Miles
12. SAFE
    Judith McClymont
13. SAFE
    Stan Applin
    KP

14. SAFE
    Jim Hingle
15. SAFE
    DH
    Philip Matthews-DMD
16. SAFE
    DH
    WML
17. SAFE
    WML
    David Rushmer

18. 17/21 Lancers Museum
    DH
19. SAFE
    RF
20. SAFE
    June O'Brien
    WML
21. WML
    DH
    Ron Biddle
22. SAFE

(22). Robert Cudmore
Ron Biddle

23. Hewett Family Papers
Brad Smith

24. SAFE
Dave Nash
Univ. of Texas

25. SAFE
DH

26. Welch Reg. Museum
Univ. of Texas

27. KP
WML

28. IWM-Q80523
Hal Egerton
Ron Biddle

29. SAFE
Gordon Smith

30. SAFE
Dave Nash
Adrian Bay

31. SAFE
Stewart Smith

32. KP
DH
WML

33. Royal Green Jackets
Lord Clifford
Muriel Monk

34. WML
Joyce Major

35. IWM
Anthony Staunton

36. SAFE
DH
Tom Miles

37. SAFE
DH
PhilipMatthews-DMD

38. Frank Franklin
Anthony Sabell
Dr Llewellyn Lloyd

39. SAFE
Alan Jordan
John Manock

40. KP
WML

41. SAFE
John Manock
Ron Biddle

42. KP
I.L.News
Steve Bench

43. WML
Dave Nash
Welch Reg. Museum

44. SAFE
RF

45. KP
Spink & Son Ltd

46. SAFE
DH
RF

47. KP
Steve Bench
Hal Egerton

48. SAFE
Dave Nash
Adrian Bay

49. Royal Green Jackets
Ron Biddle
RF

50. Royal Green Jackets
John McLeish
DH

51. Royal Engineers Mus.
RF

52. SAFE
Steve Bench
IWM-Q82646

53. Adrian Channing
DH
Lee Harvey

54. WML
Univ. of Texas

55. Ben May
Norman Irvine
I.L. News

56. KP
Alan Jordan
Univ. of Texas

57. SAFE
Dave Nash

58. Ben May
Univ. of Texas

59. IWM-Q80514
RF

60. Adrian Channing
Daniel & Steve Rouse

61. KP
Stewart Smith

62. Royal Green jackets
Mike Wade

63. SAFE
IWM
Royal Green Jackets

64. IWM-Q80548
DH
Durham L.I. Museum

65. SAFE
John Lester
Alan Jordan

66. SAFE
Daniel & Steve Rouse
RF

67. SAFE
Brad Smith

68. IWM-Q80548
Judith McClymont
I.L. News

69. IWM-Q80465
DH
Univ. of Texas

70. SAFE
John Lester

71. IWM-Q80548
John Lester

72. SAFE
Dave Nash
PhilipMatthews-DMD

73. SAFE
WML
Royal Green Jackets

74. SAFE
Doreen Naylor
Ron Biddle

75. KP
IWM
RF

76. SAFE
DH

77. Adrian Channing
RF
SAFE

78. SAFE
Steve Bench
PhilipMatthews-DMD

79. Adrian Channing
RF
SAFE

80. SAFE
Daniel & Steve Rouse
DH

81. Col.Gerald Napier
DH
Lee Harvey

82. Adrian Channing
RF
Lee Harvey

83. NMM-59/2118
DH
Bob Puffett

84. SAFE
Daniel & Steve Rouse

85. WML
Roger White
Univ. of Texas

86. KP
N. Elvines
DH

87. KP
Chris Forester

88. NMM-A-2727
Stan Applin
Spink & Son

89. Royal Marines Mus.
Joyce Major
Stan Applin

90. SAFE
Mike Wade

91. NMM-9517
Alan Jordan
PhilipMatthews-DMD

92. Adrian Channing
DH
Royal Engineers Mus.

93. KP
RF
Royal Green Jackets

94. SAFE
Univ. of Texas
PhilipMatthews-DMD

95. Major Frank Clark
DH
Dave Nash

96. Ben May
DH
PhilipMatthews-DMD

97. Scots Guards Museum
IWM

98. R.A. Historical Trust
David Rushmer
Tom Miles

99. SAFE
Stan Applin
WML

100. IWM-Q80510
Les Owen
DH

101. IWM-Q80532
Alan Jordan
Tim Day

102. Q.O.R. W. Kent Mus.
DH

103. DH
Chris Forester

104. KP
WML
Univ. of Texas

105. WML
Dave Nash

106. IWM-Q80550
RF

107. IWM-Q80508
Alan Jordan

(107). Frank Long

108. R.A.Historical Assoc.
DH

109. SAFE
Coldstream G'ds Mus.
DH

110. NMM-A1729
DH
Brad Smith

111. SAFE
Steve Bench
NMM-3404

| Chapter 2 - Indian Mutiny |

112. KP
Zoe Yalland
Tom Miles

113. KP

114. WML
Daniel & Steve Rouse
John Mannock

115. L/WML
B.A.C.S.A.

116. This England
B.S. Dureeka
KP

117. Albert Saunders
KP
Tom Miles

118. This England
Stan Applin
KP

119. IWM-Q80547
Dave Nash

120. KP
WML

121. WML
Norman Irvine

122. SAFE
RF

123. SAFE
RF
Stewart Smith

124. KP
WML

125. KP
Stan Applin
B.S. Dureeka

126. Royal Green Jackets
Eve Logan

127. This England
DH
KP

128. L/WML
DH
KP

129. Durham L.I. Museum
Brian Cornelius
KP

130. This England
RF
KP

131. Royal Green Jackets
Judith McClymont
KP

132. L/WML
Pallanza Cty Council
Col. Angelo Pacifici

133. Dennis Pillinger
KP

134. D.C.L.I. Museum
Brit. Emb.Uruguay

135. KP
Doreen Naylor
Tom Miles

136. R.A.Historical Assoc.
Steve Bench
Tom Miles

137. R.A. Historical Assoc.
RF

138. Royal Green Jackets
Alan Jordan

139. SAFE
DH
KP

140. WML
Sven A-Persson
Rotherham Art Gall'y

141. SAFE
Peter Duckers
Pat Batty

142. Gordon Highlanders
Daniel & Steve Rouse
WML

143. KP
Rotherham Art Gall'y

144. KP
Q's Own Highlanders
DH
Tom Miles

145. Ben May
DH
Dave Nash

146. SAFE
DH
Tim Pearce

147. WML
Rod Travers-Griffin

148. Q's Own Highlanders
WML
Steve Bench

149. IWM-Q80473
RF

150. Spink & Son Ltd
Robert Cudmore
WML

151. D.C.L.I. Museum
DH
KP

152. Royal Green Jackets
Cornish Times
KP

153. Gordon Highlanders
B.S. Dureeka

154. Royal Green Jackets
DH
RF

155. This England
B.S. Dureeka

156. KP
Stan Applin
B.A.C.S.A.

157. Royal Green Jackets
John Manock

158. SAFE
Mrs J. Harfield
Col. Gerald Napier

159. Robert E Salkeld
Zoe Yalland
KP

160. KP
Robert Cudmore

161. KP
B.S. Dureeka

162. KP
WML

163. KP
B.S. Dureeka

164. KP
CanadianNatArchives
Tom Miles

165. This England
Dave Nash
R.A. Historical Assoc.
166. Adrian Channing
RF
KP
167. WML
KP
RF
168. KP
B.S. Dureeka
169. Northumberland Fus.
RF
170. R.A. Historical Assoc.
RF
171. KP
Jim Hingle
172. Q'Own Highlanders
DH
KP
173. DH
RF
R.A.M.C. Museum
174. SAFE
Tom Miles
175. SAFE
Norman Irvine
176. SAFE
DH
Tom Miles
177. WML
Robert Cudmore
178. KP
Roger White
179. Q's own Highlanders
RF
180. SAFE
RF
KP
181. Northumberland Fus.
B.S. Dureeka
KP
182. Q's Own Highlanders
RF
183. KP
Stan Applin
184. R.A. Historical Assoc.
Tom Miles
185. Rotherham Art Gall'y
RF
Alan Jordan
186. KP
Stewart Smith
187. 9/12 Royal Lancers
DH
KP
188. IWM-Q80487
Joyce Major/Kannex
Tom Miles
189. KP
190. Tom Miles
KP
191. RF
KP
192. WML
DH
193. Sotheby's
KP
194. Northumberland Fus.
Pat Batty
KP
195. SAFE
RF
196. KP
John Lester

(196) WML
197. SAFE
KP
Jim Reader
198. DH
RAFGibraltar/167285
KP
199. SAFE
Daniel & Steve Rouse
Steve Bench
200. B.S. Dureeka
KP
201. This England
RF
KP
202. This England
W. Gordon Hornsby
Tom Miles
203. SAFE
Steve Bench
Tom Miles
204. KP
Tom Miles
205. Edward Burns
KP
206. KP
B.S. Dureeka
207. WML
John Chidzey
RF
208. L/WML
RF
209. KP
B.S. Dureeka
210. Spink & Son Ltd
Keith Webb BEM
211. SAFE
R. Stanley Goat
212. NMM-D437/5A
Brad Smith
213. Stan Applin
KP
214. L/WML
Norman Irvine
215. KP
RF
B.S. Dureeka
216. SAFE
RF
217. KP
M. Barnbrook
Dennis Pillinger
218. Argyll & Suth. High.
Judith McClymont
KP
219. SAFE
Norman Gordon
Stan Applin
220. RF
Ann Wilkes
221. NMM
Steve Bench
KP
222. KP
Stewart Smith
223. Roger White
DH
224. Doreen Naylor
B.S. Dureeka
225. Anthony Staunton
Judith McClymont
226. WML
Norman Irvine
M. O'Dwyer
227. SAFE

(227) Steve Bench
RF
228. Adrian Channing
G. Williams
SAFE
229. This England
Alan Jordan
SAFE
230. SAFE
Roger White
KP
231. WML
RF
Pat Doak
232. Bob Taylor
DH
233. 9/12 Royal Lancers
Daviod Rushmer
234. WML
Sue Farrington
235. Adrian Channing
DH
Royal Engineers Mus.
236. This England
Daniel & Steve Rouse
B.S. Dureeka
237. SAFE
Stan Applin
238. IWM-Q80498
RF
239. SAFE
Ron Biddle
DH
240. RF
DH
241. Argyll & Suth. High.
RF
SAFE
242. SAFE
DH
KP
243. Royal Green Jackets
Mike Wade
SAFE
244. This England
RF
245. SAFE
DH
Tom Miles
246. This England
Steve Smith
Alan Jordan
247. B.S. Dureeka
KP
248. IWM-Q88645
Alan Jordan
RF
249. Q's Own Highlanders
Stan Applin
250. WML
Lorna Alexander
251. IWM-Q80494
Brad Smith
Major M.B. Murphy
252. This England
Major M.B. Murphy
B.S. Dureeka
253. Judith McClymont
B.S. Dureeka
254. IWM-Q80482
Pat Batty
Tom Miles
255. This England
RF
Major M.B. Murphy

256. Adrian Channing
Steve Bench
SAFE
257. WML
Norman Irvine
Major M.B. Murphy
258. WML
Judith McClymont
259. IWM-Q80488
SAFE
260. KP
B.S. Dureeka
261. L/WML
RF
IWM-Q82629
262. This England
John Lester
B.S. Dureeka
263. This England
Jim Hingle
KP
264. This England
RF
265. IWM-Q81182
DH
266. IWM-Q80509
DH
Daniel & Steve Rouse
267. This England
RF
BlackWatch Reg.Mus.
268. KP
DH
269. WML
RF
James Morton
270. DH
271. David McLeish
272. WML
Ron Biddle
Alan Jordan
273. Steve Peters
KP
274. SAFE
Roy.Canadian Legion
275. Robert Cudmore
276. This England
Dave Nash
B.S. Dureeka
277. SAFE
Ron Biddle
Henry Keown-Boyd
278. L/WML
DH
279. WML
KP
280. This England
Ron Gould
L/WML
281. IWM-Q80469
Stan Applin
KP
282. This England
Dave Nash
283. SAFE
Jim Hingle
KP
284. WML
KP
285. 17/21LancersMuseu
DH
RF
286. IWM-Q80517
DH
Ron Biddle

287. Royal Green Jackets
Dave Nash
288. KP
289. SAFE
KP
290. IWM-Q80665
Stewart Smith
291. IWM-Q67053
Rod Travers-Griffin
292. Adrian Channing
DH
Royal Engineers Mus.
293. SAFE
Daniel & Steve Rouse
Steve Bench

| Chapter 3 |
| Threats to Empire |

294. This England
IWM
295. SAFE
Daniel & Steve Rouse
IWM-Q82619
296. WML
Sven A-Persson
WML
297. WML
E. Matthews
Stan Applin
298. SAFE
Joyce Major
299. SAFE
RF
IWM
300. SAFE
Geoffrey Goodyear
IWM
301. SAFE
RF
IWM
302. This England
Stan Applin
303. RF
IWM
304. IWM-Q88648
RF
305. SAFE
Roger White
306. SAFE
Geoffrey Clouder
307. KP
Joyce Major
308. Rotherham Art Gall'y
Joyce Major
309. SAFE
Joyce Major
DH
310. Ben May
DH
SAFE
311. IWM-Q80519
RF
312. IWM-Q80821
Pete Duckers
Sue Farrington
313. R.A. Historical Assoc.
Norman Gordon
Tom Miles
314. R.A. Historical Assoc.
RF
315. AlexTurnbull Library
(F3062-1/2)
Judith McClymont
AlexTurnbull Library
(F24645-1/2)

316. Ben May
  Inspector A. Donar
  PC Raymond Law
317. R.A. Historical Assoc.
  Alan Jordan
  Tom Miles
318. SAFE
  Francis Winn
  WML
319. Royal Green Jackets
  Roger White
  Norman Irvine
320. IWM
  Roger White
321. Sotheby's
  Joyce Major
  Tom Miles
322. SAFE
  DH
323. SAFE
  Alan Jordan
324. IWM-Q81179
  M. Barnbrook
  Chris Dixon
325. Adrian Channing
  Spink & Son
  John McLeish
326. Adrian Channing
  Daniel & Steve Rouse
  Royal Engineers Mus.
327. Les Perrin
  Judith McClymont
328. Stan Applin
329. SouthWalesBord.Mus.
  DH
330. Alan Jordan
  SouthWalesBord.Mus.
331. SouthWalesBord.Mus.
  Dave Nash
332. Steve Bench
  Dennis Pillinger
333. SouthWalesBord.Mus.
  C. Pat Tate
334. SAFE
  Anthony Staunton
  IWM
335. IWM
  WML
336. Gurkha Museum
  RF
337. SouthWalesBord.Mus.
  DH
  Stan Applin
338. SAFE
  Stan Applin
  KP
339. SAFE
  'Soldier' Magazine
340. Adrian Channing
  Mrs D. Miller
  Judith McClymont
341. SAFE
  RF
342. WML
343. SAFE
  Robert Cudmore
  General A.C.T. Hinds
344. SAFE
  John McLeish
  RF
345. Adrian Channing
  Steve Smith
  WML
346. Royal Engineers Mus.

(346) Judith McClymont
347. WML
  Tom Story
  Sven A-Persson
348. WML
  DH
349. 'Medal News'
  Steve Bench
350. IWM-Q80570
  RF
  ILN
351. SAFE
  RF
  WML
352. SAFE
  Steve Bench
  Ron Biddle
353. Q's Own Highlanders
  RF
  WML
354. SAFE
  Tom Miles
  B.A.C.S.A.
355. IWM-Q80534
  RF
  ILN
356. R.A.Historical Assoc.
  Daniel & Steve Rouse
  Tom Miles
357. R.A.Historical Assoc.
  Tom Miles
  DH
358. IWM-Q80490
  Gordon Highlanders
359. SAFE
  Ron Biddle

Chapter 4 - The Zulu War
360. SouthWalesBord.Mus.
  IWM
  RF
361. SouthWalesBord.Mus.
  Lt.Col. K. Plant
362. SouthWalesBord.Mus.
  Peter Ellis
  IWM
363. SouthWalesBord.Mus.
  RF
364. SouthWalesBord.Mus.
  Stan Applin
  IWM
365. Royal Engineers Mus.
  RF
366. Roy.Army Serv.Corps
  Judith McClymont
  RF
367. SouthWalesBord.Mus. R
  RF
368. SouthWalesBord.Mus.
  DH
369. SouthWalesBord.Mus.
  DH
370. SouthWalesBord.Mus.
  Dave Nash
  John Manock
371. R.A.M.C. Museum
  Jenny White
  Tom Miles
372. This England
  SouthWalesBord.Mus.
  Stan Applin
373. SouthWalesBord.Mus.
  DH
374. SAFE

(374) Ken Horton
  Lt.Col. K. Plant
375. SAFE
  DH
376. Royal Green Jackets
  Stan Applin
  DH
377. WML
  RF
  Ron Biddle
378. SAFE
  Alan Jordan
  Lt.Col. K. Plant
379. SouthWalesBord.Mus
  Sandra L. Darra
  Norman Gordon
380. 9/12 Lancers Mus.
  Dave Nash
  Sven A-Persson
381. This England
  Killie Campbell
  L/WML
382. This England
  IWM

Chapter 5
Kipling's Soldiers
383. IWM-Q80481
  Frank Franklin
384. WML
  Stan Applin
  Chris Dixon
385. WML
  Dave Nash
  Dennis Pillinger
386. L/WML
  John Lester
387. SAFE
  Stewart Smith
  Chris Dixon
388. SAFE
  M. Barnbrook
  Ron Biddle
389. SAFE
  Brig. PieterWonk
  Chris Dixon
390. SAFE
  Roger White
391. SAFE
  Stan Applin
  Brad Smith
392. SAFE
  Stan Applin
  WML
393. This England
  Norah Sanders
  IWM
394. IWM-Q80820
  DH
  Northants Reg. Mus.
395. SAFE
  Steve & Daniel Rouse
  Tom Miles
396. NMM
  Brad Smith
  SAFE
397. Royal Green Jackets
  Gordon Smith
398. IWM-Q79780
  Dave Nash
  DH
399. SAFE
  J. Blair
  WML

400. WML
  RF
  Stan Applin
401. WML
  DH
402. SAFE
  Gordon Smith
  WML
403. R.A. Historical Assoc.
  Ron Biddle
  Tom Miles
404. This England
  DH
  R.A.M.C. Museum
405. R.A.M.C. Museum
  DH
  Chris Dixon
406. Gurkha Museum
  Steve Smith
407. IWM-Q60466
  RF
  Sven A-Persson
408. IWM-Q80474
  Daniel & Steve Rouse
  Tom Miles
409. SAFE
  RF
  Stan Applin
410. SAFE
  Charles Harvey
  KP
411. SAFE
  Daniel & Steve Rouse
  Tom Miles
412. L/WML
  Brigadier S.M.A. Lee
  Steve Bench
413. SAFE
  John Carpenter
414. This England
  RF
415. Lt.Col. K. Plant
  David Hewson
416. SAFE
  RF
  Stan Applin
417. IWM-Q80464
  Stewart Smith
418. SAFE
  RF
419. This England
  Tom Story
  Stan Applin
420. Royal Engineers Mus
  Dave Nash
421. Ben May
  Roger Webster
  Gurkha Museum
422. Adrian Channing
  Gordon Smith
423. Gordon Highlanders
  W. Gordon Hornsby
424. WML
  Steve Peters
  Chris Dixon
425. Devon & Dorset Mus.
  DH
426. Gordon Highlanders
  RF
427. NAM
  DH
  IWM
428. Adrian Channing
  Steve Bench

(428) Steve Peters
429. NAM
  Hal Egerton
  Ray.Walsh (THCL)
430. Judith McClymont
  KP
431. SAFE
  Alan Jordan
  KP
  Spink & Son Ltd
432. The Royal Archives
  Alan Jordan
  Stan Applin
433. SAFE
  DH
  Q's Own Highlanders
434. IWM-Q79779
  DH
  KP

Chapter 6
The South African War
435. WML
  DH
  IWM
436. SAFE
  Robert Cudmore
  Mark Johnson
437. SAFE
  RF
  Mark Johnson
438. SAFE
  Brig. Pieter Wonk
  Lars Meyering
439. SAFE
  RF
  Mark Johnson
440. WML
  Tom Miles
  Steve Bench
441. SAFE
  Donald C Jennings
  Tom Miles
442. SAFE
  DH
443. SAFE
  RF
  Gordon Highlanders
444. SAFE
  RF
  R.A.M.C. Museum
445. Royal Green Jackets
  Ron Biddle
  Chris Forester
446. R.A. Historical Assoc.
  DH
  John Manock
447. IWM-Q79806
  John Lester
448. R.A.Historical Assoc.
  Stan Applin
  Tom Miles
449. Royal Green Jackets
  Steve Bench
450. SAFE
  Doreen Naylor
  Tom Miles
451. SAFE
  Joyce Major
452. SAFE
  Frank Franklin
453. SAFE
  Clive Roberts

(453) KP
454. SAFE
Steve Bench
Brig. Pieter Wonk
455. Royal Engineers Mus.
Steve Bench
456. Devon & Dorset Mus.
RF
457. Ray. Walsh (THCL)
John Manock
RF
458. SAFE
Steve Bench
John Manock
459. SAFE
Lars Meyering
460. L/WML
MauriceGoughPalmer
Steve Bench
461. SAFE
Sqd.Ldr. Trevor Stone
Norman Irvine
462. R.A.M.C. Museum
DH
Tom Miles
463. SAFE
Dave Rushmer
Chris Dixon
464. This England
DH
465. L/WML
RF
466. WML
Steve Bench
Tom Miles
467. Ben May
Clive Roberts
RF
468. SAFE
David Rushmer
Tom Miles
469. R.A. Historical Assoc.
RF
Tom Miles
470. L/WML
DH
471. R.A.M.C. Museum
T. McDonald
472. IWM-Q80472
DH
WML
473. Ben May
RF
474. Royal Engineers Mus.
David Rushmer
RF
475. IWM
DH
Royal British Legion
476. SAFE
Doreen Naylor
Alan Jordan
477. Ben May
Steve Bench
Gordon Highlanders
478. Ben May
RF
Chris Dixon
479. Carey Corporation
Daniel & Steve Rouse
480. SAFE
T. Pearce
481. SAFE
Dix Noonan Webb

482. SAFE
Ron Biddle
Chris Dixon
483. King'sRegimental Mus
Stan Applin
484. SAFE
Dave Nash
Alan Jordan
485. Royal Green Jackets
Stan Applin
RF
486. This England
RF
Stan Applin
487. SAFE
Judith McClymont
Tom Miles
488. SAFE
RF
DH
489. SAFE
DH
IWM
490. IWM-Q67054
Rod Travers-Griffin
491. SAFE
Dennis Pillinger
492. IWM-Q67055
DH
IWM
493. IWM-Q79795
RF
494. Scottish Regim. Mus.
Doreen Naylor
495. SAFE
Joyce Major
AlexTurnbull Library
(F-80174 - 1/2)
496. SAFE
DH
Chris Dixon
497. IWM
Steve Bench
Chris Dixon
498. WML
Lars Meyering
Major Anthony Lutz
499. IWM-Q90965
DH
WML
500. SAFE
Ron Biddle
Judith McClymont
501. K.O. Scot. Bord. Mus.
Lars Meyering
502. IWM
Judith McClymont
Anthony Staunton
503. Navy & Army Illust.
Owain Raw-Rees
KP
504. SAFE
Dave Nash
505. WML
DH
NunneryAirAmbul'ce
506. Royal Green Jackets
Alan Jordan
RF
507. WML
Trevor Dollar
508. SAFE
RF
IWM

509. SAFE
DH
Tom Miles
510. This England
Pat Doak
R.A.M.C. Museum
511. This England
Alan Jordan
Tom Miles
512. SAFE
R.A.M.C. Museum

| Chapter 7 |
| Minor Skirmishes |

513. NMM - 9/2/H2 (2)
DH
Stan Applin
514. Henry Keown-Boyd
DH
RF
515. SouthWalesBord.Mus.
RF
516. SAFE
RF
517. Royal Green Jackets
DH
Sven A-Persson
518. L/WML
Sylvia Gowardhan
519. Gurkha Museum
David Rushmer
520. This England
Alan Jordan
Stan Applin
521. D.C.L.I. Museum
RF
522. Gurkha Museum
Clive Roberts
Stan Applin

| Chapter 8 |
| First World War - 1914 |

523. IWM-Q70451
DH
Norman Irvine
524. WML
Mike Wade
IWM
525. WML
Dave Nash
Steve Bench
526. Royal Engineers Mus.
Tom Miles
WML
527. Royal Engineers Mus.
RF
WML
528. WML
W. Gordon Hornsby
Roger Firth
529. R.A.Historical Assoc.
DH
Tom Miles
530. WML
RHQ Coldstream G'ds
531. The Great War
David Redl
Steve Smith
532. R.A. Historical Assoc.
Stan Applin
Tom Miles
533. R.A. Historical Assoc.
John McLeish
Tom Miles

534. R.A. Historical Assoc.
DH
535. DH
Judith McClymont
WML
536. R.A. Historical Assoc.
DH
537. R.A. Historical Assoc.
DH
Tom Miles
538. R.A. Historical Assoc.
DH
Tom Miles
539. WML
RF
RoyReg of Wales Mus.
540. Royal Engineers Mus.
DH
541. The Great War
RF
542. The Great War
David Cairns
543. R.A. Historical Assoc.
Tom Miles
Ron Biddle
544. R.A. Historical Assoc.
Clive Roberts
RF
545. The Great War
RHQ Coldstream G'ds
546. IWM
Stewart Smith
Murdo McGregor
547. Ben May
RF
548. King's Reg. Museum
John Lester
549. Ben May
Hal Egerton
Robert Taylor
550. The Great War
RF
(512) R.A.M.C. Museum
Daniel & Steve Rouse
Tom Miles
551. The Great War
Stan Applin
IWM
552. IWM-Q50090
David Rushmer
The Great War
553. WML
DH
554. The Great War
Peter Briggs
IWM
555. Royal Green Jackets
Norah Sanders
RF
556. Royal Green Jackets
Lynne Martin
557. D.C.L.I. Museum
WML
558. The Great War
IWM
DH
559. IWM
DH
Spink & Son Ltd
560. The Great War
RF
IWM
561. The Great War
DH

562. Roy. Scots. Reg. Mus.
DH
563. WML
DH
Mike Wade
564. Royal Engineers Mus.
RF
DH
565. WML
Gordon Smith
Stewart Smith
566. The Great War
Gordon Smith
567. This England
Gerard Conway
The Border Regiment

| Chapter 9 |
| First World War - 1915 |

568. IWM
Stan Applin
Tom Miles
569. IWM
DH
Timothy S Lowry
570. The Great War
Steve Bench
IWM
571. WML
DH
572. The Great War
DH
NunneryAirAmbul'ce
573. Royal Engineers Mus.
Colonel Gerald Napier
574. Royal Green Jackets
Norah Sanders
Steve Smith
575. IWM
DH
N. Clive Dunn
576. IWM
DH
WML
577. IWM
DH
Ron Biddle
578. Royal Green Jackets
Ron Biddle
RF
579. IWM
John Chidzey
580. WML
RF
GrenadierGuards Ass.
581. IWM
DH
Steve Bench
582. L/WML
Trevor Archer
583. IWM
DH
RF
584. The Great War
DH
WML
585. Ben May
Clive Roberts
WML
586. Ben May
DH
587. This England
DH
David Rushmer

588. This England
Dolores Grant
589. IWM
DH
Rod Travers-Griffin
590. L/WML
RF
591. This England
Reg Plant
592. L/WML
DH
Tom Miles
593. This England
KP
594. This England
E.N. Finlayson
John Manock
595. IWM
DH
596. IWM
R. Stanley Goat
597. This England
Hal Egerton
Roger Firth
598. This England
Michael Kelsey
WML
599. IWM-Q79788
Daniel & Steve Rouse
David Saunders
600. Carnoustie Pub.Lib'y
Andy Bermingham
Stan Applin
601. IWM
RF
Dix Noonan Webb
602. WML
Dave Nash
Keith Webb BEM JP
603. *The Great War*
WML
IWM
604. RAF Museum
Judith McClymont
RF
605. King's Regim.Museum
Anthony Staunton
IWM
606. *The Great War*
E.N. Finlayson
Judith McClymont
607. Royal Reg. of Wales
Hal Egerton
RF
608. This England
Maire Bacon
WML
609. *The Great War*
RF
IWM-Q13352
610. Royal Marines Mus.
(10/2/P2)
Alan Jordan
611. WML
Gordon Smith
Roger Firth
612. IWM
Steve Bench
The Great War
613. St. Andrew's Pub.Lib.
RF
IWM
614. IWM
Trevor Archer
David McLeish

615. This England
David Rushmer
IWM
616. WML
RF
617. Royal Green Jackets
RF
The Great War
618. Royal Green Jackets
Stan Applin
WML
619. WML
Daniel & Steve Rouse
WML
620. IWM
Anthony Staunton
Judith McClymont
621. *The Great War*
RF
Stan Applin
622. *The Great War*
DH
Gordon Smith
623. J M A Tamplin MBE
DH
Wanda Williams
624. *The Great War*
DH
Tom Miles
625. *The Great War*
DH
Muriel Monk
626. *The Great War*
RF
WML
627. RoyalCanadianLegion
DH
WML
628. King's Regim.Museum
DH
WML
629. L/WML
RF
630. WML
KP
Roger White
Steve Smith
631. WML
Sven A-Persson
Roger White
632. This England
Roger White
DH
633. Royal Engineers Mus.
DH
RF
634. Royal Green Jackets
DH
Stan Applin
635. Ray. Walsh (THCL)
DH
RF
636. IWM
DH
Sven A-Persson
637. AlexTurnbull Library
(F35109/ -1/2)
Joyce Major
638. This England
RF
Stan Applin
639. *The Great War*
RF
John Manock
640. IWM

(640) RF
Stan Applin
641. IWM
Judith McClymont
Tom Miles
642. This England
Clive Roberts
Tom Miles
643. This England
Judith McClymont
Tom Miles
644. This England
Judith McClymont
DH
645. IWM
Brit.Emb.Copenhagen
646. Carey Corporation
Judith McClymont
Tom Miles
647. WML
Stewart Smith
Glasgow Eve. News
648. IWM
RF
Captain Tony Rogers
649. IWM
Judith McClymont
650. This England
KP
WML
651. This England
Jim Hingle
652. Royal Engineers
DH
653. Whiteley Village Club
RF
654. Gurkha Museum
WML
DH
655. K.O.S.B. Museum
RF
656. R.A.M.C. Museum
Dave Nash
Tom Miles
657. Royal Green Jackets
DH
658. Ben May
Hal Egerton
RF
659. WML
DH
Muriel Monk
660. This England
David Rushmer
Tim Day
661. WML
Ken Horton
662. WML
David Rushmer
RF
663. WML
DH
664. IWM
David Rushmer
Brad Smith
665. WML
Dave Nash
666. This England
David Rushmer
Roger Firth
667. IWM
RF
WML
668. This England
Hal Egerton

(668) DH
669. This England
Judith McClymont
Muriel Monk
670. Ben May
Steve Peters
IWM
671. IWM
DH
WML
672. RHQ Coldstream G'ds
RF
Derek Hunt
673. R.A. Historical Assoc.
Tom Miles
674. Royal Engineers Mus.
Steve Bench
675. IWM-Q85895
David Rushmer
IWM
676. IWM
Mr & Mrs R Ellis
677. WML
Jim Hingle
678. RAF Museum
Jim Hingle
RF
679. IWM
Mike Wade
Nottingham Library
680. WML
DH
681. RAF Museum
Stan Applin
682. Royal Green Jackets
Clive Roberts
RF
683. E. Lancs Reg.Museum
Pat Batty
WML
684. This England
E.N. Finlayson
Insp. A D E Lanigan

```
┌──────────────────────┐
│     Chapter 10       │
│ First World War - 1916│
└──────────────────────┘
```

685. IWM-Q98***
DH
686. This England
IWM
687. R.A.M.C. Museum
Norman Irvine
688. This England
RF
Frank Long
689. Ben May
Geoff Housego
Lee Harvey
690. King's Regim.Museum
Dave Nash
691. Roy. Army Chap.Dept.
Dave Nash
692. SouthWalesBord.Mus.
Keith Webb BEM JP
693. L/WML
C.W.G.C.
Trevor Archer
694. Roy. Army Chap.Dept.
RF
IWM
695. SouthWalesBord.Mus.
IWM
DH
696. IWM-HU37938
Steve Peters

697. This England
IWM
WML
698. King's Regim.Museum
DH
IWM
699. This England
IWM
700. This England
IWM
701. IWM
DH
C.W.G.C.
702. This England
RF
Norman Irvine
703. Roy. Star & Garter
DH
704. Royal Marines Mus.
(9/2/H3)
Ron Biddle
Stan Applin
705. L/WML
Tony Hughes
Brad Smith
706. This England
Jim Hingle
707. King's Regim.Museum
David Rushmer
Liverpool Mus.Labour
John Manock
708. IWM-Q81414
DH
IWM
709. Royal Engineers Mus.
DH
G.W. Cowles
710. IWM
Dave Nash
IWM
711. IWM
Anthony Staunton
Tom Miles
712. This England
Steve Peters
John Manock
713. Ben May
Gordon Smith
Steve Bench
714. IWM
DH
Steve Bench
715. WML
DH
Bob Puffett
716. WML
DH
Alan Jordan
717. IWM
Norah Sanders
Peter Thompson
718. WML
DH
Steve Bench
719. IWM
Norman Irvine
Steve Bench
720. RAF Museum
(PC-76/23/46)
Judith Burk
Tom Miles
721. Highlanders Museum
RF
722. IWM
Jim Hingle

723. IWM
　　DH
　　WML
724. WML
　　Sven A-Persson
725. WML
　　Ken Horton
726. IWM
　　DH
　　Jim Hingle
727. WML
　　DH
728. WML
　　DH
　　Tom Miles
729. Royal Green Jackets
　　Bob Puffett
　　Alan Jordan
730. This England
　　David Hewson
　　WML
731. IWM
　　Steve Smith
732. IWM
　　Donald C Jennings
　　John Manock
733. Devon & Dorset Reg.
　　Daniel & Steve Rouse
　　Major A Flatow
734. Carey Corporation
　　Judith McClymont
　　IWM
735. WML
　　Judith McClymont
　　DH
736. WML
　　DH
　　Tom Miles
737. Royal Green Jackets
　　Norah Sanders
　　DH
738. DH
　　RF
739. King's Regiment.Mus.
　　DH
　　Thameside Council
740. WML
　　DH
　　John Manock
741. DH
　　Bob Puffett
　　Peter Munday
742. Ray. Walsh (THCL)
　　Alan Jordan
743. DH
　　Norah Sanders
　　Doreen Naylor
744. DH
　　Judith McClymont
　　Norman Irvine
745. WML
　　Lars Meyering
746. RAF Museum
　　(PC-76/2316)
　　Dave Nash
　　Stan Applin
747. R.A.M.C. Museum
　　David Rushmer
　　Tom Miles
748. IWM
　　Judith McClymont
749. *Daily Telegraph*
　　Roger White
　　WML
750. King's Regiment.Mus.

(750) Gordon Smith
　　Doreen Naylor
751. Clarke Family Papers
　　Tom Miles
　　Dr. Simon Turner
752. Alex.Turnbull Library
　　(F-31677)
　　Norah Sanders
　　Geoff Housego
753. RHQ Coldstream G'ds
　　Bob McKenzie
　　RF
754. RHQ Coldstream G'ds
　　Steve Smith
　　WML
755. WML
　　Dolores Grant
　　Tom Miles
756. WML
　　DH
　　Helen Smith
757. Middlesex Reg.Mus.
　　DH
　　Roy.Star & Garter
758. Middlesex Reg.Mus.
　　WML
759. IWM-Q69155
　　Stan Applin
　　IWM
760. IWM
　　RF
　　Ron Biddle
761. IWM-Q114620
　　Peter Briggs
　　Gerard Conway
762. D.O.W. Reg. Museum
　　John Lester
　　WML
763. Canadian Archives
　　DH
　　Gordon Smith
764. This England
　　Dave Nash
　　WML
765. *The Glasgow Herald*
　　Stewart Smith
　　WML
766. Worcester. Reg. Mus.
　　Constantine Bonetti
　　Hal Egerton
767. IWM
　　Gus Dawson
　　DH
768. Alex.Turnbull Library
　　(F-50823-1/2)
　　DH
　　RF

| Chapter 11 |
| First World War - 1917 |

769. RAF Museum
　　DH
　　Alan Jordan
770. IWM-Q79804
　　Trevor Archer
　　Alan Jordan
771. IWM-Q80817
　　Judith McClymont
　　IWM
772. This England
　　David Rushmer
773. IWM
　　Judith McClymont
774. IWM-Q85887
　　David Rushmer

(774) Tim Pearce
775. This England
　　Stan Applin
776. WML
　　RF
777. This England
　　Manchester Eve News
　　IWM
778. Gurkha Museum
　　Stan Applin
　　Roger Firth
779. This England
　　John Manock
　　KP
780. This England
　　Alan Jordan
　　John Manock
781. Royal Green Jackets
　　Norah Sanders
　　Tom Miles
782. King's Regiment Mus.
　　Lars Meyering
　　Bob Puffett
783. This England
　　DH
　　Stewart Smith
784. WML
　　Dave Nash
785. RAF Museum
　　David Rushmer
786. IWM
　　DH
　　Judith McClymont
787. RoyalCanadianLegion
　　DH
　　Etta Walker
788. Anthony Staunton
　　Judith McClymont
　　IWM
789. Royal Marines Mus.
　　David Rushmer
　　Norman Gordon
790. R.A. Historical Assoc.
　　DH
　　Tom Miles
791. This England
　　Anthony Staunton
　　Tom Miles
792. Northumberland Fus.
　　RF
　　Jim Hingle
793. Ben May
　　DH
　　Rose Coombs MBE
794. IWM
　　Judith McClymont
　　Australian War Mem.
795. This England
　　Clive Roberts
　　David Rushmer
796. Canadian War Mus.
　　DH
　　Peter Briggs
797. IWM-Q114652
　　Judith McClymont
　　KP
798. IWM
　　Harry E Evernden
　　Rod Travers-Griffin
799. IWM-Q91474
　　David Rushmer
　　Tom Miles
800. L/WML
　　DH
　　Jim Hingle

801. This England
　　Gordon Smith
　　WML
802. IWM
　　Dave Nash
803. IWM
　　DH
　　IWM
804. IWM-Q80668
　　Jim Hingle
805. This England
　　Clive Roberts
　　Tom Miles
806. IWM-Q66180
　　Steve Bench
　　John Manock
807. WML
　　Patrick Anderson
　　Stewart Smith
808. Argyll & Suth. High.
　　RF
809. Argyll & Suth High.
　　David Rushmer
　　IWM
810. WML
　　Bob Puffett
　　Hal Egerton
811. Dennis Foster
　　RF
　　Tom Miles
812. RAF Museum P-2717
　　DH
　　Alan Jordan
813. Royal Green Jackets
　　DH
814. *Times History Gt.War*
　　RF
　　KP
815. Dorset Public Library
　　Steve Smith
816. L/WML
　　Steve Smith
　　Hal Egerton
817. IWM-Q80658
　　RF
　　KP
818. WML
　　Peter Briggs
　　Stewart Smith
819. IWM
　　DH
820. This England
　　Bob Puffett
　　C.W.G.C.
821. IWM-Q66183
　　Bill Cable
　　Spink & Son Ltd
822. IWM
　　David Hewson
823. IWM
　　Gerard Conway
　　WML
824. This England
　　Judith McClymont
　　IWM
825. IWM-Q80661
　　RF
　　KP
826. SouthWalesBord.Mus.
　　Malcolm Putney
　　RF
827. RAF Museum
　　R. Stanley Goat
828. IWM-Q80587
　　Dennis Pillinger

829. IWM-Q114621
　　Stewart Smith
　　RF
830. Carey Corporation
　　Anthony Staunton
　　Australian War Mem.
831. WML
　　RF
　　Stan Applin
832. Pat Blackett-Barber
　　Alan Jordan
　　Royal British Legion
833. Carey Corporation
　　Judith McClymont
834. IWM-Q54045
　　Alan Jordan
　　IWM-Q114643
835. This England
　　Norah Sanders
　　Norman Irvine
836. Christies(NF940-M51)
　　DH
　　IWM
837. Alex.Turnbull Library
　　(G 43325-1/2)
　　Joyce Major
838. This England
　　Malcolm Cook
　　Roger Firth
839. This England
　　David Cairns
　　Alan Jordan
840. Alex.Turnbull Library
　　(G-43326-1/2)
　　Laurie Trubshoe
841. IWM
　　John Manock
　　Donald C Jennings
842. IWM-Q54045
　　Alan Jordan
　　WML
843. IWM-Q79783
　　RF
　　Royal Engineers Mus.
844. IWM
　　Bob Puffett
　　RF
845. IWM
　　Hal Egerton
　　WML
846. This England
　　Muriel Monk
　　Clive Roberts
　　John Chidzey
847. King'sOwnRegim.Mus
　　Hal Egerton
　　John Manock
848. Gordon Highlanders
　　RF
　　IWM
849. SouthWalesBord.Mus.
　　RF
　　Doreen McGregor
850. RHQ Coldstream G'ds
　　WML
851. WML
　　Peter Briggs
　　Roger Firth
852. This England
　　DH
(743) Doreen Naylor
　　Malcolm Cook
853. P.O.W.Regim.Museum
　　Jim Hingle
　　KP

854. IWM-HU44982 Alan Jordan RF	882. Royal Scots Reg. Mus. Ron Biddle DH	(909) Peter Briggs 910. WML DH	938. This England DH IWM	963. This England Dave Nash KP
855. *The Southern Times* DH Muriel Monk	883. IWM-Q79*** Stewart Smith	911. This England DH	939. King's Regiment. Mus. Stan Applin IWM	964. Highland L.I. Museum DH IWM
856. IWM Jim Hingle WML	884. IWM Judith McClymont	912. L/WML Rod Travers-Griffin	940. IWM John Manock	965. IWM-Q94249 DH Tom Miles
857. IWM-Q20876 RF KP	885. This England Clive Roberts Tom Miles	913. WML Clive Roberts Trevor Archer	941. WML Steve Bench	966. Ben May DH IWM
858. CanadianWarMuseum Peter Briggs	886. WML Clive Roberts IWM	914. DH RF	**Chapter 12** **First World War - 1918**	967. This England Bill Cable
859. WML DH	887. IWM DH RF	915. This England Carol Fuller RF	942. RAF Museum P-1359 DH RF	968. This England Jim Hingle
860. This England DH KP	888. King's Regim.Museum Tom Miles	916. Alan Jordan This England DH	943. This England DH Dave Nash	969. IWM DH Bob Puffett
861. IWM-Q54045 Gerard Conway	889. WML RF Black Watch Museum	917. This England DH Tom Miles	944. L/WML DH Bob Puffett	970. RAF Museum (P - 76/23/9) Dennis Pillinger RF
862. IWM-Q54045 Tom Miles WML	890. IWM-Q85885 Mike Wade	918. Royal Green Jackets Ron Biddle George Fleming	945. K.S.L.I. Museum Helen Smith IWM	971. IWM Donald C Jennings KP
863. KO Scottish Borderers RF	891. WML David Rushmer DH	919. IWM-Q68324 RF Steve Bench	946. WML Gordon Smith IWM-Q60774	972. This England Judith McClymont Tom Miles
864. This England Stan Applin	892. WML Clive Roberts Tom Miles	920. IWM-Q85892 Pat Doak	947. L/WML Geoff Housego *The View*	973. L/WML DH RF
865. This England DH IWM	893. IWM-Q54252 RF Brad Smith	921. CanadianWarMuseum RoyalCanadianLegion	948. WML DH Norman Irvine	974. CanadianNat.Archives Bob Puffett RF
866. This England Hal Egerton KO Scottish Borderers	894. IWM Judith McClymont Tom Miles	922. IWM DH Hal Egerton	949. King's Regiment.Mus. DH C.W.G.C.	975. RAF Museum DH Mrs Doris Miller
867. IWM KP The Bedford School	895. *Western Daily Press* DH Ron Biddle	923. RHQ Scots Guards David McLeish KP	950. SouthAfrican National Mus. Military History DH Ron Biddle	976. IWM Ron Biddle Tom Miles
868. L/WML Norah Sanders Bob Mountney	896. Green Howards Mus. DH IWM	924. IWM-Q111824 Eve Logan DH	951. Peter M James Tim Day	977. This England David Rushmer John Manock
869. This England DH	897. This England DH WML	925. This England David Redl Pat Doak	952. Ben May RF IWM-Q5172	978. IWM Alan Jordan John Manock
870. Dolores Grant Rod Travers-Griffin *The Toronto Star*	898. This England John Manock M. Butler O'Boyne	926. IWM-Q80673 Judith McClymont	953. Ben May Roger Webster DH	979. This England Clive Roberts Sgt. Peter Johnson
871. IWM-Q50580 DH Brad Smith	899. IWM-Q79800 John Manock	927. This England Doreen Naylor	954. IWM Alan Jordan Tom Miles	980. IWM-Q80128 Peter Briggs Doreen Naylor
872. The Staff. Reg.Mus. RF	900. WML DH M H Holland	928. IWM-Q80815 DH Geoff Housego	955. L/WML David Rushmer RF	981. Gurkha Museum IWM
873. IWM-Q80816 Robert Cudmore Irish Guards Museum	901. This England Alan Ellis Family KP	929. This England John Manock Alan Jordan	956. L/WML DH Dave Nash	982. IWM Jim Hingle
874. IWM-Q81464 DH Brian Cornelius	902. Carey Corporation Hal Egerton Judith McClymont	930. L/WML RF Tom Miles	957. Sotheby's Norah Sanders IWM	983. This England DH Tim Pearce
875. IWM Judith McClymont	903. Eugene Ursual R. Stanley Goat	931. IWM-Q80670 DH Peter Briggs	958. Colonel Gerald Napier RF Hal Egerton	984. IWM DH
876. This England Bob Puffett DH	904. IWM Dennis Pillinger	932. Spink & Son Ltd DH J H West	959. This England Alan Jordan	985. WML Reg Plant
877. Royal Green Jackets RF	905. This England DH Etta Walker	933. IWM-Q80659	960. Ben May Gordon Smith IWM	986. King's Regiment.Mus. Ron Gould Mike Wade
878. IWM Norman Irvine Hal Egerton	906. L/WML DH RF	934. This England Dave Nash Tom Miles	961. This England Tom Miles Muriel Monk	987. Royal MarineMuseum (9/2/B5-(1)) Royal MarineMuseum (17/8/11-(1)) Stan Applin
879. Notts&DerbyReg.Mus. Alan Jordan *The Sentinel*	907. This England Etta Walker	935. IWM-Q80582 Tom Miles Alan Jordan	962. L/WML RF DH	988. Herbert Jenkins DH RF
880. IWM-Q79803 DH Tom Miles	908. This England DH Peter Briggs	936. WML Tom Miles IWM		
881. This England Bert Gedin *The Nottingham Press*	909. IWM-CO-2339 Sgt. Wesley Allen	937. WML DH Norman Irvine		

989. N.M.M.
Keith BEM JP
990. N.M.M.
DH
KP
991. IWM-Q*****
DH
RF
992. Royal MarineMuseum
(9/2/F2 (8))
RF
Pat Doak
Stan Applin
Ron Biddle
993. This England
DH
Tom Miles
RF
994. McKenzie Family
DH
995. IWM-Q104329
Jim Hingle
KP
996. Royal Green Jackets
Robert Cudmore
RF
997. IWM
David Hewson
Tom Miles
998. N C Dunn
Tom Miles
Hal Egerton
999. L/WML
Hal Egerton
1000. IWM
Brad Smith
Tom Miles
1001. This England
RF
IWM
1002. Royal Green Jackets
Dave Nash
RF
1003. Royal Green Jackets
Mike Wade
Dave Nash
1004. CanadianNat.Archives
Dolores Grant
Herbert Jenkins
1005. IWM-Q79805
Ron Biddle
Herbert Jenkins
1006. This England
Anthony Staunton
Australian War Mem.
1007. This England
RF
1008. IWM
Hal Egerton
John Manock
1009. WML
Dave Nash
Rod Travers-Griffin
1010. Sherwood Forest.Mus.
Michael Kelsey
KP
1011. Ron Biddle
Eric Robinson
IWM
1012. RAF Museum
DH
Hal Egerton
1013. Carey Corporation
Judith McClymont
KP

1014. Carey Corporation
David Hewson
1015. This England
Judith McClymont
Tom Miles
1016. This England
Judith McClymont
Roger Firth
1017. IWM
Anthony Staunton
Tom Miles
1018. IWM
Frank Long
Ron Biddle
1019. Alex.Turnbull Library
(F103803-3)
Dave Nash
S. Narpley
1020. IWM
Donald C Jennings
Dave Flory
DH
1021.RAF Museum
(PC76/23/10)
Alan Jordan
Steve Bench
1022. WML
Norah Sanders
C.W.G.C.
1023. IWM
Gordon Smith
1024. This England
David Rushmer
Tom Miles
1025. WML
Vernon Landry
1026. This England
Tom Miles
IWM-Q42263
1027. IWM
Norah Sanders
The Graphic
1028. RAF Museum
Dennis Pillinger
RF
1029. This England
Geoff Housego
Australian War Mem.
1030. L/WML
Etta Walker
WML
1031. IWM-Q91468
Donald C Jennings
1032. Frank Long
DH
1033. IWM
Etta Walker
Dolores Grant
1034. WML
Stan Applin
Tom Miles
1035. IWM
David Rushmer
Peter Briggs
1036. This England
Judith McClymont
Tom Miles
1037. This England
RF
Norman Irvine
1038. Spink & Son Ltd
DH
1039. This England
DH
Norman Irvine

1040. Devon & Dorset Reg.
Ken Horton
IWM-Q80671
1041. This England
Stan Applin
1042. Carey Corporation
Anthony Staunton
Tom Miles
1043. WML
Bob Puffett
IWM-Q5123
1044. Royal Engineers Mus.
DH
IWM
1045. Argyll & Suth. High.
RF
IWM
1046. L/WML
Norah Sanders
Ken Horton
1047. This England
Judith McClymont
1048. Alex.Turnbull Library
(3167-4-1/2)
Joyce Major
Alex.Turnbull Library
(F18784-1/1)
1049. The Daily Telegraph
Gary Batha
DH
1050. IWM-Q88149
Dave Nash
KP
1051. IWM
R. Stanley Goat
1052. IWM-Q81176
DH
M. Barnbrook
1053. This England
DH
Major A F Flatow
1054. Ron Biddle
Judith McClymont
IWM
1055. This England
Norah Sanders
IWM-Q6060
1056. Carey Corporation
Judith McClymont
KP
1057. Alex.Turnbull Library
(F18787-1/1)
Joyce Major
1058. This England
Judith McClymont
1059. IWM
Judith McClymont
Tom Miles
1060. Carey Corporation
DH
Tom Miles
1061. CanadianWarMuseum
Geoff Housego
IWM
1062. This England
Judith McClymont
Tom Miles
1063. Derek Hunt
Sven A-Persson
KP
1064. IWM-Q9760
Alan Jordan
Tom Miles
1065. The Daily Mirror
Tom Miles

(1065) Steven Sanday
1066. This England
DH
1067. CanadianNat.Archives
Tom Miles
IWM
1068. IWM-Q80567
Stan Applin
IWM
1069. IWM-Q9708
DH
IWM
1070. This England
DH
Tim Day
1071. IWM
DH
1072. This England
DH
Australian War Mem.
1073. This England
R Stanley Goat
The Great War
1074. Ben May
DH
RF
1075. L/WML
C.W.G.C.
IWM
1076. This England
Dave Nash
1077. Alex.Turnbull Library
(F18786- 1/1)
Joyce Major
1078. Royal Green Jackets
Ken Horton
1079. IWM-Q31304
RF
IWM
1080. Australian War. Mem.
Anthony Staunton
Tom Miles
1081. IWM-Q114614
DH
1082. This England
DH
RF
1083. IWM - 70233
Tom Miles
Alan Jordan
1084. Major A F Flatow
Frank Long
Spink & Son Ltd
1085. Carey Corporation
Judith McClymont
1086. L/WML
DH
WML
1087. Sotheby's
RF
1088. This England
RF
IWM
1089. WML
Clive Roberts
Lee Harvey
1090. RHQ Coldstream G'ds
David Rushmer
1091. IWM
Frank Long
RF
1092. CanadianNat.Archives
R Stanley Goat
DH
KP

1093. CanadianNat.Archives
DH
IWM
1094. RHQ Coldstream G'ds
John Manock
1095. The Sphere
Rod Travers-Griffin
1096. IWM-Q91471
Peter Briggs
1097. This England
John Manock
1098. K.O.S.B. Museum
DH
David Cairns
1099. Major A F Flatow
Alan Jordan
DH
1100. CanadianNat.Archives
Don McGregor
DH
1101. IWM-Q81180
DH
Tom Miles
1102. SherwoodFor.Museum
Tom Miles
1103. Alex.Turnbull Library
(F1879 - 1/1)
Joyce Major
1104. This England
Anthony Staunton
Tom Miles
1105. WML
Steve Bench
Lars Meyering
1106. WML
DH
1107. IWM-Q80568
DH
Steve Smith
1108. StaffordshireRegiment
Ken Horton
Major A F Flatow
1109. SherwoodFor.Museum
Steven Sanday
1110. Carey Corporation
Judith McClymont
DH
1111. This England
Judith McClymont
Tom Miles
1112. Derek Hunt
John Manock
IWM-Q81416
1113. SouthWalesBord.Mus.
1114. Royal Engineers Mus.
R Stanley Goat
Dennis Pillinger
1115. This England
Peter Briggs
WML
1116. WML
DH
1117. IWM-Q82410
DH
Alan Jordan
1118. RHQ Scots Guards
DH
1119. Northumberland Fus.
Stan Applin
1120. IWM-Q70039
Geoff Housego
1121. This England
Betty Collar
1122. This England
Alan Jordan

427

1123. This England
J G O'Grady
RoyalCanadianLegion
1124. Royal Scots Reg. Mus.
KP
1125. IWM-Q114045
Michael Kelsey
1126. Rotherham Museum
RF
Derek Hunt
1127. King's Regiment. Mus.
John Manock
1128. This England
Clive Roberts
IWM
1129. Derek Hunt
RF
1130. IWM
Keith Webb BEM JP
1131. This England
RF
1132. WML
DH
Alan Jordan
1133. L/WML
Candice M. da Costa
Steve Bench
1134. RAF Museum
(PC76/23/12)
DH
Dave Nash
1135. This England
RF
1136. WML
John Manock
Hal Egerton
1137. Carey Corporation
Judith McClymont
1138. Derek Hunt
Judith McClymont
1139. IWM
DH
Tom Miles
1140. Spink & Son Ltd
John Manock
1141. This England
Ken Horton
IWM
1142. Royal Engineers Mus.
RF
1143. Royal Engineers Mus.
RF
1144. SouthWalesBord.Mus.
DH
RF
1145. King's Regiment. Mus.
Gordon Smith
John Manock
1146. IWM-Q82346
Gordon Smith
Pat Batty
1147. Royal Engineers Mus.
Alan Jordan
1148. Royal Engineers Mus.
DH

Chapter 13
Between the Wars

1149. IWM-Q66160
Stan Applin
Tom Miles
1150. IWM
Judith McClymont
RF

1151. L/WML
DH
KP
1152. IWM-Q66160
Dave Nash
1153. Carey Corporation
Col. Leonid Polovtstov
RF
1154. This England
KP
1155. Spink & Son Ltd
Steve Bench
1156. King's Regiment. Mus.
Trevor Archer
RF
1157. Spink & Son Ltd
KP
1158. WML
Tony Martin
KP

Chapter 14
Second World War - 1940

1159. IWM-A29585
DH
Muriel Monk
1160. WML
Steve Bench
KP
1161. WML
Judith McClymont
IWM-A15014
1162. RAF Museum
(PC76/23/20)
John Kingsmill
RF
1163. WML
John Kingsmill
RF
1164. WML
IWM
Gallipoli Association
1165. GrenadierGuards Ass.
Mike Wade
This England
1166. IWM-1/1336
DH
RF
1167. IWM-HU2003
DH
1168. THCL -Ray. Walsh
1169. Royal Naval Museum
Steve Smith
Stan Applin
1170. E C T Wilson VC
IWM-E12375
DH
1171. RAF Museum
(PC76/23/50)
RF
1172. RAF Museum
(PC76/23/51)
Chris Forester
RF
1173. RAF Museum
Mark Cline
1174. IWM-HU1915
Stan Applin
Nat.Maritime Museum

Chapter 15
Second World War - 1941

1175. Royal Engineers Mus.
Donald C Jennings

1176. IWM-IC7126
C.W.G.C. Field Team
1177. RAF Museum
Stan Applin
Jim Hingle
1178. Ben May
Tom Miles
Judith McClymont
1179. Alex.Turnbull Library
(C-21385)
Joyce Major
Major A F Flatow
1180. This England
DH
1181. KP
T E Sentance
1182. Alex.Turnbull Library
(F125712 - 1/2)
Joyce Major
WML
1183.Alex.Turnbull Library
(F1993 - 14 DA)
John Slater
Joyce Major
1184. IWM-A7293
DH
Stan Applin
1185. IWM-HU2028
RF
1186. RAF Museum
Judith McClymont
David Hewson
1187. RAF Museum
(PC76/23/49)
David Redl
RF
1188. Carey Corporation
Judith McClymont
WML
1189. IWM
Dave Williams
RF
DH
1190. IWM-HU2046
Dave Williams
Tom Miles
1191. Royal Green Jackets
Dave Williams
IWM
1192. IWM
Dave Nash
Dr Helen Murray
1193. WML
Tom Miles
Major A F Flatow
1194.Northumberland Fus.
Tom Miles
IWM
1195. RAF Museum
Tom Miles
RF
1196. IWM-HU20575
David Rushmer
John Manock

Chapter 16
Second World War - 1942

1197. IWM-MH2587
RF
Tom Miles
KP
1198. IWM-HU2023
Tom Miles
Univ.North.Colorado

1199. RAF Museum
(PC76/23/26/1)
DH
Brad Smith
1200. IWM-A31245
Steve Bench
Doreen Naylor
1201. Royal Naval Museum
Illust.London News
DH
1202. IWM-HU1863
RF
1203. IWM-A10216
RF
KP
1204. IWM
Judith McClymont
Dr. John Laffin
1205. Royal Engineers Mus.
RF
1206. IWM-HU16542
DH
Spink & Son Ltd
1207. Royal Naval Museum
David Rushmer
RF
1208. WML
Alan Jordan
Ken Horton
1209. RAF Museum
DH
Ron Biddle
1210. This England
RF
Roger White
1211. RAF Museum
John Kingsmill
RF
1212. IWM
KP
THCL - Ray. Walsh
1213. IWM-HU2033
KP
IWM
(1183) Alex.Turnbull Lib.
John Slater
Joyce Major
1214. Alex.Turnbull Library
(F12682/ 11 DA)
Joyce Major
WML
1215. Australian War Mem.
Trevor Archer
1216. IWM-HU2010
DH
Reg Plant
1217. CanadianNat.Archives
Univ. North Colorado
1218. Dr John Laffin
Tom Miles
DH
1219. Carey Corporation
Judith McClymont
Tom Miles
1220. This England
Judith McClymont
Tom Miles
1221. Australian War Mem.
Tom Miles
1222. Carey Corporation
Michael Washbrook
1223. Royal Green Jackets
Dave Nash
RF

1224. IWM - 22225149
Dave Nash
KP
1225. RAF Museum
DH
RF
1226. Ben May
DH
Ron Biddle
1227. RAF Museum
(76/23/24)
DH
RF
1228. IWM-HU1920
Alan Jordan
Dave Nash

Chapter 17
Second World War - 1943

1229. IWM-MH2601
DH
Tom Miles
1230. This England
Judith McClymont
Australian War Mem.
1231. IWM-HU1998
Tom Miles
RF
1232. Alex.Turnbull Library
(DA 11264)
Tom Miles
KP
1233. Gurkha Museum
KP
1234. IWM-HU7994
Tom Miles
John Manock
1235. Argyll & Suth. High.
RF
Chronicle Communic.
1236. B. S. Dureeka
Tom Miles
1237. IWM-HU2027
DH
Stewart Smith
1238. IWM-HU2004
RF
1239. IWM-HU2040
DH
Alan Jordan
1240. IWM-NA6096
THCL - Ray. Walsh
Soldier Magazine
1241. Alex.Turnbull Library
(F38337 - 1/2)
Joyce Major
RF
1242. Nat.Maritime Museum
Stan Applin
1243. RAF Museum- P3578
David Redl
Tom Miles
1244. B.S. Dureeka
Dennis Pillinger
1245. Alex.Turnbull Library
(F1988 - 1/2 DA)
Chris Forester
1246. RAF Museum
C.W.G.C.
1247. Carey Corporation
Tom Miles
1248. Didy Grahame MVO
Brian Cornelius
Univ. North. Colorado

1249. Nat. MaritimeMuseum
(A-21798)
RF
Stan Applin
1250. RHQ Coldstream G'ds
DH
Major A F Flatow
1251. RAF Museum
(PC76/23/27)
RF
DH
1252. Carey Corporation
Judith McClymont
1253. CanadianNat. Archives
R Stanley Goat
Dennis Pillinger

Chapter 18
Second World War - 1944
1254. Spink & Son Ltd
Tom Miles
DH
1255. IWM-HU2051
C.W.G.C.
Univ. North. Colorado
1256. IWM
Pat Batty
RF
1257. IWM-CAN/4341
DH
Aung Thazin Studio
1258. IWM-HU2052
Aung Thazin Studio
John Wavell
1259. IWM-IND-3975
Univ. North. Colorado
1260. WML
DH/RF
1261. IWM-IND-3508
Judith McClymont
1262. Ben May
Stan Applin
1263. RAF Museum
RF
1264. This England
Judith McClymont
Gordon Drake
1265. B.S. Dureeka
Univ. North. Colorado
WML
1266. IWM-HU2056
Ron Biddle
David Rushmer
1267. This England
John Manock
1268. IWM-MH4206
Rod Travers-Griffin
1269. IWM-HU2035
Tom Miles
Stan Applin
1270. The Daily Telegraph
RF
IWM
1271. IWM-HU2037
David Rushmer
RF
1272. Dr. John Laffin
Aung Thazin Studio
Eric Francis
Dick Jordan
1273. Gurkha Museum
1274. RAF Museum
Hal Egerton
RF

1275. IWM-K9258
Tom Miles
1276. Gurkha Museum
RF
1277. RAF Museum
Mrs P Marshall
RF
1278. Gurkha Museum
Aung Thazin Studio
1279. Gurkha Museum
Major A F Flatow
1280. IWM-IND3971
Aung Thazin Studio
RF
1281. IWM-IND4056
Tom Miles
1282. Dr John Laffin
RF
1283. RAF Museum
(PC76/23/31)
Gordon Smith
Stan Applin
1284. RAF Museum
(PC76/23/32)
Etta Walker
RF
1285. IWM-HU2054
Tom Miles
RF
1286. WML
RF
The Daily Telegraph
1287. IWM
Universal Press
DH
1288. IWM-MH4204
R Stanley Goat
1289. WML
THCL - Ray. Walsh
1290. IWM-HU2049
DH
Roger Firth
1291. RF
IWM-IND4468
DH
1292. IWM-H40971
DH
Rev. Philip Frear BA
Insp. N. Kew
1293. Spink & Son Ltd
DH/RF
1294. Ben May
DH
Steve Smith
1295. IWM
DH
N C Dunn
1296. IWM - 2227330F
John Kingsmill
Jim Hingle
1297. IWM-HU2029
Stewart Smith
Univ. North. Colorado
1298. IWM-B13371
John Manock
KP
1299. WML
Major A F Flatow
DH/RF
1300. IWM-IND4515
Aung Thazin Studio
1301. Gurkha Museum
RF
1302. IWM-MH2603
KP

1303. IWM
RF
1304. WML
Tom Miles
RF/DH
1305. RAF Museum
(PC/76/23/41/2)
Brian Cornelius
RF

Chapter 19
Second World War - 1945
1306. WML
John Kingsmill
Tom Miles
1307. IWM-HU2019
Tom Miles
1308. Tom Miles
Univ. North. Colorado
1309. R.A.M.C. Museum
DH
Tom Miles
1310. IWM-HU2031
Aung Thazin Studio
Tom Miles
1311. IWM-IND4677
Aung Thazin Studio
B.S. Dureeka
1312. RAF Museum
(PC/76/23/38)
John Kingsmill
1313. WML
DH
R Stanley Goat
1314. K.S.L.I. Museum
Brian Cornelius
1315. IWM-MH4210
Rod Travers-Griffin
1316. Tom Miles
B.S. Dureeka
1317. IWM-MH2602
WML
1318. IWM-HU2050
Roy Duprey
1319. Gurkha Museum
Major A F Flatow
Lt Col. Paul Oldfield
1320. IWM-IND4713
Tom Miles
C.W.G.C.
1321. Royal Engineers Mus.
Aung Thazin Studio
1322. This England
Judith McClymont
1323. IWM
Rod Travers-Griffin
Lt Col. Andrew Webb
1324. Carey Corporation
Judith McClymont
1325. IWM-HU2048
DH
Ron Biddle
1326. RHQ Coldstream G'ds
David Redl
RF
1327. RoyalMarinesMuseum
(3696/1)
RF
Stan Applin
1328. Col. P Ladbrook MC
RF
Stan Applin
1329. IWM-IND4699
WML

1330. IWM-IND4695
KP
1331. IWM-HU2002
DH
John Manock
1332. Gurkha Museum
Lt Col.Paul Oldfield
Soldier Magazine
1333. This England
Tom Miles
Peter McKenzie
1334. Carey Corporation
THCL Ray. Walsh
1335. Australian War Mem.
Judith McClymont
1336. IWM
Judith McClymont
1337. The Belfast Telegraph
Jim Hingle
Steve Bench
1338. Royal Naval Museum
THCL Ray. Walsh
1339. Ron Biddle
DH
Brit. Embassy - Japan

Chapter 20
The Closing Episode
1340. W M Allderson
Tom Miles
DH
1341. This England
DH
Gloucester Cathedral
1342. This England
Gary Batha
Brad Smith
1343. K.O.S.B. Museum
Hal Egerton
DH
1344. Gurkha Museum
RF
1345. This England
Judith McClymont
Anthony Staunton
Tom Miles
1346. Carey Corporation
Tom Miles
1347. This England
Judith McClymont
Tom Miles
1348. WML
THCL Ray. Walsh
1349. Devon & Dorset Mus.
Mike Wade
1350. Soldier Magazine
DH
Ron Biddle
1351. DH
MajGen Pony Scherrer

Photographs used in the
INTRODUCTION
DUST JACKET
Zed Nelson Photography
I.S.N. News Group
RF
David Rushmer
Coma Roofing Company
Royal Star & Garter Home
C.W.G.C.
DH
Lt Col. K Plant
F K Horton

BRIEF HISTORY
National Portrait Gallery
WML Collection
Royal Logistic Corps
Imperial War Museum
MESSAGES/ARTICLES
Australian War Memorial
Captain Neil Blair LVO
Mrs Didy Grahame MVO
Tommy Gould VC
Imperial War Museum
Major David Jamieson VC
Lt Col Eric C T Wilson VC
Lt Col Eric Lummis
DH
Vice-Ad. Sir David Dobson
Royal Star & Garter Home

Images 1857 - 1997
WML
South Wales Bord Mus (363)
*
Great War Illustrated (672)
IWM-Q9759 (692)
IWM-NA-6093
*
Royal Engineers Mus (958)
IWM-Q68240 (998)
RHQ Irish Guards (1240)
IWM
*
Nat. Maritime Museum (66)
IWM-Q6983 (170)
Royal Green Jackets (327)
Royal Engineers (340)
*
WML
Royal Archives (376)
WML (416)
Royal Engineers (474)
*
South Wales Bord Museum
King's Regimental Museum
*
Ron Biddle
IWM Q54252
*
9/12 Royal Lancers (528)
Ron Biddle (757)
*
Paris Post (561)
IWM-HU35958 (598)
IWM-Q19625 (855)
*
IWM- Q9224
IWM-Q66160
*
Grenadier Guards Association
IWM
IWM-Q692203
*
Alexander Turnbull Library
(F1320-10)
Eugene Ursual
*
Dennis Foster
Medal Society of Ireland
*
WML (619) (1149)
Dennis Foster (811)
*
The Graphic (1212) (1279)
*

IWM- HU2056	Fairfax Photo Library	Hal Egerton (Cobbers)	KP (Nakuru)	Lancashire County Library
WML	J Harrison - Gizeh Shriners	DH (Pozieres)	Trevor Archer (Beja &	(683)
B.S. Dureeka	*	*	Knightsbridge)	Royal Star & Garter (703)
*	*Soldier Magazine*	Tom Miles (Keren)	Zimbabwe Legion (Gwelo)	*
Ron Biddle	VC & GC Asssociation	B.S.Dureeka (Kohima)	*	Ron Biddle (445)
Australian War Mem 44647	*	DH (Taukkyan)	Tom Miles (Labuan, Rabaul	*
*	Terry Duncan	*	Taiping & Yokohama	LAC Tom Harry (1213)
WML	Royal Army Medical Corps	DH (Nairobi)	*	WML (!225)
Star & Garter	*	Tom Miles (Port Moresby)	Gary Batha (Arnhem)	*
WML	Royal Green Jackets (327)	DH (Tower Hill)	DH (Berlin)	*The Daily Telegraph* (1028)
*	WML (347)	*	C.W.G.C. (St Carlos)	*
Soldier Magazine	Gordon Smith (364)	Bob Puffett (Monte Cassino)	*	*Christchurch Press* (1179)
Canadian Archives PA12903	Keith Webb BEM JP (692)	RF (St Nazaire)	John Tamplin (623)	
*		C.W.G.C. (Tyne Cot)	WML (900)	
Ron Biddle	Roy Watson (812)	*	Australian War Mem (1178)	
WML	RF (1231)	RF (Cairo) (Heliopolis)	Dr John Laffin (1237)	
M Barnbrook	Salisbury British Legion	Trevor Archer (El Alamein)		

****

The book contains numerous illustrations of VC groups and it is acknowledged that due to constraints of space in some cases not all the medals awarded to the holder are shown. The intention of the Author and Publisher in these instances was to provide further examples of the wide variety of medals awarded over the years rather than chronicle each individual's definitive awards. Also, when it has been impossible to obtain a photograph of an original group, computer imagery has been used instead.

****

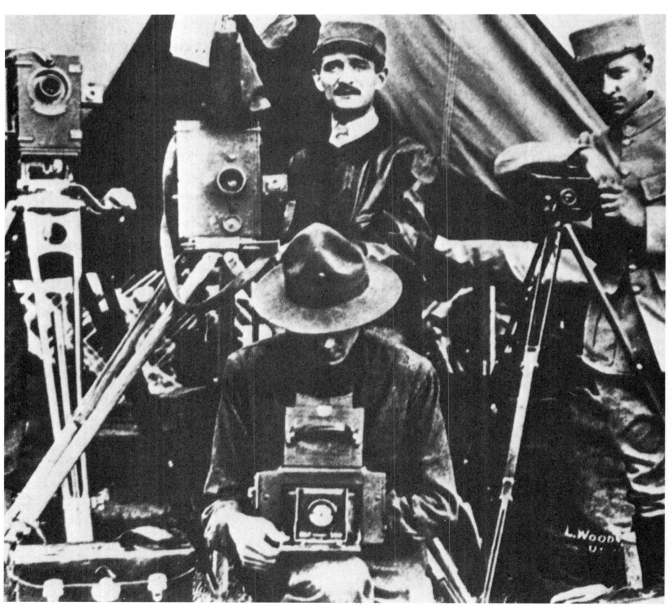

Military Photographers during the First World War, 1917

SPECIAL THANKS

I realise that this is rather an unusual addition but it would be remiss of me to not give special thanks to six people without whom '*Monuments to Courage*' would not have come to pass.

Given the length of time involved in compiling the book, coupled with the assistance I required following the accident, circumstances dictate that their help be 'specially' acknowledged. Such was their input, that I could write a chapter on each and hope they will settle for this offering, complete with photograph, by way of thanks. I list them chronologically, in line with the book!

The fact that I have been able to avoid spending much of the past seven years in hospital, thus allowing me to live a near 'normal' life, as well as being able to work full time on the book, is because I have been blessed with a remarkable sister, Pat. Having spent her entire life in every nursing capacity, she has devotedly nursed and cared for me, spending at least an hour a day tending to my needs and latest health problems as well as providing her much valued company during her visits. It is totally down to her selflessness and loving kindness that this long project has been completed; she has put her own plans aside to ensure that I have wanted for nothing and have been able to work at home, rather than struggle from a hospital bed. I will never be able to repay her for all she has done. I can, however, note her total involvement and dedicate the book to her.

Two close friends, both ex-colleagues whom I have known for almost thirty years, played an integral part in ensuring the book was finished. David Rushmer has been involved in the project since 1972, beginning to assist with trips to obtain photographs not too long afterwards, eventually making many trips to see Canon Lummis himself when I was unable to visit him personally. Until 1992, we made three or four trips each year to the Western Front, covering just about every yard from Verdun to the Channel, but drawn inexorably to the Somme, which for us has to be the most poignant region on the Front, and the final resting place of many of the subjects of this book. Knowing his loathing of hospitals, I lost count of the number of times he 'forced' himself to spend hours at my bedside, occasionally using the time well to get back at me for many (alleged) times I had 'dropped him in it' over almost quarter of a century, knowing that I was in no fit state to defend myself! Despite this, David's support was never more appreciated than during that period and the following years of convalescence when I have learned the true meaning of friendship.

Bob Fuller, the other 'old' colleague, has turned his hand to so many things for me since the accident, that it would be difficult for me to recall, let alone list them all. Having spent six months converting a derelict bungalow into the modern wheelchair-friendly house I now call home, he offered to help sort out almost 16,000 photographs that had been tossed into a couple of large boxes when friends 'packed' my belongings during my absence in readiness for the move. Noting the number relating to the Victoria Cross, Bob became interested in the subject and eventually became my 'mobile half', in much the same way I had acted as the Canon's legs thirty years previously. For four years Bob has not only travelled extensively adding to the photograph collection, but has acted as my minder on rare trips to the outside world. Not only has he hauled me safely up many flights of stairs, but on one occasion physically carried me, seated in my wheelchair, across 50 yards of an overgrown churchyard so that I could actually see a grave that I had been seeking for a number of years. (He even had the good grace to carry me back!) Without Bob's help and enthusiasm there would still be a country mile to go, which is where Bob is now heading, deciding to spend his future leisure time tracing his family tree.

In 1995, I received an enquiry out of the blue from a noted researcher in Bahrain, Kevin Patience, known only to me at that time as the author of several books on the military and transport history of East Africa and Zanzibar together with quality articles in the OMRS Journal. He asked me to locate a photograph for another book he was writing, which led to a close friendship with both Kevin and his wife Kay. Following a visit to my home in 1996, when he saw some of the VC material I had amassed, he was so enthusiastic about my efforts and research that he immediately offered to put the work into print. Considering the original plan was for a 300 page book, I am sure he did not know just quite how much work would be involved in publishing this book, which grew until its current format of two volumes and 896 pages was decided upon late in 1998. His insistence on high quality material to show the thousands of images in their best light, gave him many headaches in trying to keep the final cost 'reasonable', aware that the proceeds were being donated to the Royal Star & Garter Home, and resulted in both he and Kay generously donating much of their time and effort. Kay took over the editing, a long and thankless task and also helped to keep my spirits up when my health began to suffer badly near the end. I consider it my good fortune that in Kevin and Kay I have found two kindred spirits, sharing not only my concern about the 'forgotten heroes' but without whose hands-on support ***Monuments to Courage**' would still be on the drawing board.

Having assisted throughout the final year by translating my ramblings on the dictaphone into the English language and other vital tasks, Pat Mendes da Costa has put the icing on the cake by taking on the job of the UK distributor, stepping into the breach when previous plans had gone awry, and yet another vital member of the 'team' giving both time and effort to support the Star & Garter Home. A close friend and confidante over these past years, Pat could run her own Samaritan operation, and I am deeply grateful for her sound advice on many issues, not least of which has been '***Monuments**'.

PUBLISHER'S THANKS

Without the professional skills and extraordinary co-operation of the Dar Akbhar Al Khaleej production team *'Monuments to Courage'* may well not have come to fruition. It has taken seven months of dedicated, painstaking work by two people in particular, Manuel Paulose who ensured that the thousands of images appear in their best possible light and Anil Abraham who manipulated and set the text and photographs.

Mohammed Al-Moayyed, Press Manager; Ali Isa, Deputy Press Manager; Madhava Rao, Production Manager; Ravi T.M., Production Co-ordinator; Binny Thomas, Computer Graphic Department Head; Philip Eapen, Camera Department Head; Samuel Johnson, Printing Supervisor and John Abraham, Binding Supervisor have each contributed their expertise to the book's publication from the initial planning stage through type setting, image scanning, film production, plate making, printing, cutting, folding, stitching and binding to the presentation of the finished article in as short a time frame as possible. It has been a pleasure to work with them on the project and their input has been invaluable.

Kevin & Kay Patience
April, 1999